The Intersection of Technology and Criminal Justice

Tamara Phillips Fudge
https://orcid.org/0000-0002-8682-9711
Purdue University Global, USA

IGI Global
Scientific Publishing
Publishing Tomorrow's Research Today

Vice President of Editorial	Melissa Wagner
Director of Acquisitions	Mikaela Felty
Director of Book Development	Jocelynn Hessler
Production Manager	Mike Brehm
Cover Design	Jose Rosado

Published in the United States of America by
IGI Global Scientific Publishing
701 East Chocolate Avenue
Hershey, PA, 17033, USA
Tel: 717-533-8845 | Fax: 717-533-7115
Website: https://www.igi-global.com E-mail: cust@igi-global.com

Library of Congress Cataloging-in-Publication Data

LCCN: 2026005304 (CIP Data Pending)
ISBN13: 9798337376608
Isbn13Softcover: 9798337376615
EISBN13: 9798337376622
British Cataloguing in Publication Data
A Cataloguing in Publication record for this book is available from the British Library.

Table of Contents

Detailed Table of Contents

Law enforcement administrators wanting to improve operational and administrative effectiveness and accountability, as well as public transparency, are pressing to implement advanced technologies across the discipline. Though technology advancement is inevitable, there are several ambiguities inherent in the implementation of new technologies relative to costs and advantages for the jurisdictions involved. Prior research demonstrates the value of acknowledging front line officers' opinions on innovations and how these perspectives must be factored into administrative policies and procedures. Administrators can address officer resistance, illustrating the boundless advantages for police officers if they embrace innovative technology. Examples of technological implementation in law enforcement agencies provide insights into successes and failures of enforcement decisions informing policy and practice recommendations about the future of policing.

Conventionally, Indian police have heavily relied on traditional means of investigation, which, of late, are gradually adopting digital technology to detect, investigate, and prosecute crime, crimes in conventional as well as digital spaces. Artificial intelligence and machine learning models that enable law enforcement agencies to predict crime and act pre-emptively have assumed a prominent place in policing, for it changes the ways crimes are predicted, prevented, investigated, and prosecuted. But, achieving maximum potential of digitech in crime control requires addressing various issues related to the privacy of data, bias in algorithms, human rights, transparency, and responsibility must be addressed with the help of efficient governance structures and collaboration with stakeholders. This chapter builds a discourse inviting policymakers, technologists, and policing professionals to strive to create a balanced, responsible ecosystem of AI/ML policing that focuses on ethical standards, operational best practices, and engaging all stakeholders.

To address global scrutiny over use of force, law enforcement is replacing reactive training with proactive Virtual Reality (VR) and Generative AI (GenAI) models. This chapter evaluates how immersive simulations and Stress Inoculation Training (SIT) use real-time biometric monitoring to help officers maintain cognitive control during high-pressure crises. By utilizing AI-driven avatars, these systems create behavioral feedback loops to master de-escalation and interactions with neurodivergent individuals. While initial costs are high, VR provides a greater long-term fiscal efficiency than traditional methods. Despite risks like training scars and biometric privacy concerns, this digital evolution fosters a culture of compassion and constitutional integrity in modern policing.

This chapter addresses a central problem of a statutory vacuum created by warrantless vehicle tracking in India and South Asia which contrasts with technological capabilities of modern law enforcement. While jurisdictions like USA and UK, specific legal issues are triggered through physical trespass of a tracker or prolonged collection of location data, requiring warrants based on probable cause or RIPA authorization, India and its South Asian counterparts, base their usage of GPS technology on colonial-era statutes such as the erstwhile Telegraph Act, 1855, Telecommunications Act, 2023 or arbitrary limitless executive powers that transgress modern privacy concepts. This leads to a dual crisis – a constitutional one, whereby slap and track operations violate test of proportionality; and a civil liberty one, whereby non- existence of exclusionary rules incentivizes police overreach by admissibility of evidence obtained via invasive, warrantless tracking by the courts.

Emerging technologies, including facial recognition, biometric tracking, closed-circuit television, online monitoring, and artificial intelligence driven analytics, are rapidly reshaping the criminal justice system. The integration of modern surveillance is creating increasingly interconnected surveillance networks that enhance situational awareness, streamline decision making, and expand law enforcement's ability to identify, prevent, and respond to crime. This convergence supports more proactive policing and contributes to evolving models of public safety. Yet these developments raise significant ethical and legal concerns. Risks related to privacy breaches, discriminatory targeting, data misuse, and the erosion of civil liberties remain central to debates over the role of surveillance in criminal justice. Clear regulations, strong ethical frameworks, and democratic safeguards are essential to ensure that surveillance technologies serve the public good, uphold social justice, and support a fair and equitable society.

The new era of digital technology has brought along different cybersecurity issues, whereby automation and AI have now become the attackers' sophisticated tools, but also the protectors. By the year 2025, AI-based automated fraud with deepfakes, synthetic identity theft, and phishing has so quickly advanced that traditional security systems are struggling to cope with it. This chapter provides a critical discussion on the legal regulatory landscape of fraud ecosystems and the algorithms that threaten privacy and trust. It analyses global and Indian regulatory measures, highlights the issue of algorithmic opacity, and advocates a multi-layered governance model that combines human oversight, explainable AI, and adversarial AI defences. It has been stressed that, to counter AI-driven fraud, the coming of ethical, adaptive, and internationally harmonised regulations will not only protect innovation but also the digital ecosystems that are going to be around in the future.

Cybercrime investigation have historically been viewed as complex, both by practitioners and academics. These investigations oftentimes require collaboration across local, state, and federal agencies. Subsequently, the jurisdictional boundaries and concept associated with the crime scene, physical and digital, have become blurred. Couched within this discussion is the technological advancement shared by both investigative agencies and criminal syndicates. Put simply, as the technology advances so should the techniques and legal interpretations. Therefore, this chapter examines the evolution of cybercrime investigations and legal practices associated with investigation and prosecution of cyber-based crimes.

The expansion of cryptocurrencies and decentralized financial systems has transformed money laundering into a borderless and technologically complex form of financial crime, exposing the limits of compliance-driven enforcement. This chapter examines digital forensics as a core investigative tool in blockchain environments, focusing on transaction reconstruction, wallet attribution, and cross-chain tracing. It analyses crypto-laundering typologies such as ransomware payments, darknet marketplaces, DeFi exploits, and professional facilitation, demonstrating how forensic methods address the weaknesses of rule-based AML systems. Anchored in the criminal justice process, the chapter examines evidentiary reliability, seizure and custody of digital assets, and the admissibility of blockchain-derived evidence in court, with particular reference to India's legal framework under the Prevention of Money Laundering Act and comparative international enforcement practices.

incentives to maximize detection regardless of accuracy. The work argues fraud detection systems require transparency, contestation, and accountability standards before continuing operation in criminal justice.

The development of Artificial Intelligence has enabled the creation of artificially altered multimedia content known as deepfakes. These manipulated images, videos, and audio pose a growing threat to criminal justice systems, where the integrity of digital evidence is paramount. This chapter presents a narrative review of deepfake forensics, tracing the evolution of media manipulation from analogue techniques to modern generative models, and examining the threat landscape across political, financial, and personal domains, including non-consensual intimate imagery. Detection methodologies are surveyed, from artefact-based and statistical approaches to the operational tools accessible to law enforcement. Beyond the technical dimension, the chapter addresses chain of custody requirements, evidentiary standards across jurisdictions, the fragmented legislative landscape, and the role of Explainable AI in bridging detection outputs and courtroom admissibility. The psychological factors influencing how investigators and jurors assess synthetic media are also considered.

This chapter examines the use of tablets in correctional facilities. It argues that digital competence is essential for reentry and that incarceration intensifies the digital divide by isolating individuals from rapidly changing technologies. Using survey evidence from Cape Vincent, New York, the chapter summarizes the findings and analyzes public awareness and attitudes toward tablet functions, including education, rehabilitation, family communication, recreation, and free access. Referring to the findings, the analysis show conditional support: residents approve when tablets are framed as educational and rehabilitative infrastructure, and resist when tablets are seen as luxury items, entertainment, or “free” privileges. The chapter also addresses policy implications, privatization, surveillance, and ethical commitments to human dignity and equity. Overall, it concludes that digital rehabilitation can strengthen reintegration when tablet programs are transparent and purpose-driven.

Preface

Dr. Tamara Phillips Fudge, editor

Criminal justice is a many-layered field. It begins with policing, moves into the court system, and must take into consideration the effects on both victims and perpetrators. Some governments may use police or the courts to control political opponents, but the stated purpose of these organizations in the truly free world today is focused on keeping an area's populace safe from harm.

It is important to first note that policing and military activity have not always been separate factions. The French Gendarmerie, for example, dates back to the 1300s but by 1536, King François I designated civilian jurisdictions (NATO Stability Policing Centre, n.d.). "Policing" in the past also often included responsibilities that today are managed by other specialists; the Plymouth colony in the New World named Joshua Pratt its first constable in 1633, with the position including such tasks as maintaining the jail but also dealing with land claims and marriages (Scott & Cunningham, 1996).

While surely the concept of public control existed for many centuries, the London Metropolitan Police founded by Sir Robert Peel in 1829 is considered "the first modern police force and a model for other police forces around the world" (Honey, 2022, para. 2). Peel had noted that watchmen and "parochial police" (church-appointed watchmen) had some efficiency but were inconsistent from parish to parish; it was time for a formal, centralized, and uniformed force (Durston, 2012). Peel's Principles include maintaining order, reducing crime, being impartial, working to get the public's cooperation, and not to take the place of the court system (Williams, 2003). Officers were nicknamed "Bobbies" in deference to Peel's first name (Nix, 2025).

TOOLS

As would be expected by centuries of manifold cultural and technical changes, tools used by police have changed. Victorian era policing tools generally were lanterns, noise-makers such as whistles and ratchets, and physical restriction devices like handcuffs and leg irons (Bunce, 2022). Officers also regularly wielded wooden truncheons; these oft-decorated rods sometimes called batons, "Billy clubs," or night sticks could be as long as three feet to be able to handle crowds from horseback ("History and use," 2015) and by 1887, their use was typically directed towards arms and legs, with head-strikes only as a last attempt to subdue a suspect (Honey, 2022).

Today's systems employ far more lethal defensive weaponry, but also a cadre of technologies for maintaining order and safety, performing surveillance, and catching offenders. According to Wright (2019), police vehicles in the U.S. did not have radios until the late 1920s; today, they may be hybrid SUVs and have Kevlar-reinforced tires. Speed radar equipment, dash cams, laptops or tablets, GPS systems, and license-plate readers are among common features (Clarke, 2023), and officers often wear body cams.

OTHER FACETS TO CONSIDER

Criminal and civil infractions may require courtrooms with judges and juries, temporary housing for the accused and more long-term housing and rehabilitation for the convicted, plus assistance in various forms for victims. Prayatno et al. (2024) remind that technology must be used "in line with the principles of justice and human rights" (p. 1026).

Available technologies can strain budgets (Prayatno et al., 2024), but the question as to whether or not these various technologies always promote accuracy and timely resolutions in the courtroom must be answered (Lederer, 2023). The chronicling of cases has moved from handwritten court reporters' notes to real-time audio or video recordings of proceedings transcribed by additional technologies (Lederer, 2023). Biometrics like facial recognition may be entered into evidence (Bowers & Johnson, 2024). PowerPoint presentations may assist jurors in understanding situations, but technologies such as DNA evidence might simply be too complex for lay persons to fully comprehend (Rempel et al., 2019).

The Covid-19 pandemic taught the justice system that hearings can be held via the internet, often using Zoom. Lederer (2023) mentions the use of filters, choice of backgrounds, and the need for an adequate internet connection as points of contention. Zhuhao Wang (2025) uses the phrase "Zoom fatigue" to indicate that online proceedings can be troublesome for those with anxiety, neurodivergence, eyesight issues, or other accessibility limitations. There is also the fear of adverse publicity or depiction of video proceedings being treated as entertainment instead of a serious event in the life of human participants (Flower, 2025); care must be made to avoid allowing technology to affect outcomes. On a different note, Artificial Intelligence is suggested for courtroom simulations so that law school students may obtain experience (Rana et al., 2025).

Technology is not just a set of tools for crime detection, prevention, and indictments, of course: it presents the criminal with opportunities to *commit* crimes. Bowers and Johnson (2024) claim many types of wrongdoings may be blamed on Artificial Intelligence, such as deepfakes, phishing attacks, and the weaponization of driverless vehicles, and quantum computing might be used to compromise data or thwart encryption methods.

Croce (2025) embraces surveillance and security as benefits in correctional facilities, and meetings with lawyers, completion of educational programs, and virtual visits can be completed online, too. Maintenance is crucial to limit tech downtime in these facilities, as failures can affect the physical safety of those in the system (Croce, 2025).

Victims must not be forgotten. Online court may be helpful in ensuring physical safety and enhancing confidence in testifying, as it separates victims and witnesses from offenders (Flower, 2025). Televised court cases such as that of Johnny Depp v. Amber Heard have been said to make some domestic violence victims fear to come forward, however (Flower, 2025). De la Rue et al. (2023) list a lack of adequate resources, community, and partnerships as barriers for victims. Personal connections may be preferred by some, but there are online resources such as Victim Support Europe (n.d.), which is co-funded by the European Union; their website offers definitions, rights, protecting oneself, and other detailed directives and resources.

SIGNIFICANCE OF THIS BOOK

This volume thus addresses a wide variety of technical, legal, and ethical issues and demonstrates relevance to the system's many phases: prevention, protection, and policing, individuals' rights, gathering of evidence, courtroom issues, and lastly, movement into and out of the penal system. The layperson as well as students and professionals in technology, criminal justice, and law should be able to find content worthy of exploration, and it is hoped these ideas will spark dialogue and additional research into how these fields are interdependent – and crucial to the safety of all.

OVERVIEW OF CHAPTER CONTENT

The Evolution of Technology in the Criminal Justice System: Opportunities, Challenges, and Unintended Consequences

This chapter is an excellent way to begin this book's journey, as it starts with an historical overview of technology in the criminal justice system. This leads to exploration of the many challenges such as officer acceptance or resistance of these changes, operational barriers to use of new technologies, and the need for official oversight. In addition, there are concerns with the ethics related to tech use in monitoring and recording the populace, safeguarding collected data while still preserving privacy and the individual's civil liberties, the use of Artificial Intelligence and the power of predictive policing, and communication with the public to instill a level of trust.

Machine Learning for Smart Policing: Navigating Ethical, Legal, and Operational Realities in India

The evolution of policing in India may be represented as combination of mythological, archaeological, and historical accounts. Today's use of Artificial Intelligence and Machine Learning for prediction is described through case studies, and the need for human oversight, transparency, privacy, and other parameters must meet expected cultural values. Three technical points mentioned in this chapter are law enforcement databases transcribed from pre-computerized days, the need for human-language query capabilities, and the possibility of a variety of input such as facial recognition, text, and voice. Whether the technology should be assistive or a replacement is also explored, and ethical and legal dilemmas such as risk and accountability for both law enforcement and the court system included.

Virtually Solved: A Simulated Approach to Law Enforcement Problem Solving

Police officers encounter a myriad of volatile situations in which physical and emotional crises need quick but measured response. This chapter explains the benefits of using Virtual Reality for training, with hardware and software, adaptive environments, and other factors explored. De-escalation techniques can be acquired, and appropriate responses to mental health crises and neurodivergent encounters practiced. Training for interrogations is also possible. Biometric monitoring such as eye-tracking and heart rate is included as well as "stress inoculation training." Use of VR training provides rehearsals that also instill empathy, and through Artificial Intelligence provide useful feedback for real-life situations. That said, there are risks and other implications to study.

Digital Panopticons on Wheels: A Comparative Legal Analysis of Police Vehicle Tracking & Surveillance in India, West & South Asia

Global Positioning System (GPS) technology allows the tracking of vehicles as well as individuals, and while it only provides identity through location and movement, the data gathered might be used in a court of law. This chapter describes how the Mosaic Theory and the right to privacy as well as the proportionality principle may guide GPS use. The latter requires legal justification, specific purpose, reasoning, and necessity, and the authors divulge a "spectrum" of surveillance from warrants to authoritarian and emergency models. The lack of clearer guidance per law prompts recommendations that include specific rules for warrants, judicial oversight, data governance, and even incentives.

Digital Eyes: The Ethics of Modern Surveillance

Facial recognition and other individuals' biometrics such as fingerprints, gait, and DNA are the focus of this chapter. The sheer high numbers of police departments in large metropolitan areas using facial recognition software, for example, bring up both a social and technical problem, with great potential to negatively affect persons of color disproportionally. Consent is a continuing point of contention along with breaches and identify theft. In addition to CCTV, there is monitoring of people's digital footprint online. Artificial Intelligence can assist but there are biases to consider and characteristics such as tics that could be misinterpreted. The algorithmic biases and other ethical conundrums suggest that stronger frameworks are needed.

The Impact of Geofencing in Criminal Justice

Amber alerts and weather warnings are sent directly to smart phones within a specified perimeter called a "geofence." This kind of data is stored by companies such as Google. Law enforcement can use geofencing to warn the populace to stay away from an area where there is an active incident or to detect if a suspected criminal was indeed in proximity to a crime scene. The "geofence warrant" requesting data from non-governmental companies is a concern, as this will also pull data about persons who are not involved but happen to be nearby. This chapter explains more about how geofencing is set up as well as the problems encountered in using this technology.

Captured on Video: Methods, Case Studies, Laws, and Finding Justice

Between door cams affixed to front porches, nanny cams monitoring what is inside, workplace cameras, dash cams in vehicles and traffic cameras, drone footage, cell phone videos, officer body cams, and Closed-Circuit Television (CCTV), there are few places in the modern world which a person is not being watched. This chapter looks into specific cases where video (sometimes with audio) was used for evidence or allowed to record court proceedings. The kind of data collected includes both surroundings and people's biometrics, and both permissions and storage of collected data is a concern as is the "deepfake," with suggestions for law enforcement, the courts, and public education.

Eyes in the Sky: Balancing Public Safety and Privacy in the Drone Era

The use of drones in law enforcement is the crux of this chapter. These rather small devices are capable of entering areas that are deemed unsafe to humans and can provide a quick and wide view from above of emergencies, public events, criminal activity, or crime scenes for analysis. Initial setup may be somewhat costly but maintenance might be defended as cost-effective considering the benefits of drone use. Fears related to data management, undue trespassing, and data mismanagement are included. Types and classifications of drones and potential uses are clarified in detail, and the question as to where the line between safety and the public's civil liberties should fall is examined.

Regulating Automated Fraud: Addressing Cybersecurity Risks in the Digital Age

Artificial Intelligence increasingly is used to defraud, such as through false identity or impersonation of a real person or entity. Phishing via AI is growing at a significantly high rate in the last few years, and other incidents enabled by AI include deepfakes, ransomware, botnet farms, and other attacks. Automated fraud unfortunately works faster than detection. This chapter examines AI's use on both sides: it can be used to defraud and it can be used to detect fraud. There are digital vulnerabilities, social engineering issues, and a varying response in laws from country to country. Case studies, challenges, loopholes, and policy suggestions are surveyed, as is the culpability of technical platforms.

Tracing the Digital Trail: Modern Tools and Legal Complexities in Cybercrime Investigation

Cybercrime investigation is not an easy task; it is complicated and as this chapter indicates, requires collaboration between agencies. A brief history of cybercriminal investigation since the 1980s is outlined and today's tool limitations discussed. Cloud computing, cryptocurrency, and blockchain bring new challenges. Digital evidence is new enough that laws may not cover all instances clearly, and so there are potential issues with determining scope, serving warrants, and knowing how much evidential information is logical and legal to collect and then encrypt for safekeeping. Zero trust, data fragmentation, chain of custody, and other factors must also be considered to avoid inappropriate use of gathered digital evidence.

Digital Forensics in Financial Crime: Blockchain Analytics, Crypto Laundering, and Cross-Border Enforcement Challenges

Today's payment processors, cryptocurrency wallets and exchanges, non-fungible tokens (NFTs), and seemingly innocent "smart" contracts are increasingly subject to theft and money laundering; blockchain issues are also explained in detail in this chapter. Ransomware and other illicit operations can cost companies and their customers millions, and so analysis must include tracing the flows, evaluating system architectures, and working through several levels of complex technologies working from transaction to completed fraudulent activity. Frameworks for the law and companies in India are disclosed as well as enforcement issues when working across country borders. A strong recommendation for a shift from simple compliance to a more hands-on forensic approach is offered.

The Use of Artificial Intelligence to Improve Access to Justice

Information about the many parts of a country's justice system is not always easily obtained or understood; in addition to geographic isolation or the inability to travel, lack of funding, or even just absence of awareness, citizens and visitors alike may unknowingly run afoul of the law or suffer from not knowing legal facts related to their personal situations. A chatbot prototype is thus suggested in this chapter to provide answers to important questions about Namibian law. Ethics of such a venture, comparisons to mobile clinics and legal professionals, and a detailed explanation of each phase of development are provided along with some survey answers demonstrating effectiveness of the project.

Moving Faster than the Rules: Artificial Intelligence, Digital Evidence and the Limits of Evidentiary Standards

Evidentiary practices are uncovered in this chapter, with attention to inevitable conflict between innovation and need for fairness in the courts. While past eras relied on physical evidence (time-consuming to collect and analyze) and human testimonies (which can be fallible), Artificial Intelligence and other technologies have both made evidence-collection quick and unfortunately ethically complicated. Admissibility, electronic storage, the U.S. Federal Rule of Evidence 901, chain of custody, preservation and reliability of the evidence, and other factors are considered, as is the detection of synthetic-created content. Due process must be followed, and defendants must not have their rights violated; it is a balancing conundrum. A framework for structured integration provides a strong conclusion.

False Positives, Real Consequences: The Accuracy Crisis in Automated Criminal Accusations

Technology and automation are often an excellent method of analysis, but as this chapter reports, there can also be false positives such as accusations of fraud and criminal charges where there has not actually been any wrong-doing. These errors unfortunately cost individuals money, time, and reputation. The technology used might include racial or other biases and despite “predictive” tools, quite often fail to predict accurately. These issues are addressed in terms of technical design, laws that are not written to protect the falsely accused, and monetary benefits that result from sheer volume of accusations rather than accuracy. Michigan's MiDAS model, Deloitte's uFACTs, and other mechanisms are investigated.

Deepfake Forensics: Threats and Detection of AI-Manipulated Media

This chapter probes into the challenges of the audio-video “deepfake,” which is synthetic media made to look real by means such as Generative Adversarial Networks (GANs) and Diffusion Probabilistic Models. Included are how these are made, the typically non-consensual nature, and facets of technical detection that might or might not thwart misinformation delivery and malicious uses. Deepfake analysis may be artefact-based, statistical, or feature-based, and as the authors note, careful documentation of the tools used, parameters set, and researchers' reasoning is crucial if any conclusions are to be presented in the court room. Operational challenges, the “black box” problem and framework limitations, the legal chain of custody, jurors' perceptions, and evidentiary standards are also disclosed, with suggestions for future policies.

Punishment in a Digital Society: Tablet Use and Public Perception in Corrections

Correctional facilities are a unique situation within society. In this chapter, the tablet is recommended as a tool that can assist with rehabilitation. Unlike television, tablets are small and portable, and have manifold capabilities for education, reduction of isolation, management of behavior, and preparation to return to society along with lesser chance of re-offences. There is, however, a digital divide, as not all incarcerated individuals may have the same technological skills. The public's perception of the tablet is a problem, as tablets might be considered a "luxury," yet there are clear benefits to society. Policy implications, public awareness, and other factors such as restoring human dignity are conveyed.

Supporting the Community Reintegration of People Leaving Prison: Measuring Digital Skills as a Tool for Inclusion

This chapter provides an inside-the-walls look at how incarcerated men perceive digital literacy and the potential to gain skills that will be useful once they return to society. The Tech4PrisonLeavers project results are detailed and include both quantitative and qualitative responses plus use of voice diaries. Measurements of skill success are examined, as well as benefits such as likely changes in behavior, confidence levels, and goal-setting that can set offenders up for greater employment opportunities and far less chance to become repeat offenders. While the focus may have been on those in the prison systems, these programs may also be aimed towards other marginalized communities.

CONFLICT OF INTEREST AND REVIEW STATEMENT

Editorial board members independently handled the review process for chapters written or co-written by the editor to ensure that IGI Global's double-anonymized peer review was appropriately completed and not in any way compromised. Likewise, any chapters authored or co-authored by editorial board members were reviewed anonymously. In any instance where two reviewers' comments of a chapter were in opposition, a third reviewer was assigned to provide a logical consensus. Any peer reviews that were suspected of being written by Artificial Intelligence were removed from consideration to uphold ethical standards. Likewise, any work submitted that contained false sources or suspected AI-generated content were removed from consideration.

REFERENCES

Bowers, K., & Johnson, S. (2024, July/September). Facing the future of crime: A framework for police use of technology. *The Political Quarterly*, *95*(3), 480–488. DOI: 10.1111/1467-923X.13426

Bunce, E. C. (2022, May 2). *#MyrtleMondays: Victorian police equipment*. Elizabeth C. Bunce. https://elizabethcbunce.com/2022/05/02/myrtlemondays-victorian-police-equipment

Clarke, A. (2023, July 10). *The most overlooked feature in a police car*. CivicEye. https://www.civiceye.com/overlooked-feature-in-police-cars

Croce, J. (2025, Spring). Addressing and overcoming the top digital transformation challenges for correctional facilities. *Corrections Today*, *87*(1), 32–36.

De La Rue, L., Ortega, L., & Castro Rodriguez, G. (2023, January). System-based victim advocates identify resources and barriers to supporting crime victims. *International Review of Victimology*, *29*(1), 16–26. DOI: 10.1177/02697580221088340 PMID: 36644331

Durston, G. J. (2012). *Burglars and bobbies: Crime and policing in Victorian London*. Cambridge Scholars Publishing.

Flower, L. (2025). *The digital courtroom: Participation, attendance, engagement and consumption*. Taylor & Francis., DOI: 10.4324/9781003344643

History and use of the billy club. (2015, November 16). Police 1. https://www.police1.com/police-history/articles/history-and-use-of-the-billy-club-lCrwpOflpDTkHY2B

Honey, L. (2022, July 25). *Collecting police truncheons & tipstaves*. Homes and Antiques. https://www.homesandantiques.com/antiques/collecting-guides-antiques/experts/luke-honeys-cabinet-of-curiosities-truncheons-yipstaves

Lederer, F. I. (2023). Courtroom technology from the judge's perspective: A 2022-23 update. *Court Review*, *59*(2), 52–56.

NATO Stability Policing Centre of Excellence. (n.d.). *French Republic: Gendarmerie*. https://www.nspcoe.org/about-us/sponsoring-nations/french-republic/french-gendarmerie

Nix, E. (2025, May 27). *Why are British police officers called "Bobbies"?* History.com. https://www.history.com/articles/why-are-british-police-officers-called-bobbies

Prayatno, C., Tohari, M., & Susilowati, T. (2024, August). The impact of using technology and innovation in law enforcement in the era of digitalization. *Journal of Economics. Technology & Business*, *3*(8), 1026–1033.

Rana, P., Nagvekar, P., Agarwal, P., Savla, Y., Mishra, R., Gawade, A., & Rathod, N. (2025). AI courtroom: An AI-powered legal learning & trial prepbot. *Lex Localis: Journal of Local Self-Government*, *23*(S6), 1480–1503. DOI: 10.52152/801995

Rempel, E., Hamovitch, L., Zannella, L., & Burke, T. M. (2019, November). The power of technology: Examining the effects of digital visual evidence on jurors' processing of trial information. *Applied Cognitive Psychology*, *33*(6), 1288–1295. DOI: 10.1002/acp.3598

Scott, T., & Cunningham, C. (1996, Summer). *John Barnes of Plymouth.* The Plymouth Colony Archive Project. http://www.histarch.illinois.edu/plymouth/BARNES2.htm

Victim Support Europe. (n.d.). *Help for victims: Info for cross border victims.* https://victim-support.eu/help-for-victims/info-on-specific-types-of-victims/domestic-violence-victims

Williams, K. L. (2003, April). Peel's Principles and their acceptance by American police: Ending 175 years of reinvention. *The Police Journal*, *76*(2), 97–120. DOI: 10.1177/0032258X0307600202

Wright, I. (2019, October 8). *History of American police cars.* Car Buzz. https://carbuzz.com/features/history-of-american-police-cars

Zhuhao Wang, H. (2025). Asynchronous trials: A new approach to high-volume civil adjudication. *Denver Law Review*, *102*(3), 659–713.

Acknowledgements

SPECIAL THANKS

The editor gives thanks to each member of the board for their gracious help, which has been instrumental in ensuring the book's quality, and additionally to Dr. Holli Vah Seliskar for her expert assistance. She would also like to thank her family for putting up with the constant clacking of her keyboard in preparation for this volume. ~ Tamara Phillips Fudge

Chapter 1

The Evolution of Technology in the Criminal Justice System: Opportunities, Challenges, and Unintended Consequences

Holli Vah Seliskar
http://orcid.org/0009-0002-0411-0453
American College of Education, USA

Todd Isaacson
http://orcid.org/0009-0004-6373-5650
Purdue University Global, USA

Mary K. Lannon
Purdue University Global, USA

David Alan White
Purdue University Global, USA

ABSTRACT

Law enforcement administrators wanting to improve operational and administrative effectiveness and accountability, as well as public transparency, are pressing to implement advanced technologies across the discipline. Though technology advancement is inevitable, there are several ambiguities inherent in the implementation of new technologies relative to costs and advantages for the jurisdictions involved. Prior research demonstrates the value of acknowledging front line officers' opinions on innovations and how these perspectives must be factored into administrative policies and procedures. Administrators can address officer resistance, illustrating the boundless advantages for police officers if they embrace innovative technology. Examples of technological implementation in law enforcement agencies provide insights into successes and failures of enforcement decisions informing policy and practice recommendations about the future of policing.

DOI: 10.4018/979-8-3373-7660-8.ch001

INTRODUCTION

The criminal justice system in the United States has continued to evolve since the colonial times in the northeastern part of the United States. Post Colonial Policing was modeled after the London Metropolitan Police Service to address crime with urban development and growth. From early foot patrols with batons and call boxes on city corners, policing was scant and lacked the tools to safely confront dangerous individuals. In communities such as Jamestown, New York, policing started with the primary responsibility of fire surveillance (City of Jamestown, n.d.). The first officer killed in the line of duty in Jamestown, New York was Patrolman George Kendall, who died on June 18, 1915. Patrolman Kendall was an unarmed officer investigating a domestic incident and was confronted by Fred Shaver, who shot and killed the officer. Officer Kendall had no firearm, no radio, and no back up to adequately address the incident (City of Jamestown, n.d.). Over a century later, officers are better equipped to protect themselves and their communities with advances in tactics, weaponry, and technology (Moriarty, 2025).

Advancements in technology can be observed throughout communities in the United States, including the use of cameras and surveillance equipment. As an example, in 2015, few police departments had employed the use of body worn cameras (BWC); however, a series of high-profile police encounters that resulted in death precipitated the push for BWC (Bureau of Justice Assistance, 2025). Presently, BWC technology is commonly used within police departments. While not all police agencies have the technology, several states mandate its use. According to the National Conference of State Legislatures (2021):

> Eight states now mandate the statewide use of body-worn cameras by law enforcement officers. Those states are Colorado, Connecticut, Delaware, Illinois, Maryland, New Jersey, New Mexico and South Carolina…Prior to May 2020, South Carolina was the only state to require widespread adoption of body-worn cameras. The New Jersey and South Carolina laws make implementation of body-camera programs contingent on funding from the legislature. New Jersey appropriated funding in 2020. Before requiring statewide adoption, Colorado and Connecticut had grant programs dating back to 2015 to encourage adoption of body-worn cameras. Connecticut's 2020 law authorizes $4 million in bonds for a new grant program to fund related equipment and service purchases by municipalities. The grants can cover 30% to 50% of equipment costs as well as costs for digital storage for up to one year. The laws generally apply to all law enforcement officers who are interacting with the public. But they typically exclude officers working in courtrooms or other secure areas or confidential settings, nor do they apply to administrators or civilian staff. (para. 1)

While technology has made policing more efficient, it has also come at a significant cost to limited local budgets. For those states that do not mandate the use of BWC, the decisions to utilize the technology rest with the local law enforcement agencies. Many agencies simply are unable to afford the use of BWC and the recurring annual expenses for cloud data storage and maintenance (Maneke & Morasch, 2020). For example, Axon, a leading BWC company, charges $100 per BWC per month for cloud data storage, and for a small agency this can be problematic. Similarly, retention laws often require BWC video to be stored for a minimum of 90 days, with use of force incidents and serious investigations requiring long term storage (Bureau of Justice Assistance, 2025). This storage can be an untenable budget request in jurisdictions that have maximized their tax caps or lack the tax base to support this technology. While BWC technology has proven to be an effective tool for recording critical events in law enforcement, there are challenges associated with the number of work hours needed to process the BWC footage. This can in turn result in a reduction of availability for proactive policing and community engagement.

To highlight the lost proactive policing hours, officers utilizing BWC are required to upload, tag, and provide short narratives on incidents that were recorded during their shift (Bureau of Justice Assistance, 2025). Prior to the widespread use of BWC, officers could maintain a greater presence in the community to complete police reports, allowing for more proactive policing and community engagement. Legal requirements for securing video evidence from the BWC often requires officers to spend less time actively patrolling, sometimes up to 30 minutes prior to the end of shift. There are also significant financial burdens placed on both the offices of the prosecutors and defense attorneys due to the utilization of BWC, as they must manage the costs associated with reviewing, storing, and processing large volumes of video evidence (Bureau of Justice Assistance, 2025). This often necessitates the hiring of additional personnel in law enforcement agencies.

There are also considerations associated with requirements for timely processing of criminal cases in the courts. For example, New York State law requires processing within 14 days of an incident and prior to grand jury proceedings (New York State Senate, 2025). Thus, the increase in evidence created by BWC footage can result in the need for additional personnel in prosecutor offices. It has been argued that the current legal climate created by technology has become an advocate for criminals, rather than protecting the rights of victims (Meyers, 2023). Although the adoption of new technologies in law enforcement is both necessary and beneficial, it has also imposed significant financial obligations on law enforcement agencies, and the courts, often outpacing their available resources. If crime rates continue to increase, these technological costs will continue to escalate, presenting ongoing challenges for municipalities (Moriarty, 2025). While advances in technology have improved response times and overall effectiveness in policing, it is important to consider the unintended consequences associated with the increased reliance on technology.

ETIOLOGY AND EVOLUTION OF TECHNOLOGY IN POLICING

The past century has seen significant technological gains for law enforcement. Technology has continually influenced police work: from the beat patrol officer walking city streets through the use of new digital systems and less-lethal weapons. These changes have meant not only changes in operational procedures but also shifts in officer safety, public interactions, and the effectiveness of law enforcement agencies. In the early days of law enforcement, officers relied extensively on foot patrols – also known as beat patrols. These officers would walk assigned routes, maintain a visible presence, and report occurrences by way of call boxes or telephones placed throughout the city. The early efforts to manage community relations often suffered from slow stagnant communication and response times due to a lack of police vehicles. Two-way radios in the mid-20th century represent one of the earliest large-scale leaps in modern technology (Moriarty, 2025), enabling officers instant communication with dispatch and other officers, dramatically enhancing response efficiency and increasing interoperability. Cordner and Cordner (2025) defined interoperability as "the capacity of officers to communicate directly in the field, with other officers in their own departments, with officers or agents in different law enforcement agencies, and with fire and EMS personnel" (p. 36).

By the late 20th century, computers began to revolutionize law enforcement operations while improving efficiency and response times. Agencies turned to computerized databases for record-keeping, evidence management, booking, photo line ups, and crime analysis. These systems facilitated rapid information retrieval and sophisticated data analysis, which supported investigative work and strategic planning. Transitioning from white and green lined paper-based systems to digital platforms streamlined administrative tasks and enhanced the accuracy of police records management. The history in the field expanded into Mobile Data Terminals (MDTs) that were installed in patrol vehicles during the 1980s and 1990s. MDTs offered patrol officers real-time access to databases, dispatch information, and mapping tools. It enabled immediate background checks, warrant searches, vehicle registration checks, reducing radio traffic and increasing the effectiveness of operations in the field, and overall faster information dissemination. Thereafter, MDTs have evolved into rugged laptops and tablets, further enhancing mobile capability.

The weapons of law enforcement have also changed dramatically in the last few decades. In the early days of formalized policing, officers carried a "six shooter" revolver; fast forward to contemporary times, where officers are being issued Glock 19s with a magazine capacity of 17 rounds with extra magazines carried on officer duty belts or chest carriers. Firearms have become more reliable, accurate, and customizable, with innovations in materials and design enhancing officer safety and effectiveness. Agencies have also embraced more specialized weapons including long-range rifles and less-lethal options (Sheppard & Welsh, 2022). These advances have enabled officers to respond to a broader range of threats while reducing the risk that they pose to themselves and to the public.

Recent decades have seen a focus on less-lethal weapons, including tasers, bean bag rounds, and pepper spray. With this technology, police officers are offered options rather than lethal force, which is always safer (Moriarty, 2025). These developments underpin transparency, accountability, and situational awareness and are indicative of the shifting policing terrain in the digital age. Technological changes in policing are a double-edged sword, with both positive and negative implications. August Vollmer, known as the "father of modern policing" (Go, 2020, p. 1199), was concerned about the speed at which his officers at the Berkeley Police Department, California (BPD), could respond to calls. By 1910, each of the 25 officers was assigned a bicycle to respond to calls (Go, 2020). Four years later, Vollmer persuaded the Berkeley City Council to purchase vehicles for the department, not one for every officer as requested, but instead only a few were issued to the department.

The vehicles were not without their distractors, both internally and externally. According to Oliver (2017), Patrolman Richard Dowling stated: "Everybody will say the cops are trying to imitate millionaires" (p. 259). Externally, the citizens of Berkley and the local newspapers called the BPD "limousine police" (Oliver, 2017, p. 260). By the end of 1914, Vollmer had "created the first totally mobile patrol force in the country" (Oliver, 2017, p. 260); a trend that would expand across the country. Even as the use of automobiles spread across the country and ultimately the world, concerns persisted. O. W. Wilson, who was described by Kelling and Coles (1998) as "the dominant police theorist of the twentieth century" (p. 75), stated: "the automobile is undoubtedly the most effective and economical type of patrol when operated conspicuously by one man using superior patrol methods" (Wilson, 1950, p. 98). While this sounds like a ringing endorsement of the automobile, Wilson (1950) did list several negatives to the use of automobiles, including, but not limited to: less contact with citizens, thus neglecting public service; making inspections (such as checking doors) and making observations in general (which is difficult to do when driving). Even though the automobile was the most effective type of patrol, it still had its distractions, the double-edged sword. In the late 20th century, law enforcement agencies revisited and embraced August Vollmer's original approach to transportation by reintroducing the bicycle for patrol duties. This allowed officers to be more present and accessible within the neighborhoods they served. As a result, police departments experienced increased community interactions, fostering stronger relationships and improved communication between officers and the public.

While the automobile certainly impacted policing and advanced the capabilities of the police force, the mobile telephone has been one of the most important technological advancements in policing (Cordner & Cordner, 2025). Mobile phones provide officers with the ability to call, text, send longer messages, share their phone numbers with citizens, and provide instantaneous communication with other officers, dispatchers, supervisors, and citizens, arguably fostering greater relationships with the public and improving the services provided by law enforcement in their local communities (Cordner & Cordner, 2025). Though there are considerable advantages to these advancements in technology, there are still barriers impacting smaller and more rural law enforcement agencies who may not have access or the bandwidth to provide officers with the full extent and usefulness of these advancements. Today, those in public safety rely heavily on technology, particularly mobile phones, for everyday communication, but this reliance can come at a high cost during emergencies. During natural disasters like hurricanes and earthquakes, vital communication infrastructure—such as cell towers—can sustain serious damage. When these towers are affected, communication networks might be interrupted or become entirely unavailable. This vulnerability is not limited to cell phones alone. Mobile data terminals (MDTs), which also rely on cell towers, face the same risks. If the cell towers are damaged, MDTs could lose connectivity, further hindering emergency response efforts.

The technological evolution of policing over the past century highlights a reflective transformation from early foot patrols that were dependent on rudimentary communication equipment to patrol vehicles equipped with modern digital interface programs with limitless connectivity. While technology has impacted the adaptability and effectiveness of policing in the complex and changing world, its unburdened potential hinges on the equitable access, implementation, and overarching tenants of ethical application to ensure public trust and legitimacy of law enforcement. Thus, even with the tremendous leaps in policing technology, each has its own positive and negative implications.

POSITIVE AND NEGATIVE IMPLICATIONS OF TECHNOLOGY IN LAW ENFORCEMENT

Policing with new technology has challenges, but police administrators who adopt new technology cite significant operational benefits, including improved interactions between citizens and officers (Cordner & Cordner, 2025; Jennings et al., 2015). Additional benefits of BWC for law enforcement officers include increased transparency, faster resolution of complaints against officers, a reduction in violent incidents, providing evidence in court, and immeasurable training scenarios that result in improved officer and citizen interactions, as well as fosters self-evaluation and reflection by officers (Paoline et al., 2025). Implementing digital reporting systems and data analytics platforms simplifies administrative processes, lowers paperwork, and allows for more strategic distribution of resources (Bureau of Justice Assistance, 2018). Case management and evidence tracking tools automate processes and increase the efficiency of workflow, allowing agencies to operate with a reduced number of personnel than would be the case in a manual model (Lum et al., 2016).

BWC and GPS tracking systems have been shown to increase transparency and accountability, both internally and in interactions with the public (Paoline et al., 2025). Such improvements have been observed in local police department administrators who use captured videos from BWC to investigate citizen complaints against officers; this includes enhanced community relations and results in fewer complaints against officers (Miller & Toliver, 2014; White, 2014). For example, the Jamestown (NY)

Police Department administration would accept citizen complaints under penalty of perjury, and if the complainant citizen lacked candor, they would be charged with a Class A Misdemeanor of Filing a False Complaint. One of the authors who was a police administrator at this mid-size police agency reports that this course of action eliminated countless false complaints by over 50%, alleviating limited resources from investigating false reports.

The literature shows that technology can provide a mechanism for rebuilding public trust, after numerous well-publicized encounters involving police use of force have resulted in decreased levels of trust among the public (Skogan, 2017). While the majority of officers in studies believe BWC will not decrease their safety (>60%), only a small percentage (<20%) believe that BWC makes them feel safer (Jennings et al., 2014). Affirming findings were reported by Harris (2010) noting that technology could help reduce complaints and use of force encounters. For instance, the Rialto Assessment determined that a decrease of 88% in citizen complaints against the police after the introduction of the body-worn camera system was reported, as compared to the 2011 timeframe of 24 complaints after BWC (Ariel et al., 2015). Ariel et al. (2015) found police officer use of force declined by 60%, from 61 incidents to a mere 25 incidents. The evidence also found that shifts without BWC experienced double the number of use of force incidents as shifts with BWC (Ariel et al., 2015). All officer use of force incidents reported with deployed cameras were in a manner to indicate that force was initiated by the offender.

Although adopting new technologies in law enforcement is both necessary and beneficial, it has also imposed significant financial obligations on local governments, often exceeding their available resources. As crime rates increase, these costs continue to escalate, presenting ongoing challenges for municipalities. Law enforcement agencies across all levels of government are stretching limited budgets to acquire needed technologies with the goal of enhancing agency effectiveness and efficiency. The importance of technology in policing cannot be underscored and is growing rapidly as more efficiency, transparency, accountability, and responsiveness to community needs are mandated. BWC, cell phones, MDTs, GPS systems, and other technologies, coupled with sophisticated data analysis technology, have incredible power to change the game for law enforcement.

While there are distinct advantages to advancements in technology, there are also several issues. An issue that is seldom mentioned is that police unions must be included in negotiations regarding the implementation of new technology. According to the newly appointed chief of police for the Ludlow (MA) Police Department, Mike Brennan, "I think we have to develop the program first and put something on paper and negotiate with our unions, both patrol and supervisors" (Munson, 2026, p. 11). These collective bargaining negotiations would be required because it "would be a change in working conditions for the LPD since we don't have a body worn camera program" according to Brennan (Munson, 2026, p. 1). The use of technology in policing is not a novel and untested idea, but recent decades have witnessed a surge in both the variety and sophistication of available tools, with unprecedented costs. Lum et al. (2016), argued the reliance on technology tools such as BWC, automated license plate readers, and predictive analytics has been common but uneven across jurisdictions. The irregular implementation of technology across law enforcement jurisdictions is largely due to limited budgets.

Law enforcement jurisdictions must realize that increasing effectiveness and efficiency are not a zero-sum trade-off, and costs must be considered as new technology is implemented within the criminal justice system. Studies show that a number of law enforcement organizations have implemented innovative and new technology and that others have not, often due to structural and contextual factors, budgetary constraints, as well as differing leadership models in policing (Lum et al., 2019; Prayatno et al., 2024). Rogers' diffusion of innovations theory (2003) is an applicable theory for examining the adoption process within police organizations. According to the diffusion of innovations theory, organizational culture and leadership behavior, together with the perceived advantage of deploying technology, it influences the rate of technology diffusion. As a result, the literature also notes that technological solutions should be tailored to operational requirements and community expectations (Lum et al., 2010). This theory can be applied to small and mid-size police departments that went with a cheaper BWC system of safety vision with an internal server to upload the video data. Albeit expensive for mid-size and small agencies with limited budgets, it is a considerable savings from the current BWC system now deployed that incur annual data storage expenses that were not budget items prior to the BWC era.

One of the biggest hurdles to implementing technology in policing are budgetary constraints, and the cost of acquiring, deploying, and maintaining new systems (Prayatno et al., 2024). As described by Lum et al. (2016), budgets are often constrained, pushing agencies to prioritize the short-term operational demands over long-term technology purchases. In such cases the initial investments in hardware, software, and infrastructure are often too high, especially for smaller agencies with fewer discretionary funds (Maneke & Morasch, 2020; Miller & Toliver, 2014). Regardless of agency size, the financial burden with technology is realized with the assignment of personnel for training, data storage, managing Freedom of Information Act (FIOA) requests, and the administration of the program superseding the implementation of new technology at times.

Regardless of agency size, the financial burden with technology is realized with the assignment of personnel for training, recurring data storage costs, managing Freedom of Information Act requests, administration of the program, system upgrades and technical support (Maneke & Morasch, 2020). To alleviate some of the financial burdens, federal and/or state-funded grants can be secured, but these sources of assistance remain relatively competitive and insufficient to meet the full spectrum of expenses (Reaves, 2015). The literature further posits that problems related to resources cannot become isolated, as administrators must weigh technology investments with personnel and other essential expenses that support the community (Bureau of Justice Assistance, 2018). Police administrators and politicians argue that BWC, and other technology can save agencies money through increased professionalism that will translate into fewer confrontations, use of force encounters, and mitigating spurious lawsuits and officer complaints (Miller & Toliver, 2014). Typically, monetary judgments against officers will be taken from limited police operating budgets and from needed equipment and training programs. While this argument may have merit, the challenge is finding discretionary finances for a successful cost-benefit result. Lum and Isaac (2016) posited that "using technology can sometimes reduce efficiency and may not help achieve outcomes such as prevention or reduction of crime or the improvement of citizen trust, confidence, and satisfaction with the police" (p. 2). Ultimately, technology can prove invaluable and has the ability to transform policing for decades to come. Administrators must carefully ensure that implementation of any new technology is done with the paradigm of helping officers protect the communities they serve.

Officer Buy-In

For department initiatives to be successful, there needs to be community support, but also police officer support and buy-in. Securing internal support can be challenging, but necessary to ensure the legitimacy of the initiatives. Much resistance to these enhanced accountability mechanisms is based on concerns that they may increase officer and staff workload, limit discretion, or come with the threat of disciplinary action (Lum et al., 2019). Police culture, which is influenced by traditional practice, can create skepticism toward change, and a preference for the status quo. These cultural factors cause resistance to new tools, including technology (Lum & Isaac, 2016). Such surveillance-focused tools may also be perceived by officers as a challenge to their autonomy and an extra layer of oversight (White, 2014). Perception on technology also varied across the police ranks with commanding officers favoring technology for enhanced efficiency and productivity, whereas frontline officers viewed it as extra work and a form of "monitoring" them (Lum & Isaac, 2016). Ready and Young (2015) found that officers utilizing a BWC had heightened anxiety that supervisors would use the captured BWC videos to monitor officers.

To alleviate officer concerns, introducing new technology to officers should be done in a transparent manner with strategies that are framed as "real police work," and should highlight how it will benefit them. This approach was used at Jamestown (NY) Police Department with the introduction of BWC when police administrators established "buy in" for the program to the police union officials and how the initiative would protect officers from frivolous complaints. This "team" presentation of police administrators and union officials was a win-win, and the officers were eager to pilot the program in the county. When officers view the adoption of technology as beneficial to them, they will have then bought into the initiative (Gaub et al., 2016). To this end, the literature highlights the need for leadership involvement and participatory change management methods in order to respond to cultural factors that drive organizations (Sanders & Henderson, 2013). Ultimately, leadership in law enforcement must navigate between technology adoption and continuous advancement amidst a lack of resources, possible shortages of staffing, training of officers, privacy issues, and security concerns (Prayatno et al., 2024). While technology provides limitless potential for transparency and accountability, successful deployment requires administrators to balance the interests with both officers and the communities they serve and protect.

CHALLENGES AND ETHICAL CONSIDERATIONS OF TECHNOLOGY ADOPTION

The increased use of emerging technology in law enforcement has numerous benefits, including enhanced accountability of police officers, which can lead to an increase in public trust and confidence in policing. There are also concerns associated with the privacy rights of citizens, which must be balanced with the objectives of law enforcement. It is necessary to appropriately manage the role of technology in law enforcement, particularly given its near limitless potential and application (Cochran, 2025). It is also necessary to consider the role of human decision-making and interaction in law enforcement (Vizzini, 2022). Consideration must also be given to the long-term implications of the increasing use of technology in the pursuit of justice. The increased use of technology in law enforcement has led to public concerns about privacy and rights as citizens (Vizzini, 2022). These concerns can lead to decreased public trust in law enforcement. As such, it is important to consider the impact of technology on human interaction in law enforcement, as well as whether this creates an unintended divide between the public and law enforcement agencies (Vizzini, 2022). Recent research found that 81% of Americans are concerned about how their data are collected and used by organizations, and 71% are concerned about how their data are used by the government (Cochran, 2025). In addition, 61% of Americans do not fully understand how their data is used by organizations, and 71% have little or no understanding of how their data are used by government agencies (Cochran, 2025). Understanding privacy and balancing this with the efforts by government agencies, such as security, law enforcement, and justice has been and continues to be a continual issue facing government and law enforcement agencies. The Katz test, resulting from a 1967 Supreme Court decision, holds that an individual has a reasonable expectation of privacy if two conditions are met: first, that "the person has established an actual (subjective) expectation of privacy," and second, that "the expectation is one that society is willing to recognize as reasonable" (Cochran, 2025, p. 5).

> The [Katz] test, the Court propounded in *Katz v. United States*, examined the expectation of privacy upon which one may justifiably rely. The Court stated: What a person knowingly exposes to the public, even in his own home or office, is not a subject of Fourth Amendment protection. But what he seeks to preserve as private, even in an area accessible to the public, may be constitutionally protected. That is, the capacity to claim the protection of the Amendment depends not upon a property right in the invaded place but upon whether the area was one in which there was reasonable expectation of freedom from governmental intrusion. (Constitution Annotated, n.d., para. 3)

The more law enforcement agencies utilize technology, the less likely they are to obtain information from individuals. For example, the use of online reporting or surveillance camera footage can produce information quickly and help to effectively manage personnel and manpower. However, this also results in decreased human interaction between police officers and the public (Vizzini, 2022). Law enforcement agencies adopting increased technology to improve effectiveness and efficiency must also take steps to avoid the potential for increased disconnectedness with the community, which can erode public trust (Vizzini, 2022).

Vizzini (2022) surveyed law enforcement officers and members of the public in Florida to explore perceptions associated with law enforcement's utilization of technology and its effects on the communities they serve, particularly as related to human interaction and any potential effects. Results from law enforcement officers indicated a perceived value in police technology. Participants reported that technology is beneficial, frequent, and could increase community service (Vizzini, 2022). Results also indicated that police technology aids law enforcement efforts in preventing and solving crime. Law enforcement participants reported a concern that citizens do not understand the importance of technology, and that the community should be educated about the use of technology by law enforcement and its importance (Vizzini, 2022).

Participants from the community reported a belief that the use of technology by law enforcement benefits their communities, enhancing police performance and ability to solve crimes. Community participants also indicated that the use of technology has not harmed the community or resulted in mistrust with law enforcement (Vizzini, 2022). These results indicated that the use of technology by law enforcement is accepted and understood, although results also indicated benefit in educating the community and providing demonstrations of the technology used (Vizzini, 2022).

Vizzini (2022) concluded that the use of technology improves the ability of law enforcement officers to serve their communities. As the use of technology increases, human interaction can decrease, which can in turn create a wedge between law enforcement and the community. It appears, however, that public trust remains intact. It is recommended that communities be educated on the use of technology by law enforcement as a means of maintaining a relationship of trust with members of the community (Vizzini, 2022). Efforts should be made to demonstrate what technology is used and how this use can be of benefit to the community. Providing visual demonstrations can help to reinforce communication and interaction between law enforcement and the community, while ensuring that the community fully understands how law enforcement is utilizing technology. This approach to transparency can provide law enforcement with greater community support for obtaining and implementing technology (Vizzini, 2022).

Concerns with Monitoring and Recording of Data

The public perception of law enforcement impacts confidence and trust. Citizens are more likely to trust the use of technology by law enforcement when they believe that these efforts are truly designed to protect the community (Vizzini, 2022). As such, it is important that police agencies are clear and transparent in communicating the use, purpose, and scope of technology to citizens. Many citizens are skeptical of being monitored or recorded by BWC, facial recognition programs, drones, license plate readers (LPRs), and similar technologies. Even when these technologies are being used to detect and apprehend those who violate the law and to protect the community, they will also capture the personal, and potentially private, activities of innocent people (Vizzini, 2022). For example, drones fly above private property and record all activity in a given area, including those activities by individuals not involved in the legitimate law enforcement activity. Similarly, LPRs record license plates passing by specific locations, and store all vehicle location data (Cordner & Cordner, 2025). However, the number and proximity of these LPRs throughout a city or community can provide law enforcement agencies with enough information to know when and where vehicles travel. Again, this impacts not only those who have violated the law, but also innocent civilians moving about their daily lives, further exacerbating issues with privacy and civil liberty concerns. Many law enforcement agencies utilize LPRs without the knowledge of the public. This is further complicated by a lack of knowledge on the part of the public as to the extent of the information or data saved by law enforcement agencies and the length of time that information is stored (Vizzini, 2022).

License plate recognition (LPR) systems are widely used to monitor vehicular movement. These systems do not discriminate between individuals, meaning they record the travel patterns of all citizens, regardless of their activities. In some states, such as Washington, images and data captured by LPR systems are not only stored but also classified as public records. This designation means that the information collected—including images of vehicles and license plates—can be accessed by the public under state open records laws (Silver, 2025). The data collected in Washington was deemed to be a public record through a recent court case and because of this the Skamania (WA) County Sheriff's Office disabled their six LPRs (Silver, 2025).

The legal classification of data collected by private companies for municipal use has become increasingly relevant. A recent court decision from Washington State clarified the status of such data under public records laws. In the case of the City of Derdo-Woolley and City of Stanwood, Washington Municipal Corporations v. Jose Rodriguez, the Skagit County Superior Court examined the nature of images gathered and retained by Flock (the company that stored the data) cameras. These cameras are operated by a private company that stores data on its own servers on behalf of municipalities. The Skagit County Superior Court ultimately determined that the images collected and kept by Flock cameras were considered public records. According to Lipton (2025), this decision stated that data held by private entities, when used for municipal purposes, is subject to public records disclosure requirements. Similar concerns arise associated with the use of facial recognition technology. A 2022 poll conducted by the Pew Research Center found that 46% of respondents felt that the use of facial recognition software by law enforcement was a "good idea" for society, while 27% felt that it was a "bad idea," and 27% were unsure (Cochran, 2025). In addition, 70% of respondents felt that a positive match by facial recognition software was not sufficient justification for an arrest, particularly if there was the potential for a match that was a false positive (Cochran, 2025). The fact that there are insufficient laws governing law enforcement use of facial recognition software increases the concerns of the public associated with privacy and tracking, particularly given the large-scale surveillance made possible by this technology. In fact, some companies that manufacture these types of technology refuse to sell the software to law enforcement agencies (Vizzini, 2022). Importantly, several states and some local communities in the United States have prohibited or severely restricted the use of facial recognition software due to privacy issues, security concerns, potential biases, and concerns about error rates based on the software (Cordner & Cordner, 2025). Thus, if the public perceives that the technological capabilities of law enforcement are too broad, too loosely governed by law, and not sufficiently communicated to the public, the result will be a decrease in public trust and confidence in law enforcement and a greater divide between law enforcement and the public it serves. As such, there is a continued need to improve the perceived level of trust and transparency regarding the use of facial recognition software (Cochran, 2025).

There are also concerns associated with trade secrets held by corporations who own and operate artificial intelligence (AI) software, including facial recognition technology (Cochran, 2025; Vickers, 2024). In many jurisdictions, the law does not require criminal prosecutors to disclose the use of AI to courts or defense attorneys (Vickers, 2024). Concerns associated with its use are compounded by a lack of transparency from software companies as to how these tools work and when they are utilized. Facial recognition technology has been demonstrated as prone to bias, such as misidentifying individuals of different races (Vickers, 2024). For example, research has found concerning failure rates when facial recognition AI handles images of Black Americans, particularly Black women, by either failing to identify an individual or making a false match (Vickers, 2024). These concerns can impact whether an individual believes they are receiving a fair trial, particularly when evidence brought against them is from a machine protected by trade secrets (Vickers, 2024). As a result, many law enforcement agencies utilize facial recognition software as a lead to be followed up, rather than as evidence itself. Supporting evidence can still lead to an arrest and indictment, however, and in many cases, there is no requirement to disclose the use of AI in obtaining that evidence (Vickers, 2024). While many have called for greater transparency and measures to specify how and when these technologies are used (Cochran, 2025), doing so remains a significant challenge while the software remains protected by trade secrets, making it nearly impossible for officials to confirm whether the tools are reliable or unbiased (Vickers, 2024). This issue of reliability raises concerns regarding the Daubert Standard, which is:

> The standard that changed the admissibility criteria set forth in *Frye* was the 1993 decision in *Daubert v. Merrell Dow Pharmaceuticals, Inc.*, 509 U.S. 579; 113 S. Ct. 2786 (1993). In this landmark decision, the U.S. Supreme Court established a new standard by determining that the Federal Rules of Evidence assign the trial judge the role of gatekeeper, which allows the judge broad discretion in determining the admissibility of all scientific evidence into the courtroom.

The judge, as gatekeeper, may rule to admit expert testimony that rests on a reliable foundation and is relevant to the inquiry at hand by considering such factors as whether:

- The subject of testimony is falsifiable or testable.
- The testimony is derived from techniques with known error rates.
- The testimony has been subjected to peer review, and whether the testimony is generally accepted in the relevant scientific community. (National Institute of Justice, 2023, para. 1-2)

In 2020, the Americans Civil Liberties Union (ACLU) sued Clearview AI in Illinois, claiming that Clearview had violated state privacy laws by scraping billions of faceprints from images of individuals available online (ACLU, 2022). Clearview was accused of building a secretive surveillance and tracking tool which was then offered to law enforcement agencies at local, state, and federal levels, as well as private companies and wealthy individuals. The lawsuit underscored the potential harm associated with the collection of biometric data from individuals without their knowledge or consent. As a result of the lawsuit and subsequent settlement in 2022, Clearview was prohibited from making its faceprint data available to many businesses and private entities nationwide. In Illinois, Clearview was prohibited from selling access to its database to any entity for five years, including state and local law enforcement agencies (ACLU, 2022). Additional challenges associated with the use of AI were recently underscored during a criminal court case, in which a judge excluded facial recognition evidence in a murder trial (Daniel, 2025). With no immediate leads, investigators utilized facial recognition software to identify a suspect from surveillance video. This software was used to obtain a search warrant, during which investigators found a firearm and other evidence against the suspect. That said, prior to trial it was determined that investigators have not independently corroborated the suspect's identity prior to executing the warrant. Furthermore, investigators have not disclosed the use of facial recognition software in court documents (Daniel, 2025). Defense attorneys filed a motion to suppress the evidence obtained through the search warrant, and the judge ruled in favor of the defense, stating that the warrant was issued without sufficient probable cause. Without the evidence obtained through the search warrant, including the firearm, prosecutors have admitted it will be difficult to bring a successful prosecution or secure a conviction (Daniel, 2025). This case highlights the increasing challenges associated with the use of facial recognition software. While law enforcement and investigators argue that the software aids in expediting investigations, there are concerns associated with an overreliance on these AI tools, which can in turn lead to inaccurate identifications, lack of due process, and even wrongful convictions (Daniel, 2025).

Artificial Intelligence and Predictive Policing

Artificial Intelligence (AI) has evolved as a powerful tool with predictive policing strategies. AI enables criminal justice agencies to instantly analyze data fields to include criminal histories, geospatial information, environmental, and socioeconomic factors using machine learning algorithms that provide forecasting models of crime locations, hot-spots, times, and patterns. This new proactive approach shifts reactive response to proactive prevention, allowing for a more efficient use of limited resources (U.S. Department of Justice (USDOJ), 2024). This new capability is another technological force multiplier that can replace a team of crime analysts while freeing up additional personnel costs of salaries and benefits.

Data on the benefits of AI predictive policing models are limited due to the continued unveiling of this new technology. There are some modest benefits in the early deployment of AI predictive policing that have resulted in local reductions in targeted offenses with minor causal links to broad crime decline due to quality of data inputs and external variables (USDOJ, 2024). Some notable successes have been realized when AI is supplemented with human judgement, accentuating AI's value as a support tool rather than a standalone prevention measure (Storbeck, 2022).

Not forgoing the benefits of the use of AI tools, there are significant risks that include the use of algorithms, which focus on criminal histories and arrest data that reflect longstanding patrol strategies that focus on high-crime areas of vulnerable, low-income, and minority communities (USDOJ, 2024). When enlisting the use of AI, the mindset of the programmer is only as good as the data being input into these tools and should be the overarching paradigm when reviewing the AI produced data. Failure to consider the input of data in AI tools and the output is a frequent criticism of predictive policing for it can "amplify biases embedded in historical crime data" (USDOJ, 2024, p. 47). This type of AI predictive policing can create feedback loops, wherein policing AI hot spots target certain races and areas, further creating the impression of higher crime rates in those targeted areas, which furthers the justification of continued targeted patrols in an endless loop.

To ensure the ethical application of AI predictive policing, agencies should work with community stakeholders and relevant community organizations to align AI models to address specific community needs and expectations (USDOJ, 2024). Failure to work collectively and engage the community with the implementation of AI predictive policing models can undermine public confidence in the agency and the community at large. Similarly, police agencies should ensure that they have the resources and technical expertise necessary to employ and monitor the long-term application of predictive policing tools.

Successes and Obstacles of Using Drones

To highlight the value of embracing advancing technology, drones provide an array of mission capabilities essential for public safety agencies to increase situational awareness, improve response times, and reduce risk to personnel. Public safety agencies use drones for search and rescue, disaster response, and crime scene investigations, among other missions. Drones can cover vast areas quickly, take high-resolution images, provide live video feeds to public safety officials, and allow responders to make informed decisions without exposing themselves to potential hazards (International Association of Chiefs of Police (IACP), 2012).

The application of drones makes them a force multiplier for public safety agencies by providing extended capabilities for functions that only require limited manpower and resources (IACP, 2012). Drones allow one operator to survey a wide range of territories, track suspects, and assess dangerous situations, essentially boosting the agency's capacity and impact. Drone aerial surveillance provides real-time data during natural and manmade disasters while providing command centers with better coordination and allocation of resources.

Despite the advantages of using drones, there are significant obstacles that public safety agencies face when implementing drone, unmanned aircraft system (UAS) units within their agencies, to include complex federal regulations. Agencies must navigate the maze of federal, state, and local laws, including the Federal Aviation Administration (FAA) guidelines for unmanned aerial systems (FAA, 2026). These regulations typically necessitate that agencies secure special waivers, pilot certifications- Part 107 certification, and compliance with airspace restrictions.

> The FAA offers law enforcement agencies two options for operating UAS under 55 pounds: Operating under the small UAS rule. This rule, also called the *Part 107* rule (named after 14 C.F.R. part 107) allows entities, including law enforcement agencies, to operate UAS at or below 400 feet above ground level in operations that have "visual line of sight" of the aircraft. Receiving a certificate of authorization (COA) to function as a *public aircraft operator*. Law enforcement agencies that receive the COA are able to self-certify drone pilots to carry out official law enforcement operations. The FAA can also issue emergency authorizations to entities operating under the Part 107 rule or with a COA, allowing them to carry out specified law enforcement operations under certain conditions. An emergency authorization can include a *tactical beyond visual line of sight* waiver; while drone operators are normally required to have a visual line of sight of the aircraft, the FAA can grant an authority for law enforcement officers to operate outside of these parameters in emergency situations. (Finklea, 2023, para. 6)

Determination of such a bureaucratic process can cause delays of the deployment of drone units, causing agencies to struggle with responding quickly to new operational needs of their community (IACP, 2012).

The limitation of funding is also a major barrier for law enforcement entities to launch drone programs that start at $15,000.00. These include the outlay for purchasing a drone (and the related hardware), software for the drone, cameras, and staff for training. Aside from upfront costs, agencies need to include a budget for keeping up with maintenance, software updates, and possible insurance expenses. Agencies can already be facing budgetary constraints and may experience difficulties in justifying resources for drone units, especially as other critical public safety requirements can be at stake. For example, a mid-size police agency in Western New York sought to develop a drone unit and tasked a police captain who possessed FAA Commercial Pilot Certification to develop the program. The first step employed was to research the mission appropriate drone with capabilities that addressed the agency needs. The second step was developing a policy that would align with agency requirements. The final step to implement was selecting drone team members who were required to complete online training to secure the Part 107 Drone Operator FAA Certification.

Research and policy development can be time consuming for administrators, but lessons learned in policy development and public safety sharing networks provided many time saving shortcuts for the mid-size agency to include the IACP's policy resources. The IACP provided examples of many new drone unit policies from around the United States and templates that aligned nicely with the mid-size police agency size, community, and topography. Similarly, contact was made with a mid-size police agency administrator in a nearby state who shared policy and FAA Day Waiver procedures that facilitated a faster FAA certification for the New York drone unit. These two law enforcement departments sharing information related to drone implementation was an example of not "reinventing the wheel" and "working smarter, not harder." While challenges exist with implementing new technology, working as a collective public safety force can save valuable time and funding.

Another concern that is often encountered is that of community perception. Public perception and privacy issues can create barriers to deploying technology in law enforcement via drones (Cordner & Cordner, 2025). Concerns of increased surveillance and the potential abuse of drones to harass the public often have been discussed. Agencies must address the fears of their community by defining policies that are transparent and clear, while engaging with the community on how drones will be used. Breaking any public discontent will take a lot of communication and reassurances of citizen rights while ensuring privacy is respected with drone missions (Chen & Huang, 2021). Lastly, technical barriers can also be imposed on the deployment of drones that may present in the form of technical impediments, such as the need for data control, cybersecurity, system integration, and security challenges. Law enforcement agencies need to be assured that such drone-captured data is kept secure, accurately analyzed, with secure storage, analysis, and protection against unauthorized access or cyber threats. Much of the data concerns mirror those realized with the implementation of BWC and can be navigated using the many tools provided by the IACP and public safety partners.

FUTURE IMPLICATIONS AND RECOMMENDATIONS

The campaign for enhanced and new technologies in law enforcement presents an array of significant challenges for both operational efficiency and public trust. Emerging technology like the use of BWC, next-generation analytics, drones, artificial intelligence tools, predictive policing, and unmanned aerial systems (UAV) has the potential to increase transparency, enhance evidence collection, improve community trust in the police, and simplify investigations (Dempsey et al., 2023). There are several administrative and operational advancements that artificial intelligence can provide for law enforcement, including the automation of BWC footage, transcription of police interviews and interrogations, and the automation of surveillance footage (Cordner & Cordner, 2025). These advances, however, involve substantial financial considerations beyond the initial purchase. Agencies must assess the cost benefit ratio while factoring long term recurring costs and potential funding sources, to include public-private partnerships and grants to alleviate financial restrictions (Lum et al., 2016).

Despite the potential benefits of technology, police officers often resist technology change due to privacy issues, increased oversight, and changes in policing protocol (Ready & Young, 2015). This sort of resistance can hinder the successful introduction of new tools and systems. To mitigate officer anxiety, an array of change-management strategies must be in place, such as comprehensive training programs, communicating the benefits of the technology and putting officers in the driver's seat of decision-making processes. New developments in technology have the potential to improve overall efficiency and reduce time and expenses related to law enforcement training, by incorporating advancements that other fields have successfully utilized, such as through simulation training, Virtual Reality, Augmented Reality, and online training programs (Cordner & Cordner, 2025). When officers are part of the initial adoption process, they will take ownership of new initiatives, while encouraging agency acceptance.

Law enforcement agencies can help reduce resistance and facilitate broader cooperation by promoting a climate of cooperation and transparency around the adoption of new technological products, both internally and externally with local communities (Cordner & Cordner, 2025). Emphasizing the importance of the internet to gather and disseminate information for law enforcement agencies, as well as the use of social media platforms to build trust and rapport with local communities and provide an additional means of communication with the public cannot be underscored. Utilizing these types of technology can foster a sense of community and can bridge existing gaps between law enforcement agencies and some of its citizens, resulting in improved public service and citizen satisfaction. Agencies should also prioritize continued education and support for officers that highlight the benefits of technology and not simply issue directives on its use. Ultimately, managing costs, addressing officer resistance while promoting responsible technology deployment will be critical for the future successes of law enforcement agencies.

CONCLUSION

As technology continues to evolve, and in some instances, advances more rapidly than society can understand or effectively adapt, the criminal justice system and law enforcement agencies in particular, face ongoing challenges of ensuring technology is ethical, responsible, and is applied in an objective and fair manner. The concurrent benefits and challenges of technology adoption must be balanced with civil liberties, privacy concerns, and safeguarding personal data, especially in a digital age, in which information is increasingly becoming digitized and shared across massive networks. While digitalization of information offers greater accessibility and transferring and sharing of information, it can also increase vulnerability to cyberattacks and cyber identity thefts. In order to effectively address these ongoing advancements and subsequent challenges associated with technology, it is imperative that the criminal justice system, the legal system, and governmental agencies collaborate using transparent, multitiered and multisystemic efforts, which aim to increase public awareness, provide educational campaigns, and increase social responsibility in the use, benefits, and consideration of new technologies as they emerge into the forefront of society (Kabir & Alam, 2023; Silalahi, 2023).

REFERENCES

American Civil Liberties Union. (2022 May 11). *Court cases: ACLU v. Clearview AI.* https://www.aclu.org/cases/aclu-v-clearview-ai

Ariel, B., Farrar, W. A., & Sutherland, A. (2015). The effect of police body-worn cameras on use of force and citizens' complaints against the police: A randomized controlled trial. *Journal of Quantitative Criminology*, *31*(3), 509–535. DOI: 10.1007/s10940-014-9236-3

Bureau of Justice Assistance. (2018). *Implementing a body-worn camera program: Recommendations and lessons learned.* U.S. Department of Justice. https://www.justice.gov/iso/opa/resources/472014912134715246869.pdf

Bureau of Justice Assistance. (2025). *Implementation, body-worn camera toolkit.* https://bja.ojp.gov/program/bwc/topics/implementation

Chen, Y.-C., & Huang, C. (2021, January 6). Smart data-driven policy on unmanned aircraft systems (UAS): Analysis of drone users in U.S. cities. *Smart Cities*, *4*(1), 78–92. DOI: 10.3390/smartcities4010005

City of Jamestown. (n.d.). *Police department history.* https://www.jamestownny.gov/police-department/history

Cochran, C. (2025, September 3). *Emerging technologies in law enforcement.* Right on crime: Texas Public Policy Foundation. https://rightoncrime.com/emerging-technologies-in-law-enforcement

Constitution Annotated. (n.d.). *Katz and reasonable expectation of privacy test.* https://constitution.congress.gov/browse/essay/amdt4-3-3/ALDE_00013717

Cordner, A., & Cordner, G. (2025). Overview of law enforcement technology. In Moriarty, L. J. (Ed.), *Criminal Justice in the 21st Century*. Charles C. Thomas Publisher.

Daniel, L. (2025, January 29). Judge throws out facial recognition evidence in murder case. *Forbes.* https://www.forbes.com/sites/larsdaniel/2025/01/29/judge-throws-out-facial-recognition-evidence-in-murder-case/

Dempsey, R. P., Brunet, J. R., & Dubljević, V. (2023, March). Exploring and understanding law enforcement's relationship with technology: A qualitative interview study of police officers in North Carolina. *Applied Sciences (Basel, Switzerland)*, *13*(6), 3887. DOI: 10.3390/app13063887

Federal Aviation Administration. (2020, October 6). *Small Unmanned Aircraft Systems (UAS) Regulations, Part 107.* https://www.faa.gov/newsroom/small-unmanned-aircraft-systems-uas-regulations-part-107

Federal Aviation Administration. (2024, December 19). *Getting started.* https://www.faa.gov/uas/getting_started

Finklea, K. (2023, August 22). *Law enforcement and technology: Use of unmanned aircraft systems.* Congressional Research Service. https://www.congress.gov/crs-product/R47660

Gaub, J. E., Choate, D. E., Todak, N., Katz, C. M., & White, M. D. (2016). Officer perceptions of body-worn cameras before and after deployment: A study of three departments. *Police Quarterly*, *19*(3), 275–302. DOI: 10.1177/1098611116653398

Go, J. (2020, March). The imperial origins of American policing: Militarization and imperial feedback in the early 20th century. *American Journal of Sociology*, *125*(5), 1193–1254. DOI: 10.1086/708464

Harris, D. A. (2010, Fall). Picture this: Body worn video devices ('head cams') as tools for ensuring Fourth Amendment compliance by police. *Legal studies Research. Pittsburgh University School of Law*. https://hdl.handle.net/2346/103656

Harvard Law School & Stanford Law School. (2020). *Emerging police technology: A policy toolkit.* https://law.stanford.edu/wp-content/uploads/2020/01/Emerging-Police-Technology-A-Policy-Toolkit.pdf

International Association of Chiefs of Police. (2012, August). *Recommended guidelines for the use of unmanned aircraft.* https://www.theiacp.org/sites/default/files/all/i-j/IACP_UAGuidelines.pdf

Jennings, W. G., Fridell, L. A., & Lynch, M. D. (2014, November-December). Cops and cameras: Officer perceptions of the use of body-worn cameras in law enforcement. *Journal of Criminal Justice*, *42*(6), 549–556. DOI: 10.1016/j.jcrimjus.2014.09.008

Jennings, W. G., Lynch, M. D., & Fridell, L. A. (2015). Novmber-December). Evaluating the impact of police officer body-worn cameras (BWCs) on response-to-resistance and serious external complaints: Evidence from the Orlando Police Department (OPD) experience utilizing a randomized controlled experiment. *Journal of Criminal Justice*, *43*(6), 480–486. DOI: 10.1016/j.jcrimjus.2015.10.003

Kabir, M. S., & Alam, M. N. (2023, May). IoT, big data and AI applications in the law enforcement and legal system: A review. *International Research Journal of Engineering and Technology (IRJET), 10*(5), 1777-1789. https://www.irjet.net/archives/V10/i5/IRJET-V10I5271.pdf

Kelling, G. L., & Coles, C. M. (1998). Fixing broken windows: Restoring order and reducing crime in our communities. *Touchstone (Nashville, Tenn.).*

Lipton, B. (2025, November 12). *Washington court rules that data collected on flock safety cameras are public record.* Electronic Frontier Foundation. https://www.eff.org/deeplinks/2025/11/washington-court-rules-data-captured-flock-safety-cameras-are-public-records

Lum, C., & Isaac, W. (2016, October). To predict and serve? *Significance*, *13*(5), 14–19. DOI: 10.1111/j.1740-9713.2016.00960.x

Lum, C., Koper, C. S., & Willis, J. J. (2016). Understanding the limits of technology in policing. *Police Quarterly*, *20*(2), 1–29. DOI: 10.1177/1098611116667279

Lum, C., Merola, L., Willis, J., & Cave, B. (2010, September). *License plate recognition technology (LPR): Impact evaluation and community assessment.* Center for Evidence-Based Crime Policy, George Mason University. https://cebcp.org/wp-content/evidence-based-policing/LPR_FINAL.pdf

Maneke, J., & Morasch, C. (2020, August 3). Show-me surveillance: Law enforcement navigation of Missouri's Sunshine Law requirements. *Journal of the Missouri Bar*, *76*(4), 160–183. https://news.mobar.org/show-me-surveillance-law-enforcement-navigation-of-missouris-sunshine-law-requirements

Meyers, H. E. (2023, January 19). *Destroyed by discovery: How New York State's discovery law destabilizes the criminal justice system.* Manhattan Institute. https://manhattan.institute/article/destroyed-by-discovery-how-new-york-states-discovery-law-destabilizes-the-criminal-justice-system

Miller, L., & Toliver, J. (2014). *Implementing a body-worn camera program: Recommendations and lessons learned.* U.S. Department of Justice. https://www.justice.gov/iso/opa/resources/472014912134715246869.pdf

Moriarty, L. J. (2025). *Criminal justice in the 21st century* (4th ed.). Charles C. Thomas Publisher.

Munson, A. (2026, January 28). Mike Brennan appointed new police chief. *The Register, 82*(29). https://register.turley.com/lr-archives/LUD012826.pdf

National Conference of State Legislatures. (2021, April 30). *Body-worn camera laws database.* https://www.ncsl.org/civil-and-criminal-justice/body-worn-camera-laws-database

National Institute of Justice. (2023, August 7). *Law 101: Legal guide for the forensic expert: Daubert and Kumho decisions.* https://nij.ojp.gov/nij-hosted-online-training-courses/law-101-legal-guide-forensic-expert/pretrial/pretrial-rules-evidence/daubert-and-kumho-decisions

New York State Senate. (2025, August 8). *New York State Penal Law, Section 245.20.* https://www.nysenate.gov/legislation/laws/CPL/245.20

Oliver, W. M. (2017). *August Vollmer: The father of America policing.* Carolina Academic Press.

Paoline, E. A.III, Elligson, R., & Gau, J. M. (2025, May). Police culture and body-worn cameras: Examining how cultural values impact officers' acceptance of technology. *Policing. Policing (Oxford, England), 19,* paaf007. Advance online publication. DOI: 10.1093/police/paaf017

Prayatno, C., Tohari, M., & Susilowati, T. (2024, August 29). The impact of using technology and innovation in law enforcement in the era of digitalization. [JETBIS]. *Journal of Economics, Technology, and Business, 3*(8), 1026–1033. DOI: 10.57185/jetbis.v3i8.127

Ready, J. T., & Young, J. T. (2015, June 14). The impact of on-officer video cameras on police-citizen contacts: Findings from a controlled experiment in Mesa, AZ. *Journal of Experimental Criminology, 11*(3), 445–458. https://link.springer.com/article/10.1007/s11292-015-9237-8. DOI: 10.1007/s11292-015-9237-8

Reaves, B. A. (2015, July). *Local police departments, 2013: Equipment and technology.* Bureau of Justice Statistics. https://bjs.ojp.gov/content/pub/pdf/lpd13et.pdf

Rogers, E. M. (2003, August 16). *Diffusion of innovations* (5th ed.). Free Press.

Sanders, C. B., & Henderson, S. (2013). Police 'empires' and information technologies: Uncovering material and organizational barriers to information sharing in Canadian police services. *Policing and Society, 23*(2), 243–260. DOI: 10.1080/10439463.2012.703196

Sheppard, K. G., & Welsh, B. C. (2022, May-June). Can police use of less-than-lethal weapons reduce harm during violent police-citizen encounters? A systematic review and directions for future research. *Aggression and Violent Behavior, 64,* 101748. DOI: 10.1016/j.avb.2022.101748

Silalahi, J. A. S. (2023, May 20). The application of criminal law in the digital age: A literature review of challenges and opportunities. *Innovative: Journal of Social Science Research, 3*(2), 3658-3668. https://j-innovative.org/index.php/Innovative/article/view/678

Silver, C. (2025). Is the data collected by license plate readers public record? Here's what Florida law says. *News6*. https://www.clickorlando.com/news/local/2025/11/25/is-the-data-collected-by-license-plate-readers-public-record-heres-what-florida-law-says

Skogan, W. G. (2017). Stop-and-frisk and trust in police in Chicago. In Oberwittler, D., & Roché, S. (Eds.), *Police-citizen relations: A comparative investigation of sources and impediments of legitimacy around the world* (pp. 246–265). Routledge. DOI: 10.4324/9781315406664-11

Storbeck, M. (2022, June). *Artificial intelligence and predictive policing: Risks and challenges.* European Crime Prevention Network. https://eucpn.org/sites/default/files/document/files/PP%20%282%29.pdf

U.S. Department of Justice. (2024, December 3). *Artificial intelligence and criminal justice: Final report.* https://www.justice.gov/olp/media/1381796/dl

Vickers, C. (2024, April 7). How AI risks creating a 'black box' at the heart of US legal system. *The Hill.* https://thehill.com/business/personal-finance/4571982-ai-black-box-legal-system

Vizzini, A. (2022). The technological wedge in law enforcement. *Florida Department of Law Enforcement.* https://www.fdle.state.fl.us/getContentAsset/38e05ac5-7e0f-41b1-bfac-6738458bf7c4/73aabf56-e6e5-4330-95a3-5f2a270a1d2b/Vizzini-Anthony-paper.pdf

White, M. D. (2014). *Police officer body-worn cameras: Assessing the evidence.* Office of Community Oriented Policing Services. https://portal.cops.usdoj.gov/resourcecenter/content.ashx/cops-p289-pub.pdf

Wilson, O. W. (1950). *Police administration.* McGraw-Hill Series in Political Science.

Chapter 2
Machine Learning for Smart Policing:
Navigating Ethical, Legal, and Operational Realities in India

Vikram Singh
http://orcid.org/0000-0001-5757-9111
Chaudhary Devi Lal University, Sirsa, India

Sangeeta Rani
http://orcid.org/0009-0008-1302-6409
Chaudhary Devi Lal University, Sirsa, India

ABSTRACT

Conventionally, Indian police have heavily relied on traditional means of investigation, which, of late, are gradually adopting digital technology to detect, investigate, and prosecute crime, crimes in conventional as well as digital spaces. Artificial intelligence and machine learning models that enable law enforcement agencies to predict crime and act pre-emptively have assumed a prominent place in policing, for it changes the ways crimes are predicted, prevented, investigated, and prosecuted. But, achieving maximum potential of digitech in crime control requires addressing various issues related to the privacy of data, bias in algorithms, human rights, transparency, and responsibility must be addressed with the help of efficient governance structures and collaboration with stakeholders. This chapter builds a discourse inviting policymakers, technologists, and policing professionals to strive to create a balanced, responsible ecosystem of AI/ML policing that focuses on ethical standards, operational best practices, and engaging all stakeholders.

INTRODUCTION: SMART POLICING

The history of Indian policing comprises a mix of the modern technological innovations and the traditional sociocultural values, and it can be traced to the ancient *Vedic* era when the scriptures such as the *Rgveda* and *Atharvaveda* reigned the socio-legal pastures to fight the crime and maintain social order. Archaeological records of the *Harappan* civilization indicate of the creation of proto-police mech-

DOI: 10.4018/979-8-3373-7660-8.ch002

anisms that would protect the social coherence in the society which in effect is a primitive basis of law enforcement based on societal protection. Later, the *Mauryan Empire* can be seen as one of the critical periods of the development of policing in the Indian polity. *Arthaśāstra* by *Kautilya*, an ancient work on governance and statecraft belonging to *Mauryan* period, codifies the roles, duties, and hierarchies of organization of policing in a centralized administrative paradigm. It sheds light on extremely advanced espionage and surveillance structures and introduced roles such as *dandapāla* (general police), *durgapāla* (fortress guards) and *antpāla* (intelligence operatives). *Kautilya*, is credited to establish one of the earliest organized policing structures in the world. It is interesting to note that the role of espionage as mentioned in *Arthaśāstra* shows how a strong intelligence system is imperative in the protection of the kingdom with classes of covert agents including ascetics and merchants to highly trained spies in the art of subversion and counter-intelligence. *Arthaśāstra*, among other things, is a treatise of highly structured intelligence organization, which is the cornerstone of the first fully structured surveillance state in the world and reflects elaborate secrecy, cryptographical, and covert operations protocols (Hegde, 2017).

Later, the *Gupta* period and the medieval era are marked by the further de-centralization of Indian policing system and delegation of such powers and responsibilities to village councils (*pañcāyats*), which functioned as basic units of local control and dispute settlement, by incorporating the policing activities in these local governing bodies. The *Mughal Empire*, had however more centralized defences, but still had less direct responsibility to the people as it was more concerned with keeping the imperial authority than the local governance. Although the early systems were marked by varying degree of local policing, the *British* colonial rule provided bureaucratic centralization which restructured the relationship that existed between police and people, and triggered a transformation of Indian policing. Hierarchically disciplined and centralized police cadres dedicated to maintain law-and-order to suit the colonial administrative requirements were institutionalized by the Police Act of 1861. Instead of offering a community-based policing system, the main aim of this act was to oppress the dissent, manage the human inhabitants of the lands under its jurisdiction, and breed fear and suspicion of the government to the masses (Wahab, 2025; Singh, 2024; Attri and Tripathi, 2025). Even after gaining independence, relying upon the colonial policing legacy, the Indian policing continued to depend on manual method of investigation including human testimony and intuition, regressive social practices, and a low level of science and technology usage in investigation (Sharma & Gupta, 2022; Rohilla, 2025).

With the rapid urbanization of India and the spiralling growth of complex crimes in the digital world, the need to modernize investigation and trial of crime cannot be overstated. Apart from adoption of digital means such as creation of online crime databases, the usage of artificial intelligence (AI) and machine learning (ML) has also increased, and data-driven smart police can now analyze large crime datasets comprising features such as demographics, spatiotemporal relationships, nature and intent of the crime, modii operandi of the crime, and social indicators, etc. of the past crimes to "even" predict (and pre-empt) the crime. The implementation of predictive models that forecast crime hotspots in the real time, to provide focused patrolling and effective allocation of resources stands demonstrated by evidence of several metropolitan police districts in Delhi, Mumbai, Bengaluru, and Hyderabad. Such interventions have been linked to a high rate of crime and operation responsiveness, both (Sarkar et al., 2025). The facial recognition technology improves the process of identifying suspects and finding missing people, enhancing the investigative capabilities of police. AI-based surveillance systems like the *Jarvis* system adaptation by Uttar Pradesh are capable of processing the live video feeds received from surveillance cameras to identify unusual behaviour and provide prompt notification to the departments concerned. The AI chatbots have improved citizen participation by offering convenient police-public interfaces whereby one can report crime, creating a participatory and effective mechanism for reporting and redressing complaints. Voice analytics tools, such as *Crime GPT*, are based on complex text and voice recognition system that reveals relational connections between criminal networks, providing a new aspect of investigation ("Indian police expand," 2024; Raja, 2024).

The question of governance and federal coordination takes center stage, as the AI adoption in policing is spreading, both horizontally and vertically. The implementation of Internet of Things (IoT), big data analytics, and AI/ML defines smart policing in India, which creates a technology environment that facilitates efficiency, transparency, and flexibility. There are, however, complexities in police governance in form of the democratic system and the federal structure of India mandates police and public order as state subjects. This provincial limitation of public order leads to a patchworked and heterogenous AI/ML adoption in policing. This heterogeneity in technology adoption in policing severely affects the potential benefits that digital technologies might have yielded (Mahajan and Chaudhary, 2025). The Integrated Command and Control Centre (IC3) in Punjab and *Crime GPT* in Uttar Pradesh are two such projects that illustrate effective cooperation, in a Center-State setup, to promote technological diffusion and harmonization of policing operations. The future direction requires the development of multilevel structures of governance. These would include stringent laws and regulations, safeguarding against algorithmic bias of AI/ML solutions, and privacy protection of common citizen, transparency of AI/ML decisions, and participation of civil society, academia, technologists, and legal experts in the making of *smart police*. It is possible to reap the full benefits of AI/ML-based policing and strengthen social justice and public trust only by maintaining a balance between the innovations and ethics and ethical responsibility (Sood, 2022; Wessels, 2023).

MACHINE LEARNING INTEGRATION IN POLICING

The integration of machine-learning in policing systems has taken a global center stage in ensuring how police ensure public order, law enforcement, and the safety of the community. Politically, policing has traditionally been dependent on human judgment, local knowledge, physical presence, and operating in a reactive form based on patrols, manual records, and informal community intelligence (Bayley, 1994). Local customs and power structures have seen police making discretionary decisions with significant odds of not having access to centralized crime database and predictive models. Of late, policing departments around the world are adopting the AI/ML tools, police in India are guided by complex historical and socio-cultural dynamics that determines the adoption of such technologies.

Indian policing can be studied in mythological, archaeological, and historical contexts covering the *Ramayana* and the *Mahabharata* (mythology), *Harappan* period (archaeology), the *Vedic* and *post Vedic* ages, the *Mauryan Empire*, the *Gupta Empire*, the *Mughal Empire*, and the *British* colonial rule. The Police Act of 1861, enacted in the aftermath of 1857 uprising, still survives to remain a pillar of legal structure in the policing system of India (Wahab, 2025). It has been noted that the colonial policing system turned into the instrument of oppression and people management, which generated the strong distrust in the population (Singh, 2024; Attri and Tripathi, 2025). In India, even after more than 75 years of independence and despite the constitutional democracy and the great number of reforms, the policing system relied on the legacy of colonial policing. The police structure remains rather reactive, paper-based, and dominated by human hands, not designed to cope with the complexity of the modern-day cybercrime (Vasudev & Hansen, 2024). Being controlled by the executive, not being close to the community, and in absence of any significant police reforms, the inherited policing mechanism proved a great obstacle to the adaptation to the needs of a modern pluralistic society. With urbanization improving rapidly, more digital connectivity and more complicated crime networks, Indian policing hit a critical point of inflection. Lost opportunities apart, artificial-intelligence and machine learning technologies present a new frontier of improvement and upgradation of policing. AI/ML algorithms are used to combine large and complex data-historical records of crime, demographic variation, spatial-temporal patterns, and real-time social-media analytics to come up with predictive information regarding crime thereby potentially contributing to proactive and preventive interventions (Sarkar et al., 2025; Center for Human Security Studies, 2021). In megapolis, such as Delhi and Mumbai, ML-based crime-forecasting models are used, which have reportedly achieved over 90 percent accuracy in identifying hotspots. This helps to optimize the allocation of human resources and other infrastructure thereby contributing in crime control and reduction (Mandalapu et al., 2023).

The predictive analytics powered by AI/ML models are accompanied by data analytics that are capable of processing the live feeds received from surveillance systems in the real time. The *Jarvis*, can process the live feeds from hundreds of CCTV cameras and identify anomalous behaviour to give quick alerts. The facial-recognition technologies accelerate the identification of suspects and aid in the search of missing ones and the presence of antisocial and notorious individuals in the crowd. Citizens can also use conversational AI chatbots to gain access to cybercrime reporting channels, as also the reporting of other forms of general complaints, whereas more sophisticated voice-analytics algorithms like *Crime GPT* use audio inputs to identify criminal networks ("Indian police expand," 2024; Raja, 2024). Collectively, these new technologies form the foundation of new paradigm of smart-policing in India, leading to synergetic use of digital communication and AI/ML and data analytics algorithms to increase efficacy, responsiveness, and transparency (Press Information Bureau, 2025). Policing being a state subject in India, the realization of this synergy, however, is inconsistent due to dissimilar infrastructure, funding, policy priority, and technological preparedness across the states and union territories. Despite these disparities, there are positive examples of central-state collaborations, including the *Crime GPT* project of Uttar Pradesh and the *IC3* of Punjab, but many states still lag in reaping the benefits of these immensely potent technologies for the public good.

Having taken the initial leap in integrating AI/ML in police operations, the next few steps on sustainable improvement of policing in India may involve creating effective governance structures that integrate legal requirements, ethical regulations, algorithmic transparency, and stakeholder inclusion in the representative of socio-cultural diversity of the land. ML-driven policing systems can only be fair, just, and socially equitable by incorporating extensive ethical, legal, institutional, and community-based safeguards. This underscores the collaborative efforts amongst various stakeholders such as policymakers (legislator and executive), civil-society actors, technologists, and the judiciary in a multipronged approach towards integration of AI/ML in the making of ethically and culturally sensitive and citizen-centric policing.

MACHINE LEARNING APPLICATIONS FOR INDIAN POLICE

In continuation of the overall growth of AI/ML use in policing, the subsections below discuss two case studies of its application in India. The adoption of machine learning in real-time crime prediction, and hot spot analysis represents a paradigm shift in planning and strategizing against crime as opposed to responding to it. AI/ML-based systems utilize a broad range of multifeatured data and therefore, take into consideration past crime records, demographics, sociocultural and industrial outlook, temporal and seasonal variations, and spatial factors like population density and infrastructure. This data fusion allows creation of advanced risk-heat maps, identifying the geographical locations and areas that have high crime likelihood, leading to the deployment of pre-emptive police patrols and strategic allocation of other resources in the identified hotspots. A case in point is the Delhi Police's use of systems that combine spatio-temporal crime data and court records with offender profiles such that it can predict the possible crime areas with high precision. These predictive capabilities allow the police force to anticipate the actions of the criminals and act proactively instead of giving the traditional reactive response (Raj & Patel, 2023). On a similar note, Mumbai Police have also created and deployed ML models for processing large amounts of crime data to optimize the force's performance and resource utilization (Thacker, 2025). They claim high accuracy ratings of these predictive models, with one regression-based model reporting R-squared value close to 0.93, but these have not been independently verified (Sarkar et al., 2025). These predictive systems focus on evidence-based targeted policing as opposed to routine blanket patrolling. These models have been deployed with aims of minimizing response lag, maximizing workforce utilization, and minimizing crime instances.

Recent rise in the interest of academic and research community in explainable AI (XAI), several predictive models of policing have been equipped with explainability features to inculcate the trust of police and public in such models. The explainability models such as SHAP (SHapley Additive exPlanations) and LIME (Local Interpretable Model-agnostic Explanations) enhance clarity by providing insight into the modus operandi of an AI/ML model. In instant case, the attribute (aka feature in ML context) which might contribute more in crime may be "*Unemployment Rate*" in comparison to other features such as "*Ethnicity*"or "*Parents' Occupation.*" This deployment of predictive AI/ML models in public domains demands a strict quality control on datasets used for training and testing of these models. Ongoing calibration, and human overwatch are also needed to avoid the strengthening of historic biases and to be able to respond to changes in the crime patterns in the multifaceted urban environments in India. ML-based surveillance systems that combine the live feeds from CCTV networks with IoT sensors and data analytics to allow real-time automatic surveillance complement the predictive capabilities of AI/ML models. An example of such a trend is Jarvis, which processes video streams of public spaces in real-time and then identifies suspicious movements or objects and informs law-enforcement officers (Wahab, 2025). Such systems are more consistent and extensive as compared to human operators and provide an extensive digital record of forensic data that could be used in further investigations and prosecution in the courts of law. These deployments mark a shift from post-incident reactive analysis to anticipatory pre-emptive intervention, which is critical in areas with high population density. However, the implementation of this type of systems requires strict governance to protect privacy and to ensure the accountability of its work (Cheong, 2024).

In addition to surveillance, machine learning is changing the nature of the investigation and prosecution processes, owing mainly to the developments in digital forensics. Delhi Police now use ML-based facial-recognition algorithms capable of comparing CCTV images with data in criminal and missing-person databases, and claim to have increased search efficiency and suspects' apprehension rates (Sur, 2022). The voice analytics feature of Crime GPT identifies linguistic patterns to map intricate criminal networks through clustering techniques (Raja, 2024). Vehicle-recognition system identifies vehicles based on their features to track stolen or suspicious vehicles, and image-recognition systems help to automate the tagging of crime-scene evidence (Kishore et al., 2023). Such investigative innovations however introduce issues of bias, transparency, and accountability in the decision making assisted by such models.

All these applications characterize the changing environment of smart-policing in India, where the integration of data analytics, big data, AI, ML, and IoT can make its processes more precise and responsive. The complexity of these deployments is a positive shift from traditional manual deployments to AI/ML judgement, curated and overwatched by human expert. The transformative possibilities of AI/ML-based policing systems in the real-world situations are exemplified below.

Case Study: Jarvis

Jarvis, developed by the Gurugram-based startup Staqu for prisons department of Uttar Pradesh, is probably the most significant example of the operationalization of ML-powered surveillance system in India. It uses computer vision, object recognition, and behavioural features of the objects in the camera range to scan live feeds against security breaches, crowd behaviour, or violence. The platform integrates approximately 700 CCTV cameras in 70 prisons, covering nearly 900 square kilometers (Wahab, 2025; Bhalla, 2019). It automatically raises alarms when anomalies are detected and therefore allows a response to be made pre-emptively or proactively and generates digital forensics logs that show timestamps and object tracking to assist in investigation and prosecution. Its implementation has made Uttar Pradesh the first state in India to have an AI-assisted round-the-clock surveillance in the prison. Smartphone-based extensions of the platform enable real time situational awareness to senior officials, enhancing strategic oversight by the experts and seniors (Express Computer, 2025). In addition to the prisons, Jarvis has been deployed to protect other public places such as the temples to manage the number of visitors, track persons of interests, and ensure safety of the crowd during high traffic events like *Navaratri* festival ("UP police," 2025).

The transition from manual monitoring to ML-based systems has two main advantages: the preventive policing and digital trails, facilitating early-stage detection of potential threats and support digital forensics investigation. These benefits however raise some vital issues of privacy, informed consent, and governance of digital data. This mandates strong legal protection and transparent institutional data usage procedures to align these technologies with the Indian democratic ethos and cultural values. In the future, the issue concerning the potential occurrence of a wrongful conviction because of an error in the algorithms or biasness is crucial as it will lead to apprehension of innocent individuals and potential criminals to escape the arrest, at least for some crucial time. Apart from eroding the trust of stakeholders in these initiatives, such errors raise human and civil rights issues. Algorithms can be biased, usually reflecting socio-cultural inequalities, leading to disproportionate effects on minority demographics, which require regular auditory overwatch and training-testing datasets to be balanced and inclusive. To maintain the confidence of stakeholders of such systems, functional transparency is also paramount to ensure a human oversight and attribute accountability of decision making (Sood, 2022). Finally, the effectiveness and sustenance of the ML-based policing will rely on the hybrid human-algorithm systems, strict audits, and rights-aware governance models capable of balancing the technological innovation with the moral responsibility.

Case Study: Crime GPT

Crime GPT, another AI-based application developed by Staqu Technologies for Uttar Pradesh Police is a significant application of large language modelling (LLM) and multimodal AI tools in Indian law enforcement arena. It offers a natural language interface and voice assistants to officers for retrieving, analysing, and acting upon crime related information, thereby bridging the gap between structured crime databases and semi/unstructured audio-visual and text-based case dossiers (Raja, 2024).

At its core, Crime GPT integrates three key technical layers: (1) a large scale crime database (reportedly over 9 million digitized entries in Uttar Pradesh) inherited from its predecessor system Trinetra; (2) a retrieval augmented generation (RAG) layer that enables natural-language querying of both structured (e.g., FIRs, criminal logs) and unstructured (e.g., CCTV footage transcripts, audio intercepts) data; and (3) multimodal input interfaces supporting text, voice, and facial recognition prompts. Developers of the application claim that Crime GPT facilitates queries such as "*How many crimes committed by X in the past 24 months?*" via voice or text, and returns targeted results (Raja, 2024). Operationally, UP Police has integrated Crime GPT into their existing surveillance and criminal-database infrastructure. The system reportedly supports features such as speaker-identification, gang-network mapping, face-recognition alerts, and cross-agency data collation.

The introduction of Crime GPT has had several empirical consequences for police procedure. First, the retrieval time for relevant criminal records and investigative leads has significantly decreased, allowing frontline investigators to act on leads more swiftly. By enabling voice and text search over data lakes, the tool also expands the accessibility of criminal justice system beyond tech-savvy officers. The system additionally enhances integration across departments (e.g. judiciary, police, and prisons), enabling systematic linkage of surveillance, forensic, biometric, and crime-trend data. While Crime GPT offers clear operational advantages, it simultaneously raises important governance and ethical questions—making it a valued case for research into AI-enabled policing. Some of the issues include:

- Algorithmic transparency and explainability: Despite being built on RAG and LLM architectures, the precise decision logic (e.g., how risk scores are generated or why a suspect match is flagged) remains opaque, potentially limiting contestability of police decisions.
- Data bias risks: The core database reflects historical criminal-justice data, which may itself be skewed by socio-economic, caste or regional bias. If unmitigated, such biases can be reinforced by the system. Staqu asserts efforts to filter and audit bias, but independent verification remains limited.
- Privacy and surveillance implications: The system's ability to ingest voice, image, CCTV streams, and voice recognition for suspects raises questions about mass-surveillance, consent, data retention, and proportionality.
- Legal admissibility and accountability: Since Crime GPT delivers results in near-real-time, the chain of custody, interpretability of outputs, liability for false positives/negatives and evidence-admissibility remain open issues in Indian criminal-justice law.

ETHICAL IMPLICATIONS OF ML-BASED POLICING

Having discussed general applications and two specific deployments of AI/ML-based systems in policing, it is crucial to respond to the questions relating to ethical aspects, which in turn are vital for lending sociocultural and legal acceptance to the AI/ML-based policing systems. The swift growth of machine learning and artificial intelligence in law enforcement presents ethical dilemmas relating to equitable, accountable, and democratic policing. Several of these issues arise due to data and algorithmic bias. Since AI/ML systems are trained and tested on historical data that can tend to reflect the structural inequalities of the society, they will reproduce and reinforce the systematic injustices in predictive policing systems as well. These problems gain a special urgency in India where social stratifications of caste, religion, gender, and region have long existed. Research reveals that the marginalized groups, especially the Dalits and Muslims, are disproportionately targeted or monitored by AI/ML-based surveillance and prediction tools, further promoting the already existing marginalizations and weakening the social justice (Murugesan, 2021).

Foregoing disparities are further reinforced by facial recognition technologies. Although used in numerous police departments in India, such systems show a higher error rate with dark skinned and proletarian class people, which leads to the possibility of false identifications and wrongful arrest. Such miscarriage of justice undermines the presumption of innocence (the basic tenet of India laws) and the right to a fair trial and in the end jeopardizes the trust that the citizens have in the legal system. Tackling these issues requires not only the technical fixes but also a culturally aware governance that enables placing bias in the context of Indian socio-political realities and makes sure that the design of algorithms and training-testing datasets are inclusive and equitable.

Another critical ethical aspect of AI policing is the personal privacy of citizens. The combination of biometric, visual, and behavioural data allows mass surveillance, which threatens individual autonomy with increasing risks akin to an *Orwellian State*. Even though the legal conception of privacy in India has changed since the decision of Supreme Court of India in Puttaswamy v. Union of India case, regulatory systems are still in the transition stage. The fluidity has highlighted the necessity of explicit data usage and privacy regulations, legal data procurement methods, informed consent models, and robust safeguards against unauthorized information access and data leaks. Striking a balance between civic liberties and the safety and security of the state at large is a Herculean task; excessive surveillance may undermine the confidence of the citizens in the law enforcement and push them away in their cooperation with law enforcement officers.

Closely connected with these problems is the issue of accountability and attribution in AI/ML policing. Many AI/ML systems work in an opaque manner, in which the logic behind their decisions is not transparent to the affected individuals and cannot be explained even by the officer in-charges of these systems. This inherent opacity of AI/ML-based smart policing interferes with procedural fairness and makes it difficult to appeal against unfair outcomes, including data and algorithmic bias or identification of suspects. Such risks can be mitigated with the help of clear standards of the algorithmic auditability, interpretability, explainability, and human oversight. To avoid the errors, abuse, or prejudice against automated system, policymakers should strengthen the institutional codes of conduct and establish independent monitoring institutions.

In addition to regulation, there must be community and stakeholder involvement to build the legitimacy and trust in AI/ML-based policing. The inclusive governance should rope in the civil society, data scientists, legal professionals, and other representatives of marginalized groups at all stages of the AI/ML lifecycle: conception, design, training-testing, deployment, and assessment. The principles of citizen participation in operations and impact assessment are essential to ensure that technology does not reflect historic inequalities and imbibes democratic principles and human values. Such shared ethics can be one of the preconditions of applying AI/ML justice dispensation and it must not hit the pluralistic society of India (Rani, 2024). The ethical issues of bias, privacy, and accountability are the most crucial in AI/ML implementation in Indian policing systems. To address these issues, multipronged approach is necessary including technological innovations, regulatory protection, and participatory governance.

AI/ML can become a tool of justice delivery, provided it is supported by transparency, human rights protection, and social inclusivity.

LEGAL CHALLENGES IN ML-BASED POLICING

Apart from operational and ethical challenges to AI/ML-based policing, one needs to tread the legal and regulatory landscape upon which AI/ML integration in policing must be grounded. Introducing machine learning and artificial intelligence in Indian policing arena brings about an array of intricate legal, ethical, and procedural issues, which need to be addressed considering technological advancement, upholding the core human values, due diligence of the process, harmony of a pluralistic society, and democratic values. The developing system of data governance in India, characterized by both the Digital Personal Data Protection Act, 2023 (DPDP Act) and the upcoming operation rules (of 2025), is an essential point of nuance in this equilibrium (Akshaya and Devadharshini, 2025; Government of India, 2023).

Data-protection Laws in India

One of the most critical turning points in the changing personal data privacy environment in India is the DPDP Act of 2023, as it is the first real effort to create a set of enforceable rules concerning the management of digital personal data in the country. Codifying the major tenets of informed consent, purpose limitation, data minimization and storage limitation, the Act establishes privacy as a fundamental aspect of digital economy and digital administrative infrastructure of India. This Act seeks to conceptualize the paradigm of data fiduciary where all the parties that handle digital personal data, such as the government departments, individual companies, and other organizations handling the data, are termed as data fiduciaries who must process the personal data/information in a lawful, fair, and transparent manner (Burman, 2023). To the law enforcement departments that have increasingly been using machine-learning systems, including facial recognition databases, predictive policing systems, and real-time surveillance systems, the Act requires safeguards through encryption, data access control, data breach notifications, and purpose-based processing personal data of citizens to ensure that data are not abused and misused.

Nevertheless, the wide exemptions of the legislation on the pretext of state security, sovereignty, friendly relations with other countries, and public order creates valid concerns of overreach. Such exceptions may allow data retention for long periods of time, profiling, and surveillance in the name of national security, effectively waters down privacy protection enshrined in the Constitution of India and the DPDP Act itself. Information Technology Act, 2000 and amendments, and the accompanying rules on cybersecurity and social media intermediaries are still pillars albeit still inadequate in the regulation of autonomous or adaptive algorithmic systems. They are yet to bring up such important concerns as the transparency of algorithms, the detection of bias, or human-in-the-loop responsibility (Sood, 2022; Hanspal and Behera, 2026). The IT Act was last amended in the year 2008, when the there were no signs of AI resurgence of present times. Thus, the DPDP Act has become a significant legal breakthrough, but the overall regulatory landscape of AI/ML-driven policing in India is still fragmented, which is why more coordinated regulation is required that will allow balancing privacy protection with technological progress and democratic accountability.

Indian Courts' use of AI/ML

With the active integration of AI/ML-based systems into policing processes with their application in forensic analysis and predictive operations, the question of admissibility of digital evidences in courts of law has gained traction. In the classical Indian Evidence Act, 1872 (Bhartiya Sakshya Adhiniyam, 2023 in its new avatar), the Indian courts require that evidence exhibits provable authenticity and reliability. However, due to their opaque modus operandi, most AI/ML systems contribute little to tell-tale transparency of digital systems (Handa & Thakur, 2024). In the absence of adequate understanding of the model logic or origin of the dataset, courts are not in a good position to determine the probative value of the outputs provided by AI system, directly challenging the principles of natural justice and the right to challenge evidence.

Although evidence produced by electronic transactions and digital communications have been accepted by courts of law u/s 65B, which governs issuance of certificate of validity and admissibility of electronic records in judicial process. The certificate mentions the way the digital evidence was created, stored, and retrieved using a properly functioning device. Legal provisions of section 65B in place apart, AI/ML-specific analytics are still treated unequally in court. Some recent studies point out that the Indian courts do not have standard practices or procedures adapted specifically to algorithmic evidence, as the Frye or Daubert standards used in other jurisdictions (Ravishankar and Anand, 2023). Admissibility of AI/ML-generated digital evidence being unclear u/s 65B, some judges admit AI/ML-generated output as electronic evidence and do not require validation of models, disclosure of datasets, and descriptions of specialists, while others refuse such inputs with reference to unexplained methodology or lack of reliability. Such a disproportionate judicial environment causes a significant amount of legal uncertainty, a lack of accountability, and can damage the trust of the population in AI/ML policing.

This means that admissibility of AI/ML-assisted evidence in India requires some necessary reform in terms of judicial principles that impose the disclosure of algorithmic architecture, source and quality of dataset, domain expert opinion regarding model's error rates, strict chain-of-custody procedures, and verification by a human-in-the-loop. Until such protective measures are put in place, the adoption of AI/ML tools in policing despite its apparent technological promise is limited by the procedural and constitutional factors that should not be disregarded in the interests of efficiency.

Accountability of ML-Based Policing

Assigning accountability is paramount in terms of causation of harm, mistakes, or rights infringement in the use of artificial intelligence and machine learning systems in policing. As AI/ML gets integrated into the law enforcement processes, including the predictive algorithms for patrolling and the facial recognition systems for apprehending the suspects, the issue of responsibility in cases of malpractice becomes pressing and unresolved by the law.

In the traditional Indian law, the misconduct in policing has been held liable to identifiable human manifestations, which are officers, supervisory authorities, or institutions, and based on principles of negligence, vicarious liability, or violation of human rights and statutory laws. The AI/ML-based tools cannot fit into these frameworks well, for existing laws cannot hold and punish technology artefacts liable for any offence or crime. Since an AI/ML system does not have *mens rea* (Latin for "guilty mind") and is an autonomous system that does not necessarily follow the direct will of humans, the system works under the control of model that has been trained, tested, and validated through the historical data

(Sayyed, 2024). The AI/ML systems are not legal entities under Indian law; consequently, the owner of a system, be it an Indian developer or a deployer or a police agency are some probables to whom the responsibility might be attributed (IndiaAI, 2025).

The foregoing uncertainty is worsened in the policing situation: when a predictive AI/ML model wrongly identifies a suspect, or a surveillance system produces a false alarm, who bears the responsibility? The police force deploying can also claim that the model used by the vendor did not have sufficient protection. To circumvent the responsibility, the vendor can allege that the police have misused/abused the AI/ML system or failed to monitor it in a proper manner. In another situation, the developer could argue that the training/testing data was not under its control and it might have been unbalanced and biased. In the absence of a clear attribution of statutory liability, there will some cases and victims of AI/ML-police victimization. Indian regulators are yet to provide an AI/ML-specific liability regime. The Consumer Protection Act or the Information Technology Act do apply in cases of civil liability through product liability, but these laws do not directly cover policing-specific harms of AI/ML systems (IndiaAI, 2025; Sayyed, 2024).

To address the issues raised in the foregoing subsections, researchers and policymakers may consider shared liability schemes: schemes that would place responsibility on developers, deployers and users; compulsory liability insurance on high-risk AI/ML tools; algorithmic safety certifications; human-in-the-loop controls; and legislative clarifications/amendments to cover the unforeseen situations outlined above. It has been suggested that the strict-liability doctrine, especially when an AI/ML system inflicts severe damage despite all the foreseeable mitigation measures, should be adjusted to allow those who have suffered to seek the relief (Sayyed, 2024). Until these reforms have been introduced, the policing led by the AI/ML will run the risk of attribution of liabilities, where there are no visible culprit and rights of the vulnerable individuals are not safeguarded. Legal framework and institutional structures are necessary to make innovation accountable and ensure that people do not lose trust in AI/ML-facilitated law enforcement.

State v. Union: Regulatory Gaps

The federal system of governance in India makes it difficult to regulate the AI/ML-driven policing thus creating a conflict between technological research and protection of human rights. Since the law and order are majorly the responsibilities of the states, and every state has a great deal of freedom in policy adoption, technological implementation, and data-governance standards. They have resulted in broad differences in the level of innovation, regulatory systems, and resource bases among states (Nath and Barman, 2024). Decentralization may lead to experimentation and local innovation, but also adds to the risk of fragmented regulations, in the sense that the rights of citizens do not get equal protection and vary by their state of residence.

In the meantime, the union government in India has already embarked on large scale AI-driven policing projects, including integrated command centres and national predictive analytics programmes, which are indicative of a great deal of interest in AI/ML-driven policing (Press Information Bureau, 2025). But, the gaps in the Central and state regulations however causes a lack in harmonized and national regulatory framework, adding another dimension to already existing disparities in interstate regulations. As the less well-governed states would be implementing their robust surveillance systems with no effective protection, the more well-governed states would implement them at higher standards, creating unequal rights protection.

In response, a collective national system of governance is needed–the one based on transparency, accountability, and inclusivity. This type of framework would institute the protection of basic human rights, normalize the auditory procedures for working of algorithms, and allow the Center-State and inter-state exchange of both best practices and data fiduciary systems. It would also strike a balance between the need to be innovative and democratic by ensuring that the technological aspiration does not violate the governance structure. India can only maintain the legitimacy of AI/ML-augmented policing through harmonized regulation, both with central guidance andstate implementation, and avoid creating gaps that undermine the trust of the citizens.

AI/ML-Policing v. Legal Compliance

The robustness of regulatory mechanism of AI/ML-based policing requires incorporation of both, the aspect of legality and the aspect of community participation. India stands at the critical crossroad, necessitating not only a host of regulatory reforms, but also an institutionalized, multi-layered system of governance that instils accountability, transparency, and inclusivity at every stage of AI implementation in policing. The main point in this architecture is the legally mandated algorithmic audits by the independent regulatory bodies empowered to evaluate the AI/ML-policing systems for their accuracy, bias, and adherence to ethical norms. These audits can only be beneficial in collaboration with procedural rights such as the right of individuals to challenge, scrutinize or amend unjust recommendations of AI/ML-driven systems to enforce procedural fairness and due process.

An extensive framework that places legally binding liability clauses delineating the accountability of the AI developers, law-enforcement agencies, and system integrators to avoid accountability gaps in the case of technological failure or violation of human rights. Concurrently, the judicial and prosecutorial training programmes are essential to increase institutional literacy of digital forensics and algorithmic reasoning so that courts could be able to question AI-based evidence to uphold its integrity (Modise, 2023). At the policy level, the coherence between innovation and rights protection can be achieved through harmonization between states by model legislation and the establishment of a national AI commission for oversight of the whole gambit of AI/ML policing. This type of commission would be able to organize state-level efforts, establish standard practices in auditing, and release periodical and occasional reports on transparency in the application of AI/ML in policing. The problematic engagement of civil society, academia, and industry in governance discussions would also match technological implementation with the constitutional principles and global human-right standards.

In the absence of these precautionary measures, algorithmic policing will have the potential to support established disparities and compromise procedural justice. On the contrary, given a commitment to ethical governance, algorithmic transparency and citizen-oriented accountability, India has the chance to turn AI/ML-based policing into an example of conscientious and rights-aware technological innovation.

TECHNICAL AND OPERATIONAL ISSUES

Following the discussion on legal and ethical aspects, this section focuses on the technical and operational constraints which limit the successful implementation of the AI/ML-based policing tools in India. These issues affect the reliability, scalability, and institutional acceptance of AI/ML systems in law enforcement, and must be resolved to fully realize their potential while observing the procedural and ethical guidelines.

Operational Constraints

An underlying difficulty with the Indian policing adopting artificial intelligence and machine learning is the quality, consistency, and interoperability of underlying dataset(s). The Indian police agencies rely on heterogeneous information inherited from multiple incoherent information systems at the various levels of administration: police station, commissionerate, and state. These underlying information systems use different technology platforms and data standards. These disparities lead to mismatches in data (sources, formats, and quality) and reporting formats, hindering the creation of credible and generalizable AI/ML models (Sarkar et al., 2025). Data related issues like missing values, duplicate values, anomalies, scaling, and inaccuracies are still endemic in the datasets created from First Information Report (FIR) databases, chargesheets, and court-case decisions. These inconsistencies do not only adversely affect the precision of analysis, but also pose the threat of bias and error propagation during training and testing of predictive policing models and image processing-based surveillance algorithms. It is also important to ascertain the interoperability between dissimilar datasets comprising records of criminals, biometrics, forensics, and surveillance. The lack of standard metadata structures and common data protocols hinders the integration of state and central databases such as those which are managed by the National Crime Records Bureau of India, State Crime Records Bureaux and the Crime and Criminal Tracking Network and Systems, therefore, limiting cross-jurisdictional intelligence (Center for Human Security Studies, 2021). The practice of data silos and inconsistent data sharing agreement between departments also makes inter-agency collaboration more difficult.

The lack of these data issues is compounded with lack of infrastructural coverage especially in semi-urban and rural jurisdictions whereby network bandwidth, computing infrastructure and power reliability remain at its poorest level. The scope of using cloud-based storage and high-performance computing platforms is limited, and scalability of AI/ML applications is constrained, whereas the outdated hardware and the lack of cybersecurity support undermine the stability of operations and integrity of data ("Predictive policing," 2024). These gaps need to be bridged by developing a national data policy that, among other requirements, includes data standardization, investment in digital infrastructure, and interoperable cloud ecosystems to provide equal access to pan-India smart policing systems.

Organizational Inertia

The other aspect that is equally important in the deployment of ML-based policing systems is the organizational preparedness of law-enforcement agencies to adopt and operate these technologies. Even the most sophisticated software technology will not suffice in the absence of people with digital literacy, AI ethics, and human-in-the-loop supervision. According to recent research of the police training regimes in India, there are marked gaps in the curricula related to the technological expertise, digital forensics and investigation skills, and executive's determination (Wahab, 2024). Most states' police forces as well as central forces do not have well-organized and continuing professional police development programmes that help officers to be able to make meaning of AI and ML models' outputs, justify system-recommended actions, and supervise automated workflows. The lack of proper mechanism for periodic upskilling of police personnels weakens the work on introducing AI/ML systems in day-today processes of policing such as rounding-up and pre-emptive arrests of suspects, automatic drafting of FIR, capturing and packaging the digital evidence. Working AI/ML-based police projects that focus on the assistive qualities of artificial intelligence and machine learning in which officers still have the power to override the model's recommendations, are necessary to avoid accountability and integrity in operations; and still a few such projects are afoot in India.

The allocation of resources also adds to the complexities of AI/ML-based policing systems. Departments are not only required to invest in hardware and software, but also in training infrastructure, the change management processes, and the personnels' capacity to engage in continuous learning, that is necessary for this ever-evolving area. The present law enforcement framework requires individuals that are not only well-trained in traditional investigation and enforcement capabilities, but also those who are well versed with cybercrimes, cyber forensics, digital data management, and ethical aspects of digital age (Hanspal and Behera, 2026). Furthermore, the acceptance of technology culture requires investment in user-friendly interfaces, local language interfaces, and innovation management cells in police organizations. The policymakers should thus focus on the extensive facilities for capacity-building in digital models to make sure that AI/ML-based systems enhance but not overpower law-enforcement processes and agencies. Smart policing can be operationally feasible, but with no real organizational preparedness, the promise of such technological capability can be confined to the realm of technological possibilities.

AI/ML as Assistant v. Replacement

The satisfactory implementation of AI/ML-enabled policing systems can only be achieved with not only technical expertise but a purposeful design of the human overwatch and machine support. The human-in-the-loop paradigm considers the ML as an aid that will not replace the human decision-makers but allow the officers to check, modify, or veto the suggestions made by the machine learning algorithms. This protection is necessary to avoid blatant abuse of human rights and ultimately the loss of trust in ML-based policing systems. Automation in policing processes can be incredibly efficient, yet the integration of situational awareness, ethical consciousness, contextual insight, and critical judgment in algorithmic systems may not be an easy task. Such systems maintain responsibility and protect integrity of enforcement by incorporating human control at critical decision points within the system. The institutionalization of this protection is associated with critical design and governance challenges: it is clear where automated alerts should be discussed by a human; officers should be trained to identify the weaknesses of algorithms; procedures must be provided to be able to intervene in cases of machine error; workflows need to be designed to ensure that human confirmation is an obligatory step prior to taking high-stakes actions such as charging life imprisonment or capital punishment (Galante et al., 2023).

This kind of balanced model creates trust among the citizens and officers, enhances the acceptability of advanced tools and organizational preparedness to this seemingly radical change in policing systems. Without meeting the foregoing prerequisites, the police agencies will end up over-automating and relegating the human responsibilities to algorithms. Human-in-the-loop guarantees are not an operational choice only, rather they are a part of creating a policing system where algorithmic decisions in critical domains are curated by a human expert so ensure that AI/ML-policing are effective, ethical, and equitable.

Scaling and Jurisdictional Challenges

Having addressed the issues of organizational preparedness and human-machine coordination, the next phase in the realization of AI/ML-based policing is the scaling and adaptation of the artificial intelligence and machine learning technology in policing systems in India–a large and diverse legal jurisdiction. The pan-India implementation of AI/ML-based policing presents some unique challenges, primarily originated due to diversity of states, languages, crime patterns, and administrative structures in India. Localization of AI/ML models' capabilities presents a significant limitation in that crime trends in metro cities such as Bengaluru are radically different than that of a predominantly rural district of Bihar or Jharkhand. The AI/ML systems need to take into consideration the linguistic diversities, religious civil laws, state legislations, differences in data-availability and socio-economic factors to make meaningful predictions (Chhina, 2025). A failure in addressing the abovementioned localization requirements poses a threat of poor model performance, mistrust of the citizens and accentuated operational error rates. The other obstacle is the differences in infrastructure and governance among states and union territories. Some administrative jurisdictions might have developed surveillance systems, cloud computing, and policy framework, while others might not have sufficient network bandwidth, computing resources, or institutional preparedness to support a successful changeover to smart policing. Such differences impede the countrywide and uniform adoption of AI/ML-based policing systems ("Predictive policing," 2024). Pilot projects in Delhi, Punjab, Maharashtra, and Uttar Pradesh demonstrate the potential and restriction: where it has worked in one state, it may not necessarily work in another as the capacity and regulations are different.

Scaling also requires the involvement of stakeholders and a continuous refinement protocol. Another drawback of deployment in the absence of feedback loops is that the system may lag the projection, or fail to keep pace with the changing needs of legal frameworks, crime evolution, and community demands. This will make it necessary to ensure sustainable adaptation by guaranteeing inclusive governance, scalable training programmes, and adaptive AI/ML models. Lastly, there are jurisdictional risks which pose regulatory and ethical risks. Diverse state level data-governance regimes, divergent privacy protections, inconsistent consumer protection, and inadequate legal framework establish a patchwork of protections that can fail to build trust among the populace and accountability among the operating personnels. These risks may be reduced through a gradual, incremental rollout strategy, beginning with smaller units, assessing the results, and modifying the practice and then expanding it, as this is likely to adjust AI/ML-based systems to the social and institutional diversity of India.

CONCLUSION AND PROSPECTS

The introduction of artificial intelligence and machine learning in Indian policing is at a cross-road, with both the unprecedented opportunities and immense governance and ethical issues to be addressed. The ability of machine learning to improve predictive power, improve investigative accuracy, and better allocation of resources has re-construed the possibility of law enforcement in solving intricate, data-driven crime ecosystems. Predictive analytics allow police to be more proactive in predicting upcoming crime patterns and transform Indian policing from reactive enforcement patterns to pre-emptive policing. Through the synthesis of large amounts of historical data, including crime trends, demographics, geography, and socio-economic factors, AI/ML systems help the process of identifying crime hotspots. Developers of these software tools have claimed acceptable accuracy rates; however, their claims have not yet been validated by independent evaluators. Such insights allow the targeted and pre-emptive patrolling and strategic resource allocation in the metropolitan areas to reinforce the evidence-based policing practices.

In addition to prediction, AI/ML-based surveillance and investigation technologies have transformed the public order enforcement. Computing systems capable of processing live feeds from thousands of CCTV cameras to identify anomalies and alert the field officers on the imminent threat. Facial recognition makes the process of identifying a suspect at crowded places and recovering missing persons faster, whereas applications such as Crime GPT use voice analytics to deanonymize criminal or criminal communication networks. These innovations make situational awareness and response capabilities much better in highly populated and fast-urbanizing settlements. The citizen-centered AI/ML interfaces and chatbots have facilitated ease of filing complaints, provided participatory involvement, as well as strengthened the democratic aspect of police institutions.

Amidst these developments, there arise serious ethical and legal issues. Algorithmic and data bias present an issue, because machine learning algorithms trained on biased data will discriminate against certain disadvantaged groups, especially under-represented ones. The disproportionate targeting of vulnerable populations and gender or skin-colour related errors in the facial recognition technology are indications of why the use of AI/ML should be reasonably adjusted to embrace fairness and equity (Basheer, 2025; Sood, 2022). Equally, AI/ML-driven surveillance is accompanied by acute privacy issues that require a robust data governance infrastructure, a clear consent mechanism, and legal responsibility to ensure proper use of personal digital data including social media profiles and video footage. Most AI/ML systems are opaque, which also complicates transparency and interpretability as well as the right to challenge automated decisions. All these complications necessitate the establishment of institutional check and balance systems, algorithmic auditing protocols, and binding ethical standards to provide procedural justice and societal confidence.

Community involvement and multi-stakeholder partnership is also paramount for success of application of AI/ML policing systems in the long run. AI governance should be inclusive of civil society, technologists, legal experts, and representative of marginalized sections in policy-making and review processes. This participatory arrangement will make the use of AI/ML to strengthen the principles of democracy and not contribute to strengthen the existing inequalities. The federal system in India makes it challenging to harmonize the situation at the state level, as the digital infrastructure, resource distribution, and legal preparedness vary among different states. The efforts must mainly be focused on balancing innovation and control, interoperability, and responsibility without compromising the state autonomy and a national strategy.

The realization of transformative potential of AI/ML in law enforcement and delivery of justice requires development of sturdy and multipolar governance frameworks that integrate ethico-legal processes, technological innovations, algorithmic accountability, and continuous learning in the law enforcement institution. This will necessitate simultaneous investments in infrastructure modernization, capacity building, algorithmic auditability, and culturally adaptive AI/ML model design. The future developments also envision a smart integrated public order and justice ecosystem that goes beyond policing to judicial and correctional services spanning legal data analytics, blockchain-secured digital evidence management, and AI/ML-based decision-making systems.

The artificial intelligence and machine learning based decision support systems provide Indian policing with a significant chance to move to the systems of data-driven, rights-observing, and participatory public safety. Its long-term use, however, does not solely rely on using technologies but incorporating

REFERENCES

Akshaya, R., & Devadharshini, V. V. (2025, April 26). An analysis on artificial intelligence and data privacy in India. *Indian Journal of Law and Legal Research, 7*(2), 4917–4921. https://3fdef50c-add3-4615-a675-a91741bcb5c0.usrfiles.com/ugd/3fdef5_0a790d1ad05548dfa0758fd7c6586057.pdf

Attri, A., & Tripathi, M. K. (2025). Police reform and human rights: Bridging the gap in protection of minority communities. *International Journal of Political Science and Governance, 7*(8, 8A), 27–32. DOI: 10.33545/26646021.2025.v7.i8a.617

Basheer, I. P. (2025, January). Bias in the algorithm: Issues raised due to use of facial recognition in India. *Journal of Development Policy and Practice, 10*(1), 61–79. Advance online publication. DOI: 10.1177/24551333241283992

Bayley, D. H. (1994). *Police for the future.* Oxford University Press. DOI: 10.1093/oso/9780195091168.001.0001

Bhalla, K. (2019, November 8). Gurugram startup Staqu develops AI surveillance system for monitoring Uttar Pradesh prisons. *Inc42.* https://inc42.com/buzz/gurugram-startup-staqu-develops-ai-surveillance-system-for-uttar-pradesh-prisons/

Burman, A. (2023, October 3). *Understanding India's new data protection law.* Carnegie Endowment for International Peace. https://carnegieendowment.org/research/2023/10/understanding-indias-new-data-protection-law?lang=en&utm_source=chatgpt.com

Center for Human Security Studies. (2021, October 19). *Using Artificial Intelligence for smart policing.* https://chss.org.in/using-artificial-intelligence-for-smart-policing/

Cheong, B. C. (2024, July 2). Transparency and accountability in AI systems: Safeguarding wellbeing in the age of algorithmic decision-making. *Frontiers in Human Dynamics, 6*, 1421273. DOI: 10.3389/fhumd.2024.1421273

Chhina, M. A. S. (2025, March 13). How Mohali police are integrating AI into day-to-day crime detection and resolution. *The Indian Express.* https://indianexpress.com/article/cities/chandigarh/mohali-police-integrating-ai-crime-detection-resolution-9884590

Delhi Police. (2019, July 24). *Best practices in Delhi Police.* https://delhipolice.gov.in/doc/Best_practices-English.pdf

Galante, N., Cotroneo, R., Furci, D., Lodetti, G., & Casali, M. B. (2023). Applications of artificial intelligence in forensic sciences: Current potential benefits, limitations and perspectives. *International Journal of Legal Medicine, 137*(2), 445–458. DOI: 10.1007/s00414-022-02928-5 PMID: 36507961

Government of India. (2023, August 11). *The Digital Personal Data Protection Act, 2023* (Act No. 22 of 2023). https://www.meity.gov.in/static/uploads/2024/06/2bf1f0e9f04e6fb4f8fef35e82c42aa5.pdf

Handa, S., & Thakur, S. (2024, November). Role of artificial intelligence in admissibility of electronic evidence. *International Journal of Research Publication and Reviews, 5*(11), 1323–1328. https://ijrpr.com/uploads/V5ISSUE11/IJRPR34777.pdf

Hanspal, M. S., & Behera, B. (2026). Privacy and data protection in AI-driven legal services: An analysis of India's emerging challenges and solutions. *Journal of Trends and Challenges in Artificial Intelligence, 3*(1), 73–82. https://jai.aspur.rs/archive/v3/n2/2.php

Hegde, M. (2017, April 10). Espionage in Kautilya's Arthaśāstra. *Pragyata.* https://pragyata.com/espionage-in-kautilyas-arthasastra

Indian police expand AI facial recognition system, arrest 70 suspects in Delhi. (2024, December 24). ID Tech Wire. https://idtechwire.com/indian-police-expand-ai-facial-recognition-system-arrest-70-suspects-in-delhi

Kishore, M. B., Reddy, S., Sujihelen, L., Sivasangari, A., & Christy, A. (2023, May). Artificial Intelligence based detection of traffic violations by two-wheeler vehicles. [Conference paper]. *2023 7th International Conference on Intelligent Computing and Control Systems (ICICCS)* (pp. 1788-1792). https://doi.org/ DOI: 10.1109/ICICCS56967.2023.10142605

Mahajan, S., & Chaudhary, R. (2025, July). Technological evolution of Indian policing from traditional to SMART technology. *International Research Journal of Multidisciplinary Scope*, *6*(3), 800–812. DOI: 10.47857/irjms.2025.v06i03.04072

Mandalapu, V., Elluri, L., Vyas, P., & Roy, N. (2023, June 14). Crime prediction using machine learning and deep learning: A systematic review and future directions. *IEEE Access : Practical Innovations, Open Solutions*, *11*, 60153–60170. Advance online publication. DOI: 10.1109/ACCESS.2023.3286344

Modise, J. M. (2023, June). Community engagement in policing: A path to more meaningful, knowledgeable, and successful public consultation. *International Journal of Innovative Science and Research Technology*, *8*(6), 3894–3906. DOI: 10.5281/zenodo.10060950

Murugesan, R. (2021, April 16). *Predictive policing in India: Deterring crime or discriminating minorities?* LSE Human Rights Blog. https://blogs.lse.ac.uk/humanrights/2021/04/16/predictive-policing-in-india-deterring-crime-or-discriminating-minorities

Nath, S., & Barman, A. (2024). AI-Policing in India - Existing research and where to begin future research? [IJIRCST]. *International Journal of Innovative Research in Computer Science and Technology, 12*(5), 14–23. DOI: 10.55524/ijircst.2024.12.5.3

Press Information Bureau, Government of India. (2025, February 25). *Integrating AI in India's judiciary and law enforcement.* [Press release]. https://www.pib.gov.in/PressReleasePage.aspx?PRID=2106239

Predictive policing: Leveraging AI and Machine Learning for crime prevention. (2024, November 18). New Media Communication. https://newmediacomm.com/predictive-policing-leveraging-ai-and-machine-learning-for-crime-prevention

Raj, R., & Patel, H. (2023, December). Predictive policing and the emerging contours of law enforcement in India: A study. *International Journal of Innovative Science and Research Technology*, *8*(2), 16–29. https://rru.ac.in/wp-content/uploads/2024/04/Volume-8-Issue-2-SMART-Policing-Innovations.pdf

Raja, A. (2024, April 26). Meet Crime GPT, the UP Police Department's AI tool for fighting crime. *India AI.* https://indiaai.gov.in/article/meet-crime-gpt-the-up-police-department-s-ai-tool-for-fighting-crime

Rani, M. (2024, September 12). Impacts and ethics of using Artificial Intelligence by the Indian Police. *Public Administration and Policy*, *27*(2), 182–192. DOI: 10.1108/PAP-06-2023-0081

Ravishankar, K., & Anand, P. (2023, August 8). *AI judges: The question of AI's role in Indian judicial decision-making*. Centre for Comparative Constitutional Law and Administrative Law. https://www.calj.in/post/ai-judges-the-question-of-ai-s-role-in-indian-judicial-decision-making

Rohilla, N. (2025, June). History and evolution of police system in India. *Journal of International Research for Engineering and Management*, *5*(6), 1. https://joirem.com/wp-content/uploads/journal/published_paper/volume-05/issue-6/J_mbEhydGj.pdf

Sarkar, A., Mishra, A. K., Singh, U. P., Hassan, S., Munda, G. S., & Singh, P. (2025, July). Real-Time crime prediction in India using machine learning. *International Journal for Research in Applied Science and Engineering Technology*, *13*(7), 641–646. DOI: 10.22214/ijraset.2025.73053

Sayyed, H. (2024, April). Artificial intelligence and criminal liability in India: Exploring legal implications and challenges. *Cogent Social Sciences*, *10*(1), 2343195. DOI: 10.1080/23311886.2024.2343195

Sharma, A., & Gupta, S. (2022). Origin of police system in India and the world. *International Journal of Law, Management, &. Humanities (Washington)*, *5*(2), 792–806. https://doij.org/10.10000/IJLMH.112900

Singh, R. K. (2024). The evolution of the Indian police: From colonial legacy to contemporary challenges. *International Journal of Multidisciplinary Trends*, *6*(8, 8A), 50–54. DOI: 10.22271/multi.2024.v6.i8a.467

Sood, Y. (2022, October 30). Addressing algorithmic bias in India: Ethical implications and pitfalls. SSRN *Electronic Journal*. https://dx.doi.org/DOI: 10.2139/ssrn.4466681

Sur, A. (2022, January 19). Delhi Police deploys facial recognition systems, CCTV cameras ahead of Republic Day: Report. *Medianama*. https://www.medianama.com/2022/01/223-facial-recognition-systems-republic-day-report

Thacker, H. (2025, April 17). How Mumbai Police are using technology to prevent crime. *The CSR Journal*. https://thecsrjournal.in/mumbai-police-artificial-intelligence-ai-technology-prevent-crime/

Vasudev, E., & Hansen, T. B. (2024, March 1). *Citizens and the state: Policing, impunity, and the rule of law in India*. The Hindu Centre for Politics and Public Policy. https://www.thehinducentre.com/profile/author/Eklavya-Vasudev-17224

Wahab, M. I. (2025, July 10). *AI in policing: Trends, applications, and challenges*. Legal Service India. https://www.legalserviceindia.com/Legal-Articles/ai-in-policing-trends-applications-and-challenges

Wessels, M. (2023). Algorithmic policing accountability: Eight sociotechnical challenges. *Policing and Society*, *34*(3), 124–138. DOI: 10.1080/10439463.2023.2241965

Chapter 3
Virtually Solved:
A Simulated Approach to Law Enforcement Problem Solving

Kathi Nicholson
http://orcid.org/0009-0003-5423-5294
Purdue University Global, USA

Lara C. Lucas
http://orcid.org/0009-0007-8758-7519
Purdue University Global, USA

Cassie Longhart-Thomas
http://orcid.org/0000-0002-2683-405X
Purdue University Global, USA

ABSTRACT

To address global scrutiny over use of force, law enforcement is replacing reactive training with proactive Virtual Reality (VR) and Generative AI (GenAI) models. This chapter evaluates how immersive simulations and Stress Inoculation Training (SIT) use real-time biometric monitoring to help officers maintain cognitive control during high-pressure crises. By utilizing AI-driven avatars, these systems create behavioral feedback loops to master de-escalation and interactions with neurodivergent individuals. While initial costs are high, VR provides a greater long-term fiscal efficiency than traditional methods. Despite risks like training scars and biometric privacy concerns, this digital evolution fosters a culture of compassion and constitutional integrity in modern policing.

INTRODUCTION

As law enforcement agencies face unprecedented scrutiny regarding use of force, particularly during mental health crises and high-risk encounters, traditional training methodologies are being supplemented by Virtual Reality (VR) and Generative Artificial Intelligence (GenAI). The transition from reactive to proactive leadership in training design is thus to be examined, including the neurobiological benefits of stress inoculation through biofeedback, and the tactical applications of immersive simulations (DHS,

DOI: 10.4018/979-8-3373-7660-8.ch003

2024). Drawing on recent empirical research and departmental pilots, this study evaluates the efficacy of VR in building mental muscle memory and narrowing the validity gap in multisensory reliability (Stubbs, 2025). It also critically addresses ethical vulnerabilities regarding biometric data privacy and the implementation of dark patterns, deceptive design interfaces that can manipulate user consent, in emerging surveillance and training technologies (Chowdhary et al., 2023).

The evolution of training in law enforcement has historically been a reactive process. From the earliest days of American policing, external societal expectations, ranging from the Founding Fathers' vision of civic responsibility to modern demands for equity, have shaped what officers must learn. The modern era requires a proactive approach, however. The tension between the ideal of proactive leadership and the historical reality of a reactive system is most evident in how officers are prepared for high-risk, low-frequency events (Stubbs, 2025).

According to Muñoz et al. (2024), officers are frequently unprepared for the rapid escalation of emotions during a crisis, a deficiency rooted in a historical reliance on reactive training models that fail to bridge the gap between theory and field reality. Traditional classroom settings often falter because they do not successfully mimic the unpredictable needs of the field, where physiological stress often overrides cognitive recall. VR offers a proactive choice for leadership to prioritize human outcomes over procedural checklists. By utilizing VR to simulate these high-stakes environments, agencies can move beyond response mechanisms and toward a model of anticipatory readiness.

TECHNICAL MECHANICS OF IMMERSIVE SIMULATIONS

Modern policing requires a diverse set of skills that are notoriously difficult to hone within traditional classroom or static range environments. To address these complexities, law enforcement training has undergone a significant technological metamorphosis, transitioning from simple "shoot-don't-shoot" simulators to complex, multi-layered Virtual Reality (VR) environments that prioritize situational awareness and cognitive agility. These sophisticated ecosystems leverage high-fidelity graphics and spatial computing to replicate the atmospheric tension of real-world patrol work, ensuring that the trainee feels a sense of psychological presence that static training cannot replicate (Shuai et al., 2025). By integrating interconnected hardware and software layers, these systems move beyond linear video playback to provide a fully navigable, 360-degree theater of operations.

This technological shift is predicated on the necessity of multisensory fidelity. For a simulation to be effective in law enforcement, it must do more than simply present a visual stimulus; it must evoke the same autonomic nervous system responses that an officer would experience in a live incident. The mechanics of these simulations, ranging from the precision of motion capture to the integration of biometric feedback, are specifically engineered to narrow the validity gap between the training hall and the field (Stubbs, 2025). By creating a high-fidelity action-perception loop, these systems allow officers to build the mental muscle memory required to make split-second, ethical decisions under extreme physiological stress (Yebra et al., 2019).

The shift toward non-linear, AI-driven environments allows for a level of investigative and tactical sophistication previously reserved for high-cost live exercises. The technical architecture of modern VR platforms supports the objective evaluation of an officer's omnispective performance, allowing for a level of data-driven debriefing that was physically impossible in the master-apprentice models of the past (Department of Homeland Security [DHS], 2024). It is helpful to detail the specific hardware and software integrations that make this level of immersive precision possible, focusing on how these mechanical tools translate into measurable professional competence.

Hardware and High-Fidelity Integration

According to the Sacramento Police Department pilot, tactical execution simulations require a specialized kit. Officers are typically equipped with head-mounted displays (HMDs) and full-body motion capture trackers on their arms, feet, and back (Melendez & Christoff, 2024). To ensure skill transfer, officers use replica firearms that provide haptic feedback, accounting for physical weight and recoil. Crucially, the data from these integrated trackers allows for a comprehensive after-action review (AAR), where instructors can utilize 3D replays to analyze exact sighting lines and movement paths with mathematical precision (DHS, 2024). This reinforces the critical decision-making model by showing officers exactly where they may have missed a de-escalation cue or failed to utilize cover (Melendez & Christoff, 2024).

Generative AI and Adaptive Environments

The integration of Generative AI (GenAI) and VR marks a fundamental shift from scripted, branching narratives to living training environments. While traditional simulations rely on preset verbal commands, the integration of large language models (LLMs) allows officers to speak freely, creating a realistic engagement where an AI-driven avatar analyzes tone, word choice, and volume in real-time. For example, if an officer uses aggressive language, a GenAI persona simulating a mental health crisis may react with increased agitation; conversely, empathetic prompts can lead the avatar to de-escalate. This creates a high-fidelity action-perception loop where the officer's behavior directly dictates the digital environment's response, reinforcing the neural pathways required for effective real-world de-escalation (Muñoz et al., 2024).

Muñoz et al. (2024) identify critical gaps in training for volatile mental health events, noting that officers often struggle with extreme emotions or the rapid escalation of a situation, which frequently leads to a higher use of force. VR allows for the rehearsal of de-escalation strategies, such as active listening and offering choices, against AI-driven avatars capable of simulating various psychological states. This immersive rehearsal helps bridge the gap between theoretical knowledge and the high-stress application required in the field (Kleygrewe et al., 2024). This leads directly to specialized applications where environmental fidelity is paramount for officer safety and community trust.

SPECIALIZED TRAINING APPLICATIONS

The move toward specialized training applications represents the practical culmination of the hardware and software integrations already examined. While general patrol maneuvers and basic tactical drills form the foundation of academy life, the complexities of modern policing demand a more nuanced approach to human-centric encounters. Specialized applications in virtual reality are not merely digital versions of existing lectures; they are purposefully engineered environments designed to target specific cognitive and behavioral gaps that have historically led to tragic outcomes in the field. This transition is driven by the train as you fight philosophy, which posits that training environments must mimic the physiological and psychological stressors of real-world encounters to be effective (Muñoz et al., 2024).

By moving beyond a one-size-fits-all training philosophy, agencies can now deploy targeted simulations that address the most volatile and high-liability aspects of public service. This shift into specialized domains is rooted in the recognition that an officer's greatest tool is often their ability to communicate effectively under extreme duress. Traditional methods frequently fail to provide the repetitive, high-stakes rehearsal necessary to master these soft skills in an environment that truly mimics the atmospheric tension of a street-level crisis. Consequently, specialized VR modules allow for a high degree of pedagogical precision, isolating variables such as tone, body language, and environmental distractions to ensure that the trainee is learning to manage their internal state while simultaneously managing external factors (Muñoz et al., 2024).

Next, the specific domains need to be explored, where immersive technology is currently seeing the most significant institutional adoption. From the delicate nature of mental health crisis intervention to the comparative data provided by successes in the medical and aviation sectors, these applications demonstrate a paradigm shift in professional development. By prioritizing these specialized tracks, law enforcement leadership can ensure that officers are not just technically proficient with their equipment but psychologically prepared for the diverse and unpredictable human interactions that define the contemporary criminal justice landscape. This ensures that when an officer encounters a specialized crisis in the real world, the experience is encoded as a manageable digital memory rather than an overwhelming, novel stressor (Muñoz et al., 2024).

VR-Based De-escalation and Mental Health Crisis Intervention

The application of VR for training is showing promise to help officers respond effectively to high-stress situations such as mental health crises. These particular encounters require advanced communication skills, emotional intelligence, and rapid decision-making under pressure, skills that are difficult to develop in a traditional classroom setting. The use of VR-based training provides experiential learning that allows officers to practice de-escalation techniques in a more controlled environment. Modern research suggests that for these simulations to be effective, they must trigger the same psychophysiological responses found in real-world encounters (Muñoz et al., 2024). By replicating the physiological and psychological stress of suicidal ideations or psychotic episodes, VR helps officers build the situational awareness and muscle memory essential for crisis intervention.

The integration of GenAI enhances VR training through adaptive scenarios. In a traditional environment, an officer might do role-play exercises based on a given scenario. With GenAI-driven simulations, scenarios can be modified to mimic real-life behaviors and escalation levels in real-time based on the trainees' reactions. The use of GenAI can provide a wider range of outcomes, provide immediate feedback, and learn from the officers' responses to provide relevant training that is tailored to the officers' needs. Continuous exposure can improve the officers' judgement, empathy, and confidence in acting in various situations.

Cross-Industry Efficacy of VR Training

The following examples from various industries demonstrate the potential VR has for successful training and the applicability to law enforcement:

- In 2025, a study was conducted to explore the effectiveness of using VR training for high-risk safety situations in health and occupational safety in Industry 4.0 (Qawqzeh et al., 2025).
- In 2024, research showed that VR training helps promote de-escalation techniques in high-stress encounters among law enforcement officers (Muñoz et al., 2024).
- Another study in 2019 highlights the improvement VR has made in enhancing medical education (Pottle, 2019).
- A study by Pallavicini et al. (2016) examined the use of VR to assess stress and the potential for high-stress behaviors.
- Research conducted by Lohre et al. (2020) studied orthopedic surgeon residents' knowledge and metrics after using VR training compared to video instruction.
- VR is now a tool that is being used to compliment flight training (Pierobon, 2025).
- A 2025 study demonstrates how VR can be used in a variety of fields including agricultural educations (Pulley et. al, 2025).
- A 2002 study was conducted that demonstrated the use of pedestrian safety training in children using VR (McComas et. al., 2002).

These studies demonstrate the promise VR tools have on providing a learning environment in various settings for assorted training purposes such as flight training, surgical simulations, and safety practice. VR shows increasing promise for training law enforcement officers in stressful situations such as mental health crisis.

TACTICAL APPLICATIONS IN VR

The integration of immersive technology into the tactical domain represents a fundamental evolution in how law enforcement agencies approach high-stakes preparedness. Historically, tactical proficiency was measured through the mastery of isolated physical skills, marksmanship, defensive tactics, and building clearance, often practiced in controlled, predictable environments. However, real-world operational success is rarely determined by physical mechanics alone; it is dictated by the officer's ability to maintain cognitive clarity while under extreme physiological load. Tactical applications in VR are specifically engineered to address this action-perception loop, ensuring that an officer's technical skills do not degrade the moment a situation becomes volatile (Yebra et al., 2019).

There is a shift from rote, repetitive drills to a model of stress inoculation that prioritizes the human element of tactical engagement. By leveraging high-fidelity simulations, agencies can move beyond the logistical constraints of traditional force-on-force (FoF) training to provide frequent, consequence-driven rehearsal. The goal of this pedagogical shift is to build mental muscle memory, a state where an officer's brain has already processed a digital version of a high-stress encounter. This reduces the novelty of the threat and narrows the arousal-action gap, the critical moment where heightened physiological arousal can cause the emotional brain to override rational judgment, thereby reducing the likelihood of catastrophic errors in the field (Muñoz et al., 2024).

The application of VR in tactical training allows for a degree of empathetic perspective-taking that was previously difficult to achieve in traditional curricula. By utilizing role-play scenarios and AI-driven feedback loops, officers can practice the delicate art of de-escalation within a tactical framework, learning that their verbal presence is as critical as their physical positioning (Jenkins & Shields, 2024). As these systems become more standard in departmental pilots, they provide a scalable solution for building a force that is not only tactically proficient but also emotionally aware. This marriage of tactical execution and behavioral conditioning ensures that the lessons of the virtual theater translate into safer, more compassionate outcomes in the community (Melendez & Christoff, 2024).

The Shift from Linear to Non-Linear Tactical Training

The integration of VR into high-risk tactical training represents a paradigm shift from static, linear drills to fluid, non-linear engagement. Traditional tactical training often relies on FoF exercises using marking rounds; while valuable, these are logistically demanding, requiring elaborate physical training facilities and a significant number of role-players (DHS, 2024). VR provides a proactive choice for leadership to supplement these methods with high-frequency, low-cost tactical rehearsal that can be conducted in a much smaller footprint. By simulating high-stakes environments, agencies move toward a model of anticipatory readiness. This is particularly critical for high-risk, low-frequency events, such as active shooter responses, where officers must perform complex tasks under extreme physiological stress. VR allows for the creation of multi-layered environments that challenge an officer's ability to maintain tactical 360-degree awareness while simultaneously managing communication and de-escalation (Melendez & Christoff, 2024).

AI-Driven Feedback

In high-risk tactical scenarios, these AI-driven environments provide immediate feedback tailored to an officer's specific verbal and physical cues. This interaction fosters autonoetic consciousness, the neurological capacity for an officer to mentally relive a simulation and recognize exactly how their specific behaviors dictated the outcome (Muñoz et al., 2024). Unlike static training, these scenarios can be modified in real-time based on the trainee's reactions, ensuring that the range of possible outcomes remains as unpredictable as a real-world encounter (Jenkins & Shields, 2024).

BEHAVIORAL CONDITIONING FOR MENTAL HEALTH CRISIS INTERVENTION

VR training offers the law enforcement agencies the ability not only to provide life-like scenarios, but the ability to provide role-playing scenarios. This allows the officer the ability to experience a mental health crisis from the perspective of the individual who experiences a mental health illness. Role-play can improve the officer's empathy for mental health crises, reduce stigma, and promote compassionate responses during real-life encounters. VR training can save the organization long-term cost and liability risk, promote trust within the community, and foster confidence in responding to high-stress situations, in addition to consistency in training from new recruits to senior staff. According to Qawqzeh et al. (2025), VR allows for the integration of simulation-based training into everyday practice and become a regular occurrence. With VR training, students can feel at ease making mistakes while learning and improving performance. This can prevent the officer from making mistakes in the field, especially under stressful situations, where their action might have a negative outcome.

Law enforcement officers spend extended periods of time on alert, working hard to keep the community in which they serve safe. Over time, then, the officers may lose the ability to be empathetic, compassionate, or objective when faced with a mental health crisis. The use of VR can help officers interact with various scenarios that can improve or build upon empathy or compassion. According to Riches et. al., (2022), VR technology transports users into a position and perspective of another individual, which optimizes opportunities for learning and increases staff understanding of service user experience. This study reflects the ability that VR has to fine tune the soft skills needed to properly approach a mental health crisis.

According to Forbes Human Resources Council, VR helps to develop human-centric leaders through practice, reflection, and interactions that can promote behavior changes ("Revolutionizing employee training," 2023). The ability of VR to provide real-life scenarios will allow the officer to reflect on their initial reaction and access alternative methods to respond to high-stack situations. According to Muñoz et al. (2024), in addition to the highly personalized scenarios, controlled environment, realism, and deep immersivity, VR has the ability to collect data from the interaction to debrief with the trainee. This data can help provide further training opportunities, establish strengths and weaknesses, and improve situational awareness.

Over the past several decades, the possibility of police encountering people with a mental or behavioral health crisis has nearly doubled. According to Mental Health America (2024), about 10% of law enforcement contacts consist of a person with serious mental illnesses. Mental health can come in a variety of different forms and can present differently based on the type of illness and whether or not the symptoms are controlled or uncontrolled. According to Substance Abuse and Mental Health Services Administration (2023), mental health includes emotional, psychological, and social well-being, and can impact how one thinks, feels, and acts in a stressful situation. Mental health illness can include a person with various symptoms, including mood swings, erratic behavior, fighting, and harming oneself or others. Often, law enforcement is dispatched to calls that might appear to be an act of violence but turn out to be a mental health crisis. According to Muñoz et al. (2024), officers are often unprepared for the quickly changing and volatile events during a mental health crisis and cite gaps in the training. This lack of preparedness is exacerbated by the diverse forms mental illness can take, and this can lead to a higher use of force, (often lethal), than in situations not involving mental health crises.

Emphasis on de-escalation within training programs could help improve positive outcomes for events involving people in crisis. Advances in technologies are allowing for the development of training exercises with immersive experiences that allow officers to actually practice the classroom theories (Muñoz et al., 2024). The use of VR for training is showing promise to help officers in times of stress to better de-escalate. Recent audits of the technology provide examples of VR being successfully applied to prepare professionals for high-stress situations before they are exposed to them in the field. While earlier iterations of this technology were utilized for medical residency simulations using haptic force-feedback, the modern technical architecture now allows for the replication of complex mental health scenarios and behavioral crises in law enforcement training. These systems use high-fidelity AI and spatial audio to simulate the physiological and psychological pressures of a real-world encounter, allowing officers to practice verbal de-escalation in a risk-free environment (DHS, 2024).

BIOMETRIC MONITORING AND INVESTIGATIVE SOPHISTICATION

The emergence of biometric monitoring and precision analytics represents a shift in law enforcement training from subjective observation to empirical validation. While traditional training relies on the limited perspective of a human instructor to evaluate performance, immersive technologies allow for the recording and analysis of a trainee's internal physiological state. This investigative sophistication refers to the ability to decode the complex relationship between an officer's physical responses and their cognitive decision-making. By capturing data that is invisible to the naked eye, such as micro-fluctuations in heart rate or subtle shifts in gaze patterns, agencies can move beyond simply assessing what an officer did and begin to understand why they did it (Muñoz et al., 2024).

An exploration of how the integration of biometric sensors transforms VR from a mere visual simulator into a sophisticated diagnostic tool is prudent. Through psychophysiological monitoring, instructors can identify the exact moment an officer loses cognitive control, providing a roadmap for stress inoculation training (SIT) that is tailored to the individual's unique stress thresholds. This data-driven approach is not limited to tactical field maneuvers; it is equally transformative in the realm of investigative interviews and interrogations. In these high-stakes human interactions, the ability to maintain emotional equilibrium and read subtle behavioral cues is paramount (Shuai et al., 2025).

As VR systems become more granular, they offer a repository of analytics that facilitate a loop of action, feedback, and immediate retry. This iterative process ensures that successful behaviors are not just discussed in a classroom but are encoded into the officer's professional habits through autonoetic consciousness, the ability to mentally relive and learn from a digital experience as if it were a real-world memory (Muñoz et al., 2024). By leveraging these insights, departments can refine the sophisticated communication and analytical skills essential for modern crime detection, ultimately fostering a higher standard of investigative integrity and officer resilience.

Psychophysiological Monitoring and Stress Inoculation

A core advantage of VR in high-risk training is its ability to record the trainee's nervous system through psychophysiological monitoring. Advanced systems now integrate cardiovascular and electrodermal activity sensors to monitor heart rate (HR) and heart rate variability (HRV) during tactical entries. Beyond simple pulse tracking, this integration facilitates a more sophisticated action-perception loop (Yebra et al., 2019). By being consistently exposed to high-stress digital stimuli while reviewing their biometric data, officers develop the ability to recognize the early physical warning signs of high-arousal states. This data allows instructors to identify the defensive-dynamics dichotomy, the precise physiological threshold where a trainee's stress response may trigger tunnel vision or auditory exclusion, fundamentally overriding their cognitive control and de-escalation training (Melendez & Christoff, 2024).

Through stress inoculation training (SIT), VR provides officers with the opportunity to manage their physiological responses in real-time. By viewing their own biofeedback data, such as heart rate and heart rate variability (HRV), via a heads-up display (HUD) inside the goggles, officers can learn to utilize tactical breathing to lower their arousal levels and maintain situational awareness while inside a high-intensity simulation (Muñoz et al., 2024). The potential of VR for police training under stress is rooted in ensuring high-fidelity tactical realism. Because VR creates an environment of total immersion where the adversary is unpredictable, it forces the officer to stay in a constant state of tactical observation. This increases the cognitive load to ensure that when they face a real-world threat, their brain has already processed a digital version of that stressor, thereby preventing the habituation of errors, often termed training scars, that occur when simulations lack multisensory depth (Stubbs, 2025).

Precision Analytics and Pedagogical Intervention

Post-training data provided by VR systems offers a level of insight that traditional observation cannot match. This includes granular data on eye tracking and gaze patterns, showing exactly where an officer was looking, or what they missed, during a tactical entry (Jenkins & Shields, 2024). Instructors can review a full 3D replay of the simulation, analyzing exact sighting lines and movement paths to correct errors in positioning or cover usage (Kleygrewe et al., 2024). The ability to pause the simulation for immediate pedagogical intervention creates teachable moments while the experience is fresh in the trainee's memory, allowing for an immediate reset that anchors correct tactical choices (DHS, 2024). This loop of action, feedback, and immediate retry ensures that successful tactical behaviors are encoded into the officer's professional habits, reducing the likelihood of complacency in the field (Melendez & Christoff, 2024).

The Transformation of Investigation and Interrogation Training

The integration of immersive technology into law enforcement is not limited to tactical field-based scenarios or high-stress combat execution. While physical readiness remains a cornerstone of police work, the modern officer must also possess sophisticated communication and analytical skills to navigate complex legal and social landscapes. Consequently, VR is rapidly expanding into the interview and interrogation arena. As VR technologies become more sophisticated, there is an ever-growing trend of adoption across diverse law enforcement disciplines, especially in training genres that have traditionally been cost-prohibitive or logistically difficult to execute with high frequency (DHS, 2024). By shifting the focus from the street to the interview room, agencies are utilizing these innovative tools to refine the soft skills that are essential for successful crime detection and prosecution (Melendez & Christoff, 2024).

The application of VR in law enforcement training extends far beyond high-stress field maneuvers. It is rapidly transforming the interview and interrogation arena as well. Because traditional interrogation training is both expensive and time-consuming, agencies are increasingly adopting these sophisticated technologies to simulate complex human interactions. This immersive experience is achieved by tricking the brain into perceiving a digital world as reality, providing a level of psychological presence that static training cannot match (Shuai et al., 2025).

While popular police dramas often depict intense, high-stakes interrogations as a matter of routine, the reality of mastering this skill is far more nuanced. Traditionally, officers have learned these techniques through role-playing simulations. However, these methods require immense resources and typically provide a restricted experience because multiple human-led sessions are logistically taxing and expensive (DHS, 2024). Incorporating VR and AI into this curriculum changes the dynamic entirely, allowing for the repeated practice of interrogation techniques backed by objective, data-driven feedback (Muñoz et al., 2024). The scenarios can be quickly altered to reflect various investigative needs, offering scalable benefits to officer training (Jenkins & Shields, 2024). Specifically, high-fidelity environments can simulate the physiological and psychological pressure of an interview, forcing the officer to manage their own stress responses while maintaining the cognitive effort necessary to identify deception (Muñoz et al., 2024).

Central to this immersion is the use of a headset that blocks physical vision to display stereoscopic 3D images. By presenting slightly different viewpoints to each eye, this technology leverages stereopsis, the neurological process of merging two images to create a sense of depth. This ability to see in stereo is a critical element for trainees, as it provides the realistic depth perception required to accurately read a suspect's body language and spatial presence during a simulated questioning (DHS, 2024).

Simultaneously, integrated sensors track head and hand movements with high precision, updating the digital environment in real-time to maintain a seamless sense of being there (DHS, 2024). This visual stage is complemented by spatial audio, which replicates how sound travels in a physical room, presenting an immersive and believable experience. This high-fidelity training allows officers to practice reading body language and other subtle micro-expressions that can indicate deception, stress, and other psychological indicators during an interview or interrogation (Shuai et al., 2025). Considering the logistical and financial challenges of creating a realistic questioning scenario with professional live actors, VR presents a promising and scalable opportunity to train officers in this delicate art.

A primary benefit of using VR for officer interrogation training is the capacity for timely feedback and dynamic analytics. Unlike a human role-player who may struggle to maintain consistency across dozens of sessions, the characters in a VR simulation remain consistent and can be adapted in real-time by the software or an instructor (Muñoz et al., 2024). Within the VR equipment resides the capability to track eye movements, gaze patterns, and voice inflections with mathematical precision (Jenkins & Shields, 2024). This level of detail is essential because high-fidelity environments increase the suspect's motivation to remain deceptive, forcing the officer to utilize these precise cues to detect inconsistencies (Melendez & Christoff, 2024).

As the trainee's tone changes, the AI-driven character adapts its demeanor instantly, becoming helpful, hostile, aggressive, or evasive based on the officer's input. This immediate response allows the officer to witness the direct impact of their tone and verbal signals on a suspect's willingness to cooperate. By identifying which cues trigger defensive or deceptive behaviors, officers develop autonoetic consciousness, the ability to mentally relive the scenario and recognize how their own specific behavior dictated the suspect's outcome. This self-reflection allows officers to improve their interview tactics, de-escalation skills, and build the confidence necessary for real-world encounters (Muñoz et al., 2024). This iterative process can be done repeatedly in a virtual environment with little to no risk to the officer, the agency, or an active investigation. The data can then be reviewed afterward for additional feedback and insights (DHS, 2024).

The VR systems provide a vast repository of data post-training, offering a level of insight that traditional observation cannot match. This includes granular data on where an officer was looking at any given second and how quickly they were able to make critical decisions during the simulation (Melendez & Christoff, 2024). These metrics allow for an objective evaluation of an officer's investigative instinct and situational awareness (DHS, 2024).

These systems allow for immediate pedagogical intervention. An instructor can pause the simulation at any moment to review a specific decision made by the officer, allowing for an immediate reset that anchors correct tactical choices (DHS, 2024). This creates a teachable moment while the experience is still fresh, facilitating autonoetic consciousness, the ability to mentally represent and relive past experiences, as the officer reflects on how their specific behavior dictated the outcome (Muñoz et al., 2024). The officer can then immediately correct mistakes and retry the scenario, providing an instant understanding of successful interactions versus incorrect procedures. By repeating this cycle of action and feedback, officers can ensure that effective interrogation tactics become a permanent part of their professional repertoire, allowing for more consistent results in real-world interviews (Melendez & Christoff, 2024).

An additional training area showing promise and potential growth is de-escalation. This, along with previously discussed area, relies heavily on soft skills that are notoriously difficult to master through observation alone (Melendez & Christoff, 2024). In de-escalation situations, emotions are typically running high and there is much unknown. Adding VR training lets officers experience these situations through a VR lens without the risk associated with these encounters. Realistic, high-stakes scenarios allow officers to familiarize themselves with high-pressure dialogue and practice advanced communication techniques without the danger or repercussions of real-life situations (Muñoz et al., 2024). This creates a state of psychological presence where the brain responds as if the threat is real, allowing for effective stress inoculation without actual physical harm (Shuai, 2025).

Interrogation and de-escalation training curriculum for officers typically contains a mix of software solutions and live exercises. While these current tools enhance training, they frequently become dated as criminal tactics evolve and need to be constantly refreshed (Jenkins & Shields, 2024). Training during live exercises also involves extensive resources and high costs, these simulations are limited by the physical and logistical constraints of coordinating role-players. As highlighted by the implementation of VR systems in modern agencies, shifting to immersive platforms provides a safer, more controlled environment for high-intensity de-escalation and interrogation, reducing the inherent risks associated with traditional field-based drills (Melendez & Christoff, 2024).

Specialized Training for Neurodivergent Encounters

One area getting attention is de-escalation training for encounters with neurodivergent individuals. Typical training for de-escalation is often the worst protocol for someone who is neurodivergent as the commands often trigger a sensory overload. This is an example where it would be unethical to ask a neurodivergent person to participate in high-stress training exercises, and asking other officers to role-play the part often lacks the necessary behavioral nuance (Oh & Son, 2022).

This is a primary use case for VR, as virtual interactions with people on the autism spectrum allow officers to practice techniques without compromising the health and safety of these individuals. Oh and Son (2022) describe a classic A-B test scenario where officers participated in one of three training methods: video training, practice with VR, or both video and VR practice. They report that data indicates significantly more effective training and better retention of de-escalation skills when practicing in the VR setting (Oh & Son, 2022). VR training allows research about neurodivergent behaviors to be incorporated into the simulation in a realistic manner (Oh & Son, 2022). This is particularly true when AI is added to ensure the avatar responds dynamically to the officer's tactics (Muñoz et al., 2024).

CRITICAL CHALLENGES

Technical Limitations, Ethics, and Physical Risks

While the transformative potential of immersive technology in law enforcement is undeniable, the transition from traditional methodologies to high-fidelity simulations introduces a complex array of institutional and ethical risks. These challenges are not merely technical hurdles to be overcome by better hardware; they represent fundamental concerns regarding the intersection of human rights, physiological privacy, and operational readiness. As agencies move toward permanent departmental integration, leadership must grapple with the unintended consequences of behavioral conditioning and the legal vacuum surrounding the collection of biometric data. A critical examination of these vulnerabilities is essential to ensure that the adoption of VR and GenAI enhances public safety without compromising the constitutional or psychological integrity of the officers involved (Chowdhary et al., 2023).

At the forefront of these psychological risks is the validity gap, where the digital environment fails to accurately translate to the physical reality of the street. If simulations lack multisensory fidelity, they risk fostering negative transfer, the encoding of dangerous habits that could prove fatal in a high-stakes encounter (Stubbs, 2025). The persuasive power of immersive technology necessitates a rigorous ethical framework. Without intentional guardrails, a heavy reliance on threat-centric scenarios may inadvertently reinforce a tactical-response bias, fundamentally shifting an officer's default reaction from community engagement toward physical defense (Muñoz et al., 2024).

Technical, psychological, and physical risks defining the current frontier of immersive training provides clearer insight. From cybersickness to the ethical dilemmas of biometric reviews, these challenges highlight the need for robust data governance. By addressing these vulnerabilities, the criminal justice system can move toward a data lifecycle management model that prioritizes human-centric design and institutional accountability (Jenkins & Shields, 2024).

Mechanical Risks and the Phenomenon of Negative Transfer

While the benefits of immersive tactical training are significant, the transition must address mechanical risks that lead to training scars. At the heart of this issue is the physiological discrepancy between simulated performance and real-world behavior. This gap is often fueled by a lack of perceptual realism. If the digital environment does not elicit a genuine autonomic nervous system response, the training fails to provide necessary stress inoculation (Muñoz et al., 2024). A primary technical driver of this failure is latency jitter, the micro-delays between an officer's physical movement and the visual update in the headset (Stubbs, 2025). For example, if a VR system has even a 20-millisecond lag during a holster draw, an officer may subconsciously adjust their mechanics to compensate. In a real-world shootout, where survival is measured in milliseconds, this trained delay can be fatal (DHS, 2024).

In cognitive psychology, this result is known as negative transfer, occurring when a training environment reinforces ineffective or dangerous habits. Because the brain processes these immersive experiences through autonoetic consciousness, the ability to mentally represent and relive past events, it may treat a flawed digital interaction as a primary survival memory (Stubbs, 2025). When mental muscle memory is built on incomplete data, such as the absence of realistic haptic recoil or tactile feedback, agencies risk the development of permanent mechanical training scars (DHS, 2024). A lack of high-fidelity facial micro-expressions in a simulation can hinder the social recognition skills required for de-escalation, potentially leading to incorrect social judgments or a failure to perceive intent in the field (Shuai et al., 2025).

Psychological Risks and Behavioral Conditioning

A significant psychological risk of VR integration is the potential for unintended conditioning. Immersive simulations are inherently persuasive because they utilize psychological presence to trick the brain's amygdala into responding to digital stimuli as if they were real threats (Shuai et al., 2025). If the majority of VR training scenarios are designed with a threat-centric focus, the technology may inadvertently reinforce a stress-induced behavioral default, where trainees prioritize tactical force over verbal de-escalation strategies (Muñoz et al., 2024).

This primes officers to perceive danger in ambiguous situations, potentially bypassing higher-order cognitive reasoning. To mitigate this, agencies must ensure a balanced scenario library where de-escalation is the primary path to success. The integration of GenAI ensures environments mimic the unpredictability of real-life situations, preventing officers from gaming the system by memorizing scripted NPC patterns (DHS, 2024). This variability is essential to narrowing the validity gap, ensuring that the officer's biological stress response remains authentic to the tactical challenge rather than the simulation's limitations (Stubbs, 2025).

Ethical Risks and Biometric Data Privacy

The collection of involuntary biological data, such as heart rate, pupil dilation, and gaze tracking, creates a legal vacuum. When a department mandates VR training, it is essentially searching through the officer's internal physiological state. Because training is a condition of employment, consent to biometric monitoring is often misleading; if an officer must submit to a VR stress test to keep their badge, the data collection may be viewed as a warrantless search of their biological effects (Chowdhary et al., 2023). Many VR systems utilize dark patterns, manipulative interfaces that goad users into sharing data, increasing the risk that sensitive biometric profiles could be stored or breached by third-party vendors (Chowdhary et al., 2023).

Physical Risks and Operational Readiness

The physical health of the officer must also be protected, particularly regarding cybersickness. This disorientation is caused by a sensory conflict where the eyes perceive motion the body does not feel. To maintain operational readiness, training programs should utilize a combination of behavioral and software-based mitigations, such as mandatory cool-down periods and field-of-view (FOV) vignetting, which restricts peripheral vision during high-velocity digital movement to reduce nausea (Oh & Son, 2022). Emerging hardware solutions like galvanic vestibular stimulation (GVS) are being explored to align the user's vestibular system with the visual display via low-level electrical impulses to the inner ear. For individuals unable to participate in immersive environments due to medical conditions such as chronic eye strain or persistent headaches, organizations must provide alternative training modalities to ensure equitable professional development (Northern Illinois University, 2021).

Organizational Barriers and Data Governance

Another concern with using VR is the security of the data collected. The organization would need to ensure there is strong data governance in place to ensure the correct permissions are granted to the correct individuals and proper security measures are in place to prevent unauthorized access. This is especially critical because biometric data is immutable. Unlike a password, an officer cannot change their heart rate variability or gaze patterns if they are leaked in a breach (Chowdhary et al., 2023).

A principled approach to AI in policing requires that agencies maintain transparency regarding how this data is stored and who has the right to audit it (Jenkins & Shields, 2024). If an officer's stress response data is used for performance reviews or promotional decisions without their explicit consent, it creates a pre-crime ethical dilemma where an individual is judged on their physiological potential for failure rather than their professional actions. To avoid this, departments must implement a data lifecycle management policy that dictates when biometric files are encrypted, how long they are retained, and under what specific legal conditions they can be accessed by third-party vendors or internal affairs. By establishing these guardrails early, agencies can build the institutional credibility necessary to win over late adopters who may otherwise be skeptical of the technology's intrusive potential.

SYNTHESIS AND THE FUTURE OF IMMERSIVE POLICING

The training opportunities inherent in VR represent a transformative frontier for interview techniques, interrogation strategies, and de-escalation protocols. While these technologies are currently in the emerging stages of institutional adoption, the potential for industry-wide growth is substantial. To transition from pilot programs to widespread implementation, law enforcement agencies must continue to substantiate the objective effectiveness, pedagogical superiority, and long-term fiscal sustainability associated with immersive simulations. Significant progress is already visible on the horizon. For example, the 2026 acquisition of specialized VR training pods by the Tampa Police Department signals a definitive shift toward permanent departmental integration (Tampa Police Department, 2026). This shift is driven by a multidisciplinary leap in capability that addresses several long-standing gaps in traditional police academies. The future of this field is anchored in four primary pillars of innovation:

1. Psychophysiological Mastery: Allows for stress inoculation training (SIT), where biofeedback prepares officers for the defensive dynamics dichotomy, the physiological threshold where cognitive control is often lost to tunnel vision (Melendez & Christoff, 2024).
2. Cognitive and Ethical Advancement: Overcomes the engagement gaps of passive learning by utilizing the action-perception loop to strengthen the encoding of episodic memories (Yebra et al., 2019). These objective, immersive environments further provide a platform for identifying and mitigating implicit bias through perspective-taking exercises (Melendez & Christoff, 2024).
3. Tactical and Investigative Sophistication: Utilizes high-fidelity environments and AI to enhance investigative interviews and decision-making speed (Jenkins & Shields, 2024).
4. Logistical and Economic Efficiency: VR offers a scalable solution to the high recurring costs and logistical burdens associated with traditional FoF training facilities and role-player expenses (DHS, 2024).

As the VR industry moves toward multisensory fidelity, integrating scent generators, galvanic vestibular stimulation (GVS), and AI-driven coaching, the focus remains on a balanced marriage of standard practices and modern technology. By utilizing these tools to create high-fidelity digital memories, agencies can ensure that officers are prepared for the physical reality of the street. The goal is to refine an officer's autonoetic consciousness, ensuring they can carry the lessons of the virtual world into the physical one without compromising their constitutional or psychological integrity (Muñoz et al., 2024).

Advanced Biofeedback and Stress Management

As VR systems become more sophisticated, incorporating wearable devices that track heart rate, breathing, and even cortisol levels provides a comprehensive biofeedback loop. Instructors can modify the scene and audio sounds in real-time within the VR scenario to intentionally increase the officer's stress levels. By reviewing these biometric data points alongside a 3D replay of the simulation, instructors can facilitate autonoetic consciousness in the trainee, allowing them to recognize the exact point where their internal physiological state dictated an external tactical error (Muñoz et al., 2024).

Addressing Implicit Bias and Promoting Compassion

Training scenarios can be specifically tailored to identify and address implicit biases by providing officers with diverse scenarios involving suspects of different races, ages, and abilities. These immersive simulations enable officers to recognize signs of crisis, such as neurodiversity or a mental health emergency, and choose the appropriate path of de-escalation. Because the digital environments are consistent, instructors can utilize objective data, such as gaze-tracking heatmaps, to determine if an officer's focus patterns change based on a suspect's demographic profile, providing a mathematical foundation for discussing bias that traditional observation cannot provide (Jenkins & Shields, 2024).

This transition from a reactive to a proactive system is most evident in the recent implementations within the Seattle and Phoenix Police Departments. By allowing officers to step into the shoes of community members, VR facilitates a high degree of perspective-taking and empathy. Internal evaluations conducted during these deployments found that 81% of participating officers reported that VR scenarios effectively prepared them to adapt their approach to a call, while 60% reported an increase in perspective-taking ("How virtual reality is transforming," 2022). This success is rooted in the creation of a durable digital memory that officers can relive through autonoetic consciousness, ensuring that the lessons of compassion and de-escalation are encoded as personal experiences rather than just academic concepts (Muñoz et al., 2024).

Overcoming the Pedagogical Engagement Gap

Research has shown that most people have short attention spans, particularly when presented with passive information. Traditional training methods, such as lectures and textbook reading, often fail to encode information to episodic memory (Muñoz et al., 2024). Without the emotional and sensory hook provided by active participation, the lessons are often lost before an officer reaches the field (Muñoz et al., 2024). The intense stimulation and activity associated with training in virtual environments offer much promise for these law enforcement training scenarios because they force the brain to live the experience rather than just read about it (Stubbs, 2025).

Investigative Sophistication through AI and VR Integration

One of the most powerful features of these systems is the ability to quickly create new scenarios, add what-if variables to the mix, and change the training environment in real-time in response to the trainee's specific actions (Jenkins & Shields, 2024). Furthering the synergy between AI and VR, modern training programs can analyze a trainee's verbal responses, tone, and even gaze patterns to offer immediate, data-driven feedback and specific recommendations for further training (Muñoz et al., 2024).

Melendez and Christoff (2024) highlight how VR can simulate suspects participating in a crime to advance an officer's investigative capabilities. Their research indicates that high-fidelity VR environments increase the fundamental motivation of the simulated suspect to remain deceptive, thereby requiring the officer to invest significantly more cognitive effort in the interview. This increased engagement in the simulation leads to a more effective transfer of deception detection and investigative skills to real-world scenarios, ensuring successful tactical behaviors are encoded into the officer's professional repertoire.

Resource Allocation and Comparative Logistical Benefits

Agencies must decide how to allocate limited resources to achieve the best tactical outcomes. While traditional FoF training is logistically heavy and limited by physical set designs, VR training allows complex drills to be conducted in a smaller footprint with a significantly lower cost per repetition. The financial impact of these methods scales differently over time, as the software-driven nature of VR allows for instant resets and eliminates the high recurring costs associated with marking rounds and role-player pay (DHS, 2024). Safety profiles also vary significantly. While traditional training carries an inherent risk of physical injury from projectiles and high-stress physical encounters, VR allows officers to train in a controlled environment where risks are primarily limited to physiological side effects like cybersickness (Stubbs, 2025).

This shift toward a digital medium does more than just mitigate physical risk. It unlocks a level of data-driven feedback that is impossible to replicate in a physical space. The depth of feedback and variety of training environments also favor digital solutions in several key areas. While traditional training reviews typically rely on the subjective notes and limited memory of a human instructor, the digital environment offers a persistent, objective record. By leveraging 3D spatial data, the system allows for an omnispective review, the technical capability for an instructor to detach from the trainee's viewpoint and move freely through the frozen digital scene. This allows for a 360-degree evaluation of an officer's positioning from the suspect's perspective, ensuring that tactical movements are evaluated with empirical data rather than observation alone (DHS, 2024).

Future Outlook: Multisensory Fidelity and AI-Driven Coaching

To reach the full potential of VR, the industry is moving toward multisensory fidelity and hyper-personalized learning. Future systems are exploring the integration of scent generators to provide olfactory cues, such as the smell of gunpowder or narcotics, which can trigger danger recognition faster than visual cues alone. The use of hardware like galvanic vestibular stimulation (GVS) is being developed to align the officer's inner ear with the digital environment. While these specialized tools represent the frontier of the field, current high-fidelity platforms already leverage integrated weapon systems and 360-degree environments to ensure officers treat digital threats with real-world gravity (DHS, 2024). This level of immersion ensures the brain registers tactical mistakes with a high degree of neural urgency, bridging the gap between simulation and field performance (Stubbs, 2025).

The next generation of VR training will include AI coaches that analyze an officer's performance against thousands of other data points. Instead of a human instructor simply saying, you were too slow, the AI can provide a heatmap of the officer's eye gaze, showing exactly where they missed a concealed weapon or a de-escalation cue (Jenkins & Shields, 2024). The integration of VR and GenAI represents a transformation of the capabilities available in criminal justice. A close examination of the advantages, such as logistical efficiency and stress inoculation, balanced against the weaknesses, such as conditioning and the Fourth Amendment implications of biometric privacy, can guide the future toward a more ethical model (Chowdhary et al., 2023).

CONCLUSION

The integration of Virtual Reality (VR) and Generative Artificial Intelligence (GenAI) into law enforcement represents a fundamental shift from historically reactive training models to a paradigm of proactive, anticipatory readiness. These immersive technologies address the unprecedented scrutiny surrounding use-of-force by providing a high-fidelity platform for mastering both tactical execution and sophisticated soft skills. By simulating high-risk, low-frequency events, such as active shooter responses or volatile mental health crises, VR allows officers to build mental muscle memory and emotional resilience in a controlled, risk-free environment (Stubbs, 2025). Central to this transformation is the neurobiological benefit of Stress Inoculation Training (SIT). Through real-time psychophysiological monitoring and biofeedback, officers can learn to recognize the early physical warning signs of heightened physiological arousal and utilize tactical breathing to maintain cognitive control under extreme stress (Muñoz et al., 2024). The synergy between VR and GenAI creates living training environments where adaptive adversaries respond dynamically to an officer's tone, volume, and word choice (Muñoz et al., 2024). This behavioral feedback loop is particularly valuable for de-escalation training and specialized encounters, such as those involving neurodivergent individuals, where traditional protocols may inadvertently trigger sensory overload (Oh & Son, 2022).

Despite these significant advantages, the transition to immersive training is not without its challenges. Agencies must critically address the validity gap and the potential for training scars caused by technical issues like latency or a lack of multisensory fidelity (Stubbs, 2025). There are also vital ethical considerations regarding biometric data privacy, the risk of cybersickness, and the substantial upfront costs that may be prohibitive for smaller departments (Muñoz et al., 2024). As evidenced by pioneering programs like those in the Sacramento and Tampa Police Departments, the long-term investment in VR systems can lead to significant logistical efficiencies, a reduction in liability risks, and enhanced community trust (Tampa Police Department, 2026). Ultimately, the goal of this digital evolution is to ensure that officers are better prepared for the physical and psychological realities of the street, fostering a culture of policing that is characterized by calm, compassionate, and effective crisis intervention.

As the marriage of standard practices and modern technologies matures, the focus remains on ensuring the digital world prepares officers for the physical reality of the street. This objective must be achieved without compromising the psychological well-being of the personnel or infringing upon their fundamental constitutional rights. Consequently, future training frameworks will require a rigorous balance between the immersive power of synthetic environments and the ethical guardrails of biometric data privacy. By prioritizing human-centric design alongside technical innovation, the criminal justice system can leverage these tools to uphold the highest standards of public safety and professional integrity.

REFERENCES

Chowdhary, S., Kawakami, A., Gray, M. L., Suh, J., Olteanu, A., & Saha, K. (2023, June). *Can workers meaningfully consent to workplace wellbeing technologies?* [Conference paper]. ACM Conference on Fairness, Accountability, and Transparency (pp. 569-582). https://doi.org/DOI: 10.1145/3593013.3594023

Department of Homeland Security. (2024, January). *Virtual Reality (VR) training systems for first responders market survey report.* System Assessment and Validation for Emergency Responders (SAVER) Program. https://www.dhs.gov/sites/default/files/2024-07/2024_0709_st_vrmsr%20%282%29.pdf

How virtual reality is transforming the way Phoenix PD trains. (2026, February 24). Axon Enterprise. https://www.axon.com/resources/articles-source/how-virtual-reality-is-transforming-the-way-phoenix-pd-trains

Jenkins, M., & Shields, C. (2024, April 10). *Taking a principled approach to AI in policing.* Police Chief Online. https://www.policechiefmagazine.org/principled-approach-ai

Kleygrewe, L., Hutter, R. I. V., Koedijk, M., & Oudejans, R. R. D. (2024, July). Changing perspectives: Enhancing learning efficacy with the after-action review in virtual reality training for police. *Ergonomics, 67*(5), 628–637. DOI: 10.1080/00140139.2023.2236819 PMID: 37440434

Lohre, R., Bois, A. J., Pollock, J. W., Lapner, P., McIlquham, K., Athwal, G. S., & Goel, D. P. (2020). Effectiveness of immersive virtual reality on orthopedic surgical skills and knowledge acquisition among senior surgical residents. *JAMA Network Open, 3*(12), e2031217. DOI: 10.1001/jamanetworkopen.2020.31217 PMID: 33369660

McComas, J., MacKay, M., & Pivik, J. (2002). Effectiveness of virtual reality for teaching pedestrian safety. *Cyberpsychology & Behavior, 5*(3), 185–190. DOI: 10.1089/109493102760147150 PMID: 12123238

Melendez, H., & Christoff, T. (2024). *Sacramento (California) Police Department's virtual reality system: Addressing crime through innovative technology.* Office of Community Oriented Policing Services. https://portal.cops.usdoj.gov/resourcecenter/content.ashx/cops-r1174-pub.pdf

Mental Health America. (2024, September 16). *Responding to behavioral health crises.* https://mhanational.org/position-statements/responding-to-behavioral-health-crises

Muñoz, J. E., Lavoie, J. A., & Pope, A. T. (2024, September 4). Psychophysiological insights and user perspectives: Enhancing police de-escalation skills through full-body VR training. *Frontiers in Psychology, 15.* Advance online publication. DOI: 10.3389/fpsyg.2024.1390677 PMID: 39295763

Northern Illinois University Continuing and Professional Education. (2021, June 15). *Virtual reality and lean…the good, the bad, and the ugly.* https://cpelearn.niu.edu/virtual-reality-and-leanthe-good-the-bad-and-the-ugly

Oh, H., & Son, W. (2022). Cybersickness and its severity arising from virtual reality content: A comprehensive study. *Sensors (Basel), 22*(4), 1314. DOI: 10.3390/s22041314 PMID: 35214216

Pallavicini, F., Argenton, L., Toniazzi, N., Aceti, L., & Mantovani, F. (2016, December). Virtual reality applications for stress management training in the military. *Aerospace Medicine and Human Performance*, *87*(12), 1021–1030. https://asma.kglmeridian.com/downloadpdf/view/journals/amhp/87/12/article-p1021.pdf PMID: 28323588

Pierobon, M. (2025, December 10). *Training with virtual reality*. Flight Safety Foundation. https://flightsafety.org/asw-article/training-with-virtual-reality

Pottle, J. (2019, October). Virtual reality and the transformation of medical education. *Future Healthcare Journal*, *6*(3), 181–185. DOI: 10.7861/fhj.2019-0036 PMID: 31660522

Pulley, J., Claflin, K., & Thompson, A. (2025, August 4). A review of virtual reality applications in agriculture education and recommendations for future research. *Journal of Agricultural Education*, *66*(3), 15. DOI: 10.5032/jae.v66i3.3195

Qawqzeh, Y., Shraah, A. A., Rizwan, A., Sánchez-Chero, M., More, L. A. V., & Shabaz, M. (2025, August 7). Exploring the effectiveness of virtual reality-based training for sustainable health and occupational safety in Industry 4.0. *Scientific Reports*, *15*, 28930. DOI: 10.1038/s41598-025-14173-y PMID: 40775014

Revolutionizing employee training: six benefits of virtual and augmented reality in the workplace. (2023, May 11). *Forbes*. https://www.forbes.com/councils/forbeshumanresourcescouncil/2023/05/11/revolutionizing-employee-training-six-benefits-of-virtual-and-augmented-reality-in-the-workplace

Riches, S., Iannelli, H., Reynolds, L., Fisher, H. L., Cross, S., & Attoe, C. (2022, July 19). Virtual reality-based training for mental health staff: A novel approach to increase empathy, compassion, and subjective understanding of service user experience. *Advances in Simulation (London, England)*, *7*, 19. DOI: 10.1186/s41077-022-00217-0 PMID: 35854343

Shuai, T., Beng, S., Khalid, F. B., & Rahmat, R. W. B. O. K. (2025, October 8). Advances in facial micro-expression detection and recognition: A comprehensive review. *Information (Basel)*, *16*(10), 876. DOI: 10.3390/info16100876

Stubbs, G. (2025, June 12). Addressing the potential for training scars: Investigating the risk of using extended reality in police training. *Policing. Journal of Policy Practice*, *19*, paaf019. Advance online publication. DOI: 10.1093/police/paaf019

Substance Abuse and Mental Health Services Administration. (2023, April 24). *What is mental health?* https://www.samhsa.gov/mental-health/what-is-mental-health

Tampa Police Department. (2026, January 8). *New year, new tech for Tampa Police Department* [Press release]. https://www.tampa.gov/news/2026-01/new-year-new-tech-tampa-police-department-178786

Yebra, M., Galarza-Vallejo, A., Soto-León, V., Gonzalez-Rosa, J. J., de Berker, A. O., Bestmann, S., Oliviero, A., Kroes, M. C. W., & Strange, B. A. (2019, August 6). Action boosts episodic memory encoding in humans via engagement of a noradrenergic system. *Nature Communications*, *10*(1), 1–12. DOI: 10.1038/s41467-019-11358-8 PMID: 31388000

KEY TERMS AND DEFINITIONS

Action-perception loop: A neurological process where physical movement during a simulation triggers the brain's noradrenergic system, deeply encoding the sensory experience into long-term episodic memory. This ensures that tactical lessons learned in VR are more effectively retained than those from passive instruction (Yebra et al., 2019).

After-action review (AAR): A structured review process of a training task that allows trainees to discover for themselves what happened, why it happened, and how to sustain strengths and improve on weaknesses. In VR, this often includes a 3D digital replay of the session (Jenkins & Shields, 2024).

Autonoetic consciousness: The neurological capacity to mentally relive past experiences and recognize oneself as the causal agent in those. In VR training, this facilitates deep learning by allowing officers to understand how their specific behaviors dictated a simulation's outcome (Muñoz et al., 2024).

Biometric data privacy: The ethical and legal framework governing the collection, storage, and use of a trainee's physiological data, such as heart rate or gaze patterns, during simulation (Muñoz et al., 2024).

Cybersickness (VR sickness): Nausea, disorientation, or headaches caused by a sensory conflict where the eyes see movement that the body does not physically experience (Oh & Son, 2022).

Dark patterns: Manipulative software interfaces designed to goad users into sharing private data or consenting to complex privacy policies without a full understanding of the implications (Chowdhary et al., 2023).

Defensive dynamics dichotomy: The physiological threshold during a high-stress encounter where an individual loses cognitive control and reverts to tunnel vision or instinctual survival behaviors (Melendez & Christoff, 2024).

Electrical muscle stimulation (EMS): A haptic technology that uses localized electrical impulses to trigger involuntary muscle contractions. In a tactical VR environment, EMS provides a physiological consequence for perceived hits or tactical errors, ensuring that digital threats are treated with real-world gravity and mitigating the invincibility bias often found in lower-fidelity simulations (DHS, 2024).

Episodic memory: A category of long-term memory that involves the recollection of specific events, situations, and experiences. VR aids in encoding this by allowing the brain to live the scenario through physical action, which triggers the release of norepinephrine to stabilize the memory trace (Yebra et al., 2019). This ensures that tactical lessons learned in a simulation are more readily accessible during real-world high-stress encounters.

Force-on-force (FoF): Traditional tactical training involving live exercises with non-lethal marking rounds (DHS, 2024).

Galvanic vestibular stimulation (GVS): A non-invasive technique that applies low-level electrical currents to the mastoid processes behind the ears to stimulate the vestibular nerve. By simulating the sensation of motion or imbalance, GVS aligns the inner ear's physical equilibrium with the visual movement of a virtual display, thereby mitigating the sensory conflict that leads to cybersickness (Oh & Son, 2022).

Generative artificial intelligence (GenAI): A form of AI capable of creating dynamic, non-scripted content in real-time (Jenkins & Shields, 2024). In law enforcement training, it allows AI-driven avatars to analyze an officer's tone and word choice to generate realistic, unpredictable responses (Muñoz et al., 2024).

Haptic feedback: The use of tactile sensations, such as vibration, recoil, or pressure, to provide physical feedback to the user. In tactical simulations, this technology enhances realism by allowing officers to feel the operation of a firearm or the resistance of digital objects, thereby reinforcing muscle memory during high-stress drills (DHS, 2024).

Heatmap (gaze): A data visualization tool showing the intensity and location of an officer's eye fixations, revealing whether they identified threats or missed de-escalation cues (Jenkins & Shields, 2024).

Latency: The micro-delay between an officer's physical movement and the subsequent visual update in the VR headset, technically referred to as motion-to-photon latency (DHS, 2024). When this delay exceeds the threshold of human perception (typically 20 milliseconds), it creates a sensory mismatch between the vestibular system and the visual cortex, which is a primary cause of cybersickness (Oh & Son, 2022).

Mental muscle memory: The reinforcement of critical decision-making models and physical movements through repetitive, high-fidelity rehearsal in a virtual environment (Melendez & Christoff, 2024).

Multisensory fidelity: The degree to which a simulation engages multiple sensory modalities, including visual, auditory, olfactory, and haptic inputs, to achieve high-fidelity immersion. High multisensory fidelity is a technical requirement for reducing the validity gap between simulated and real-world tactical environments (DHS, 2024).

Olfactory cues: Environmental scents (e.g., gunpowder, narcotics, or fire) integrated into simulations to trigger rapid neural recognition of threats. By engaging the olfactory system, which has a direct anatomical link to the amygdala and hippocampus, simulations enhance ecological validity and ensure the brain processes digital threats with the same neural urgency as real-world encounters (Stubbs, 2025).

Omnispective review: A technical feature of high-fidelity VR systems that allows an instructor to view a recorded simulation from any angle or position within a persistent 3D environment. Unlike 2D video playback, an omnispective review enables the analysis of sighting lines, muzzle vectors, and cover usage from any perspective, including the suspect's, providing a mathematically precise evaluation of tactical positioning (DHS, 2024).

Psychological presence: A state achieved when immersive technology tricks the brain into perceiving a digital world as reality, providing a level of emotional and cognitive realism that static training cannot match (Shuai et al., 2025).

Sighting lines (digital): Visual vectors generated during a 3D after-action review (AAR) that display the mathematically precise path of an officer's weapon aim or eye gaze (DHS, 2024). These markers allow instructors to evaluate muzzle discipline, target acquisition speed, and the accuracy of scanning and breathing techniques during high-stress simulations.

Stress inoculation training (SIT): A pedagogical method where trainees are exposed to increasing levels of stress in a controlled environment to build resilience to high-stakes pressure (Muñoz et al., 2024).

Training scars/negative transfer: Unintended or maladaptive habits acquired during simulation that can have harmful repercussions in real-life encounters (Stubbs, 2025).

Validity gap: The psychological and physiological discrepancy between an officer's performance in a simulated environment and their subsequent behavior in a high-stakes, real-world encounter. This gap occurs when a simulation fails to produce the necessary level of neural urgency, leading to the encoding of flawed survival memories that do not translate to field success (Stubbs, 2025).

Chapter 4
Digital Panopticons on Wheels:
A Comparative Legal Analysis of Police Vehicle Tracking and Surveillance in India, West, and South Asia

Bhagyashree Agarwal
http://orcid.org/0009-0008-4969-5102
University of Petroleum and Energy Studies, Dehradun, India

Siddharth Saxena
http://orcid.org/0009-0003-1664-9568
Maharashtra National Law University, Nagpur, India

ABSTRACT

This chapter addresses a central problem of a statutory vacuum created by warrantless vehicle tracking in India and South Asia which contrasts with technological capabilities of modern law enforcement. While jurisdictions like USA and UK, specific legal issues are triggered through physical trespass of a tracker or prolonged collection of location data, requiring warrants based on probable cause or RIPA authorization, India and its South Asian counterparts, base their usage of GPS technology on colonial-era statutes such as the erstwhile Telegraph Act, 1855, Telecommunications Act, 2023 or arbitrary limitless executive powers that transgress modern privacy concepts. This leads to a dual crisis – a constitutional one, whereby slap and track operations violate test of proportionality; and a civil liberty one, whereby non- existence of exclusionary rules incentivizes police overreach by admissibility of evidence obtained via invasive, warrantless tracking by the courts.

INTRODUCTION: MOVING TOWARDS SURVEILLANCE THROUGH ALGORITHMS

Global Positioning System (GPS) technology has completely transformed various vehicular operations. The integrations of GPS technology into law enforcement represents a transformative shift from physical manual patrolling to automated algorithmic surveillance. The police vehicle has transformed from a mode of transport into a "rolling surveillance platform" which is capable to perform continuous,

DOI: 10.4018/979-8-3373-7660-8.ch004

retroactive and predictive monitoring of the individual (Ferguson, 2017). The Global Positioning System (GPS) technology is the enabler mechanism behind this transformation which assists the real-time tracking of the location of vehicles with exceptional accuracy. Prior to this technology, the police surveillance systems relied on humans and their observations which were limited due to geographical constraints as well as temporal weaknesses. Post the emergence of GPS technology, law enforcement officials have been gifted with the blessing of real time awareness (Koops et al., 2019). Every single movement of the marked vehicle can be reconstructed and cross-verified through other telecommunication patterns and financial transactions. This also contains the possibility of predicting future patterns of conduct with a certain level of objectivity.

This technological advancement is a major characteristic of the digital age where predictability of behavioural patterns and its commodification is on the rise (Zuboff, 2019). An emergence of the new economic and political order is seen with the collection of the data by the big-tech giants and even utilised by the state as a part of the surveillance apparatus. This approach termed as "surveillance capitalism" is focused on translating the extracted data into predictive behaviour results by using machine learning and shaping the various ideas behind human conduct. This has extended its reach from the Silicon Valley and permeated the state infrastructure dealing with policing, surveillance and maintenance of law and order.

Modern policing mechanisms have been promoting data-backed and algorithmic surveillance tactics for identifying individuals in the "heat list" and for "person-based predictive modelling." These mechanisms integrate varied datasets such as location, financial transactions, telecommunications for monitoring on a pre-emptive basis (Ferguson, 2017). This data is considered to be objective as it is not tainted by socially divisive elements such as race, caste, class and even apolitical in nature. Even then, these datasets are said to have inherited certain biases, though the discriminatory elements under these surveillance systems pass-off as rational and objective elements under the policing systems.

The tracking of the police vehicles by the GPS monitoring system is a culmination of various elements altogether. A simple process of tracking the latitudes and longitudes helps the information required by the police vehicles. Recognition of the locational data, as distinct from other forms of data, has been recognized by the courts in several jurisdictions. Justice Alito in the case of *United States v. Jones* 565 U.S. 400 (2012) has stated that aggregated location over a period of time is actually "a picture of a person's life that is quite detailed and comprehensive". Wherever the location is, it establishes the presence of the individual at hospitals, religious sites, political spaces, private relationships and other places where the details of the private life of an individual can be traced and trailed. This data serves as an enabling factor for establishing the "mosaic theory" (Kerr, 2012) of the Fourth Amendment as given by Orin Kerr – this data reveals what just individual observations are incapable of presenting such as identity, personal associations and attitudinal patterns.

In India and South Asia, this problem is acute in nature due to the intersections of institutional, technological, administrative and legal factors which are peculiar to this geographical region. The policing system in the United States of America and the United Kingdom has been democratic as it has developed through various legal frameworks which has limited the tracking done by the police such as the Fourth Amendment requirements in the United States and Regulation of Investigatory Powers Act, 2012 in the United Kingdom (Varner et al., 2021). Similar legislations do not seem to find a place in India and other South Asian countries. In India, modernization of the policing infrastructure has been promoted through the CCTNS – Crime and Criminal Tracking Network and Systems (Dhir & Sarraf, 2016) – which serves as an integrated database for the history of criminals, data of the crimes reported, registration of vehicles and geolocations across police stations in the country. This advancement in infrastructure unfortunately fails to find a legislative backing and suffers from judicial oversight.

This legislative vacuum is a leading cause of concern for the constitutional and civil liberties violations in the country which are amplified by the lack of democratic policing structures. The Supreme Court of India, in the monumental case of *K.S. Puttaswamy v. Union of India* AIR 2017 SC 4161, state that the right to privacy is a fundamental right under the Article 21 of the Indian Constitution which talks about the right to life and personal liberty. This judgement and the following *K.S Puttaswamy II* AIR 2018 SC (SUPP) 1841, espoused the proportionality principle with much detail stating that any infringement or derogation of the right to privacy by the state must satisfy certain given conditions like – authorized by the legal mechanisms, rational connection between the means and the end, and necessity as no other alternative available. The current GPS tracking carried out by the police vehicles fails to satisfy the condition of legality as it is practiced without expressed statutory authority. India has no exclusionary principle in law of evidence for those obtained after violations of privacy after the judgement in *Pooran Mal v. Director of Inspection* 1974 AIR 348. The consequence of it being that a constitutional right to privacy may be violated by the police for evidentiary reasons (Gautam, 2017). If relevant evidence is obtained through an unwarranted tracking by the GPS, it is considered to be admissible as evidence in court. Thereby, the protection given to the right to privacy by the Constitution is nullified. This transformation, however, is at an acute scale in India, where the privacy jurisprudence is in a nascent stage, being recently affirmed as a fundamental right by Supreme Court of India in *Justice K.S. Puttaswamy v. Union of India (2017)* ("Puttaswamy"). India has been heavily investing in modernizing its policing infrastructure through various initiatives like Crime and Criminal Tracking Network and Systems (CCTNS), yet the legal framework governing these technologies remains fragmented and ambiguous in comparison to other established jurisdictions. While CCTNS acts as a central point for data access integrating locations with criminal histories and vehicular information, there are no data retention standards in place. Without any oversight and retention protocols, this GPS data remains retained indefinitely leading to permanent profiling which is way beyond the necessity prong outlined in the test of proportionality in KS Puttaswamy. This coupled with mosaic theory shows graver consequences – for instance, a vehicle tagged with a GPS tracker can be searched as a stationary vehicle under Section 102 of Bharatiya Nagrik Suraksha Sanhita, 2023, however, prolonged tracking with the tracker goes beyond the actual requirement and generates a profile which is illustrated by Mosaic theory.

The Pakistan Telecommunication Reorganization Act of 1996, in Section 54, warrants that surveillance may be authorized without judicial warrant enabling their tracking system of Lawful Intercept Management System (LIMS) (Zaib et al., 2025). Even in Bangladesh, the Digital Security Act of 2018, gives power to arrest on mere suspicion to the polices for offences in the digital world which are not conducive for the current political regime. In such situations, locational data hold importance to justify the arrest for instances of dissent and hate speech (Taher, 2025). In Sri Lanka, where emergency powers have been under operation, the Prevention of Terrorism Act of 1979 (Gunawardana, 2023) allows arrest without judicial safeguards for extended periods. In all these three countries in South Asia, the colonial legislation – the Telegraph Act 1885 is still maintained and used as a mechanism to justify unnecessitated surveillance by the police (Prasad & Aravindakshan, 2021).

In China, where the authoritarian rule of the government exists, privacy is subordinate to the state security and various technological advancements are put in place for bringing it into effect such as the facial recognition technology and location and vehicle tracking. This has also been referred to as "techno-authoritarianism" (Hoffman, 2022). The Chinese model of surveillance is used by other countries on the pretext of it being a security-first model of governance by the state. Automation in flagging of content against the state and prioritization of the state security over individual interests and comprehensive data collection are the elements of this Chinese surveillance technology.

India's privacy jurisprudence may be juxtaposed against three models – the *warrant-centric proceduralism* of United States of America (USA) and the United Kingdom (UK), the *authoritarian predictive policing* model of China, and the *emergency-power-driven* model of India's South Asian neighbours like Pakistan, Bangladesh and Sri Lanka (Privacy International, 2019). The understanding of these distinctive yet comparative frameworks becomes essential for policymakers to navigate the tension between technological efficiency through these technologies and preserving civil liberties in digital public spaces (Zuboff, 2019).

The existing legal scholarship on police surveillance fixates on two extremes – the robust Fourth Amendment jurisprudence in USA with its foundation in *United States v. Jones* or a critique on mass surveillance in various authoritarian jurisdictions. There is however a scarcity of scholarship that contextualize India as a base jurisdiction rather than a peripheral jurisdiction; comparative scholarship that analyses regional trend of surveillance in South Asia; and *systemic* nature of vehicle surveillance and its integration with other systems not just the isolated act.

The central problem of a statutory vacuum created by *warrantless* vehicle tracking in India and South Asia contrasts with technological capabilities of modern law enforcement. While jurisdictions like USA and UK, specific legal issues are triggered through physical trespass of a tracker or prolonged collection of location data, requiring warrants based on *probable cause* or RIPA authorization (Kerr, 2012), India and its South Asian counterparts, base their usage of GPS technology on colonial-era statutes such as the Telegraph Act, 1855 or arbitrary limitless executive powers that transgress modern privacy concepts. This leads to a dual crisis – a constitutional one, whereby *slap and track* operations violate test of proportionality in Puttaswamy; and a civil liberty one, whereby non-existence of exclusionary rules incentivizes police overreach by admissibility of evidence obtained via invasive, warrantless tracking by the courts. The influence of Chinese models adds fuel to fire whereby exported surveillance tech comes often bundled with logic that prioritizes state security over individual civil liberties without checks and balances found in democracies (Greitens, 2020).

This brings four objectives: (1) to evaluate the constitutionality of warrantless GPS tracking in India by police by applying test of proportionality laid down in Puttaswamy, supplemented by High Court interpretations such as *Frank Vitus v. Narcotics Control Bureau* (2024); (2) to contrast Indian framework with *warrant* requirement jurisprudence in US+A (*United States v. Jones*) and UK (Regulation of Investigatory Powers Act, 2000) to identify safeguards that India lacks; (3) to analyse how emergency-power-driven models in jurisdictions like China, Sri Lanka employ national security exceptions to bypass judicial oversight for tracking of vehicles; and (4) to propose amendments or practices for India that can be integrated into existing frameworks to balance right of privacy with investigative efficacy drawing upon the best practices inferred through the comparative analysis.

For fulfilling these objectives, a doctrinal research methodology is employed to analysis primary legal sources such as Constitution of India, 1950, Bharatiya Nagarik Suraksha Sanhita, 2023, Digital Security Act and other secondary sources such as books, journal articles etc. A *functionalist* approach draws comparison between jurisdictions on how state intrusion is regulated in movement of individuals.

The models can be placed on a spectrum of surveillance – *judicial oversight models* (USA and UK), *statutorily ambiguous* models (India), and *state prerogative* models (China). A test of proportionality is to be laid in Puttaswamy specifically to police vehicle technology dealing with GPS duration, data retention and real-time vehicular monitoring. The shared legislative heritage of South Asian nations is to be examined to contribute to the under-researched field of comparative South Asian privacy law, exemplifying shared history does not result in shared constitutional values and futures. To be noted (1) Theoretical and constitutional framework for evaluating the GPS tracking systems adopted by the police and incorporation of the mosaic theory of the Fourth Amendment of the United States along with the proportionality principle of the Indian Constitution. (2) A comparative approach of warrant centric countries, hybrid systems of legislative ambiguity and security first countries. (3) The Indian approach to police surveillance and the right to privacy jurisprudence in detail while referring to the Telegraph Act and the Bharatiya Nagarik Suraksha Sanhita and the impact of the *Frank Vitus v. Narcotics Control Bureau* (2024) judgement. (4) The exclusionary principle which conflicts with the civil liberties and the constitutional guarantees. (5) Certain statutory amendments and reforms that would strike a balance between the investigative requirements and the constitutional guarantees drawing on the best practices after a comparative analysis.

THE THEORETICAL AND CONSTITUTIONAL FRAMEWORK: MOSAIC THEORY, RIGHT TO PRIVACY AND PROPORTIONALITY PRINCIPLE

In a liberal democratic governance set up, the police surveillance through GPS possesses a constitutional challenge and creates a fundamental issue as to how can the legislation reconcile the state interest of prevention of crime with the individual's right to privacy. Consent or voluntarily disclosing information is not enough for smooth policing mechanisms in a democracy. There is a certain need of coercive power to search, detain and seizure. However, this power cannot be uncontained. Constitutional limitations exist such as judicial authorization, rules of evidence and standards of proportionality, necessity and reasonableness.

Indian Constitution and the Principle of Proportionality

In India, with the Puttaswamy judgement, the proportionality principle was crystallized along with the recognition of the right to privacy as a fundamental right under Articles 14, 19 and 21 of the Constitution of India. This judgement further recognized the concept of informational privacy, stating that right to privacy also extents to control over *digital* shadows, including geospatial data. This decision was pivotal in overturning the earlier decisions of M.P. Sharma v. Union of India (1954) and Kharak Singh v. State of Uttar Pradesh (1963) which prioritized surveillance and state security mechanisms (Bhandari & Lahiri, 2020). Even if the language of the Indian Constitution did not resonate with the Fourth Amendment of the United States, the Supreme Court of India interpreted the constitutional provisions to incorporate privacy protection.

After a comparative constitutional analysis of whether the infringement of privacy by the state may be constitutionally justified, the Bench espoused a test of proportionality which was based on four elements (Sinha & Dutta, 2025). They are as follows:

i. Legality: For any restriction to be constitutionally justified, it requires the backing of a legislation. Any administrative discretion or delegated legislation with weak legislative powers cannot be sufficient for derogation of right to privacy.

ii. Legitimate Aim: The rationale behind the restriction of privacy must be for a purpose to promote the democratic aims of the country such as preventing crime, maintaining law and order and protecting rights of individuals.
iii. Rationale Connection: For the means and the end, there should be a suitable and rationale connection. The measures that are undertaken to achieve the objectives should be suitably related to each other for it to surpass the justification of infringement of right to privacy.
iv. Necessity and Proportionality: The measure undertaken by the state should be such that no other alternative, which is less intrusive in nature, existed apart from the it which is as effective as the current one. The measure is also seen to be proportional to the objective the action aims to achieve for it to pass the given test.

The 2018 Aadhar judgement further refined this concept while examining India's biometric data collection for an identification and social security scheme. For satisfying the test of necessity, the state has to undertake the task of evaluating other alternatives available and their outcomes to choose the one with the greater effectiveness which justifies its intrusiveness too. In the dissenting opinion, it was stated that the necessity test was not satisfied by the Aadhar scheme as mandatory data collection could be made voluntary for it to achieve better results in terms of privacy protection (Arun, 2021). Even though the articulation of the proportionality test in the judgements has been precise, achieving the given application becomes challenging for the law enforcement agencies in the country. The GPS vehicular tracking fails on the necessity requirement for prolonged tracking due to like *less intrusive* methods such as CCTV can achieve the same ends regardless.

The Meaning of the Mosaic Theory

The mosaic theory of the Fourth Amendment lends a constitutionally relevant significance to the tracking by GPS as developed in the case of *United States v. Jones* in 2012 and further elaborated by Orin Kerr. This theory states that individual situations may not highlight the importance of protecting it, but an aggregation of all such situations reveal as to the necessity of the protection granted.

In the 2012 *Jones* case (Slobogin, 2012), it was held that the continuous tracking of the vehicle was to be considered as a Fourth Amendment search which had to be mandates by a warrant. It highlighted by Justice Scalia that placing a GPS device on the vehicle constitutes as physical trespass. Justice Alito argued that if the state acquires such continuous locational data – it is a violation of the right to privacy under the Fourth Amendment as with the assembling of locational data and other data with the law enforcement, it can chalk out the complete daily routine of a person.

The scholarly interpretation of the mosaic theory by Orin Kerr distinguishes between two approaches to the Fourth Amendment: the sequential approach which understands each action of the police in isolation and the mosaic approach which calculates a series of actions in totality. Prolonged collection of data can reveal patterns about a person's associations and behavioural characteristics which furthers the comprehension of their identity, beliefs and actions (Bellovin et al., 2014).

The Supreme Court further endorsed this theory in the case of *Carpenter v. United States* 585 U.S. 296 wherein it held that the access to the cell-site location information (CSLI) for a period of 127 days is a violation of Fourth Amendment which has to be mandated with a warrant. The Court even rejected the third-party doctrine where is willingly the information is given to a third-party, there should not be a reasonable expectation of privacy by the individual who has so consented (Fairbanks, 2021). Even if held as business records, such private information has the capacity to be seen as surveillance because of the data being comprehensive in nature.

According to Ferguson (2021), scholars have analysed this decision of the Court as a significant change in the understanding of the Fourth Amendment and its jurisprudence. Technological exceptionalism has been embraced as specific technologies which are comprehensive and conduct continuous data collection possess the necessity of heightened constitutional protection. Newer technologies do not need to fit into the criteria and requirements laid down by older legislations. Laws have to adapt to technological advancements, and such constitutional principles have to be developed to suit the digital age surveillance mechanisms.

Application to Police Vehicle Tracking by GPS

The proportionality principle and the mosaic theory when applied to the police vehicle tracking by the GPS, it establishes various constitutional positions.

In India, as the police vehicle tracking is practiced, it fails the test of legality which has been laid down in the Puttaswamy judgement. In the Telegraph Act, 1885, surveillance for national security and public order have been allowed for any messages that are being transmitted. To understand location tracking in the Act as given, is an incorrect interpretation of the legislation and the terms given such as "interception" and "transmission." This scope of interpretation was extended by the court in the case of *R.M Malkani v. State of Maharashtra* 1973 AIR 157 where the meaning of telegraph was extended to mean telephonic conversations encompassing communication through electronic means. This interpretation was meant to be evolutionary in nature as it adapted a colonial legislation to the technology that advanced later. Such interpretation and reasoning, cannot be overly stretched, however. Telegraph regulation and location tracking cannot be used as analogous terms while interpreting the colonial legislation. It is not a form of communication or transmission and there is no interception involved. The Telegraph Act, in whichever way, cannot authorise vehicle and locational tracking.

The Bharatiya Nagarik Suraksha Sanhita, 2023, has discussed the modernization of the criminal proceedings in the country, though it misses to address surveillance by digital means in an expressed manner. Section 102 allows the police to search movable properties that includes vehicles on the basis of suspicion and in some cases without a warrant too. This provision specifically deals with a stationary search of the vehicle, not constant continuous moving vehicles such as done by the tracking through GPS. In Section 69 of the Information Technology Act, 2002, which allows the government to instruct the intermediaries to permit surveillance for national security and public law and order, even that applies to electronic communications and not geolocation tracking (Bailey & Parsheera, 2021).

The gap in the statutes is confirmed that no Indian legislation explicitly deals with the authority of the law enforcement officials to affix GPS devices in vehicles and collect geolocation data from them for continuous periods. This legal gap is violative of the test of legality as laid down in the Puttaswamy judgement. Masquerading a practice by improvisation, which is not authorized by law, is violative of the constitutional principles.

Mosaic Theory: Prolonged GPS locational tracking by the police vehicles does not qualify the touchstone of necessity and proportionality as there is no adequate justification for such data collection for continuous periods. If there is suspicion and tracking is even required for crime-scene investigations, a narrow time limit may be permissible with the scope of tracking defined. This would also respect the right to privacy as per the constitutional terms. Contrary to this, police vehicle surveillance is a continuous routine and unwarranted action. The aggregation of the geolocation data collection constructs mosaics of an individual's life in detail with patterns being recognized in movement, affiliations and behaviour which any investigative procedure may be incapable of achieving (Zuboff, 2019).

The difference between geolocation tracking of vehicles as a form of surveillance by the police and other forms of surveillance have been highlighted by the mosaic principle. A singular instance of a person being in a particular location is not protected by the constitution, but continuous observations of locational patterns is. Limited and brief duration GPS tracking may be permissible, but prolonged indefinite tracking is a constitutional violation. The requirement of necessity for the proportionality principle is not satisfied in this case as conventional methods such as financial records, communication records, CCTV footages are to be explored as less intrusive alternatives first.

THE COMPARATIVE ANALYSIS OF THE SPECTRUM OF SURVEILLANCE

There are specifically three distinct models which can be identified for understanding police surveillance in a spectrum from maximum state security actualization to minimum judicial intervention.

The Warrant-Centric Model of Surveillance

In the United States, through various judgements on constitutional principles, prerequisite necessity of a warrant has been recognized for GPS surveillance as it is considered as intrusive and violative of privacy. In the 2012 *Jones* case, all the judges agreed that placing a device on a vehicle for tracking purposes constitutes a violation of the Fourth Amendment, even though they were divided on the reasoning behind the violation – whether it was for privacy considerations or physical trespass of the individual. They agreed that such prolonged continuous tracking systems have to be substantiated by a warrant (Millcarek, 2012).

The Fourth Amendment has various levels of protection that it offers. Pre-authorization as a requirement where the state has to establish a reasonable cause behind the intervention and procure a warrant before any activity of surveillance is conducted. Specific judicial scope and temporal limitation which limits the surveillance powers, even if pre-authorized, to a specific location, time and vehicle preventing any misuse or abuse of the authorized power. Also, the exclusion principle which provides that the admissibility of evidence is questioned if it is obtained post-violation of the Fourth Amendment which acts like a deterrent for deviant police behaviour.

Additional qualifications get imposed in certain state and federal legislations. The Omnibus Crime Control and Safe Streets Act, 1968, creates a special procedure for issuing a warrant in cases of electronic surveillance. There is an additional layer of "necessity within necessity" added in this scenario where the government has to project that other normal investigative mechanisms have failed or are likely to fail before warrant for such surveillance is issued. This makes it a last resort mechanism of surveillance when everything else seems to have failed or are inadequate. On a presumptuous basis, location tracking is considered as intrusive, hence judicial permission is warranted.

The United Kingdom's Regulation of Investigatory Powers Act, 2000, has certain protections which are analogous to United States legislations, however, they differ in their constitutional principles. Certain structured safeguards are provided to surveillance measures that are given under the legislation for preventing abuse of such power. "Directed surveillance" as given in the legislation has the prerequisite of written authorisation from a specific designated public official. The means have to proportional to the ends being achieved and it should be necessary for purposes of national security, maintenance of law and order and public health and safety. The authorization has to be periodically reviewed so that it may not be carried out for longer than required (Brown, 2012). In "intrusive surveillance," authorization requirements are stricter and even require judicial authority approvals before permitting it. Executive and judicial permissions have to be justified and not merely be done as a matter of protocol.

In this legislation, transparency and accountability have to be taken into account for all the authorizations given for surveillance. The state is answerable to the legislature and independent regulatory authorities if there is any doubt about unlawful exercise of powers. The result is such that standards operating procedures are such developed so that presumptively longer duration of surveillance requires constant and periodic approvals for it to not be excessive in nature.

The Authoritarian Model of Surveillance

The complete antagonistic approach to surveillance has been undertaken by China where it is not treated as an exception, but a compulsory governance mechanism. Tracking of phones, locations, facial recognition, vehicle monitoring and predictive policing are all considered to be a part of the ways in which law enforcement is carried out in the country. Major cities have various cameras installed for surveillance purposes which are enabled with facial recognition as a detection mechanism for crime prevention and control. Police officials have vast powers such as locational tracking, procuring financial records and vehicle tracking with very relaxed procedures. Even telecom industries and internet service providers have been controlled to ease surveillance under the garb of national security (Hicks, 2022).

Not just for tracking criminals, but even for political dissenters or critiques of the state and the government, minority communities are all under the umbrella of surveillance in such an authoritarian model. Identification of individuals with the help of geolocation, as to who attended protests, visited religious places or is associated with political groups and attended meetings of the same, is undertaken as a way to intervene with any activity threatening the power of the government. After identification, restrictions are imposed such as travel clearance, denial of services and defamation in the society – all of which are interventions for non-abiding behaviour.

For China, state security triumphs privacy of a person. If surveillance is necessary for state security, that is deemed sufficient for curtailment of freedom. Privacy and security are considered to be antithetical in a authoritarian model of the state governance. Geopolitical considerations have even heightened the need for such a system, and this technology has been developed and shared with other countries by China. The logic behind this is the need to prioritize the needs of the state over the rights of an individual for a state to function without any glitches. Privacy is treated as some sort of luxury with does not coexist with state security (Hoffman, 2022).

The Emergency Model of Surveillance of South Asia

The middle ground of surveillance mechanisms has been undertaken by South Asia. Democratic countries with privacy and other constitutional values interact with emergency provisions, exceptions for state security and administrative discretion. This is also known as "emergency exception model" of surveillance where day-to-day processes are suspended in exceptional circumstances while exercising emergency powers by the state.

In Pakistan, privacy is recognized as a constitutional right. The Pakistan Telecommunication Reorganization Act (PTRA), 1996, gives the power to the central government to grant surveillance powers if needed for national security without any judicial authorization being needed. There is also a Lawful Intercept Management System (LIMS) in place for surveillance of the people in the country without any warrant. Discretionary powers with state security and intelligence agencies assert the power given in the legislation without any judicial control (Shahid et al., 2007).

The "emergency" exception for Pakistan seems to be invalid as the surveillance mechanisms is treated as the norm. No limits for the timeline, place and purpose of surveillance exits, so unchecked power to carry out measures for state security is the norm for the law enforcement officials.

In Bangladesh, the Digital Security Act, 2018, gives power to the police officials to arrest in cases of suspicious activity in digital platforms including fake news, seditious activities, hate speech, etc. Even though formal processes exist, weak enforcement is the practice to suppress dissent in the country (Rahman & Rashid, 2020). Under Sections 41 and 43 of the Act, even seizure of devices, locational data and "any other information" is accessible by the police while doing investigations. Suspicion gives unbridled power for surveillance. The colonial legislations – the Telegraph Act, 1885 and the Wireless Telegraphy Act, 1933 are still in force in Bangladesh which are given creative understandings to allow modern techniques of surveillance with the help of these laws.

Sri Lanka has been under emergency for such a prolonged period due to the unrest in the state. The Prevention of Terrorism Act, 1979, which was legislated as a temporary action, still is in force. Detention for extended durations without proper safeguards are permitted under this Act. Ambiguous provisions which are vague and broad in nature give extended powers to the police for search, seizure and surveillance. Emergency regulations are also issued from time to time to restrict speech, movement and associations in the country. Emergency as a measure has been normalized in Sri Lanka as even though an exceptional measure, it has become routine in the country (Coomaraswamy & Reyes, 2004).

Across South Asia, reliance on colonial legislations is a routine, even though creative interpretation to accommodate modern surveillance is seen. An exception for state security interests is present all across the countries, even in functional democracies. Courts seem to rarely exercise their power to control unbridled actions by police under the garb of state security. Even though this model differs from China in theory with the retention of democratic institutions, in practice, it imitates it by using surveillance as a mode of political control.

THE INDIAN CRISIS: A STATUTORY VACUUM

India is surrounded by diverse and distinct models of vehicular tracking in its neighbourhood yet confronts a different crisis from its neighbours' adopting models of *warrant-centric* in democracies and *security-first* in South Asian neighbourhood. India's position in this context of GPS-based vehicular tracking is a deeply paradoxical one. On one end of the rope, the Supreme Court of India, in its landmark judgement of KS Puttasawamy, has laid down one of the most sophisticated and right centric (protective) privacy frameworks in the global south building the framework from the foundations of Article 14, 19 and 21 and incorporating a test of proportionality in the adjudication (K.S. Puttaswamy v. Union of India (2017) 10 SCC 1; K.S. Puttaswamy v. Union of India (Aadhaar) (2018) 10 SCC 1). On the other end, the statutory framework that functions on the ground level has its foundations in the colonial era telegraph legislation and various provisions of the Information Technology Act, 2000, currently in process of repealing by the newly enacted Indian Telecommunication Act, 2023 (Indian Telegraph Act 1885; Information Technology Act 2000; Indian Telecommunication Act 2023). This arrangement is not simply defective technically. It leads to a legal structural crisis. Police and executive bodies have routinely deployed GPS-based tracking along with database integration and analysis through algorithms without any statutory authorization or procedural safeguards and lack of judicial oversight and yet are not prevented by the law to rely on the output material in the court (George, 2025; Malhotra & Goyal, 2025).

Historically, the foundation of the surveillance framework was based on Section 5 of the erstwhile Telegraph Act, 1955. This enactment was drafted to regulate the telegraph lines in the 19th century; however, the provision was subsequently reinterpreted to make accommodation for the coverage of the interception of telephone calls and other forms of electronic communication. Most notably, the case of RM Malkani v State of Maharashtra, the Supreme Court of India read down the word "telegraph" to include modern telephony under the scope (R.M. Malkani v. State of Maharashtra (1973) 1 SCC 471). Despite successive efforts of interpretation to widen the scope of the Section 5, it did not sit comfortably with the GPS-based vehicular tracking. As the geographical coordinates of a vehicle do not constitute "messages brought for transmission by or transmitted or received by any telegraph" in the ordinary course. In addition, the act of affixing a device to the vehicle and collecting its geographical location over time does not fit in the language of the Act that covers communication between senders and recipients. These differences between statutory text and practice at ground level leads to serious concerns under the privacy framework laid down in the Puttaswamy case that demands clear and statutory authorization to intrude into any person's privacy.

The recent enactment of Indian Telecommunications Act, 2023 does not resolve the problem but complicates it. It repeals the erstwhile Indian Telegraph Act, 1855 and the Indian Wireless Telegraphy Act, 1933, and formalizes a modern and technologically neutral framework for the telecommunication services as per the modern needs. It takes an expansive defining and interpretation of the term "telecommunication" to mean –

> "telecommunication" means transmission, emission or reception of any messages, by wire, radio, optical or other electro-magnetic systems, whether or not such messages have been subjected to rearrangement, computation or other processes by any means in the course of their transmission, emission or reception. (Indian Telecommunications Act, 2023)

This definition clearly underlines and covers the conventional modes of communications (calls) and internet-based communications. It expands the scope of the term, however, to include a wider range of machine-to-machine communications as well as the Internet of Things data that generally transmit and received through telecom networks. In principle, the data relayed by GPS devices (geographical coordinates) through telecom networks to servers fall under the ambit of the Indian Telecommunications Act, 2023.

The Indian Telecommunications Act, 2023 also re-enacts and lays down the structure of the interception powers of the authorities. For instance, under Section 20, Central or State Government can *direct* the interception, monitoring or blocking of any message or class of messages between two or more persons or relating to any subject, being transmitted or received through telecommunication services, on the occurrence of public emergency or in the interest of public safety. Further grounds include necessity or expediency in the interests of the sovereignty and integrity of India and the security of the State or friendly relations with foreign States, public order or for preventing the incitement to the commission of an offence. This provision also supports the *temporary* suspension of telecom services operating in the area by providing statutory backing for internet shutdowns which were executed and implemented through executive orders under delegated legislation. Scholars have been critical of this move and have underlined the potential and continuity of the newer framework. Scholars have described the regime under the Indian Telecommunications Act, 2023 to be *regressive* and *authoritarian* based on the centralization of the discretion in the executive and continued reliance on broader abstract grounds such as *public order* and *public emergency* without any existence of oversight (Arun, 2025; George, 2025).

The Government of India has issued the Telecommunications (Procedures and Safeguards for the Lawful Interception of Messages) Rules under the Indian Telecommunications Act, 2023, which *reproduce* the erstwhile authoritative model under the Rules 419 and 419A of the Indian Telegraph Act, 1855. These orders are generally issued by Union or State Home Secretary with approval and review by executive committees, but there is no oversight or any one to authorize or audit interception. This is exacerbated by no prior judicial warrant as well as no individual notification or *ex post* remedy for those under surveillance. The colonial era foundations for interception have been modernized but the substance of the same is preserved in the newer enactment. The qualities of erstwhile Indian Telegraph Act, 1855 – executive control, weak transparency and no external review still remain the qualities of the newer Indian Telecommunications Act, 2023, now India's interception regime.

When these foundations are applied to GPS-based vehicular tracking, it becomes problematic. While it is no longer accurate to claim the non-existence of an Indian statute on the interception or monitoring of data streams, given the scope of Indian Telecommunications Act, 2023 and the generality of Section 20, an argument can be drawn up by the State that geographical coordinates transmitted by GPS over the networks is a particular application of the message interception power under the newer statute, provided the conditions laid down under Section 20 are met. Though, in a limited sense, the gap existing under the Indian Telegraph Act, 1855 has partially filled yet the current regime still remains unsuitable to address the constitutional mandates and harms posed by the GPS-based vehicular tracking.

The Indian Telecommunications Act, 2023 does not refer to the affixing of the tracking devices to the privately owned vehicles. It does not draw a distinction between interception of specific communications and sustained, regular and automated monitoring of the movement of a person over the time. It lays down no thresholds of suspicion on the individual, no maximum duration of tracking and no physical limitations of locational surveillance. It does not incorporate *necessity* as *last resort standard* found in the United States Title III, which requires the government to exhibit that conventional methods of investigation have failed or are too dangerous before a resort to electronic surveillance is made. Nor it creates an oversight body (judicial or quasi-judicial) as seen in United Kingdom's Investigatory Powers Commissioner, to have an oversight or authorise or audit the forms of tracking. The Indian Telecommunications Act, 2023, instead, treats interception as an executive function characterised by loosely necessity and expediency standards and leaves the safeguards to the whims of the executive.

From the perspective of the proportionality framework under the Puttaswamy judgement, there is deficiency in two aspects. First, the legality demands that not only a law exists, but that law must be sufficient to direct a precise, foreseeable and specific intrusion in question. The Indian Telecommunications Act, 2023 reproduces the interception logic of the Indian Telegraph Act, 1855 and does not satisfy this condition whereby the intrusion is not specific, continuous and high resolution of individuals or vehicles leading to long term profiling of the individuals (Gautam, 2017; George, 2025; *K.S. Puttaswamy v Union of India*, 2017). The second aspect is that even if the requirement is met at a lower threshold, the necessity and balance is not. The Indian Telecommunications Act, 2023 does not identify *mosaic* harms due to long term location tracking as identified in the US judgements of – *United States v. Jones* and *Carpenter v. United States*, and it does not require the State to show that less intrusive techniques would be inadequate, hence, a resort to GPS surveillance (United States v. Jones 565 US 400, 2012; Carpenter v. United States 585 US 296, 2018; Kerr, 2012).

Judicial engagement in India with GPS-based surveillance has been mostly through bail conditions rather than court doing the investigations. The Supreme Court of India in its judgement of *Frank Vitus v. Narcotics Control Bureau,* considered a bail condition that required the accused to live location through digital means as a precondition for bail. While the court accepted that bail orders can be restrictive in nature and restrict liberty of the individual to ensure the presence at trial and prevent the obstruction of justice, it also recognized that continuous electronic monitoring leads to different intrusion in the privacy of the individual, since every movement of the individual would be exposed to the authorities *(Frank Vitus v. Narcotics Control Bureau,* 2024). This intrusion falls under the scope of the Puttaswamy's notion of privacy under the Article 21 of the Constitution of India.

In *Frank Vitus*, brought live location sharing under the ambit of Article 21 of the Constitution of India. The SC held that such measure of live location sharing must be backed by compelling reasons, proportionate to the aim of securing attendance at the trial in addition to examination of less intrusive measures. Semiotically, this judgement resists the normalization of electronic surveillance as a condition for bail but conceptualizes the monitoring as an exceptional measure (George, 2025; Malhotra & Goyal, 2025). Academic discourse has expanded this reason beyond the bail condition context, arguing that if limited location monitoring is intrusive enough to trigger Article 21, long term vehicular tracking must also satisfy the proportionality test under Article 21 (George, 2025; Singh et al., 2025).

Evidence law further compounds this issue. The Indian Evidence Act, 1872, now Bharatiya Sakshya Adhiniyam, 2023, makes admissibility dependent on the relevance to the facts in issue rather than the means of the collection of evidence. The means of evidence collection thus has no effect on the admissibility of the evidence, whether illegal or legal. The Supreme Court of India in *Pooran Mal v. Director of Inspection,* has held that evidence collected through unconstitutional means through searches or seizures can be admitted on the principle that courts exist to ascertain the truth of the matter, not to punish investigative lapses (*Pooran Mal v. Director of Inspection*, 1974). Later decisions have followed this line and illegally obtained evidence largely remains admissible in the court (Gautam, 2017; Varma, 2019).

Recent scholarship on the issue has been largely critical. Khagesh Gautam's analysis of the unfair operation principle has traced instances whereby Indian courts have excluded evidence to be admitted on grounds of fairness, even though there is no rule of exclusion, and argues that these exclusionary instances can be developed into a robust fairness doctrine for cases that violate rights during surveillance (Gautam, 2017). The Law Commission of India's 94th report had recommended 40 years ago, that Indian law must be amended to include or adopt a limited exclusionary rule for serious constitutional violations, relying on deterrence as well as moral imperative to deny the State the fruits of its own wrongdoing in investigation. A more recent scholarship on the issue has consistently pressed for a context specific/ sensitive exclusionary doctrine for digital evidence that is collected through disproportionate or unlawful means or monitoring to be included under the interception powers of the Indian Telecommunications Act, 2023 in the light of the Puttaswamy judgement.

The interaction between an executive controlled regime under the Indian Telecommunications Act, 2023 and the admissibility criteria under the Indian Evidence Act, 1872 and now the Bharatiya Sakshya Adhiniyam, 2023 leads to a dual crisis. At the structural level, state agencies are equipped with modern technologies which are powerful and enjoy the legality to track movements and communications. On the other hand, Puttaswamy judgement requires that any restriction or intrusion in the privacy must be sanctioned in substantive sense by the law. At the remedial level, there is no exclusionary rule or sanctions, leaving the criminal process no incentive to restrain itself or regulate these practices. At the judicial level, however, the courts have recognized certain surveillance measures as unconstitutional or disproportionate, yet admit the evidence so collected through these measures. This arrangement does not actualize the constitutional imperative of right to privacy as enshrined under the Article 21 of the Constitution of India and widens the gap between rights discourse and lived experiences (Gautam, 2017; Malhotra & Goyal, 2025; Varma, 2019). GPS-based vehicular tracking becomes a pragmatic instance of surveillance of movement, and these contradictions and interactions exhibit how a system that proclaims strong privacy commitments can have internal problems in surveillance infrastructure leading the rights to privacy to not operationalize due to statutory and evidentiary doctrines (Kavenna, 2019).

RECOMMENDATIONS AND BRIDGING THE GAP

A survey of legal responses to GPS-based surveillance reveals a stark divergence in strategies in reconciling the two ends of the rope – effective policing and protection of right to privacy under the Article 21 of Constitution of India. Warrant-centric systems as seen in jurisdictions of USA and UK have recognised that prolonged real time monitoring and tracking of individuals and vehicles leads to revealing of mosaic of personal life and is subject to strict *ex ante* judicial control leading to temporal limits and exclusionary remedies (United States v. Jones 565 US 400, 2012; Carpenter v. United States 585 US 296, 2018; Kerr, 2012). On the other end of the spectrum, authoritarian or *emergency-driven* models of jurisdictions of China and South Asian States, have led to normalization of movement monitoring as a routine with no judicial oversight using broader justifications of national security or public order (Greitens, 2020; Zuboff, 2019).

India occupies an uncomfortable position in the spectrum. The constitutional jurisprudence in India has evolved considerably after the Supreme Court of India's judgement in Puttaswamy, is aligned *rhetorically* with rights protective models that seriously consider the threats posed by prolonged location data and analysis through algorithms (Gautam, 2017; K.S. Puttaswamy v. Union of India, 2017). At the same time, at statutory and institutional levels, semiotically security first approach can be seen. The Indian Telecommunications Act, 2023, repealing the Indian Telegraph Act, 1855, re-enacts and re-introduce interception powers without any judicial oversight. The Bharatiya Sakshya Adhiniyam, 2023, along with erstwhile the Indian Evidence Act, 1872, does not make admissibility dependent on the means of collection of evidence during the investigation, hence, making illegally obtained material admissible in the court. Constitutional rights have therefore been given effect yet statutorily constitutional violations erode the legitimacy of policing practices (George, 2025; Malhotra & Goyal, 2025; Singh et al., 2025).

To improve these issues, three improvements can be done. Judicial oversight can be included in the Indian Telecommunications Act, 2023 and the Bharatiya Nagarik Suraksha Sanhita, 2023. The experience of Title III in USA shows that specialized warrant regime can go beyond the normal search warrants by leveraging *demonstrable* necessity, *heightened* judicial scrutiny and *strict temporal* and substantive limitations Omnibus Crime Control and Safe Streets Act 1968, Title III; Kerr 2012). The UK's layered distinction between *directed, intrusive* and *interception* of communications with different authorization procedures for each of them, exhibits that corresponding proportional legal protection can be given to degrees of intrusiveness (Regulation of Investigatory Powers Act 2000; Police and Criminal Evidence Act 1984, s 78). In Indian context, prolonged vehicular tracking through GPS-based, should not be left to the general interception power under the statutes. Therefore, a different category with judicial oversight and authorization with narrowing of investigative powers with limitation on duration and scope with mandatory review and termination after the purpose is served.

The governance of data infrastructures where GPS-data is fed especially through CCTNS has to be robust as a second improvement. GPS data once collected rarely remains confined to the particular investigation during which the same was collected. Instead, the same is fed into large databases linked to various vehicular records, criminal history records and even Aadhaar linked systems available for multiple agencies for analysis. The comparative experience shows that this happens with no limitations and retention leads to the data becoming tools of general social control. The principles underlying the Digital Personal Data Protection Act, 2023 namely data minimisation, storage limitation, data localisation with clearly proportional articulated purposes can be incorporated into CCTNS to govern GPS-derived data for law enforcement (Digital Personal Data Protection Act 2023; George, 2025). This would lead to both technological measures leading to access controls and automated deletion coupled with legal measures causing proportionate control and access.

For a third improvement, remedies and incentives have to be included for instances of disproportionate instances of access. Indian courts have stayed with the principle of relevancy to determine admissibility, so there is no incentive for investigative agencies to comply with constitutional constraints. Experiences from varied jurisdictions such as Canada, UK and regional human rights system show that robust proportionate doctrines of exclusion that weigh the violations of human rights on the adjudication as well as investigation show that these measures can protect fairness of trial and legitimacy of the system (Gautam 2017; Law Commission of India 1983). This unfairness principle can be used as foundation for Indian Courts to develop context-specific exclusionary rule for digital evidences collected through disproportionate means or unlawful surveillance whereby less intrusive techniques of investigation could be employed and violation reflects institutional ignorance to constitutional mandates. The test of proportionality under Puttaswamy judgement can act as an anchor for building upon this foundation for exclusionary doctrine. This means that where surveillance would not fulfil the tests of suitability in the case, reliance on the evidence will not bear the fruits of wrongdoing in the case for the State. A principled approach would be best instead of arbitrary sanction.

Institutional arrangements can determine whether the legal reforms can be effective or not. Independent oversight bodies in the form of data protection authority with effective jurisdiction over processing of data or a special body in the form of executive such as commissioner can be tasked with reviewing and oversight of tracking and interception are indispensable if executive self-regulation is to be replaced with accountability (George, 2025). Training programs for law enforcement agencies can be updated to build capacity building and increase exposure and sensitization for constitutional mandates of data protection and data surveillance. Without investments in capacity building, well-built infrastructure through statutes cannot be realized on the ground.

These recommendations together can form a concrete path for effective interplay of India's constitutional mandates and ground lived experiences of surveillance practices. The Indian Telecommunications Act, 2023 is not neutral in this aspect. It removes the colonial era principles of interception but re-enacts them without any kind of oversight proportional safeguards or independent body of oversight. It threatens the pre-existing executive cantered, surveillance that is ill-equipped to measure the specific issues of GPS-based vehicular tracking and algorithmic policing.

CONCLUSION

Police vehicles with location tracking technology and usage of the data so collected for analysing certain trends in criminal behaviour is reflective of the contemporary changes in constitutionalism in the digital age. Such advancement in technology is helpful in monitoring a huge number of individuals and their daily routes, which would have been impossible to carry out with precision using traditional methods of policing and surveillance. Also, such monitoring using technology blurs the difference between targeted surveillance and generalised policing for social control. With every police car exercising a vigilant check on the movement of each vehicle, the differentiation between the efforts to maintain law and order and intrusion of private lives is difficult to draw (Zuboff, 2019).

In liberal constitutionalism, the issue is seen through the metaphor of the panopticon, where an omnipresent mode is observing all actions which requires every subject to act in discipline and self-control. In GPS tracking, this metaphor is not a mere rhetoric. Even if the data collection is by the police vehicles of the location they travel to and the routes taken, it gives away a picture of the entire lives of the individual and their respective associations. After a significant period of time, this data reveals the behavioural patterns, associations, individual beliefs and connections of the person, revealing detailed information about their private life. As the jurisprudence developed by United States, such collection of information is different from isolated instances on a qualitative basis. There is a deeper penetration to an individual's private life affecting their autonomy as well as identity (United States v. Jones 565 US 400, 2012; Carpenter v. United States 585 US 296, 2018; Kerr, 2012).

In India, post the Puttaswamy judgement, the constitutional jurisprudence reflects the privacy debate integration in the Indian constitution. Recognition of informational privacy is seen as an integral part of the right to life and personal liberty of an individual. For asserting any restriction on a constitutional right, proportional principle was espoused featuring elements of legality, legitimate aim, necessity and suitability (K.S. Puttaswamy v. Union of India, 2017). Even though these principles find a way in judicial pronouncements, to strengthen them into practice, they have to be translated into practice with effective standard procedures and regularization of the GPS tracking by police vehicles. The principles so developed have to exist with a matured criminal justice system which is capable of sustaining the constitutional principles.

India has a choice to make between the security-first model and a warrant-centric model. For security-first model, modernization of surveillance technology is seen to dominated by the law on telecommunications and such actions are justified for public order and national security. For a warrant-centric control, greater judicial control and statutory safeguards have to be in place to prevent any chance of misuse of power by the police. Whichever direction is taken, not only will it shape the criminal behaviour and the judicial system around it, but also the various interpersonal interactions and associations in the society.

Regulating GPS technology usage by the police does not imply that it does not have any investigative worth or that a pre-digital past was a better way to deal with criminal behaviour. GPS technology provides great assistance to the law enforcement bodies in the country by optimising their functioning in emergency situations and matters which require precision and detail. It also enhances accountability on the part of the officials, and it provides a trail of their movements and associations as well, which help in identifying cases of misconduct and abuse.

The major question of concern is the manner in which GPS technology is to be used, the purpose it serves and the safeguards and remedies available against it. For achieving a constitutionally aligned adaptation of this technology, statutory provisions clearly stating the instances in which they might be used, independent bodies regulating such usage and repercussions that follow for violation of the given standards is needed. Apart from this, awareness in the public is needed which does not see surveillance as a way of hindrance which is confined to law enforcement officials, but it includes welfare of each element of the society symbolizing democracy in practice.

The trajectory undertaken by India as a response to the GPS tracking will also determine the test of constitutional perspectives to adapt to modern digital age. As the current regime with the Telecommunications Act tilts towards extensive interception and tracking powers, with lesser judicial protection for warrantless activities undertaken by police, it thus leads to grave violations of rights and lesser trust in the democratic and administrative institutions of the country (Indian Telecommunication Act, 2023; Pooran Mal v. Director of Inspection, 1974; Gautam, 2017). If, in an opposite manner, the current statutory changes are made for a proportionate regulatory framework to realign the investigative powers of the police with the right to privacy and dignity of individuals, India's approach would be applauded and recognized as an example to balance technology with rights.

The choice is not just limited to the privacy discourse in the country anymore. It affects the kind of political establishments are envisioned in the future as data is not just a resource but also a mechanism of control. When police vehicles function as digital panopticons on wheels with no legal restraint or judicial control, it normalises a certain form of governance which does not function on transparency and accountability. The purpose of law enforcement officials is not just detection and punishment of crime, but also preservation of a social decorum where persons exist freely without the fear of constant watch or shadow being maintained over them.

REFERENCES

Arun, P. (2021). In pursuit of personal data: A survey on state surveillance and democracy in India. In P. R. deSouza, Mohd. S. Alam, & H, Ahmed (Eds.), *Companion to Indian democracy: Resilience, fragility, ambivalence* (pp. 234-255). Routledge India. https://doi.org/DOI: 10.4324/9781003219477

Arun, P. (2025). Regressive and authoritarian: Surveillance powers in the Telecommunications Act 2023 and Post Office Act 2023. *Indiana Law Review*, *9*(1), 80–96. DOI: 10.1080/24730580.2024.2440943

Bailey, R., & Parsheera, S. (2021, October). Data localization in India: Paradigms and processes. *CSI Transactions on ICT*, *9*(3), 137–150. DOI: 10.1007/s40012-021-00337-4

Bellovin, S. M., Hutchins, R. M., Jebara, T., & Zimmeck, S. (2014). When enough is enough: Location tracking, Mosaic theory, and Machine Learning. *New York University Journal of Law & Liberty*, *8*(2), 555–628.

Bhandari, V., & Lahiri, K. (2020). The surveillance state: Privacy and criminal investigation in India: Possible futures in a post-Puttaswamy world. *University of Oxford Human Rights Hub Journal, 3*(2), 15-46. https://papers.ssrn.com/abstract=3580630

Brown, I. (2012, November). Government access to private-sector data in the United Kingdom. *International Data Privacy Law*, *2*(4), 230–238. DOI: 10.1093/idpl/ips018

Coomaraswamy, R., & de los Reyes, C. (2004, April). Rule by emergency: Sri Lanka's postcolonial constitutional experience. *International Journal of Constitutional Law*, *2*(2), 272–295. DOI: 10.1093/icon/2.2.272

Dhir, S., & Sarraf, S. (2016, January-June). Crime and criminal tracking networks & systems using agile methodology. *BVICAM's. International Journal of Information Technology : an Official Journal of Bharati Vidyapeeth's Institute of Computer Applications and Management*, *8*(1), 930–933. https://www.proquest.com/openview/b2e2634c6c517fa3ad98ff1e939bebca/1?pq-origsite=gscholar&cbl=2034493

Fairbanks, R. (2021, June 23). Masterpiece or mess: The Mosaic theory of the Fourth Amendment post-Carpenter. *Berkeley Journal of Criminal Law, 26*(1), 71-119. https://doi.org/DOI: 10.15779/Z38DZ03287

Ferguson, A. G. (2017). *The rise of Big Data policing: Surveillance, race, and the future of law enforcement*. NYU Press. DOI: 10.18574/nyu/9781479854608.001.0001

Ferguson, A. G. (2021). Facial recognition and the Fourth Amendment. *Minnesota Law Review, 105*(3), 1105–1210. DOI: 10.24926/265535.4104

Gautam, K. (2017, October 12). The unfair operation principle and the exclusionary rule: On the admissibility of illegally obtained evidence in criminal trials in India. *Indiana International & Comparative Law Review*, *27*(2), 147–189. DOI: 10.18060/7909.0049

George, P. (2025, February 6). *India's surveillance landscape after the DPDPA*. IAPP. https://iapp.org/news/a/india-s-surveillance-landscape-after-the-dpdpa

Greitens, S. C. (2020). Surveillance, security, and liberal democracy in the post-COVID world. *International Organization*, *74*(S1), 169–190. DOI: 10.1017/S0020818320000417

Gunawardana, V. (2023, June). Criminalising dissent: Sri Lanka's Prevention of Terrorism Act and its use in suppressing social movements - 2022. *Asian Journal of Management Studies, 1*(1), 83–99. http://repo.lib.sab.ac.lk:8080/xmlui/handle/susl/4050

Hicks, J. (2022, August 1). *Export of digital surveillance technologies from China to developing countries* [Report]. Institute of Development Studies. https://doi.org/DOI: 10.19088/K4D.2022.123

Hoffman, S. (2022, April). China's tech-enhanced authoritarianism. *Journal of Democracy, 33*(2), 76–89. DOI: 10.1353/jod.2022.0019

Kavenna, J. (2019, October 4). Shoshana Zuboff: 'Surveillance capitalism is an assault on human autonomy.' *The Guardian*. https://www.theguardian.com/books/2019/oct/04/shoshana-zuboff-surveillance-capitalism-assault-human-automomy-digital-privacy

Kerr, O. (2012). The Mosaic theory of the Fourth Amendment. *Michigan Law Review, 111*(3), 311–354. https://repository.law.umich.edu/mlr/vol111/iss3/1. DOI: 10.36644/mlr.111.3.mosiac

Koops, B.-J., Newell, B. C., & Škorvánek, I. (2019, March 1). Location tracking by police: The regulation of "tireless and absolute surveillance." *UC Irvine Law Review, 9*(3), 635–698. https://escholarship.org/uc/item/62r710t0

Malhotra, D., & Goyal, K. (2025, March 5). Balancing liberty and surveillance: The intersection of digital monitoring and bail jurisprudence in India. *SSRN, 1*, 163–197. https://jccj.in/2025/03/05/balancing-liberty-and-surveillance-the-intersection-of-digital-monitoring-and-bail-jurisprudence-in-india/. DOI: 10.2139/ssrn.5589250

Millcarek, L. (2012, July). Eighteenth century law, twenty-first century problems: *Jones*, GPS tracking, and the future of privacy. *Florida Law Review, 64*(4), 1101–1111. https://scholarship.law.ufl.edu/flr/vol64/iss4/7

Prasad, S. K., & Aravindakshan, S. (2021). Playing catch up – privacy regimes in South Asia. In Çınar, Ö., & Vanberg, A. D. (Eds.), *The right to privacy revisited.* Routledge. DOI: 10.4324/9781003252191-5

Privacy International. (2019, January 26). *State of privacy Pakistan.* https://privacyinternational.org/state-privacy/1008/state-privacy-pakistan

Rahman. Md, A., & Rashid, H.-O. (2020, July 15). Digital Security Act and investigative journalism in Bangladesh: A critical analysis. *CenRaPS Journal of Social Sciences, 2*(2), 216–236. DOI: 10.46291/cenraps.v2i2.32

Shahid, M. K., Shou-lian, T., & Liu, C. (2007). Competition and liberalization policies and regulations for telecommunications industries in China and Pakistan: A comparative analysis. *International Journal of Management Science and Engineering Management, 2*(4), 268–277. DOI: 10.1080/17509653.2007.10671026

Sinha, N., & Dutta, M. (2025). Proportionality in Indian and South African review jurisprudence – A comparative analysis. *Global Journal of Comparative Law, 14*(3), 326–358. DOI: 10.1163/2211906X-14030004

Slobogin, C. (2012, June). Making the most of United States v. Jones in a surveillance society: A statutory implementation of Mosaic theory. *Duke Journal of Constitutional Law & Public Policy*. https://scholarship.law.vanderbilt.edu/faculty-publications/260

Taher, M. A. (2025). Right to access the internet vis-à-vis freedom of expression: Bangladesh in context. In *The Asian Yearbook of Human Rights and Humanitarian Law* (pp. 35–60). Brill Nijhoff., DOI: 10.1163/9789004748736_003

Varma, B. (2019, March 15). Column: Fruit of the poisonous tree. *Bar and Bench*. https://www.barandbench.com/columns/column-fruit-of-the-poisonous-tree

Varner, C., Wood, D. P., & Young, D. (2021, August 19). A report from the 2015 United States–United Kingdom legal exchange. *Judicare International, 100*(2). https://judicature.duke.edu/articles/a-report-from-the-2015-united-states-united-kingdom-legal-exchange/

Zaib, H. U., Shaheen, M. B., & Chaudhary, H. K. (2025, July-September). Constitutional validity of surveillance technologies in Pakistan: Reconciling national security with individual privacy rights in the digital age. *Social Science Review Archives*, *3*(3), 1653–1665. DOI: 10.70670/sra.v3i3.991

Zuboff, S. (2019). *The age of surveillance capitalism: The fight for a human future at the new frontier of power*. PublicAffairs.

Chapter 5
Digital Eyes:
The Ethics of Modern Surveillance

Vernice J. Moody
http://orcid.org/0009-0003-8422-0122
Purdue University Global, USA

Jaylen B. Moody
http://orcid.org/0009-0007-6902-611X
Bowie State University, USA

ABSTRACT

Emerging technologies, including facial recognition, biometric tracking, closed-circuit television, online monitoring, and artificial intelligence driven analytics, are rapidly reshaping the criminal justice system. The integration of modern surveillance is creating increasingly interconnected surveillance networks that enhance situational awareness, streamline decision making, and expand law enforcement's ability to identify, prevent, and respond to crime. This convergence supports more proactive policing and contributes to evolving models of public safety. Yet these developments raise significant ethical and legal concerns. Risks related to privacy breaches, discriminatory targeting, data misuse, and the erosion of civil liberties remain central to debates over the role of surveillance in criminal justice. Clear regulations, strong ethical frameworks, and democratic safeguards are essential to ensure that surveillance technologies serve the public good, uphold social justice, and support a fair and equitable society.

INTRODUCTION

Surveillance technologies are fundamental aspects of everyday life, increasingly present in various forms, shaping individuals' interaction with their surroundings and how organizations monitor activities (Cindrapole & Rosmini, 2024). These technologies interconnect systems designed to enhance situational awareness and facilitate more informed and efficient decision-making. Key technologies include facial recognition, biometrics, closed-circuit television (CCTV), online data monitoring, and artificial intelligence (AI)-powered analytics. Law enforcement agencies continually seek out and adopt these tools to improve their ability to detect crimes and support the prosecution of offenders (Almeida et al., 2022).

Surveillance technologies offer a range of benefits, but their adoption and use pose significant ethical challenges. The ethical debate centers on balancing the imperative of public safety with the protection of

DOI: 10.4018/979-8-3373-7660-8.ch005

individual privacy rights (Okandeji, 2024; Wheatley, 2024). These challenges include wrongful identification, erosion of public trust, disproportionate targeting of certain groups, and questions of regulatory oversight. As these technologies integrate into criminal justice systems, the need to balance public safety with individual privacy rights becomes urgent and contested (Wang, et.al, 2024).

BACKGROUND ON SURVEILLANCE TECHNOLOGIES AND THE CRIMINAL JUSTICE SYSTEM

Facial recognition, biometric tracking, CCTV, online data monitoring, and AI-powered analytics shape daily routines and contribute to contemporary security and data-management practices. In criminal justice, these tools support crime prevention and investigation by expanding agencies' ability to identify individuals, monitor spaces, and analyze information at scale.

A leading example of this shift involves facial recognition, which evolved in step with broader advances in computing and automated identification. Facial recognition technology underwent significant evolution since its inception. In the 1960s, early systems relied on manual measurements of facial features. Over time, advances in statistical modeling and neural networks improved accuracy and efficiency, enabling precise mapping of the human face (Qinjun et al., 2023).

Related identification systems extend beyond facial features to other biological and behavioral markers, making biometrics a broader foundation for modern monitoring. Biometric tracking uses unique physical or behavioral traits to identify individuals, providing a reliable basis for personal identification (North-Samardzic, 2020).

While biometrics focus on identifying individuals, CCTV broadens surveillance by continuously monitoring environments and recording activity over time. CCTV uses video cameras to monitor activities in public and private spaces. The technology supports proactive and reactive crime control by enabling authorities and organizations to observe, document, and respond to incidents as they occur (Oloke et al., 2024).

Surveillance extends beyond physical spaces into digital environments, where online activity can be captured, analyzed, and connected to other data sources. Online data monitoring evolved from early computer-logging practices in the 1980s into today's AI-driven, large scale surveillance systems (Ehrlinger & Wöß, 2022). In this context, artificial intelligence (AI) refers to machines that perform tasks that typically require human cognitive abilities, such as recognizing patterns, classifying information, and generating predictions (Stockwell et al., 2024).

Together, these technologies enable a more data-intensive model of policing, where decisions are increasingly shaped by continuous monitoring and automated analysis. As technology advances, surveillance tools become increasingly central to responsive policing ("The use of surveillance," 2023). These innovations streamline efforts to solve crimes, apprehend offenders, and deliver justice, contributing to broader goals of public safety and societal well-being (Loux & Loux, 2025). Predictive and identification oriented systems illustrate a shift toward policing models in which risk assessment, pattern detection, and automated alerts shape priorities and practices, sometimes outpacing existing legal and ethical safeguards (Stiernströmer, 2026).

As surveillance becomes more pervasive and predictive, concerns about rights, fairness, and accountability grow increasingly difficult to separate from debates about effectiveness. The integration of surveillance technologies into criminal justice systems also sparked profound ethical debate, particularly around the tension between public safety and individual privacy. A prominent concern involves privacy violations, including the collection of sensitive information without individuals' knowledge and the lack of informed consent regarding the use of data (Okandeji, 2024).

An examination of Chicago, Houston, New York City, Los Angeles, and Washington, D.C., along with a national case from Japan, show how jurisdictions adopt surveillance technologies to support law enforcement in practice. These cases represent heavily surveilled and technologically advanced environments where scale, crime challenges, and political complexity make surveillance central to monitoring public spaces, deterring criminal activity, and supporting investigations ("Atlas of Surveillance," n.d.). Japan provides an international comparison in which the extensive use of CCTV and biometric systems reflects a technologically advanced but culturally distinct approach, highlighting how legal frameworks and societal norms shape surveillance adoption and oversight ("A Novel Solution," 2024).

LITERATURE REVIEW

To better understand how surveillance technologies integrated into law enforcement, this literature review examines major surveillance tools and their potential effects on law enforcement outcomes.

Haley (2025) noted the evolution of surveillance spans from basic observational methods to advanced AI systems that automatically detect suspicious behavior. Over the past decades, surveillance technologies have advanced rapidly, shifting from traditional CCTV systems to AI-driven networks that integrate biometrics, predictive analytics, and large-scale data aggregation. Recent scholarship increasingly questions not only the operational effectiveness of these systems but also their broader implications for civil liberties, algorithmic fairness, and public trust.

Prior to the 1970s, policing operated predominantly as a reactive enterprise, relying on routine patrols, responses to emergency calls, and post-incident investigations. Over time, both practitioners and scholars observed that these reactive strategies exerted limited influence on overall crime rates. This recognition contributed to a gradual reorientation of policing toward proactive, analytically informed, and data-driven approaches (Brayne & Christin, 2021). This shift toward proactive policing increased demand for technologies that deliver real-time intelligence, automate pattern detection, and expand agencies' ability to anticipate and respond to crime.

Modern surveillance technologies increasingly support law enforcement and criminal justice efforts to reduce violent crime. Haley (2025) noted that these systems combine biometric data, facial recognition, and machine learning to improve identification and monitoring processes. Surveillance tools may prevent violence by enabling faster response, increasing situational awareness, and expanding analytic capabilities within justice departments. Real-time monitoring and alerts, automated evidence collection, and AI-assisted case prioritization are additional benefits supported by modern sensors and biometric technologies (Haley, 2025).

CCTV stands as one of the oldest and most widely adopted surveillance technologies, with its presence established across many sectors (Oloke et al., 2024). Building on this foundation of visual monitoring, facial recognition technology played a central role in contemporary identity-management systems, enabling verification, identification, and investigation. (Erickson & Merkle, 2025). Complementing facial recognition, biometric tracking drew on characteristics such as fingerprints, facial structure, iris patterns, voice, and even walking style (North-Samardzic, 2020). As surveillance expanded beyond physical spaces, online data monitoring highlights the growing complexity and scope of monitoring in the digital age (Ehrlinger & Wöß, 2022). AI-powered analytics replicated or simulated aspects of human intelligence to address problems and execute activities that otherwise requires human decision-making and thought processes (Stockwell et al., 2024).

While surveillance technologies offer powerful tools for enhancing public safety, their integration into criminal justice systems raises profound ethical challenges. ical (2025) noted that these technologies require careful governance. Key concerns include data privacy, information security, system accuracy, and broader ethical implications.

Within surveillance studies, facial recognition technology emerges as one of the most contested modes of police monitoring. Wang et al. (2024) emphasized that facial recognition raises concerns related to privacy, ethical governance and regulatory oversight.

Additional concerns include the disproportionate targeting of certain groups, which can reinforce societal biases and enable unequal treatment. Collected data may also be misused or repurposed beyond its original intent, and widespread surveillance can erode civil liberties and diminish public trust (Okandeji, 2024; Wheatley, 2024). These ethical tensions are not abstract; they take shape differently depending on local policy choices, governance capacity, and the scale of deployment in specific jurisdictions.

Related critiques extend to AI-powered surveillance tools more broadly; Richardson et al. (2019) explained how "dirty data" produced through racially disparate policing and the uneven surveillance of marginalized communities can distort predictive outputs and reinforce existing structural inequities.

Research conducted in the United States suggests that installing video surveillance systems does not significantly impact overall crime rates. Biale (2008) found that the presence of such systems had an insignificant effect on deterring crime. This finding indicates that while surveillance may serve other purposes such as aiding investigations or providing a sense of security its direct influence on reducing crime can be limited.

Across the literature, three themes recurred: policing increasingly depends on integrated surveillance infrastructures; predictive and biometric systems can embed bias, prompting calls for audits, open data standards, and regulatory oversight; and these technologies influence police and community relations, civil-liberties protections, and perceptions of legitimacy.

Surveillance Technology Deployment in the US and Japan

In cities such as Chicago, Houston, Washington, D.C., Los Angeles, New York City and globally in Japan, surveillance technologies increased the perceived certainty of apprehension and transform the relationship between state and the public. To ground these broader claims, the following cases outline how specific jurisdictions have adopted surveillance tools to address local public safety priorities.

Chicago, with an estimated population of nearly 2.7 million people, comprises 50 wards, 77 community areas, and 100 neighborhoods ("City of Chicago," n.d.). The city faced persistently elevated levels of violence for decades. To address these challenges, the Chicago Police Department established Real-Time Crime Centers (RTCCs), which are equipped with advanced technologies to support crime control and prevention initiatives (Arietti, 2024). Another policing technology used by the Chicago Police Department involves ShotSpotter. First tested in 2012 and implemented in 2018, ShotSpotter provides AI sensors in the detection of gunshots (Piza, 2024).

While Chicago highlights real-time analytics and gunshot detection, Houston shows how surveillance expansion can align with organizational strategies for addressing disorder. Houston's estimated population totals approximately 2.4 million people ("Houston," n.d.). A key component of the Houston Police

Department's organizational structure involves the Differential Response Team, tasked with targeting and addressing both social and physical disorder within the city (Zhao & Zhang, 2022).

New York City also shows how large departments combine surveillance capabilities with mobile and information-access technologies to support street-level decision-making. New York City's estimated populations totals 2.4 million people ("New York," n.d.). The city's large and diverse population presents unique challenges for maintaining public safety and addressing crime effectively.

The New York City Police Department (NYPD) implemented several innovative tools aimed at improving public safety and responding to these challenges. Among these initiatives, the NYPD Mobility Platform equips field officers with smartphones and tablets. This technology enhances officers' ability to access vital information, communicate efficiently, and respond quickly to incidents ("Technology," n.d.).

Los Angeles provides a related but distinct example, emphasizing mobile-first platforms and modernization efforts designed to improve operational flexibility Los Angeles' estimated populations totals 3.9 million residents, reflecting its status as one of the largest urban centers in the United States ("Los Angeles," n.d..).

The city took significant steps to modernize its approach to crime prevention. Central to this effort, the Los Angeles Police Department (LAPD) shifted away from using bulky laptops in favor of more versatile cell devices. This transition represents part of the department's Mobility First strategy, which equips officers with advanced technology to enhance their efficiency and effectiveness in the field (Calams, 2024).

Washington, D.C. illustrates how surveillance adoption can be shaped by the demands of incident response, investigative support, and interagency coordination. Washington, D.C., the capital of the United States, estimated population totals 702,300 residents ("Washington, District of Columbia," n.d.). The city's efforts to maintain public safety are closely tied to its use of advanced technologies, particularly in support of criminal investigations and incident response (Perry, 2024).

The Metropolitan Police Department (MPD) in Washington, D.C., oversees law enforcement throughout the city. To enhance its capabilities in managing and resolving criminal activity, the MPD established the RTCC (Perry, 2024). The RTCC plays a crucial role in supporting investigations and responding to ongoing criminal incidents. By leveraging innovative technology, the center provides real-time assistance, helping law enforcement personnel address cases more efficiently and effectively (Perry, 2024).

Japan adds a national point of comparison and highlights distinct governance and cultural conditions. Japan's estimated population totals 123 million people ("Japan," n.d.). Japan adopted technological advancements to enhance its crime prevention strategies. One significant development involves the creation of Crime Nabi, a predictive tool designed to promote citizen engagement in crime prevention efforts. Initially, this tool aimed to encourage active participation from the public in maintaining safety and security across communities ("A Novel Solution," 2024).

These jurisdictional examples show how surveillance technologies are woven into day-to-day policing through real-time monitoring, data-driven coordination, and prevention-oriented strategies. The question of where these tools are deployed shifts to a closer examination of how the surveillance technologies shape contemporary investigations and ongoing debates about privacy, bias, and oversight. It is helpful to first define each technology and outline its use in policing.

Facial Recognition Technology

Facial recognition technology rapidly emerged as one of the most consequential tools reshaping contemporary policing, enabling new forms of suspect identification and large-scale analysis of visual data.

Dauvergne (2022) noted that law enforcement agencies adopted facial recognition technologies to identify victims, support criminal investigations, and locate suspects. In practice, agencies captured images and feed them directly into recognition systems, streamlining operational processes (Okandeji, 2024). As these systems integrated with real-time analytics, facial recognition functioned as a force multiplier by increasing the speed and efficiency of identification and decision-making for both law enforcement officials and city managers (Ly, 2025).

Despite these operational benefits, facial recognition technology raised critical concerns about privacy, surveillance, and the ethical governance of biometric data (Tuhin, 2025). Algorithms underpinning these systems can be susceptible to racial and gender bias, increasing the risk of misidentification and discrimination. Notably, facial recognition systems showed higher misidentification rates among people of color, which can exacerbate racial bias and contribute to unjust outcomes (Tuhin, 2025; Wheatley, 2024).

In *USA: Amnesty International, S.T.O.P. Lawsuit Reveals NYPD Surveillance Abuses* (2025), Amnesty International highlights infringements on privacy rights, noting that large-scale image collection can occur without individuals' knowledge or consent. This type of deployment also diminished the public's sense of safety, particularly when authorities use these tools to suppress or punish (Zalnieriute, 2025). Without clear regulations, facial recognition may become a mechanism for mass surveillance and social control (Okandeji, 2024).

Research conducted by Johnson et al. (2024) provides valuable insights into the impact of facial recognition technology on public safety and privacy. Their study was guided by three main questions:

1. How does the adoption of facial recognition technology affect the reduction of violent crimes within police forces?
2. Does technology contribute to increased arrests or racial disparities?
3. How does facial recognition enhance the judicial system?

The findings highlighted facial recognition may be more effective as a targeted investigative tool than as a broad deterrent for crime. Johnson et al. (2024) found statistically significant reductions in certain violent crimes, particularly homicide and felony violence, although the effects were modest and not substantial. The study also found no evidence that facial recognition increased arrest rates or exacerbated racial disparities in violent criminal cases (Johnson et al., 2024).

Chicago serves as a prominent testing ground for the implementation of modern surveillance technologies in law enforcement, particularly predictive-policing systems and body-worn camera programs. These technologies have enhanced crime prevention, improved accountability, and increased the efficiency of police operations; empirical research shows that their effects are mixed and often controversial (Saunders et al., 2016; Williams et al., 2021).

One of Chicago's most notable surveillance initiatives was the Strategic Subject List, a predictive policing tool designed to identify individuals identified as high risks of involvement in gun violence. Evaluations of the Strategic Subject List program indicated that individuals on the list experienced increased police attention, but the initiative had minimal impact on crime or victimization. Instead, predictive surveillance frequently intensified police contact without delivering measurable public safety benefits, raising concerns about fairness and effectiveness in particular communities subjected to heavy policing (Saunders et al., 2016).

The broader ethical and societal issues of algorithmic reconnaissance in Chicago law enforcement are brought to light by recent studies. An analysis of predictive policing tools found that discussions about algorithmic bias, evidentiary requirements, and fairness were heavily influenced by these factors. The public's trust declined because of divergent perceptions of what constitutes reliable evidence and fair policing. Ultimately, it influenced the city's decision to end its predictive policing initiatives, demonstrating how surveillance technology can undermine law enforcement's legitimacy and governance (Ziosi & Pruss, 2024).

Facial recognition technology exerts a substantial impact on operations and decision-making within New York City's criminal justice system. The NYPD committed millions of dollars to acquiring and deploying these advanced systems ("USA: Amnesty International," 2025). Facial recognition technology emerged as a prominent example of expansive law-enforcement use of technology, with the NYPD conducting approximately 10,000 searches to assist in generating leads (Jones, 2021).

The NYPD utilizes facial recognition technology to solve crimes and promote public safety. This technology plays a key role in identifying suspects captured on camera during incidents such as robberies, burglaries, assaults, shootings, and other serious offenses. Facial recognition also assists the department in identifying individuals who may be experiencing memory impairment or in recognizing deceased persons whose identities remain unknown (New York City Police Department, 2023).

The implementation of facial recognition technology in New York City also affects civil liberties. Wang (2025) reported the NYPD's repeated use of these technologies, subjecting residents to surveillance practices. The accuracy and fairness of such practices are topics of ongoing debate among scholars and policymakers. The NYPD's approach to criminal justice continues to evolve, guided by reforms that focus on enhancing fairness and transparency within the system.

Broader social and constitutional implications impact New York City through the vast access to databases, highlighting the unregulated expansion of facial recognition technology leading to civil liberties and deepening historical patterns of discriminatory policing. Biases, including algorithms and racial disparities in law enforcement practices, increase the likelihood that this technology will reinforce unequal injustices instead of mitigating them (Jones, 2021).

Since 2009, the LAPD used facial recognition software almost 30,000 times as noted by a report from Rector and Winton (2020). The LAPD repeatedly asserted that it maintains no records pertaining to facial recognition systems and at various points, denied employing such technology (Rector & Winton, 2020). This pattern of denial complicated efforts to assess the scope of biometric surveillance in one of the nation's largest police jurisdictions and underscores broader challenges in obtaining transparency from law-enforcement agencies regarding emerging surveillance practices.

Washington, D.C., as the nation's capital, serves as a critical benchmark for evaluating the impact of modern surveillance technologies on law enforcement and national security (La Vigne et al., 2011). Facial recognition technology constitutes one of the principal tools influencing the district's policing methods. Comparing live or recorded photos to extensive databases of faces enables agencies to identify people quickly, leading to faster identification and greater investigative effectiveness. The technology offers operational advantages, improving public safety and speeding up investigations ("How policing agencies use AI," 2024). Law enforcement's use of facial recognition technology closely examines ethical deployment, potential bias, and legal oversight. These systems are integrated into intricate regulatory frameworks. In Washington, D.C., where federal law enforcement and agencies frequently work together, these technologies strengthen the power and accountability of policing institutions.

Beyond operational effectiveness, facial recognition technology significantly shaped public trust and governance by revealing that face recognition in law enforcement functions as a social, as well as a technical, problem (Hill et al., 2022). When implemented without clear policies or significant public involvement, it can worsen already-existing gaps in law enforcement and disproportionately harm communities of color. Facial recognition affects community views of legitimacy and fairness. Tensions that have historically existed between law enforcement and marginalized groups run the potential of undermining trust and increasing public mistrust. Co-constructed policymaking was suggested as a risk-reduction tactic, arguing that involving public stakeholders in the creation and management of surveillance programs enhances accountability and increases public acceptability of these technologies (Hill et al., 2022).

A controversial deployment of live facial recognition technology by a private company in Japan analyzed the social, legal, and ethical implications of its use. A focus on the July 2021 implementation by East Japan Railway Company (JR East) introduced a facial recognition system at major train stations to identify individuals flagged by authorities as suspicious. While the system aimed to improve safety in response to increasing attacks on trains, JR East's failure to disclose operational procedures, data storage policies, and usage guidelines triggered public criticism and social concern. The controversy illustrates how the deployment of sensitive biometric technologies without transparency can undermine public trust and provoke backlash (Ozaki, 2022).

The JR East study highlighted the emphasis on challenges with data protection, privacy, and fairness related to live facial recognition technology. Biometric data collection in public places poses serious ethical and legal issues since it might identify people without their knowledge or consent. Ozaki (2022) noted no comprehensive legislative framework governing the use of live facial recognition technology by private businesses in public locations. The JR East case highlights a broader regulatory void in Japan. This regulatory ambiguity raises the possibility of abuse, illegal surveillance, and human rights breaches. Ozaki (2022) argues that the ethical application of facial recognition technology requires careful balancing of social consent, privacy rights, and public safety goals.

As reported by Willey (2024), the Houston Police Department approved an agreement focused on expanding and maintaining its network of surveillance cameras. This initiative contributes to the department's ongoing efforts to support crime prevention and strengthen public safety across the city. The police department emphasized that the surveillance cameras being deployed do not incorporate AI technologies. Officials stated these cameras are not utilized for facial recognition purposes, addressing potential privacy concerns within the community (Willey, 2024).

Despite extensive research, no peer-reviewed research was gathered for Houston to address current facial recognition technology and law enforcement and further its impact on the law enforcement sector.

Biometric Tracking

Biometric tracking emerged as a key component of contemporary policing, enabling identification through fingerprints, facial features, gait, and other physiological markers. Smith and Miller (2021) noted biometric tracking systems can operate in two primary modes. For *one-to-many*, an unknown individual's biometric data undergoes comparison against a database of stored profiles to determine identity, a common practice in criminal investigations. For *one-to-one*, verification involves confirming whether an individual matches who they claim to be by comparing their biometric data with a single, pre-enrolled reference profile..

Stockwell et al. (2024) noted biometric tracking methods can make inferences about a person's psychological or emotional states, verify identity, and classify individuals. Interpreting subtle biometric signals, such as facial expressions or physiological responses, can provide insights into an individual's mental or emotional condition.

Biometric data plays a critical role in modern policing and law enforcement practices by transforming how agencies identify individuals, solve crimes, and support community safety (Erickson, 2025). In practice, police commonly employ fingerprint and DNA analysis to identify suspects who may have been present at crime scenes and to link individuals to specific events or locations, providing crucial evidence in criminal cases (Stockwell et al., 2024). Biometric identification emerged as a routine investigative practice, enhancing both accuracy and efficiency.

Rapid advances in surveillance technologies contributed to a complex and often unexamined reality of involuntary biometric observation. As these tools become more prevalent, individuals are increasingly subject to monitoring in public spaces without explicit consent. Modern surveillance systems are multifaceted and include tools such as gunshot detection systems, surveillance cameras, drones, and automatic license plate readers. Across these applications, biometric capabilities identify and track individuals in public environments (Haley, 2025).

Haley (2025) noted that implementing biometric surveillance systems improve public safety, in part by enabling authorities to respond more effectively to incidents. By continuously monitoring environments and collecting data, agencies increase situational awareness and shorten response times. At the same time, the widespread use of these technologies raises important questions about privacy and the societal implications of constant observation.

Biometric systems are increasingly important in crime-control efforts because their ability to uniquely identify individuals sets them apart from traditional manual identification methods (Stockwell et al., 2024). Because these systems rely on distinctive physical or behavioral characteristics such as fingerprints or facial recognition they can offer greater accuracy and reliability and reduce the risk of mistaken identity.

In some contexts, biometric recognition systems identify individuals more reliably than human operators, helping to safeguard against errors that can occur in human decision-making (Stockwell et al., 2024). This level of precision proves especially valuable when accurate identification becomes critical, as it can minimize misidentification and enhance security. By automating parts of the identification process, biometric systems can also reduce mistakes arising from human judgment and inconsistency (Stockwell et al., 2024).

Despite the security and convenience biometrics can offer, biometric tracking presents significant ethical challenges. Key concerns include protecting biometric data from breaches, reducing the risk of identity theft, and establishing governance frameworks and regulations that limit misuse (ical, 2025).

The deployment of biometric identity systems by law enforcement sparked public debate, particularly regarding privacy, civil liberties, and the potential misuse of sensitive biometric data. Critics argued that widespread use may enable unwarranted surveillance and infringe on individual rights. These concerns underscored the need for careful ethical evaluation and regulatory oversight as biometric technologies continue to evolve (Jansen et al., 2021).

Comprehensive searches across peer-reviewed articles, journals, and academic databases identified limited scholarship on current biometric tracking use in law enforcement for Houston, Chicago, Los Angeles, New York City, Washington, D.C., and Japan. This lack of peer-reviewed evidence limits the ability to assess effectiveness, ethical implications, and operational outcomes at the municipal level. It also constrains evidence-based policymaking and highlights the need for more rigorous academic evaluation of biometric technologies in law enforcement.

CCTV

CCTV became a core element of contemporary policing, providing continuous visual monitoring and supporting investigations. Bandara (2023) highlighted that CCTV systems increasingly use machine-learning algorithms to support pattern recognition across three primary detection types designed to enhance security and situational awareness. Behavior detection analyzes an individual's movements to determine whether actions are suspicious or deviate from normal patterns, helping personnel identify potential threats based on conduct within a monitored area.

Object detection focuses on identifying specific items such as guns and other weapons within the camera's view so the system can alert authorities quickly and support swift intervention. Intrusion detection safeguards restricted areas by monitoring unauthorized access attempts and helping ensure only individuals with proper clearance enter secure zones, protecting sensitive locations and assets (Bandara, 2023).

Saluja et al. (2023) noted CCTV systems are commonly installed in locations such as schools, banks, and shopping facilities. Businesses also leverage CCTV to monitor activity in and around their premises. In these settings, cameras can deter shoplifting, safeguard employees, and help track entries and exits within the establishment (Saluja et al., 2023).

Research identifies several benefits associated with CCTV deployment, particularly because visible surveillance can discourage unlawful or harmful behavior. Reported advantages include preventing and identifying theft, deterring personal attacks and vandalism, and reducing fights in monitored areas (Saluja et al., 2023).

Houston implemented outdoor surveillance cameras as required by a city ordinance in 2022. These cameras help law enforcement to get tough and solve crimes (Newberry, 2022). Businesses must operate the cameras in well-lit areas, operate 24 hours a day, and have footage available for the Houston Police Department to review within 72 hours of the request (Nuckolls, 2023).

Japan traditionally relied on active community participation for crime prevention, with residents monitoring neighborhoods, reporting suspicious activity, and fostering collective responsibility for public safety (Yang et al., 2024). As the population aged, sustaining this model became more difficult, increasing demand for more durable crime-prevention tools. In response, CCTV gained prominence as a reliable solution that could support public safety despite demographic change. Japan expanded camera installations across urban areas and integrated CCTV into smart-city development, enabling real-time monitoring that can improve the ability to detect and respond to criminal activity (Yang et al., 2024).

Several major U.S. cities implemented extensive surveillance camera networks to enhance public safety and security. Bischoff (2024) note the difficulty of estimating the number of CCTV cameras, as sources provide inconsistent figures and limited public information, leaving true totals potentially higher or lower than commonly cited. With that limitation, Bischoff (2024) estimated approximately 48,283 cameras in Chicago, 11,714 in Houston, 70,882 in New York City, and 39,790 in Los Angeles (Bischoff, 2024).

An estimated 35,082 cameras monitor public spaces in Washington, D.C (Bischoff, 2024). The Washington Metropolitan Area Transit Authority oversees a surveillance system that extends beyond the city into neighboring jurisdictions, including Montgomery County, MD, and Prince

George's County, MD. This regional integration expands coverage and strengthens coordination among transit and public safety agencies across the metropolitan area (Bischoff, 2024).

Yang et al. (2024) noted that Japan does not maintain an official, centralized count of surveillance cameras because systems are owned and operated by a wide range of entities, including individuals, businesses, government agencies, and private organizations. This decentralized ownership makes comprehensive tracking difficult. Even without an official tally, reports suggest Japan operates more than five million surveillance cameras, reflecting extensive deployment across sectors and settings.

Despite its advantages, CCTV raises ethical concerns, including the erosion of anonymity in public spaces, the potential misuse of recorded footage, and insufficient oversight of surveillance practices. These risks can intensify as camera networks expand and monitoring becomes more diffuse, underscoring the need to balance security objectives with privacy, accountability, and transparent governance (Okandeji, 2024).

CCTV remains a widely deployed policing tool that supports investigations and situational awareness, increasingly enhanced by machine-learning features such as behavior, object, and intrusion detection (Bandara, 2023). At the same time, large-scale camera networks can strain monitoring capacity and raise persistent concerns about privacy, data misuse, and oversight, underscoring the need for transparent governance that aligns security objectives with accountability (Okandeji, 2024; Hopkins & Mahr, 2024).

Online Data Monitoring

Online data monitoring became an important element of policing, enabling the tracking of digital communications, social-media activity, and online behavior. Every action performed on digital platforms—browsing, sharing content, or completing online transactions—leaves traces. These traces, commonly described as digital footprints, reflect a user's behavior, preferences, and interactions in the digital realm (Yadav & Varshney, 2024). Online data monitoring builds on these footprints through the tracking, logging, analysis, and storage of user activity, communications, and behavior across digital networks. As these practices have expanded, they highlight the growing complexity and scope of monitoring activities in the digital age (Ehrlinger & Wöß, 2022).

As digital platforms proliferate, the volume and diversity of user data increase, contributing to the continual expansion of individual and collective digital footprints (Yadav & Varshney, 2024). Within this environment, online data monitoring plays a key role in maintaining data quality and reliability. This work includes testing data pipelines for integrity, tracking system health to detect and address issues, and using anomaly-detection techniques to identify irregularities as part of broader data-quality measurement and observability efforts (Ehrlinger & Wöß, 2022).

The rapid growth of social media platforms transformed global communication by enabling instant connectivity across borders and real-time information sharing. This scale and speed also create opportunities for online crime, making digital surveillance techniques increasingly important for monitoring, detecting, and responding to cyber threats. Social media patrolling refers to the systematic monitoring of digital platforms to identify suspicious behaviors and detect potential cybercrime, enabling timely intervention to prevent incidents from escalating and to protect online communities (Ganguli, 2025).

Social media platforms become hotspots for cybercriminal activity, including identity theft, financial fraud, cyberbullying, misinformation and disinformation campaigns, and even terrorism (Ganguli, 2025; Haley, 2025). In response, law enforcement agencies have expanded online data monitoring to support detection and prevention efforts in digital spaces. These practices raise important ethical concerns because surveillance conducted without informed consent, creating difficult tradeoffs between individual privacy and collective safety (Okandeji, 2024; Zalnieriute, 2025).

The evolving nature of cybercrime on social media presents significant obstacles for traditional law enforcement methods. Detecting and apprehending offenders grows more complex as criminals conceal identities and move quickly across platforms (Ganguli, 2025).

Police intelligence involves the development and application of tools designed to assist government agencies and law enforcement in the general detection of crime. This area encompasses a broad range of problem categories related to criminal acts, with a primary focus on supporting efforts to address and solve crime (Edwards et al., 2015).

Edwards et al. (2015) noted that the primary interest within police intelligence lies in two key domains: the investigation of criminal organizations and the spatially restricted prediction of criminal activity. While these domains are the central concerns, police intelligence addresses other, lesser crimes, thereby contributing to a comprehensive approach to crime prevention and detection.

A sizable portion of work in this field concentrates on strengthening police investigations through technology that filters knowledge from web-based news sources. The main objective of this approach centers on giving investigators situational awareness and keeping them informed about relevant public information. By systematically analyzing online news sources, police intelligence supports law enforcement professionals in keeping updated on developments that may impact ongoing investigations or highlight emerging trends within the public domain (Edwards et al., 2015).

Block (2023) noted that the Chicago Police Department employs online data monitoring practices to systematically scrape and analyze information drawn from individuals' social media accounts, integrating these digital traces into broader intelligence and investigative activities.

Ayoub and Griffiths (2023) noted that officers within the NYPD have used social media platforms for a wide range of purposes, including monitoring public gatherings and tracking individuals and their social connections in the absence of any demonstrated evidence of criminal wrongdoing.

Dwyer (2021) reported internal records indicate that the LAPD conducts extensive surveillance of social-media platforms. Officers routinely collect social-media account information from individuals during in-person encounters. The department then aggregates these data along with information drawn from multiple external sources into centralized databases designed to expand its surveillance reach and enhance its analytical capabilities.

Dyson et al. (2024) reported internal documents reveal that law enforcement agencies in Washington, D.C., use online surveillance tools to systematically monitor individuals' social media activity, collect information on users and their associated social networks, and track data related to public demonstrations. These records further show that the agencies relied on software from multiple vendors to scan millions of websites, process large volumes of unfiltered social media content, and conduct behavioral and network analyses of individuals' online interactions.

Surveillance technologies and electronic monitoring have become increasingly integrated into everyday life in Japan. The Japanese public's lack of opposition can be attributed to a lack of trust in the media, discouraging critical discourse regarding government surveillance practices. The framing of such technology as necessary for public safety further introduces privacy concerns (Abe, 2004).

Despite extensive research, no peer-reviewed research was gathered for Houston to address current online data tracking technology and law enforcement and further its impact on the law enforcement sector. The absence of scholarly literature highlights a gap within the empirical research addressing the localized use and consequences of integrating modern technology in policing practices worldwide.

Online data monitoring extends surveillance into digital life by transforming expanding digital footprints and social media activity into actionable intelligence for investigations and prevention efforts (Yadav & Varshney, 2024; Ganguli, 2025). Documented practices across major jurisdictions show both the operational value of these tools and the persistent ethical tradeoffs they create, particularly when monitoring occurs at scale without clear consent, transparency, or oversight (Okandeji, 2024; Zalnieriute, 2025).

AI-Powered Analytics

AI-powered surveillance reshapes modern policing by enabling the analysis of vast data streams and the detection of patterns beyond human capacity. These systems guide decision-making and monitor public spaces.

AI processes and analyzes immense volumes of public and private data, enabling detailed information extraction at an unprecedented scale (Wheatley, 2024). AI-powered analytics propel rapid technological advancement, transforming operational processes and reshaping the landscape of innovation (Williams et al., 2023).

AI-powered analytics emerged as a promising approach for detecting and preventing criminal activity (Kaur & Saini, 2024; Wheatley, 2024). AI's impact on crime detection and prevention stands out within the broader expansion of AI across sectors (Williams et al., 2023). The deployment of AI technologies continues at an unprecedented pace, with law enforcement agencies using these tools in targeted locations to forecast crime and optimize resource allocation (Davies & Krame, 2023; Haley & Burrell, 2023). As these technologies become more embedded in routine policing practices, they are transforming collected information, interpreted, and acted upon within the criminal justice system (Epstein & Emerson, 2024).

The integration of AI presents complex ethical challenges, including algorithmic bias, insufficient accountability, and opaque decision-making processes (Wheatley, 2024). When ethically governed, however, AI can also support internal investigations by auditing processes, uncovering hidden patterns of misconduct, and enhancing transparency within organizations and law enforcement agencies (Haley & Burrell, 2025).

Across the United States, law enforcement agencies are integrating AI-powered analytics to support investigative decision-making and enhance operational efficiency (Epstein & Emerson, 2024). However, these technologies have often been implemented without sufficient disclosure or community consultation, raising public concern (Haley & Burrell, 2025). Related complaints about excessive force, wrongful arrest, and profiling have surfaced, underscoring the need for responsible AI deployment and clear safeguards (Haley & Burrell, 2025).

AI-powered surveillance systems have become increasingly sophisticated and can recognize people within monitored environments (Almeida et al., 2022). Building on this capability, these systems may infer behaviors and predict potential risks as situations unfold. For example, AI-based camera systems can learn to flag unusual behavior—such as repeated scanning of surroundings—by analyzing patterns associated with suspicious activity, supporting more proactive surveillance strategies (Bandara, 2023).

AI-powered predictive policing represents a major step forward in the evolution of law-enforcement technology (Raji & Sholademi, 2024). Predictive policing draws on data-intensive methods to uncover hidden patterns and anticipate where crimes might occur, who could be involved, and which individuals may be at risk (Raji & Sholademi, 2024). Examples of enabling technologies include machine learning, big-data analytics, and geospatial analysis tools that map crime incidents and reveal patterns across locations (Raji & Sholademi, 2024).

Chicago offers a clear example of how predictive approaches are applied at the municipal level. Chicago implemented innovative systems designed to analyze vast amounts of data ("Transforming urban living," 2025). These systems identify emerging crime hotspots by recognizing patterns and trends, enabling police departments to allocate resources strategically and respond proactively to potential threats.

The data-driven and preventive approach represents a shift in how law enforcement operates. By intervening earlier in the crime cycle, agencies can address issues before they escalate, leading to enhanced public safety. The proactive deployment of resources contributed to measurable reductions in crime rates, illustrating the effectiveness of predictive policing in Chicago ("Transforming urban living," 2025).

Beyond identifying predictive hotspots, Houston shows how AI can also support community-focused operational planning. The Houston Police Department recognized several advantages in adopting AI within its operations. AI serves as a valuable tool for identifying, categorizing, and prioritizing public safety concerns voiced by residents. By leveraging these AI capabilities, the department can support data-driven approaches to community planning, ensuring that the most pressing issues are addressed efficiently (Dominguez, 2025).

The data generated through AI analysis further enables the Houston Police Department to develop targeted strategies for social media outreach. These efforts are specifically designed to heighten public awareness and improve community education regarding safety matters. Through focused digital engagement, the department works to keep residents informed and involved, ultimately supporting safer and more informed communities (Dominguez, 2025).

While Houston's examples emphasize operational planning and community engagement, New York City demonstrates AI use in high-traffic public-transit environments. In response to increasing safety concerns, New York City took significant steps to expand its use of AI surveillance within the subway system (Harris, 2025). The AI system continuously monitors behavioral patterns and identifies those deemed potentially suspicious. Examples of such behaviors include unattended objects and abrupt or aggressive movements. The system operates under intentional programming that prevents the identification of specific individuals, focusing instead on behavior-based detection. This approach, termed "predictive prevention," seeks to identify potential threats by analyzing observable actions rather than relying on personal identification (Harris, 2025).

Critics raised concerns about the risks associated with this type of surveillance within New York City, despite the intended benefits. They warn that these systems could enable large-scale behavioral policing, as the underlying algorithmic models may inadvertently replicate existing human biases. Harmless actions, such as nervous tics, could be misclassified as indicators of potential threats. These critics argue that such practices not only jeopardize individual privacy but contribute to the gradual normalization of pervasive surveillance in public spaces (Harris, 2025).

While New York City emphasizes behavior-based monitoring in public transit, Los Angeles shows how AI can be embedded within broader smart-city infrastructure. Los Angeles adopted smart city strategies to modernize its urban environment. These initiatives leverage advanced digital systems with the goal of improving multiple aspects of city life, including traffic management, public safety, and the efficiency of municipal services ("AI-powered cameras in LA," 2025). A central component of Los Angeles's smart city strategy entails the deployment of AI-enabled traffic cameras. These advanced systems are designed to provide real-time monitoring of traffic conditions and support operational decision-making for city officials (("AI-powered cameras in LA," 2025).

By integrating AI technologies, Los Angeles enhanced its ability to respond promptly to changing traffic patterns, incidents, and emergencies ("AI-powered cameras in LA," 2025). The adoption of these digital solutions reflects Los Angeles' broader commitment to data-driven urban governance. By utilizing AI-powered tools and real-time data collection, the city aims to make more informed decisions that benefit residents and improve the effectiveness of municipal operations ("AI-powered cameras in LA," 2025).

While Los Angeles highlights AI embedded in smart-city infrastructure, Washington, D.C. demonstrates AI-enabled surveillance designed to extend remote monitoring and incident response. In Washington, D.C., the MPD expanded its technological infrastructure through the adoption of a comprehensive aerial-surveillance program ("How policing agencies use AI," 2024). This initiative includes the deployment of unmanned aerial systems. The aircraft carries infrared imaging and advanced geospatial-mapping systems that enhance operational awareness and support real-time decisions. Together, these platforms constitute a substantial enhancement of the department's remote-monitoring capacity ("How policing agencies use AI," 2024).

Beyond U.S. municipal deployments focused on physical space monitoring, Japan demonstrates the application of AI to digital security on a national scale. Japan's strategic shift toward incorporating AI into its cybersecurity and information-warfare capabilities marked a deliberate effort to modernize and strengthen its digital defense posture (Hoang Hop, 2025). AI no longer functions merely as a supporting technology but now plays a central role in reshaping how Japan anticipates, detects, and counters cyber threats. This shift enables Japan to maintain a proactive and adaptive posture in an increasingly complex digital security landscape (Hoang Hop, 2025). Japan's use of predictive analytics enables AI-driven models to anticipate potential attack vectors by analyzing historical incident data, assessing contemporary geo-political dynamics, and identifying recurring patterns in cybercriminal activity. This approach enhances the capacity of security systems to detect emerging threats before they materialize (Hoang Hop, 2025).

One major concern centers on the potential for AI systems to uncover personal details about individuals. These details may originate from a variety of datasets, some of which individuals may not even be aware exist or have not explicitly agreed to share. As a result, AI can inadvertently expose sensitive information without the person's knowledge or consent (Wheatley, 2024).

These surveillance systems often operate without meaningful human oversight. This lack of direct human involvement raises important questions about accountability, transparency, and the potential for misuse (Almeida et al., 2022). Wheatley (2024) noted the ability of AI to aggregate and interpret diverse data sources raises important questions surrounding privacy and consent. Careful evaluation of how these technologies affect personal privacy, along with the ethical implications of disclosing information without an individual's consent, remains essential.

Ly (2025) emphasized the need to establish clear boundaries for the acceptable uses of AI systems. By clearly outlining these boundaries, organizations can ensure that AI technologies are utilized in a responsible and ethical manner. This practice supports the preservation of trust and integrity throughout AI deployment. Setting clear limits on the application of AI helps to prevent misuse and reduces the risk of unintended consequences. By proactively establishing these guidelines, stakeholders can promote the responsible advancement of AI while protecting individuals and society (Ly, 2025).

AI-powered analytics extend surveillance from observation to inference by enabling agencies to forecast risks, automate pattern detection, and accelerate operational decision-making across contexts ranging from predictive policing and real time camera analysis to community planning and cybersecurity (Raji & Sholademi, 2024; Bandara, 2023; Hoang Hop, 2025). The same scale and capacity that make these systems powerful also heighten concerns about privacy, bias, and accountability, underscoring the need for transparent oversight and clearly defined limits on acceptable use (Wheatley, 2024; Haley & Burrell, 2025; Ly, 2025).

CONCLUSION

Surveillance technologies have become deeply embedded in law enforcement and criminal justice systems, offering powerful tools for monitoring, analyzing, and interpreting community behavior. By supplying agencies with extensive streams of information, these systems support more data-driven forms of decision making and play a growing role in preventing, detecting, and prosecuting crime. Facial recognition, biometric identification, and CCTV networks enhance personal identification and real time monitoring, while online data surveillance and AI-enabled analytics expand predictive capabilities and resource allocation.

The integration of these technologies into policing also raises significant ethical and governance challenges. Concerns regarding algorithmic bias, systemic limitations, and accountability highlight the risks of relying on opaque or error-prone systems. Issues of consent, data misuse, and the potential erosion of personal freedoms underscore broader tensions between public safety and individual rights.

As surveillance tools continue to evolve, the need for robust regulatory frameworks, transparent oversight, and sustained public engagement becomes increasingly urgent. Ethical and responsible deployment of these systems supports the protection of civil liberties and the preservation of public trust in democratic policing.

Statement

The authors declare no competing interests. This research received no specific grant from any funding agency in the public, commercial, or not-for-profit sectors; the authors covered funding for this research.

REFERENCES

Abe, K. (2004, June). Everyday policing in Japan: Surveillance, media, government and public opinion. *International Sociology*, *19*(2), 215–231. DOI: 10.1177/0268580904042901

AI-powered cameras in LA: Are DUI arrests going high-tech? (2025, April 30). Werksman Jackson Quinn, Los Angeles Criminal Defense Blog. https://werksmanjackson.com/blog/ai-powered-cameras-in-la-are-dui-arrests-going-high-tech

Almeida, D., Shmarko, K., & Lomas, E. (2022, August). The ethics of facial recognition technologies, surveillance, and accountability in an age of artificial intelligence: A comparative analysis of US, EU, and UK regulatory frameworks. *AI and Ethics*, *2*(3), 377–387. DOI: 10.1007/s43681-021-00077-w PMID: 34790955

Arietti, R. (2024, January-February). Do real-time crime centers improve case clearance? An examination of Chicago's strategic decision support centers. *Journal of Criminal Justice*, *90*, 102145. DOI: 10.1016/j.jcrimjus.2023.102145

Atlas of surveillance. (n.d.). Electronic Frontier Foundation. https://atlasofsurveillance.org

Ayoub, E., & Griffiths, H. (2023, November 20). *We're suing the NYPD to uncover its online surveillance practices*. Brennan Center for Justice. https://www.brennancenter.org/our-work/analysis-opinion/were-suing-nypd-uncover-its-online-surveillance-practices

Bandara, P. (2023, July 21). *Japan tests 'minority report' style cameras to stop crime before it happens*. PetaPixel. https://petapixel.com/2023/07/21/japan-tests-minority-report-style-cameras-to-stop-crime-before-it-happens

Biale, N. (2008, June 25). *What criminologists and others studying cameras have found*. ACLU Technology and Liberty Program. https://www.aclu.org/sites/default/files/images/asset_upload_file708_35775.pdf

Bischoff, P. (2024, January 8). *CCTV surveillance in the most populated cities in the United States*. Comparitech. https://www.comparitech.com/blog/vpn-privacy/us-surveillance-camera-statistics

Block, A. (2023, November 8). *What we know about CPD social media technology and monitoring*. ACLU Illinois. https://www.aclu-il.org/en/news/what-we-know-about-cpd-social-media-technology-and-monitoring

Brayne, S., & Christin, A. (2021, August). Technologies of crime prediction: The reception of algorithms in policing and criminal courts. *The Sociological Review*, *68*(3), 608–624. DOI: 10.1093/socpro/spaa004 PMID: 38250480

Calams, S. (2024, February 13). *Leading the digital beat: LAPD's deputy chief talks technology's role in shaping the future of policing*. Police1. https://www.police1.com/tech-pulse/leading-the-digital-beat-lapds-deputy-chief-talks-technologys-role-in-shaping-the-future-of-policing

Cindrapole, A. C., & Rosmini, S. (2024, May). The legal and ethical implications of surveillance in criminal law: A literatur review. *eScience Humanity Journal* *4*(2), 448-455. https://doi.org/DOI: 10.37296/esci.v4i2.164

City of Chicago. (n.d.). *Facts & statistics.* https://www.chicago.gov/city/en/about/facts.html

Dauvergne, P. (2022). Facial recognition technology for policing and surveillance in the Global South: A call for bans. *Third World Quarterly, 43*(9), 2325–2335. DOI: 10.1080/01436597.2022.2080654

Davies, A., & Krame, G. (2023, December 13). Integrating body-worn cameras, drones, and AI: A framework for enhancing police readiness and response. *Policing. Policing (Oxford, England), 17*, paad083. Advance online publication. DOI: 10.1093/police/paad083

Dominguez, C. (2025, October 19). How is AI used in Houston law enforcement? The sheriff's office and a prosecutor weigh in. *Houston Chronicle.* https://www.houstonchronicle.com/news/houston-texas/trending/article/montgomery-county-ai-crimes-21017304.php

Dwyer, M. P. (2021, September 8). *LAPD documents reveal use of social media monitoring tools.* Brennan Center for Justice. https://www.brennancenter.org/our-work/analysis-opinion/lapd-documents-reveal-use-social-media-monitoring-tools

Dyson, I., Milner, Y., & Griffiths, H. (2024, April 30). *Documents reveal how DC police surveil social media profiles and protest activity.* Brennan Center for Justice. https://www.brennancenter.org/our-work/analysis-opinion/documents-reveal-how-dc-police-surveil-social-media-profiles-and-protest

Edwards, M., Rashid, A., & Rayson, P. (2015, September). A systematic survey of online data mining technology intended for law enforcement. *ACM Computing Surveys, 48*(1), 1–54. DOI: 10.1145/2811403

Ehrlinger, L., & Wöß, W. (2022, March 30). A survey of data quality measurement and monitoring tools. *Frontiers in Big Data, 5*, 850611. DOI: 10.3389/fdata.2022.850611 PMID: 35434611

Epstein, B., Emerson, J. J., & Chat, G. P. T. (2024, April 3). *Navigating the future of policing: Artificial intelligence (AI) use, pitfalls, and considerations for executives.* Police Chief Online. https://www.policechiefmagazine.org/navigating-future-ai-chatgpt

Erickson, D., & Merkle, D. (2025, July 24). *How facial recognition assists criminal investigations.* Police1. https://www.police1.com/police-products/police-technology/police-software/facial-recognition/facial-recognition-is-solving-crimes-heres-how-to-use-it-the-right-way

Erickson, P. (2025, September 18). *Biometrics for law enforcement: Transforming public safety with fast, accurate identification.* HID Global Corporation. https://blog.hidglobal.com/biometrics-law-enforcement-transforming-public-safety-fast-accurate-identification

Ganguli, P. (2025). Digital policing: Using social media surveillance to tackle cybercrime. *Indian Journal of Legal Review, 5*(1), 324–334. https://ijlr.iledu.in/wp-content/uploads/2025/02/V5I136.pdf

Haley, P. (2025, May 16). The impact of biometric surveillance on reducing violent crime: Strategies for apprehending criminals while protecting the innocent. *Sensors (Basel), 25*(10), 3160. DOI: 10.3390/s25103160 PMID: 40431950

Haley, P., & Burrell, D. N. (2025). Integrating artificial intelligence into law enforcement: Socioeconomic and ethical challenges. *SocioEconomic Challenges, 9*(2), 60–77. https://armgpublishing.com/wp-content/uploads/2025/07/SEC_2_2025_4.pdf

Harris, L. (2025, May 3). *New York MTA quietly turns to AI surveillance to predict crime before it happens.* Newstarget. https://www.newstarget.com/2025-05-03-mta-turns-to-ai-surveillance-to-predict-crime.html

Hill, D., O'Connor, C. D., & Slane, A. (2022). Police use of facial recognition technology: The potential for engaging the public through co-constructed policy-making. *International Journal of Police Science & Management*, *24*(3), 325–335. DOI: 10.1177/14613557221089558

Hoang Hop, H. (2025, February 28). *The peace of Japan and the AI.* Japan Up Close. https://japanupclose.web-japan.org/policy/p20250228_1.html

Hopkins, M., & Mahr, J. (2024, September 29). *Many cameras. Little focus. Blurry results.* Illinois Answers Project. https://illinoisanswers.org/2024/09/29/chicago-police-camera-surveillance-fail-deliver-promise-fight-crime

Houston. (n.d.). World Population Review. https://worldpopulationreview.com/us-cities/texas/houston

How policing agencies use AI. (2024, November 12). Policing Project. https://www.policingproject.org/ai-explained-articles/2024/9/6/how-policing-agencies-use-ai

Jansen, F., Sánchez-Monedero, J., & Dencik, L. (2021, July). Biometric identity systems in law enforcement and the politics of (voice) recognition: The case of SiiP. *Big Data & Society*, *8*(2), 20539517211063604. Advance online publication. DOI: 10.1177/20539517211063604

Japan. (n.d.). World Population Review. https://worldpopulationreview.com/countries/japan

Johnson, T. L., Johnson, N. N., Topalli, V., McCurdy, D., & Wallace, A. (2024, December). Police facial recognition applications and violent crime control in U.S. cities. *Cities (London, England)*, *155*, 105472. DOI: 10.1016/j.cities.2024.105472

Jones, C. (2021, October). Law enforcement use of facial recognition: Bias, disparate impacts on people of color, and the need for federal legislation. *North Carolina Journal of Law & Technology*, *22*(4), 777–814. https://scholarship.law.unc.edu/ncjolt/vol22/iss4/6

Kaur, M., & Saini, M. (2024, July). Role of Artificial Intelligence in the crime prediction and pattern analysis studies published over the last decade: A scientometric analysis. *Artificial Intelligence Review*, *57*(8), 202. DOI: 10.1007/s10462-024-10823-1

La Vigne, N. G., Lowry, S. S., Markman, J. A., & Dwyer, A. M. (2011). *Evaluating the use of public surveillance cameras for crime control and prevention.* U.S. Department of Justice, Office of Community Oriented Policing Services. Urban Institute, Justice Policy Center. https://www.urban.org/sites/default/files/publication/27556/412403-evaluating-the-use-of-public-surveillance-cameras-for-crime-control-and-prevention.pdf

Los Angeles (n.d.). World Population Review. https://worldpopulationreview.com/us-cities/california/los-angeles

Loux, M., & Loux, B. (2025, October 28). *Technology in criminal justice: Efficiency and fairness.* American Military University. https://www.amu.apus.edu/area-of-study/criminal-justice/resources/technology-in-criminal-justice

Ly, D. (2025, August 21). Facial recognition in policing and smart cities: Balancing innovation with responsibility. *Forbes*. https://www.forbes.com/councils/forbestechcouncil/2025/08/21/facial-recognition-in-policing-and-smart-cities-balancing-innovation-with-responsibility

New York City Police Department. (2023, October 26). *Facial recognition: Impact and use policy*. https://www.nyc.gov/assets/nypd/downloads/pdf/public_information/post-final/facial-recognition-nypd-impact-and-use-policy_10.26.23.pdf

New York. (n.d.). World Population Review. https://worldpopulationreview.com/us-cities/new-york/new-york

Newberry, B. (2022, July 19). New ordinance requires some Houston businesses to have surveillance cameras, share footage if HPD asks. *Click2Houston*. https://www.click2houston.com/news/local/2022/07/19/new-ordinance-requires-some-houston-businesses-to-have-surveillance-cameras-share-footage-if-hpd-asks

North-Samardzic, A. (2020, December). Biometric technology and ethics: Beyond security applications. *Journal of Business Ethics*, *167*(3), 433–450. DOI: 10.1007/s10551-019-04143-6

A novel solution to public security: Japan's AI-based crime prediction. (2024, June 7). KIZUNA. https://www.japan.go.jp/kizuna/2024/06/japans_ai-based_crime_prediction.html

Nuckolls, C. (2023). Houston security camera ordinance: Reasonable safety measure or Orwellian surveillance. *SMU Science & Technology Law Review*, *26*(1), 8. DOI: 10.25172/smustlr.26.1.8

Okandeji, E. (2024, October 2). *The ethics of surveillance technologies*. Federal Character. https://federalcharacter.com/the-ethics-of-surveillance-technologies

Oloke, O. C., Keke, O. V., Mushanga, S., & Nwokolo, B. O. (2024, December). Efficacy of closed circuit television in security management of commercial properties in Lagos Metropolis, Nigeria. *International Journal of Safety and Security Engineering*, *14*(6), 1719–1727. DOI: 10.18280/ijsse.140607

Ozaki, A. (2022, September). The use of live facial recognition technology by private entities in public places: A study of recent case in Japan. [Conference paper]. In D. Kreps, R. Davison, T. Komukai, & K. Ishii (Eds.), *Human choice and digital by default: Autonomy vs digital determination. 15th IFIP International Conference on Human Choice and Computers* (pp. 27–35). Springer. https://doi.org/DOI: 10.1007/978-3-031-15688-5_3

Perry, N. (2024, September 3). *How D.C. police launched a real time crime center in 8 months*. Police1. https://www.police1.com/tech-pulse/how-d-c-police-launched-a-real-time-crime-center-in-8-months

Piza, E. L. (2024, February 21). *Learning about ShotSpotter and gun violence - from Chicago*. Vital City. https://www.vitalcitynyc.org/articles/learning-about-shot-spotter-from-chicago

Qinjun, L., Tianwei, C., Zhao, Y., & Yuying, W. (2023). Facial recognition technology: A comprehensive overview. *Academic Journal of Computing & Information Science*, *6*(7), 15–26. DOI: 10.25236/AJCIS.2023.060703

Raji, I., & Sholademi, D. B. (2024). Predictive policing: The role of AI in crime prevention. *International Journal of Computer Applications Technology and Research, 13*(10), 66–78. DOI: 10.7753/IJCATR1310.1006

Rector, K., & Winton, R. (2020, September 21). Despite past denials, LAPD has used facial recognition software 30,000 times in last decade, records show. *Los Angeles Times*. https://www.latimes.com/california/story/2020-09-21/lapd-controversial-facial-recognition-software

Richardson, R., Schultz, J., & Crawford, K. (2019, May). Dirty data, bad predictions: How civil rights violations impact police data, predictive policing systems, and justice. *Big Data & Society, 10*(1), 192–233. https://ssrn.com/abstract=3333423

Saluja, D., Kukreja, H., Saini, A., Tegwal, D., Nagrath, P., & Hemanth, J. (2023, November). Analysis and comparison of various deep learning models to implement suspicious activity recognition in CCTV surveillance. *Intelligent Decision Technologies, 17*(4), 917–942. DOI: 10.3233/IDT-230469

Saunders, J., Hunt, P., & Hollywood, J. S. (2016, August). Predictions put into practice: A quasi-experimental evaluation of Chicago's predictive policing pilot. *Journal of Experimental Criminology, 12*(3), 347–371. DOI: 10.1007/s11292-016-9272-0

Smith, M., & Miller, S. (2021). *Biometric identification, law and ethics*. Springer., DOI: 10.1007/978-3-030-90256-8

Stiernströmer, E. (2026, January). Facial recognition technology in law enforcement- a scoping review of existing empirical studies. *Police Practice and Research, 1*(25), 1–25. Advance online publication. DOI: 10.1080/15614263.2026.2627208

Stockwell, S., Hughes, M., Ashurst, C., & Ní Loidcáin, N. (2024, March). *The future of biometric technology for policing and law enforcement: Informing UK regulation*. Centre for Emerging Technology and Security (CETaS), Alan Turing Institute. https://cetas.turing.ac.uk/sites/default/files/2024-03/cetas_research_report_-_the_future_of_biometric_technology_for_policing_and_law_enforcement_0.pdf

Technology. (n.d.). New York City Police Department. https://www.nyc.gov/site/nypd/about/about-nypd/equipment-tech/technology.page

ical, G.-M. (2025). Facial recognition and biometric systems: Benefits and challenges for law enforcement. *Land Forces Academy Review, 30*(2), 249–259. DOI: 10.2478/raft-2025-0024

Transforming urban living: The expansion of smart city infrastructure in Chicago. (2025, April 15). The Chicago Journal. https://thechicagojournal.com/the-expansion-of-smart-city-infrastructure

Tuhin, M. (2025, April 9). What is facial recognition technology? How it works and why it matters in 2025. *Science News Today*. https://www.sciencenewstoday.org/what-is-facial-recognition-technology-how-it-works-and-why-it-matters-in-2025

USA: Amnesty International, S.T.O.P. lawsuit reveals NYPD surveillance abuses. (2025, November 13). Amnesty International. https://www.amnesty.org/en/latest/news/2025/11/amnesty-and-s-t-o-p-reveal-nypd-surveillance-abuses

The use of surveillance technology in law enforcement. (2023, February 23). Criminal Justice - iResearchNet. https://criminal-justice.iresearchnet.com/criminal-justice-process/impact-of-technology/the-use-of-surveillance-technology-in-law-enforcement

Wang, X. (2025, November 14). Rights groups claim 2,700 NYPD documents disclosed in lawsuit reveal 'surveillance abuses'. *JURISTnews.* https://www.jurist.org/news/2025/11/rights-groups-claims-2700-nypd-documents-disclosed-from-lawsuit-reveal-surveillance-abuses

Wang, X., Wu, Y. C., Zhou, M., & Fu, H. (2024, July 2). Beyond surveillance: Privacy, ethics, and regulations in face recognition technology. [REMOVED HYPERLINK FIELD]. *Frontiers in Big Data, 7,* 1337465. DOI: 10.3389/fdata.2024.1337465 PMID: 39027377

Washington, District of Columbia. (n.d.). World Population Review. https://worldpopulationreview.com/us-cities/district-of-columbia/washington

Wheatley, M. C. (2024, November). Ethics of surveillance technologies: Balancing privacy and security in a digital age. *Premier Journal of Data Science, 2024.* Advance online publication. DOI: 10.70389/PJDS.100001

Willey, J. (2024, June 13). Houston city council OKs $178K to expand HPD's surveillance network. *ABC13 Houston.* https://abc13.com/post/houston-police-artificial-intelligence-video-surveillance-airship-ai/14942179

Williams, M. C., Jr., Weil, N., Rasich, E. A., Ludwig, J., Chang, H., & Egrari, S. (2021, March). *Body-worn cameras in policing: Benefits and costs (Working Paper No. 2021-38).* Becker Friedman Institute. University of Chicago. https://bfi.uchicago.edu/wp-content/uploads/2021/04/BFI_WP_2021-38.pdf

Williams, R., Ali, S., Devasia, N., DiPaola, D., Hong, J., Kaputsos, S. P., Jordan, B., & Breazeal, C. (2023, August). AI+ ethics curricula for middle school youth: Lessons learned from three project-based curricula. *International Journal of Artificial Intelligence in Education, 33*(2), 325–383. DOI: 10.1007/s40593-022-00298-y PMID: 35935456

Yadav, R., & Varshney, R. (2024, July-December). Right to be forgotten amidst data protection, right to privacy and cyber security. *Library Progress International, 44*(2), 1750–1757. https://bpasjournals.com/library-science/index.php/journal/article/view/2092

Yang, S., Nakajima, H., Yang, Y., Shin, Y., & Koizumi, H. (2024, November 15). The impact of surveillance cameras and community safety activities on crime prevention: Evidence from Kakogawa City, Japan. *Sustainable Cities and Society, 115,* 105858. DOI: 10.1016/j.scs.2024.105858

Zalnieriute, M. (2025). Facial recognition surveillance and public space: Protecting protest movements. *International Review of Law Computers & Technology, 39*(1), 116–135. DOI: 10.1080/13600869.2023.2295690

Zhao, J., & Zhang, Y. (2022, June). A longitudinal study of police differential response team impact on crime in Houston: A test of broken windows thesis. *Police Quarterly, 26*(2), 143–168. https://doi.org/ DOI: 10.1177/10986111221092947

Ziosi, M., & Pruss, D. (2024, June). Evidence of what, for whom? The socially contested role of algorithmic bias in a predictive policing tool. [Conference proceedings] In *Proceedings of the 2024 ACM Conference on Fairness* (pp. 1596–1608). Accountability, and Transparency., https://dl.acm.org/doi/pdf/10.1145/3630106.3658991 DOI: 10.1145/3630106.3658991

KEY TERMS AND DEFINITIONS

Artificial Intelligence Powered Analytics: The application of artificial intelligence (AI), such as machine learning, to automatically process and analyze data to find insights, patterns, and relationships.

Biometric Tracking: The process of using biological or behavioral traits, fingerprints, face ID, voice ID, etc., to automate collection and analysis of measurable human characteristics to personalize data collection for identification.

Closed-Circuit Television: Video surveillance technology systems utilizing video signals though a closed loop to a limited set of monitors, allowing for private networks.

Facial Recognition: Biometric technology used to analyze images or video to detect a face, extract patterns and features, and compare against a stored database to identify and verify personnel.

Law Enforcement: A government organized system for enforcing laws, maintaining public order, and preventing/detecting crime through agencies, such as police and sheriffs, that patrol, investigate, and arrest offenders to protect laws.

Online Data Monitoring: Systems used to collect, analyze, and track online activity and digital signals from web browsing, social media, applications, geolocation, and metadata.

Privacy: A legal concept used to protect individuals from intrusive or unwanted observation, collection, use, or disclosure of personal data.

Surveillance Ethics: A branch of ethics focusing on the moral evaluation of surveillance practices by studying the issues surrounding monitoring people, balancing security while protecting individual rights.

Transparency: The principle of processing or functions that operate in the background without the user's knowledge and clearly communicate which data the system collects, why, for how long, and who can access it.

Chapter 6
The Impact of Geofencing in Criminal Justice

Tamara Phillips Fudge
http://orcid.org/0000-0002-8682-9711
Purdue University Global, USA

Susan Shepherd Ferebee
http://orcid.org/0000-0002-3616-634X
University of Phoenix, USA

ABSTRACT

Geofencing is a technology in which an outlined geographic area gathers data for a specific purpose. Freight logistics, emergency alerts, and other practices already use this technology. However, when it is used by law enforcement, there are concerns, even though such "geofence warrants" must first be approved by a judge. Perpetrators have been caught due to the nets cast by these warrants, which means they provide some value in protecting people. Laws are supposed to protect from undue search and seizure, but privacy and prior permission are nearly impossible to guarantee. Innocent people can be potentially misidentified as criminals, and the role of for-profit tech companies in supplying personal location data is of particular concern. Fortunately, laws are being interpreted, tech companies are being cautious with sharing data, and other issues are coming to the fore to settle how these situations can best be managed. Geofence warrants that adhere to particularity, breadth, and probable cause along with clear guidance from governments can continue to help ensure public safety.

INTRODUCTION

Geofencing technology creates virtual boundaries around distinct areas and has become an increasingly important tool in criminal justice systems. It is used for various purposes, including monitoring offenders, enhancing surveillance, and improving public safety by mapping geographic boundaries around locations where mass shootings or other dangerous crimes are or may be occurring. Individuals about to enter an active crime area can also be warned on their smartphones. Despite its growing application,

DOI: 10.4018/979-8-3373-7660-8.ch006

the implications of geofencing on privacy, legal frameworks, and its overall efficacy in reducing crime remain subjects of debate (Raflesia et al., 2021).

Recent scholarly literature has examined the benefits and drawbacks of geofencing in criminal justice. Scholars such as Sawyers (2022) have highlighted the technology's potential to enhance law enforcement capabilities by providing real-time location data to help track offenders and prevent crimes. Studies have additionally shown that geofencing can improve the speed of identifying suspects within a geofenced crime scene (Malik et al., 2022).

There are, however, concerns regarding privacy and ethical implications. Özdal Oktay et al. (2023) suggest that geofencing and other geolocation services may infringe on individual privacy rights, as continuous monitoring can lead to intrusive surveillance practices and affect innocent bystanders. Google's previous role in receiving such requests also needs further exploration (Amster & Diehl, 2022).

BACKGROUND

Geofencing technology establishes virtual boundaries and tracks boundary crossings using RFID, GPS, WiFi, and cellular networks. It triggers location-specific actions and has evolved rapidly over the last several decades. Geofencing emerged in the 1990s and its technology has improved steadily from RF-based systems to GPS-driven monitoring (Murphy, 1997). Other advances include context-aware systems (Lee et al., 2013) biometrics integration, and temporal geofences (Garzon & Deva, 2014).

The earliest known geofencing applications were in fleet management and transportation logistics, where it tracked vehicles, monitored entry and exit routes in restricted places, and enforced regulatory compliance for heavy goods vehicle control (Reclus & Drouard, 2009). This early use laid the groundwork for geofencing operations feasibility for real-time monitoring in changing environments. From its use in logistics, geofencing rapidly expanded into retail and marketing industries. The research into mobile apps and location-based advertising showed how geofencing could engage users in geofenced areas, market in proximity to users, and offer personalized services (Brown & Harmon, 2014).

Moving beyond commercial use, the health and safety industries adopted geofencing for tracking Alzheimer patients within a predetermined area (Pratama et al., 2020), contributing to its later use in criminal justice to improve offender compliance and excluded area enforcement. Geofencing was also reliable for spatial hazard detection in safety-critical scenarios (Wawrzyniak & Hyla, 2016). Adaptive, dynamic geofencing provided the capability for geofencing boundaries to change in real time depending on behavioral or environmental data (Pongpaichet et al., 2013). The evolution of geofencing in other domains paved the way for geofencing technology to aid criminal justice professionals in various ways, improving suspect identification, protecting citizens from dangerous locations and individuals, and monitoring and controlling offenders.

Geofencing Technology

Geofencing is the designation of "virtual perimeters" of real-time locations of people, pets, or things. It works in conjunction with other technologies such as the Global Positioning System (GPS) (Raflesia et al., 2021), RFID chips, and/or with drones and mounted security cameras (Ashe, 2023). An antenna technology called frequency diverse arrays may be used to boost signal security and limit interference

(Del Prete et al., 2025) and indoor 5G small cells can be employed, advantageous since it is widely available (Famili et al., 2025).

Programs for setting up geofences may use latitude and longitude specifications, Google Earth, or other web-based mapping (Awati, 2022). Geometric and geographic data is stored in a relational database; the interdependency of this data is crucial with this 2-dimensional spatial data that must represent a 3-dimensional reality (Hasan & Vijayaraghavan, 2019). Once a geofence is programmed, an alert is generated as a device or tagged object crosses over the edge into the area or when it exits, and these are picked up by a broadcast receiver. The activity does not have to trigger an immediate alert; a specific period of time to "dwell" before notification can be programmed as a "loitering delay" ("Create and monitor," 2024).

There are several programming algorithms used for geofencing, including point-in-polygon, where the criteria is whether or not a device is within the geofence's polygon; distance-based, when the distance between the geofence's center point and the device is calculated as a means to determine if the device is truly inside the fence; and cellular and Wi-Fi fingerprinting, where cell tower signals and Wi-Fi determine the true location ("Geofencing: An in-depth," 2024). Programming can be done in Java, Python, or other languages, and there are easy-to-use apps available especially for circular geofences. It should be added that not only can organizations and companies set up geofences, so can individuals who want to set reminders or alarms when moving about and entering an area of their designation. This kind of command would be set in a "if-then" programming format (Awati, 2022).

The areas to be covered can be circular or polygonal in shape, or it may set as isochrone, in which time determines distance ("Geofence API," n.d.). Vector data in the form of points, lines, and other shapes, is specified and digitized; raster data is used to store satellite and other continuous imagery (Hasan & Vijayaraghavan, 2019). Analysis must consider clusters, hot spots, and patterns, plus which data is redundant, unnecessary, and/or in error; this uses a combination of skills in computer science, spatial science, math, and statistics. Even when programs provide tables, maps, dendograms, bar charts, scatter plots, graphs, etc., the persons drawing conclusions must understand all of these relationships (Hasan & Vijayaraghavan, 2019).

In Figure 1, a circular geofence is shown. Areas are defined with a radius around specified latitude and longitude points ("Create and monitor," 2024). This geofence design is the easiest to implement (Ricci, 2022), and it is possible to set up more than one and overlap them in order to cover a reasonable expanse of ground.

Figure 1. Circular geofence

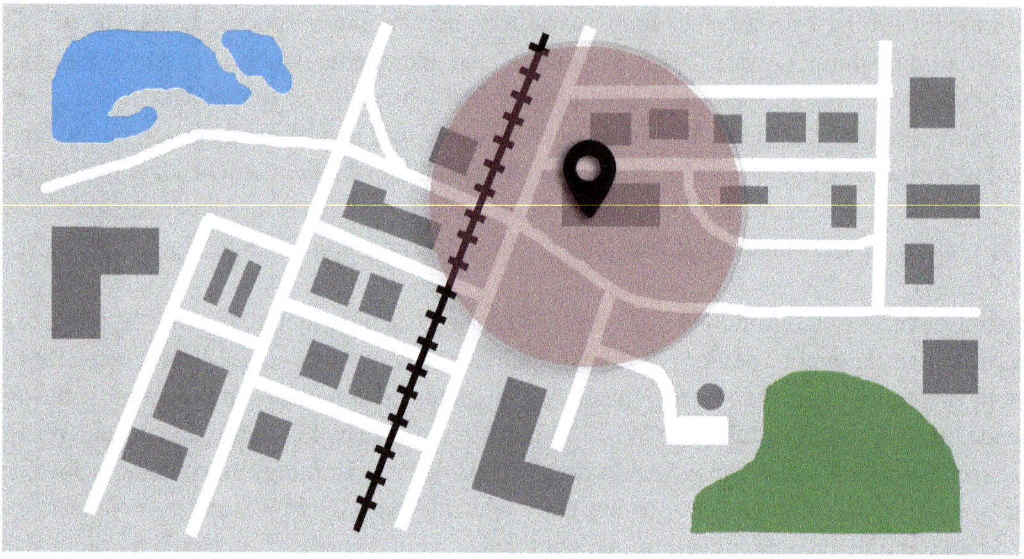

(Fudge, 2026a)

Figure 2 shows a polygonal geofence, which is more difficult to set up. It can add expense to the project, according to Ricci (2022), and thus may be less common (Awati, 2022). As shown below, this kind of geofence can be shaped in many ways, using multiple latitude/longitude points of reference. The polygons can be convex, concave, or compound (Ketzner et al. (2022).

Figure 2. Polygonal geofence

(Fudge, 2026c)

Lastly, there is an isochrone geofence. The purpose of an isochrone is to determine "areas you can reach within the same time from a source location by a particular mode of transport under normal circumstances" (Hasan & Vijayaraghavan, 2019, p. 125). Since this relies on time and not all terrain can be traversed on foot or in a vehicle with the same speed, the fence's field is not a simple circle nor simple lines. Figure 3 relates to someone walking or running rather than focusing on a vehicle which should only navigate on roadways. The railroad clearly poses a barrier for the time allowed.

Figure 3. Isochrone geofence

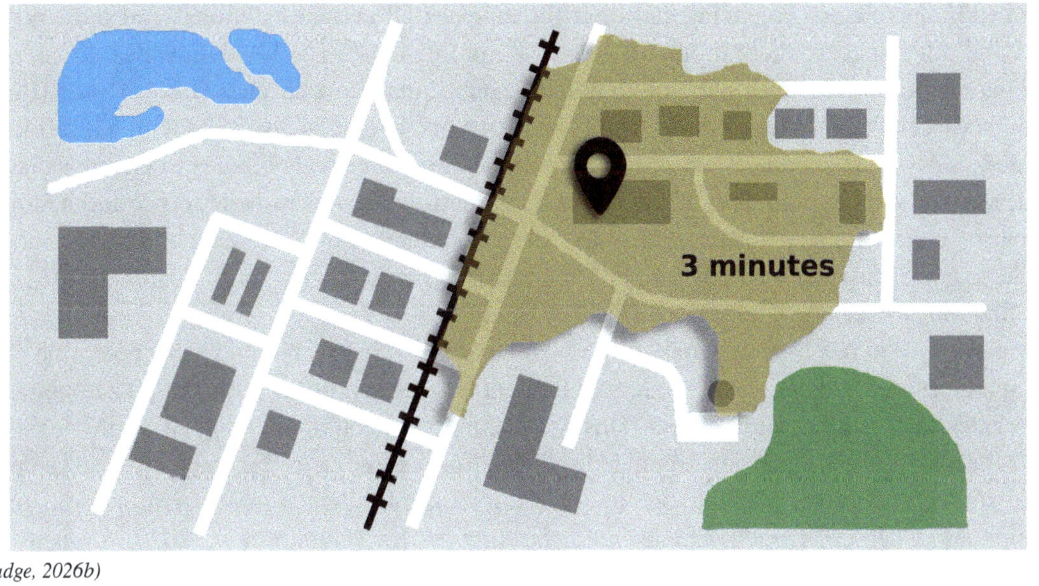

(Fudge, 2026b)

Geofences may also be defined as static or dynamic; the former is for those which are fixed and the latter for those which change according to identified parameters such as weather or movement of objects (Arora & Deswal, 2025). Yu and Scheidegger (2025) additionally mention corridor or motion-planning representations.

Technologies often combine, such as those explained by O'Malley and Smith (2022). Closed-captioned TV, geofencing, facial recognition, LED lighting controls, and other mechanisms are part of the *Switching on Darwin* program in Australia creating a "smart" city. This is similar to programs all over the world, and attempts to assist with traffic control and street lighting, weather monitoring, and other things related to public safety, including monitoring public benches with smart sensors (O'Malley & Smith, 2022). Concerns include racial discrimination and the fact that marginalized populations may not have the same level of access to technologies as those who hold more power. Public perception is fed positive ideas, of course, portraying big data as statistical, automated, and impersonal is a strategy to deflect public fears (O'Malley & Smith, 2022).

LITERATURE REVIEW

A Wide Variety of Uses

Geofencing is already used in several fields and is currently being developed in others. The technology is used for freight transportation on land and water, with a benefit of better "truck turn times" (Ashe, 2023). Curvey (2024) describes this as arrival and departure times, including loading, unloading, and other necessary activities; slow movement negatively affects the supply chain and product availability to the consumer.

Ricci (2022) explains geofencing can limit the airspace allowance for drones and thereby protect airports and other spaces where drone usage may be problematic. The FAA regulates drone use, but geofencing offers more feasible safety solutions for the public than Beyond Visual Line of Sight (BVLOS) restrictions (Ricci, 2022). Molnar et al. (2024) adds that geofencing is also used with aircraft to avoid designated no-fly zones and is combined with collision avoidance technologies to ensure safety. Late in 2024, reports of a large number of rather large unidentified drones in New Jersey and nearby U.S. states caused concern; the government claimed there is no danger but is investigating, and since most drones have geofencing software, they should not be able to enter no-fly zones (Milliner, 2024). As of this writing, no answer is available regarding this situation.

Autonomous vehicles have cameras, LiDAR, and various radar technologies for operation (Fudge, 2022), and Gurumurthy et al. (2021) reiterates that geofencing can be used for shared autonomous vehicle services such as Uber and Waymo. This would limit the geographic range of a vehicle's service, help alleviate congestion, and balance demand and wait times. Regular traffic could also use geofencing, roadside sensors, and other technologies in tandem to control traffic signals during periods of great congestion and when emergency vehicles need the right-of-way (Ghouri et al., 2020). In many cities, geofencing is used with ebike rentals as well. The city of Darwin, Australia explains this is to control speed, keep the bikes within a certain locale, prevent their use in particular areas, and ensure that the rental is returned to an appropriate spot ("E-scooters & e-bikes,", n.d.). Caggiani et al. (2025) studied geofencing with community escooters for monitoring speed and location, including the use of Fuzzy Inference Systems to keep track of accidents within the geofence.

The EU introduced the ReVeAL (Regulating Vehicle Access for Improved Liveability) Project in 2020, which examined ways to address Urban Vehicle Access Regulations (UVARs). The goal is to reduce the number of cars and emissions in urban areas. Geofencing was one of the proposed measures. Geofencing was proposed for speed reduction. The proposal discussed alerting drivers to reduce their speed when they enter a geofenced urban area. A second proposal was that the geofence would trigger automatically switching the car from gas use to electric power. A certified geofencing device in the vehicle would be required to enter a geofenced urban area (Sadler, 2020).

Companies dealing with hazardous materials can benefit from geofencing, according to Alexander (2021). The WirelessHART device invented just a few years ago can be clipped to a worker's shirt and provide alerts when the person has moved into a zone designated as hazardous (Alexander, 2021). Similarly, the United Kingdom's Network Rail approved the use of Tended's wearable geofencing device in 2022; this followed two years of testing and includes a dashboard for analyzing any boundary breaches ("Wearable," 2022). Tended's website claims that the accuracy is "down to the centimetre," the wearer receives immediate alerts to ensure their safety, and companies in the construction and utilities sector also benefit from this geofencing ("A new era," n.d.; "Wearable," 2022).

Microchips provide pet identification, but do not emit signals to specify pet location. Real-time tracking with GPS and "safety zones" set via geofencing are available in tracker devices which can be affixed to the pet's collar (McMennamy, 2024).

Otaki et al. (2025) promote the use of geofencing for tourism, as a means to help visitors find points of interest. Sasaki et al. (2025) take the idea further by suggesting geofencing technologies for "location-based storytelling" (p. 99).

Hyperlocal Mobile Alerts are cell phone messages sent within a geofence using wireless technologies, GPS, and/or cellular networks. The resulting text or audio messages can warn people on a school campus or an entire city about serious weather events such as tornadoes, fires, missing people alerts, or terrorist activities. Bender (2013) and others documented its use well over a decade ago, and Yu and Scheidegger (2025) label this as a passive/active function. Similar uses include tracking of inventory location and text messages for marketing (Raflesia et al., 2021) plus dissemination of political statements and some questionable use in healthcare for advertising (Thomas, 2020).

The United States has a system for alerts called the Integrated Public Alert and Warning System (IPAWS), and this includes Wireless Emergency Alerts (WEA) and Emergency Alert System (EAS) messaging (FEMA, 2024). Polygonal and circular geofences are used by WEAs, and the fence must be sent to within 1/10 mile of the expected message delivery (FEMA, 2023). Some older phones may receive a message even if moved out of the fence area, but as of 2022, 60% of smartphones allow "Geo-Targeting" (FEMA, 2023, inset), which means they will only receive the alert if within the fence. Amber Alerts use WEA and it has proven effective in recovering many missing children. Tornado warnings are posted on television stations via Emergency Alert System (EAS) messaging (FEMA, 2024).

Other wide-area alerts are possible. Raflesia et al. (2021) present three main concerns: permission, privacy, and preference. When a school sets up weather alerts, for example, parents or students are asked to "opt-in" or "opt-out." Instructions should explain how any gathered data will be used and may offer preferences such as text messaging or phone calls to receive such alerts. Opt-in boundaries require an application to be opened and are called "active" geofences using GPS technology, whereas "passive" geofences are those which use cellular data and wi-fi connections and are set to be in operation at all times (Awati, 2022). The idea of a wide-area passive geofence is where the technology's use in policing can be questioned.

GEOFENCING AND THE LAW

Some uses for this technology assist companies without affecting innocent individuals; for example, geofencing can be used to thwart motor vehicle theft. Gantenapalli et al. (2024) explain their combination of an Arduino-based module using GPS and GSM (Global Systems for Mobile Communications) which is then programmable via mobile app and designates a geofence. If a thief is able to move the vehicle out of the geofenced area, an immediate alert would go to the owner's phone. The owner then can call authorities, plus the system provides tracking information in real time for observing the route. The owner can opt to have the system programmed for remotely shutting the engine down when leaving the geofence as well, which would aid significantly in recovery of the vehicle (Gantenapalli et al., 2024). Likewise, construction areas can use geofencing to reduce theft of heavy equipment. Because frequent moving of excavators and other equipment is impractical, these vehicles often remain on the job site and can be the target for thieves. As an example, telecommunications company Cable East Inc. said that when their equipment is stolen, insurance claims take weeks and jobs are put behind schedule (Gillin, 2024). According to the company's risk management director, thieves usually steal items from locations that are less visible by other means (Gillin, 2024). They began using tracking devices programmed with geofencing and monitored by satellite, and in early 2024 claimed that successful recovery through use of this system has saved them $2.5 million (Gillin, 2024).

Geofencing can actually help a person who has been wrongly accused. Kelly (2021) described a case where his client had been injured by a train and the prosecution claimed she had opened a locked gate to access the area wherein she was hurt. Smartphone photos are generally "geotagged" with time and location and paid platforms such as Geofeedia and Snaptrends can be used to search by time and location for posted items (Kelly, 2021). A photo was located from this kind of search and proved the gate was unlocked. Subsequent interviews with witnesses corroborated and even said the gate was usually unlocked. The client won her case (Kelly, 2021).

The internet itself is not immune to geofencing needs, as humans attempting to defraud ecommerce are indeed existing in a physical world. According to Mazzanti (2022), a municipality's website in New Jersey was hacked, so a cybersecurity company was employed; the solutions included IP addresses of incoming network traffic and can thus identify a physical location. Using geofencing, traffic from specific locations can then be blocked (Mazzanti, 2022). A well-designed geofence can prevent Distributed Denial of Service (DDoS) attacks, or allow access from unusual locations – such as a European entity trying to access a U.S. company – by setting "challenge questions" for authentication (Mazzanti, 2022). While there are definitely benefits, there can also be unjustified blocking, which could be used to deny goods or services to groups of people. To combat this in the European Union, a regulation was written in 2018 that prevents this discrimination in Europe based on country, language, or other barriers (Regulation (EU) 2018/302, 2018).

A controversial use of geofencing is found in the potential for geofences to be placed around women's clinics and shelters in an attempt to prosecute women who obtain an abortion or related care, or those who cross state lines for the procedure (Auteri, 2023).This potential became realized with the outcome of *Dobbs v. Jackson Women's Health Organization* in the U.S., which overturned *Roe v. Wade*. To protect this kind of data, tech companies reacted: "Google responded that it would automatically delete its users' location history after visiting sensitive locations such as abortion clinics or domestic violence shelters. Other BigTech companies are expected to take similar actions" (Auteri, 2023, p. 182).

THE GEOFENCE WARRANT

Another highly debated use of this technology is found in the geofence warrant. The first federal such warrants in the United States were conducted in 2016, although the general public was not made aware via news coverage until two years later, according to Tursi (2023). These warrants operate on an assumption that the criminal being sought was carrying their phone on their person at the time the crime was perpetrated, and they are often simply issued for "probable cause," which can be difficult to justify (Elm, 2020). These authorizations are reverse-location warrants permitting law enforcement to search databases for active mobile devices within a defined geographic area. These warrants are controversial because they can provide law enforcement access to personal user data stored by tech companies like

Google, which in the past had collected application and website activity on the person's phone as well as a history of the device's location (Damon, 2025).

Critics argue that geofence warrants are unconstitutional as they may violate the Fourth Amendment's protections against general warrants, which require probable cause and specificity. For instance, a federal court deemed a geofence warrant unconstitutional because it did not establish probable cause to search every Google user within the specified area. There are also assertions that individuals have a reasonable expectation of privacy regarding their location information and other personal data (National Association of Criminal Defense Lawyers, n.d.). While geofencing has identified murderers and robbers, it is troublesome, as Stender (2024) claims, that it has also been used to identify women seeking abortions, surely an overreach.

Of additional concern is that the mapping company contracted by law enforcement must divulge to investigators whatever data they have collected for whichever devices are covered under a geofencing warrant; this "unmasking" can include names, a variety of contact information, and even payment details (Amster & Diehl, 2022). To illustrate the extent of the problem, it is notable that in 2020 alone, Google received 11,554 requests from law enforcement, each warrant asking for personal data (Bathke, 2024).

THE TECH INDUSTRY'S ROLE

Google has had the largest share of these warrants. The process has included a policy to require probable cause, and to work through the warrant in three steps designed to narrow down potential crime perpetrators or victims while protecting as many others as possible: 1) The "initial data dump" wherein devices are listed only by a device ID, and time stamps/locations are collected. This is shared with the law enforcement requestor. 2) "Selective expansion" is the addition of other data for specific devices as requested by law enforcement after the first step. 3) "Unmasking" is where the list has been pared down the most, and names, addresses, email, phone numbers, and other personal information connected with the time and location is made available (Bathke, 2024). The plan was to check location history (which updates every two minutes or so) and use of applications such as Google Maps and Images, all within a given timeframe. Google then provided user's location history saved in Google's Sensorvault, which also contained information that identified accounts (Schembri, 2023). This was related to a person's Google account, not their device.

That said, as of December 2023, the company announced they are changing how location history works in Maps, so they will not be executing these broad warrants. Law enforcement can still request highly revealing data about specific individuals from information retained for long periods of time (Farivar & Brewster, 2023). Elm (2024) claims that Google was saving data for over a decade in their Sensorvault. With the changes, individuals may now store location information right on their devices or upload to the cloud with the caveat that Google would not have access to it (Elm, 2024).

Recently, Google changed how it stores users' location history data. They are moving the data storage from centralized databases to encrypted storage on people's devices, which means new data will no longer be accessible to Google (Chowdri, 2204). What data is still in Sensorvault can still be shared with law enforcement, however (Marathe, 2024). Google's decisions were likely prompted by lawsuits as well. In late 2022, Arizona announced that there was an $85 million settlement due to the company's deceptive practices in continuing to collect location data even when users tried to opt out or disable location settings (Arizona Attorney General, 2022). Apparently the "Web & App Activity" setting still collected locations, assisting Google in selling targeted advertisements, and thus making profits using location data (Arizona Attorney General, 2022). According to Tursi (2022), many other states and the District of Columbia also took umbrage and went to court; $392 million was paid out to forty states.

Google has tried to safeguard privacy along the way, according to Bathke (2024). The company realized their opt-in for location information can be confusing to users. Cell Site Location Information, also known as CSLI, obviously collects more than just location; it targets individual devices (Bathke, 2024). The for-profit status of Google, suggests the possibility of the organization inappropriately cooperating with public agencies (Bathke, 2024).

Location history data is said to be still available from other companies. Apple claims it does not store location data in such a manner; it is on the users' devices, rendering a warrant unhelpful – yet they have gotten a few requests (Marathe, 2024). Snapchat regularly deletes much of user content within a short, set time period, but can answer a warrant for law enforcement to gather personal information, some communications, the user's connections list, and geolocation data ("Snap Inc.," 2025). Lyft's policy insists on probable cause and also has a set policy for warrants, which can include GPS location information ("Lyft's law enforcement support," n.d.). Uber, like other companies, will disclose information requested within the law, will supply data pertinent to their services, and may permit law enforcement access ("Law enforcement requests," n.d.). While geofencing and location data are not specifically listed in their website, the fact this is a transportation company means that location and time stamps will be part of the reports if a warrant is honored.

LIMITATIONS OF THE TECHNOLOGY AND POTENTIAL SOLUTIONS

Geofencing must be accurate, reliable, and available to be effective for criminal just use. Currently, several technological limitations exist. Because geofencing relies on the user's device, the device must be compatible with GPS capability. Watts (2024) explains that adaptive, active geofencing relies on GPS constantly, quickly draining a device's battery, which might encourage users to turn off location services, rendering the geofence useless. Users must install the appropriate app, or the geofencing will not work. In criminal justice, an offender with an ankle bracelet could be required to have the app installed. For determining who and where the suspects might be during a crime, the potential of an app having been installed on the perpetrator's device to divulge this information is unlikely. Law enforcement can set boundaries that trigger actions when a device either exits or enters the boundary. This does not require active geofencing or any knowledge or action by a user (Watts, 2024).

In Apple smartphones, geofencing works through the use of Apple's Core Location Framework and a tool called CLRegion. The tools are powerful but limited. For example, the Core Location is limited to monitoring 20 regions simultaneously ("Geofencing iOS," 2024). Core Location provides good location accuracy in offline scenarios; real-time monitoring in changing environments can reduce precision, particularly when tall structures or weak GPS exist. Latency is another problem. An entrance or exit event might not trigger instantly. These limitations are particularly relevant in a law enforcement environment.

Radar is a geofencing platform that offers more options for creating the geofence area. Unlike Core Location, Radar can monitor millions of geofences at the concurrently, offers location accuracy to 5 meters, and has lower latency. While Core Location and CLRegion only work on iOS, Radar works across iOS and Android ("Geofencing iOS," 2024). Overall, artificial intelligence (AI) and the Internet of Things (IoT) will add powerful predictive analytics to geofencing technology. 5G technology is also said to lead to quicker, more accurate location tracking (Williams, 2024).

RELEVANT LAWS AND REGULATIONS IN CRIMINAL JUSTICE

Using geofencing and "geofencing warrants" in criminal justice has indeed in recent years sparked considerable debate, particularly concerning privacy rights and the Fourth Amendment. As this technology becomes more prevalent, various court cases, laws, and regulations have emerged that shape and define its legal boundaries. Unfortunately, existing law is also applied to new technology that it might not have been intended to cover.

FOURTH AMENDMENT (UNITED STATES)

The Fourth Amendment of the United States Constitution is often cited in conflict with technology activities such as geofencing. In 2012, Supreme Court Justice Sonia Sotomayor suggested location data and privacy rights were connected to this Amendment (Elm, 2020), which reads:

> The right of the people to be secure in their persons, houses, papers, and effects, against unreasonable searches and seizures, shall not be violated, and no warrants shall issue, but upon probable cause, supported by oath or affirmation, and particularly describing the place to be searched, and the persons or things to be seized. (U.S. Const. Amend. IV)

It is noted that this only consists of 54 words and was written well before any modern technology existed. Fan (2024) suggests that the concepts set forth must evolve since the interpretation is too often vague and awkward in modern times. The original searches were physical, whereas technology is now virtual. The third-party exposure doctrine identifies information that has already been shared with a third party; this weakens the Fourth Amendment claims of those whose phone or bank data is requisitioned by law enforcement (Fan, 2024).

U.S. State Consumer Privacy Laws

- ***Connecticut***: Effective July 1, 2023, Connecticut expanded the Connecticut Act Concerning Personal Data Privacy and Online Monitoring (CTDPA) to make it unlawful to use a geofence to create a virtual space within 1750 feet of any reproductive or sexual healthcare facility or any mental healthcare facility to collect data, track, identify, or send any message to a consumer about the consumer's health data (O'Connor & Giovannini, 2024).
- ***New York***: Creating a geofence around a healthcare facility is unlawful to send digital ads, profile consumers, or infer consumers' health conditions or the treatment of any person within or at a specific medical facility. The law was effective July 2, 2023 (O'Connor & Giovannini, 2024).
- ***Washington***: The Washington My Health My Data Act, effective July 22, 2023, makes it unlawful for anyone to create a geofence around any organization that provides in-person health services for a) identifying or tracking consumers obtaining healthcare services, b) collecting individual's health data, or c) send messages or ads to individuals related to their health data or services (O'Connor & Giovannini, 2024).

- ***Nevada:*** On March 31, 2024, Nevada implemented the Nevada Consumer Health Data Privacy Law, which prohibited geofences within 1750 feet of any healthcare facility or entity offering in-person healthcare or selling health products (O'Connor & Giovannini, 2024).

U.S. State Criminal Procedures

- ***Utah***: A provision was added to the Utah Code of Criminal Procedure stating that law enforcement was prohibited from obtaining reverse-location information for devices inside a geofence unless they obtain a search warrant and the investigation is for a class A or B misdemeanor or a felony, involves the risk of harm or existing harm to an individual, relates to the unlawful possession of protected wildlife, is included in a pattern of crimes, or there is an ongoing threat to public safety (O'Connor & Giovannini, 2024).

U.S. Court Cases

Ybarra v. Illinois 1979

Ybarra v. Illinois (1979) is a significant case in understanding the legal implications of geofencing warrants, particularly concerning the Fourth Amendment's protection against unreasonable searches and seizures. In Ybarra (1979), the Supreme Court held that simply being present where a search warrant is executed does not automatically subject an individual to a search without probable cause specific to that person. This precedent is relevant to geofencing warrants, which involve collecting data from all devices within a specified area to identify potential suspects. Applying the principles from this case, the indiscriminate data collection from all individuals within a geofenced area could be seen as a violation of their Fourth Amendment rights if there is no specific probable cause linking them to the alleged crime (Asgari, 2024).

Carpenter v. United States 2018

Carpenter v. United States (2018) is a landmark case with significant implications for geofencing warrants, particularly regarding the Fourth Amendment's protection against unreasonable searches and seizures. In Carpenter, the Supreme Court ruled that the government needs a warrant to access historical cell site location information (CSLI) from a cell phone, as individuals can reasonably expect privacy in their physical movement (National Association of Criminal Defense Lawyers, n.d.). This decision is directly relevant to geofencing warrants, which involve gathering location data from all devices within a specified area to identify potential suspects. The ruling in Carpenter emphasizes that accessing such detailed location information without a warrant violates the Fourth Amendment (*Carpenter v. United States*, 2018). When law enforcement seeks to use geofencing technology, they must therefore demonstrate probable cause and obtain a warrant to ensure compliance with constitutional protections. Carpenter sets a precedent that reinforces the need for judicial oversight and privacy protection in the digital age, making it a critical reference point in discussions about the legality and application of geofencing warrants (National Association of Criminal Defense Lawyers, n.d.)

United States v. Chatrie 2020

United States v. Chatrie (2020) is also a crucial case in the context of geofencing warrants, providing significant insight into the legal challenges and implications. In this case, law enforcement used a geofencing warrant to obtain location data from Google, capturing information from all devices within a specified area to identify a robbery suspect. The court scrutinized the warrant's breadth and the lack of particularized probable cause, highlighting the tension between effective law enforcement and privacy rights. As stated in *United States v. Chatrie* (2020), individuals "simply cannot forfeit the protection of the Fourth Amendment for years of precise location information by selecting 'YES I'M IN,'" at the time they accept an applications' terms and conditions (Section 4).

Warrants must be specific enough to allow officers to exercise minimal judgment in deciding what items to seize (*United States v. LaChance*, 1986). When evaluating the constitutionality of a search, courts must consider its reasonableness, which is the central concern of the Fourth Amendment. This involves balancing the extent to which the search intrudes on an individual's privacy against the necessity of the search for advancing legitimate government interests (*United States v. Knights*, 2001).

Geofence Warrant served in Washington, DC on January 6, 2021

Four acres around the U.S. Capitol building were covered by what Elm (2024) calls the largest geofence warrant to date. From 2:00-6:00 pm on that date, the FBI had access to location data from 5,723 devices within that area; this was narrowed down to 1,518 (Elm, 2024). By using this technology, the FBI was able to map details about the movement of these individuals during the attack and ultimately asked Google for additional data regarding 1,498 devices (Elm, 2024). In *United States v. Rhine* (2023), a defendant was accused of four misdemeanors related to the riot. A tip received by the FBI implicated the defendant, saying there were text messages between him and his wife during this time, and the warrant showed 26 instances of his cellphone being within the geofence, including 22 pings inside the building itself, after a margin of error was calculated. He challenged the peculiarity and claimed the geofence warrant was overbroad, but the court upheld the warrant due to the unusual nature of these events, stating that "suppression [of the geofence data] is inappropriate under the good faith exception to the exclusionary rule" (*United States v. Rhine*, 2023, p. 66).

State of Minnesota v. Contreras-Sanchez, Appeal 2024

The Minnesota Court of Appeals determined that geofence warrants are not categorically prohibited by either the U.S. or state constitutions; they are to be assessed for each case's merit (*State v. Contreras-Sanchez Appeal*, 2024). In this case, an informant implicated others and said they all had cell phones when a victim was murdered. The accused murderer's phone data indicated he was at the location at the time the person's body was discarded in a rural farm culvert. A geofence warrant was set up around the crime scene and data requested for a time period starting the date the victim was reported missing until the discovery of the body. Twelve devices were identified, but most did not dwell long in the area, likely just traveling through. The accused's phone, however, clearly spent much time right at the culvert on one occasion. Law enforcement then asked Google for identifying information and found the phone belonged to Ivan Contreras-Sanchez. His appeal was based solely on the geofencing, but the court ruled that the warrant met constitutional requirements and was served properly (*State v. Contreras-Sanchez Appeal*, 2024).

United States v. Jamarr Smith, Thomas Iroko Ayodele, Gilbert McThuinel II 2024

In this case, constitutionality under the Fourth Amendment played a diminished role in whether law enforcement acted in good faith. The Fifth Circuit Court of Appeals reviewed the defendant's appeal regarding their motion to suppress evidence gathered unconstitutionally from a geofence warrant. The final holding stated:

> We hold that geofence warrants are modern-day general warrants and are unconstitutional under the Fourth Amendment. However, considering law enforcement's reasonable conduct in this case in light of the novelty of this type of warrant, we uphold the district court's determination that suppression was unwarranted under the good-faith exception. (*United States of America v. Jamarr Smith*, 2024, IV. Conclusion)

The fact that the technology used was novel carried much weight in this appeal (*United States v. Smith*, 2024). Unlike the Fourth Circuit ruling in *United States v. Chatrie,* which ruled that ordering Google to look through its entire location history for accounts close to a crime was not a search because people voluntarily agreed to have their location tracked, the Fifth Circuit stated that individuals often do not know they have volunteered to share that data. The *United States v. Smith* ruling breaks from the previous rulings, in that the ruling specifically stated that geofence warrants are inherently unconstitutional and sets the precedent for a landmark Supreme Court Fourth Amendment appeal soon ("Fifth Circuit rules," 2024).

The *United States v. Smith* also split with the Fourth Circuit, holding that law enforcement's accessing location – even when limited by time and specific geographical location – violates a person's reasonable expectation of privacy and is, in fact, a Fourth Amendment search. About geofence search warrants being a clear violation of the Fourth Amendment, the Fifth Circuit stated that the places being searched included a third-party provider's entire universe of a user's historical location movements, and that can never be adequately particularized to legally justify the intrusion (Holtzblatt et al., 2024).

Other Countries' Laws and Additional Crime-Related Geofence Examples

Brazil

Brazil's LGPD law, Lei Geral de Proteção de Dados Pessoais (2018) covers the safety of personal data. It does not specifically mention geofencing but protects personal and anonymized data, its collection, processing, consent, shared use, and other parameters, and the description includes use of available technologies – thereby including geofencing. There is a clause excluding purposes such as public safety, national security, and criminal investigations, and special rules for data relating to minor children (Lei Geral, 2018).

Tozi (2024) describes that the use of geofencing by Uber and 99/DiDi, the two most-often used ride sharing companies in Rio de Janiero, as a means of excluding areas considered more dangerous. The result is "urban algorithmic inequalities," because drivers are more likely to go to the more affluent parts of the city and lower-income people may not be able to get a ride home if they live in a risk zone as defined by the geofence (Tozi, 2024, pp. 44-45).

India

India's Digital Personal Data Protection Act of 2023 addresses the collection of geospatial data, requiring consent except in cases of court orders, medical emergencies, and the like, although Tavawalla and Majumdar (2024) argue that both consent and notification can be difficult to obtain and verify.

Devi and Radha (2024) reported that during every 16 minutes of 2019, a woman was raped. They suggest use of a geofencing app to alert women when they have crossed out of safe limits and to help keep children within safe boundaries when away from home. Their example shows geofencing can be used by individuals to thwart personal crime.

Nigeria

The Nigeria Data Protection Act (2023) is a plan that includes location data as a subset of personal datasets. While geofencing is not specified in the verbiage, personal data is controlled through cybersecurity rules, breach protocol, registration for persons who control and process data, legal recourse, and other requirements. A warrant can be issued if there is a reasonable suspicion that a crime has been or is being committed (The Nigeria Data Protection Act, 2023).

The country sees a high number of kidnappings, and Bello et al. (2023) suggest several technical means such as smart phone and smart watch applications that can help locate and thus rescue victims. The system the authors designed sends an SMS report to authorities when triggered, and updates are sent should the victim be moved (Bello et al., 2023). While it is not perfectly clear how geofencing might be legally controlled, this example demonstrates that the technology could be used to solve crime.

Australia

Each state in Australia has its own regulations on surveillance-related systems. In New South Wales, the Surveillance Devices Act of 2007 is still active; this covers both the person and the device as being protected from surveillance except in cases of warrants or emergency authorization (Surveillance Devices Act, 2024). Installation, recording, and monitoring are included, and permission must be granted for use. A surveillance device warrant can be obtained via magistrate or judge and requires information such as the alleged crime, device(s) to be used, name of the person(s) being observed if known, and other information, including specifying a time limit of no more than 90 days. This focuses on devices, related equipment, and transmission connections, plus invokes the Commonwealth's Telecommunications (Interception) Act of 1979 (Surveillance Devices Act, 2024).

The theft of livestock is a prevalent problem in Australia – for example, New South Wales alone reported 16,700 sheep and 1,800 cattle were stolen annually between 2015 and 2020 (Mulrooney & Harkness, 2023). The remote locations of many farms means that law enforcement may not be able to reach victims within a reasonable time, and some farmers have given up reporting such thefts. Mulrooney and Harkness (2023) conducted an experiment by first tagging twenty sheep with special tags and then setting up a geofence. This was followed by mock theft of the sheep; real-time data was available and two tags were identified as outside the perimeter of the geofence. This prevention, intervention, tracking, and recovering stolen livestock is made possible using geofencing (Mulrooney & Harkness, 2023), establishing additional crime-deterrent possibilities.

United Kingdom

In the U.K, the Human Rights Act ensures a right to individual privacy, including being protected from "interference by a public authority," although there is a caveat about public safety and prevention of crime (Bengart, 2024, p. 668). As this was considered rather vague and new technologies present new challenges, the Regulation of Investigatory Powers Act of 2000 was developed to help limit law enforcement's reach, and this was followed by the Investigator Powers Act of 2016 and the Data Retention and Acquisition Regulations of 2018. The combination of acts allow for location data to be collected if it is related to public safety or national security, or if there is knowledge or prevention of a serious crime, with a few other caveats. The Office for Communications Data Authorizations receives warrant requests first and determines if all laws are being followed before the request may proceed (Bengart, 2024).

A case study in 2022 used geofencing to monitor workspaces within the Ministry of Defense, turning off laptop features such as the webcam unless the device was in a secured area and testing device location in buildings and vehicles ("Case study: Geofencing," 2022). While the newfound mobility of the workforce worldwide since the Covid-19 pandemic has encouraged work from home, geofencing can thus be used to protect military intelligence.

FURTHER DISCUSSION

Policing and the Geofencing Warrant

There are various ways in which this technology can be used by law enforcement. Crime may be prevented by some geofencing through warning citizens of dangers and providing emergency contact information (Raflesia et al., 2021). Malik et al. (2022) clarifies a combination of technologies such as RFID, GPS, Wi-Fi, and Call Record Data (CRD) interface well with geofencing in the quest to apprehend criminals. Once the crime scene and potential search zone has been determined, anyone who has been in the area can be identified. Kidnappings are one area of interest; while minors may not have a phone or other electronic device, the kidnapper likely is in possession of one or uses the internet for some purpose.

Timeliness of police response is crucial. This may include traffic control via technology for emergency responders (as mentioned previously) and setting up a geofence to attempt keeping criminals inside a perimeter and innocent bystanders safely outside (Sullivan, 2021).

Not all criminals are known to the police, and so a geofencing warrant can be issued. This must be first approved by a judge, technically set up, and the activity tied to data stored by a tech company.

Problems With Geofencing Warrants

A few terms help to understand warrant requests: "particularity," which requires the warrant clearly identify what information is sought, and "breadth," which provides limits to the scope of requested data (Owsley, 2022). "Overbreadth" is when too many items are requested than deemed necessary (Elm, 2020). This can be difficult to determine since laws have not kept up with technology, and those that are used to justify actions may be said to be beyond the original scope of the original data collection ("Overbreadth," 2023). Warrants failing to meet particularity and breadth are thus subject to scrutiny.

Obviously, geofencing warrants do not request permission from the person who is the subject of inquiry, nor do they consider privacy and preference. A warrant can bring up data for hundreds or thousands of devices (Schembri, 2023); of course, not all people with those devices are guilty of a crime. Schembri (2023) agrees that geofencing can affect the privacy of a large number of people.

A concern can be voiced that judges are not technically educated about these kinds of surveillance techniques; this leads to inconsistency in decisions (Marathe, 2024). Browning (2020) argues that judges must be educated about ethical use of current technologies, yet in a 2019 survey, only 30% felt their understanding was satisfactory. The Model Code of Judicial Conduct in the U.S. states that "competence in the performance of judicial duties requires the legal knowledge, skill, thoroughness, and preparation reasonably necessary to perform a judge's responsibilities of judicial office" (Browning, 2020), verbiage which is repeated in many states' version of a code of conduct. This points to knowledge about many kinds of circumstances, and would include those that are based on or have elements of technological events.

Of genuine concern is that innocent people can be accused of crimes. There was the plight of a bike rider who looped through his neighborhood and was accused of burglary because he was simply in proximity to a burgled home; the man's exercise app had sent data to Google who shared it with law enforcement. Another man was accused of murder because he gave a phone to another person without logging out of his Google account; the true culprit was using said phone. The innocent man lost his job due to the damage to his reputation (Amster & Diehl, 2022; Joseph, 2023). In another case, U.S. Magistrate Judge David Weisman presided over a case in which pharmaceuticals were stolen in a large and densely populated large city (Owsley, 2022). A law enforcement geofence was requested for a 100-meter radius; this boundary included businesses, medical offices, restaurants, residences, and fitness centers. Weisman agreed there was probable cause for a geofence, but was concerned about the tremendous amount of data collected regarding innocent people. He finally declared that "the warrant application is completely devoid of any meaningful limitation" (Owsley, 2022, p. 841).

Technologically, device settings, unreliable network connections, and the potential for alerts arriving 2-6 minutes after an event can render the results less valid ("Create and monitor," 2024), however, results can pinpoint locations within a 3-6 feet (Elm, 2024).

Recommendations Regarding Geofence Warrants

Geofence warrants have value in catching criminals, and as Elm (2020) suggests, have been mostly granted for serious crimes such as killings, drive-by shootings, residential burglaries, arsons, armed theft, and kidnappings (Malik et al., 2022) and missing persons (Bender, 2013). To facilitate appropriate use of the technology, Chowdri (2024) says law enforcement investigators should do the following to ensure the court supports the warrant and stays within legal and logical boundaries:

- **Narrow the geographic location and time**. The geofence should be as small as possible so the warrant is seen as being particularized. An example of a geofence warrant was in *Price v. The Superior Court of Riverside County* (2023). In this case, the geofence warrant was narrowed to the front porch of the house and two house lengths north and south of the street in front of the house between 10:00 p.m. and 10:22 p.m. The court labeled this geofence warrant as the epitome of particularity in time and location (Chowdri, 2024).

- **Justify each step**. In the warrant, document the reasoning used to narrow down an original list so that the intent is not simply probing for any information available (Chowdri, 2024).
- **Involve the prosecuting attorney**. When drafting the geofencing warrant, work with the prosecutor and the agency attorney to ensure its completeness.

While these are important steps for law enforcement, the law itself needs clarity. A Geolocation Privacy and Surveillance (GPS) Act has been proposed in the U.S. Senator Ron Wyden of Oregon's website explains this would create a standard legal framework for the use of geofences (and therefore geofencing warrants); based somewhat on current wiretapping laws, it includes strict rules for obtaining a warrant, prohibits the use of unlawfully gained geolocation information in court cases, provides instructions for emergency use, and defines fraud in connection with warrant requests ("GPS Act," n.d.). This was proposed in 2017 and movement of the bill is currently uncertain; similar bills have been considered since about 2011.

According to Tobler (1970), "everything is related to everything else, but near things are more related than distant things" (p. 236). This "first law of geography" as it is called in other geography literature is invoked in cases of looking for a person's proximity to a crime scene. Walker (2021) reminds that physical geography typically does not change quickly, but human geography does; also mentioned is that such theories and application of them modify over time through paradigm shifts, gradual changes, and applying context. Change is thus inevitable in the human realm, and must be expected in governance.

Lastly, the exploration of other options may be recommended. "Tower dumps," for example, are networks of antenna systems and ground equipment that deliver and receive cell phone signals at specific locations (Glaser, 2025). Glaser (2025) explains that phone company logs of calls and text messages sent over wireless services can provide law enforcement with location information and time stamps, although more sparsely populated areas may not result in as much precision as cities where there are more densely positioned cell sites.

CONCLUSION

Geofencing technology became a significant tool in criminal justice, offering numerous benefits such as enhanced surveillance, real-time monitoring, and improved public safety. Google's departure from most geofencing warrants has changed this, and it has yet to be seen what other tech companies may do. Geofencing can monitor offenders and crime scenes as well as issue timely alerts in emergencies, which showcases its versatility and potential in maintaining law and order. The use of geofencing is not without challenges and controversies. Privacy concerns, the ethical implications of constant surveillance, the potential for innocent individuals to be accused of crimes, and the legal frameworks governing its use remain pressing issues. Particularity and breadth must be better defined and regulated. The debates around geofence warrants, particularly regarding their alignment with the Fourth Amendment, highlight the need for a balanced approach which would safeguard individual rights while leveraging technological advancements for public safety. As the technology evolves, continuous dialogue among legal experts, technologists, policymakers, and the public will be essential to ensure that geofencing can still be used by law enforcement, but used responsibly and effectively, within the bounds of the law.

REFERENCES

Alexander, A. (2021, July). Location monitoring for greater plant safety: Location monitoring devices and geofencing can help reduce risks of injury or exposure for plant personnel. *Processing*, *34*(7), 26–27.

Amster, H., & Diehl, B. (2022, February). Against geofences. *Stanford Law Review*, *74*(2), 385–445.

Arizona Attorney General. (2022, October 4). *Attorney General Mark Brnovich achieves historic $85 million settlement with Google*. [Press release]. https://www.azag.gov/press-release/attorney-general-mark-brnovich-achieves-historic-85-million-settlement-google

Arora, P., & Deswal, S. (2025, March 10). Geofence-based boundary violation detection algorithms in Unmanned Aerial Vehicles. *International Journal of Communication Systems*, *38*(4), 1–11. DOI: 10.1002/dac.6035

Asgari, S. (2024, March 27). *The threat of geofence warrants: Why courts should deem geofence warrants unconstitutional under the Fourth Amendment*. NYU Proceedings. https://proceedings.nyumootcourt.org/2024/03/the-threat-of-geofence-warrants-why-courts-should-deem-geofence-warrants-unconstitutional-under-the-fourth-amendment

Ashe, A. (2023, September 25). Digital perimeters. *Journal of Commerce*, *24*(20), 37–38.

Auteri, S. (2023). The ripple effect of Dobbs on geofence warrants. *Northern Kentucky Law Review*, *50*(2), 181–203.

Awati, R. (2022, December). *Geofencing*. TechTarget. https://www.techtarget.com/whatis/definition/geofencing

Bathke, B. (2024, Spring). Google and the role of surveillance intermediaries in geofence warrants. *Tulane Journal of Technology and Intellectual Property*, *26*, 111–134.

Bello, I. A., Bashir, A., Kamba, M. I., Ibahim, S., & Bena, A. A. (2023, November). Smart watch technology as a solution to insecurity in northern Nigeria: A case study of kidnapping. *The 9th National Conference on skill acquisition as a solution to insecurity and unemployment in Nigeria, Kebbi.*

Bender, J. (2013, February 17). *Good "geofences" make good neighbors in age of mobile alerts.* New England Board of Higher Education. https://nebhe.org/journal/good-geofencing-makes-good-neighbors-the-age-of-mobile-alerts

Bengart, A. A. (2024). Always a suspect: Law enforcement's violative use of geofence warrants and geolocation data in criminal investigations and proceedings. *Cardozo International & Comparative Law Review*, *7*(2), 639–673.

Brown, R. L., & Harmon, R. R. (2014, October). Viral geofencing: An exploration of emerging big-data driven direct digital marketing services. *Proceedings of PICMET '14 Conference: Portland International Center for Management of Engineering and Technology; Infrastructure and Service Integration*, Kanazawa, Japan, pp. 3300-3308.

Browning, J. G. (2020, July). Should judges have a duty of tech competence? *St. Mary's Journal on Legal Malpractice & Ethics, 10*(2), 176-196.

Caggiani, L., Camporeale, R., Di Bari, D., & Ottomanelli, M. (2025, July). A geofencing-based methodology for speed limit regulation and user safety in e-scooter sharing systems. *Journal of Intelligent Transport Systems*, *29*(4), 401–416. DOI: 10.1080/15472450.2023.2201681

Carpenter v. United States. 484 U.S. 19 (2018). https://casetext.com/case/carpenter-v-united-states-10

Case study: Geofencing technology trialled with Defence Digital. (2022, January 13). GovUK. https://www.gov.uk/government/case-studies/geofencing-technology-trialled-with-defence-digital

Chowdri, P. (2024, January 4). *Emerging tech and law enforcement: What are geofences and how do they work?* Lexipol. https://www.lexipol.com/resources/blog/emerging-tech-and-law-enforcement-what-are-geofences-and-how-do-they-work

Const, U. S. Amend. IV. https://constitution.congress.gov/constitution/amendment-4

Create and monitor geofences. (2024, June 17). Android Developers. https://developer.android.com/develop/sensors-and-location/location/geofencing

Curvey, E. (2024, June 27). *Tips for improving truck turn times.* Tideworks Technology. https://tideworks.com/tips-for-improving-truck-turn-times

Damon, S. (2025). The constitutionality of geofence warrants. *Student Journal of Information Privacy Law, 3*(1), 76-98. https://digitalcommons.mainelaw.maine.edu/sjipl/vol3/iss1/6

Del Prete, S., Barbiroli, M., & Fuschini, F. (2025, February). Frequency diverse array for signal geofencing in wireless communications: Does it work? *IEEE Open Journal of Antennas and Propagation*, *6*(1), 51–63. DOI: 10.1109/OJAP.2024.3465652

Devi, G. G., & Radha, R. (2024, September 20). Smart alerting services; Safeguarding women and children in the digital age. *The Scientific Temper*, *15*(3), 2683–2691. DOI: 10.58414/SCIENTIFICTEMPER.2024.15.3.36

E-scooters & e-bikes. (n.d.). City of Darwin. https://www.darwin.nt.gov.au/community/about-darwin/getting-around/e-scooters-e-bikes

Elm, D. L. (2020, Summer). Geofence warrants: Challenging digital dragnets. *Criminal Justice*, *35*(2), 7–13.

Elm, D. L. (2024, August 8). Are geofence warrants headed for extinction? *Criminal Justice*, *39*(2), 48–60.

Famili, A., Sun, S., Atalay, T., & Stavrou, A. (2025). Harnessing Meta-Reinforcement Learning for Enhanced Tracking in Geofencing Systems. *IEEE Open Journal of the Communications Society*, *6*, 944–960. DOI: 10.1109/OJCOMS.2025.3531318

Fan, M. D. (2024, April). Big data searches and the future of criminal procedure. *Texas Law Review*, *102*(5), 877–936.

Farivar, C., & Brewster, T. (2023, December 14). Google just killed warrants that give police access to location data. *Forbes*. https://www.forbes.com/sites/cyrusfarivar/2023/12/14/google-just-killed-geofence-warrants-police-location-data

FEMA. (2023, February 22). *Geographic accuracy of Wireless Emergency Alerts (WEAs).* https://www.fema.gov/emergency-managers/practitioners/integrated-public-alert-warning-system/public/wireless-emergency-alerts/geographic-accuracy-wea

FEMA. (2024, April 4). *IPAWS myths vs. facts.* https://www.fema.gov/emergency-managers/practitioners/integrated-public-alert-warning-system/public/myths-facts

Fifth Circuit rules that geofence warrants are inherently unconstitutional. (2024, August 13). EPIC. https://epic.org/fifth-circuit-rules-that-geofence-warrants-are-inherently-unconstitutional

Fudge, T. P. (2022, October). Ethics and risks associated with self-driving automobiles. In Fudge, T. P. (Ed.), *Exploring ethical problems in today's technological world* (pp. 289–314). IGI Global., DOI: 10.4018/978-1-6684-5892-1.ch015

Fudge, T. P. (2026a, January 2). *Circular geofence.* [Image]. Fudgelink: The simple geometry of geofencing. https://fudgelink.com/geofencing

Fudge, T. P. (2026b, January 2). *Isochrone geofence.* [Image]. Fudgelink: The simple geometry of geofencing. https://fudgelink.com/geofencing

Fudge, T. P. (2026c, January 2). *Polygonal geofence.* [Image]. Fudgelink: The simple geometry of geofencing. https://fudgelink.com/geofencing

Gantenapalli, S. R., Choppala, P. B., & Teal, P. D. (2024, June). Securing vehicles with Arduino: Implementing geo-fencing technology for theft prevention. *IEEE International Conference on Information Technology, Electronics and Intelligent Communication Systems (ICITEICS),* Karnataka, India. https://doi.org/DOI: 10.1109/ICITEICS61368.2024.10625496

Garzon, S. R., & Deva, B. (2014, September). Geofencing 2.0: Taking location-based notifications to the next level. *UbiComp '14: Proceedings of the 2014 ACM International Joint Conference on Pervasive and Ubiquitous Computing*, pp. 921-932. https://doi.org/DOI: 10.1145/2632048.2636093

Geofence API. (n.d.). NetBillion.ai. https://docs.nextbillion.ai/docs/tracking/api/geofence

Geofencing: An in-depth overview. (2024, August 2). NetBillion.ai. https://nextbillion.ai/post/geofencing

Geofencing iOS: Understanding the limitations. (2024, September 18). Radar. https://radar.com/blog/limitations-of-ios-geofencing

Ghouri, M. F., Malahim, M., Shaikh, S. M., & Fattima, Z. (2020, December 17). GSM and IoT based smart traffic system with geofencing. *Journal of Independent Studies and Research on Computing*, *18*(2). Advance online publication. DOI: 10.31645/16

Gillin, P. (2024, February 25). *Geofencing helps construction firm avoid $2.5M in equipment theft.* Silicon Angle. https://siliconangle.com/2024/02/25/geofencing-helps-construction-firm-avoid-2-5m-equipment-theft

Glaser, P. (2025, October 1). Dumping the fence: Unifying tower dumps and geofence searches as reverse location searches. *University of Baltimore Law Review*, *54*(2), 5. https://scholarworks.law.ubalt.edu/ublr/vol54/iss2/5

GPS Act. (n.d.). Ron Wyden, United States Senator for Oregon. https://www.wyden.senate.gov/priorities/gps-act

Gurumurthy, K. M., Auld, J., & Kockelman, K. (2021). A system of shared autonomous vehicles for Chicago: Understanding the effects of geofencing the service. *Journal of Transport and Land Use*, *14*(1), 993–948. DOI: 10.5198/jtlu.2021.1926

Hasan, A., & Vijayaraghavan, J. (2019, May). *Geospatial data science quick start guide*. Packt. https://research.ebsco.com/linkprocessor/plink?id=22cfc18b-1285-31e3-8a0f-1fc176486ed2

Holtzblatt, A., Varghese, G. P., Aiken, E., Russell, W., & Gelbort, H. (2024, August 27). *The impact and future of the Fifth Circuit's new hard-line stance on geofence warrants*. WilmerHale. https://www.wilmerhale.com/en/insights/client-alerts/20240827-the-impact-and-future-of-the-fifth-circuits-new-hard-line-stance-on-geofence-warrants

Joseph, S. (2023, Spring). The unconstitutionality of geofence warrants. *University of Central Florida Department of Legal Studies Law Journal*, *6*, 71–112.

Kelly, S. P. (2021, Winter). Internet searching, geo-tagging, geo-fencing and open source investigations: A plaintiff's perspective. *Trial Journal*, *23*(1), 32–39.

Ketzner, R., Ravindra, V., & Bramble, M. (2022, October). A robust, fast, and accurate algorithm for point in spherical polygon classification with applications in geoscience and remote sensing. *Computers & Geosciences*, *167*, 105185. DOI: 10.1016/j.cageo.2022.105185

Law enforcement requests. (n.d.). Uber Transparency Report. https://www.uber.com/us/en/about/reports/transparency/law-enforcement

Lee, G.-L., Yun, N.-Y., & Park, S.-H. (2013, October 1). A smart electronic tagging system based on context awareness and machine to machine internetworking. *International Journal of Distributed Sensor Networks*, *9*(10), 392083. Advance online publication. DOI: 10.1155/2013/392083

Lei Geral de Proteção de Dados Pessoais. Law n. 13.709/2018 (2018, August). https://www.lgpdbrasil.com.br/wp-content/uploads/2019/06/LGPD-english-version.pdf

Lyft's law enforcement support. (n.d.). Lyft. https://help.lyft.com/hc/ko/all/articles/115012925607-Lyft-s-law-enforcement-support

Malik, A. A., Azeem, W., & Asad, M.Dr Aftab Ahmad MalikDr Waqar AzeemDr Mujtaba Asad. (2022, September 10). The child kidnapping and abuse by gang criminals and the legitimate custody of minors to parents after rescue and use of geo-fencing to arrest the absconding criminals. *International Journal for Electronic Crime Investigation*, *6*(3), 3–10. DOI: 10.54692/ijeci.2022.0603136

Marathe, I. (2024, August 30). *Tech providers, not courts, may have last word on geofence warrants*. LegalTech. https://www.law.com/legaltechnews/2024/08/30/tech-providers-not-courts-may-have-the-last-word-on-geofence-warrants

Mazzanti, C. (2022, March 28). Securing the perimeter: How geofences can make good neighbors. *Regional Business News*, *35*(12), 7.

McMennamy, A. (2024, May 15). *GPS pet tracking devices versus microchips: Which tracks pets better?* Tracki. https://tracki.com/blogs/post/pet-gps-tracking-devices-vs-microchipping

Milliner, C. (2024, December 13). New Jersey drone mystery: What to know and what can be done. *ABC News*. https://abcnews.go.com/US/new-jersey-drone-mystery/story?id=116719847

Molnar, T. G., Kannan, S. K., Cunningham, J., Dunlap, K., Hobb, K. L., & Ames, A. D. (2024, March). Collision avoidance and geofencing for fixed-wing aircraft with control barrier functions. *IEEE Transactions on Control System Technology*. https://doi.org//arXiv.2403.02508DOI: 10.48550

Mulrooney, K., & Harkness, A. (2023, September 27). Farm crime and security: Evaluating smart tag technology for preventing, tracking and recovering stolen livestock. *International Journal of Rural Criminology*, *8*(1), 108–123. DOI: 10.18061/ijrc.v8i1.9619

Murphy, J. H. (1997, February 14). Feasibility demonstration of a second-generation electronic monitoring system. *SPIE Conference Proceedings,* 2935, pp. 143-152. https://doi.org/DOI: 10.1117/12.266794

National Association of Criminal Defense Lawyers. (n.d.). *Geofence warrant primer.* https://www.nacdl.org/getattachment/816437c7-8943-425c-9b3b-4faf7da24bba/nacdl-geofence-primer.pdf

A new era of safety. (n.d.). Tended. https://www.tended.co.uk

The Nigeria Data Protection Act of 2023. (2023, July 1). *Federal Republic of Nigeria Official Gazette, 110*(119), A719-758. https://cert.gov.ng/ngcert/resources/Nigeria_Data_Protection_Act_2023.pdf

O'Connor, M., & Giovannini, A. V. (2024, January). *USA: New geofence technology laws*. OneTrust DataGuidance. https://www.dataguidance.com/opinion/usa-new-geofence-technology-laws

O'Malley, P., & Smith, G. J. D. (2022, February). 'Smart' crime prevention? Digitization and racialized crime control in a Smart City. *Theoretical Criminology*, *26*(1), 40–56. DOI: 10.1177/1362480620972703

Otaki, K., Okada, A., Matsumori, T., & Yoshida, H. (2025, September 29). Data-driven discrete geofence design using binary quadratic programming. *ArXiv*. https://doi.org//arXiv.2509.24679DOI: 10.48550

Overbreadth. (2023, July). Cornell Law School Legal Information Institute. https://www.law.cornell.edu/wex/overbreadth

Owsley, B. L. (2022, June 1). The best offense is a good defense: Fourth Amendment implications of geofence warrants. *Hofstra Law Review*, *50*(4), 829–894.

Özdal Oktay, S., Heitmann, S., & Kray, C. (2023). Linking location privacy, digital sovereignty and location-based services: A meta review. *Journal of Location Based Services*, *18*(1), 1–52. DOI: 10.1080/17489725.2023.2239180

Pongpaichet, S., Singh, V. K., Jain, R., & Pentland, A. (2013, October). Situation fencing: Making geofencing personal and dynamic. In V. K. Singh, T. Chua, R. Jain (Eds.), PDM '13 *Proceedings of the 1st ACM International Workshop on Personal Data Meets Distributed Multimedia* (3-10). ACM. https://doi.org/DOI: 10.1145/2509352.2509401

Pratama, E. R., Renaldi, F., Umbara, F. R., & Djamal, E. D. (2020, September). Geofencing technology in monitoring of geriatric patients suffering from dementia and Alzheimer. In D. Sensuse, E. C. Djamal, A. A. Agus, F. Nugraha, & L. M. Hasani (Eds.), *2020 3rd International Conference on Computer and Informatics Engineering (IC2IE),* Yogyakarta, Indonesia, pp. 106-111. IEEE. https://doi.org/DOI: 10.1109/IC2IE50715.2020.9274637

Price v. The Superior Court of Riverside County 93 Cal. App. 5th 13 (2023). https://casetext.com/case/price-v-the-superior-court

Raflesia, S. P., Taufiqurrahman, T., Lestarini, D., & Bardadi, A. (2021, March). A context-aware mobile-based system for crime prevention and emergencies. [IJEEI]. *Indonesian Journal of Electrical Engineering and Informatics*, *9*(1), 153–162. DOI: 10.52549/ijeei.v9i1.2624

Reclus, F., & Drouard, K. (2009). Geofencing for fleet & freight management. *2009 9th International Conference on Intelligent Transport Systems Telecommunications (ITST),* Lille, France, pp. 352-356. https://doi.org/DOI: 10.1109/ITST.2009.5399328

Regulation (EU) 2018/302 of the European Parliament and of the Council. (2018, February 28). Official Journal of the European Union. LI 60/1. https://eur-lex.europa.eu/legal-content/EN/TXT/?uri=CELEX:32018R0302

Ricci, J. (2022). No drone zones: Assessing the FAA's role in implementing geofencing and the future of drone regulations in the United States. *University of Illinois Journal of Law. Technology & Policy, 2022*(1), 161–181.

Sadler, L. (2020, October 22). *Geofencing guidance for Urban Vehicle Access Regulations* (working document). ReVeAL Project. https://civitas-reveal.eu/wp-content/uploads/2020/08/Note-on-Geofencing-for-UVAR_Lucy-Sadler-Sadler-Consultants-1.pdf

Sasaki, I., Arikawa, M., Lu, M., Utsumi, T., & Sato, R. (2025, September). *Activating location-based storytelling in a city: Geofence identification from crowdsourced mobile sensing.* [Conference paper]. The International Archives of the Photogrammetry, Remote Sensing and Spatial Information Sciences, *48*(4), 9th International Conference on Smart Data and Smart Cities. https://doi.org/DOI: 10.5194/isprs-archives-XLVIII-4-W16-2025-99-2025

Sawyers, R. (2022, Spring). For geofences: An originalist approach to the Fourth Amendment. *George Mason Law Review, 29*(3), 787–826. https://lawreview.gmu.edu/print__issues/for-geofences-an-originalist-approach-to-the-fourth-amendment

Schembri, T. J. (2023, Autumn). The rise of technology and its effect on search and seizure analysis: The constitutionality of geofencing warrants under the Supreme Court's Fourth Amendment jurisprudence. *SSRN, 75*(1), 129–154. DOI: 10.2139/ssrn.4430269

Snap Inc. law enforcement guide. (2025, July 1). Snapchat. https://www.snapchat.com/lawenforcement

State v. Contreras-Sanchez, A22-1579, 5 N.W.3d 151 (Minn. Ct. App. 2024). https://casetext.com/case/state-v-contreras-sanchez

Stender, S. (2024). Circumventing the Fourth Amendment: The unconstitutional nature of geofence warrants. *Utah Law Review*, *2024*(3), 733–759. DOI: 10.63140/rv3lhh.e-i

Sullivan, D. (2019, November 8). *Digital transformation and law enforcement: How smart technology can reduce response times, improve public safety and save lives.* LinkedIn. https://www.linkedin.com/pulse/digital-transformation-law-enforcement-how-smart-can-reduce-sullivan

Surveillance Devices Act 2007 No 64. (2024). New South Wales Government. https://legislation.nsw.gov.au/view/whole/pdf/inforce/2024-07-01/act-2007-064

Tavawalla, H., & Majumdar, A. (2024, August 19), Impact of India's new privacy law on the geospatial industry. *The National Law Review, XIV*(336). https://natlawreview.com/article/impact-indias-new-privacy-law-geospatial-industry

Thomas, A. (2020, Winter). No place to hide: Private implications of geolocation tracking and geofencing. *SciTech Lawyer*, *16*(2), 20–23.

Tobler, W. R. (1970, June). A computer movie simulating urban growth in the Detroit region. *Economic Geography*, *26*, 234–240. DOI: 10.2307/143141

Tozi, F. (2024, June). Ride-hailing corporations, territorial selectivity, and urban algorithmic inequalities in Brazil. In Vale, M., Ferreira, D., & Rodrigues, N. (Eds.), *Geographies of the Platform Economy. Economic Geography* (pp. 33–48). Springer., DOI: 10.1007/978-3-031-53594-9_3

Tursi, R. (2023, March). Gone fishing: Casting a wide net using geofence warrants. *Washington Law Review (Seattle, Wash.)*, *98*(1), 323–362.

United States of America v. Jamarr Smith, Thomas Iroko Ayodele, Gilbert McThunel II (2024, August 29). US Court of Appeals, Fifth Circuit. No. 23-60321. https://caselaw.findlaw.com/court/us-5th-circuit/116472182.html

Const, U. S. Amend. IV. https://constitution.congress.gov/constitution/amendment-4

United States v. Chatrie, 590 F. Supp 3d 901 (2022). https://casetext.com/case/united-states-v-chatrie

United States v. Knights, 534 U.S. 112 (2001). https://supreme.justia.com/cases/federal/us/534/112

United States v. LaChance, 788 F.2d 856 (1986). https://casetext.com/case/united-states-v-lachance

United States v. Rhine, 652 F. Supp. 3d 38 (2023). https://casetext.com/case/united-states-v-rhine-11

Walker, R. T. (2021, April). Geography, Von Thünen, and Tobler's first law: Tracing the evolution of a concept. *Geographical Review*, *112*(4), 591–607. DOI: 10.1080/00167428.2021.1906670

Watts, K. (2024, November 4). *Geofencing demystified: Understanding the virtual boundaries in marketing.* Raincross. https://raincross.com/what-is-geofencing

Wawrzyniak, N., & Hyla, T. (2016, June). *Application of geofencing technology for the purpose of spatial analysis in focuses on geofencing in mobile navigation for hazard alerts.* Inland mobile navigation. 2016 Baltic Geodetic Congress (BGC Geomatics), Gdansk, Poland, pp. 34-39. https://doi.org/DOI: 10.1109/BGC.Geomatics.2016.15

Wearable geofencing approval. (2022, November). *Railway Gazette International, 178*(11), 16.

Williams, C. (2024, December 10). *How geofencing technology is transforming business in 2024.* Tech-Times. https://www.techtimes.com/articles/308656/20241210/how-geofencing-technology-transforming-business-2024.htm

Ybarra v. Illinois, 444 U.S. 85 (1979). https://casetext.com/case/ybarra-v-illinois

Yu, Y., & Scheidegger, S. (2025, November 19). PCARNN-DCBF: Minimal-intervention geofence enforcement for ground vehicles. *ArXiv*. https://doi.org//arXiv.2511.15522DOI: 10.48550

KEY TERMS AND DEFINITIONS

Geofence warrant: A kind of search warrant meant to gather mobile device geographic information from companies such as Google.

Geofence: An area designated to identify movement in or through a geographic location. These may be circular, polygonal, or isochrone (a complex shape) and multiple geofences could be set up to cover more area if needed.

Hyperlocal Mobile Alerts: Messages sent to phones that are located within a specified geofence using GPS, cellular networks, or wifi. These may include weather notifications, Amber alerts, or other time-sensitive messages.

Static vs. Dynamic geofencing: The former is a geofence that does not change once it is set. The latter is a geofence that may be changed to meet parameters such as changes in weather, movement, or other requirements,.

Chapter 7
Captured on Video:
Methods, Case Studies, Laws, and Finding Justice

Tamara Phillips Fudge
http://orcid.org/0000-0002-8682-9711
Purdue University Global, USA

ABSTRACT

Video technology has become an important facet of both crime prevention courtroom evidence. The methods to create videos today are many, including law enforcement body-worn cameras, vehicle dashcams and traffic cameras, news helicopter and drone video, doorbell cameras and "nanny" cams in the home, Closed-Circuit Television in many public places, and the smartphone held in many a citizen's hand at any given moment. Court proceedings may be recorded, televised, or held on an online platform such as Zoom. Case studies demonstrate how video has been and continues to be used in crime investigations and courts, often composed of many hours gathered from a network or a combination of methods. A brief discussion of how laws in various places may affect admissibility of video in courts is included, as are some recommendations for law enforcement, the courtroom, and public education, including the fact that all persons should consider that no matter their location and whether for better or worse, they may be subject to video surveillance.

INTRODUCTION

Video evidence gathered by law enforcement and subsequently used in court can clearly make a difference in the outcome of a trial. Exploring methods for video capture is a first step, and the study of a variety of court cases in which video evidence has been successfully or unsuccessfully employed helps to paint another part of the picture of this powerful technology. The kinds of data potentially collected and how/where it is stored makes a difference in the privacy concerns of ordinary citizens, and relevant laws explored to better understand the uses and potential abuses of this technology in the realm of criminal justice.

DOI: 10.4018/979-8-3373-7660-8.ch007

LITERATURE REVIEW

As with any new invention, the purpose and uses for video have evolved. The birth of "moving pictures" and television unleashed the potential for entertainment and many other uses. In the 1880s, a mechanical device able to capture a series of images to display movement when presented in succession was invented; this system was shortly thereafter combined with cathode ray tubes, thus moving towards electronic television, which would come to be in 1927 but not commercially available for another decade and not broadcast to the public for yet another decade (Lucas, 2016). The terminology can be confusing; WeVideo explains "film" uses celluloid film stock and the term typically refers to artful endeavors or movies; the word "video" originally meant analog or digital recordings on magnetic tape and is now typically used for any digital capture of an event as it occurs ("Understanding the nuances," 2024). It is this latter definition used today in the realm of criminal justice, although "filming" is also accepted to describe the action of making video recordings.

Today, video monitoring in public places, financial institutions, and schools, on public transportation, and in other locations is a growing trend and is intended to help identify who is at fault in accidents, recognize emergency situations, and prevent or mitigate illegal activities (Gupta & Agarwal, 2023). Interpretation of video – which might be accompanied by coordinated audio – is crucial. Video can be altered, so it may not present a complete narrative of an event. Parry et al. (2021) suggest video evidence be coordinated with interview questions and rating methods to ensure the validity for the courtroom. Wu et al. (2021) indicate video surveillance effectiveness in preventing crime needs to come from "public willingness to cooperate" in both formal and informal interactions (p. 433).

It is first important to realize how many different ways video may be captured and under a variety of circumstances.

Body-Worn Cameras: Video from Law Enforcement Officers

Hansen Löfstrand and Backman (2021) explain law enforcement body-worn cameras especially in the United States are meant to provide a means for public accountability. These devices may also be useful in law enforcement education (András & Bélai, 2025). Video from these cameras can be used as evidence when prosecuting crimes such as domestic violence, but problems may occur if the video is misread and the mere act of recording may cause a perpetrator to respond with additional violence (Iliadis et al., 2024). A hesitant victim might feel compelled into pressing charges due to the captured video despite physical safety apprehensions (Iliadis et al., 2024). Thompson et al. (2025) raise further concerns if or when an officer's audio is muted or indiscernible, the camera lens is obstructed, or the camera is simply not activated during an encounter with the public.

In countries such as Spain and Sweden, bodycams are perceived more as protection for the officers themselves, who may be subject to harassment (Hansen Löfstrand & Backman, 2021). In Hungary they are said to be intended for the officers' personal safety, for border police to record criminal offenses, and for the Parliamentary Guard to verify their location (András & Bélai, 2025). Thompson et al. (2025) state their use might result in "enhanced scrutiny by supervisors, the courts and the general public" (p. 2). A somewhat minor effect of adding this technology to a police force is the wearer's tendency to be more mindful of language and professionalism (Thompson et al., 2025). With this in mind, officers who work alone may feel safer when wearing a bodycam since it provides evidence of their work and also may deter attacks (András & Bélai, 2025).

Smartphone Recordings: Video by Alert Citizens or Criminals Themselves

Rizzo et al. (2023) explored incidents in which smartphone video was taken of violent events and shared online, creating viral and disturbing content. The underlying reasons may be to humiliate, distort situations, or take revenge, and intervention may be necessary to instead promote personal and societal accountability, respect, and empathy (Rizzo et al., 2023). The killings of two university students from Norway and Denmark in Morocco in 2018 was recorded on video, where the killers also filmed themselves uttering political-religious declarations (Libell et al., 2018). A 2025 murder of three young women in Buenos Aires, Argentina was live-streamed, possibly as a warning from a drug cartel (Ionova, 2025).

Other illegal but less deadly activities might also be recorded by those committing crimes, such as an incident in which a hundred-year-old historic tree located on Hadrian's Wall in Northumberland, England was cut down in 2023 by one person while an associate "filmed the act of 'mindless' vandalism" (Leatherdale & Lake, 2025, para. 6). It was reported the phone's metadata pointed to the site where the vandalism occurred, which along with social media posting of the video aided in the perpetrators' prosecution.

Onlookers might record incidents using their phones as well. The quality of the recording may affect admissibility, and audio might not be allowed without both parties' consent (Worgul, 2025); in fact, recording could violate wiretapping laws and cause legal issues for the videographer (Ratzan, 2021). Not all jurisdictions are permissive of smartphone recordings. For example, in New South Wales, Australia, Benson (2021) says the Surveillance Devices Act disallows smartphone recordings unless there is consent granted or the recording is deemed necessary for the person's protection; recording may be subject to jailtime or a fine. There is also "desirability of admitting the evidence [when it] outweighs the undesirability of doing so" (Benson, 2021, para. 5). The person who wishes to record videos on a phone should understand the laws at the location of the alleged crime.

Vehicle Dashcams and Traffic Cameras: Video on the Roads

Dashcams record the date, time, and auditory elements of an incident, and can include travel speed and GPS coordinates (Daraghmi & Shawahna, 2023). Ezzat (2025) explains alarms can be set up with Amber Alerts and law enforcement can be notified about the location of vehicles which have been stolen. Lallie (2023) adds the route taken and its surroundings can be important in reconstructing events, and such recordings may become even more important when autonomous vehicles are involved.

Wang et al. (2019) provide insight into traffic cameras capturing video that helps to recognize anomalies in vehicle behavior, including location of stalled vehicles as well as those which are moving at abnormal speeds. The European Transport Safety Council (2019) note road deaths connected to speed above posted limits is clearly a concern – for example, 55% of European Union road fatalities occur on rural roads where studies indicate up to 63% of observed speeds were excessive, and approximately one-third of accidents resulting in death are related to inappropriately high speeds.

Not all citizens appreciate roadway surveillance, however. In mid-2024, police in Portland, Oregon were vexed by a vigilante destroying traffic cameras by shooting them; perpetrator Chase Grijalva was seen in disguise on surveillance cameras and ultimately caught through an anonymous tip. His excuse was perceiving these cameras as governmental "eyes of extortion" (Iboshi, 2025, para. 9). The ownership of collected data can also be questioned, as explained by Ezzat (2025): while cameras might be owned by local governments, private companies are often employed to manage the data. Lum et al. (2025) declare "targeting, testing, and tracking" are necessary to prove if the implementation of traffic cameras are cost-effective (p. 3).

Helicopters and Drones: Video from the Sky

Still photographs from above the earth started in the U.S. Civil War era, first from balloons and later with cameras attached to kites and even pigeons, and by around 1911, pictures were taken from airplanes (National Air and Space Museum, 2023). Wartime reconnaissance, review of disaster zones, and the monitoring of geographical changes were finally possible. To cover a large area, photographs were carefully pasted together (National Air and Space Museum, 2023). McClain (1996) states aerial cinematography using a mix of hand-held cameras and those affixed to the planes was popular in early Hollywood, with blockbusters such as 1927's *Wings* showing harrowing stunts. Thirty years later, the show *Whirlybirds* introduced helicopters to television audiences, and inventions such as the Tyler Major Mount made it possible to control vibrations from the flying machine (McClain, 1996). Video taken from helicopters can be used to monitor traffic, and Ulvin et al. (2023) suggest using live video connections in medical helicopters for enhanced patient care when en route to the hospital.

Drones can be employed where large crowds are expected such as music festivals, sporting arenas, and planned rallies and parades. Royo et al. (2022) state this is a cost savings especially compared to helicopter use, and an environmentally friendly way to surveil places where problems might endanger attendees. The lack of human presence at the point of video capture might be connected to distancing needs during the Covid-19 pandemic, yet the savings as well as the potential for a broad overview from above have made drones useful for these events (Royo et al., 2022). More recently, some cities such as Denver, Colorado have considered using drones as first-responders for 911 calls when the area is remote and difficult to access quickly (Bradbury, 2024). Drones can also be useful in other ways, including "searching for missing people, mapping crime or crash scenes, providing overhead surveillance during SWAT operations, or tracking fleeing suspects" (Bradbury, 2024, para. 5).

Doorbell and Nanny/Granny Cams: Video at Home

Cameras set up at a home's exterior and especially the front door allows homeowners to communicate remotely with someone outside the home, and related apps such as Amazon's Ring Neighbors can alert neighbors to incidents; the idea is to deter theft or break-ins, and still allow for communication with expected visitors. However, the door cam apps may unfairly identify people of color as acting suspicious and even using "racialized language," adding to the potential for unwarranted gatekeeping (Calacci et al., 2022, p. 21). Delgado (2024) points out crime might be deterred, although delivery persons, joggers, and others simply traveling through or dropping off someone in the neighborhood may be unethically targeted by alarms set off by these systems and could encourage microaggressions. Calacci et al. (2022) assert when a homeowner sets up a doorbell cam, it can act as a neighborhood watch but affects everyone within proximity and does so without asking permission.

Doorbell cams include not only video but two-way audio; motion detection tells the system when to begin recording, and wireless connectivity will stream the activity to the user's device such as through an app on a smartphone (Grant, 2024). The two-way audio makes this kind of video recording different than other forms.

The so-called "nanny" cam is a very small device set up inside a home to surveil the activity of childcare workers; "granny" cams are the same except for the purpose of monitoring elderly persons. In both cases, the idea is to be able to watch for abuse or lack of adequate care, but lack of consent can be a legal problem depending on the jurisdiction (Mulkerrin & O Keeffe, 2025). These cams are often hidden within another item or placed on a shelf out of view (Peeler, 2022). Mulkerrin and O Keeffe (2025) explain while relatives are likely to agree to this monitoring of elderly patients in nursing homes, the persons being watched may not have retained mental capacity to agree to the intrusion. Location of the camera must not infringe upon the dignity of any person, such as placement in bathrooms or clothes changing areas, and in most places, recording audio at the same time may violate wiretapping laws (Mulkerrin & O Keeffe, 2025; Peeler, 2022).

Closed-Circuit Television (CCTV): Video Nearly Anywhere

CCTV is often installed in high-crime areas and are perceived by many as a measure of safety, yet also an invasion of privacy for those who live in the area and are not part of the criminal community (Narayan, 2023). These can be set up in a myriad of locations, from street corners and parking lots to those pointed at Automatic Teller Machines. Dywaba et al. (2025) explain CCTV helps in investigating ATM fraud, and the presence of these cameras is a deterrent to potential crime. This being said, image quality must be clear to assist in investigations; the study by Dywaba et al. (2025) in South Africa recommends court orders be executed quickly and a chain of custody be established both to acquire video recordings legally but also to have access before recordings are erased or destroyed.

The October 2025 crown jewel theft at the Louve in Paris is an example of what happens when CCTV does not comprise enough of the security measures in public places; it was reported only renovated rooms of the famed museum had cameras, leaving many without (Solomon, 2025). Despite a bucket-lift vehicle outside the building, alarms being set off, personnel alerted, and museum visitors present in the building during the quick although fruitful four-minute heist (Adamson, 2025; Solomon, 2025), there does not seem to be any video evidence to bring the perpetrators to justice.

CCTV can capture the physical act of a crime and also can assist investigators with facial recognition of offenders (Narayan, 2023) and other biometric characteristics such as gait and estimated height and weight. Wu et al. (2021) studied people in China and determined the presence of cameras provide a perception of security and can cover areas where there is little access to other protections. A study by Kansal et al. (2025) indicated with continual use of video surveillance, facial recognition is considered the top risk in the Netherlands, Indonesia, Philippines, Singapore, and Vietnam, whereas security of personal belongings the top concern in Germany and Thailand. Other concerns in that study include behavior and location (Kansal et al., 2025).

Post Crime: Video in Court

The use of video in courtrooms extends well beyond using it as evidence. Since the COVID-19 pandemic, Zoom and similar online platforms have been used in lieu of in-person participation, although Feigenson (2023) notes jury trials held fully online and cases in which there is complicated evidence may not work as well as simple cases. A noteworthy limitation is that communication online limits the feeling of "co-presence," as it lacks the breadth of normal physical cues of when people are in the same room together; the self-conscious participant might also unwittingly affect final outcomes from "Zoom fatigue" (Feigenson, 2023, p. 464). Bild et al. (2021) identifies "cognitive interruptions" and poor video or audio quality as other factors which could lead to negative court outcomes.

Another way in which video might be used in courts is with news coverage, when allowed by the presiding judge. Hetzel and Strickland (2025) claim this can keep participants more aware of their behavior as well as educate the public about how a trial is conducted. Historically, however, uncontrolled filming has sometimes been a problem: when Bruno Hauptmann was on trial in 1935 for the kidnapping and murder of Charles Lindbergh's baby, for example, there were as many as 120 cameramen among the 700 or so members of the media in attendance, creating a flurry of distractions (Hetzel & Strickland, 2025).

SELECTED CASE STUDIES

After the debacle of excessive media coverage in the Lindbergh case, a committee of law makers in Chicago developed a rule called *Canon 35* in response to the media frenzy, which Kielbowicz (1979) deemed an important outcome. This reads:

> Proceedings in court should be conducted with fitting dignity and decorum. The taking of photographs in the courtroom, during sessions of the court or recesses between sessions, and the broadcasting of court proceedings, degrade the court and create misconceptions with respect thereto in the mind of the public and should not be permitted. (Kielbowicz, 1979, p. 14)

Photography had already been under scrutiny since a 1927 incident in which a murder suspect was photographed in jail (Kielbowicz, 1979), but this new rule – although not adopted in all jurisdictions and not meant to be a worldwide mandate – was meant to set expectations. These expectations did not last long, as in 1937, the U.S. House of Representatives proposed to allow video use in federal courts (Eckman, 2016). The overall history of allowing broadcasted video of court proceedings in the United States shows both reluctance and permission, from rules which prohibited cameras to pilot programs permitting them, to recommendations they be allowed under certain circumstances (United States Courts, n.d.).

Videography distraction in the courtroom has occasionally affected outcomes, as in the 1965 case of Billie Sol Estes v. Texas where the television coverage was deemed so disruptive that the Supreme Court overturned the conviction (Hetzel & Strickland, 2025). Among other concerns are whether or not the presence of cameras compromise individuals' privacy (Eckman, 2016). Hetzel and Strickland (2025) said the U.S. Supreme Court decided in 1981 that the outright banning of trial broadcasts is not justifiable. Today, laws about video use for law enforcement and in the court systems vary per geographic boundaries, whether they be local, state/province, country, or a collective. The multiple methods of obtaining video translate to multiple uses, as evidenced in the cases examined below.

1985: Murder of Derek and Nancy Haysom

Bedford County, Virginia, USA, with ties to England, Canada, and Germany

Elizabeth Haysom and her then-boyfriend Jens Söring were accused and convicted of murdering her parents, retirees Derek and Nancy Haysom. Upon learning they were suspects, Söring and Haysom left the United States and ended up living in England for a short time, and then were arrested there for cheque fraud. While in custody, Söring admitted to the murders; despite this, he fought extradition (Lillich, 1991). With the promise the death penalty would not be considered, the couple was extradited back to

Virginia (Connolly, 2016). Söring later said he admitted guilt only to try to keep Haysom from the death penalty, while Haysom said "he isn't innocent, he is just as guilty as I am;" she entered a plea of guilty and was sentenced as an accessory (Connolly, 2016, para. 18). Despite his claim he had a psychiatric syndrome causing delusions, he went to trial for first-degree murder and was convicted of the charge (Lillich, 1991). The trial hinged on physical evidence such as a bloody sock print, photographic evidence, and an alibi that did not fully hold up (Connolly, 2016). Both were sentenced to prison, although Söring requested and was granted a transfer to his home country of Germany. Both were paroled in 2019, with Haysom sent back to her home country of Canada, and neither being allowed to enter the United States again (Turyn, 2025).

Videos of the crime scene and excerpts from the courtroom can still be found online (see "Nova Scotia's 1990 report," 2023). The court proceedings were not as widely televised as the Simpson trial, but people in the Lynchburg, VA area were fully aware of daily events through television news reports. More directly, this case was reexamined in a 2017 documentary *Killing for Love* (also known as *The Promise*) which mixes real courtroom video with reenactments yet does not come to a conclusive answer as to Söring's guilt or innocence (Connolly, 2016).

Evaluation: Video was taken of the aftermath of the crime and in the courtroom, and at least snippets remain available online. A recent documentary mixes real video with reenactment, which may or may not be accurate since the filmmakers and actors were not involved in the event itself in 1985, yet the film may affect public opinion.

1994: Road Chase and Murder Trial of O. J. Simpson

Brentwood, Los Angeles, California, USA

The murders of Nicole Brown Simpson and Ronald Goldman were well publicized, with her ex-husband, Orenthal James (O. J.) Simpson accused. First came the televised, 60-mile, rather slow freeway chase with Simpson as a passenger, in a white Ford Bronco; Chang (2024) reported nearly 100 million people watched this as the event unfolded. The trial's televised proceedings lasted for over a year, despite the lack of a murder weapon and little physical evidence (Hastie & Pennington, 1996). Among the stories were that the real culprits were drug dealers, the investigators mishandled the scene, and a lead detective was considered prejudiced due to racial motivations; the jury had to decide based on interpretations and reasonable doubts, and surely after a year wanted to close deliberations quickly (Hastie & Pennington, 1996). The trial ended with acquittal, which led to a civil suit. Video had already played a major role – in fact, Passalacqua (1995) had already predicted the demise of daytime soap operas since they were largely pre-empted by live trial video. A few years later, Shaath (2019) noted soap operas had been greatly reduced in number, replaced with reality television, and the trial was deemed to have been at least partially to blame.

Evaluation: The sensationalism of the live video of the freeway chase (taken from a news helicopter) and continued live coverage of the trial on television were notable, but it is not known if the publicity could have been the cause for the trial's long length. The effects overall were long-lasting, not only for the jury who had to spend an inordinate time away from family and careers, but also for the television industry and viewers.

2016: Truck Terrorism/Murder at Christkindlmarket in Berlin

Breitscheidplatz Square, Berlin, Germany

An outdoor Christmas market was the target for a terrorist attack on December 19, 2016, when a truck drove directly into the scene, hitting people and kiosks; while fingerprints in the truck identified the person responsible, a taxi's dashcam recorded the event, providing law enforcement with visual proof of the truck's high speed and implying intent ("Dashcam shows truck," 2016). The large semitrailer truck carried 25 tons of construction steel (Pieper, 2021). Thirteen people died and 48 were injured (Czymara et al., 2023); the truck had been hijacked and its original driver was among the dead. Police at the time asked the public not to take and share video of the aftermath to protect the privacy of the victims ("Truck plows through crowd," 2016). A Tunisian with an Italian criminal history was deemed responsible, and three days after the killings, was located and killed by police in Milan, Italy (von Münchow, 2017). It was later determined to be a political Islamist attack with the possibility it was orchestrated by someone other than the Tunisian himself (Pieper, 2021).

The attack prompted cries for better video surveillance and criminal history checks for those crossing borders (von Münchow, 2017). It also highlighted the need for robust victim assistance, and authorities now place concrete barriers around Berlin festivals to physically stop such attacks (Pieper, 2021). Czymara et al. (2023) reported a rise in the number of abusive comments responding to related YouTube videos after such attacks, and fortunately the platform is known to remove content deemed hateful (p. 548); post-event public scrutiny can be driven by video recordings.

Evaluation: Dashcam video shows the event, and bystander phone video is assumed in existence. It was unclear if CCTV was in place, but calls for better surveillance indicate any CCTV assumed in use was inadequate. This event also highlights the need to connect other factors with video evidence, such as fingerprints and other biometrics, criminal record databases, and physical barriers around vulnerable areas. Lastly, public opinion of shared online videos presents its own dangers.

2017: Prolific "Ninja" Burglar Caught

Osaka, Japan

Jordan (2017) reported a burglar dressed as a ninja vexed Japan for several years, with a loss of items and cash worth 30 million yen taken from over 250 different thefts. The thief, dubbed "the Ninja of Heisei," apparently used an abandoned apartment to change into his all-black costume. He was caught on camera many times traversing roofs and nimbly moving through Osaka with his face was obscured by his costume – until police reviewing footage found he had let his mask slip once. Police then surveilled him during daytime and noted no criminal behavior, but one night the string of thefts ended: 74-year-old Mitsuaki Tanigawa was caught after stealing from an electronics store, and, realizing the spree was over, was quoted as saying that stealing was easier than working (Jordan, 2017).

Evaluation: CCTV revealed manifold theft incidents; the thief was caught when his disguise slipped one time and his face was shown on camera. Since the thefts occurred over a long time and in a rather wide area, the use of CCTV was important in bringing the spree to an end. It must also be noted vigilance on part of the police was necessary to carefully review and monitor the recordings.

2019: Jussie Smollett's Hate Crime Hoax

Streeterville neighborhood, Chicago, Illinois, USA

Actor Jussie Smollett claimed he was the target of a racist attack in Chicago. Babwin and Tareen (2019) explain police bodycams show a small rope around Smollett's neck, which he claimed he left in place just so police would see it; in the video he said bleach had been poured over him, and at that point, he asked the officers to turn off their bodycams. For the investigation, 90 hours of video were collected, much of it from CCTV; notably, the camera facing the alleged crime scene itself was not working (Babwin & Tareen, 2019). The network of CCTV cameras in Chicago helped to identify two alleged perpetrators, and working retroactively through time using private, public, and vehicle video, they were able to ascertain the two alleged perpetrators may have been hired by Smollett to stage the alleged attack (Ferguson, 2025). The State of Illinois indicted Smollett with felony disorderly conduct due to falsely reporting the situation, with community service and bond forfeiture requirements (People of the State of Illinois v. Jussie Smollett, 2024). While the initial charges were dropped, they were reinstated and in late 2021 Smollett was sentenced to jail for 150 days plus 2 1/2 years of probation, finding him guilty of felony disorderly conduct (Flowers, 2025). This outcome was then overturned due to "prosecutorial issues," however, the city sued because of the high cost of the investigation, and in mid-2025, a settlement was reached; news reports said Smollett promised to give $60,000 to certain charities (Flowers, 2025).

Evaluation: A network of CCTV devices, private surveillance video, and vehicle video provided 90 hours of video evidence a crime had not been committed. It is noted settling out of court is not an admission of guilt, and the accusation levied by some it was contrived for the sake of publicity has not been verified. The time and personnel costs of gathering and determining relevant evidence from a wide swath of networks and devices includes time law enforcement could have spent on other cases. The grappling of the courts as to whether or not charges could be made is far more a procedural problem than related to the event unfolding on Chicago streets.

2020: Murder of George Floyd

South Minneapolis, MN, USA

This well-publicized case centered over the detainment of a citizen who died after a police officer had knelt on the victim's neck for a lengthy time. Officer Derek Chauvin's body cam footage as well as that of other officers was shown in court, and included victim George Floyd's imploring to be able to get off the ground and he was not able to breathe; Chauvin's bodycam had fallen off the officer at one point, however, so the physical set up of knee-on-neck was not included (Levenson & Cooper, 2021). A crowd had gathered, and a teenager who filmed the incident on her phone later expressed survivor guilt (Hernandez, 2021), but her video was helpful in showing a different perspective. A juror told the *Minnesota Star Tribune* that the bodycam video and audio from the officers on scene were critical, as well as expert testimony from medical personnel (Walsh, 2021).

Evaluation: Multiple law enforcement bodycams and a bystander's smartphone video provided damning evidence for the courtroom. The inclusion of Floyd's voice allowed him to be a witness on his own behalf. In this case, the law enforcement bodycams could not protect officers from their own wrong-doing.

2022: Detainment and Imprisonment of Content Creators

Alexandria, Egypt

In this case, a video created simply as entertainment and posted on TikTok unknowingly was a crime. Basma Hegazy, Mohamed Hossam el-Dien, and Ahmad Ali el-Kholi's video story *The Visit* is about a bumbling petty criminal who is visited in jail by his savvy fiancée, and their discussions include talk about the persons in power ("Egypt: Three TikTok," 2023; "The detention," 2023). The Association for Freedom of Thought and Expression explain the country's courts found the creators as well as others to be guilty of "joining a terrorist group, committing the crime of financing terrorism, spreading false news and information, and using social media accounts to spread false news and information" ("The detention," 2023) and some creators are accused of human trafficking, although it is unclear how this could be applied (Fangary & Mahfouz, 2025). Egypt's Interior Ministry has arrested a number of social media creators in the last five years for failing to meet expectations of what they deem as public morals; Fangary and Mahfouz (2025) mention that women appear to be targeted most often, and an Egyptian lawyer claims the cybercrime laws of his country are vague, rendering the charges to be unconstitutional.

Evaluation: Video was created for the purpose of entertainment; it may well have also been intended to be a social commentary. The creators may or may not have known it would violate morals clauses in their country's laws, and the apparent gender bias is of concern. While there has been some outcry of unfairness, this case illustrates the need to understand local laws when making videos, whether they are posted on the internet or elsewhere.

2025: Murder of Michael Boschetto

Villafranca Padovana, Veneto, Padua, Italy

On April 27, 2024, Michael Boschetto was stabbed and killed, and his longtime friend, Giacomo Friso, was subsequently suspected. The assailant stole the victim's phone and returned to his own home, where he recorded a 20-second "selfie" video. A police chase ensued, and when Friso was caught, his hands still had blood on them (Gómez Fuentes, 2025). When Boschetto's phone was confiscated, police were unable to unlock it, and months later, it was given to the victim's father, who hoped to find photos of his son on the phone. With the assistance of his son's girlfriend, they were able to unlock the device. Federico Boschetto was quoted in news reports describing a video on his son's phone "of Friso filming himself as he walked into his house, dancing and making a victory sign … The face of that man, who had just been arrested for my son's death, was on his phone, wearing a mocking smile" (Nunes, 2025, paras. 7-8). The prosecutor was promptly given the phone with this new evidence, and the video was slated to be shown in court ("Spunta il video selfie," 2025). Friso's demeanor aside, the video gave evidence that the story originally given did not match what had been told (Nunes, 2025). As of this time, the court is apparently awaiting audio/video recording transcripts of several interrogations related to the case. Despite positive drug tests on the day of the murder and a history of violence, Friso was declared competent to stand trial ("Morte di Michael Boschetto," 2025).

Evaluation: The discovery of a video made of oneself after a crime, and there is the fact the device was found with the accused after the event may be used to influence a judge or jury. Law enforcement might have asked family to help them unlock the phone earlier, but not all facts about this case are available yet.

2025: Bondi Beach Massacre

Bondi Beach, greater Sydney metropolitan area, Australia

The recent mass murder of Jewish people holding a Hanukkah celebration at Bondi Beach demonstrates a variety of video implementations can work together to explain a situation. First, a dashcam video recorded the murder of Boris and Sofia Gurman, who saw one of the gunmen get out of a vehicle and attempted to tackle him, only to be shot and killed. Drone footage of the area included the bridge the perpetrators used as their shooting vantage point (Aliieva & Gao, 2025). Ahmed Al Ahmed successfully tackled one shooter a short time later; it is not clear from news reports if the widely disseminated recording was caught on CCTV or on a smartphone, but there was at least one bystander who apparently recorded on a phone providing a somewhat different view (Trigger, 2025). After the attack, additional video instances include CCTV recordings of the two perpetrators in the Philippines previous to the event are being analyzed (Butler, 2025), a phone video of the older shooter verifying his religious and political ideology, and the younger shooter making his first court appearance by video (McGuirk, 2025).

Evaluation: A mix of vehicle cams, drone footage, CCTV, and smartphone video provided a rather full account of the incident, including perpetrators, heroes, and victims. As the surviving assailant is put on trial, undoubtedly video will play a large evidentiary part, along with factors such as fingerprints, shell casings, and other physical evidence.

Ongoing since at least 2022: Russians Drones Violating Norwegian Airspace

Oslo, Norway and other locations

Over the last few years, Russian citizens have been accused of flying drones over airports and other restricted airspace in Norway; arrests in 2022 included the son of a Vladimir Putin associate (Singh, 2022). Singh (2022) explained drone use in airport space results in temporary shutdowns, and sabotage was suspected. Edvardsen (2025) stated other NATO countries such as Estonia, Finland, Latvia, Lithuania, Poland, and Romania have experienced the same violations instigated by Russian drone users, heightening the fear of war – and at the same time, Russia maintains its innocence.

Evaluation: Video from drones could reveal state secrets to enemies; the devices themselves obstruct airplane takeoff and landing patterns and present a physical danger. Diplomacy may be able to solve the problems, but is not likely as seen from an historical vantage point.

FURTHER DISCUSSION: DATA FROM VIDEO AND OTHER PROBLEMS

Kansal et al. (2025) state "in practice, most surveillance cameras capture data in raw format that can be easily understood by humans" (p. 6). While this sounds simple, this includes a great deal of data, including:

Surroundings

- Location – may include GPS coordinates and a path

- Time and duration of events – may also reveal speed of movement
- Physical properties of objects such as size, shape, and colors

People

- Facial recognition – a geometric matching of facial characteristics
- Voiceprint – sound waves analyze a person's speaking where audio is allowed
- Lip-reading analysis – also called "visual speech recognition" (Feigenson & Carney, 2025, p. 32)
- Gait and posture – walking style or patterns, body alignment
- Gender and/or race identification
- Height, weight, age estimation
- Clothing choices and how the clothing is worn
- Right- or left-handedness and manner in which objects are handled

(Alrashoud, 2025; Daraghmi & Shawahna, 2023; Feigenson & Carney, 2025; Kansal et al., 2025; Lezama, 2022)

Where audio is allowed and sensors are in place, gunshot analysis from video might also be possible to clarify location origin via triangulation (Feigenson & Carney, 2025). Notably, Lezama (2022) describes video analytics as the automatic documentation of time and space for an event; it might look for historical insight and unexpected behaviors, but computerized systems also need human monitoring and evaluation.

Storage

Collected data must be stored somewhere. Door cams, nanny cams, and dashcams send streaming video and/or recordings through an app, wherein data is accessible later – and is stored somewhere. For example, Amazon's Ring in particular is known to have a very large database containing facial recognition data and other activity (Calacci et al., 2022), and collection, storage and use of this data is not clear and surely not shared with passers-by. This is a worldwide issue, as Ring is available in the U.S.A. and large parts of Canada, plus more than three dozen countries in Europe, United Arab Emirates, and South Africa ("Ring Alarm," 2024), and the Neighbors app allows owners to post recordings (Ng, 2022). News reports in mid-2022 claimed the company had provided footage to law enforcement without asking owner permission at least 11 times that year but notified the owners; these were instances wherein serious crimes had occurred or suspected (Ng, 2022).

It is not just home video collecting data, of course. A smartphone video is stored on the device; it could be uploaded to YouTube and then becomes part of their database. CCTV recordings are maintained by law enforcement or businesses, depending on the location of the cameras. Data storage presents challenges since the questions of privacy, permission, control of its use, and right to "forget" the data are at stake.

Modern Problems

The "deepfake" video is of great concern, as it is a false representation created by machine learning algorithms (Weikmann et al., 2025). These AI-enhanced videos might be created for entertainment, political, or other purposes but erode trust and can provide advantages or disadvantages in court when compared to verifiable facts (Feigenson & Carney, 2025). Alrashoud (2025) notes the technology needed to create these is readily available and constantly improving, making detection rather challenging. Convolutional Neural Networks can be applied to visual elements and there are datasets to evaluate speech inconsistencies; nonetheless, time and expertise can be thwarted by poor video quality and file compression techniques (Alrashoud, 2025). A somewhat different version is a "cheapfake," video which has only been slightly altered (Weikmann et al., 2025), making detection of fake elements more difficult.

Akumba et al. (2021) include splicing and resampling pieces of real videos may be nearly indiscernible to viewers; even the removal or insertion of a few frames could alter the meaning. Several methods might be used to detect consistency or lack thereof, with a Lucas Kanade optical flow producing perhaps the highest precision (Akumba et al., 2021). Ölvecký et al. (2025) compared open-source and commercial tools, finding the latter more successful with deepfake detection.

Modern Solutions

Registration of cameras with law enforcement is one logical step. Callaghan (2025) explains registering a door cam or dashcam with Western Australia's law enforcement's CAM-MAP enables quick response by law enforcement, as they can virtually be on site and respond to incidents quickly.

Technology is already used for data analytics in various ways, such as facial recognition using computer coordinates and voiceprints showing frequency, amplitude, and time in wave forms and spectrograms. Some solutions are the result of large-scale efforts: in São Paulo, Brazil, a large network of 25 thousand CCTV cameras dubbed "Smart Sampa" has enabled law enforcement to locate fugitives and missing persons, and to catch crimes in progress thanks to facial recognition followed by officer verification (Galarraga Gortázar, 2025). Other solutions may be forthcoming: the European Transport Safety Council (2019) proposes Intelligent Speed Assistance, which uses a combination of video and GPS technologies and can control the speed of a vehicle through limiting the power provided by the engine itself, and Darwis et al. (2025) suggest using steganography to hide sensitive data yet preserve the quality and integrity of the video.

Falcón-López et al. (2025) explain that deep learning methods can be used with high accuracy to detect alterations in videos; the use of substantial datasets and training for such models helps with a variety of multimedia types, and there are quite a few commercial tools available to forensic analysts.

RELEVANT LAWS: EXAMPLES

Each political region has the right to establish laws regarding the use of video as it relates to law enforcement and courts within their jurisdictions. Just a few are mentioned below to provide definitions and to demonstrate the vagueness which must be evaluated by adjudicators for individual cases, with final decisions about admissibility and/or permissions likely also contingent upon non-video facts also in evidence.

The European Union's General Data Protection Regulation (GDPR) is considered one of the strongest protections worldwide for data permissions, collection, storage, use, and eventual destruction of said data; it is applicable to citizens of EU countries. Videography is not specifically mentioned, but the data therein may be included in some of Article 4's Definitions:

(1) 'personal data' means any information relating to an identified or identifiable natural person ('data subject'); an identifiable natural person is one who can be identified, directly or indirectly, in particular by reference to an identifier such as a name, an identification number, location data, an online identifier or to one or more factors specific to the physical, physiological, genetic, mental, economic, cultural or social identity of that natural person;
(2) 'processing' means any operation or set of operations which is performed on personal data or on sets of personal data, whether or not by automated means, such as collection, recording, organisation, structuring, storage, adaptation or alteration, retrieval, consultation, use, disclosure by transmission, dissemination or otherwise making available, alignment or combination, restriction, erasure or destruction. (GDPR, Article 4)

Per the GDPR, personal data must be "collected for specified, explicit and legitimate purposes" (Article 5.1.b), accurate, and retained no longer than necessary (Article 5.1.d-e). Restrictions are in place in the event of a country's or the public's security, and "the prevention, investigation, detection or prosecution of criminal offences or the execution of criminal penalties, including the safeguarding against and the prevention of threats to public security … [as well as] the protection of judicial independence and judicial proceedings" (Article 23.1.a-c-d-f).

In Hong Kong, the Personal Data (Privacy) Ordinance (2022) mentions video, audio, and other electronic data (Section 66J-electronic message section) but is not specific for their use, only that those acting in an official capacity "must have regard to the safeguards under the common law to protect the privacy of a person in the circumstances in which a power to access an electronic device is exercised" (PDPO, Section 66G.10). The Ordinance was amended as recently as 2022, and even clearer guidelines for CCTV, drone use, and vehicle cams were issued in December 2025 by the Office of the Privacy Commissioner for Personal Data (Kennedy & Wong, 2025), Kennedy and Wong (2025) explain these guidelines include the need for lawful purpose and necessity when setting up cameras, the use of low resolution is recommended unless facial recognition is deemed necessary, and CCTV audio must be disabled "unless there is a clearly justified and compelling need" (para. 5).

In India, Kalaam (2025) explains any filming in public, whether staged, on-the-street interviews, or at public events, is subject to several statutes, including the Indian Penal Code wherein videography may be considered an annoyance or denigration of someone's character. The Information Technology Act of 2000 is more explicit in its concerns about privacy and obscenity; other rules allow for filming police activity such as some restricted areas requiring permission (Kalaam, 2025).

In the United States, video capture might be subject to the Constitution's First Amendment's protection of freedom of speech and the Fourth Amendment's declaration "the right of the people to be secure in their persons, houses, papers, and effects, against unreasonable searches and seizures, shall not be violated" (Amendment IV, 1791). Hetzel & Strickland (2025) mention the First Amendment as a call for media persons gaining access to court recordings.

As the U.S. is a federalist country, each state may have its own controls; as one example, Illinois' Biometric Information Privacy Act (2024) focuses on biometrics, which are defined in this law as "any information, regardless of how it is captured, converted, stored, or shared, based on an individual's biometric identifier," and lists eye scans, facial geometry, and voiceprints among the data that is protected – but specifically disallows photographs, height and weight, hair color, and tattoos (BIPA, Section 10), which could also be present in videos. Graves (1979) noted each state may determine whether or not cameras are allowed in courtrooms, with many testing the allowance in the 1970s.

RECOMMENDATIONS AND CONCLUSION

Awareness of video methods, combinations and uses, and legalities help lead to some simple recommendations for law enforcement and the courts, plus through public education.

Law Enforcement

Officer body-worn cameras are an important investment for creating evidence for trials and also to supervise officer behavior. Clear rules needs to be set by the agency about camera positioning, when it is allowed to turn the camera off, how long it is appropriate to record, appropriate verbiage when being recorded, and so on.

Required training would alleviate any confusion and fears about wearing the camera and should also include an understanding of local laws so citizen video activity is understood and treated lawfully on the street.

The Courtroom

Videos used as evidence in many places must be relevant, authentic, and clearly unaltered, all of which must be verified through a legal chain of custody ("Role of video evidence," 2025).

- Relevance ensures the case's evidence is not obfuscated by video content that does not specifically relate to the incident.
- Authentication is a measure of accuracy. The court in Christopher Mooney v. The State of Maryland (2024) stated authentication requires "testimony by a witness with personal knowledge of the content of the video or testimony concerning the method of production of the video" (para. 1). The options for authentication are "pictorial testimony" (a person present during the event verifies the video's content), "silent witness" (evaluation of the video process), and self-authenticating business records (Aracri, 2024).
- Integrity means the video has not been altered by any means. Verification may require the use of detection tools.

Where not mandated to use video as part of courtroom proceedings, judges must weigh the benefits and drawbacks, and consider how cameras may affect participant behavior and ultimate case outcomes. Zoom sessions when appropriate should have stipulated rules about behavior and surroundings to lessen misunderstandings.

Perhaps most important is the effect videos can have on judges and juries. Myhand (2023) points out that once a video has been viewed, human perception and the emotions involved are very difficult to change. Since witnesses cannot be expected to know when a deepfake or altered video is presented, the authentication process must occur well before showing it as evidence in court. Vakhitova et al. (2022) aptly state, "viewers are never neutral ... the footage will be read and responded to based on individual, social, political, ideological and cultural factors which influence interpretation" (p. 182).

The U.S. Federal Rule of Evidence 901(a) requires "authentication" for the courts but does not provide much specific guidance (Myhand, 2023). Authentication means a lawyer has the responsibility to ensure the video was not altered in any way, and the device and time for the video capture are precisely identified (Rind, 2026). Rind (2026) further explains this might be done through witness testimony or more accurately through metadata, patterns, and other means of digital forensic analysis such as confirmation of the cryptographic hash values completed at each transfer point, which then results in a "chain of custody" log.

In the State of Iowa v. Terrence Edward Manning Jr. (Case No. 23-1390), the defendant successfully petitioned for a new trial based on lack of proper authentication of a video purportedly showing him in a store parking lot inflicting injury to another person. The video in question was a surveillance video captured by a law enforcement body cam and submitted under the "silent witness" doctrine. The court proclaimed, "We find substantial evidence of Manning's specific intent. But because the district court erred in admitting the surveillance video without proper authentication, and that error was not harmless, we reverse Manning's conviction and remand for a new trial" (Court of Appeals, p. 2). Apparently the officer whose body cam captured the security camera footage did not know how many cameras were focused on the event and the store personnel showing the video zoomed in and changed some viewing angles during this footage, calling the officer's view into question. Ultimately, the victim's testimony, although he was briefly unconscious, authenticated enough of the video for it to be entered legally into evidence, and the original conviction was affirmed (Iowa Supreme Court, 2025).

Public Education

Care should be taken to understand local laws and regulations regarding the use of smartphone videos. The homeowner who opts to install a door cam or nanny cam must be aware of where their data is going to be stored and for what length of time; discussion with neighbors and others who may be filmed prior to installation may ease any tensions. Purpose should be determined and personal identification such as license plates of parked cars or faces of children might be best obscured before posting videos to an app, YouTube, or elsewhere online.

Sharing dashcam footage of road incidents with victims and authorities should be a priority before sharing with online groups, as local laws may disallow video in court which has been widely disseminated. Knowing local laws about smartphone video recording likewise would be wise to avoid issues such as arrest for violating someone else's rights. As stated above, any video meant for a court case should be left unedited, even if it is unduly long.

Final Words

For the last century and a half, moving pictures have been part of the world, with audio added about 100 years ago. The video of today comes in various formats, created by an abundance of devices and methods and meant for a myriad of reasons, not the least of which is public and personal safety. This does not go without problems, with deepfakes and altered videos offering malicious intent, and permission, collection, storage, use, and destruction of video data not always considered. The average person must realize that no matter where they are, there is a high likelihood they are being surveilled by video.

For the sake of the criminal justice system, important next steps for both technologists and law makers should be to strengthen authentication methods, secure data storage methods, and improve documentation. Company and community responsibilities include publicizing privacy policies about the capture of video from phones, door cams, and other personal devices so the public acts legally and ethically; this in turn will assist law enforcement but also protect the individual from undue data sharing. Each of the players – the citizen, law enforcement, communities, companies, and the courts – must follow the law but also needs to recognize how their efforts may be used for good or for harm.

REFERENCES

Adamson, T. (2025, October 19). Thieves steal crown jewels in 4 minutes from Louvre Museum. AP News. https://apnews.com/article/france-louvre-museum-robbery-a3687f330a43e0aaff68c732c4b2585b

Akumba, B. O., Iorliam, A., Agber, S., Okube, E. O., & Kwaghtyo, K. D. (2021, April). Authentication of Video evidence for forensic investigation: A case of Nigeria. *Journal of Information Security, 12*(2), 163–176. DOI: 10.4236/jis.2021.122008

Aliieva, E., & Gao, L. (2025, December 16). Video shows elderly couple trying to stop and disarm Bondi gunman. *NBC News.* https://www.nbcnews.com/world/australia/new-video-shows-elderly-couple-disarm-bondi-beach-gunman-rcna249446

Alrashoud, M. (2025, June). Deepfake video detection methods, approaches, and challenges. *Alexandria Engineering Journal, 125*, 265–277. DOI: 10.1016/j.aej.2025.04.007

Amendments I and IV. (1791, December 15). Constitution of the United States. https://constitution.congress.gov/constitution

András, H. L., & Bélai, G. (2025). The impact of recordings of police actions on organisational culture. *Academic Journal of Internal Affairs / Belügyi Szemle, 73*(6), 1287–1300. https://doi.org/DOI: 10.38146/bsz-ajia.2025.v73.i6.pp1287-1300

Aracri, C. (2024, September 12). *Supreme Court of Maryland discusses authentication of video evidence.* Maryland State Bar Association. https://www.msba.org/site/site/content/News-and-Publications/News/General-News/Supreme-Court-of-Maryland-Discusses-Authentication-of-Video-Evidence.aspx

Babwin, D., & Tareen, S. (2019, June 25). Chicago police release more than 1,000 files from Smollett investigation. *PBS/Associated Press.* https://www.pbs.org/newshour/nation/chicago-police-release-more-than-1000-files-from-smollett-investigation

Benson, J. (2021, February 15). *Smartphone recordings as evidence in family law proceedings.* Berryman Partners. https://www.berrymanpartners.com.au/smartphone-recordings-as-evidence

Bild, E., Redman, A., Newman, E. J., Muir, B. R., Tait, D., & Schwarz, N. (2021, October). Sound and credibility in the virtual court: Low audio quality leads to less favorable evaluations of witnesses and lower weighting of evidence. *Law and Human Behavior, 45*(5), 481–495. DOI: 10.1037/lhb0000466 PMID: 34871019

Biometric Information Privacy Act. (740 ILCS 14, Section 10). (2024, August 2). Illinois State Government. https://www.ilga.gov/Legislation/ILCS/Articles?ActID=3004&ChapterID=57

Bradbury, S. (2024, May 26). Police drones responding to 911 calls in Colorado? “This really is the future of law enforcement.” *The Denver Post.* https://www.denverpost.com/2024/05/26/colorado-police-drones-first-responders

Butler, J. (2025, December 29). CCTV suggests alleged Bondi shooters acted alone and did not receive training in Philippines, AFP says. *The Guardian.* https://www.theguardian.com/australia-news/2025/dec/30/alleged-bondi-shooters-did-not-receive-training-philippines-ntwnfb

Calacci, D., Shen, J. J., & Pentland, A. (2022, November 11). The cop in your neighbor's doorbell: Amazon Ring and the spread of participatory mass surveillance. *Proceedings of the ACM on Human-Computer Interaction, 6*(CSCW2), 400. https://doi.org/DOI: 10.1145/3555125

Callaghan, R. (2025, February). *How home CCTV can help keep our suburbs safer*. Horizons. https://rac.com.au/horizons/lifestyle/perth-cctv-program

Chang, R. (2024, April 11). *What happened to the white Ford Bron*co. Biography. https://www.biography.com/crime/oj-simpson-bronco-chase-car-museum

Christopher Mooney vs. State of Maryland. (2024, August 13). Maryland Courts. https://www.mdcourts.gov/data/opinions/coa/2024/32a23.pdf

Connolly, K. (2016, November 5). Documentary casts doubt on guilty verdict in 1990 Virginia murder trial. *The Guardian*. https://www.theguardian.com/us-news/2016/nov/05/jens-soring-elizabeth-haysom-virginia-murders-documentary

Court of Appeals in Iowa. (2025, February 19). State of Iowa v. Terence Edward Manning Jr. (Case 23-1390). Iowa Courts. https://www.iowacourts.gov/courtcases/22746/embed/CourtAppealsOpinion

Czymara, C. S., Dochow-Sondershaus, S., Drouhot, L. G., Simsek, M., & Spörlein, C. (2023, January). Catalyst of hate? Ethnic insulting on YouTube in the aftermath of terror attacks in France, Germany and the United Kingdom 2014–2017. *Journal of Ethnic and Migration Studies*, *49*(2), 535–553. DOI: 10.1080/1369183X.2022.2100552

Daraghmi, Y.-A., & Shawahna, I. (2023, August). Digital forensic analysis of vehicular video sensors: Dashcams as a case. *Sensors (Basel)*, *23*(17), 7548. DOI: 10.3390/s23177548 PMID: 37688004

Darwis, D., Fernando, Y., Mehta, A. R., Wamiliana, , & Setiawansyah, . (2025, October). Metadata-based video steganography: Development of a new model for secure information embedding. *Engineering, Technology &. Applied Scientific Research*, *15*(5), 27076–27088. DOI: 10.48084/etasr.11937

Dashcam shows truck rushing towards Berlin Christmas market. (2016, December 22). *Reuters*. https://www.reuters.com/article/world/exclusive-dashcam-shows-truck-speed-into-berlin-christmas-market-idUSKBN14B2FG

Delgado, R. (2024, Winter). Doorbell monitors, pest alarms, neighborhood chat groups, and a second fundamental contradiction. *Case Western Reserve Law Review*, *75*(2), 521–529.

Detention of four defendants was renewed, including Chocalata and Warda; and activist Wessam Salah was released, The. (2023, May 21). Association for Freedom of Thought and Expression (AFTE) Egypt Weekly Legal Bulletin. https://afteegypt.org/en/legal-profiles-en/weekly-legal-bulletin-en-2/2023/05/21/34502-afteegypt.html

Dywaba, Z., Horne, J., & Thenga, G. (2025, March 27). Unlocking the investigative potential: The role of Closed-Circuit Television footage in combating ATM card fraud. *OIDA International Journal of Sustainable Development*, *18*(6), 53–70.

Eckman, S. J. (2016). Video broadcasting from the federal courts: Issues for Congress. In M. Davis (ed.), *Cameras in Federal Courts* (pp. 1-25). Nova Science.

Edvardsen, A. (2025, October 1). *Russia's violations of Norwegian and allied airspace: "Sign of desperation," says professor.* High North News. https://www.highnorthnews.com/en/russias-violations-norwegian-and-allied-airspace-sign-desperation-says-professor

Egypt: Three TikTok influencers arrested after parody video of jail visit. (2023, January 30). Middle East Eye. https://www.middleeasteye.net/news/egypt-tiktok-influencers-arrested-parody-video-jail-visit

European Transportation Safety Council. (2019, February 18). *In-vehicle technology vital to tackling speeding in Europe.* [Press release]. https://etsc.eu/in-vehicle-technology-vital-to-tackling-speeding-in-europe

Ezzat, W. (2025, December 30). New petition targets license-plate reader cameras in the Quad Cities. *KWQC News.* https://www.kwqc.com/2025/12/31/new-petition-targets-license-plate-reader-cameras-quad-cities

Falcón-López, S. A., Tobarra, L., Robles-Gómez, A., & Pastor-Vargas, R. (2025, November 29). Forensic analysis of manipulated images and videos. *Applied Sciences (Basel, Switzerland), 15*(23), 12664. DOI: 10.3390/app152312664

Fangary, F., & Mahfouz, S. (2025, August 3). *Seven TikTokers arrested on immorality charges as authorities respond to campaign against 'vulgar' content.* Mada. https://www.madamasr.com/en/2025/08/03/news/u/seven-tiktok-creators-arrested-on-moral-charges-as-authorities-respond-to-campaign-against-vulgar-content

Feigenson, N. (2023, Spring). Adjudication on Zoom and beyond: Human interaction in virtual courts. *Washburn Law Journal, 62*(3), 461–506.

Feigenson, N., & Carney, B. (2025). Generative AI as courtroom evidence: A practical guide. *Mitchell Hamline Law Review, 52*(1), 3.

Ferguson, A. G. (2025, May). Video analytics and Fourth Amendment vision. *Texas Law Review, 103*(6), 1253–1319.

Flowers, V. (2025, May 24). Jussie Smollett to make charitable donations to settle Chicago's hoax attack lawsuit. *NBC News.* https://www.nbcnews.com/news/us-news/jussie-smollett-settle-chicago-lawsuit-rcna208880

Galarraga Gortázar, N. (2025, May 10). In São Paulo, 'Big Brother' is watching, with 25,000 cameras and facial recognition technology. *El País.* https://english.elpais.com/international/2025-05-10/in-sao-paulo-big-brother-is-watching-with-25000-cameras-and-facial-recognition-technology.html

Gómez Fuentes, Á. (2025, June 3). Un padre desbloquea el móvil de su hijo apuñalado en Italia y encuentra al asesino. *ABC.* https://www.abc.es/sociedad/padre-desbloquea-movil-hijo-apunalado-italia-encuentra-20250602191600-nt.html

Grant, S. (2024, November 3). *How does a doorbell camera work?* Abode. https://goabode.com/blog/how-doorbell-camera-works

Graves, D. (1979, June-July). Cameras in the courts: The situation today. *Judicature, 63*(1), 24–27.

Gupta, N., & Agarwal, B. B. (2023, April). Recognition of suspicious human activity in video surveillance: A review. *Engineering, Technology &. Applied Scientific Research, 13*(2), 10529–10534. DOI: 10.48084/etasr.5739

Hansen Löfstrand, C., & Backman, C. (2021). Control or protection? Work environment implications of police body-worn cameras. *New Technology, Work and Employment, 36*(3), 327–347. DOI: 10.1111/ntwe.12201

Hastie, R., & Pennington, N. (1996). The O.J. Simpson stories: Behavioral scientists' reflections on the people of the State of California v. Orenthal James Simpson. *University of Colorado Law Review, 67*(4), 957–976.

Hernandez, J. (2021, May 26). Read this powerful statement from Darnella Frazier, who filmed George Floyd's murder. *NPR.* https://www.npr.org/2021/05/26/1000475344/read-this-powerful-statement-from-darnella-frazier-who-filmed-george-floyds-murd

Hetzel, D., & Strickland, R. A. (2025, March 31). *Cameras in the courtroom.* Middle Tennessee State University Free Speech Center. https://firstamendment.mtsu.edu/article/cameras-in-the-courtroom

Iboshi, K. (2025, July 22). Why former US Army soldier went 'sword in hand' in alleged traffic cam shooting spree across Portland. *KGW8 News.* https://www.kgw.com/article/news/investigations/portland-man-chase-grijalva-allegedly-shoot-traffic-cameras/283-e86307df-49ec-4393-85df-4b3874e97cbb

Iliadis, M., Harris, B., Vakhitova, Z., Flynn, A., & Tyson, D. (2024, November). Police body-worn cameras as a response to domestic and family violence: Practitioner insights into the consequences for victim/survivors. *Violence Against Women, 30*(14), 3536–3557. DOI: 10.1177/10778012231185541 PMID: 37487222

Ionova, A. (2025, October 3). Brutal killing of 3 women, livestreamed on social media, shocks Argentina. *The New York Times.* https://www.nytimes.com/2025/09/26/world/americas/argentina-women-murder-instagram.html

Iowa Supreme Court. (2025, October 3). State of Iowa v. Terence Edward Manning Jr. (No. 23-1390). Iowa Courts. https://www.iowacourts.gov/courtcases/22746/embed/SupremeCourtOpinion

Jordan, A. (2017, October 27). "Ninja" burglar revealed to be 74-year-old man. *Tokyo Weekender.* https://www.tokyoweekender.com/japan-life/ninja-burglar-revealed-74-year-old-man

Kalaam, S. A. (2025, July 8). *The legality of public filming and pranks in India.* LawBro. https://www.lawbro.net/blog/law-5/the-legality-of-public-filming-and-pranks-in-india-18

Kansal, K., Wong, Y., & Kankanhalli, M. S. (2025, July). Implications of privacy regulations on video surveillance systems. *ACM Transactions on Multimedia Computing Communications and Applications, 21*(7), 1–27. DOI: 10.1145/3706108

Kennedy, G., & Wong, J. K. C. (2025, December 15). *Hong Kong issues new PCPD guidelines and leaflets on CCTV, drones and in-vehicle cameras.* Mayer Brown. https://www.mayerbrown.com/en/insights/publications/2025/12/new-guidance-on-cctv-drones-and-in-vehicle-cameras-in-hong-kong

Kielbowicz, R. B. (1979, June-July). The story behind the adoption of the ban on courtroom cameras. *Judicature*, *63*(1), 14–23.

Lallie, H. S. (2023, July). Dashcam forensic investigation guidelines. *Forensic Science International Digital Investigation*, *45*, 301558. DOI: 10.1016/j.fsidi.2023.301558

Leatherdale, D., & Lake, E. (2025, April 30). Video shows felling of much-loved tree, jury told. *BBC.* https://www.bbc.com/news/articles/c3v90z17k74o

Levenson, E., & Cooper, A. (2021, March 31). Derek Chauvin's body camera video shows his reaction just after George Floyd left in an ambulance. *CNN.* https://www.cnn.com/2021/03/31/us/derek-chauvin-trial-george-floyd-day-3

Lezama, F. (2022, August 28). A guide to video analytics: Applications and opportunities. TryOLabs. https://tryolabs.com/guides/video-analytics-guide

Libell, H. P., Sorensen, M. S., Alami, A., & Callimachi, R. (2018, December 22). Video of tourist's killing in Morocco is most likely real, Norway says. *The New York Times.* https://www.nytimes.com/2018/12/22/world/europe/scandinavian-tourists-morocco.html

Lillich, R. B. (1991, January 1). The Soering Case. *The American Journal of International Law*, *85*(1), 128–149. DOI: 10.1017/S0002930000011398

Lucas, K. (2016, January 26). *Stay tuned for a brief history of television. Video* Caption Corporation. https://www.vicaps.com/blog/brief-history-television

Lum, C., Koper, C. S., Lee, H., Nagin, D. S., & Sherman, L. (2025, December 11). Measuring the cost-effectiveness of new technologies in policing: The case of automatic license plate readers (ALPR). *Cambridge Journal of Evidence-Based Policing*, *9*(1), 1–19. DOI: 10.1007/s41887-025-00099-y

McClain, S. (1996, Spring/Summer). A history of aerial cinematography. *The Operating Cameraman*, *6*(1), 32–49.

McGuirk, R. (2025, December 22). Australian police release documents showing Bondi Beach shooting suspect conducted firearms training with his father. *PBS.* https://www.pbs.org/newshour/world/australian-police-release-documents-showing-bondi-beach-shooting-suspect-conducted-firearms-training-with-his-father

Morte di Michael, B. in aula Giacomo Friso si avvale della facoltà di non rispondere. (2025, December 12). *Padova Oggi.* https://www.padovaoggi.it/cronaca/udienza-processo-friso-boschetto-padova-11-dicembre-2025.html

Mulkerrin, E. C., & Keeffe, O, S. T. (2025, September 18). In-room surveillance of residents in long term care: It's complicated. *Irish Medical Journal*, *118*(8), 127. PMID: 40982312

Myhand, T. (2023). Once the jury sees it, the jury can't unsee it: The challenge trial judges face when authenticating video evidence in the age of deepfakes. *Widener Law Review*, *29*(2), 171–189.

Narayan, S. (2023). CCTVs and the criminal city. *Surveillance & Society*, *21*(4), 363–374. DOI: 10.24908/ss.v21i4.15779

National Air and Space Museum. (2023, June 21). *The beginnings and basics of aerial photography.* Smithsonian. https://airandspace.si.edu/stories/editorial/beginnings-and-basics-aerial-photography

Ng, A. (2022, July 13). *Amazon gave Ring videos to police without owners' permission.* Politico. https://www.politico.com/news/2022/07/13/amazon-gave-ring-videos-to-police-without-owners-permission-00045513

Nova Scotia's 1990 report about 'grisly trial' of Jens Soering. (2023, November 8). [Video]. CBC News. https://www.cbc.ca/player/play/video/1.7022295

Nunes, E. (2025, June 3). Selfie killer: I unlocked my murdered son's phone after his death…& found his grinning 'killer' posing in selfie moments after stabbing. *The Sun.* https://www.thesun.co.uk/news/35227135/unlocked-murdered-sons-phone-grinning-killer

Ölvecký, M., Huraj, L., & Brlej, I. (2025, February). Evaluating the Effectiveness of Deepfake Video Detection Tools: A Comparative Study. *TEM Journal, 14*(1), 64–77. https://doi.org/DOI: 10.18421/TEM141-07

Parry, M. M., Dario, L. M., & Moule, R. K.Jr. (2021, July). Is seeing believing? On the content validity of video recordings for use in criminological research. *Deviant Behavior*, *42*(7), 807–820. DOI: 10.1080/01639625.2019.1699259

Passalaqua, C. (1995, August 15). Post-Trial, Is There Life for the Soaps?: Television: The past decade has seen steadily dropping ratings for daytime soap operas. Simpson trial has only caused further erosion. Los Angeles Times. https://www.latimes.com/archives/la-xpm-1995-08-15-ca-35367-story.html

Peeler, T. (2022, September 19). *Nanny/babysitter cam law.* LegalMatch. https://www.legalmatch.com/law-library/article/babysitternanny-camera-legality.html

People of the State of Illinois v. Jussie Smollett. (2024, November 21). https://law.justia.com/cases/illinois/supreme-court/2024/130431.html

Personal Data (Privacy) Ordinance. Cap. 486. (2022, January 10). Hong Kong e-Legislation. https://www.elegislation.gov.hk/hk/cap486!en-zh-Hant-HK.pdf

Pieper, O. (2021, December 19). *Germany remembers Christmas market attack victims.* Deutsche Welle. https://www.dw.com/en/5-years-later-germany-remembers-victims-of-berlin-christmas-market-terror-attack/a-60148540

Ratzan, S. (2021, May 17). *Cell phone videos are ubiquitous, but are they admissible?* Ratzan Weissman & Bolt. https://www.rwblawyers.com/news/cell-phone-videos-are-ubiquitous-but-are-they-admissible

Regulation 2016/679 OJ L 119 of the European Parliament and of the Council of 27 April 2016 on the protection of natural persons with regard to the processing of personal data and on the free movement of such data, and repealing Directive 95/46/EC (General Data Protection Regulation). *Official Journal of the European Union, 59,* 1-88. https://eur-lex.europa.eu/legal-content/EN/TXT/PDF/?uri=CELEX:32016R0679

Rind, A. (2026, February 25). *Video evidence Authentication: Standards courts expect in 2026*. Vidizmo Digital Evidence Management System. https://digitalevidence.ai/blog/video-evidence-authentication-standards-courts

Ring Alarm monitoring services for your location. (2024, March 7). Ring. https://ring.com/gb/en/support/articles/xk0je/Ring-Alarm-availability-in-Europe

Rizzo, A., Princiotta, E., & Iuele, G. (2023, December). Exploring the link between smartphone use, recorded violence, and social sharing in 80 case studies in Italy. *Psych*, *5*(4), 1241–1255. DOI: 10.3390/psych5040082

Role of video evidence in modern legal practices, The. (2025, July 28). Marko Law. https://www.markolaw.com/post/the-role-of-video-evidence-in-modern-legal-practices

Royo, P., Asenjo, À., Trujillo, J., Çetin, E., & Barrado, C. (2022, November 17). Enhancing drones for law enforcement and capacity monitoring at open large events. *Drones (Basel)*, *6*(11), 359. DOI: 10.3390/drones6110359

Shaath, S. (2019, March 27). Decline of soap operas: was OJ Simpson to blame? *BBC*. https://www.bbc.com/news/world-us-canada-47585335

Singh, I. (2022, October 19). *Norway detains 7 Russian drone pilots, including Putin associate's son*. Drone DJ. https://dronedj.com/2022/10/19/norway-russian-drone-pilot-arrest

Solomon, T. (2025, October 20). French audit reveals that major parts of the Louvre have no cameras, and other security flaws. *Art News*. https://www.artnews.com/art-news/news/french-audit-louvre-robbery-security-flaws-no-cameras-1234757968

Spunta il video selfie choc del killer con il rivale ancora Morente. (2025, June 3). *Padova Oggi*. https://www.padovaoggi.it/cronaca/villafrancapadovana-video-delitto-processo-3-giugno-2025.html

Thompson, S. K., Sandhu, A., & Koziol, C. (2025, June). 'History is written by the victor ... but in some cases, it's also now written by the recordings': Body-worn cameras and the double-edged nature of police visibility. *Theoretical Criminology*, •••, 1–20. DOI: 10.1177/13624806251342569 PMID: 41799372

Trigger, R. (2025, December 14). Moment Ahmed Al Ahmed disarms gunman Sajid Akram captured on film. *ABC News*. https://www.abc.net.au/news/2025-12-14/bondi-shooter-tackled-and-disarmed-by-possible-civilian/106141690

Truck plows through crowd at Christmas market in Berlin, killing 12. (2016, December 19). *CBS News*. https://www.cbsnews.com/news/truck-plows-through-crowd-christmas-market-berlin-germany

Turyn, N. (2025, October 23). Convicted killer Jens Soering reacts to Netflix docuseries 'Till Murder Do Us Part'. *ABC13 News*. https://wset.com/news/local/convicted-killer-jens-soering-reacts-to-netflix-docuseries-till-murder-do-us-part-november-2023

Ulvin, O. E., Skjærseth, E. Å., Krüger, A. J., Thorsen, K., Nordseth, T., & Haugland, H. (2023, October 3). Can video communication in the emergency medical communication Centre improve dispatch precision? A before–after study in Norwegian helicopter emergency medical services. *BMJ Open*, *13*(10), e077395. DOI: 10.1136/bmjopen-2023-077395 PMID: 37899141

Understanding the nuances between 'film,' 'movie,' and 'video.' (2024, June 12). WeVideo. https://www.wevideo.com/blog/film-movie-video-comparison

United States Courts. (n.d.) *History of cameras, broadcasting, and remote public access in courts.* https://www.uscourts.gov/court-records/access-court-proceedings/remote-public-access-proceedings/history-cameras-broadcasting-and-remote-public-access-courts

Vakhitova, Z., Iliadis, M., Harris, B., Tyson, D., & Flynn, A. (2022, June 22). The merits and risks of body-worn camera footage in domestic and family violence incidents and legal proceedings: A study of police perceptions and experiences. *Policing and Society, 33*(2), 170–186. DOI: 10.1080/10439463.2022.2082421

von Münchow, S. (2017, July). *Aftermath of the terror attack on Breitscheid Platz Christmas Market: Germany's security architecture and parliamentary inquiries.* George C. Marshall European Center for Security Studies, Occasional Papers, No. 028. https://www.marshallcenter.org/en/publications/occasional-papers/aftermath-terror-attack-breitscheid-platz-christmas-market-germanys-security-architecture-and

Walsh, P. (2021, June 10). 2nd Derek Chauvin juror who deliberated comes forward, breaks down what worked for prosecution and what didn't for defense in George Floyd murder case. *Minnesota Star Tribune.* https://www.startribune.com/2nd-derek-chauvin-juror-who-deliberated-comes-forward-breaks-down-what-worked-for-prosecution-and-wh/600066839

Wang, C., Musaev, A., Sheinidashtegol, P., & Atkison, T. (2019, June 20). Towards detection of abnormal vehicle behavior using traffic cameras. In K. Chen, S. Seshadri, & L.-J. Zhang (Eds.), *Big Data – BigData 2019. Lecture Notes in Computer Science* (pp. 125-136), 11514. Springer. https://doi.org/DOI: 10.1007/978-3-030-23551-2_9

Weikmann, T., Egelhofer, J. L., & Lecheler, S. (2025, December). Beyond credibility: The effects of different forms of visual disinformation. *Journalism & Mass Communication Quarterly, 102*(4), 1020–1043. DOI: 10.1177/10776990251357299

Worgul, M. (2025, October 22). *Can cell phone video be used as evidence in court?* Worgul, Sarna & Ness. https://www.pittsburghcriminalattorney.com/can-cell-phone-video-be-used-as-evidence-in-court

Wu, Y., Sun, I. Y., & Hu, R. (2021, January). Cooperation with police in China: Surveillance cameras, neighborhood efficacy and policing. *Social Science Quarterly (Wiley-Blackwell), 102*(1), 433–453. https://doi.org/DOI: 10.1111/ssqu.12903

KEY TERMS AND DEFINITIONS

Body cam: A video camera worn on the person, typically a police officer, with footage saved to ensure legitimacy of interaction with the public as well as to serve as proof of criminal activity.

Closed-Circuit Television (CCTV): Video cameras set up to cover large swaths of areas such as streets, parking lots, inside stores, etc. The footage is viewable by those authorized and recordings typically kept for a specific period of time.

Dash cam: A video camera affixed to a vehicle with views to the front and/or back. Footage can be saved via an app for sharing with law enforcement or other purposes.

Deepfake: Video (sometimes with audio) that has been altered or created by AI or other technological means.

Doorbell cam: A camera attached to a home, typically on the front, to capture audio and video activity and to be able to communicate with visitors remotely via an app.

Drone camera: A video camera affixed to an Unmanned Aerial Vehicle (UAV), a device that can fly into otherwise dangerous spaces or show incidents from the sky. Note that these are strictly regulated.

Nanny (or Granny) cam: An inside-the-home camera set up to be able to monitor caretakers.

Chapter 8
Eyes in the Sky:
Balancing Public Safety and Privacy in the Drone Era

Cassie Longhart-Thomas
http://orcid.org/0000-0002-2683-405X
Purdue University Global, USA

Kathi Nicholson
http://orcid.org/0009-0003-5423-5294
Purdue University Global, USA

ABSTRACT

The rapid advancement in technology such as Unmanned Aircraft Systems (UAS), has significantly transformed law enforcement operations through improving situational awareness, expanding operational reach, and improving efficiency in high-stress situations. As drones become more popular, accessible, cost-effective, and sophisticated, the interest by law enforcement agencies have increased. While the use of drones offers a clear operational advantage, particularly in remote areas, their increased use raises ethical, legal, and social concerns centered around privacy, civil liberties, and appropriate use. This work provides a comprehensive framework for understanding the history of UAS, the governance, legal constraints, and ethical considerations necessary to balance the rights of the public and the objectives of public safety with the expansion of drone technology.

INTRODUCTION

The advancement of Unmanned Aircraft Systems (UAS), commonly known as drones, represents a significant technological shift that is rapidly redefining the operational capabilities of modern institutions, particularly in the realm of law enforcement. According to the International Trade Administration (n.d.), a UAS consists of an aircraft with no pilot on board, a remote pilot station, a command and control link, and a payload specific to the intended operation or application, which could include a camera or other sensor to collect data for analysis. As these devices become smaller, cheaper, and more sophisticated, they offer undeniable advantages, from rapidly covering large geographic areas during search and rescue operations to providing a crucial aerial perspective in tactical situations. According to Finklea (2023),

DOI: 10.4018/979-8-3373-7660-8.ch008

an estimate from 2020 indicates that more than 1,500 state and local public safety agencies (over 70 percent work in law enforcement) have acquired drones, an increase of more than 500 agencies from the 2018 estimate. According to Enemark (2021), governments today are making armed and unarmed drones available to police for border control, criminal investigations, rescue missions, traffic management, and monitoring of public events.

Drones are being utilized to access areas that might be deemed unsafe for personnel to enter, such as fires or hazardous environments. According to Fudge and Ferebee (2024), the use of drones for search and rescue is cost-effective in comparison to traditional techniques. This especially applies when searching in remote areas, where resources would otherwise be limited. Given the ability of drones to access these remote areas, drones can be effective in increasing a victim's chance of survival compared to other methods of rescue that do not incorporate drones. The increased integration of drones into daily police work simultaneously introduces profound ethical and social dilemmas regarding the balance between public safety and civil liberties. According to COPS (2020), before implementing a drone program, state and local agencies must consider the impact of their program, federal, state, and local laws and regulations, conduct community outreach, funding, and the appropriate drone.

A systematic review explores this tension, beginning with the examination of diverse applications of drones in law enforcement, including utility in surveillance and emergency response. In an emergency situation, the use of an armed drone could increase the chances of innocent bystanders being injured. Enemark (2021) argues that while military ethics may permit a calculated risk to civilians during combat, domestic police ethics strictly forbid any use of force that endangers innocent bystanders. Several concerns are centered around using a drone for malicious purposes, including spying or accessing unauthorized areas. Discussions are occurring about police using drones in situations that ultimately violate citizens' rights. According to Gips et al. (2025), civil liberty advocates are concerned that law enforcement is using or will use drones for improper usage, such as observing groups that are peacefully gathering or to surveil marginalized communities without probable cause. These concerns lead to the questions pertaining to what the legal requirements or policies are centered around the use of UAS, particularly surrounding law enforcement use.

The core of this analysis shifts to the legal and policy landscape, investigating how the deployment of these technologies intersects with fundamental rights, specifically concerning the right to privacy, the protections guaranteed by the Fourth Amendment against unreasonable searches, and the emerging challenges posed by data aggregation and algorithmic policing.

According to the Congress Constitution Annotated (n.d.), the Fourth Amendment is the right of the people to be secure in their persons, houses, papers, and effects against unreasonable search and seizures, shall not be violated, and no Warrants shall issue, but upon probable cause, supported by Oath or affirmation, and particularly describing the place to be searched, and the persons or things to be seized.

The populace should be able to gather in public, at their home, or on paper without the fear of misuse of UAS without probable cause. According to Enemark (2021), the use of drones has generated concerns for intrusiveness of police surveillance and the impact on individual privacy and freedom. This has caused panic among the community increasingly on the privacy of the community. According to the Office of Community Oriented Policing Services (COPS) (2020), community members have voiced concerns about the use of drone videos and individual privacy. Given the capability of drones to capture more than the intended images and to access areas law enforcement could not otherwise legally breach, it is important for public safety agencies to understand the methodology and governance behind the use of drones in daily practice. The Federal Aviation Administration (FAA) has authority over the safety of the airspace. While federal regulations governing the use of drones by law enforcement at the federal, state, and local levels are limited, officers still have the lawful duty to uphold the constitutional rights of the public. Ultimately, this analysis aims to provide a comprehensive framework for understanding and addressing the complex governance required by this transformative technology. How do these policies or legislation(s) protect the citizen's right as guaranteed by the Fourth Amendment?

THE DRONE

History

Drones have been used for quite some time. According to Gillis et al. (2024), drone use can be dated back to 1849 in Italy when Venice was fighting for their independence from Austria when a hot-air balloon was equipped with bombs. While this was not officially classified as a drone then, it staged the idea of utilizing airspace to carry items without a human present. Later in 1917 the U.S. Army created the Kettering Bug that was an experimental unmanned flying bomb aircraft, that was never operationally used (Gillis et al., 2024). The military has been one of the biggest supports of using drones since the early 1900s, given the ability for surveillance, protection, search and rescue, damage assessment, and weapon utilization. Over the past several decades the drone has become more advanced and widely used for a variety of reasons. The following are a few examples of how drones have been used since 1973.

- In 1973 the Israel Air Force (IAF) first employed UAVs in the Yom Kippur War (Rodman, 2010).
- Customs and Boarder Protection employed the Predator B to enhance law enforcement operations at the border in 2005 (U.S. Customs and Border Protection, 2023).
- In 2020 NASA launched Ingenuity Mards Helicopter FL and it landed in 2021 on Mars (NASA, n.d.).
- In 2021, Zipline, Pfizer, and BioNTech collaborate and deliver COVID-19 vaccinations to Ghana ("Zipline, Pfizer," 2021).
- Since 2022, both Russia and Ukraine have used cheap drones and unmanned robotics in war (Bendett and Kirichenko, 2025).

Types of Drones and Uses

A drone is a piece of smart technology that can be controlled remotely by humans. According to the Federal Aviation Administration (2025b), an unmanned aircraft system (UAS) is defined as an aircraft that is operated without direct human intervention from within or on the aircraft. A drone is operational by using onboard computers, sensors, and GPS technology. There are several different types of drones that include hobbyist (hobby), midsize military and commercial, large military, and stealth combat. The following explain what each drone type.

- Hobbiyst drones: are readily available to purchase, pre-assembled or assembled, and do not require formal training (Sayler, 2015).
- Midsize military and commercial drones: considered to be middleweight drones between 1-600kg and are not available to the general public.

- Large military drones: include armed drones, and not available to the public (Sayler, 2015).
- Stealth drones: are highly sophisticated technology and used in the military only (Sayler, 2015).

The hobbyist drones have been around for a while, come in a variety of customizable assembles, and can be controlled by a phone and taking photos. The hobbyist drone is one of the most popular types of drones among many different recreation hobbies such as photography, sports, and entertainment. According to Termanini (2023), the U.S. Navy's experiment with Radio Controlled Aircraft led to the invention of the Curtiss N2C-2 DRONE in 1937 that led to the influence of new UAVs combat training tools. Midsize military and commercial drones are being used for commercial or military activities. According to Sayler (2015), the midsize commercial and military drone is being used for agriculture to survey or spray crops, and retailers like Amazon are considering the use for delivery of goods. Compared to the hobbyist drones, these drones are larger in size, which means they can carry more weight such as that of an explosive device or retail packages. This makes it appealing to retail organizations for timely and efficient delivery of customer orders.

One of the most sophisticated drones is that of the stealth combat drone. This drone is at the top of the advanced technology chain. These stealth drones allow the military the ability to penetrate airspace at greater altitudes for longer periods of time. According to Ryan (2025), Lockheed Martin's Vectis, is capable of precision strike, electronic warfare, intelligence, surveillance, and the ability to counter air missions. While stealth drones are beneficial in a war setting, they might not be appropriate use for recreation, retail, or law enforcement needs. For law enforcement agencies, the use of smaller drones can allow officers the ability to access locations that might be hard for humans to access.

Classification of UAV

Drones can be classified by their rotor configuration and size. The type of rotor configuration is important in use and features of the drone. According to the Drone Pilot Ground School, the rotor configuration of a drone has a direct impact on the characteristics of its flight, stability, and its overall use. There are 4 main types of rotor configuration which include multi-rotor, fixed-wing, single-rotor, and fixed-wing hybrid. The cheapest of the rotor types is the multi-rotor and commonly used for photography or recreational purposes. While the most expensive of the group would be the fixed-wing hybrid and can range on the higher side of over 200,000 (Dukowitz, 2026). The fixed-wing hybrid is used for search and rescue, combines vertical takeoff and landing, and is versatile for diverse environments. The fixed-wing hybrid is ideal in law enforcement to help navigate areas where a larger surface area with little resources available like that of a missing person on a mountain. This drone can help cover more area in a shorter period of time (Dukowitz, 2026).

The size of the drone helps determine the functionality, capability, and application. The 5 main classifications drone sizes such as nano, small, medium, large, and heavy-lift. According to Abdullah (n.d.), very small UASs include insect-size drones up to 50 centimeters in length and are exceptionally lightweight, making longer distances operational. These tiny, structured drones make it easier to maneuver in and out of tight spaces and remain in flight for longer periods of time. Larger drones include those that are used by the military such as the Predator. According to Abdullah (n.d.), the large UASs are typically equipped with state-of-the-art payloads, sophisticated sensors, targeting equipment, long-range communication systems, and can travel longer distances. These larger drones make it ideas for military use of carrying bombs, making it safer for soldiers and prevents fatalities due to combat. The most expensive heavy-lift drone cost more than 100,000 but can carry heavier loads such as film equipment. Dukowitz (2026) explains the heavy-lift drone is engineered to carry heavy equipment, large delivery packages, and specialized tools, therefore making them best for logistics, film, transportation, and construction tasks.

Modern Day Use of Drones

Drones are transforming the way business is done, from the military, public safety, and commercial delivery, to medical aid. According to Sauser (2025), the use of UASs in the Battle of Avdiivka in 2024 has created new possibilities for deep strikes and operational shaping, allowing commanders to affect the battlefield across multiple domains and distances. What this means is the military can attach multiple locations at the same time with no human interaction from a remote setting. This has proven drones can go where humans cannot and perform otherwise dangerous tasks that could be lethal to human life.

Outside of military use, drones are being used to save lives with AEDs. According to Avive, in the state of GA the Northside Hospital Foundation, Northside Hospital Heart Institute, Avive Solutions, and Forsyth County Fire Department have teamed up to deliver AEDs to the community during a 911 activation of a cardiac arrest ("Forsyth County," 2025). The purpose of this initiative is to help emergency responders to provide defibrillation sooner rather than later to those who are suffering a life-threatening emergency where their heart has stopped. This demonstrates the ability of a drone to deliver packages quickly and avoid high congestion areas that otherwise would slow down the response of emergency vehicles.

The military and medical fields are not the only industries utilizing drones in modern society, eCommerce is using drones to deliver goods to customers. Amazon is currently using drones in their logistics infrastructure. According to Amazon, their drones are fully electric and produce zero exhaust emissions during flights and can carry items up to 5 pounds ("Drone delivery FAQs," n.d.). The use of drones has made it easier to reduce carbon emissions, reduce waiting times, and safely deliver items to location. Increase the options of delivery in a wider area.

Drone Use in Law Enforcement

According to the Federal Aviation Administration (2025b), as of August 2024 the use of drones is growing with over 860,000 registered drones with the FAA. It is clear that drones provide safer and better options to access remote locations and areas that humans should be go due to various reasons such as terrain, danger, or hazardous conditions. Drones are intelligent technology that help companies collect data, communicate, or operate in an efficient manner. According to Finklea (2023), there is limited specific legislation that prohibits tools and technology such as UAV used by federal law enforcement agencies to help aid investigations. Drone as First Responder (DFR) is the common term that is being used to identify the use of drone in public safety. Law enforcement agencies are using drones for various reasons including traffic control, search and rescue, and access to dangerous areas with hostiles. According to the U.S. Department of Homeland Security (2025) a DFR system include launch stations, rapid, remote UAS deployment to an incident, and transmission of critical information back to emergency teams in real time, allowing better-informed decision-making. The following are current use cases.

- In 2018, Chula Vista in CA began deploying drones from the rooftop of the police department for 911 calls including fires, traffic, and dangerous suspects (City of Chula Vista, n.d.).

- In 2021, Lexington County Sheriff's Department deployed their drone unit with SWAT using small drones for search and rescue (Lexington Sheriff's Department, n.d.).
- In 2024, the Redmond Police Department deployed a First Responder drone to access 911 calls before the ground unit arrives (Redmond Washington, n.d.).
- In 2025, Dunwoody Policy in GA started their pilot program and soon after used a drone to survey a scene of a tussle between law enforcement and a suspect and chaotic radio traffic and the status of the officers (Ridderbusch, 2025).

Drones are becoming increasingly popular for their rapid response, versatility, and functionality. Drones can provide a quicker response than motorized vehicles. Making it easier to surveillance locations for safety, entry points, and number of suspects or victims.

Benefits of Using UAS in Law Enforcement

Sending a patrol unit can take time based on time of day, traffic, road closures, etc., regardless of the call type. The ability to operate a drone can provide live feedback without delays and help determine the nature and extent of the 911 activation. UASs provides a way for law enforcement to scope out the area and a matter of minutes to help determine what type of resources are needed and how much. The benefits of drones have shown promise in many areas such as search and rescue, surveillance, tactical use, traffic management, and locating a suspect. The use of drones in traffic management alone is projected to grow from \$42.3 billion in 2023 to \$72.5 billion by 2028 (DSLRPros, 2025). Officers cannot monitor high risk areas 24/7. According to Christoff and Patterson (2025), as part of planning a targeted enforcement operation, drones can help agencies identify areas where speeding rates are higher or disregarding a traffic light, increasing informed approach (p. 9). The use of UASs in traffic management can decrease the changes of a serious incidents, especially in high-speed pursuits by providing alternative routes, and blocking intersections to allow safe passing of vehicles or pedestrians not involved in the incident.

According to Johnson et al. (2023), according to a 2020 survey by the Police Executive Research Forum (PERF), the most common use of drones in law enforcement is for search and rescue for missing persons. This has proven to be beneficial in covering a lot of ground and live footage which allows the department to reduce ground labor and increase the potential rescue time. Search and rescue might be the most common use of drones, however other practical benefits include reduced community violence and crime rate through surveillance and integrated facial recognition, and increased officer awareness and preparedness. Deploying drones before a portal unit arrives increases the safety of the office by situation awareness.

Currently the cost of implementing drone use is a controversial topic. Some research indicates that the use of drones is more cost effective. According to DSLRPros (2025), drones might only dent a budget of a few thousand dollars but might be more cost-effective than refueling a helicopter and recruiting a pilot. On the other hand, some research indicates the start-up, and on-going cost can range up to 30,000 or more. According to Christoff and Petterson (2025), a report in 2024 from Beverly Hills Police Department in CA, indicated the departments potential investment included the initial cost of \$114,811for 25 drones and the maintenance cost of \$48,800 across five years (lifespan of each drone) (p. 6). It appears to be mixed opinions of the cost analysis of drone applications. More research and data are needed to determine the true return-on-investment (ROI). While drones offer many different benefits to law enforcement, their use also raises important legal and ethical considerations that must be carefully addressed.

LEGAL AND POLICY FRAMEWORKS

The Fourth Amendment

The current judicial framework for UAS is deeply rooted in the plain view doctrine, a legal principle holding that law enforcement does not conduct a search under the Fourth Amendment when they observe items or activities in plain view from a location where they have a legal right to be. Historically, this doctrine was applied to the skies during the 1980s as manned flight became a common tool for drug interdiction. In the pivotal case of California v. Ciraolo (1986), the Supreme Court addressed whether a warrant was required for police to observe a suspect's backyard from a fixed-wing aircraft. The defendant had grown marijuana in a yard shielded by two high fences, explicitly manifesting a subjective expectation of privacy. The Court ruled that because the officers were flying at 1,000 feet in public navigable airspace, any member of the public could have peered down and seen the same activity. Chief Justice Burger famously noted that the Fourth Amendment simply does not require the police traveling in the public airways to obtain a warrant in order to observe what is visible to the naked eye (*California v. Ciraolo*, 1986). This established that the navigable airspace essentially functioned as a public highway, where privacy expectations were diminished.

This precedent was pushed further in Florida v. Riley (1989), where the surveillance occurred from a helicopter hovering at only 400 feet. In *Riley*, the Court held that even at this lower altitude, the surveillance was constitutional because the helicopter was operating within the FAA's lawful limits for rotary-wing aircraft. These cases created a bright-line rule based on altitude. If an officer is in public airspace, their observations, regardless of the privacy barriers on the ground, do not constitute a search (*Florida v. Riley*, 1989). As modern drones frequently operate at altitudes as low as 30 feet, the legal community is debating whether these navigable airspace rules can survive the transition from high-altitude planes to low-altitude robotics (Kilbane, 2019).

To understand why drones pose a unique threat to the Fourth Amendment, one must examine the curtilage doctrine. Originating in English common law, the curtilage is the area immediately surrounding and associated with the home, which is treated as part of the home itself for Fourth Amendment purposes. The Supreme Court established a four-factor test in United States v. Dunn (1987) to determine if an area falls within this protected zone:

- Proximity: How close the area is to the dwelling.
- Enclosure: Whether the area is included within an enclosure surrounding the home.
- Nature of Use: The specific activities for which the area is used.
- Privacy Steps: The measures taken by the resident to shield the area from public view (*United States v. Dunn*, 1987).

Historically, the curtilage was protected by a horizontal boundary, such as fences, walls, and hedges. Drones, however, introduce a vertical curtilage conflict. An area that satisfies all four *Dunn* factors (e.g., a fenced-in back patio used for private family gatherings) remains shielded from ground-level eyes but is completely exposed to a drone hovering just above the roofline. As Koerner (2015) observed, drones do not merely pass through the sky like a plane. They occupy the vertical curtilage, creating an intrusive presence that interferes with the quiet enjoyment of the property (Khalil, 2023). This necessitates a redefinition of the curtilage from a 2D plot of land to a 3D privacy box that extends upward, protecting the home from low-altitude vertical encroachment (Kilbane, 2019).

As UAS technology transitioned from basic optics to advanced sensor suites, the Supreme Court's focus shifted from where the officer was to what technology they were using. Kyllo v. United States (2001) established the sense-enhancing technology standard. The court ruled that using thermal imaging to detect heat signatures emanating from a home constituted a search. Justice Scalia argued that to allow the government to use technology not in general public use to discern the intimate details of a home would leave the homeowner at the mercy of advancing technology (*Kyllo v. United States*, 2001). For UAS, this means that while a drone might legally fly at 400 feet, the use of zoom lenses, LIDAR, or infrared sensors to peer through windows or into shielded areas likely requires a warrant (Villasenor, 2013).

The mosaic theory further complicated this, which emerged from United States v. Jones (2012) and Carpenter v. United States (2018). The theory suggests that while a single instance of observation in public might be legal, the pervasive and tireless collection of data over time creates a comprehensive mosaic of an individual's private life. Chief Justice Roberts noted in *Carpenter* that the ever-watchful eye of digital technology can track a person's movements with a precision that was previously impossible, revealing their religious, political, and social associations. As Finklea (2023) highlights, when this theory is applied to Drone as a First Responder (DFR) programs that maintain a constant presence over a city, the resulting exhaustive, continuous tracking constitutes a search, regardless of whether the person is in plain view (Alvarado, 2024).

The Fifth Amendment

Beyond the Fourth Amendment, UAS technology intersects with the Fifth Amendment, specifically regarding the collection of communicative evidence. Modern drones are often equipped with parabolic microphones and AI-driven gait analysis software, such as those developed by Versaterm ("2026 trends," 2026), which increasingly rely on algorithmic probable cause (Kilbane, 2019). If a drone passively records an individual making incriminating statements in an area they believed was private, the defense may argue a violation of the privilege against self-incrimination. The Fifth Amendment protects individuals from being compelled to be witnesses against themselves, ensuring the government adheres to established standards of procedural fairness (Constitution Annotated, n.d.).

Historically, the distinction between communicative and physical evidence distinction in Schmerber v. California (1966) determined that physical evidence, such as a blood sample, is not protected, whereas testimony is. As Villasenor (2013) suggests, a drone's pervasive presence could create a form of constructive compulsion. If suspects are aware they are being watched by a drone 24/7, they may feel compelled to speak or act in a way that is not voluntary. This use of drones to prompt a reaction, such as hovering low to induce a flight response, may be challenged as a coercive tactic designed to bypass the suspect's right to remain silent (Kilbane, 2019).

The Drone as a First Responder (DFR)

The Drone as First Responder (DFR) model is redefining the social contract between police and the community. In traditional models, drones are reactive. In DFR, they are proactive, launched the moment a 911 call is placed. Programs in cities like Chula Vista have demonstrated that drones can arrive at a scene 2-3 minutes before patrol cars 70% of the time (Chula Vista Police Department, n.d.). This speed provides a critical benefit, tactical de-escalation. By providing live situational awareness, drones allow supervisors to see if a man with a gun is actually a man with a cell phone or if a suspect has already left the area. This prevents the adrenalized response that often occurs when officers rush into an unknown situation, thereby reducing the likelihood of lethal force (Enemark, 2021). The psychological cost, however, is high. As Versaterm notes regarding the deployment of these persistent systems, citizens in over-policed neighborhoods may view the constant overhead eye as an occupying force rather than a safety tool, leading to a negative impact on public life ((“2026 trends,” 2026; Gips et al., 2025).

Line of Sight

The traditional regulatory framework for UAS has historically been anchored in the requirement for the pilot to maintain a Visual Line of Sight (VLOS) with the aircraft. This physical constraint served as a natural tether that limited the geographic scope of drone operations and ensured a high level of pilot accountability. The 2025 Federal Aviation Administration's (FAA) Beyond Visual Line of Sight (BVLOS) Rule has fundamentally altered this landscape, allowing law enforcement to operate drones miles away from the pilot via cellular networks and satellite links.

From a Fourth Amendment perspective, BVLOS operations expand the geographic footprint of government surveillance. When an officer is limited by Visual Line of Sight (VLOS), the surveillance is localized and finite. Under BVLOS, a single pilot in a centralized command center can manage multiple drones patrolling entire municipal sectors. This force multiplier effect raises concerns regarding the officer-to-observation ratio. As drones become increasingly autonomous, the level of direct human oversight decreases, leading to what legal scholars call autonomous probable cause (Kilbane, 2019). If a drone operating BVLOS identifies a suspicious activity via an AI algorithm and initiates a pursuit, the court must determine if the reasonable suspicion belongs to the pilot, the algorithm, or the agency's operational policy.

BVLOS flight further complicates the passing through versus occupying debate. In *California v. Ciraolo* (1986), the aircraft was a transient entity in the sky. In contrast, BVLOS drones can loiter indefinitely over a neighborhood, effectively occupying the public airspace. As Koerner (2015) observed, this loitering capability is a core component of the mosaic theory, as it enables the type of long-term, exhaustive tracking that the Supreme Court cautioned against in *Carpenter v. United States* (2018). The shift to BVLOS necessitates a new notice of surveillance standard, where citizens are alerted to the presence of wide-area drone patrols, much like the requirements for fixed CCTV networks in urban centers (Kilbane, 2019).

Every UAS flight generates a massive volume of telemetry data, a second-by-second log of GPS coordinates, battery levels, motor RPMs, and pilot inputs. In a legal setting, this data is treated as a digital fingerprint. Under the Federal Rules of Evidence, forensic investigators use this data to authenticate the chain of custody. If a police department cannot produce the telemetry logs for a specific flight, the defense may argue a spoilation of evidence, claiming the data was deleted to hide officer misconduct (“2026 trends,” 2026). New 2026 mandates for end-to-end encryption (E2EE) ensure that this data cannot be tampered with between the drone and the cloud server (“2026 trends,” 2026). Forensic tools like MD-DRONE are now used by prosecutors to reconstruct flight paths and prove exactly what a drone saw at the time of an arrest, providing a level of objective truth that often surpasses human testimony (Liju, 2025).

The United States stands as a global outlier in the realm of aerial privacy due to its highly decentralized patchwork of state-level statutes, which creates a significant lack of jurisdictional uniformity. This contrasts sharply with the harmonized approach of the European Union, which has seamlessly integrated UAS governance into the robust framework of the General Data Protection Regulation (GDPR). Within the European model, any high-resolution imagery capturing identifiable human faces is classified as sensitive biometric data, triggering stringent protection protocols. Before a single rotors-on operation can commence, European law enforcement agencies are statutorily required to conduct an exhaustive Data Protection Impact Assessment (DPIA). This forensic self-audit must definitively prove that the intended surveillance is not only legally authorized but also strictly proportionate and necessary to achieve a specific public safety objective, thereby ensuring that the state's interest does not unnecessarily override individual privacy rights (National Conference of State Legislatures [NCSL], 2023).

The United Kingdom has pioneered a model of radical transparency overseen by the surveillance camera commissioner. Under the UK's 2026 Surveillance Camera Code of Practice, which emphasizes policing by consent, there is a rigorous mandate that all police drone deployments be logged in real-time on public-facing digital dashboards (Information Commissioner's Office [ICO], n.d.). This systemic approach prioritizes institutional accountability over operational anonymity, providing citizens with the means to scrutinize the flight paths and mission justifications of governmental aircraft ("2026 trends," 2026).

Whereas the European Union's GDPR utilizes the principle of Data Minimization. Under Article 5 of the GDPR, personal data must be adequate, relevant, and limited to what is necessary in relation to the purposes for which they are processed (General Data Protection Regulation [GDPR], 2016). As noted by the NCSL (2023), for European drone operators, this means that even if a flight is legally authorized via a Data Protection Impact Assessment (DPIA), the resulting footage must be redacted or anonymized in real-time if it captures third parties not involved in the investigation.

In stark contrast, the American model remains void of a comprehensive federal Drone Privacy Act, leaving a legislative vacuum that has forced individual state legislatures to act as the primary defenders of Fourth Amendment values. States such as Florida, Illinois, and Virginia have emerged as leaders in this filling of the void, albeit with varying degrees of stringency. According to the NCSL (2023), these jurisdictions have largely adopted a search by default stance, wherein the deployment of a UAS for evidence gathering is legally categorized as a search and seizure. Consequently, law enforcement must secure a judicial warrant based on probable cause unless the flight falls under specific, narrowly tailored exigencies. These exceptions are typically restricted to immediate life-safety scenarios, such as the recovery of missing children via AMBER Alerts, high-stakes search and rescue missions in remote terrain, or the mitigation of imminent threats to life or property (Virginia Law, n.d.). This divided landscape means that an American citizen's reasonable expectation of privacy from aerial intrusion is currently determined more by state boundaries than by a unified national constitutional standard.

Data Management and Retention Protocols

The legal journey of a UAS-captured data points does not conclude when the drone lands. Rather, it enters a complex forensic lifecycle governed by increasingly stringent data sovereignty standards. In the United States, the 2026 Blue UAS Executive Order has fundamentally transformed the hardware and software landscape for domestic law enforcement. This mandate requires agencies to utilize only vetted UAS platforms, those manufactured within the United States or by approved allied nations, to ensure that sensitive surveillance data is not backdoored or transmitted to foreign servers. This shift is a direct response to national security concerns regarding data leakage, but it also has profound implications for individual privacy. By ensuring that data remains within a domestic, encrypted closed-loop system, agencies can more easily adhere to court-ordered chain-of-custody requirements ("2026 trends," 2026).

The storage of this data remains a significant point of constitutional friction. While the Fourth Amendment protects against unreasonable seizure, the long-term retention of non-evidentiary footage is viewed by privacy advocates as a form of perpetual seizure. In response, state legislatures in Florida and Illinois have implemented rigorous data purging protocols. Under these statutes, any UAS footage that does not contain specific evidence of a crime or is not part of an active investigation must be permanently deleted within a window typically ranging from 30 to 60 days (National Conference of State Legislatures [NCSL], 2023).

Comparing this to the international paradigm, the European Union's GDPR utilizes the principle of Data Minimization. Under Article 5 of the GDPR, personal data must be adequate, relevant, and limited to what is necessary in relation to the purposes for which they are processed. As noted by the NCSL (2023), for European drone operators, this means that even if a flight is legally authorized via a DPIA, the resulting footage must be redacted or anonymized in real-time if it captures third parties not involved in the investigation. The technical cost of this privacy by design is substantial, requiring onboard AI processors to blur faces and license plates before the data is even written to the drone's internal storage (Christoff & Patterson, 2025).

The forensic integrity of this data is additionally protected by metadata and telemetry logs. As Versaterm specifies, every second a drone is in flight, it records its precise GPS coordinates, altitude, motor temperature, and pilot control inputs ("2026 trends," 2026). In a court of law, this metadata serves as the digital fingerprint of the flight. If an agency fails to preserve this telemetry, or if the telemetry contradicts the officer's testimony regarding the drone's position, the defense may move for the spoliation of evidence. Under the Federal Rules of Evidence, the loss of this metadata can lead to the suppression of the entire video record, as the court cannot verify if the drone was operating within a plain view altitude or if it had secretly crossed into a vertical encroachment zone over private curtilage (Kilbane, 2019).

With a move toward a unified federal standard, the debate continues over whether the United States should adopt a GDPR-style mandatory anonymization for all police UAS feeds. Versaterm suggests that critics in law enforcement argue that such requirements would stifle the real-time utility of DFR programs ("2026 trends," 2026). Meanwhile, supporters argue that without such safeguards, the mosaic theory of surveillance will inevitably lead to a society where no movement in public remains truly private (Gips et al., 2025).

The integration of UAS into the daily fabric of urban life introduces a phenomenon often described by sociologists as the panoptic effect. Derived from Jeremy Bentham's eighteenth-century architectural design for a prison, the Panopticon, this theory suggests that when individuals believe they might be watched at any moment, they begin to self-regulate their behavior, effectively becoming their own overseers. As Enemark (2021) observes in the context of modern policing, the persistent presence of a DFR or an autonomous patrol unit creates a psychological environment where the overhead eye is perceived as omnipresent. This leads to a documented suppression of expression, where citizens refrain from exercising constitutionally protected rights, such as peaceful assembly, religious practice, or anonymous social interaction, out of a fear that their actions are being permanently recorded and algorithmically analyzed (Gips et al., 2025).

Public Anonymity

Historically, the Fourth Amendment has focused on the protection of private spaces, such as the home or the curtilage (*United States v. Dunn*, 1987). Sociologists, on the other hand, argue that a vital component of a free society is public anonymity, the ability to move through public spaces without being identified or tracked by the state. UAS technology, particularly when paired with re-identification (Re-ID) and gait-analysis algorithms, effectively strips this anonymity away. When a drone can follow a citizen across multiple city blocks and link their movements to a digital profile, the public nature of the street is fundamentally altered ("2026 trends," 2026). This persistent overwatch transforms the street from a space of social liberty into a space of state-managed compliance ("Marginalized community," n.d.).

The psychological burden of UAS surveillance is not distributed equally across society. Studies in predictive policing suggest that drones are often deployed more frequently in neighborhoods with lower socio-economic status or higher concentrations of marginalized communities. When these communities are subjected to constant aerial monitoring, it reinforces a surveillance feedback loop. Versaterm identifies that the data gathered by drones in these areas, such as frequent loitering or non-criminal street gatherings, is fed back into predictive algorithms, which then recommend even more drone patrols for those same areas ("2026 trends," 2026). This creates a psychological sense of being under a robotic occupation, which significantly erodes the legitimacy of law enforcement and damages community-police relations ("Marginalized community," n.d.).

The Loss of Human Intuition

From an operational psychology perspective, the shift toward tele-present policing through drones may lead to the de-skilling of the police force. When officers rely on a high-definition 4K zoom lens from 200 feet in the air to assess a situation, they lose the vital sensory cues, such as body language, tone of voice, and environmental context, that are only available through human-to-human interaction. As Enemark (2021) suggests, this distance can lead to cognitive detachment, where the remote pilot views the citizens on the ground as digital targets rather than community members. This detachment is a primary driver behind the ethical movement to ban weaponized payloads on domestic drones, as the psychological barrier between the officer and the use of force is dangerously lowered when that force is delivered via a remote interface (Christoff & Patterson, 2025).

To mitigate these psychological harms, many agencies are moving toward a model of radical transparency. This involves more than just having a privacy policy. It requires active community engagement through public flight maps and audit logs. By allowing citizens to see exactly why a drone was launched (for example, searching for a missing senior versus general patrol), agencies can begin to rebuild the social contract. However, as the National Conference of State Legislatures (2023) has observed regarding 2026 legislative sessions in states like Illinois and Virginia, transparency alone may not be enough. The ultimate psychological protection for the citizen may only be found in strict, warrant-based limitations that prevent the drone from becoming a permanent witness to public life (Virginia Law, n.d.).

As the courts move deeper into the 2020s, a new legal front has emerged that challenges the plain view doctrine by shifting the focus from optics (what the drone sees) to emissions (what the drone produces). While *California v. Ciraolo* (1986) and *Florida v. Riley* (1989) were decided based on the premise that aerial observation is a passive act, modern litigation in 2024 and 2025 has begun to categorize low-altitude UAS operations as a form of physical intrusion. This evolution is rooted in the property-based approach to the Fourth Amendment revived in *United States v. Jones* (2012), which holds that a search occurs when the government physically occupies private property for the purpose of obtaining information. Building on this theory, Kilbane (2019) argues that drones hovering at low altitudes over a home's curtilage constitute a physical trespass through their unique acoustic signatures and luminous interference. In several 2025 appellate rulings, defense attorneys successfully argued that drones hovering at altitudes of 50 to 100 feet over a home's curtilage constitute a physical trespass through their emissions (Liju, 2025). Unlike high-altitude fixed-wing aircraft, a quadcopter drone produces significant Acoustic signature (noise) and luminous interference (flashing strobe lights) required by FAA Part 107 for night operations (Federal Aviation Administration, 2025c).

Under modern interpretations of physical trespass, if a drone's rotors create a downwash of air that disturbs property or if its noise prevents the quiet enjoyment of a backyard, the drone has physically entered the curtilage, similar to an officer stepping over a fence. As Khalil (2023) notes, these sensory intrusions are increasingly viewed as a violation of the Ad Coelum Doctrine, an ancient common law principle stating that a landowner's property rights extend "up to the heavens". While the Supreme Court limited this in *United States v. Causby* (1946) to allow for high-altitude flight, the 2025 lower court trend suggests that the immediate reaches of the envelope above a home (the first 200 feet) remain the private domain of the resident (Kilbane, 2019).

A pivotal 2024 Ohio appellate case, *State v. Miller*, addressed whether a police drone hovering for twenty minutes over a suspect's driveway constituted an unreasonable seizure of the curtilage. The court ruled that while passing through the airspace might be permissible, stationary loitering at a low altitude interferes with the occupancy rights of the homeowner. This ruling suggests that time is a critical factor in Fourth Amendment reasonableness. The court noted that a drone's ability to remain fixed in space creates a constructive fence that prevents the homeowner from using their property without being subjected to state scrutiny. As Alvarado (2024) highlights, this loitering-as-search standard effectively bridges the gap between the mosaic theory of long-term tracking, and the trespass theory of physical presence (Kilbane, 2019).

The courts are also grappling with multi-spectral sensors that capture data outside the human visible spectrum. In 2025, the use of Optical Gas Imaging (OGI) and light detection and ranging (LIDAR) on police drones has been challenged under the *Kyllo v. United States* (2001) framework. Because these sensors allow police to see through certain materials or detect chemical signatures emanating from inside a structure, they go far beyond the naked eye observation permitted in *Ciraolo*. The emerging consensus in 2026 is that the moment a UAS utilizes any sensor other than a standard RGB camera, the plain view exception evaporates, and a warrant becomes a constitutional necessity ("2026 trends," 2026).

As courts wrestle with the vertical encroachment of UAS technology, a parallel movement has emerged within the 119th Congress of 2026 to establish a federal floor for aerial privacy. This legislative push is driven by the perceived inadequacy of the current state-level patchwork, which has left millions of citizens with inconsistent Fourth Amendment protections depending on their geographic location. The center of this storm is the proposed No-Fly Zones for Law Enforcement (NFZ-LE) Act of 2026, a bill that seeks to codify the above and below surface property rights for the digital age (Villasenor, 2013). The NFZ-LE Act proposes a radical shift in how navigable airspace is defined. Under this framework, any operation by a government UAS below 200 feet over private residential property would be classified as a categorical search. As Finklea (2023) argues, this creates a statutory bubble of privacy around the home to resolve the ambiguity of the plain view doctrine (NCSL, 2023). Conversely, Enemark (2021) notes that opponents in urban law enforcement argue such rigid limits would cripple DFR programs that require low-altitude flight to navigate urban canyons ("2026 trends," 2026).

Integral to the 2026 landscape is the maturation of the Blue UAS policy. As of 2026, the Department of Justice has implemented a total ban on the use of federal grant money for UAS manufactured in covered foreign jurisdictions. As the Federal Aviation Administration (2025c) outlines, this policy acknowledges that UAS are flying data nodes. The concern is that metadata and biometric signatures could be harvested to build a digital twin of American infrastructure. By mandating hardware sovereignty, the framework ensures the chain of custody for surveillance data is secured from the moment of capture ("2026 trends," 2026).

Perhaps the most forward-looking component of the 2026 regulatory shift is the requirement for algorithmic auditing. As UAS move from being human-piloted to autonomous processors, the reasonable suspicion standard is being transferred to the software. 2026 proposed standards require that any AI model used for behavioral detection or target re-identification undergo a third-party audit to identify and mitigate algorithmic bias ("2026 trends," 2026). In previous years, vendors shielded these algorithms as intellectual property (IP). A growing body of 2025 case law has however suggested that secret probable cause is an affront to due process. The new mandate requires that if an algorithm triggers a law enforcement intervention, the logic behind that trigger must be explainable and discoverable by the defense. This ensures that the Sixth Amendment right to confront one's accuser extends to the digital accusers flying overhead ("Marginalized community," n.d.).

As drones become essential tools for law enforcement, they have also become tools for criminal enterprise, used for smuggling contraband into prisons, industrial espionage, or disrupting public events. This has forced the development of counter-unmanned aircraft systems (C-UAS), or interdiction technology. Under the FY26 National Defense Authorization Act (NDAA), the IACP (2026) notes that state and local law enforcement have been granted expanded authority via the Safer Skies Act to neutralize drones deemed a credible threat to critical infrastructure and mass gatherings. As McKinnon (2026) points out, however, the method of neutralization carries significant legal weight:

- Electronic Interdiction (Jamming): Disrupting the radio frequency (RF) link between the drone and the controller. This is often viewed as a seizure of digital communications under the Wiretap Act, requiring a high threshold of proof that the drone is engaged in illegal activity (McKinnon, 2026).
- GPS Spoofing: Overriding the drone's navigation to force it to land. This represents a seizure of the aircraft itself, which, under FAA regulations, is treated as a civilian aircraft. Disabling an aircraft in flight is a federal crime, creating a conflict where local police might violate federal aviation law to enforce local safety (McKinnon, 2026).

The primary Fourth Amendment concern in C-UAS is the collateral seizure of data. Jamming or spoofing a drone's signal can inadvertently interfere with civilian cell signals, Wi-Fi networks, and even medical devices in the vicinity. If a police C-UAS operation causes a nearby civilian's drone to crash or disrupts their private communications, it creates a third-party seizure claim. Legal scholars argue that C-UAS protocols must include a least intrusive means test, requiring officers to attempt to identify and contact the pilot before resorting to electronic or physical interdiction (U.S. Department of Justice et al., 2020).

CONCLUSION

The evolution of UAS governance between 1986 and 2026 represents a full circle in American legal thought. A plain view standard that allowed the state to gaze down from the heights of the Cold War era (California v. Ciraolo, 1986) provided a start. Citizens have arrived at a point where the state's eyes can hover at windows, listen to whispers, and predict movements through mathematics. The balancing act of the next decade will not be found in a single court ruling or a single law, but in the continuous effort to harmonize the innovation of public safety with the immutability of the Bill of Rights. As Justice Scalia warned in *Kyllo*, the government must not be allowed to use technology to shrink the realm of guaranteed privacy (*Kyllo v. United States*, 2001).

The trajectory of UAS development, from the experimental Kettering Bug of 1917 to the sophisticated stealth and life-saving AED delivery systems of 2026, demonstrates a tool of unparalleled versatility (Govindarajan et al., 2025). The same efficiency that allows a drone to reach a search-and-rescue victim in remote terrain or a medical emergency in minutes also grants the state an unprecedented vantage point for surveillance (Starks, 2025). The challenge for modern governance is to protect the operational utility of drones, which has proven indispensable in medical, commercial, and tactical settings, while simultaneously fortifying the legal barriers against their potential for intrusiveness. The Fourth Amendment was written to protect the home as a sanctuary, whether that sanctuary remains intact in an age of 5,000-foot optical zooms and autonomous patrols is the defining legal challenge of today.

FUTURE RECOMMENDATIONS

While the use of UAS in law enforcement has demonstrated significant success in search and rescue operations, research remains limited on critical issues such as the safe operation of drones around citizens, standardized training, and public safety regulations. Given ongoing concerns related to privacy, ethics, and security, the development of clear regulatory frameworks is essential. According to Dolata and Schwabe (2023), police drone policies must be subject to the mandate of the force, ensuring fairness and legality in an area of public life while preserving law and order. This suggests that drone policies should be held to the same rigorous standards that officers must follow in person. As West et al. (2018) first observed, current research suggests that many of these policies are still developed without adequate public input (Dolata & Schwabe, 2023). As technology continues to advance, future research should examine how law enforcement agencies protect the Fourth and Fifth Amendment rights of the public while addressing the ethical standards governing autonomous policing.

REFERENCES

Abdullah, Q. A. (n.d.). GEOG 892- Geospatial applications of Unmanned Aerial Systems: Classification according to size. *PennState College of Earth and Mineral Science.* https://courses.ems.psu.edu/geog892/node/642

Alvarado, A. (2024). The mosaic theory in Fourth Amendment jurisprudence: The last bastion of privacy in a camera-surveilled world. *St. Mary's Law Journal*, *55*(3), 849–884. https://commons.stmarytx.edu/thestmaryslawjournal/vol55/iss3/5

Bendett, S., & Kirichenko, D. (2025, January 10). *Battlefield drones and the accelerating autonomous arms race in Ukraine.* Modern War Institute at West Point. https://mwi.westpoint.edu/battlefield-drones-and-the-accelerating-autonomous-arms-race-in-ukraine

California v. Ciraolo, 476 U.S. 207. (1986, May 19). *Justia U.S. Supreme Court.* https://supreme.justia.com/cases/federal/us/476/207

Campbell, C. (n.d.). *What is 'smart' technology?* Williams College Office for Information Technology. https://oit.williams.edu/ats-posts/what-is-smart-technology

Carpenter v. United States, 585 U.S. 296. (2018, June 22). *Oyez.* https://www.oyez.org/cases/2017/16-402

Christoff, T., & Patterson, Q. (2025, September). *Drones as first responders (DFR): National landscape, operational considerations, and future directions.* CNA Corporation. https://www.cna.org/reports/2025/09/Drones-as-First-Responders.pdf

Chula Vista Police Department. (n.d.). *Drone as first responder (DFR) operations and de-escalation dashboard.* Retrieved March 30, 2026 from https://app.powerbigov.us/view?r=eyJrIjoiNWNiYmI5ZTEtMzVjZi00NjNjLTkzNzgtNjg5NDQ3Yzk1NzEzIiwidCI6IjU2ZmM0NjE4LWM4M2QtNDAxZS1hNTMxLWZlYTEyNGI2NDZhNyJ9

City of Chula Vista. (n.d.). *Drone program.* https://www.chulavistaca.gov/departments/police-department/programs/uas-drone-program

Department of War. (n.d.). *Privacy, civil liberties, and transparency.* https://pclt.defense.gov/DIRECTORATES/Privacy-and-Civil-Liberties-Directorate/Civil-Liberties

Dolata, M., & Schwabe, G. (2023, October). Moving beyond privacy and airspace safety: Guidelines for just drones in policing. *Government Information Quarterly*, *40*(4), 101874. DOI: 10.1016/j.giq.2023.101874

Drone delivery FAQs. (n.d.). Amazon. https://www.amazon.com/gp/help/customer/display.html?nodeId=T3jxhuvPfQ629BOIL4

Dukowitz, Z. (2026, January 3). *Selfie drones: A comprehensive guide for drone pilots.* Drone Pilot Ground School. https://www.dronepilotgroundschool.com/selfie-drone

Enemark, C. (2021, June 19). Armed drones and ethical policing: Risk, perception, and the Tele-present officer. *Criminal Justice Ethics*, *40*(2), 124–144. DOI: 10.1080/0731129X.2021.1943844 PMID: 34413570

Federal Aviation Administration. (2025a, August 6). *Beyond visual line of sight (BVLOS): Normalizing drone operations in the national airspace*. https://www.faa.gov/newsroom/beyond-visual-line-sight-bvlos

Federal Aviation Administration. (2025b, May). *Drone integration: concept of operations.* https://www.faa.gov/uas/resources/policy_library/Drone-Integration-Concept-of-Operations-May-2025.pdf

Federal Aviation Administration. (2025c, March 19). *Remote ID for drone pilots: Compliance and enforcement standards.* https://www.faa.gov/uas/getting_started/remote_id

Finklea, K. (2023). Law enforcement and technology: Use of unmanned aircraft systems. *Library of Congress.* https://www.congress.gov/crs-product/R47660

Florida v. Riley, 488 U.S. 445. (1989). *Justia U.S. Supreme Court.* https://supreme.justia.com/cases/federal/us/488/445

Forsyth County, GA and Avive Solutions celebrate a life saved by citizen volunteer through Avive's 4 minute community program. (2025). Avive. https://www.avive.life/news/forsyth-county-avive-life-saved

Fudge, T. P., & Ferebee, S. S. (2024). Search and Rescue drones: Balancing security & privacy with preserving life. In Shah, I., & Jhanjhi, N. (Eds.), *Cybersecurity issues and challenges in the drone industry* (pp. 108–127). IGI Global., DOI: 10.4018/979-8-3693-0774-8.ch005

Gillis, A., Lutkevich, B., & Earls, A. (2024). *What is a drone (UAV)?* TechTarget. https://www.techtarget.com/iotagenda/definition/drone

Gips, M., Goldenberg, P., & Grantham, D. A. (2025). A response to the concerns of civil liberties groups on law enforcement's use of uncrewed aerial systems. https://www.scribd.com/document/849957571/Drone-White-Paper

Govindarajan, B., Jaganraj, R., Srinivasan, V., & Kumaran, T. (2025). Evolution of UAV technology: From early innovations to future horizons. In Mellal, M. (Ed.), *Innovations and developments in Unmanned Aerial Vehicles* (pp. 53–94). IGI Global., DOI: 10.4018/979-8-3693-8462-6.ch004

Hazardous. (n.d.) Merriam-Webster. https://www.merriam-webster.com/dictionary/hazardous

Illinois General Assembly. (2024, June 14). Freedom from Drone Surveillance Act (725 ILCS 167). https://www.ilga.gov/Legislation/ILCS/Articles?ActID=3520&ChapterID=54

Information Commissioner's Office. (n.d.). Video surveillance (including guidance for organisations using CCTV). https://ico.org.uk/for-organisations/uk-gdpr-guidance-and-resources/cctv-and-video-surveillance/guidance-on-video-surveillance-including-cctv

International Trade Administration. (n.d.). Unmanned aircraft systems. https://www.trade.gov/unmanned-aircraft-systems

Johnson, A., Egan, E., & Londoño, J. (2023, January 9). Police tech: exploring the opportunities and fact-0checking the criticisms. *Information Technology & Innovation Foundation.* https://itif.org/publications/2023/01/09/police-tech-exploring-the-opportunities-and-fact-checking-the-criticisms

Khalil, R. F. (2023). Aerial trespass and the Fourth Amendment. *Michigan Law Review, 121*(7), 1269–1299. https://repository.law.umich.edu/mlr/vol121/iss7/4. DOI: 10.36644/mlr.121.7.aerial

Kilbane, S. M. (2019, January 30). Drones and Jones: Rethinking curtilage flyover in light of the revived Fourth Amendment trespass doctrine. *Capital University Law Review*, *42*, 249–285. https://www.capitallawreview.org/article/7273-drones-and-jones-rethinking-curtilage-flyover-in-light-of-the-revived-fourth-amendment-trespass-doctrine

Koerner, M. R. (2015). Drones and the Fourth Amendment: Redefining expectations of privacy. *Duke Law Journal*, *64*(6), 1129–1172. https://scholarship.law.duke.edu/dlj/vol64/iss6/3

Kyllo v. United States, 533 U.S. 27. (2001). *Oyez*. https://www.oyez.org/cases/2000/99-8508

Lexington Sheriff's Department. (n.d.). *Taking flight: meet the team controlling the drones at LCSD.* https://joinlcsd.com/taking-flight-meet-the-team-controlling-the-drones-at-lcsd

Liju, A. (2025, September 5). *Recovering metadata & telemetry from drones & legal implications of seizing UAV evidence*. Cyint Technologies. https://www.cyint.in/post/recovering-metadata-telemetry-from-drones-legal-implications-of-seizing-uav-evidence

Marginalized community surveillance. (n.d.). Sustainability directory. https://lifestyle.sustainability-directory.com/area/marginalized-community-surveillance/resource/1

McKinnon, M. E. (2026, January 5). Counter-drone technology coming to your town. *Fox Rothschild: Plane-ly Spoken.* Fox-Rothschild. https://plane-lyspoken.foxrothschild.com/2026/01/05/counter-drone-technology-coming-to-your-town

NASA. (n.d.). *Ingenuity Mars helicopter*. https://science.nasa.gov/mission/mars-2020-perseverance/ingenuity-mars-helicopter

National Conference of State Legislatures. (2023, March 27). *Current unmanned aircraft state law landscape*. https://www.ncsl.org/transportation/current-unmanned-aircraft-state-law-landscape

Office of Community Oriented Policing Services. (2020). *Drones: A report on the use of drones by public safety agencies – and a wake-up call about the threat of malicious drone attacks*. U.S. Department of Justice. https://portal.cops.usdoj.gov/resourcecenter/content.ashx/cops-w0894-pub.pdf

Pandian, M. P. (2010). RFID issues. *RFID for Libraries: A Practical Guide* (p. 133-149). https://doi.org/ DOI: 10.1016/B978-1-84334-545-9.50005-7

Parten, J. L. (2022, June). *Police use of drone surveillance technology.* Law Enforcement Management Institute of Texas (LEMIT). https://hdl.handle.net/20.500.11875/4139

Redmond, Washington. (n.d.). *Drone program.* https://www.redmond.gov/2161/Drone-Program

Regulation (EU) 2016/679 of the European Parliament and of the Council of 27 April 2016 on the protection of natural persons with regard to the processing of personal data and on the free movement of such data, and repealing Directive 95/46/EC (General Data Protection Regulation). (2016). *Official Journal of the European Union*, L119, 1–88. https://gdpr-info.eu/art-5-gdpr

Ridderbusch, K. (2025, August 25). Case study: How Dunwoody Police use drones to speed response and improve officer safety. *Police (Springfield)*, *1*, •••. https://www.police1.com/drones/case-study-how-dunwoody-police-use-drones-to-speed-response-and-improve-officer-safety

Rodman, D. (2010, September). Unmanned aerial vehicles in the service of the Isreal Air Force: "They will soar on wings like eagles.". *Middle East Review of International Affairs (Online)*, *14*(3), 77–87.

Ryan, M. (2025, September 22). *Lockheed Martin unveils stealth combat drone.* AVWeb. https://avweb.com/aviation-news/lockheed-martin-new-stealth-combat-drone

Sauser, M. K. (2025, July-August). Unmanned aircraft and the revolution in operational warfare: Preparing the U.S. Army for the age of unmanned systems. *Military Review*, •••, 54–64. https://www.armyupress.army.mil/Journals/Military-Review/English-Edition-Archives/July-August-2025/Unmanned-Aircraft-Revolution

Sayler, K. (2015, June). *A world of proliferated drones: A technology primer.* Center for a New Americal Security. https://drones.cnas.org/wp-content/uploads/2016/03/CNAS-World-of-Drones_052115.pdf

Schmerber v. California, 384 U.S. 757. (1966). *Justia U.S. Supreme Court.* https://supreme.justia.com/cases/federal/us/384/757

Shavers, B. (2013). Physical investigations. *Placing the suspect behind the keyboard: using digital forensics and investigative techniques to identify cybercrime suspects.* (p. 53-84)(. https://doi.org/DOI: 10.1016/B978-1-59-749985-9.00003-4

Starks, M. A. (2025, November 19). Integration of drone-delivered AEDs into emergency response: A multi-center trial. *Cardiovascular Business.* https://cardiovascularbusiness.com/topics/clinical/heart-rhythm/drones-deliver-aeds-first-time-united-states

Termanini, R. (2023). *Drone delivery methods and how to communicate with the destination.* Biomedical Defense Principles to Counter DNA Deep Hacking., DOI: 10.1016/B978-0-323-99914-4.00004-7

2026. *trends every public safety leader should watch.* (2026). Versaterm. https://www.versaterm.com/resource/2026-trends-every-public-safety-leader-should-watch

United States v. Causby, 328 U.S. 256. (1946). *Justia U.S. Supreme Court.* https://supreme.justia.com/cases/federal/us/328/256

United States v. Dunn, 480 U.S. 294. (1987). *Jusita U.S. Supreme Court.* https://supreme.justia.com/cases/federal/us/480/294

United States v. Jones, 565 U.S. 400. (2012). *Oyez.* https://www.oyez.org/cases/2011/10-1259

U.S. Customs and Border Protection. (2023, August 18). *Air and marine operations' unmanned aircraft system.* https://www.cbp.gov/about/history/cbp-20-20-establishment/air-and-marine-operations-unmanned-aircraft-system

U.S. Department of Homeland Security. (2025, July). *TechNote: Drone as first responder.* https://www.dhs.gov/sites/default/files/2025-07/25_0708_st_dfrtn.pdf

U.S. Department of Justice. Federal Aviation Administration, Department of Homeland Security, & Federal Communications Commission. (2020, August). *Advisory on the application of Federal laws to the acquisition and use of technology to detect and mitigate Unmanned Aircraft Systems.* https://www.faa.gov/sites/faa.gov/files/uas/resources/c_uas/Interagency_Legal_Advisory_on_UAS_Detection_and_Mitigation_Technologies.pdf

Villasenor, J. (2013). Observations from above: Unmanned aircraft systems and privacy. *Harvard Journal of Law & Public Policy, 36*(2), 457–517. https://journals.law.harvard.edu/jlpp/wp-content/uploads/sites/90/2013/04/36_2_457_Villasenor.pdf

Virginia Law. (n.d.). *Code of Virginia § 19.2-60.1. Use of unmanned aircraft systems by public bodies; search warrant required.* https://law.lis.virginia.gov/vacode/19.2-60.1

West, J. P., Klofstad, C. A., Uscinski, J. E., & Connolly, J. M. (2018). Citizen support for domestic drone use and regulation. *American Politics Research, 47*(1), 119–151. DOI: 10.1177/1532673X18782208

What are carbon emissions & why do they matter? (n.d.). Constellation. https://www.constellation.com/energy-101/energy-innovation/what-are-carbon-emissions.html

What is an unmanned aircraft system (UAS)? (n.d.). Federal Aviation Administration. https://www.faa.gov/faq/what-unmanned-aircraft-system-uas

Wolfrum, R. (2015, September). Combatants. *Max Planck Encyclopedias of International Law (MPIL).* https://opil.ouplaw.com/display/10.1093/law:epil/9780199231690/law-9780199231690-e272

Zipline, Pfizer and BioNTech collaboration paves the way for automated, on-demand delivery of first mRNA COVID-29 vaccines in Ghana. (2021, November 11). Pfizer. https://www.pfizer.com/news/press-release/press-release-detail/zipline-pfizer-and-biontech-collaboration-paves-way

2026. *trends every public safety leader should watch.* (2026). Versaterm. https://www.versaterm.com/resource/2026-trends-every-public-safety-leader-should-watch

KEY TERMS AND DEFINITIONS

Ad coelum Doctrine: An ancient common law principle stating that a landowner's property rights extend "up to the heavens." In modern litigation, this doctrine is used to argue that low-altitude UAS operations constitute a physical trespass when they interfere with the immediate reaches of the airspace above a home (Kilbane, 2019).

Aerial Surveillance: near invisibility of investigators for suspect mobile surveillance from the air covering a greater land space (Shavers 2013).

Beyond Visual Line of Sight (BVLOS): Drone operations where the aircraft is operated past the pilot's ability to maintain direct visual contact. Under the 2026 FAA updates, these operations are increasingly facilitated by cellular networks and satellite links to ensure safe integration into the national airspace (Federal Aviation Administration, 2025a).

Blue UAS: A federal mandate and hardware sovereignty policy requiring law enforcement to utilize only vetted UAS platforms manufactured domestically or by approved allied nations to ensure evidentiary integrity and data security ("2026 trends," 2026).

Carbon Emissions: is the admission of carbon into the atmosphere through CO2 molecules from fuel, gasoline, coal, or wood that is burned ("What are carbon emissions," n.d.).

Civil Liberties: are the fundamental rights and freedoms protected by the Constitution of the United States (Department of War, n.d.).

Combatants: is attributed to members of the regular armed forces of a State, who manifest the Sate's monopoly on the use of legitimate forces in the pursuit of its interests. Combatants along have the right to take direct part in hostilities and may not be prosecuted for their participation in hostilities (Wolfrum, 2015).

Counter-Unmanned Aircraft Cystems (C-UAS): Technology and protocols such as electronic jamming, GPS spoofing, or kinetic capture, used by law enforcement to detect and neutralize unauthorized drones deemed a threat to safety (McKinnon, 2026).

Curtilage: The area immediately surrounding and associated with a home that receives the same Fourth Amendment protections as the home itself. In modern drone litigation, this definition is being expanded to include a vertical curtilage conflict, where low-altitude UAS flights are challenged as an unconstitutional physical intrusion into the immediate reaches of the private airspace above the home (United States v. Dunn, 1987).

Data Minimization: A privacy principle requiring that personal data captured by UAS be adequate, relevant, and limited to only what is strictly necessary for the intended public safety objective (GDPR, 2016).

Data Protection Impact Assessment (DPIA): An exhaustive forensic self-audit required under European law to prove that a drone surveillance operation is legally authorized, proportionate, and necessary (GDPR, 2016).

Fifth Amendment: A section of the U.S. Constitution providing protections against self-incrimination and guaranteeing due process. It governs the procedural fairness of how drone-captured communicative evidence is managed (Constitution Annotated, n.d.).

Fourth Amendment: The part of the U.S. Constitution that protects citizens against unreasonable searches and seizures and requires warrants to be supported by probable cause (Constitution Annotated, n.d.).

Hazardous: involving or exposing one to risk. as of loss or harm ("Hazardous," n.d.).

Intrusiveness: infringing on a person's civil rights and unlawful searches and seizures (Parten, 2022).

Mosaic Theory: A legal theory suggesting that while individual public observations are legal, the pervasive and tireless collection of data points over time creates a comprehensive mosaic of private life. In the context of UAS, this long-term tracking constitutes a search that the Supreme Court cautioned against in its landmark ruling (Carpenter v. United States, 2018).

Panoptic Effect: A psychological phenomenon where the perceived omnipresence of surveillance causes individuals to self-regulate and suppress constitutionally protected behaviors. In modern policing, the persistent presence of drone patrols creates an environment where citizens act as their own overseers out of a fear of being constantly recorded (Enemark, 2021).

Return On Investment (ROI): is a measure used to evaluate the efficiency of an investment or to compare the efficiencies of number of investments. The ROI is calculated by dividing the benefit of the investment by the cost of the investment and the result is expressed as a percentage or ratio (Pandian, 2010).

Smart technology: is the integration of telecommunication, networked technology, computing, automation, and adaptive functionality into items that previously did not have such potential. Remote operation or access is a hallmark of smart devices (Campbell, n.d.).

Surveilled marginalized communities: refers to the monitoring or collecting of data directed at populations already disadvantaged by systemic inequalities, often under guise of security, efficiency, or compliance ("Marginalized community," n.d.).

Telemetry Data: A digital fingerprint of a UAS flight, recording second-by-second logs of GPS coordinates, altitude, and pilot inputs used to authenticate the chain of custody in legal proceedings ("2026 trends," 2026).

Unmanned Aircraft Systems (UAS): air vehicles and associated equipment that do not carry a human operator but is operated remotely or fly autonomously. A UAS generally consists of an aircraft with no pilot on board, has a remote station, a command-and-control link, and a payload specific to the intended application/operation, which often includes specialized cameras or sensors to collect data for analysis (International Trade Administration, n.d.).

Chapter 9
Regulating Automated Fraud:
Addressing Cybersecurity Risks in the Digital Age

Jyoti
http://orcid.org/0009-0009-9435-438X
School of Law, Bennett University, Greater Noida, India

Naresh Prajapati
http://orcid.org/0000-0002-0752-3651
School of Law, Bennett University, Greater Noida, India

Pradeep Kulshreshtha
School of Law, Bennett University, Greater Noida, India

Anwesha Ghosh
http://orcid.org/0000-0003-4167-2121
Amity Law School, Amity University, Mumbai, India

ABSTRACT

The new era of digital technology has brought along different cybersecurity issues, whereby automation and AI have now become the attackers' sophisticated tools, but also the protectors. By the year 2025, AI-based automated fraud with deepfakes, synthetic identity theft, and phishing has so quickly advanced that traditional security systems are struggling to cope with it. This chapter provides a critical discussion on the legal regulatory landscape of fraud ecosystems and the algorithms that threaten privacy and trust. It analyses global and Indian regulatory measures, highlights the issue of algorithmic opacity, and advocates a multi-layered governance model that combines human oversight, explainable AI, and adversarial AI defences. It has been stressed that, to counter AI-driven fraud, the coming of ethical, adaptive, and internationally harmonised regulations will not only protect innovation but also the digital ecosystems that are going to be around in the future.

DOI: 10.4018/979-8-3373-7660-8.ch009

INTRODUCTION

The swift incorporation of automation and Artificial Intelligence (AI) into current cyber environments has drastically changed aspects of fraud, security risks, and digital governance in cyberspace. Initially aimed at improving workflow and protecting digital transactions, AI technologies have gradually been used as potent weapons by cybercriminals. To achieve their objectives by 2025, fraudsters will utilise the power of AI largely by carrying out many scam activities that are difficult to detect and huge in size, through tricks like pretending to be someone famous using deepfake technology, coming up with fake but almost real identities, and running large-scale phishing attacks very quickly and silently, targeting unsuspecting victims (Ali et al., 2025).

The AI threats that are now taking over the digital world rely on highly sophisticated algorithms that mimic human activities to such a high degree that they go undetected by the security measures and the detection systems of the past. One application of this is the use of deepfake technology to impersonate a CEO and thereby have a fraudulent transaction approved (Ehtesham, 2025). Another example is synthetic identities, which mix genuine and invented data to commit account-opening fraud, resulting in considerable losses for banks and consumers. On the other hand, the production of phishing attacks via AI has become so sophisticated that the perpetrators can send out a volume of personalised emails and messages simultaneously, thereby enhancing the chance of deceiving the victims ("Synthetic identity fraud," 2025). The latest statistics show that there is a frightening rise of such fakes: the number of cases with AI involvement has risen sharply, and the number of phishing reports has increased by more than 46%. Phishing emails generated by AI have now accounted for more than 82% of all phishing attempts. Moreover, social engineering methods that incorporate AI have almost tripled, and along with that, a bogus call centre has been employing AI for real-time voice modulation and multilingual communications. A survey of financial institutions reveals that more than 90% of fraud cases they encounter are linked to AI technologies, and identity fraud through synthetic means is the fastest-growing area of financial crime. In different parts of the world, the total amount of money lost every year due to AI scams is already in the billions of dollars, and this figure is likely to see a steep increase in the future (Martin, 2025).

AI's dual role as a fraud perpetrator and a fraud-fighting tool at the same time points to the paradox in security governance. Current regulatory and technical controls often go obsolete since criminal innovations are always faster than the pace at which the finance and cybersecurity sectors are making huge investments in AI-based detection systems to keep pace. Hence, it is critically important that there are adaptive, ethical, and multi-layered approaches to regulation and technological measures to properly protect digital ecosystems in the new era. These challenges must look at how governance models, policy reforms, and advancing technologies interact with the changing landscape of automated fraud through AI in 2025 and beyond (Butler, 2025).

An examination of the global and Indian contexts of automated fraud is thus warranted, focusing on the development of AI governance frameworks such as the proposed U.S. Artificial Intelligence Accountability Act 2025, the EU's AI Act, and ongoing reforms to India's cybersecurity policy. The analysis has trans, sectoral applicability, assessing how generative AI, cross-border digital flows, and the innovation of new policies implicate state and organisational capacities in regulating digital risk and accountability.

Figure 1. AI-driven fraud incidents

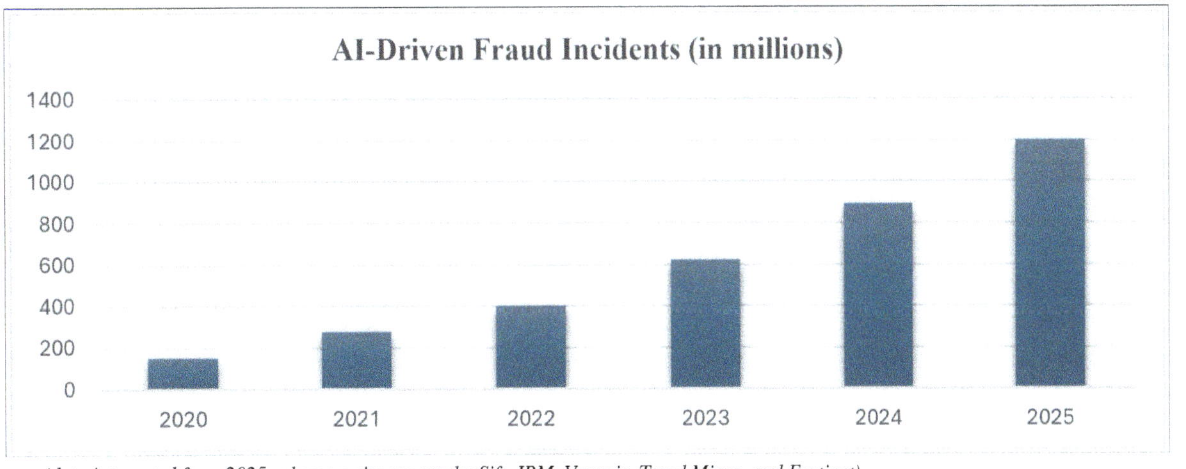

(data integrated from 2025 cybersecurity reports by Sift, IBM, Varonis, Trend Micro, and Fortinet)

Figure 1 depicts the significant growth of global AI-related cyber fraud incidents anticipated between 2020 and 2025. This growth is catalysed by technological advancements in generative AI, enabling fraudsters to replicate and automate fraud schemes, from deepfake impersonations to synthetic identity fraud to AI phishing. These frauds are much more sophisticated and move at a pace where legacy detection programs are challenged to flag risks. The result is financial loss and degraded trust in digital platforms. The data is synthesised from several leading cybersecurity companies and research organisations and showcases an urgent need for flexible legal frameworks and governance models to support technological exploitation.

RESEARCH METHODOLOGY

A qualitative doctrinal research method is adopted, centring on a thorough investigation of secondary data, which is composed of legal texts, regulatory frameworks, policy documents, and current scholarly and industry reports on AI-powered automated fraud and cybersecurity, mainly. The purpose is to critically assess the international and Indian legal approaches to AI fraud by employing a comparative and thematic analysis to reveal the regulatory trends, algorithmic transparency difficulties, and governance voids. The methodology allows for a detailed comprehension of the existing legal treatment of the new AI danger and gives guidance to the proposal of adaptable and efficient digital governance in the continuously changing cyber environment (Bhat, 2020).

CONCEPTUAL AND THEORETICAL FRAMEWORK

A conceptual and theoretical framework plays a significant role in clarifying the concepts that influence a specific issue, in this case, automated fraud during the time of artificial intelligence. The framework presents the perspective to examine the creation of fraud, the behaviour of algorithms, the failure of traditional systems, and the principles that should guide regulation. Rather than merely recounting the events, this forms the groundwork for comprehension of the more profound forces behind AI facilitated cons: algorithmic autonomy, dual-use risks, algorithmic opacity, cyber risk theory, social engineering, and governance models. The mentioned concepts not only guide but also connect the reader to the practical fraud cases and the larger legal and technological theories (Salawu et. al., 2023).

Automation and Autonomous Systems

Automation is the term that refers to such digital systems that can carry out tasks with no or minimal human assistance, and it is the main factor behind the fraud ecosystem that is driven by AI today. In 2025, automated systems are not plain rule-based programs anymore; they are adaptive, self-improving, and decision makers at the speed of human fraudster pace that cannot even be matched. Autonomous AI tools can generate fake identities, impersonate humans, mimic real voices, and conduct up to hundreds of coordinated fraud attempts in seconds. The human-controlled scam-to-machine-operated fraud transition has not only increased cybercrime in terms of scale but also sophistication. And one of the main reasons why automation is so powerful is its ability to operate at scale. The power of a single algorithm can be used to its fullest extent in the case of sending thousands of personal phishing messages, running multiple synthetic identity applications, or even manipulating digital systems across borders in real-time. A whole criminal gang that used to disappear and fly under the radar can now easily be replaced by a single person using automated software. The high-volume aspect of the activity is what makes it very difficult for the traditional fraud detection systems to handle, as they were designed for the detection of occasional, human-paced attacks rather than the constant machine-driven activity (Kotagiri & Bammidi, 2024).

The autonomous systems are even capable of adapting and learning. The present malware and botnet can even monitor the defences that will successfully detect them, thereby changing their patterns to eliminate future detection. This property of self-learning makes automated fraud very difficult to contain. The systems are so human in their interaction that the victims cannot tell if it is a real person or an automated scam. They also point to the necessity of regulatory frameworks being updated to recognise how automation has radically altered the crime scenario in digital systems (Wazzan et al., 2021).

The Dual-Use Theory of Artificial Intelligence

The dual-use theory indicates that artificial intelligence has two polar identities. In fact, the same technology that enhances security, increases efficiency, and facilitates digital transformation can be used to execute cybercrime at unprecedented levels. This dual-use quality sits at the core of the automated fraud proposition in 2025. AI tools developed for neutral or helpful purposes, where the intent is to enrich the end user (i.e., voice synthesis, generative images, automated conversations, behaviour modelling, data patterns), are readily repurposed into tools for deception, coercion, and financial crime. This creates tension for regulators: promote innovation and growth in AI without exposing individuals and institutions to automated fraud (Ueno, 2023).

The dual-use characteristics of AI can be observed in various aspects of cybercrime. Deepfake technology, developed for entertainment and creative purposes, is being used in ways to fake a CEO's voice, impersonate family members, and generate realistic "digital arrest" video scams against victims. The dual-use aspect of AI presents a further challenge for legal and policy systems. Regulatory structures typically assume an easy demarcation between hazardous and beneficial technologies, but the pervasive nature of AI blurs this line. One tool can be both productive and harmful depending on how it is deployed, leading lawmakers to rethink conceptions of accountability, risk, and oversight. Regulations cannot simply prohibit the technology, as there is industry dependence on the technology, and they must develop adaptable governance structures that anticipate misuse, demand transparency, and necessitate protective measures such as human oversight, explainability, and auditing (Vaseashta, 2025).

Algorithmic Opacity and Black -Box Decision- Making

Algorithmic opacity is a term used for the feature of artificial intelligence systems that lack transparency in their decision-making processes. Many of today's AI models, particularly those in deep learning, have the characteristics of "black box" operation. They analyse an enormous volume of data and yield results, yet the reasoning behind those results remains ambiguous to the users, regulators, and even the developers. The lack of transparency, in this case, becomes a great issue in automated fraud, since, for instance, fraud detection, risk assessment and identity verification these days very much depend on the algorithmic systems. When the systems do not give reasons for their actions, it then becomes more difficult to spot weaknesses, make corrections, or decide who is liable in case of damage (Chiao, 2019).

Explainable AI (XAI) as a Governance Requirement

Explainable AI, commonly known as XAI, is gaining prominence as a major necessity in the governance of AI, particularly in critical domains like fraud detection, financial transactions, identity verification, and cybersecurity. The stakes are very high as people's rights and finances may be at risk due to automated systems making the decisions. Regulators thus are insisting that the AI models justify their decisions in an intelligible manner (Potluri, 2025).

Digital Vulnerability and Cyber Risk Theory

The cyber risk theory describes how digital environments today are an interconnected ecosystem in which vulnerabilities appear at a rate that is difficult to manage. Fraud thrives well in such environments since an attack on one platform can spread to other platforms very fast. With the increasing level of complexity of digital systems, even minor vulnerabilities, including old-fashioned software, poor authentication, or incorrectly set up APIs, become a point of entry into large-scale AI-based fraud (McKay, 2026).

Behavioural and Social Engineering Theories

Behavioural and social engineering theories have to do with the way human psychology steers vulnerability in digital spaces. Automated fraud succeeds not simply because of the advancement in technology, but because it targets predictable human behaviours. Social engineering is based on the concept that people can be manipulated into revealing sensitive information, making payments, or granting access when they believe the request to be legitimate. In 2025, social engineering uses AI to shift to an even more precise and personalised form of manipulation, making fraud attempts far more convincing and much harder to detect.

Finally, social engineering theories outline why awareness and digital literacy are essential to cybersecurity governance. No amount of automation or regulation can fully immunise against the human factor. The objective is clear: behavioural resilience becomes as vital as technical defences (Montañez et al., 2020).

Global Digital Governance and Multi-Level Regulation

Global digital governance refers to the shared rules, standards, and cooperative mechanisms through which countries and institutions manage digital risks. Automated fraud has made this more important than ever. Because AI-driven scams operate across borders, no single country can regulate or contain them alone. A deepfake scam created in one country, hosted on servers in another, and executed against victims in a third shows how global the problem has become. Multi-level regulation tries to address this by building coordination across national, regional, and international layers. The first big complication is that different countries regulate AI and cybersecurity differently. These differences ensure disparate levels of protection and let fraudsters take full advantage of the resulting loopholes to operate from jurisdictions with weak oversight. Furthermore, multilevel regulation underlines the need for coordination among jurisdictions. The prosecution of automated fraud cases involves multiple legal systems. Coordinated frameworks, such as mutual legal assistance treaties (MLATs), cybersecurity MoUs, and rapid digital evidence protocols, are useful to investigators in accessing information more rapidly. Without these mechanisms, automated fraud investigations would stall at jurisdictional boundaries (Hanisch et al., 2023).

Figure 2. Indexed growth of AI-based fraud categories in the digital ecosystem, 2020–2025

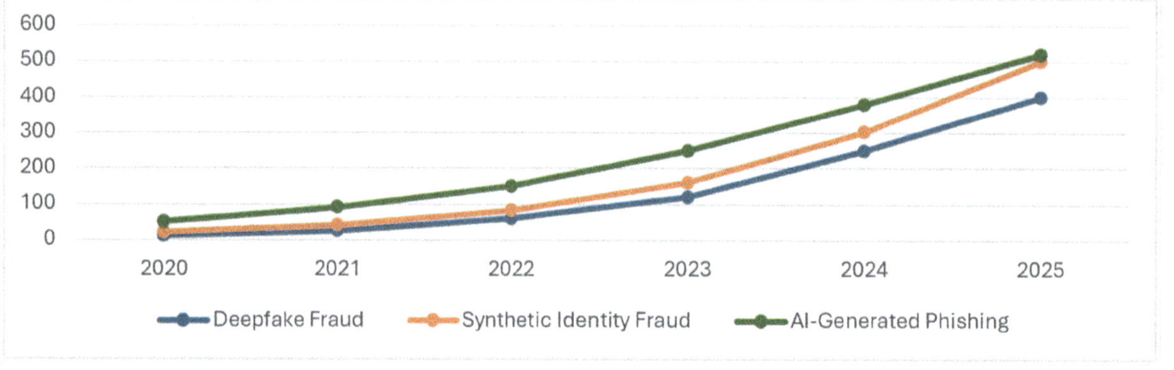

(data integrated from major threat intelligence reports, including IBM X-Force Threat Intelligence Index 2025, Trend Micro GenAI risk forecasts, and Sift Digital Trust Index Q2 2025)

Figure 2 indicates an increasing trend in AI-driven fraud methods between 2020 and 2025. Deepfake-based scams, synthetic identity fraud, and AI-generated phishing demonstrate tremendous growth, especially beyond 2022, since generative AI tools have become more accessible and powerful. The indexed values provide a comparison of the relative increase in each type of fraud, with phishing remaining the most widespread but exhibiting the least acceleration from the two others, synthetic identity fraud and deepfake scams. This pattern reflects criminals' increasing reliance on automation, the expanding attack surface within digital ecologies, and the constraints of using traditional systems for fraud detection. All in all, the trend indicates an urgent need for adaptive regulation, cross-border coordination, and strong AI governance frameworks (Muhly et al., 2025).

INTERNATIONAL AND DOMESTIC CYBERSECURITY ENVIRONMENT

Rapid digitalisation, cross-border data flows, and the accelerating use of artificial intelligence by defenders and cybercriminals alike shape the 2025 cybersecurity environment. Automated fraud has emerged as one of the big global threats that operate beyond national boundaries, is fast-evolving, and exploits the differences between regulatory systems. Both the international and domestic cybersecurity landscapes need to be understood in analysing the laws' response to AI-enabled fraud and where the gaps remain (Jones, 2023).

Global Cybersecurity Landscape

Fast-growing generative AI tools, cross-border data flows, and the growth of automated fraud networks drive the global cybersecurity environment in 2025. Today's cybercriminals utilise deepfakes, synthetic identity engines, and bot-driven phishing systems across multiple countries at machine speed. Many of these attacks originate in one jurisdiction, are run on servers in another, and victimise people worldwide. Thus, it has become challenging for enforcement. There is an added layer of anonymity brought about by cloud infrastructure, encrypted messaging, and digital payment platforms created in this very complex international environment (World Economic Forum, 2025).

Countries react to this with different approaches: from the strong regulatory EU AI Act, imposing strict standards on high-risk AI systems, with particular emphasis on transparency, explainability, and human oversight, to more enforcement-based approaches in the United States, anchored in actions against deceptive or unsafe AI systems taken by agencies such as the FTC and SEC. Hybrid models combine cybersecurity standards with AI ethics guidelines, as in Singapore, Japan, and Australia. Global regulation remains uneven despite the beginning of cooperation using networks like Europol, Interpol, and UN cybercrime groups. These gaps let fraud networks move their operations to weaker jurisdictions, and stronger, harmonised international governance against AI-enabled crime is needed (Cancela-Outeda, 2024).

Figure 3. Frequency of major AI-enabled cyberattack types globally

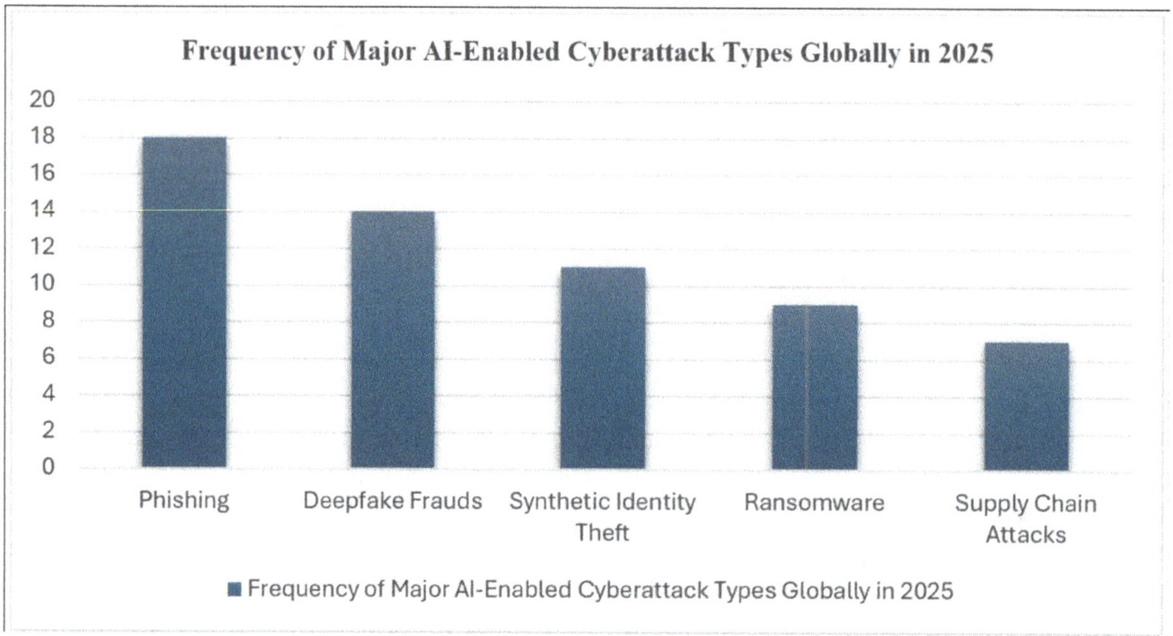

(data integrated from So Safe Cybercrime Trends Report, 2025; World Economic Forum, 2025; NIST AI Cyberattack Analysis, 2025)

Data shown in Figure 3 points toward an increasing sophistication and diversification of cyber threats made possible using artificial intelligence. This underlines the urgent need for globally implemented advanced measures regarding cybersecurity and adaptive regulatory frameworks.

Table 1. Comparison of global AI cybercrime regulatory policies (2024-2025)

Jurisdiction	Main Legislative Act	Year	Focus Area	Enforcement	Challenges
US	AI Account Act	2025	Transparency and Auditing	Federal Trade Commission	Coordination and Compliance
EU	AI Act	2025	Risk Management and Rights Protection	European Commission	Enforcement across member States
India	Cyber Security Framework	2024-2025	Digital Infrastructure Protection	Ministry of Electronics and Information Technology	Capacity and Coordination

(data integrated from U.S. Artificial Intelligence Accountability Act, 2025; European Union AI Act, 2025; Indian Ministry of Electronics & IT Draft Cybersecurity Policies, 2024-25)

Table 1 compares three major global AI cybercrime regulatory policies of the United States, the European Union, and India. In this table, each jurisdiction's key legislative act, year of enactment, focus areas of cybersecurity, enforcement bodies, and notable challenges are presented. Such a comparison will provide a deeper understanding of the different regulatory approaches, underlining how transparency, risk management, and implementation vary among them. It serves to place in context the increasingly global effort to fight AI-driven cyber threats with appropriate and coordinated legal responses.

India's Domestic Cybersecurity Environment

India's domestic cybersecurity landscape in 2025 is characteristic of rapid digital growth, juxtaposed with increased vulnerability to AI-enabled fraud. With the world's largest digital payment ecosystem and extensive Aadhaar-linked services, India has emerged as one of the world's most significant targets for deep fake scams, synthetic identity fraud, automated phishing, and voice cloning-based extortion. The existing legal framework, the Information Technology Act, 2000, and the IT Rules, 2021, provide the basic structure for cyber offences, intermediary liability, and digital platform regulation, but these laws have been drafted long before generative AI became mainstream. Consequently, India has developed regulatory lacunae in areas related to algorithmic manipulation, misuse of biometric data, deep fake-based impersonation, and automated bot-driven cybercrime ("Understanding India's cybersecurity policy frameworks," 2025).

In a bid to strengthen domestic protection, India has been gradually updating its governance approach. The Digital Personal Data Protection Act, 2023, introduces stronger safeguards around personal data, something quite crucial given that synthetic identity fraud relies heavily on stolen or leaked information. Agencies like CERT-In have expanded their mandate to include rapid reporting of AI-related cyber incidents, mandatory log retention, and coordination with banks, telecom companies, and government platforms during large-scale cyberattacks (Chaturvedi, 2025). The United States has enacted a comprehensive framework which governs both artificial intelligence operations and cybersecurity protection efforts. The proposed Artificial Intelligence Accountability Act together with its legislative initiatives mandates organisations to provide algorithmic transparency while assessing risks and establishing responsibility for their automated decision-making systems. The Federal Trade Commission (FTC) and the Cybersecurity and Infrastructure Security Agency (CISA) from the United States work together with private technology companies to identify and prevent AI-based fraud activities. The United States model shows more established procedures for enforcement and cooperation between government and private companies than India's developing regulatory system (Sokler et al., 2024).

Recent cases, like *ED v. Dubai Digital Arrest Syndicate in 2025*, along with increasing incidents of deepfake impersonation, reveal how domestic threats are getting connected with global cybercrime networks. The regulatory spotlight has thus fallen on India's need for enhanced digital identity protection, improved verification mechanisms, and collaboration with international agencies. Even as the progress is in the offing, India's domestic cybersecurity environment still needs clearer rules on AI accountability, biometric safety, automated fraud detection standards, and cross-platform data sharing frameworks if the scale and speed of AI-driven cybercrime are to be handled effectively (Khanna, 2025).

Key Case Laws Illustrating the Cybersecurity Environment

AI Deepfake Fraud Cases in India (2025)

In India, deepfake technology was reported on as a major tool for financial fraud in 2025. Criminals, for instance, made use of face-swap and voice-cloning software to come up with very realistic videos of people, such as employees and executives and further used these altered clips for requesting money transfers or passing digital verification checks. Such incidents proved that deepfakes had already become so advanced that they could easily overcome the most basic security checks and were able to take advantage of the communication based on trust. The cases of 2025 were a wake-up call for banks and other financial institutions, as well as government agencies, to revamp their verification systems, invest in deepfake-detection tools, and incorporate multi-layer authentication for the prevention of identity theft (Josey, 2025).

SEBI v. Algorithmic Manipulators (2024)

In this situation, the *Securities and Exchange Board of India (SEBI)* acted against brokers and traders who were misusing automated algorithmic trading systems to manipulate the market. During the inquiry, it was discovered that these market participants had written codes for their algorithms to perform high-speed order and cancellation, order creation at the same time, thus causing misrepresentation in the form of fake volume and supply and demand signals, which were misleading. SEBI, after this case, also revised its regulatory framework for algorithmic trading and, at the same time, strengthened real-time monitoring to ensure more efficient detection of abnormal automated trading patterns (Shekhar, 2025).

Challenges in the Cybersecurity Ecosystem

The cybersecurity ecosystem has several important issues due to the advances of AI-enabled fraud that have become more sophisticated and harder to detect. One of the principal challenges is the speed of automated attacks: fraud systems built with machine learning, deepfake generators, and synthetic identity engines function much more quickly than human investigators or conventional security products. Institutions have difficulty keeping up with automated attacks because their validation, evidence collection, and cross-checks are still oriented toward slower, manual versions of crime. As a result, fraud practitioners can take advantage of a minor vulnerability and expand their attack across multiple platforms within seconds (Soni et al., 2023).

Another substantial issue is that the law and the laws it interprets are often fragmented. Cybercrime often operates across borders, but regulations do not. Each country has its own level of data protection, accountability of artificial intelligence, digital evidence, and platform liability. Fraud operations exploit this process by routing calls and payments through jurisdictions with weak enforcement laws. Even within a country, sector-specific laws, for example, banking, telecommunications, digital identity, and AI products, often exist in silos. These divided laws lead to contradictions and inconsistent outcomes, which criminals take advantage of, making coordinated governance difficult and slow to respond to significant fraud events. There are also notable resource and technological infrastructure limits. Many institutions are not equipped with leading AI-detection tools, deepfake detection systems, and real-time monitoring platforms (Admass et al., 2024).

Lastly, the ecosystem is impeded by a shortage of cybersecurity professionals with adequate training. The skills needed to identify and analyse AI, synthesised fraud, like machine learning forensics, algorithm audits, and biometric / risk assessment, are still emerging. Organisations rely on old detection models, which cannot detect synthetic profiles or identify AI-synthesised phishing. The human skill gap, coupled with rapid technological change, makes it difficult for governments and institutions to be able to maintain a consistent defence capability. These challenges highlight the extreme urgency of needing updated laws, further digital resilience, AI-enabled forensic capability, and improved collaboration between local and international agencies. Without a legislated solution, the cybersecurity ecosystem will always be behind and vulnerable to the scale, speed, and sophistication of automated fraud (Jha, 2025).

Significance of a Cybersecurity Contextual Comparison

A contextual comparison of the cybersecurity environment is important because AI-enabled fraud does not remain in a single nation. Automated scams, impersonations through deep fakes, and synthetic identity networks operate across multiple jurisdictions concurrently. Different standards on AI accountability, data protection, and procedures for handling digital evidence in each respective country provide cybercriminals with opportunities to exploit weaknesses. Analysing global or domestic frameworks will identify gaps and illustrate whether and how those gaps affect national security, financial systems, and public safety. A comparative approach also spotlights best practices. Leading regions like the European Union, the United States, and parts of the Asia Pacific have developed sophisticated models for AI governance, market accountability, and cyber incident reporting. These could provide the necessary lessons for countries like India while building their own regulatory structures. Comparative study ensures that new laws are not made in isolation but are tuned to global standards, hence allowing for easier collaboration with international agencies. At the end, a comparative perspective strengthens cross-border enforcement. Cybercrime investigations increasingly depend upon access to foreign servers, digital logs, cloud accounts, and international payment systems. The more varied legal systems are understood, the better the facilitation of evidence, sharing, coordination with global regulators, and building joint responses in the case of large-scale fraud incidents. In an age where AI-driven crimes spread faster over borders, a comparative analysis of cybersecurity is crucial to establishing a resilient, future-ready governance framework that combats sophisticated threats (Zhang, 2024).

ROBOTIC FRAUD SYSTEMS AND LOOPHOLES

The robotic fraud systems refer to an automated network that operates fraud without any human involvement, using AI, machine learning, and bots. These systems run large-scale scams by combining deepfake tools, identity, generation engines, phishing bots, and automated transaction scripts. They operate at machine speed, enabling them to execute thousands of attempts in mere seconds. Fraudsters program these tools in such a way that they could adapt themselves, observe security patterns, and keep modifying to avoid detection. Because of this, automated fraud has become much faster, complex, and dangerous compared to conventional manual scams (Furnell, 2017).

The biggest reason for their success in robotic systems is the loopholes present in digital ecosystems. Weak KYC systems, outdated mechanisms for verification, a lack of coordination across platforms, and a lack of real-time monitoring make the fraud operation much more powerful. Many times, banks, fintech platforms, and government portals operate in fragmentation, where fraud detected on one platform does not reach another platform. It is this delay that bots use to their advantage while creating synthetic identities, deepfake impersonation, and routing funds instantly using automated laundering. These structural weaknesses make robotic fraud systems unstoppable, making their regulation and investigation quite challenging (Tanimu & Abada, 2025).

Automated Botnets and Identity Farms

Large-scale automated botnets and identity farms are the backbones of modern robotic fraud systems. Botnets are large networks of infected or remotely controlled devices, computers, phones, servers, and

IoT devices that execute commands automatically without the user's knowledge. In financial and cyber fraud, these botnets are programmed for high-volume tasks; the creation of fake accounts, the generation of login attempts, scraping personal data, and the launching of coordinated phishing or credential stuffing attacks. Because thousands of devices can act at once, botnets overwhelm security systems, repeatedly testing verification barriers in search of which combinations of data successfully pass fraud filters. This level of automation gives fraudsters unprecedented power, especially when institutions still rely on outdated or manual detection processes (Lefoane et al., 2025).

Identity farms work in close connection with these botnets. Using AI models, these farms create realistic synthetic identities in bulk, complete with fabricated photographs, digital documents, behaviour patterns, and even simulated browsing histories. Quite often, criminals combine fragments of real data, part of Aadhaar, PAN formats, email patterns, or social media details with AI-generated content to generate apparently legitimate identities. Using those identities, automated tools apply for loans, open bank accounts, activate SIM cards, create social media profiles, or register on fintech platforms. Because identity farms work 24/7, a single system can generate hundreds or thousands of identities in a day (Schmitt & Flechais, 2024).

Such botnets and identity farms are dangerous because they combine speed, scale, and stealth. Bots operate around the clock without human fatigue, test millions of variations in credentials, and adapt instantly when a method does not work. Identity farms then use those validated combinations and spread them across digital ecosystems before institutions can respond. Together, they form an extremely efficient fraud pipeline that bypasses traditional security systems and takes advantage of fragmented regulations. As these technologies continue to improve, identifying fake digital activity is becoming even more complex, making future cybersecurity require even stronger AI-based verification and cross-platform cooperation (Wu et al., 2024).

Deepfake-Driven Impersonation Systems

Deepfake-based impersonation systems rely on the most sophisticated AI technologies to produce human-like voices, mimic facial expressions, and generate full video appearances to a very high degree of accuracy. With the help of these tools, deceitful individuals can assume the identities of others, such as police officers, bankers, judges, corporate executives, or even family members, in a manner that appears genuine to the targeted person. The integration of voice cloning and face-synthesis technologies has turned impersonation into one of the most powerful avenues of robotic fraud. The transition from text-based scams to the use of deceptive, immersive, real-time audio and video has rendered many victims unable to differentiate between genuine communication and artificial intervention (Klepper, 2025).

Pornographic deepfake extortion cases have been a major issue in India over the years 2024-2025, and it was one of the most important events in the country. The scammers got hold of a woman's normal pictures from different social media platforms and then used AI to creatively put her face on XXX videos. After making the videos, the criminals would threaten the victims that they would show the video to the victims' families, workmates, and public platforms unless a certain amount of money was paid. This kind of deepfake impersonation not only impersonates an individual but also turns the person's digital presence into a weapon targeting that person's dignity, reputation, and emotional vulnerability. The quickness, as well as the total automation with which these videos are made, and the use of deepfake tools, show the psychological dimension of fraud they have extended (Furizal et al., 2025).

Deepfake impersonation systems, for instance, make the most of the weaknesses in institutional verification systems. Up to now, a lot of banks, fintech firms, and service providers have been using old-fashioned methods like voice-based authentication, selfie video verification, or appearance-matching techniques. These methods very often fail when an AI impersonation can mimic the original person very accurately. A scammer might create several deepfake versions and run them through the verification process several times until one pass. This is how it might result in unauthorised transactions, account takeovers, or falsely verified identities. The other issue that comes with deepfake impersonation is the huge scale they could operate. Fraud networks can change their identities instantly and perform multilingual impersonation campaigns in different areas (Diel et al., 2025). Daily, fake calls from so-called bank managers, police officers, or human resources are introduced as an example of impersonation becoming a mass-scale operation rather than a single case, as shown in Table 2.

Table 2. Deepfake examples

Type of Deepfake	Target	Purpose	Example
Voice Cloning	Corporate Employees	Fake Payment Authorisation	UK CEO Case (2023)
Video Deepfake	Government/Authority	Coercion and Intimidation	Singapore Govt Deepfake Scam
Face Swap Videos	Individuals	Extortion	India Deepfake Extortion Cases
Real-Time Deepfake Calls	Bank Officials	Fund Transfer	Hong Kong Bank Heist

(data integrated from CERT-In advisories, State Cyber Police reports, documented deepfake fraud incidents from 2024–2025)

Automated Phishing and Behavioural Manipulation Engines

AI-enabled fraud has been perpetrated through automated phishing and behavioural manipulation engines. Large language models, behavioural analytics, and automated delivery tools are used by these systems to create volumes of personalised phishing messages. Traditional phishing relied on generic emails that were sent to thousands of people, hoping a few would respond. AI-driven phishing engines analyse a person's social media activity, browsing habits, communication style, location, or recent online behaviour to create messages that feel highly specific and believable. This shift away from mass phishing toward precision-targeted manipulation has made detection significantly harder (Rao & Pais, 2017).

Modern phishing engines use a combination of automated data gathering and adaptive message generation. Bots scrape publicly available information like recent posts, likes, job roles, friends, and even writing tone. AI models then convert that information to customised phishing scripts. Instead of "Click here to update your bank account," AI engines send messages like, "We noticed an unusual login attempt near your college campus at 5:10 pm today. Please verify your identity." Since the message is reflective of the victim's context, they respond sooner. These engines create thousands of such messages every hour, constantly modifying vocabulary and structure to bypass spam filters and detection algorithms (Qabajeh et al., 2018).

A second layer of these systems involves behavioural manipulation, where AI predicts when and how a user is most likely to respond. Fraud programs bots to track the pattern of online activity of the victim, what time they are active, what device they use, how fast they reply, and what type of alerts they usually open. Once patterns are identified, phishing attempts are sent at the exact moment the victim is least attentive or most emotionally vulnerable. This heightens the chances that the victim will act without giving it a second thought, whether it be clicking a malicious link, entering banking details, or sharing OTPs and documents (Kim & Im, 2025).

Most of the attacks today involve AI-generated voices or chat responses, while the bots can handle an entire conversation from end to end. The moment the victim initiates a response, the automatic system further keeps interacting by adjusting the tone and responses in real time, which creates the illusion of speaking with a real person, thereby further lowering suspicion.

Another major issue is that automated phishing engines evolve continuously. While a security system blocks one type of message, the AI instantly generates alternative versions. Some phishing systems make use of feedback loops: if a victim does not respond, the AI optimises the message structure, urgency, or emotional tone for better effectiveness. That self-correcting behaviour makes them more efficient than human scammers and faster than most detection technologies (McKenna, 2024).

All in all, automated phishing and behavioural manipulation engines are revolutionising digital fraud through a combination of psychological insight and machine automation. They have found vulnerabilities in email security, rely on the publicly available digital footprint, and scale at levels and speeds no conventional cybersecurity system currently maintains. Their rise underlines the urgent need for stronger behavioural authentication, AI-driven detection tools, and public awareness across the board to reduce vulnerability to highly personalised digital manipulation (Manky & Baram, 2025).

Synthetic Identity Generation Loopholes

Synthetic identity generation has emerged as one of the most sophisticated and undetectable forms of AI-enabled fraud. In this process, fraudsters combine pieces of actual personal information with AI-generated details to establish new digital identities that seem valid. Unlike stolen identities, synthetic identities are partially fabricated and thus partially real, which makes it very challenging for institutions to raise an alarm. These generally include AI-generated photos, fake addresses, manipulated ID numbers, and contrived digital histories combined in such a manner that can easily pass through outdated verification systems. Because the "person" does not actually exist, tracing responsibility becomes extremely hard. These arise due to weaknesses in Know Your Customer (KYC) frameworks, fragmented databases, and inconsistent verification standards across institutions. AI tools take advantage of this by creating thousands of identity permutations and automatically testing these through bot-driven registration systems. Once one combination works, the same synthetic identity is then duplicated across banks, fintech applications, telcos, and even e-commerce sites. The repetition makes this identity acquire an artificial "history," thereby strengthening its credibility over time (Gu et al., 2025).

Synthetic identities are particularly dangerous because they circumvent the most critical assumption of digital security that every identity maps to a real human. Fraudsters use these profiles to get loans, open bank accounts, activate SIM cards, or get digital wallets in their name. They keep these accounts responsibly serviced for months to gain trust; it is only after they have a credible digital footprint that they pull off large-scale fraud, such as loan defaults, chargebacks, or money mule operations. Because the identity is not linked to any real individual, law enforcement agencies face an extraordinary challenge in tracking the fraud back to a source. The explosion of synthetic identity fraud in 2024-2025 has been directly linked to generative AI tools that automate this entire process. These systems unceasingly test multiple KYC portals to find out which institutions have weaker verification checks. At the end, synthetic identity generation loopholes have shown the shortcomings of legacy KYC systems in an AI-driven environment. The ability to automate identity creation, testing, and deployment at scale has turned synthetic identities into a core component of robotic fraud networks. The solution to this problem lies in stronger biometric authentication, cross-platform data integration, fraud-detection AI, and uniform national-level verification standards that can prevent false identities from gaining systemic acceptance (Diel et al., 2025).

Machine-Speed Transaction Routing and Laundering

Machine-speed transaction routing and laundering refer to the use of automated systems, bots, and AI tools for moving money across digital platforms at a pace much faster than human monitoring can keep up with. For traditional financial fraud, many steps must be performed manually: logging into accounts, transferring funds, and waiting for clearances. But with AI-enabled laundering, this is no longer an issue. Automated scripts can transfer money between multiple accounts, wallets, and crypto platforms within mere seconds; the movement is virtually untraceable in real time. The goal is simple: move stolen or fraud-generated funds so fast and across so many channels that by the time authorities catch the fraud, it is already dispersed (Crispin, 2025).

These automated systems employ smurfing methods whereby large sums are broken down into smaller-than-regulatory-reporting-threshold amounts. The AI tool automatically splits the sum of money stolen into hundreds of micro-transfers, automatically routing it through wallets, prepaid cards, gaming platforms, crypto mixers, or international fintech apps. What used to take hours or days now happens in less than a minute. Bots monitor the success rate for transactions and instantly reroute failed transfers using backup accounts. Such agility provides criminals with ways around security layers dependent on watching unusual patterns or detecting high-risk transfers ("Smurfing in money laundering," 2025).

Crypto-based laundering has become a major element of machine-speed routing: AI bots convert stolen money into digital assets such as stablecoins, privacy coins, or tokenised vouchers, scattering them across multiple blockchain wallets. Some automatically use cross-chain bridges, making forensic tracking all but impossible. Fraud rings often combine such tools with automated identity farms, harnessing synthetic identities to open dozens of temporary wallets or accounts used exclusively for money flow. By the time law enforcement tries to freeze the funds, the trail has already shifted across multiple platforms, often beyond national jurisdiction. Meeting this challenge will take real-time transaction monitoring, cross-platform alert systems, stronger Anti-Money Laundering (AML) algorithms, and coordination among regulators if fraud proceeds are to be prevented from disappearing in an instant into complex digital networks (M, 2025).

Lack of Cross-Platform Coordination

One of the greatest reasons why robotic fraud systems succeed is the lack of coordination between banks, fintech platforms, telecom operators, social media companies, and crypto exchanges. Each platform has its own verification and security process; however, these systems seldom share information in real time with each other. When the fraud gets transmitted, this piece of information mostly stays restricted to one institution, giving automated fraud networks enough time to move money, switch identities, or delete traces before any collective response is possible. This delay becomes a huge loophole that AI-driven scams use quite effectively (Godwin, 2025). Fraudsters use this gap to their advantage. A synthetic identity rejected by one bank may sail through onboarding at another, simply because their databases do not talk to one another. Similarly, money stolen through UPI or wallet fraud is often routed through a chain of apps before the victim's bank raises an alert. This lack of integrated fraud-alert systems lets machine-speed routing, deepfake impersonation, and botnet activity cascade across platforms without setting off immediate alarms. Even telecom and social media platforms, playing a part in OTP delivery and identity verification, stay compartmentalised, which helps fraudulent accounts remain active for a longer time (Shoemaker, 2025).

Aggregately, poor cross-platform coordination has created a fragmented digital ecosystem in which institutions detect fraud much more slowly than automated systems can act. This systemic gap in coordination enables the rapid scaling of most robotic fraud techniques, whether deepfake impersonations, phishing engines, or synthetic identities. A far stronger, unified, and real-time coordination framework across financial, digital, and communication platforms is required to lower the success rate of AI-enabled fraud in 2025 and beyond (Wegner et al., 2023).

NEW GOVERNANCE MODELS AND ETHICAL REGULATION

The recent rise in automated and AI-driven fraud has thus brought to the forefront a series of fundamental gaps in the traditional models of cyber governance clear need for new and adaptive frameworks of regulation. Laws written for manual or less sophisticated crimes in cyberspace are frankly out of place with such rapid developments as deepfakes, synthetic identities, and real-time automated phishing attacks. Thus, governance will need to be flexible, proactive, and insert ethical standards into this "AI paradox," wherein AI systems are both defenders and enablers of fraud ("Impact of Artificial Intelligence," 2023).

Algorithmic Transparency and Auditability

Algorithmic transparency and auditability have gained a central place in the regulation of systems driven by AI applications, particularly those concerning financial transactions, proof of identity, or automated decisions. Advanced fraud rings use opaque algorithms in trading bots, KYC systems, and content filters to find weak points that regulators cannot see. New governance frameworks compel organisations to reveal how their algorithms work, what data they use, and how they make decisions. This new approach, from regulating outcomes to regulating technology itself, helps ensure that automated tools do not operate in a "black box" where mistakes, manipulation, or partiality stay hidden. Transparency also helps regulators examine whether an AI system follows ethical standards, avoids misuse, and ensures fairness in digital processes (Gao et al., 2025).

A key example that reinforces this need is *SEBI v. Algorithmic Manipulators, 2024,* in which unregistered trading bots manipulated stock prices by executing high-speed automated trades. Without transparency, regulators could hardly detect unusual patterns until significant damage had already been caused. This case pushed SEBI to insist on mandatory bot registration, real-time disclosures, and audit trails for algorithmic trading platforms (Joshi, 2025).

Platform Accountability and Duty of Care

Platform accountability and the duty of care have become central elements of modern AI governance because digital platforms now play a direct role in enabling or preventing fraud. Many AI tools, such as voice-cloning models, deepfake generators, automated chat systems, and content personalisation engines, are built and distributed by large technology companies. When these tools are misused for impersonation, extortion, or large-scale fraud, platforms cannot simply shift blame to users. New approaches to regulation demand that AI developers and digital intermediaries embed safety layers into their technology. These include watermarking, real-time misuse detection, identity verification for high-risk models, and clear guardrails that limit how AI can be used. The core idea is that platforms must take proactive responsibility instead of reacting only after harm occurs (Price, 2021).

This is reflected in FTC v. AI Technologies (2025), in which the U.S. Federal Trade Commission held an AI company liable for failing to take adequate steps to prevent its generative tools from being used in impersonation scams. It also emphasised that AI platforms must consider high-risk misuse and embed protective mechanisms into their models. It also marked a signal to the rest of the international regulators, including India and the EU, that the platforms bear legal and ethical responsibility to monitor harmful activity, disclose system risks, and cooperate with law enforcement when investigations are undertaken. This means that, in the context of the rise in deepfake fraud and automated phishing campaigns, platform accountability can ensure that the responsibility for digital safety is shared across the entire technological ecosystem and not left solely to users or law enforcement agencies ("FTC proposes new protections," 2024).

Multi-Stakeholder Coordination on Fraud Prevention

Multi-stakeholder coordination has emerged as one of the most important elements in modern AI governance, given that no single institution can handle AI-enabled fraud on its own. Pieces of information from banks, fintech platforms, telecom operators, social media companies, and government agencies are all exploited by fraud networks. When these systems operate in silos, automated scams move faster than any response time of a particular platform. New models of governance, therefore, emphasise real-time data sharing, joint fraud-alert systems, and cross-platform verification networks. Such a multi-stakeholder coordination enables suspicious identities, deepfake misuse, bot-driven money routing, or abnormal behavioural patterns to be flagged across multiple platforms at once, hence closing the gap that AI-driven fraud thrives on. This has acquired momentum in the wake of the AI-driven fraud incident surge in India in 2025, covering deepfake extortion, synthetic identity operations, and machine-speed transaction routing. To this end, regulators are pushing for integrated fraud registries, unified KYC protocols, and collaborative monitoring systems that connect financial institutions, communication networks, and cybercrime cells. Multi-stakeholder coordination strengthens digital resilience by ensuring that fraud alerts travel as fast as the automated threats they seek to stop (De Donà, 2025).

Ethical AI Design and Misuse Safeguards

Ethical AI design has become key in reducing the misuse of advanced technologies, as fraud networks increasingly rely on generative models, deepfake tools, and automated decision systems. Ethical design requires developers to build AI systems with safety checkpoints from the beginning rather than treating misuse as an afterthought. It means running risk assessments, monitoring model behaviour, stopping damaging outputs, limiting high-risk functionality, and keeping sensitive capabilities out of the reach of unverified users. Misuse guards like watermarking, output traceability, content authenticity verification, and identity-based access controls minimise the opportunities for impersonation, the creation of synthetic identities, and automated manipulations. If integrated at the design stage, these safeguards can limit how easily their tools can be turned into instruments of fraud (Jedličková, 2024).

Stronger Data-Privacy and Identity Protection Laws

With AI-driven fraud increasingly relying on large volumes of scraped or leaked personal data, stronger data privacy and identity protection laws are becoming crucial. After all, synthetic identities, deepfake impersonation, behavioural phishing, and automated fraud systems all require access to someone's photos, ID details, voice samples, location data, and browsing patterns. Weak data protection gives fraud networks the raw material they need to build highly convincing fake identities or manipulate victims. For this reason, new governance models focus on limiting unnecessary data collection, enforcing strict consent-based processing, and holding platforms accountable for data leaks or misuse. When data exposure reduces, the capacity of fraud systems to generate realistic deepfakes or personalised phishing messages also drops significantly (Kulhari, 2018).

CONCLUSION AND POLICY IMPLICATIONS

The development of artificial intelligence functions as a dual force which helps and hinders the ongoing battle against digital fraud. AI technologies use advanced data analytics together with automated monitoring systems to improve fraud detection capabilities while simultaneously providing criminals with new methods to execute cyberattacks. The research shows how AI-enabled fraud presents both regulatory problems and technological obstacles which governments must overcome.

Different countries have developed unique methods to handle regulatory matters. The United States has created operational systems and value exchange systems which enable enforcement organisations to work together, but India needs to build its regulatory systems and policy methods for handling the upcoming AI dangers which will emerge in the future.

The research results indicate that better regulatory cooperation needs to happen together with technological defense improvements and international partnerships to reduce financial crimes which use artificial intelligence. The development of transparent AI governance frameworks together with advanced cybersecurity systems and international regulatory collaboration needs to become the primary focus for policymakers to protect against the rising danger of automated fraud in the digital economy.

REFERENCES

Admass, W. S., Munaye, Y. Y., & Diro, A. A. (2024). Cyber security: State of the art, challenges and future directions. *Cyber Security and Applications*, *2*, 100031. DOI: 10.1016/j.csa.2023.100031

Ali, S., Wang, J., & Leung, V. C. M. (2025, June). AI-driven fusion with cybersecurity: Exploring current trends, advanced techniques, future directions, and policy implications for evolving paradigms- A comprehensive review. *Information Fusion*, *118*, 102922. DOI: 10.1016/j.inffus.2024.102922

Bhat, P. I. (2020, January 23). Doctrinal legal research as a means of synthesizing facts, thoughts, and legal principles. In *Idea and Methods of Legal Research* (pp. 143-168). DOI: 10.1093/oso/9780199493098.003.0005

Butler, R. (2025, February 7). *2025 Predictions: How will the interplay of AI and fraud play out?* Thomson Reuters Institute. https://www.thomsonreuters.com/en-us/posts/corporates/2025-predictions-interplay-fraud-ai

Cancela-Outeda, C. (2024, October). The EU's AI act: A framework for collaborative governance. *Internet of Things : Engineering Cyber Physical Human Systems*, *27*, 101291. DOI: 10.1016/j.iot.2024.101291

Chaturvedi, S. (2025, March 5). The DPDP rules unveiled: Progress, shortcomings and the road ahead. *Harvard Journal of Law & Technology*. https://jolt.law.harvard.edu/digest/the-dpdp-rules-unveiled-progress-shortcomings-and-the-road-ahead

Chiao, V. (2019, June 20). Fairness, accountability and transparency: Notes on algorithmic decision-making in criminal justice. *International Journal of Law in Context*, *15*(2), 126–139. DOI: 10.1017/S1744552319000077

Crispin, M. (2025, October 16). *Fraud Detection with Machine Learning & AI*. SEON. https://seon.io/resources/fraud-detection-with-machine-learning

De Donà, M. (2025, December). Multistakeholder governance through epistemic authority: exploring the role of the Climate and Clean Air Coalition in the global climate regime. *International Environmental Agreements Politics Law and Economics*. DOI: 10.1007/s10784-025-09708-7

Diel, A., Lalgi, T., Mellis, F. S., Teufel, A., & Bäuerle, A. (2025, December). The harm of deepfakes: A scoping review of deepfakes' negative effects on human mind and behavior. *AI & Society*. Advance online publication. DOI: 10.1007/s00146-025-02774-0

Ehtesham, H. (2025, December 25). *AI cyberattack statistics 2025: What the data warns us about*. All About AI. https://www.allaboutai.com/resources/ai-statistics/ai-cyberattack

FTC proposes new protections to combat AI impersonation of individuals. (2024, February 15). [Press release]. Federal Trade Commission. https://www.ftc.gov/news-events/news/press-releases/2024/02/ftc-proposes-new-protections-combat-ai-impersonation-individuals

Furizal, N., Ma'arif, A., Maghfiroh, H., Suwarno, I., Prayogi, D., Kariyamin, N., Lonang, S., & Sharkawy, A. (2025). Social, legal, and ethical implications of AI-Generated deepfake pornography on digital platforms: A systematic literature review. *Social Sciences & Humanities Open, 12*, 101882. DOI: 10.1016/j.ssaho.2025.101882

Furnell, S. (2017). The evolving landscape of technology-dependent crime. In McGuire, M. R., & Holt, T. J. (Eds.), *The Routledge Handbook of Technology, Crime and Justice* (pp. 65–77). Routledge., DOI: 10.4324/9781315743981-4

Gao, M., Peng, J., & Wang, H. (2025, December). Algorithmic transparency, financial stability, and enterprise digital transformation. *Finance Research Letters, 86*(B), 108481. DOI: 10.1016/j.frl.2025.108481

Godwin, F. O. (2025, April 26). The role of Artificial Intelligence and Robotic Process Automation (RPA) in fraud detection: Enhancing financial security through automation. *International Journal of Finance, 10*(3), 80–100. DOI: 10.47941/ijf.2671

Gu, H., Chandrasegaran, S., & Lloyd, P. (2025, January 27). Synthetic users: Insights from designers' interactions with persona-based chatbots. *Artificial Intelligence for Engineering Design, Analysis and Manufacturing, 39*, e2. DOI: 10.1017/S0890060424000283

Hanisch, M., Goldsby, C. M., Fabian, N. E., & Oehmichen, J. (2023, July). Digital governance: A conceptual framework and research agenda. *Journal of Business Research, 162*, 113777. DOI: 10.1016/j.jbusres.2023.113777

Impact of artificial intelligence on fraud and scams. (2023, December). Stop Scams UK. https://www.pwc.co.uk/forensic-services/assets/impact-of-ai-on-fraud-and-scams.pdf

Jedličková, A. (2024, August). Ethical approaches in designing autonomous and intelligent systems: A comprehensive survey towards responsible development. *AI & Society, 40*(4), 2703–2716. DOI: 10.1007/s00146-024-02040-9

Jha, A. C. (2025, June 10). A comprehensive review of challenges in cybersecurity systems across digital infrastructures. In A. C. Jha & S. K. Dandapat (Eds.), *CyberFusion: The Strategic Integration of Cybersecurity for Digital Transformation in Tech Environment* (pp. 16-25). QTanalytics. DOI: 10.48001/978-81-980647-2-1-2

Jones, E. (2023, Spring). Digital disruption: Artificial intelligence and international trade policy. *Oxford Review of Economic Policy, 39*(1), 70–84. DOI: 10.1093/oxrep/grac049

Josey, V. (2025, August 10). Deepfake: The new face of financial fraud. *Deccan Herald.* https://www.deccanherald.com/opinion/deepfake-the-new-face-of-financial-fraud-3674748

Joshi, N. (2025, February 4). *Sebi takes its investor-protection crusade to algo trading turf.* Mint. https://www.livemint.com/market/sebi-framework-algo-algorithmic-trading-rules-retail-investors-api-market-11738681654852.html

Khanna, R. (2025, June 2). ED slaps PMLA in 1,500-crore digi-arrest fraud run from Dubai. *The Times of India*. https://timesofindia.indiatimes.com/city/kolkata/ed-slaps-pmla-in-1500-crore-digi-arrest-fraud-run-from-dubai/articleshow/121576275.cms

Kim, T., & Im, I. (2025, January). Understanding users' AI manipulation intention: An empirical investigation of the antecedents in the context of AI recommendation algorithms. *Information & Management, 62*(1), 104061. DOI: 10.1016/j.im.2024.104061

Klepper, D. (2025, July 28). Scammers are impersonating CEOs and Trump officials using AI deepfakes. *AP News.* https://apnews.com/article/artificial-intelligence-deepfake-trump-espionage-hack-scammers-da90ad1e5298a9ce50c997458d6aa610

Kotagiri, A., & Bammidi, T. R. (2024). Sustainable safeguarding: Implementing fraud defense systems for authorized push payments through robotics process automation and AI integration. [Conference paper]. In P. Whig, N. Silva, A. A. Elngar, N. Aneja, & P. Sharma, P. (Eds.), *Sustainable Development through Machine Learning, AI and IoT. Communications in Computer and Information Science, 2196* (pp. 130–140). DOI: 10.1007/978-3-031-71729-1_13

Kulhari, S. (2018). Data protection, privacy and identity: A complex triad. In *Building-Blocks of a Data Protection Revolution: The Uneasy Case for Blockchain Technology to Secure Privacy and Identity* (1st ed., pp. 23-37). Nomos Verlagsgesellschaft mbH. https://www.jstor.org/stable/j.ctv941qz6.7

Lefoane, M., Ghafir, I., Kabir, S., & Awan, I.-U. (2025, April). Internet of Things botnets: A survey on Artificial Intelligence based detection techniques. *Journal of Network and Computer Applications, 236,* 104110. DOI: 10.1016/j.jnca.2025.104110

M, R. (2025, October 5). *Blockchain crime typologies: 32 case studies bridging traditional and crypto laundering (Part-1).* LinkedIn. https://www.linkedin.com/pulse/blockchain-crime-typologies-32-case-studies-bridging-traditional-m-45epc

Manky, D., & Baram, G. (2025, January 16). *Beyond Phishing: Exploring the rise of AI-enabled cybercrime.* University of California Berkeley Center for Long-Term Cybersecurity. https://cltc.berkeley.edu/2025/01/16/beyond-phishing-exploring-the-rise-of-ai-enabled-cybercrime/

Martin, K. (2025, May 27). *AI cyber attack statistics 2025.* Tech Advisors. https://tech-adv.com/blog/ai-cyber-attack-statistics

McKay, C. (2026). Digital criminology, vulnerability theories and digital vulnerability. In *Digital Vulnerability in Criminal Justice Vulnerable People and Communication Technologies* (pp. 23–43). Palgrave MacMillan., DOI: 10.1007/978-3-032-10028-3_2

McKenna, F. (2024, December 17). 5 AI scams set to surge in 2025: What you need to know. *Forbes.* https://www.forbes.com/sites/frankmckenna/2024/12/16/5-ai-scams-set-to-surge-in-2025-what-you-need-to-know

Montañez, R., Golob, E., & Xu, S. (2020, September 29). Human cognition through the lens of social engineering cyberattacks. *Frontiers in Psychology, 11,* 1755. DOI: 10.3389/fpsyg.2020.01755 PMID: 33101096

Muhly, F., Chizzonic, E., & Leo, P. (2025, February 24). AI-deepfake scams and the importance of a holistic communication security strategy. *International Cybersecurity Law Review, 6*(1), 53–61. DOI: 10.1365/s43439-025-00143-7

Murugesan, B. (2025, March 10). AI-driven phishing and deep fakes: The future of digital fraud. *Forbes*. https://www.forbes.com/councils/forbestechcouncil/2025/03/10/ai-driven-phishing-and-deep-fakes-the-future-of-digital-fraud

Potluri, S. (2025, July 12). Policy-Aware secure data governance in distributed information systems using explainable AI models. *International Journal of AI, BigData. Computational and Management Studies*, *6*(3), 1–10. DOI: 10.63282/3050-9416.IJAIBDCMS-V6I3P101

Price, L. (2021). Platform responsibility for online harms: Towards a duty of care for online hazards. *Journal of Medicine and Law*, *13*(2), 238–261. DOI: 10.1080/17577632.2021.2022331

Qabajeh, I., Thabtah, F., & Chiclana, F. (2018, August). A recent review of conventional vs. automated cybersecurity anti-phishing techniques. *Computer Science Review*, *29*, 44–55. DOI: 10.1016/j.cosrev.2018.05.003

Rao, R. S., & Pais, A. R. (2017, April). Detecting phishing websites using automation of human behavior. [Conference proceedings]. *3rd ACM Workshop on Cyber-Physical System Security* (pp. 33–42). DOI: 10.1145/3055186.3055188

Salawu, R. O., Bolatito, A.-O. S., & Masibo, S. (2023). Theoretical and conceptual frameworks in clarification. *European Chemical Bulletin*, *12*(12), 2103–2117. DOI: 10.48047/ecb/2023.12.12.139

Schmitt, M., & Flechais, I. (2024, October). Digital deception: Generative artificial intelligence in social engineering and phishing. *Artificial Intelligence Review*, *57*(12), 324. DOI: 10.1007/s10462-024-10973-2

Shekhar, C. (2025, July 12). *Jane Street case marks a turning point in SEBI's index governance strategy.* Zenodo (CERN European Organization for Nuclear Research). DOI: 10.2139/ssrn.5341047

Shoemaker, P. (2025, November 6). *Deepfakes and identity verification: What's at risk.* Identity. https://www.identity.org/the-growing-threat-of-deepfakes-to-identity-verification-processes

Smurfing in money laundering: Understanding smurfing techniques and AML responses across regulated sectors. (2025, June 12). Dilisense. https://dilisense.com/en/insights/what-is-smurfing-in-money-laundering

Sokler, B. D., Hecht, A., Fjeld, C. R., & Tikhonovsky, M. (2024, October 3). *FTC launches Operation AI Comply with five enforcement actions involving AI misuse -AI: The Washington Report.* Mintz. https://www.mintz.com/insights-center/viewpoints/54731/2024-10-03-ftc-launches-operation-ai-comply-five-enforcement

Soni, T., Kaur, R., Gupta, D., Sharma, A., & Gupta, G. (2023, April). The cybersecurity ecosystem: challenges, risk and emerging technologies. [Conference paper]. *7th International Conference on Trends in Electronics and Informatics (ICOEI), Tirunelveli, India* (pp. 699–703). DOI: 10.1109/ICOEI56765.2023.10125775

Synthetic identity fraud & its importance in a digital world. (2025, February 18). Moody's. https://www.moodys.com/web/en/us/kyc/resources/insights/synthetic-identities-and-why-they-are-important-in-todays-digital-landscape.html

Tanimu, J. A., & Abada, W. (2025, December). Addressing cybersecurity challenges in robotics: A comprehensive overview. *Cyber Security and Applications*, *3*, 100074. DOI: 10.1016/j.csa.2024.100074

Ueno, H. (2023). Artificial Intelligence as dual-use technology. In Hatzilygeroudis, I. K., Tsihrintzis, G. A., & Jain, L. C. (Eds.), *Intelligent systems reference library* (pp. 7–32)., DOI: 10.1007/978-3-031-22371-6_2

Understanding India's cybersecurity policy Frameworks: IT Act, national cybersecurity policy, and strategy. (2025, January 10). RSM India. https://www.rsm.global/india/insights/consulting-insights/cybersecurity-policy-frameworks

Vaseashta, A. (2025). Dual-use Artificial Intelligence: Trends, security challenges, and mitigation strategies. In Vaseashta, A., & Rocha, A. (Eds.), *Information systems engineering and management, 6* (pp. 3–37). Springer., DOI: 10.1007/978-3-032-00202-0_1

Wazzan, M., Algazzawi, D., Bamasaq, O., Albeshri, A., & Cheng, L. (2021, June). Internet of Things botnet detection approaches: Analysis and recommendations for future research. *Applied Sciences (Basel, Switzerland)*, *11*(12), 5713. DOI: 10.3390/app11125713

Wegner, D., Borba da Silveira, A., Marconatto, D., & Mitrega, M. (2023, September). A systematic review of collaborative digital platforms: Structuring the domain and research agenda. *Review of Managerial Science*, *18*(9), 2663–2695. DOI: 10.1007/s11846-023-00695-0

World Economic Forum. (2025, January). *Global cybersecurity outlook 2025*. https://reports.weforum.org/docs/WEF_Global_Cybersecurity_Outlook_2025.pdf

Wu, G., Wang, X., & Zhang, J. (2024, May). PeerG: A P2P botnet detection method based on representation learning and graph contrastive learning. *Computers & Security*, *140*, 103775. DOI: 10.1016/j.cose.2024.103775

Zhang, L. (2024, January 9). *Deciphering cybersecurity vulnerabilities requires context*. Security Boulevard. https://securityboulevard.com/2024/01/deciphering-cybersecurity-vulnerabilities-requires-context

Chapter 10
Tracing the Digital Trail:
Modern Tools and Legal Complexities in Cybercrime Investigation

Tyler Cranmore
Southeast Missouri State University, USA

Joshua Todd Shadwick
http://orcid.org/0000-0003-1934-4594
Southeast Missouri State University, USA

ABSTRACT

Cybercrime investigation have historically been viewed as complex, both by practitioners and academics. These investigations oftentimes require collaboration across local, state, and federal agencies. Subsequently, the jurisdictional boundaries and concept associated with the crime scene, physical and digital, have become blurred. Couched within this discussion is the technological advancement shared by both investigative agencies and criminal syndicates. Put simply, as the technology advances so should the techniques and legal interpretations. Therefore, this chapter examines the evolution of cybercrime investigations and legal practices associated with investigation and prosecution of cyber-based crimes.

INTRODUCTION

In 2013 federal investigators dismantled the Silk Road, an online black market operating on the dark web that facilitated illegal drug sales, money laundering, and weapon transactions. The owner of the Silk Road, Ross Ulbricht, was ultimately convicted on multiple counts marking one of the most significant cybercrime prosecutions in United States history. The investigation relied on tracing digital evidence such as blockchain transactions, encrypted communications, and hidden metadata (*United States v. Ulbricht*, 2014). The Silk Road case demonstrated how forensic techniques and cyber-intelligence tools can be used to uncover criminal activity concealed within complex digital infrastructures.

DOI: 10.4018/979-8-3373-7660-8.ch010

Figure 1. Process of Dark Web moving towards suspect arrest

(image by the authors)

Cybercrime investigations are inherently complex and often require collaboration among federal agencies, cybersecurity experts, and private technology companies. The boundaries between physical and digital crime scenes have been blurred, as digital data becomes an increasingly important form of evidence gathered through complex data mining techniques (Sayal et al., 2024). Yet, as the same technologies that are used in criminal investigations improve, so do the technological capabilities of cybercriminals. Indeed, modern law enforcement agencies face an expanding battleground where evidence goes beyond the physical, existing in lines of code rather than strands of DNA.

Tension exists between technological innovations and the legal or ethical boundaries which exist to guide law enforcement agencies. The Silk Road investigation effectively illustrates the dilemma, as law enforcement agencies gain the capability to penetrate encrypted networks, scrape communications, and trace transactions how far should digital investigations extend – at what point do these investigations cross the line and erode individual privacy and constitutional protections?

Digital evidence has become an integral part of modern criminal investigations; therefore, understanding how law enforcement navigates this evolving terrain is essential. It is important to examine the tools and techniques that enable cybercrime investigation in the United States, as well as the legal and ethical frameworks that shape their use. Drawing on cases such as the Silk Road prosecution, federal statutes, and forensic practice guidelines, this analysis highlights both the expanding capabilities of investigative technologies and the constitutional constraints that govern them. The following discussion situates these developments within the broader evolution of cybercrime investigation and the ongoing debate over privacy and state authority in digital spaces.

The rise of digital ecosystems has fundamentally transformed not only the nature of crime but also the methodologies employed to investigate it. The Silk Road case marked a watershed moment in cybercrime history by showing how digital footprints could be traced and deconstructed to prosecute large-scale criminal networks. This development was not isolated; it signaled a broader shift in the landscape of law enforcement, where traditional tools are often inadequate to address offenses occurring in distributed, virtual spaces. From ransomware groups hiding behind layers of anonymity to state-sponsored attacks on critical infrastructure, modern cybercrime has globalized threats and necessitated an equally sophisticated investigative response.

Understanding the mechanics of these investigations is not only a matter of technical knowledge but a critical exercise in legal reasoning. As technology outpaces regulation, the boundaries between public safety and civil liberty become increasingly contested. Positioning at that intersection shows where analyzing the modern tools, institutional structures, and judicial doctrines define how the U.S. responds to digital crime. Through detailed case examples, legal frameworks, and an exploration of investigative technologies, this work maps out a dynamic and often contentious space where privacy, power, and evidence converge. It further seeks to contextualize cybercrime investigations as part of a broader sociotechnical evolution, wherein digital evidence is not merely supplemental, but central to prosecutorial success. To understand how contemporary investigative practices developed, it is first necessary to examine the historical evolution of cybercrime investigation in the United States.

THE HISTORICAL EVOLUTION OF CYBERCRIME INVESTIGATION

Early Computer Crime and Digital Evidence (1980s – 1990s)

As personal computing and networked systems became commonplace in the late twentieth century, law enforcement agencies began encountering offenses that could not be effectively addressed using traditional investigative methods. Enacted in 1984, the Computer Fraud and Abuse Act (CFAA) became the first major cybercrime statute criminalizing unauthorized computer usage (18 U.S.C. § 1030). One of the first major hacking cases prosecuted under the CFAA was *United States v. Morris* (1991), which involved the release of what is widely regarded as the first internet worm (*United States v. Morris, 1991).*

Investigators initially relied on traditional analog methods supplemented by improvised digital techniques, often operating with limited training, jurisdictional uncertainty, and no centralized forensic infrastructure. Indeed, practitioners soon realized that digital evidence required new procedures. Early efforts highlighted the inadequacy of traditional approaches and emphasized the need for specialized expertise in handling digital evidence. Recognizing the growing complexity of digital offenses, federal agencies soon established specialized units to investigate cybercrime and standardize the digital evidence practices.

Institutional Response and the Rise of Cyber Units (1990s – 2000s)

The limitations of early investigative efforts established a clear necessity for a structured response that led into the creation of specialized federal units designed to handle digital offenses in the 1990s. One of the earliest specialized units, the Federal Bureau of Investigation's National Computer Crime Squad, was established in 1991 and later evolved into the National Cyber Investigative Joint Task Force (NCIJTF) in 2008 (Steinmetz et al., 2025). Policymakers also recognized the importance of public reporting in cyber incidents, leading to the creation of the Internet Crime Complaint Center (IC3) in 2000 as a centralized mechanism for reporting cybercrime and disseminating annual trend analyses (Internet Crime Complaint Center [IC3], n.d.).

The creation of federal infrastructure reinforces the shift from ad-hoc responses into structured federal infrastructure for cyber-criminal investigations. A new importance was placed onto public reporting and federal partnerships, while cyber threats are now viewed as national security issues. The movement toward intelligence-sharing and joint operations builds into a robust digital infrastructure. As investigative techniques become formalized, digital forensics emerges as a recognized discipline in law enforcement and the broader field of criminal justice.

Figure 2. A simple timeline of cybercriminal investigation in the U.S.

(image by the authors)

The emergence of Digital Forensics (2000s – 2010s)

While the 2000s marked the early professionalization of digital forensics, the transformation from an improvised technical skill into a recognized investigative science accelerated in the 2010s. Digital evidence became standardized. The creation of NIST (National Institute of Standards and Technology) SP 800-86 in 2006 developed guidelines for digital evidence handling (Kent et al., 2006). Chain of custody requirements became the focus of law enforcement agencies handling digital evidence.

Common forensic software tools, such as EnCase, FTK, and Autopsy, are found in law enforcement agencies (see Agboola et al. 2024; Mandela et al., 2024). Indeed, professional training and certification programs began to familiarize agencies with digital threats. Specialized labs and forensic examiners popped up at the federal, state, and local levels with courts increasingly recognizing the importance of digital evidence reliability. The professionalization of digital forensics thus created the technical and institutional foundation upon which modern cybercrime investigations are built. Previous iterations of standards and tools have paved the way for increasingly sophisticated tools and collaborative approaches to digital evidence analysis.

Modern Investigative Methods and Technologies

Finally, modern cybercriminal investigations include analytical tools, standardized processes, and collaborative models to extract and analyze data. Analytical tools can image devices at the bit-level, hashing (a cryptographic process that produces a unique value to verify integrity of data) the data to ensure integrity for criminal proceedings. File system analysis, log analysis, and remote data acquisitions have become commonplace investigative methods. These methods represent the foundation of contemporary cybercrime investigations and are worthy of detailed examination. The professionalization of digital forensics ultimately created the technical and institutional foundation upon which modern cybercrime investigations are built.

MODERN INVESTIGATIVE TECHNIQUES

Digital Forensic Imaging and Analysis

Forensic imaging is the cornerstone of modern cybercriminal investigations, due to the nature of digital evidence. Digital evidence begins at the bit level, where a series of zeroes and ones create the interface and data seen today. The goal of forensic imaging is to create an exact bit-level replica of the target system for subsequent analysis. The target cellphone, computer, or smart device is copied and examined using complex forensic analysis tools such as Cellebrite, EnCase, or Autopsy. The key here is to ensure evidence remains intact and kept in the original state on the device, to prevent tampering for future analysis and ultimately, use in court. It is crucial that imaging techniques ensure the integrity (in this case, integrity means that the data remains without changes from its original form) of evidence for future analysis. Contemporary cybercrime investigations rely on a combination of analytical tools, standardized processes, and collaborative models to acquire and analyze digital evidence.

As forensic imaging serves as the foundation of modern cybercrime investigations, write blockers represent a critical safeguard within the imaging process. A write blocker is a hardware or software tool designed to prevent data from being written to a storage device during examination, allowing investigators to access information while preserving the original evidence in an unaltered state (Roffel & Lin, 2023). By restricting write commands, write blockers preserve the condition of the data when a device is seized or received by authorities. In practice, the use of a write blocker renders the device effectively "read-only," ensuring that timestamps, file structures, and system data remain unchanged throughout the investigative process.

Figure 3. An example write blocker forensic flow

(image by the authors)

Once write-blocking measures are in place, forensic bit-level imaging is used to create a complete copy of the device. This process captures all data stored on the system, including active files, deleted information, slack space, and metadata. Commercial forensic tools commonly used by law enforcement agencies support this process. Cellebrite, for example, is frequently employed in the extraction and analysis of mobile device data (Aljahdali et al., 2021), while software such as EnCase and Autopsy is widely used for imaging desktop and laptop computers (Chidambaram et al., 2022). Through bit-by-bit copying, these tools produce an exact replica of the device as it existed at the time of acquisition, allowing investigators to conduct analysis without risking contamination of the original evidence. Maintaining the integrity of digital evidence is essential for its admissibility in court, and additional verification steps are therefore required. Hashing techniques are used to generate a unique digital fingerprint for both the original device and its forensic image. Hash values are calculated before and after imaging and then compared to verify that the forensic copy remains identical to the original data source.. When the hash values match, investigators can demonstrate that the evidence has retained its integrity and reliability throughout the imaging process. Although multiple hashing algorithms exist, they all rely on mathematical functions that transform data into a fixed value used to validate the authenticity of digital evidence. The widespread adoption of cloud computing has introduced distinct investigative and evidentiary challenges for law enforcement conducting cybercrime investigations.

Despite their effectiveness, modern investigative tools are not without limitations: many of the technologies used in cybercrime investigations, including forensic software, blockchain analysis platforms, and AI-assisted systems, rely on proprietary processes that are not always transparent to courts or defense counsel. This lack of transparency can raise concerns regarding evidentiary reliability and the ability to challenge findings in adversarial proceedings. Additionally, the rapid pace of technological advancement often outstrips the development of legal standards, creating uncertainty about how digital evidence should be interpreted, validated, and admitted in court. These limitations highlight the importance of not only expanding investigative capabilities, but also critically evaluating their constraints to ensure alignment with legal and constitutional safeguards.

Cloud and Network Evidence

The widespread adoption of cloud computing has introduced significant challenges for law enforcement officials conducting cybercrime investigations. When data is no longer stored locally on a physical device but instead housed within cloud-based services, investigators must determine how to access that information in a manner that is both lawful and ethically sound. Criminal activity increasingly occurs across networked environments and cloud platforms, complicating the identification, acquisition, and preservation of digital evidence (Wall, 2017). Recognizing these challenges, the National Institute of Standards and Technology (NIST) has issued guidance addressing the unique forensic difficulties associated with cloud computing, including issues related to data volatility, shared infrastructure, and third-party control (Herman et al., 2024). Where earlier investigative practices focused primarily on physical devices owned by suspects or victims, cloud-based environments present fundamentally different obstacles. As a result, investigators often rely on network logs, server records, and cloud-stored data controlled by private service providers, creating additional jurisdictional, legal, and procedural complexities.

Accessing data over cloud systems can provide law enforcement with unique challenges, and so it is imperative that effective tools are used. Investigators cannot directly seize cloud data. Subpoenas, search warrants, and court orders are the most effective tools to request data for investigators, unlike personal devices access is provided indirectly and must be legally mediated. The cloud data is often controlled by internet service providers who create and manage the cloud platforms; therefore, provider cooperation is required for data access. These companies must comply legally while maintaining regulations and privacy responsibilities creating unique positions to manage (see Tang et al., 2016). This cooperation can take time and might be narrow in scope, as it is shaped by company policies and governmental regulations, thus evidence access is not immediate or even guaranteed in some cases. Jurisdictional complexities create additional complexities as the cloud service providers might store data across states or countries (Segall, 2013; Jaeger et al., 2009). Overall, access to evidence in clouds might be limited due to privacy concerns, proper due process procedures, and the scope of the authority requesting the data. Technical access can blur the lines of constitutionality in cases creating diverse challenges for investigators to manage. Effective investigators must be able to navigate the balance between individual rights, legal compliance, and data necessity to effectively navigate the cloud environment.

Figure 4. An example investigative process diagram for cloud investigations

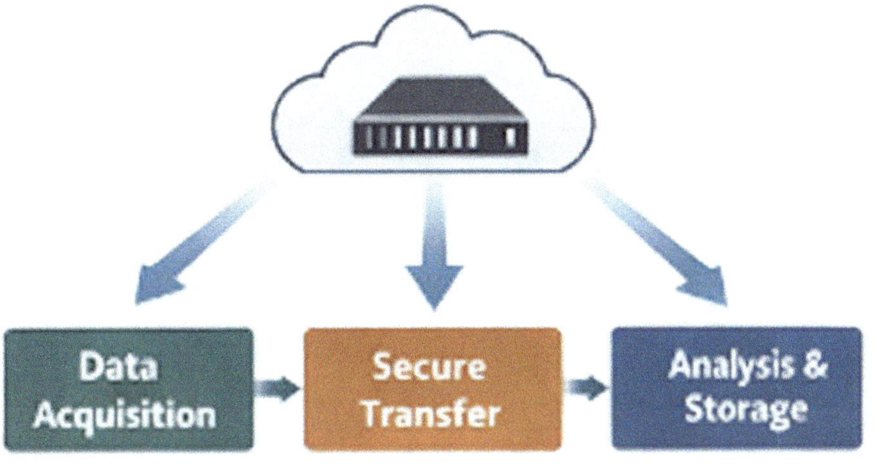

(image by the authors)

The forensic recovery of network and cloud evidence often hinges on capturing transient data states, such as logs, RAM snapshots, or cached session data, which may be lost if not preserved quickly. Network traffic analysis can help identify command-and-control server interactions, malware propagation paths, and unauthorized data exfiltration. Deep packet inspection (DPI) is one method that provides granular insight into data flow across networks, though its use raises ethical and legal questions related to privacy and warrant requirements.

The elasticity of cloud infrastructure (its ability to scale dynamically) means that virtual machines and storage containers may exist only briefly. Evidence can become inaccessible if forensic capture does not occur in real time. Tools like FROST and cloud API integrations with platforms such as AWS and Microsoft Azure have become essential to incident response teams. In addition to technical challenges, investigators must work within the contractual and jurisdictional frameworks dictated by cloud service providers' terms of service and national privacy regulations. Ensuring evidentiary compliance often requires collaboration with legal teams, cloud architects, and data governance officers.

CRYPTOCURRENCY AND BLOCKCHAIN ANALYSIS

Cryptocurrency has become increasingly prevalent within cybercriminal circles, serving as a common medium for online transactions, dark web marketplaces, and ransomware payments. As a result, digital currency now plays a central role in many cybercrime ecosystems and is frequently encountered by investigators. Cryptocurrencies are particularly attractive to offenders due to the perception that transactions provide a degree of anonymity. Unlike traditional financial systems, cryptocurrency transactions do not rely on centralized banking records and instead operate through pseudonymous addresses, complicating conventional financial investigations. This shift disrupts traditional investigative methods and requires law enforcement agencies to adopt new approaches to financial tracing. Despite perceptions of anonymity, cryptocurrency transactions are often recorded on public blockchains, enabling investigators to identify transactional patterns and trace illicit activity, as demonstrated in cases such as the Silk Road investigation.

Figure 5. An example Blockchain transaction

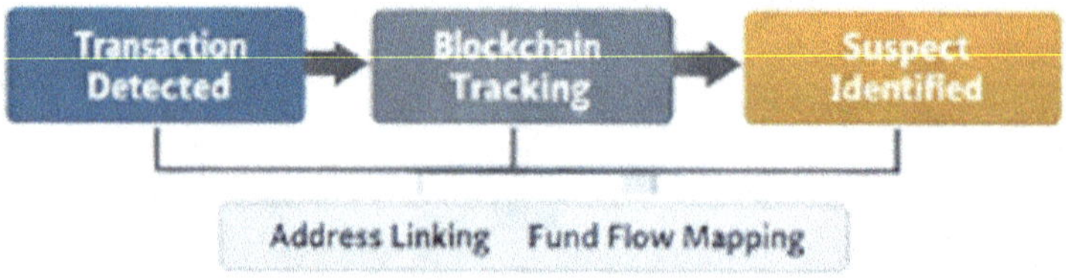

(image by the authors)

While cryptocurrencies are often believed to provide complete anonymity, law enforcement agencies have developed investigative techniques to trace transactions across blockchain networks. Blockchain technology functions as a public ledger, recording each transaction in a permanent and time-stamped manner (Nofer et al., 2017). Investigators can analyze transaction flows, wallet addresses, and patterns of activity to identify connections between accounts and trace the movement of illicit funds. These methods allow law enforcement to follow the digital trail of transactions as they move across wallets and exchanges, sometimes linking activity back to identifiable individuals or services (Sathilkumar & Graham, 2018). Specialized analytical tools are frequently used to assist in this process, enabling investigators to visualize transaction networks and identify suspicious behavior. Although blockchain analysis requires technical expertise and significant resources, it has become an increasingly valuable tool in cybercrime investigations involving cryptocurrency.

Despite the growing effectiveness of blockchain analysis, cryptocurrency investigations remain limited by several technical and legal challenges (Dyson et al., 2019). Cybercriminals increasingly rely on privacy-enhancing tools, such as mixing services and tumblers, which are designed to obscure transaction trails and complicate tracing efforts. Certain cryptocurrencies also prioritize anonymity by design, reducing the visibility of transaction data available to investigators. Jurisdictional barriers further complicate cryptocurrency investigations, as digital exchanges and wallet services often operate across international borders. Accessing relevant records may therefore require cooperation from foreign governments or private companies, introducing delays and legal uncertainty. These limitations illustrate the ongoing challenge law enforcement faces in balancing evolving investigative techniques with increasingly sophisticated methods used to conceal illicit financial activity while protecting individual's privacy (Dyson et al., 2019).

Artificial Intelligence and Investigative Tools

As the volume and complexity of digital evidence continue to grow, law enforcement agencies have increasingly incorporated artificial intelligence and automated tools into cybercrime investigations. These technologies are used to assist investigators in managing large datasets, identifying patterns, and prioritizing relevant information across digital systems. Automated tools can support tasks such as log analysis, malware classification, and open-source intelligence collection, allowing investigators to process evidence more efficiently (Faqir, 2023). Rather than replacing human judgment, artificial intelligence is commonly applied as a support mechanism to reduce investigative workload and enhance analytical capacity. The integration of these tools reflects a shift toward data-driven investigative practices designed to keep pace with the scale of modern cybercrime (Faqir, 2023).

While artificial intelligence offers clear advantages in efficiency and scale, its use in cybercrime investigations also raises important concerns. Automated systems rely on underlying data and programmed parameters, which can influence how information is prioritized or interpreted during an investigation. This reliance introduces the potential for bias, error, or overreliance on algorithmic outputs if human oversight is insufficient (Završnik, 2021). The use of automated tools may also reduce transparency in investigative decision-making, making it more difficult to explain how conclusions were reached. These concerns highlight the need for careful oversight, validation, and accountability when artificial intelligence is integrated into law enforcement practices. As such, the use of automated investigative tools must be balanced with professional judgment and adherence to legal and ethical standards (Završnik, 2021).

Another notable area where artificial intelligence is gaining traction involves facial recognition and image classification, particularly in cases involving digital surveillance or leaked imagery. Facial recognition software such as Clearview AI or NEC's facial identification system has been utilized by law enforcement to match suspects captured in stills or video feeds to known databases. These tools have drawn significant criticism for potential racial bias, false positives, and lack of transparency in their algorithmic processes, however. In response, some jurisdictions have placed moratoriums on facial recognition use by police agencies, citing due process and civil liberties concerns.

While artificial intelligence offers clear advantages in efficiency and scale, its use in cybercrime investigations also raises significant legal and evidentiary concerns. Courts and legal scholars have increasingly questioned the reliability of algorithmically generated outputs, particularly when these systems function as "black boxes" that cannot be easily examined or explained. This lack of transparency complicates due process protections, as defendants may be unable to meaningfully challenge how they were identified or prioritized during an investigation. There are also concerns surrounding algorithmic bias that suggest automated tools may unintentionally reinforce existing inequalities if trained on incomplete or skewed datasets (Završnik, 2021). As a result, while artificial intelligence enhances investigative capabilities, its use must be carefully evaluated to ensure consistency with constitutional protections and evidentiary standards.

Metadata and Digital Evidence

Metadata is not a single, uniform category of information. Its form and evidentiary value vary depending on the type of digital artifact involved and the system that produced it. In email systems, metadata can include sender and recipient addresses, subject lines, timestamps, and server relay paths. These details may establish timelines, infer intent, or suggest coordination among actors. Documents often contain revision histories, author identifiers, and save locations that reveal how and when a file was created or altered. Image files similarly contain EXIF metadata capable of disclosing GPS coordinates, device identifiers, time zones, and even the software used to process an image. Taken together, these embedded layers provide investigators with inferential value that extends well beyond visible content.

Courts have shown an increasing willingness to treat metadata as primary evidence rather than merely contextual support. In *United States v. Sedaghaty* (2011), metadata analysis played a central role in demonstrating that certain financial documents had been intentionally modified to obscure records. In that case, metadata functioned not only to authenticate files but also to support inferences of concealment. What ultimately mattered was not the presence of metadata itself, but the ability of forensic examiners to clearly document and explain how it was generated, preserved, and interpreted. As digital environments become more mobile and fragmented, metadata is likely to play an even greater role in reconstructing events that leave few physical traces.

Metadata remains a critical, yet often underestimated, component of digital evidence in cybercrime investigations. Commonly described as data about data, metadata supplies the contextual information necessary to establish timelines, verify authenticity, and correlate activity across devices or accounts. Email metadata, for example, can reveal routing paths and read status even when message content has been deleted. Embedded image metadata may disclose when and where a photograph was taken, along with the make and model of the capturing device. These details can bridge the gap between digital activity and physical actors, strengthening investigative narratives where direct evidence is limited.

Extracting and analyzing metadata requires specialized forensic tools and careful handling. Programs such as ExifTool and FTK allow investigators to retrieve metadata from documents, emails, images, and file systems, but the information they uncover is particularly sensitive to inadvertent alteration. Routine actions, such as opening a file, copying it improperly, or changing storage environments, can modify metadata fields. For that reason, metadata analysis is tightly bound to preservation protocols and chain of custody requirements. Courts have increasingly acknowledged the probative value of metadata, particularly in cases where it corroborates testimony or contradicts a defendant's account. In cybercrime investigations, metadata can become the linchpin that connects a suspect to a specific action when little else is available.

Inter-agency and Public-Private Collaboration

Modern cybercrime investigations rarely occur in isolation and instead rely on extensive collaboration among law enforcement agencies, private organizations, and international partners. Cyber offenses frequently span multiple jurisdictions and technological platforms, making cooperation essential for effective investigation and enforcement. Federal agencies often work alongside state and local authorities, as well as specialized task forces, to share intelligence and coordinate responses to cyber incidents. Private technology companies and internet service providers also play a critical role as owners of digital evidence, network infrastructure, and user data. These partnerships allow investigators to access technical expertise and information that would otherwise be unavailable through traditional investigative methods. As cybercrime continues to evolve, collaborative frameworks have become a foundational component of modern cybercrime enforcement efforts.

Information-sharing mechanisms have become essential to facilitating collaboration across agencies and sectors involved in cybercrime investigations. Task forces, reporting centers, and joint investigative initiatives allow law enforcement to aggregate intelligence, identify trends, and coordinate responses to cyber threats more effectively. Bodies such as federal task forces and public reporting systems support the appropriate exchange of information between government agencies and private organizations.

Reliance on collaborative frameworks also presents challenges, including differences in organizational priorities, legal obligations, and data-sharing limitations (Tóth & Gáspár, 2020). Private companies must balance cooperation with law enforcement against regulatory requirements and user privacy expectations, while agencies must ensure that shared information is used appropriately and lawfully. Despite these challenges, effective collaboration remains critical to addressing the scale and complexity of modern cybercrime investigations.

LEGAL AND ETHICAL CONSIDERATIONS IN CYBERCRIME INVESTIGATIONS

Fourth Amendment Protections and Digital Searches

The rapid expansion of digital evidence has required courts and law enforcement agencies to reconsider how traditional Fourth Amendment protections apply within cybercrime investigations. The Fourth Amendment was designed to guard against unreasonable searches and seizures, yet its application becomes more complex when searches involve digital devices and data rather than physical spaces (Donohue, 2015). Unlike traditional searches, digital searches often expose vast amounts of personal information unrelated to the underlying investigation, increasing the potential for intrusion. Devices such as smartphones and computers can contain years of communications, location data, and personal records, often exceeding the informational scope of traditional physical searches. As a result, courts have increasingly recognized that digital evidence requires heightened constitutional consideration. These concerns underscore the tension between effective cybercrime enforcement and the preservation of individual privacy rights in the digital age.

Figure 6. The multi-faceted challenges facing digital evidence

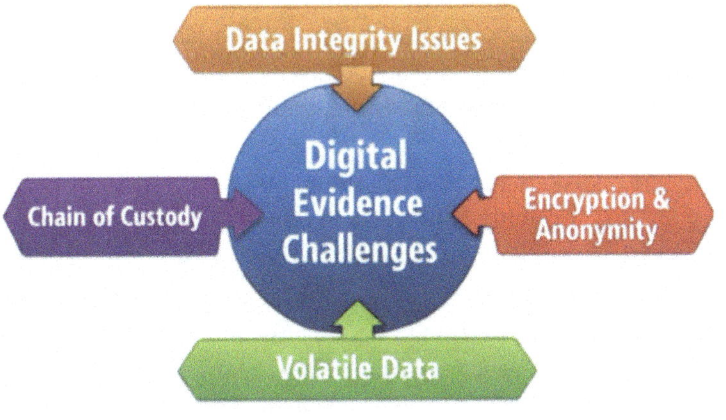

(image by the authors)

While the Fourth Amendment traditionally focused on physical spaces such as homes, papers, and effects, digital searches challenge these categories by concentrating vast amounts of personal information into a single device or account. A single search of a smartphone or computer can reveal intimate details about an individual's life, including communications, financial activity, location history, and associations. This breadth of information raises concerns that digital searches may become overly expansive if not carefully constrained. Unlike physical searches, where officers are limited by physical boundaries, digital searches risk exposing data far beyond the scope of the suspected offense. As a result, courts have increasingly emphasized the need for clear limits and particularity when authorizing searches of digital devices. These distinctions highlight why digital searches require a different constitutional analysis than traditional investigative methods.

The Supreme Court directly addressed these concerns in *Riley v. California* (2014), a decision that significantly reshaped how digital searches are evaluated under the Fourth Amendment. In *Riley*, the Court held that law enforcement officers generally must obtain a warrant before searching the digital contents of a cellphone seized during an arrest. The decision recognized that modern cellphones are not merely physical objects but repositories of extensive personal data, capable of revealing far more information than traditional items carried on an individual (*Riley v. California*, 2014). The Court emphasized that the depth, breadth, and sensitivity of digital information necessitate greater constitutional protection than that afforded to physical searches alone. By distinguishing digital data from other forms of evidence, this case established an important precedent limiting warrantless searches in the digital context: the ruling has had significant implications for cybercrime investigations, reinforcing the principle that technological capability does not override constitutional safeguards.

Building on the principles established in *Riley*, the Supreme Court further refined Fourth Amendment protections in *Carpenter v. United States* (2018), a case addressing the collection of historical cell-site location information. In this case the Court ruled that law enforcement generally must obtain a warrant to access detailed location data held by third-party service providers, recognizing that such records reveal deeply personal patterns of movement and behavior (*Carpenter v. United States*, 2018). This decision marked a significant departure from traditional third-party doctrine, which had previously allowed certain records held by external entities to be obtained with less judicial oversight. The Court acknowledged that advances in technology had altered the nature of privacy expectations, particularly where digital data can provide comprehensive insight into an individual's daily life. For cybercrime investigations, this underscored the importance of judicial authorization when accessing sensitive digital records, especially those maintained by private companies. Together, *Riley* and *Carpenter* illustrate how constitutional doctrine is evolving to address the realities of digital evidence and technologically enhanced investigations.

Subsequent lower court decisions have continued to test and refine the principles established in Carpenter, particularly in cases involving large-scale digital data collection. In *United States v. Chatrie* (2020), the court examined the use of geofence warrants, which allow law enforcement to obtain location data from all devices within a defined geographic area during a specified time period. This investigative technique raised significant concerns regarding overbreadth, as it may capture data from numerous individuals who are not suspected of any wrongdoing. The case highlights the growing tension between investigative efficiency and Fourth Amendment protections, particularly as emerging technologies enable broad and highly detailed data collection. While courts have not reached uniform conclusions on the constitutionality of such practices, cases like *Chatrie* demonstrate that the legal system is still actively grappling with how to apply traditional constitutional safeguards to modern digital investigations.

Warrants, Scope, and Overcollection

Although warrants are a central safeguard in digital investigations, the scope of authorized searches presents unique challenges in cybercrime cases. Unlike traditional warrants that target specific physical locations or objects, digital warrants often authorize searches of devices or accounts that contain vast amounts of unrelated personal information. A single warrant for a computer, smartphone, or cloud account may expose years of communications, photographs, financial records, and location data. As discussed in cases previously, this raises concerns about overcollection, where investigators lawfully obtain access to information far beyond what is necessary for the underlying investigation. The risk of overcollection is particularly pronounced in cybercrime cases, where relevant evidence is often intermingled with large volumes of personal data. As a result, courts and law enforcement agencies must carefully consider how digital warrants are structured and executed to ensure compliance with constitutional principles. In an attempt to address the risks associated with overcollection, courts have emphasized the importance of particularity and minimization in digital search warrants.

The Fourth Amendment requires that warrants clearly specify the scope of the search and the types of data subject to seizure, yet applying this requirement in digital environments remains challenging. Investigators may encounter relevant evidence interspersed with vast quantities of unrelated personal information, making it difficult to isolate data tied directly to the suspected offense. Minimization procedures are therefore increasingly used to limit exposure to irrelevant data and reduce unnecessary intrusion into private information. However, traditional doctrines such as plain view become more complicated in digital contexts, where investigators may unintentionally encounter unrelated evidence while conducting lawful searches. These challenges illustrate the ongoing difficulty of translating established warrant principles of modern cybercrime investigations.

Cloud Data and Privacy Expectations

The increasing reliance on cloud-based services has further complicated how privacy expectations are evaluated in cybercrime investigations. Traditionally, the third-party doctrine suggested that individuals have a reduced expectation of privacy in information voluntarily shared with external entities, such as service providers. In the digital context, however, this principle becomes more difficult to apply, as cloud services routinely store extensive amounts of personal data that users rely on for daily communication, storage, and computing functions (Hemdan & Manjaiah, 2016). Unlike limited transactional records, cloud-stored data may include private documents, communications, photographs, and location information that extend far beyond the scope of any single investigation. As a result, determining whether users maintain a reasonable expectation of privacy in cloud data presents significant legal challenges. These issues place cloud service providers in a difficult position, functioning as custodians of sensitive information while simultaneously responding to lawful requests from law enforcement agencies.

The Supreme Court's decision in *Carpenter v. United States* (2018) further complicated the application of the third-party doctrine in cases involving cloud-stored data. While earlier doctrine assumed that individuals relinquished privacy interests by sharing information with third parties, *Carpenter* acknowledged that modern digital records can reveal far more detailed and sensitive information than traditional business records (*Carpenter v. United States*, 2018). In cloud-based environments, users may not meaningfully choose to disclose personal data but instead rely on service providers as a practical necessity of digital life. As cloud services continue to function as extensions of personal storage and communication, courts must increasingly assess privacy expectations based on the nature and sensitivity of the data rather than solely on its possession by a third party. These developments signal an evolving legal landscape in which traditional doctrines are being reconsidered to reflect the realities of digital dependency and data centralization.

Encryption, Law Enforcement Access, and "Going Dark"

The widespread adoption of encryption technologies has introduced additional challenges for cybercrime investigations and intensified debates surrounding law enforcement access to digital evidence. Encryption is designed to protect data by rendering it unreadable without proper authorization, safeguarding communications, stored files, and cloud-based information from unauthorized access. While these protections serve important privacy and security functions, they can also limit investigators' ability to obtain evidence, even when lawful authority exists (Atwood, 2015). Law enforcement agencies have expressed concern that strong encryption may impede investigations by preventing access to critical information, a challenge often described as the "going dark" problem (Walden, 2018). At the same time, encryption has become an essential component of modern digital security, protecting individuals, businesses, and governments from cyber threats. This tension places encryption at the center of ongoing legal and policy discussions regarding the balance between public safety and individual privacy.

Efforts to address the investigative challenges posed by encryption have generated significant debate over whether and how law enforcement should obtain lawful access to encrypted data. Suggestions such as exceptional access mechanisms or encryption backdoors are often framed as solutions that would allow investigators to access evidence when authorized by a court. Despite these concerns, critics argue that weakening encryption could create systemic vulnerabilities, increasing the risk of unauthorized access, cyberattacks, and misuse. From an investigative perspective, the absence of access can hinder evidence collection, while from a privacy standpoint, weakened encryption threatens data security for all users. These competing concerns illustrate the difficulty of reconciling investigative necessity with the broader implications of altering encryption standards (Walden, 2018). As a result, encryption remains an unresolved issue in cybercrime investigations, requiring careful consideration of legal authority, technological risk, and ethical responsibility.

Judicial Interpretation and Scope

Cases such as *United States v. Ganias* and *United States v. Moore Bush* further illustrate the unresolved tensions surrounding digital evidence and prolonged surveillance. In *Ganias*, the Second Circuit raised concerns regarding the government's retention of non-responsive data beyond the scope of a warrant, highlighting how digital storage capabilities can conflict with traditional limitations on search scope. Although the decision was later vacated, the case underscored the legal risks associated with overcollection and long-term data retention in digital investigations. Similarly, *Moore Bush* addressed the constitutionality of prolonged pole camera surveillance, raising questions about whether persistent monitoring over time (when aggregated) constitutes a search under the Fourth Amendment. The case reflects broader judicial uncertainty regarding how duration and technological enhancement affect expectations of privacy. Together, these cases demonstrate that courts are still grappling with how to apply established constitutional principles to modern forms of digital surveillance and evidence collection.

Figure 7. Courts must often balance privacy issues and efficiency in cybercriminal cases

(image by the authors)

Courts have also placed renewed emphasis on minimization requirements in digital warrants. Investigators are increasingly expected to demonstrate that search protocols are structured to limit exposure to non-relevant personal data. Decisions like this reflect a growing expectation that digital warrants incorporate filtering mechanisms, keyword constraints, or post search review processes. The message from courts is clear. Technological capability does not excuse imprecision: crafting constitutionally sound digital search protocols now requires both technical literacy and legal restraint.

Judges play a central role in shaping how cybercrime investigations proceed by interpreting how constitutional protections apply in evolving technological contexts. Judicial rulings influence not only whether warrants are issued, but how specific they must be and what forms of digital evidence may ultimately be admitted. As statutory reform lags technological change, courts have increasingly acted as de facto regulators of investigative scope. Post Carpenter decisions addressing real time location tracking, cloud-based records, and browsing history illustrate the uneven and case specific nature of this evolution. Together, these rulings form a patchwork that guides investigative practice while leaving substantial uncertainty. The principle of particularity has proven especially difficult to apply in digital searches. Judges now frequently require warrants to include explicit minimization strategies designed to prevent general searches of personal data. Failure to demonstrate meaningful boundaries can result in suppression, particularly where warrants resemble the broad exploratory searches the Fourth Amendment was designed to prohibit. This evolving jurisprudence underscores the need for ongoing training among investigators, prosecutors, and judges alike. As digital evidence becomes more central to criminal cases, legal education focused on cybercrime issues will play an increasingly important role in aligning investigative practices with constitutional expectations.

Ethical Boundaries, Surveillance, and Investigative Oversight

Beyond constitutional and statutory requirements, cybercrime investigations raise broader ethical questions concerning surveillance, proportionality, and institutional oversight. As investigative technologies become more powerful, law enforcement agencies gain the ability to collect, analyze, and retain vast amounts of digital information, often extending beyond the immediate scope of a criminal inquiry. These capabilities raise concerns about mission creep, where tools designed for specific investigative purposes are gradually expanded into broader surveillance practices. Ethical considerations therefore require investigators to assess not only whether an action is lawful, but whether it is appropriate given the level of intrusion involved. Maintaining clear boundaries around data collection and use is essential to preserving public trust and ensuring that technological advancement does not erode fundamental civil liberties. In this context, ethical oversight functions as a necessary complement to legal regulation in modern cybercrime investigations. Effective oversight mechanisms play a critical role in addressing the ethical risks associated with technologically enhanced cybercrime investigations. Internal policies, judicial supervision, and external review processes are designed to ensure that investigative practices remain consistent with legal standards and ethical expectations. Training requirements and professional guidelines further help investigators understand the appropriate use of digital tools and the limits of their authority. Transparency in investigative practices, where possible, also contributes to public accountability by clarifying how digital evidence is collected, analyzed, and retained. Without meaningful oversight, advanced investigative technologies risk undermining public confidence and perceptions of legitimacy. Accordingly, ethical governance structures are essential to balancing investigative effectiveness with respect for individual rights in the digital age. Ethical considerations therefore require investigators to assess not only whether an action is lawful, but also whether it is proportionate given the level of intrusion involved.

FUTURE TRENDS AND EMERGING CHALLENGES IN CYBERCRIME INVESTIGATION

As technology continues to evolve, cybercrime investigations are expected to face increasingly complex challenges that extend beyond existing investigative frameworks. For example, advances in computing, automation, and digital infrastructure continue to reshape both criminal activity and law enforcement responses. While existing tools and legal doctrines provide a foundation for modern cybercrime investigations, emerging technologies will require investigators, policymakers, and courts to continually reassess investigative practices and regulatory boundaries. Future developments will test the adaptability of law enforcement agencies as well as the resilience of constitutional and ethical safeguards in the digital environment.

Artificial Intelligence Expansion and Investigative Automation

Artificial intelligence is expected to play an increasingly prominent role in future cybercrime investigations as data volumes continue to grow. As cybercrime generates vast quantities of logs, communications, and digital artifacts, investigators may rely more heavily on automated systems to triage evidence, identify patterns, and prioritize investigative leads (Marturana et al., 2012). Machine learning models can assist in malware classification, anomaly detection, and network traffic analysis, allowing agencies to respond more efficiently to increasingly complex threats (Mishra et al., 2018). These tools may also support predictive analytics, helping investigators anticipate emerging criminal techniques or identify high-risk digital environments.

Increased reliance on artificial intelligence introduces new challenges related to transparency, accountability, and oversight. Automated systems may obscure decision-making processes, making it more difficult to explain how investigative conclusions are reached. Errors in training data or algorithmic design can also influence outcomes, potentially reinforcing bias or producing inaccurate results. As artificial intelligence becomes more deeply integrated into investigative workflows, law enforcement agencies will need to ensure that human judgment remains central to decision-making. Balancing efficiency with accountability will be essential to maintaining public trust and ethical legitimacy in future cybercrime investigations.

Encryption, Privacy Technologies, and the Investigative Arms Race

The continued expansion of encryption and privacy-enhancing technologies is likely to intensify the ongoing tension between digital security and law enforcement access. As individuals and organizations increasingly rely on end-to-end encryption, anonymization services, and decentralized platforms, investigators may encounter greater obstacles in obtaining usable evidence (Pisarić, 2020). These technologies can limit access to communications, stored data, and transactional records, even when lawful authority exists (Pisarić, 2022). From an investigative standpoint, this trend raises concerns about evidence loss and investigative blind spots. At the same time, privacy technologies serve legitimate purposes, protecting users from cyber threats, unauthorized surveillance, and data breaches. Efforts to weaken encryption for investigative access risk creating vulnerabilities that could be exploited by malicious actors. This dynamic reflects an ongoing tension between investigative capability and technological innovation, where advancements on one side often prompt countermeasures on the other. Future cybercrime investigations will likely require alternative strategies that emphasize intelligence gathering, metadata analysis, and cooperative partnerships rather than direct access to encrypted content.

Jurisdictional Fragmentation and Globalized Cybercrime

Cybercrime increasingly operates across national borders, complicating jurisdictional authority and legal enforcement. Digital infrastructure allows offenders to exploit differences in legal systems, data protection laws, and enforcement capabilities across countries. Evidence may be stored in one jurisdiction, controlled by a provider in another, and linked to criminal activity originating elsewhere. These complexities challenge traditional models of territorial jurisdiction and raise questions about sovereignty, cooperation, and legal harmonization. International collaboration will become increasingly important in future cybercrime investigations. Mutual legal assistance treaties, cross-border task forces, and shared intelligence platforms may play a greater role in addressing transnational cyber offenses. Differences in legal standards, privacy protections, and political priorities can hinder effective cooperation, however. As cybercrime continues to globalize, law enforcement agencies must adapt to an investigative landscape where jurisdictional boundaries are less clear and cooperation is both essential and difficult to achieve.

Training, Resources, and Institutional Adaptation

The effectiveness of future cybercrime investigations will depend heavily on the availability of trained personnel and institutional resources. As investigative tools become more specialized and technologically advanced, agencies must invest in ongoing training and professional development to ensure investigators possess the necessary technical and legal expertise. Resource disparities between agencies may create uneven investigative capacity, particularly at the state and local levels. Smaller agencies may struggle to keep pace with evolving cyber threats without access to specialized tools or expertise.

Institutional adaptation will also require updating policies, procedures, and oversight mechanisms to reflect technological change. Agencies must continually evaluate whether existing practices remain appropriate for new forms of digital evidence and investigative techniques. Failure to adapt risks both ineffective enforcement and erosion of public trust. By prioritizing training, collaboration, and ethical governance, law enforcement agencies can better prepare for the evolving challenges that will define the future of cybercrime investigation.

The evolution of cybercrime investigations underscores the convergence of law, technology, and governance in increasingly intricate ways. Whereas earlier eras of policing relied primarily on physical evidence and direct observation, the digital age demands interpretive and technical expertise that bridges disciplines. Investigators today must be part forensic analyst, part legal theorist, and part systems architect. The criminal justice system's ability to adapt to these challenges is not guaranteed; it requires intentional policy, continuous education, and institutional innovation.

Zero Trust and Data Fragmentation

The growing adoption of zero trust architectures within corporate and government networks presents a new challenge for cybercrime investigations. Under zero trust models, no device or user is automatically trusted, and access is continuously verified through layered security controls. While this approach is effective at limiting unauthorized access and lateral movement, it also fragments visibility for investigators. Logs may be compartmentalized, credentials short lived, and access records distributed across multiple systems, complicating traditional evidence collection. From an investigative standpoint, these environments require a shift toward forensic readiness rather than reactive acquisition. Effective investigation increasingly depends on proactive logging, integration with endpoint detection systems, and clearly documented access hierarchies. Evidence may no longer reside in a single repository but instead be spread across microservices, containerized applications, or dynamic endpoints. Understanding how zero trust architectures shape evidence trails is becoming essential in cases involving insider threats, corporate cybercrime, and large-scale data breaches. As these systems become more common, training in their structure and implications will be critical for both digital forensic practitioners and cybersecurity professionals engaged in criminal investigations.

Chain of Custody and Legal Integrity

Judicial scrutiny of chain of custody documentation has intensified, particularly in cases where digital evidence is outcome determinative. Courts increasingly evaluate digital forensic methods using standards associated with scientific evidence, including reproducibility, peer review, and known error rates. In *United States v. Ganias* (2014), the Second Circuit raised concerns about the prolonged retention of data beyond a warrant's scope, highlighting how technical evidence handling can intersect with Fourth Amendment protections. Although the decision was later vacated, it underscored the legal consequences of improper evidence management.

Breakdowns in chain of custody have resulted in the suppression of digital evidence in numerous cases. Failures such as incomplete forensic logs, altered timestamps, or unsecured storage environments can undermine evidentiary reliability. Even seemingly minor oversights, such as storing forensic images on shared networks without appropriate access controls, may be sufficient to raise reasonable doubt. To address these risks, many agencies have adopted digital evidence management systems that track every interaction with forensic data using immutable logs and role based permissions. These systems provide audit trails that can be presented in court to demonstrate procedural compliance.

Maintaining the integrity of digital evidence is not merely a technical concern. It is a legal requirement grounded in evidentiary standards and procedural fairness. Chain of custody refers to the chronological documentation of how evidence is seized, transferred, analyzed, stored, and presented. In cybercrime investigations, where data can be easily altered or duplicated, preserving an unbroken and transparent chain is essential. Courts often require proof that evidence remains in substantially the same condition as when it was first obtained, placing a premium on meticulous documentation. Chain of custody obligations extend beyond physical devices to include network logs, cloud stored data, and metadata obtained from third parties. When evidence is acquired from service providers, each step from request to receipt to analysis must be carefully documented. Challenges frequently focus on whether evidence was altered or whether procedural shortcuts compromised its reliability. As cybercrime cases increasingly rely on decentralized and remote data sources, standardizing chain of custody practices across agencies and jurisdictions will become even more important.

Cross-Border Cybercrime Enforcement

Cybercrime does not respect national boundaries. As offenses increasingly occur across digital infrastructure that spans continents, international cooperation has become a cornerstone of effective enforcement. The Budapest Convention on Cybercrime, established by the Council of Europe in 2001, remains the primary international treaty aimed at harmonizing national laws, improving investigative techniques, and fostering international collaboration in cybercrime cases. Although widely adopted by Western nations, its reach is limited, with key global players such as Russia and China remaining non-signatories. This lack of global consensus on cybercrime norms has created enforcement blind spots and jurisdictional tension.

Even among countries that are party to the Budapest Convention, disparities in privacy law, evidentiary standards, and constitutional protections can hinder cooperation. Mutual Legal Assistance Treaties (MLATs) are often slow and bureaucratic, creating investigative delays that reduce the timeliness and effectiveness of digital evidence acquisition. For instance, if a cybercriminal operating in Brazil uses servers in Sweden to launch an attack against a U.S. target, investigators may need to navigate three distinct legal systems just to access critical logs or user information. These complexities introduce uncertainty that can be exploited by offenders and may undermine prosecution.

Recent efforts have aimed to address these limitations through bilateral agreements and the development of more streamlined data-sharing protocols. The U.S. CLOUD Act, for example, allows for reciprocal arrangements with certain foreign governments to expedite access to data stored by tech companies. However, critics argue that such agreements risk undermining due process protections or allowing surveillance regimes to bypass domestic legal safeguards. Striking a balance between efficiency and accountability remains an unresolved tension in the international legal framework surrounding cybercrime. Future progress will require both technological standardization and legal harmonization, alongside the development of transnational oversight bodies capable of mediating privacy and enforcement priorities in a consistent manner.

Investigative Overreach and Possible Misuse

The deployment of advanced investigative tools, while essential for modern law enforcement, also raises the risk of overreach and misuse. The power to extract, analyze, and store vast quantities of personal data must be constrained not only by law but by ethical and institutional safeguards. Historical instances where surveillance tools were misapplied, such as the use of Stingray devices without proper warrants or improper deployment of malware in non-target systems, underscore the potential for rights violations when oversight is lax.

The risk of investigative error or abuse increases in environments where digital tools are poorly understood or where operational pressures incentivize shortcuts. For example, automated algorithms used in suspect identification or behavior prediction can reinforce existing biases or rely on flawed data, leading to wrongful suspicion or prosecution. As agencies increasingly rely on private vendors for digital investigative tools, concerns have emerged regarding transparency, accountability, and vendor-driven limitations on disclosure. In some cases, proprietary software has been shielded from judicial review due to trade secret protections, preventing defendants from assessing or challenging the basis of evidence used against them. To mitigate these risks, law enforcement agencies must prioritize transparency, procedural safeguards, and regular audits of digital investigative processes. Independent review boards, clear usage policies, and technological literacy among both practitioners and judicial actors are essential. Ethical missteps in digital investigations can have far-reaching consequences—not only for individual rights, but also for the perceived legitimacy of law enforcement and judicial outcomes. Ultimately, the credibility of cybercrime enforcement hinges not only on its technical capabilities, but on the integrity of the legal and ethical boundaries that shape its use.

CONCLUSION

Digital evidence is no longer auxiliary; it is foundational to contemporary cybercrime investigation. From the chain of custody protocols governing cloud data to the artificial intelligence tools guiding threat assessments, every aspect of cybercrime enforcement reflects a paradigm shift in how society conceptualizes both crime and justice. While the deployment of increasingly powerful tools offers new avenues for accountability, it also creates new risks of abuse, overreach, and systemic bias. Hence, maintaining transparency, protecting privacy, and enforcing legal boundaries are not optional: they are the very criteria by which legitimacy in this domain must be judged. In the near future, law enforcement agencies, legal institutions, and private-sector partners must co-evolve to meet the threats posed by emerging technologies and transnational criminal networks. Robust collaboration, technological literacy, and ethical oversight will determine whether cybercrime investigations serve the public interest or erode it. The ideas thus presented provide a snapshot of current capabilities and a call to future-proof investigative and legal architectures for a world increasingly defined by its digital terrain.

The evolution of cybercrime investigation reflects a broader transformation in how crime, evidence, and enforcement are understood in the digital age. From early computer misuse cases addressed through improvised investigative strategies to the highly specialized, technology-driven practices employed today, cybercrime investigations have expanded alongside the growth of digital infrastructure. As illustrated by the Silk Road prosecution, modern investigations increasingly rely on the ability to trace digital artifacts such as encrypted communications, blockchain transactions, and metadata across complex technological environments (*United States v. Ulbricht*, 2014). These developments demonstrate both the potential and the limits of technological innovation in uncovering criminal activity concealed within digital systems.

There is value in tracing the historical progression of cybercrime investigation in the United States, highlighting how legal frameworks, and reviewing institutional responses and how forensic practices have adapted to emerging digital threats. Early reliance on traditional investigative methods proved insufficient as offenses moved beyond physical spaces and into networked environments, prompting the creation of specialized cyber units and the professionalization of digital forensics (Steinmetz et al., 2025; Kent et al., 2006). Over time, standardized procedures, forensic tools, and training programs have strengthened the reliability and admissibility of digital evidence, establishing cybercrime investigation as a recognized and essential component of modern criminal justice practice.

At the same time, the expansion of investigative capabilities has introduced new legal and ethical challenges. The integration of cloud computing, cryptocurrency, artificial intelligence, and encryption technologies has fundamentally altered how evidence is stored, accessed, and analyzed. Investigators must now navigate jurisdictional boundaries, third-party data control, and increasingly sophisticated privacy-enhancing technologies that complicate evidence collection (Wall, 2017; Dyson et al., 2019). While technological tools enable more effective investigations, they also raise concerns about overcollection, surveillance, and the erosion of individual privacy if not carefully regulated.

Judicial decisions such as *Riley v. California* (2014) and *Carpenter v. United States* (2018) reflect an evolving constitutional approach to digital evidence, recognizing that traditional Fourth Amendment doctrines require reconsideration in light of modern technologies. These cases underscore the principle that investigative authority must remain bounded by constitutional safeguards, even as digital evidence becomes central to criminal enforcement. Similarly, debates surrounding encryption and lawful access highlight the difficulty of balancing public safety interests with the need to preserve secure digital environments for individuals and institutions (Walden, 2018; Pisarić, 2020). These tensions illustrate that technological capability alone cannot determine investigative practice; legal and ethical considerations must remain central to cybercrime enforcement.

Collaboration has emerged as another defining feature of contemporary and future cybercrime investigations. Effective enforcement increasingly depends on coordination among federal, state, and local agencies, as well as cooperation with private technology companies and international partners. Information-sharing mechanisms, task forces, and public reporting systems such as the Internet Crime Complaint Center play a critical role in addressing the scale and complexity of cybercrime (Tóth & Gáspár, 2020). These collaborative frameworks also require careful governance to ensure accountability, transparency, and respect for privacy obligations.

Moving forward, cybercrime investigations will continue to evolve in response to emerging technologies, globalized criminal activity, and shifting legal standards. Advances in artificial intelligence, encryption, and digital infrastructure will likely intensify the challenges faced by investigators, while simultaneously offering new tools for analysis and detection (Faqir, 2023; Završnik, 2021). The effectiveness of future cybercrime enforcement will depend not only on technological innovation, but on sustained investment in training, oversight, and ethical governance. As digital evidence becomes increasingly pervasive, maintaining public trust and constitutional legitimacy will remain essential to the long-term success of cybercrime investigations. Ultimately, the intersection of technology and criminal justice demands a careful balance between innovation and restraint. Cybercrime investigations must adapt to an evolving digital landscape while remaining grounded in legal principles and ethical responsibility. By examining the tools, techniques, and legal complexities that define modern cybercrime investigation, the importance of aligning investigative capability with constitutional protections in an era where the digital and physical worlds are inseparably intertwined is underscored.

REFERENCES

Agboola, V., Osamor, J., & Olajide, F. (2024). Evaluating the efficiency of FTK, autopsy, and mobile forensic tools: A comparative study in criminal investigations. [IJICR]. *International Journal of Intelligent Computing Research, 15*(1), 1279–1291. DOI: 10.20533/ijicr.2042.4655.2024.0156

Aljahdali, A., Alsaidi, N., Alsafri, M., Alsulami, A., & Almutairi, T. (2021). Mobile device forensics. *Romanian Journal of Information Technology & Automatic Control, 31*(3), 81–96. DOI: 10.33436/v31i3y202107

Atwood, J. R. (2015). The encryption problem: Why the courts and technology are creating a mess for law enforcement. *Saint Louis University Public Law Review, 34*(2), 407–434.

Chidambaram, A. S., Suthendran, K., & Kumar, M. S. (2022, March). Forensic investigation on electronic evidences using encase and autopsy. *Sustainable Development in Engineering and Technology*, 117-124.

Donohue, L. K. (2015). The Fourth Amendment in a digital world. *Annual Survey of American Law, 71*, 553–685.

Dyson, S., Buchanan, W. J., & Bell, L. (2019, July 29). The challenges of investigating cryptocurrencies and blockchain related crime. *ArXiv.* https://doi.org//arXiv.1907.12221DOI: 10.48550

Faqir, R. S. A. (2023, December). Digital criminal investigations in the era of artificial intelligence: A comprehensive overview. *International Journal of Cyber Criminology, 17*(2), 77–94.

Hemdan, E. E.-D., & Manjaiah, D. H. (2016, October). A cloud forensic strategy for investigation of cybercrime. In *2016 International Conference on Emerging Technological Trends (ICETT)* (pp. 1-5). IEEE. https://doi.org/DOI: 10.1109/ICETT.2016.7873667

Herman, M., Iorga, M., Salim, A. M., Jackson, R. H., Hurst, M. R., Leo, R. A., Mishra, A. K., Landreville, N. M., & Wang, Y. (2024, July). *NIST Cloud Computing Forensic Reference Architecture* (NIST Special Publication 800-201). National Institute of Standards and Technology. https://doi.org/DOI: 10.6028/NIST.SP.800-201

Internet Crime Complaint Center. (n.d.). *Internet Crime Complaint Center.* Federal Bureau of Investigation. https://www.ic3.gov

Jaeger, P. T., Lin, J., Grimes, J. M., & Simmons, S. N. (2009, April 8). Where is the cloud? Geography, economics, environment, and jurisdiction in cloud computing. *First Monday, 14*(5). Advance online publication. DOI: 10.5210/fm.v14i5.2456

Mandela, N., Manna, F., Garibado, D. A., Musaka, S., Mutara, M., & Mistry, N. R. (2024, February). Exploring the use of Tails Operating System in cybercrime and its impact on law enforcement investigations. *In 2024 11th International Conference on Computing for Sustainable Global Development (INDIACom)* (pp. 1109-1114). IEEE. https://doi.org/DOI: 10.23919/INDIACom61295.2024.10499122

Marturana, F., Tacconi, S., Bertè, R., & Me, G. (2012, June). Triage-based automated analysis of evidence in court cases of copyright infringement. In *2012 IEEE International Conference on Communications (ICC)* (pp. 6668-6672). IEEE. https://doi.org/DOI: 10.1109/ICC.2012.6364819

Mishra, P., Varadharajan, V., Tupakula, U., & Pilli, E. S. (2018). A detailed investigation and analysis of using machine learning techniques for intrusion detection. *IEEE Communications Surveys and Tutorials, 21*(1), 686–728. DOI: 10.1109/COMST.2018.2847722

Nofer, M., Gomber, P., Hinz, O., & Schiereck, D. (2017). Blockchain. *Business & Information Systems Engineering, 59*(3), 183–187. DOI: 10.1007/s12599-017-0467-3

Pisarić, M. (2022, March). Communications encryption as an investigative obstacle. *The Journal of Criminal Law & Criminology, 60*(1), 61–74. DOI: 10.47152/rkkp.60.1.4

Pisarić, M. M. (2020). Encryption as an obstacle for criminal investigation and evidence collection. *Zbornik Radova, 54*(3), 1079–1094. DOI: 10.5937/zrpfns54-26929

Riley v. California, 573 U.S. 373 (2014).

Roffel, M., & Lin, X. (2023, August). Write Blocker for Internet of Things Flash technologies. In *2023 20th Annual International Conference on Privacy, Security and Trust* (PST) (pp. 1-10). IEEE. https://doi.org/DOI: 10.1109/PST58708.2023.10320158

Sathilkumar, A., & Graham, N. (2018). Cryptocurrency: Law enforcement challenges and opportunities. A risk perspective. *Australia and New Zealand Society of Evidence Based Policing, 3*(1), 11–13.

Sayal, A., Gupta, A., & Vasundhara, C., M, Y. B., Gupta, V., & Maheshwari, H. (2024, April). Crime detection using data mining techniques. In *2024 Sixth International Conference on Computational Intelligence and Communication Technologies (CCICT)* (pp. 200-204). IEEE. https://doi.org/DOI: 10.1109/CCICT62777.2024.00041

Segall, S. (2013). Jurisdictional challenges in the United States government's move to cloud computing technology. *Fordham Intellectual Property. Media and Entertainment Law Journal, 23*(3), 1105–1153.

Steinmetz, K. F., Schaefer, B. P., & Kurtz, D. L. (2025). Computer crime units and task forces. In *Policing the Digital Void: Cybercrime Investigations in the US* (pp. 47-59). Springer Nature Switzerland. https://doi.org/DOI: 10.1007/978-3-031-98040-4_4

Tang, J., Cui, Y., Li, Q., Ren, K., Liu, J., & Buyya, R. (2016, June 6). Ensuring security and privacy preservation for cloud data services. *ACM Computing Surveys, 49*(1), 1–39. DOI: 10.1145/2906153

Tóth, D., & Gáspár, Z. (2020, December 1). Jurisdictional challenges of cybercrime. *Journal of Eastern European Criminal Law, 7*(2), 101–118.

United States v. Chatrie, 590 F. Supp. 3d 901 (E.D. Va. 2020).

United States v. Morris, 928 F.2d 504 (2d Cir. 1991)

United States v. Ulbricht, 31 F. Supp. 3d 540 (S.D.N.Y. 2014).

Walden, I. (2018, August). 'The Sky is Falling!'–Responses to the 'Going Dark' problem. *Computer Law & Security Review, 34*(4), 901–907. DOI: 10.1016/j.clsr.2018.05.013

Wall, D. S. (2017, May 13). Towards a conceptualisation of cloud (cyber) crime. In *International Conference on Human Aspects of Information Security, Privacy, and Trust* (pp. 529-538). Springer International Publishing. DOI: 10.1007/978-3-319-58460-7_37

Završnik, A. (2021). Algorithmic justice: Algorithms and big data in criminal justice settings. *European Journal of Criminology*, *18*(5), 623–642. DOI: 10.1177/1477370819876762

Chapter 11

Digital Forensics in Financial Crime:

Blockchain Analytics, Crypto Laundering, and Cross-Border Enforcement Challenges

Smruti Ranjan Sahoo
http://orcid.org/0009-0001-2910-7982
KIIT University, India

Puranjoy Ghosh
KIIT University, India

ABSTRACT

The expansion of cryptocurrencies and decentralized financial systems has transformed money laundering into a borderless and technologically complex form of financial crime, exposing the limits of compliance-driven enforcement. This chapter examines digital forensics as a core investigative tool in blockchain environments, focusing on transaction reconstruction, wallet attribution, and cross-chain tracing. It analyses crypto-laundering typologies such as ransomware payments, darknet marketplaces, DeFi exploits, and professional facilitation, demonstrating how forensic methods address the weaknesses of rule-based AML systems. Anchored in the criminal justice process, the chapter examines evidentiary reliability, seizure and custody of digital assets, and the admissibility of blockchain-derived evidence in court, with particular reference to India's legal framework under the Prevention of Money Laundering Act and comparative international enforcement practices.

INTRODUCTION

Financial crime is transforming with the decentralised digital finance. The money laundering scenario has gone beyond bank-centric techniques and has now evolved to platform-based and protocol-driven money laundering techniques. In the past, criminals laundered illicit funds by using cash businesses, casinos, or shell companies; however, they are now taking advantage of online payment processors, cryptocurrency exchanges, decentralised finance (DeFi) services, and even algorithmic smart contracts to conceal the sources of funds ("Illicit finance risk," 2023). Bank accounts that played a central role in

DOI: 10.4018/979-8-3373-7660-8.ch011

laundering in the past have been replaced by pseudonymous cryptographic wallets and automated protocols that hide ownership. The speed and the anonymity of these new systems make them very difficult to detect and require a fundamental change in how an investigation is carried out ("Cryptocurrencies: Tracing the evolution," 2021).

Emerging technologies are a double-edged sword for financial crime cryptocurrencies (e.g., Bitcoin or privacy coins) and stablecoins enable value to flow throughout the world without disclosing the identity of users. DeFi applications on blockchain networks allow users to swap tokens, lend money, or receive yields without involving traditional intermediaries, according to the U.S. Department of Treasury. Trading in non-fungible tokens (NFTs), non-fungible items that are unique to each owner, has also become a way to park illicit money across jurisdictions. Each innovation cuts overreliance on regulated gatekeepers and can ruin conventional monetary surveillance. Yet these same advances offer new tools for enforcement. Artificial intelligence and big data analytics can be used to identify hidden trends within large transactions datasets, whereas digital forensics can be used to systematically extract and analyse the electronic evidence (Mohanta et al., 2025). Incorporating these methods into anti-money laundering (AML) efforts could lead to earlier detection of illegal activity and better enforcement results ("Updated guidance," 2021).

Still, today's anti-money laundering architecture is largely mired in static, compliance-based rules. Traditional monitoring systems detect transactions above certain thresholds or similar to known patterns, which is not ideal for decentralised and fast-changing networks. Sophisticated criminals utilise techniques such as mixers, privacy coins, and cross-chain "chainhopping" to obfuscate transactions and avoid detection ("Illicit finance risk," 2023). Such static systems are incapable of adapting to new typologies or of discovering hidden links in complex data. As a result, analysts are overloaded with false positives, and purified, novel laundering schemes frequently escape detection. Simply filing suspicious transaction reports after the fact rarely disrupts criminal networks or recovers assets. To effectively tackle modern threats like avoiding sanctions through crypto-trafficking, there is a need for more active investigation tools than what traditional compliance methods offer.

Advanced digital forensics is emerging as a must for this field. Blockchains will give you unalterable records of the transaction, but pseudonymous addresses will conceal the human identities behind the addresses, and illegal money can be fragmented and combined through innumerable wallets and protocols. This tension between transactional transparency and identity concealment gives rise to what can be termed the forensic paradox, a concept to be explored in detail. Forensic experts have now used transaction graph analysis, address clustering heuristics, and other methods to link addresses that do not seem to be related to real people (Lenahan-Pfahlert, 2024). Combined with data from cryptocurrency exchanges, these links can often be corroborated by investigators, allowing them to pierce the pseudonymous veil. Such methods have been used to map complex laundering networks from darknet marketplaces to ransomware operations and have enabled high-value asset seizures. In short, the ability to trace illicit cryptographic flows end-to-end is increasingly considered not optional but essential to effecting law enforcement.

The next challenge is to connect these technological tools with justice on the ground. In practice, though, investigators need to be able to trace illicit crypto flows, as well as acquire digital evidence that can hold up in court. They often encounter roadblocks in freezing/seizing cryptocurrency at the cross-border level, as rapid cooperation from crypto exchanges and international partners is required to prevent suspects from transferring assets (Renuka, 2026). After the investigative stage, lawyers for the prosecutor must translate advanced blockchain analyses into clear and admissible evidence. Courts are now struggling with the reliability of such high-tech evidence, but recent rulings within the US have ruled that blockchain tracing analysis is admissible as long as rigorous methods are used (Lenahan-Pfahlert, 2024). Ultimately, successful prosecutions of crypto-related money laundering are about combining state-of-the-art forensic methods and applying more traditional standards of proof.

Legal and institutional frameworks are starting to evolve to cope with this changing threat. Many jurisdictions are revising laws and procedures to consider virtual assets. In India, for example, in 2023 an amendment to the Prevention of Money Laundering Act (PMLA) included virtual asset service providers (e.g., cryptocurrency exchanges) under anti-money laundering requirements (Press Information Bureau, 2025). Such an amendment is a critical step, but enforcement is a difficult one without commensurate capacity for investigation.

Other major jurisdictions are also increasing enforcement, but criminals are still taking advantage of gaps between countries. Differences in the definition and regulation of crypto assets in different nations and varying privacy laws pose a barrier to cross-border evidence sharing and cooperation (Renuka, 2026). Investigators require specialised training regarding blockchain analytics, and judges need an understanding of digital evidence in order for the courts to appropriately consider it. In this context a “forensic-first” approach has been advocated, an approach based on a logic of proactive investigation and technical analysis in parallel with regulation. Especially for India's burgeoning crypto market, if there is a dire need to highlight the need for forensic rigour right from the beginning, it would bolster the battle against financial crime considerably in the decentralised era.

EVOLUTION OF FINANCIAL CRIME AND CRYPTO-LAUNDERING TYPOLOGIES

Financial crime typologies have changed from traditional bank-based financial crimes to crypto-driven schemes that implement the use of wallets, protocols, and cross-border digital rails (Levi & Soudijn, 2020). Three stages of classic money laundering are typically used to define money laundering, namely placement, layering, and integration (Levi & Reuter, 2006). Placement is the act of inserting illegal money into the formal economy through banks, casinos, currency exchanges, trade, or cash-heavy businesses. The money's origin is disguised by layering shell companies, offshore accounts and complex transfers. Integration converts the cleaned money into seemingly legitimate assets such as real estate, businesses or financial instruments (Levi & Reuter, 2006). These steps were reliant on regulated intermediaries that could document, report and provide points of investigation. Virtual assets and blockchain systems alter that logic by shifting the key laundering activities away from institutions and into user-controlled wallets and automated protocols, limiting the effectiveness of routine compliance checks (Financial Action Task Force, 2019).

Virtual assets transform each stage, instead of replacing the whole framework. Placement now can occur when criminal proceeds transfer into digital assets through peer-to-peer markets, cash brokers, mules, or exchange accounts through deception or collusion. Layering is used to expand funds by making rapid moves between addresses and spreading money across various addresses and using services like mixers or privacy tools that make it difficult to easily trace. Integration might be cashing out through compliant or non-compliant exchanges, converting to high-resolution, high-value goods, or utilising crypto to get assets that can be resold at a later time. These pathways often prove to be too much for compliance-first models because rule-based monitoring is anchored to identifiable intermediaries, traditional account histories and static red-flag thresholds. Blockchain forensics, by contrast, has the potential to trace flows, even with limited visibility of compliance, because transactions leave permanent on-chain traces which can be analysed as a linked graph of value movement (Financial Action Task Force, 2019).

Cryptocurrency-enabled crime has been on the rise, due to digital assets, for a combination of speed, global reach, and operational pseudonymity. Ransomware also shows the interconnectivity of extortion and laundering in the same pipeline. Often, threat actors request money in cryptocurrency and then attempt to cover the trail by rapid transfers, swaps, and obfuscation services (Financial Crimes Enforcement Network, 2021). Darknet markets also rely on virtual assets to settle contraband and stolen data, such as being able to use escrow and reputation systems but keep participants off traditional rails. These typologies avoid routine compliance because no bank transfer is required, and suspicious activity reporting on initial movement may be missing. Yet they remain vulnerable to forensic inquiry because the fundamental aim of laundering, moving, consolidating and transforming money leads to identifiable patterns and convergence points which can be analysed through transaction graph analysis and attribution-supported tracing (Financial Action Task Force, 2023).

In an example of ransomware-DeFi laundering, a victim's payment might enter a group of addresses controlled by an attacker and pass through automatic services created to segregate attribution. The money may be exchanged into a high-liquidity token on a decentralised exchange, sent through a mixer to make it harder to trace the money, bridged to another chain, and deposited into a lending protocol. Withdrawals from said protocol can seem far away from the initial input. Compliance monitoring fails here because there is little correlation between protocol-level activity and institutional reporting, and static rules are unable to comprehend multi-step, cross-chain sequences. Forensic reconstruction concentrates on aspects overlooked by existing regulations, such as connecting hops, sequencing events by time, clustering indicators, and identifying exit points like centralised exchanges and fiat off-ramps. It also involves examining service wallets where cooperation and evidence might be acquired (Financial Action Task Force, 2023).

Decentralised finance renders typological complexity even worse by multiplying laundering-compatible actions while limiting centralised control. DeFi protocols enable swaps, loans, and yield strategies using smart contracts and liquidity pools, often without identity checks at the protocol level (Harvey et al., 2020). Composability permits value to pass in multiple protocols in a single transaction sequence, making it difficult for threshold-based compliance filters to interpret. DeFi also supports "layering by design"; through liquidity provision, staking, and routing, inputs could become different outputs while concealing provenance by contract interactions. These factors make it more difficult to enforce, especially when there is no operator who can be forced to conduct KYC or freeze suspicious funds. Forensics can still help; given that DeFi interactions are recorded on-chain, they can help find repeated patterns of exploitation, touchpoints of a contract, and clusters of wallets that are repeated across incidents. Cross-referencing exchange data and open-source intelligence can help increase attribution and evidentiary reliability.

NFT markets offer opportunities for laundering by their valuation opacity and by self-dealing. NFTs are portable stores of value, and there is no standardised pricing, to the extent that NFTs can be laundered in the same way as the art market. Wash trading, where a party repeatedly sells one NFT among wallets under common control to create an appearance of legitimate wealth generation and market provenance, creates an appearance of legitimate wealth generation and market provenance. Compliance-first approaches miss this because NFT platforms may not always perform necessary identity checks, and the transaction is billed as a sale of the items rather than a financial transfer. Forensic approaches analyse the money trail rather than the story, analysing the funding sources of the wallets, clustering indicators, fast resale patterns and connections between the buyer and the seller addresses to identify artificial valuation and circular movement of value (Bonifazi et al., 2023).

In an NFT-based obfuscation scenario, illegal proceeds can be converted into crypto and then used to "buy" an NFT from a cooperating seller at an inflated price (Sifat et al., 2024). The seller may run the proceeds through additional wallets and later exchange value through separate transaction streams, while the buyer refers to an on-chain record of a legitimate sale and makes the expense appear as an investment. Compliance controls may break down because the activity is not subject to normal banking surveillance and because marketplace documentation may appear commercially plausible. Forensic reconstruction views the NFT as the transport vehicle, not as the evidence of legitimacy, as it studies circular funding, correlated wallets and uncharacteristic pricing relationships in trading history to distinguish real market movement from transfer in laundering-orientated (Bonifazi et al., 2023).

Structural drivers are the way in which these typologies proliferate and persist. Regulatory fragmentation leads to uneven obligations between jurisdictions, while the investigative capacity varies. Actors take advantage of permissive environments, delays in mutual legal assistance and inconsistencies in data retention and platform cooperation to facilitate the cross-border movement of laundering activities faster than legal processes can keep up. Economic asymmetries are also important. The strong legitimate demand for crypto in a setting of currency instability drives up the background level of activity, providing cover for illicit flows and making their detection difficult. In light of these conditions, the typologies are not simply "known"; they are constantly evolving. The analytical value is in determining what each typology tells us about the limitations of enforcement and possibilities for forensics. Compliance screening tends to be best where identity is least available, and forensic reconstruction best where transaction data is most persistent and linkable. That divergence is the justification for a forensic-first focus (Financial Action Task Force, 2023).

BLOCKCHAIN TECHNOLOGY AND THE FORENSIC PARADOX

Blockchain technology operates through distributed ledgers that record transactions across a network of participants rather than through a single central authority. Each transaction is permanently recorded and made visible to all network users, creating a system that is transparent by design. This transparency distinguishes blockchain-based financial systems from traditional banking infrastructures, where transaction visibility is largely confined to regulated intermediaries and supervisory authorities. At the same time, blockchain systems do not record real-world identities in the manner of bank accounts. Participants transact through cryptographic addresses, which function as persistent identifiers but do not directly reveal personal information. This architectural choice generates a distinctive evidentiary environment in which transactional data are openly accessible while the identity of the actor remains concealed. Legal and regulatory scholarship has long recognized that this removal of centralized intermediaries reduces institutional oversight and complicates conventional enforcement models, even as it enhances data integrity and auditability (Ducas & Wilner, 2017).

The tension between openness and concealment gives rise to what is commonly described as the forensic paradox. Blockchain ledgers disclose the full history of value transfers, including timestamps, transaction amounts, and address interactions, yet they do not disclose who controls the addresses involved. In public discourse, this feature is often described as anonymity; however, from an investigative standpoint, blockchain systems are more accurately characterized as pseudonymous. Addresses are stable over time, and repeated use generates behavioural patterns that can be examined and compared. Investigators can trace how funds move across addresses, identify clusters of activity, and reconstruct transaction pathways over extended periods. Digital forensic practice relies on correlating these on-chain patterns with off-chain data sources, such as exchange records, seized devices, communications metadata, or open-source intelligence, to infer the likely human actors behind transactions (Ombu, 2023). The paradox lies in the fact that blockchains simultaneously provide an unusually rich transactional record and an incomplete account of legal identity.

This paradox has significant implications for criminal justice. Offenders exploit the gap between traceability and attribution by fragmenting funds across multiple addresses, using privacy-enhancing services, or routing transactions through decentralized platforms that lack customer identification requirements. Empirical studies of cryptocurrency-linked crime have shown that pseudonymity and global accessibility make blockchain systems attractive for money laundering, ransomware payments, and illicit trade (Kethineni & Cao, 2019). At the same time, those activities still generate observable trails. Investigative success increasingly depends on the ability to analyse these trails in context, rather than on detecting isolated suspicious transactions. Blockchain data alone can reveal how funds moved, but it cannot, by itself, establish who controlled those funds at a legally sufficient standard. As a result, attribution derived from blockchain analysis remains an evidentiary inference rather than direct proof, and that distinction is critical when cases proceed to court.

Differences across the virtual asset ecosystem further shape the evidentiary landscape. Centralized exchanges and custodial wallet providers maintain internal records linking customers to addresses, making them key points of contact between blockchain activity and legal identity. These entities often provide liquidity, fiat on-ramps, and asset custody, which brings them within the scope of regulatory oversight and lawful process. From an enforcement perspective, such intermediaries can supply corroborating evidence that supports attribution and strengthens prosecutorial cases. Decentralized exchanges and non-custodial wallets, by contrast, allow users to transact without surrendering control or identity information to a service provider. While this design enhances autonomy and resilience, it reduces institutional visibility and limits the availability of documentary evidence. Compliance obligations are unevenly distributed across these systems, creating environments in which illicit actors can deliberately avoid regulated entry points.

Wallet architecture further complicates attribution. Custodial services concentrate control within providers that may respond to subpoenas or freezing orders, whereas non-custodial wallets place control entirely in the hands of users. When non-custodial wallets are used exclusively, investigators must rely on circumstantial and corroborative evidence to link addresses to individuals. Such evidence may include device seizures, transaction timing correlated with known activities, reuse of addresses across services, or eventual interaction with regulated platforms. Forensic analysis therefore operates within a broader evidentiary framework in which blockchain records are one component rather than a standalone solution. Reliable attribution depends on careful documentation, cross-verification, and procedural safeguards that meet evidentiary standards (Ombu, 2023).

Interoperability tools and cross-chain bridges introduce additional layers of complexity. These mechanisms allow value to move between blockchains, often through wrapped assets or external validators, enabling rapid shifts across technical environments. From an investigative perspective, cross-chain movement fragments transaction histories and requires reconstruction across multiple ledgers with different data structures. Regulatory discussions have emphasised that technological innovation in this area frequently outpaces supervisory capacity, creating opportunities for laundering strategies that exploit technical novelty and jurisdictional lag (Ducas & Wilner, 2017). The evidentiary burden increases as investigators must demonstrate continuity of value across chains and explain complex mechanisms to courts that may be unfamiliar with such systems.

Beyond individual investigations, blockchain architecture raises broader regulatory and security concerns. Financial stability risks emerge when opaque practices, leverage, or interconnected platforms amplify systemic shocks. National security risks arise when value can be transferred across borders with minimal friction and limited oversight. Analyses of enforcement outcomes, including those informed by the FinCEN files, illustrate that effective responses depend not only on reporting but on institutional co-ordination, investigative quality, and the ability to translate complex financial data into legally actionable evidence (D'Avino, 2022). Comparative studies further show uneven implementation of compliance and investigative practices across jurisdictions, enabling regulatory arbitrage and undermining cross-border cooperation (Renda & Caneppele, 2023).

Ultimately, blockchain systems produce a form of evidence that is abundant yet incomplete. They reveal how value moves with unprecedented clarity, while concealing the identities that criminal justice systems must ultimately establish. The forensic paradox underscores that inference drawn from blockchain analysis cannot substitute for legal proof of identity and intent. Courts require corroboration, procedural integrity, and clear explanations of analytical limits. Effective governance in this space therefore depends on integrating blockchain transparency with robust forensic practice, institutional cooperation, and evidentiary discipline, rather than treating technical traceability as a substitute for legal attribution.

DIGITAL FORENSICS METHODOLOGIES IN BLOCKCHAIN INVESTIGATIONS

Digital forensics has moved beyond the physical realm to the blockchain ledger analysis in financial crime investigations. In systems based on blockchain technology, evidence is not represented as files on a single device, but in the form of transaction records on an immutable ledger. Thus, the ledger itself becomes a primary object of forensic analysis with each transaction being a clue to financial behaviour. Traditional forensic principles have been modified for this context, recognizing that blockchain evidence is persistent, publicly available and cryptographically secured, but is often devoid of direct links to real-world identity (Ombu, 2023).

Unlike traditional digital forensics where a physical device may be taken, blockchain forensics is dependent on data collection from network nodes and third-party services. Investigators frequently run their very own full nodes to bring back transaction histories by themselves and confirm the integrity of blocks. Extracting data directly from the ledger maintained by consensus guarantees the evidence is representative of the true state of transactions and not manipulable by any intermediary. In practice, the amount of data on the blockchain often means using special analytics platforms or APIs. While these tools can speed up analysis, there are some potential reproducibility issues. To address such concerns, investigators cross-check outputs from analytics tools with data from their own nodes to verify consistency (Atlam et al., 2024). They also record every step in the data extraction and analysis process by noting the data software versions, parameters and timestamps to create an audit trail that is conducive to reproducibility. Such rigour ensures that blockchain evidence can be independently checked by repeating the steps of the analysis, as is increasingly expected by courts.

At the core of blockchain forensics are transaction graph analyses, which are used to build up how the funds move through the network. Every transaction can be represented as part of a directed graph in which addresses are nodes and transactions are edges where value is transferred from nodes to nodes. By charting these interactions, investigators have a visual and mathematical representation of how illegal money could have moved. Graph techniques help to detect patterns such as long chains of transactions, several sources converging into one address or spreading from one address into many outputs. Timing data also provides another dimension. Certain patterns, such as rapid sequences of hopping, cyclic transfers or long, dormant periods followed by sudden movements, can point to laundering techniques. Recent literature confirms that analysis of transaction graphs is one of the pillars of cryptocurrency investigations (Atlam et al., 2024).

Building on the concept of transaction graphs, forensic analysts use heuristics based on clustering algorithms to determine which addresses might be under the control of the same entity. One popular method is the multi-input heuristic which states that if multiple addresses appear as inputs on the same transaction, then it is likely they all belong to one owner. Other behaviour-based heuristics look for patterns in the way that addresses handle change outputs, reuse addresses or pay transaction fees. This approach simplifies the follow-the-money process by reducing the number of addresses to a lower number of inferred wallets. However, it is important to realize that these techniques are probabilistic (not deterministic). Sophisticated users can subvert heuristics on purpose; for example, by using CoinJoin mixing protocols that combine the inputs from different users into one transaction to avoid the multi-input assumption. Empirical studies indicate that both false positives and false negatives occur that investigators can mistakenly merge together unrelated addresses or fail to draw links between addresses that are actually connected (Conti et al., 2023). Therefore, analysts consider the results of clustering as hypotheses that need additional confirmation. Any conclusions based on heuristic methods must be verified by other forms of evidence or techniques to prevent an overstatement of confidence in attributions.

The ability to attribute blockchain activity to real-world entities is still one of the most difficult parts of cryptocurrency investigations. Investigators search forums, social media and dark web marketplaces for clues that link blockchain addresses to user aliases or organizations. Investigators additionally use leaked data or public records linking addresses and identities. Another important avenue is through regulated cryptocurrency exchanges and services. When law enforcement obtains exchange records, it is sometimes possible to link addresses that are being used in the trials with customer accounts. Case studies of dark web market take-downs show that even users who tried to remain anonymous were revealed from the correlation of on-chain transaction behaviour and off-chain data (Mas'ud et al., 2021). Thus, investigators are unlikely to present such findings as definitive proof of identity in a judgment or as a definitive link to a criminal act but instead include such discoveries as probabilistic linkages with multiple indicators (Ombu, 2023) to avoid presenting more evidence of forensic certainty in legal proceedings than is appropriate.

Advanced laundering tactics, such as peel chains, mixers/tumblers, and cross-chain hops, aim at making it difficult to trace and emphasising the limitations of forensic techniques. Criminals use these methods to break the trace of funds for example by moving illicit cryptocurrency across multiple blockchains or converting into privacy coins. Detecting such schemes involves correlating activities across ledgers, for example, spotting points where value leaves one chain and turns up elsewhere on another. Specialized analytics tools can help flag probable instances of this chain-hopping, but any conclusions that are drawn need to be taken with some caution, as not all similar transactions are linked and coincidences can be misleading. No matter how advanced the analytics skills are, there are inherent reliability constraints. Heuristic approaches have a potential for error. An analysis might identify a non-suspicious cluster of transactions as suspicious because it matches a pattern, or a cunning launderer might go undetected because he avoided known patterns. False positives can lead investigators into false directions and implicate others who are not actually guilty, while false negatives could let illicit money fly through undetected. Therefore, it is important to support each analysis finding with external sources of evidence. Investigators can validate on-chain results by cross checking with exchange records or sources from the open-source intelligence (OSINT). A holistic approach merging on-chain analysis with off-chain data ultimately leads to more confident and defensible conclusions (Jahankhani et al., 2019).

Ensuring the reproducibility and transparency of the investigative process is an essential component of blockchain forensics (Alqahtany & Syed, 2024). Legal cases can be decided on complex blockchain evidence, and investigators should work hard to preserve the data and methods used. Maintaining these records and following principles of repeatability is so that anyone can repeat the analysis if necessary. With reproducibility, the credibility of findings is strengthened while also aligning investigations within blockchain with traditional standards of forensic science where conclusions by an expert can be independently tested (Ombu, 2023).

CRYPTO-LAUNDERING CASE TYPOLOGIES AND FORENSIC RECONSTRUCTION

Crypto-laundering investigations benefit from case studies that show real-life scenarios of how forensic blockchain analysis is being used for real-world investigations (Wollerton, 2023). One prominent example is the Colonial Pipeline ransomware attack in 2021, where a group of cybercriminals (DarkSide) extorted a ransom of 75 Bitcoin from a U.S. pipeline operator. The criminals tried to launder the ransom by transferring the money through a series of wallets, but investigators quickly traced the money on Bitcoin's public ledger. Using transaction graph analysis the FBI identified a particular address that contained 63.7BTC, the bulk of ransom and crucially obtained that wallet private key (U.S. Department of Justice, 2021). These findings enabled the agents to confiscate the funds, which were established to be "proceeds traceable to a computer intrusion and property involved in money laundering". The results of the trace evidence of Bitcoins and also the seized private key were important in the legal aspect and the U.S. Department of Justice obtained a warrant to seize the Bitcoins and managed to retrieve about $2.3 million of the ransom money. This Colonial Pipeline case proved that even the best ransomware attack operators can be stopped with timely blockchain forensics (U.S. Department of Justice, 2021). In India, this type of operation would be strengthened by the Prevention of Money Laundering Act (PMLA) which, since 2023, is used to catch crypto transactions, meaning the Indian law enforcement would be able to seize crypto assets that were involved in illegal dealings the same way.

Another instructive case was the taking down in 2013 of the Silk Road darknet marketplace, which brings up crypto-laundering and online illicit economies (Ahmad et al., 2023). Silk Road is described as a market hidden in the Tor network for narcotics and criminal services, where all deals were paid for in Bitcoin. Vendors and the site's operator amassed significant profit from their cryptocurrency, frequently attempting to clean the money through cryptocurrency mixing services, or by switching between multiple addresses. Forensic reconstruction using blockchain played a crucial role in unravelling these activities, however. After Silk Road's servers were confiscated, the investigators used the logs of transactions on the marketplace and the ledger blocks of Bitcoin to trace hundreds of thousands of bitcoins in illegal payments back to wallets controlled by Ross Ulbricht (the site's founder). One of the FBI analysts used this method to trace more than 700,000 BTC from Silk Road addresses to Ulbricht's laptop, linking

Ulbricht directly to the illicit funds (Turner et al., 2020). This laundering trail was revealed because Ulbricht had concentrated his illicit income in a relatively small collection of addresses without completely anonymizing those addresses (van Roomen, 2025). The integration of graph analysis from the blockchain with traditional digital evidence involves several steps. This combination of forensic methods and blockchain graph analysis elucidates the actions taken by the agents who apprehended Ulbricht (Ron & Shamir, 2014). The agents arrested Ulbricht while he was logged into his account as an admin user, allowing them to acquire certain unencrypted wallet files and wallet keys from his account. Agents seized Ulbricht's laptop computer with his Bitcoin wallets, which forensic analysis revealed to have been funded by Silk Road dealings. In court this evidence supported money laundering charges on top of the charges of drug trafficking thereby emphasising that crypto-tracing techniques were admissible and persuasive to the jury. The Silk Road case, which was prosecuted in the U.S. had international dimensions as well (e.g. servers in Iceland) which also highlights that international cooperation is often necessary. Indian authorities would deal with a similar situation under cyber laws and PMLA, in line with the standards of international anti-money laundering law.

Decentralized finance (DeFi) exploitation and crypto mixers are a more recent type of crypto-laundering crime, as seen in the 2022 Axie Infinity Ronin Bridge Hack. In that case, a North Korean state-sponsored hacking group (Lazarus) stole approximately $600 million in cryptocurrency from a blockchain "bridge" used in a video game ecosystem. The thieves then laundered a large portion of the stolen Ether using an Ethereum mixing service called Tornado Cash. This technique involved breaking the trail of the funds by mixing the stolen Crypto with other user deposits so as to render the origins invisible. Blockchain forensic experts retaliated by tracing the movement of the stolen funds in and out of the Tornado Cash (Nadler & Schär, 2023). They found out that more than $455m of the money the hack yielded was channelled through Tornado Cash and through forensic analysis of the patterns in the money flow, authorities were able to eventually identify some of the withdrawal addresses of the launderers (U.S. Department of the Treasury, 2022). The findings generated by this on-chain investigation were serious enough that the U.S. Treasury's Office of Foreign Assets Control publicly blamed Lazarus for the laundering and issued sanctions on Tornado Cash in August 2022. This was unprecedented legally. An entire mixer service was legally sanctioned for facilitating crime. The Ronin hack case made clear that even "anonymity tools" in DeFi is not outside the reach of the law enforcement. Internationally, anti-money laundering bodies have been calling for tighter control of such mixers. India's regulators have also included mixer-linked transactions in the list of high-risk transactions under the PMLA compliance regime. This instance thus demonstrates the impact of advanced forensic tracing and regulatory action to combat new types of crypto laundering schemes that make use of decentralized technologies.

Finally, some crypto-laundering schemes involve professional enablers in the legal or financial sector to cover up the illegal funding. One US attorney was found guilty in 2019 for helping to deliver a cryptocurrency fraud (the OneCoin scheme) by laundering the proceeds of the fraud (around $400 million) through shell companies and overseas bank accounts. Forensic investigators discovered that he established some bogus investment funds to disguise the origin of the money (U.S. Attorney's Office, 2019). He was duly convicted of money laundering, thereby proving that even professionals can get in trouble if they facilitate crypto-related money laundering. Such conduct is equally culpable under Indian law; for example, complicit lawyers or accountants would be prosecutable under laws such as the PMLA.

A more recent example further demonstrates the integration of blockchain analytics with traditional investigative methods. In 2025, Chinese authorities tracked a $20 million laundering scheme by combining on-chain analytics with exchange records (Whitaker, 2025). By maintaining Know Your

Customer records, authorities accessed transaction logs from eight different cryptocurrency platforms. This enabled them to link wallet addresses to real identities and trace the flows from fiat currency to cryptocurrency. Investigators found that even when coins had been passed through mixers, forensic reconstruction could partially or fully reconstruct flows. The case underscores that combining blockchain forensics with traditional financial intelligence and cross-border data sharing is essential to countering evolving criminal tactics.

These cases collectively illustrate that whether through ransomware, darknet markets, DeFi exploits, professional networks, or state-level enforcement operations, crypto-laundering leaves trails which can be unravelled through forensic reconstruction. Each typology required investigating tools (from blockchain analytics to classic financial tracing) to obtain evidence admissible in court, stating that robust forensic means combined with legal frameworks can overcome the perceived anonymity of cryptocurrency transactions.

INDIAN LEGAL AND INSTITUTIONAL FRAMEWORK FOR CRYPTO-FORENSICS

India's legal response to crypto-forensics has been through its existing financial crime architecture, rather than a special cryptocurrency statute. The Prevention of Money Laundering Act, 2002 (PMLA) is still the main law used to investigate and prosecute money laundering crimes, and it now clearly applies to digital assets through updates in regulations rather than new laws. A decisive development was witnessed in March 2023, when the Ministry of Finance issued a notification to amend the activities involving virtual digital assets as covered under PMLA, thereby bringing cryptocurrency exchanges, custodial services, and asset transfer platforms under the ambit of anti-money laundering regulation (Press Information Bureau, 2025). This notification recognised that crypto-asset intermediaries increasingly carry out functions similar to traditional financial institutions and may further the concealment or movement of proceeds from crime if they are allowed to remain unregulated.

Following this extension, virtual asset service providers were determined to be reporting entities and held to be subject to customer due diligence, record maintenance, and suspicious transaction reports. These requirements are an attempt to carry over traditional compliance requirements into the crypto world, forcing exchanges and custodians to sort out identities and maintain histories of transactions for investigative purposes. This approach, however, faces structural limitations. Many crypto transactions are carried out on decentralised or offshore platforms that are beyond India's regulatory reach, and self-custodial wallets enable users to transact without involving any institutional intermediaries. As a result, even though the PMLA allows for investigating money laundering related to crypto, simply following rules is not enough to handle direct transfers between users or international trading on the platforms being investigated, which is very important.

Institutional responsibility of crypto-forensics is allocated by mainly two different authorities, such as the Financial Intelligence Unit-India and the Enforcement Directorate. FIU-IND is the national financial intelligence centre with inputs from reporting entities regarding suspicious transactions, and it processes them via pattern matching to identify suspicious laundering activities. Since the inclusion of virtual assets under the PMLA, FIU-IND has issued advisories and taken enforcement actions against non-compliant crypto platforms, signifying more assertive oversight. Nevertheless, the efficiency of FIU-IND in crypto cases is limited by a lack of uniform reporting criteria and data access, making crypto transaction starvation and the provision of financial intelligence less than optimal (Press Information Bureau, 2025).

The Enforcement Directorate exercises powers to carry out its functions, investigative and prosecutorial, under the PMLA, including search, seizure and attachment of property and arrest. Actions by the Indian government have increasingly found crypto-assets to be an attachable property and the proceeds of crime. The execution of seizure and attachment orders in relation to digital assets, however, has certain novel challenges. Control over crypto-assets lies in the access to the private keys instead of accessing or possessing a physical possession of it, and wallets may be scattered over devices or can be outside India. Crypto-assets are also extremely volatile, which raises issues about valuation at the time of attachment and responsibility for preserving value during the proceedings' pendency. Indian agencies are tackling these issues by partnering with regulated exchanges to safely hold crypto-assets that are taken by authorities, using tools like multi-signature wallets to keep the assets secure and stop any unauthorised transfers. These practices reflect a developing understanding of how traditional notions of seizure and possession will have to be adapted to decentralised financial instruments.

The evidentiary treatment of material derived from Blockchains represents one of the complex issues in Indian crypto-forensics, particularly concerning the admissibility of the evidence obtained from Blockchains. The Indian Evidence Act, 1872, regulates the admissibility of electronic records and blockchain transaction data; results of forensic analytics and wallet attribution reporting clearly fall under this ambit. Section 65B of the Evidence Act extends the requirement of a certificate attesting to the integrity, the manner of production and the reliability of electronic records being submitted in court (Raj Goyal & Prasad Mali, 2025). In *Arjun Panditrao Khotkar v. Kailash Kushanrao Gorantyal* (2020), the Supreme Court reiterated that compliance with Section 65B is compulsory and that only properly certified electronic evidence is admissible (Chadha & Sivaraman, 2024). This ruling has an immediate effect on evidence of crypto-forgery, as blockchain evidence is created by unidentifiable computer systems controlled by a network, an approach that differs from the generation process of centralised networks.

Applying Section 65B to blockchain evidence leaves some open questions about who can issue the required certificate and how the integrity of the system should be established. In practice, investigators are dependent on forensic analysts or exchange compliance officers that extract the blockchain data using verified nodes or analytical software and certify the extraction process, software environment, and data integrity. Courts are also increasingly using expert testimony to elucidate the workings of blockchains, trace methodologies, and attribution logic. Such expert evidence is essential to bridge the technical gap between the data relating to cryptographic transactions and legal standards of proof, but it should be proffered with caution. Blockchain analysis often leads to likely conclusions rather than certain identification, so courts need additional proof, like device seizures, exchange records, or communication logs, to support these conclusions (Fröwis et al., 2020).

Institutional capacity challenges complicate the crypto-forensic framework in India further. Law enforcement organisations are struggling with a shortage of staff with the skills needed to analyse blockchains and process smart contracts, as well as trace cross-chains. Investigative practices are still fragmented across jurisdictions with little standardisation on evidence collection and documentation. Dependence on foreign exchanges and private analytics providers raises concerns about data sovereignty and transparency of procedures. Mutual legal assistance mechanisms, although legally available, are frequently too slow to keep up with the speed of moving crypto-assets, thereby affecting chances of timely asset recovery.

India's legal and institutional framework for crypto forensics therefore represents a period of transition. Statutory inclusion of virtual assets in PMLA is a necessary first step, but successful enforcement relies on procedural adaptation, evidentiary clarity, and sustained capacity building. The Indian experience emphasises that crypto-forensics cannot be based only on compliance obligations and technological suppositions of transparency but must combine a spirit of forensic rigour with principles of criminal procedure and evidence law that are well established in Indian legal regimes.

CROSS-BORDER ENFORCEMENT AND GLOBAL COOPERATION CHALLENGES

Cryptocurrency's borderless nature poses a fundamental problem for law enforcement agencies that are divided according to national lines. Transactions on blockchain networks are not approved by any one country's financial system but are approved globally, obviating the traditional link between financial activity and jurisdiction. A single crypto transfer could come from a wallet in one country to an exchange in another, and the infrastructure could be located in multiple areas. This fragmentation tends to blur lines of investigative authority and applicable law considerably. These ambiguities are compounded by inconsistent regulation of virtual asset service providers (VASPs) across the world. Some countries strictly regulate and monitor crypto businesses, while others have little oversight. Illicit actors take advantage of this patchwork by moving to permissive jurisdictions and constraining funds through platforms that resist foreign legal requests. International assessments warn that such varying regimes open up opportunities for regulatory arbitrage and make it difficult to oversee the global cryptocurrency market (Financial Stability Board, 2025).

Getting evidence and seizing assets across borders are impeded due to sluggish legal processes. Mutual legal assistance treaties (MLATs) are currently a key method of cross-border evidence sharing, but they are not well-suited for the speed of cryptocurrency transactions. Formal MLAT requests require diplomatic and judicial measures that typically require many months, while the illicit funds can be scattered across numerous addresses in minutes. Practitioners report that asking for foreign cooperation is an onerous, time-consuming process; in fact, a 2023 survey showed that 60% of investigators cited multi-jurisdictional hurdles as a major challenge. By the time foreign account information is generated under an MLAT target, foreign assets might already have been shifted into untraceable channels. Conflicting data localisation laws also make it harder to receive timely access to records, with privacy and disclosure rules varying between jurisdictions, and can cause the release of important material to grind to a halt. Such legal frictions make it difficult for investigators to maintain the ephemeral evidence trails in the case of crypto-laundering (“Tackling crypto crime,” 2023).

In response to these shortcomings, enforcement agencies are looking to public-private partnerships and advanced analytics to increase the strength of cross-border investigations. Specialised blockchain analysis firms are currently working together with investigators from around the world to trace illicit flows of crypto in real time, effectively bypassing some of the delays involved in access to formal legal aid. Surveys show that 92% of law enforcement personnel regard cooperation with blockchain analytics companies and major exchanges as essential to solving crypto cases. These partnerships can quickly determine suspects and assets by using global datasets and expert tools. For instance, cross-border investigative “sprints” facilitated by private analytics firms have demonstrated considerable success. In 2025, a collaborative initiative involving Canadian and American authorities, supported by a blockchain analytics company, uncovered over $74 million in cryptocurrency fraud and assisted in freezing tens of millions in illicit funds (“The US and Canada join forces,” 2025). Such collaborations are a new model for agile international enforcement that can counter the crypto crime even when formal cooperation is lacking.

Table 1. Comparative overview of crypto-forensic enforcement agencies and capabilities

Agency / Jurisdiction	Primary Forensic Powers	Data Access Mechanism	Operational Strength	Structural Limitation in Crypto Cases
FinCEN (United States)	Financial intelligence collection; AML supervision; coordination with criminal agencies	Mandatory Suspicious Activity Reports (SARs) from VASPs; regulatory examinations	Early detection through compliance intelligence; strong domestic reporting ecosystem	SAR-based intelligence is reactive; limited direct control over decentralised protocols
IRS–Criminal Investigation (United States)	Criminal investigation; asset tracing; seizure and forfeiture	Blockchain analytics tools; subpoenas to exchanges; inter-agency data sharing	Deep forensic capability and prosecutorial integration	Jurisdictional reach depends on exchange cooperation and MLAT timelines
Department of Justice (United States)	Prosecution; forfeiture; negotiated compliance settlements	Court orders; deferred prosecution agreements; global coordination	Ability to impose extraterritorial pressure (e.g., Binance settlement)	Enforcement leverage weak against non-custodial or fully decentralised actors
National Crime Agency (United Kingdom)	Financial investigation; crypto seizure; operational coordination	Blockchain analytics; cooperation with FCA-regulated firms	Integrated crime–regulatory model; early intervention	Asset recovery constrained when wallets or keys are offshore
Financial Conduct Authority (United Kingdom)	Regulatory supervision; market access control	Licensing, audits, and compliance reporting	Preventive gatekeeping through market exclusion	No direct investigative or prosecutorial authority
Europol (European Union)	Intelligence coordination; analytical support; joint investigations	Shared intelligence platforms; Joint Investigation Teams (JITs)	Cross-border pattern recognition and pooled expertise	Dependent on member-state participation and data quality
FIU-IND (India)	Financial intelligence analysis; STR dissemination	Reporting entities under PMLA; exchange reporting	Centralised intelligence repository; growing crypto oversight	Limited visibility into offshore and decentralised platforms
Enforcement Directorate (India)	Search, seizure, attachment, prosecution under PMLA	Court-authorised seizure; exchange cooperation; MLATs	Statutory authority to attach crypto as proceeds of crime	Practical difficulty in controlling private keys and cross-chain assets

Note. This comparative overview demonstrates that while national agencies possess significant statutory authority, effective crypto-forensic enforcement increasingly depends on analytics partnerships, regulatory leverage over custodial gateways, and coordinated intelligence sharing, rather than on traditional mutual legal assistance mechanisms alone.

Several jurisdictions have also turned to multi-agency enforcement models to do more than step onto national territory. In the United States, crypto-related financial crime is dealt with using a unified approach between regulatory, investigative, and sanctions agencies. FinCEN (the US financial intelligence unit) collects financial intelligence from suspicious activity reports, IRS-CI traces illegal blockchain transactions, and the Office of Foreign Assets Control (OFAC) freezes illegal assets through sanctions. Together, this intelligence, investigation, and sanctions toolkit of powers increases the reach of enforcement. In 2023, Binance, the world's largest cryptocurrency exchange, admitted to wilful violations of anti-money laundering and sanctions laws and agreed to a $4.3 billion settlement with the Justice Department, FinCEN, OFAC, and other regulators (Mortlock et al., 2025). The Binance case represented a significant way in which two US enforcement bodies can use compliance data, criminal prosecution, and sanctions to hold a global platform accountable for its operations spanning across many different countries.

Other countries and regions are working on similar collaborative frameworks. In the United Kingdom, the National Crime Agency is responsible for crypto-related investigations, and specialised blockchain units work on crypto-related cases, while the Financial Conduct Authority oversees the crypto business landscape to ensure compliance and prevent the misuse of their platforms. This mixture of policing and oversight is intended to not only disrupt laundering but also to prevent future abuse by raising the standards of the industry. European authorities have strengthened cross-border cooperation through the intelligence sharing of Europol and the establishment of joint investigation teams, which permit investigators from several countries to work in a single legal framework. These initiatives have led to an improvement in the ability of the collective to trace cryptocurrency flow from one nation to another, although success hinges on consistent participation of all member states and timely data availability from these states. In addition, regular international conferences hosted by Europol, the Financial Action Task Force and others provide platforms for investigators and regulators to exchange typologies and techniques, strengthening informal cooperation across jurisdictions (Ilbiz & Kaunert, 2022).

Despite these advances, there are still critical gaps in the global enforcement of crypto-crimes (Sneha et al., 2024). Some jurisdictions lack the legal frameworks and political will to regulate crypto markets and cooperate on investigations, creating de facto safe havens for exchanges and wallet services facilitating laundering. Even among willing states, privacy laws and sovereignty concerns limit the data sharing to real time, like authorities being often hesitant to expose sensitive financial information to foreign counterparts without protracted procedures. In the absence of binding international obligations, much of the cross-border coordination still depends on voluntary alignment and goodwill, which can falter in cases of divergence of national interest. These dynamics have resulted in a fragmented enforcement landscape that sophisticated criminals exploit, operating in areas where oversight is minimal. Addressing this challenge will necessitate more than sporadic efforts. Regulators and law enforcement authorities need to collaborate to harmonise the key regulations to reduce arbitrage loopholes, simplify the legal assistance process to accelerate access to evidence, and build trust through constant partnership. Ultimately a sustained and structured response at a global level will be required to keep up with the transnational nature of cryptocurrency-enabled financial crime.

COMPLIANCE VS. FORENSICS: RETHINKING AML IN CRYPTO MARKETS

Anti-money laundering (AML) efforts in finance have traditionally been based on a compliance-first model involving procedures and compliance over actual investigation results. Under this approach, banks and other institutions spend significant resources conducting customer due diligence, transaction monitoring, and suspicious activity reporting primarily to meet regulatory requirements. Commentators have argued that this compliance-centric regime promotes a culture of formalism, or "tick-box" compliance, that is more concerned about paperwork than impact (Pol, 2018). Pol (2018) notes that institutions prefer to show their ability to comply with the laws rather than doing any substantive analysis of risks that affect their customers and transactions. This dynamic creates an avalanche of reports that may swamp enforcement agencies with information of little investigative value and ultimately defeats the purpose of effective enforcement.

In the case of cryptocurrency markets, in which transactions occur over networks that are decentralised and do not involve traditional financial intermediaries, the shortcomings associated with compliance-driven AML are particularly pronounced. Even when virtual asset service providers (VASPs) are subject to AML regulations, visibility into the context of the transactions is often fragmentary. Kethineni and Cao (2019) recognise that automated red flag systems can identify suspicious crypto transactions but cannot easily explain how illicit money moves through the chains of multiple wallets, mixers and exchanges.

As such, while risk indicators may be identified, the risk indicators may not give investigators the means for reconstructing the laundering scheme behind the risk or for identifying the ultimate beneficiaries.

The enforcement of AML in the crypto field is greatly hindered by inconsistencies in regulation and poor data quality issues. Many jurisdictions have not yet fully implemented the FATF's AML standards for virtual assets, leaving regulation gaps for illicit actors who are relocating their operations to countries with lax regulation (Renda & Caneppele, 2023). The quality of suspicious reporting also varies greatly. A couple of large exchanges report thousands of alerts, while many smaller platforms report very little, creating a flood of low-value "defensive" reports, and the few meaningful leads are lost in the noise (Pol, 2018).

At this point, the distinction between compliance-first and forensic-first AML models can be seen as analytically salient. A compliance-first approach measures success based on procedural measures such as customer verification, transaction volumes that trigger due warnings, and the number of suspicious activity reports registered. Its prime institutional goal is regulatory defensibility more than investigative resolution. By contrast, a forensic-first framework measures effectiveness in terms of substantive results, such as reconstruction of illicit transaction flows, identification of controlling actors, asset tracing, and evidentiary usability in criminal proceedings. While compliance-first AML is preventive by nature and form-driven, forensic-first AML is investigative and evidence-driven and leans toward analytical depth rather than procedural volume. This is especially important in crypto markets, where decentralisation and pseudonymity are threatening the assumptions underlying traditional compliance regimes.

The above challenges have led to admonitions to rethink crypto AML enforcement from a "forensic-first" perspective. Unlike the compliance-first paradigm, where the judge considered successful outcomes in procedural terms (e.g., number of reports filed) and the filing of a suspicious activity report was an end in itself, a forensic-first style mechanism considers suspicious activity reports as a starting point for investigation, while a successful outcome is measured by concrete results such as funds traced or criminal networks disrupted. In a forensic-driven model, analysts do not have to stop at flagging an anomalous transaction but rather follow the money trail across a number of wallets, exchanges, and jurisdictions in an effort to build a full picture of the laundering scheme. Experts highlight that government success in financial crime control will depend on mapping these transaction networks as a whole instead of identifying isolated red flags (Ombu, 2023). By reconstructing entire illicit flow pathways, rather than focusing merely on cataloguing suspicious transactions, enforcement agencies can identify intervention targets with much greater precision and effect than is possible under a compliance-first regime.

A forensic-first approach does not imply avoiding basic compliance checks; rather, it redeploys them as a springboard to investigations. Banks, exchanges, and other VASPs will have to bring in their compliance teams to work with forensic analysts so that red flags will generate collaborative follow-up rather than routine filing. Reporting requirements should be adjusted to reflect more complex contextual data such as associated transactions and behavioural patterns instead of simplistic triggers on thresholds. Regulators would also begin to assess institutions on demonstrable accounts of crime disruption outcomes (e.g., cases solved or illicit assets seized) rather than box-ticking adherence. Empirical analyses have suggested that such outcome-orientated supervision can significantly enhance the effectiveness of AMLs by aligning institutional incentives with crime prevention goals (Ahmed et al., 2022). This kind of oversight would spur institutions to go beyond complying with the bare minimum and actively help unpack illicit economic networks.

Advanced analytics and artificial intelligence (AI) can be powerful investigative tools in a forensic-first approach and not become a tool of mass surveillance (Mohanta et al., 2024). Machine learning systems now have the ability to sift through large datasets of blockchain data and find complex patterns and hidden correlations that are beyond the reach of humans. For instance, AI models can be used to cluster cryptocurrency addresses to identify networks of interlinked actors, detect suspicious transaction patterns (such as those indicative of coin-mixing or tumbling services), and prioritise alerts based on the likelihood of illicit activity, a set of capabilities increasingly being adopted in AML efforts (Ahmed et al., 2022). These technologies, if properly harnessed, can dramatically extend the scope of investigators to unravel sophisticated laundering operations that would otherwise be undetected.

At the same time, the implementation of AI in AML should be coupled with transparency, rigorous validation, and human oversight to prevent biased or erroneous results. Algorithms that are trained on historical enforcement data can perpetuate existing biases or lead to false positives that disproportionately affect certain groups. Legal scholars emphasise that explainability is necessary when AI outputs are used for enforcement decisions where punitive sanctions or criminal charges may be a consequence (D'Avino, 2022). In a forensic-first approach, AI should be used to augment human investigative capacity and efficiency as well as to maintain accountability and due process, rather than serve as an opaque black box judge of suspect behaviour.

POLICY AND INSTITUTIONAL ROADMAP FOR INDIA

India's response to crypto-enabled financial crime needs a clear, time-bound policy roadmap that enables the building of specialised capacity and coordination. Given the decentralised, cross-border nature of blockchain transactions, simple amendments to existing laws are not good enough. The government has already mobilised resources; as of late 2025, more than 2100 law enforcement officers have been trained in advanced cyber forensic techniques, and new forensic labs and coordination teams were set up across the country. Comparative experiences have indicated that the coordination at the central level enhances the outcome of investigation; in line with this, the Indian Cybercrime Coordination Centre (I4C) of India established seven Joint Cyber Coordination Teams (JCCTs) to enhance the interstate management of the cases ("Cybercrime roadmap," 2025). Investigators also caution that cross-border crypto cases are not simple to handle and formal mutual assistance processes can be "onerous" ("Tackling crypto crime," 2023). A phased roadmap should therefore clearly reinforce specialised units and better cross-agency and cross-border information sharing.

In the short term (1-2 years), dedicated units for blockchain forensics and training expansion should be formalised in India. Specialised units in enforcement agencies can provide centres of excellence for tracing cryptocurrency transactions, attribution of wallet addresses and validation of digital evidence under standardised procedures. India is already investing in training. In the FY 2022-23 more than 2,800 officers participated in cryptocurrency investigation-related courses, and the Home Ministry has proposed a national cryptocurrency exchange database by 2024 (Pessarlay, 2023). These efforts need to be incorporated into the permanent curricula. For example, national forensic academies and I4C should enshrine modules that address blockchain architecture and crypto tracing tools and digital evidence law. Crucially, the training of judges needs to be a fundamental pillar and not a sideline. Explicitly, courses have been built for law enforcement and judiciary officers for cryptocurrency crimes (Press Information Bureau, 2025). Making such training mandatory for courts dealing with the cases involving PMLA and cybercrime will take away the scepticism of the blockchain evidence and avoid procedural delays.

In the medium term (3-5 years), focus should move to integrating data and tightening regulations for forensic readiness. Disparate data environments need to give way to an integrated analytics platform. This platform, overseen by I4C or a similar agency, would ingest data from the blockchain ledgers, exchange transaction records and intelligence inputs, enabling it to find and track the illicit flow of funds in real time and provide comprehensive cross-case analysis. Such centralisation is not of power but of access coordinated with proper legal protection. On the regulatory front, virtual asset service providers should be made to maintain detailed logs of transactions and assist proactively in conducting forensic analyses. Scholars observe that AML measures for crypto are still "not optimal" without effective collaborative frameworks (Renda & Caneppele, 2023); mandates for forensic data retention and immediate cooperation with investigators will balance compliance benefits with evidence collection. India should also increase international cooperation. Criminals abuse the lack of jurisdiction, and law enforcement surveys highlight the fact that mutual legal assistance is often slow for crypto cases ("Tackling crypto crime," 2023). Through seeking bilateral agreements on the sharing of data with major crypto centres and through multilateral enforcement networks, India can accelerate access to foreign exchange and wallet data. Joint investigations and sharing of typologies by international task forces will improve preparedness further.

In the long term (beyond 5 years) these capacities should be fully institutionalised and regularly updated. Specialised forensic units and cyber coordination teams would regularly deal with sophisticated crypto cases, and prosecutors and judges would be familiar with blockchain evidence with minimum delays in trials. Regulatory and legal frameworks need to adapt constantly. Targeted changes can be made to require traceability measures (e.g., wallet registry or chain-analysis support) for new crypto applications, while protecting privacy and due process. International partnerships will become a regular feature of the investigation, with protocols for the data flows across borders established. By following this time-phased roadmap and prioritising forensic capability, India can move from being reactive in complying to proactive in preventing crypto-enabled financial crime, all the while maintaining accountability, legal integrity and public trust.

CONCLUSION

Digital forensics is now known as the core of modern financial crime enforcement. But by analysing information from public ledgers, investigators can fill in illicit flows that would elude traditional probes. Blockchain is a double-edged sword. Criminals take advantage of the pseudonymity and the tools, such as coin mixers, but each transaction is recorded on-chain and cannot be altered forever. In a historic case, analysts copied the Silk Road marketplace's servers and combed its data for the one thing that would link the pseudonymous operator with Ross Ulbricht. Similarly, a cryptocurrency mixer service known as Tornado Cash was sanctioned by US authorities after investigators traced it to North Korean hackers belonging to the Lazarus Group laundering stolen digital assets. These cases demonstrate that with the correct tools, law enforcement can use blockchain's transparency against illegal actors.

Today's anti-money laundering model needs to shift from one of passive compliance to a proactive forensic approach. Exchanges and wallets will continue to onboard customers and file information, but there should be an active push and pull on the part of agencies that will mine real-time into that information. The case studies examined demonstrate that when on-chain analytics are combined with exchange records, KYC data, and cross-border intelligence sharing, investigators can link wallet addresses to real identities and trace the flows from fiat currency to cryptocurrency. Even when coins have been passed through mixers, forensic reconstruction can partially or fully reconstruct flows. This integration of blockchain analytics with traditional evidence and international data sharing is imperative to get ahead of evolving criminal tactics.

Regulators and lawmakers are also caught up. Courts stress that enforcement must be balanced with legal protections. For instance, India's Supreme Court overturned an absolute ban on cryptocurrencies, stating that regulation should be "reasonable, evidence-based and minimally invasive" and stressing that the mere possession or trading of virtual assets is "not illegal". In March 2023, India amended its laws, specifically the PMLA, to designate crypto exchanges and other virtual asset service providers as reporting entities. These measures allow authorities to force data from exchanges and seize illegal assets under the law. Issues in evidence handling continue to remain such as Indian courts generally require a Section 65B certificate in the case of electronic records, which is problematic in the case of blockchain data, which is spread across borders. In *Arjun Panditrao Khotkar v. Kailash Kushanrao Gorantyal* (2020), the Supreme Court reiterated that compliance with Section 65B is compulsory and that only properly certified electronic evidence is admissible. This requirement presents a particular challenge for blockchain-derived evidence, which originates from decentralised systems rather than centralised computer networks. With these constraints in consideration, India and others will need to strengthen forensic capacity, investing in labs at home, in training analysts and developing best practices while ensuring that investigations are conducted with complete respect for due process and privacy.

Looking to the future, global cooperation and clear norms will be key. International forums (such as the UNODC-Europol crypto-asset conferences) are creating a community to communicate best practices and new techniques ("9th global conference," 2025). Progress remains inconsistent, as certain jurisdictions lack clear regulations regarding cryptocurrencies or impose restrictions on cross-border data sharing for privacy reasons. Harmonisation of definitions, improvements to mutual legal assistance treaties and data sharing agreements will be necessary to close down enforcement gaps. All of enforcement needs to be balanced with core rights and principles. The guarantee of due process that nobody can be deprived of liberty without fair procedures applies in full force to digital evidence. Tools like AI-driven transaction monitoring should be employed in a proportionate way, focusing on real threats instead of mass surveillance. This discipline ensures the legitimacy of the criminal justice system for maintaining public confidence in anti-money laundering efforts. The analysis demonstrated how digital forensics can use the transparency of blockchain to address illicit finance, and can match technical tools to legal protections and international collaboration. By doing so, India and other jurisdictions can transform blockchain from a criminal risk into a powerful asset to financial integrity to create a resilient and rights-respecting enforcement regime.

REFERENCES

9th global conference on criminal finances and cryptoassets. (2025, October). Basel Institute on Governance. https://baselgovernance.org/9crc

Ahmad, A. A., Jusoh Yusoff, A. F., Mat Zain, M. N., & Ahmad, S. (2023, June 30). Conspiracy of Silk Road: Dread Pirate Roberts to cybercrime and money laundering. [MJSSH]. *Malaysian Journal of Social Sciences and Humanities*, *8*(6), e002354. DOI: 10.47405/mjssh.v8i6.2354

Ahmed, S., Alshater, M. M., El Ammari, A., & Hammami, H. (2022, October). Artificial intelligence and machine learning in finance: A bibliometric review. *Research in International Business and Finance*, *61*, 101646. DOI: 10.1016/j.ribaf.2022.101646

Alqahtany, S. S., & Syed, T. A. (2024, February 12). ForensicTransMonitor: A comprehensive blockchain approach to reinvent digital forensics and evidence management. *Information (Basel)*, *15*(2), 109. DOI: 10.3390/info15020109

Atlam, H. F., Ekuri, N., Azad, M. A., & Lallie, H. S. (2024, September 7). Blockchain forensics: A systematic literature review of techniques, applications, challenges, and future directions. *Electronics (Basel)*, *13*(17), 3568. DOI: 10.3390/electronics13173568

Bonifazi, G., Cauteruccio, F., Corradini, E., Marchetti, M., Montella, D., Scarponi, S., Ursino, D., & Virgili, L. (2023, February 20). Performing wash trading on NFTs: Is the game worth the candle? *Big Data and Cognitive Computing*, *7*(1), 38. DOI: 10.3390/bdcc7010038

Chadha, V., & Sivaraman, J. (2024, June 25). Critical analysis of the law on admissibility of electronic evidence in India. *Jindal Global Law Review*, *15*(1), 119–132. DOI: 10.1007/s41020-024-00219-1

Conti, M., Kumar, G., Lal, C., & Saha, R. (2023, August). Blockchain-based distributed and secure digital forensic investigation systems. *Advances in Information Security*, *105*, 337–362. DOI: 10.1007/978-3-031-32146-7_11

Cryptocurrencies: Tracing the evolution of criminal finances. (2021, December). Publication Office of the European Union: Europol. https://doi.org/DOI: 10.2813/75468

Cybercrime roadmap 2026: Nearly 2,500 law enforcement personnel trained on latest forensic tools, techniques. (2025, December 31). *The Economic Times.* https://economictimes.indiatimes.com/tech/technology/cybercrime-roadmap-2026-nearly-2500-law-enforcement-personnel-trained-on-latest-forensic-tools-techniques/articleshow/126270912.cms

D'Avino, C. (2022, November 6). Money laundering and AML regulatory and judicial system regimes: Investigation of FinCEN files. *European Journal of Law and Economics*, *55*, 195–223. DOI: 10.1007/s10657-022-09756-3

Ducas, E., & Wilner, A. (2017, December). The security and financial implications of blockchain technologies: Regulating emerging technologies in Canada. *International Journal (Toronto, Ont.)*, *72*(4), 538–562. DOI: 10.1177/0020702017741909

Financial Action Task Force. (2019, June). *Guidance for a risk-based approach to virtual assets and virtual asset service providers.* https://www.fatf-gafi.org/en/publications/Fatfrecommendations/Guidance-rba-virtual-assets.html

Financial Action Task Force. (2023, March). *Countering ransomware financing: Report of the Financial Action Task Force.* https://www.fatf-gafi.org/content/dam/fatf-gafi/reports/Countering-Ransomware-Financing.pdf.coredownload.pdf

Financial Crimes Enforcement Network. (2021). *Financial trend analysis: Ransomware trends in bank secrecy act data.* https://www.fincen.gov/system/files/2022-11/Financial%20Trend%20Analysis_Ransomware%20FTA%202_508%20FINAL.pdf

Financial Stability Board (FSB). (2025, October 16). *Thematic review on FSB global regulatory framework for crypto-asset activities.* https://www.fsb.org/uploads/P161025-1.pdf

Fröwis, M., Gottschalk, T., Haslhofer, B., Rückert, C., & Pesch, P. (2020, June). Safeguarding the evidential value of forensic cryptocurrency investigations. *Forensic Science International Digital Investigation, 33*, 200902. DOI: 10.1016/j.fsidi.2019.200902

Harvey, C. R., Ramachandran, A., & Santoro, J. (2020). DeFi and the future of finance. SSRN *Electronic Journal.* https://doi.org/DOI: 10.2139/ssrn.3711777

Ilbiz, E., & Kaunert, C. (2022, May 27). Sharing economy for tackling crypto-laundering: The Europol associated 'Global Conference on Criminal Finances and Cryptocurrencies.'. *Sustainability (Basel), 14*(11), 6618. DOI: 10.3390/su14116618

Illicit finance risk assessment of decentralized finance. (2023, April). U.S. Department of the Treasury. https://home.treasury.gov/system/files/136/DeFi-Risk-Full-Review.pdf

Jahankhani, H., Kendzierskyj, S., Jamal, A., Epiphaniou, G., & Al-Khateeb, H. (2019). Blockchain and clinical trial. In *Advanced sciences and technologies for security applications.* Springer International Publishing., DOI: 10.1007/978-3-030-11289-9

Kethineni, S., & Cao, Y. (2019, February). The rise in popularity of cryptocurrency and associated criminal activity. *International Criminal Justice Review, 30*(3), 325–344. DOI: 10.1177/1057567719827051

Lenahan-Pfahlert, K. A. (2024, March 18). *Blockchain analysis and related expert testimony admissible in criminal trial.* Money Laundering Watch. https://www.moneylaunderingnews.com/2024/03/blockchain-analysis-and-related-expert-testimony-admissible-in-criminal-trial

Levi, M., & Reuter, P. (2006). Money laundering. *Crime and Justice, 34*(1), 289–375. DOI: 10.1086/501508

Levi, M., & Soudijn, M. (2020). Understanding the laundering of organized crime money. *Crime and Justice, 49*, 579–632. DOI: 10.1086/708047

Mas'ud, M. Z., Hassan, A., Shah, W. M., Abdul-Latip, S. F., Ahmad, R., Ariffin, A., & Yunos, Z. (2021, January). A review of digital forensics framework for blockchain in cryptocurrency technology. [Conference paper]. *2021 3rd International Cyber Resilience Conference (CRC).* DOI: 10.1109/CRC50527.2021.9392563

Mohanta, A. Sneha, Garikapati, K., Mohanty, S., & Samanta, S. (2025, June). Forensic linguistics and DBN: Automating the analysis of witness statements and testimonies in AI-driven policing. In M. A. Abdelmottlep (Ed.), *AI-Driven Policing and Urban Security in Smart Cities* (pp. 171-202). IGI Global. https://doi.org/DOI: 10.4018/979-8-3373-0245-4.ch007

Mohanta, A., & Garikapati, K. Sneha, Mohanty, S., & Shreya. (2024, December). Predictive justice in criminal proceedings: The role of AI jurimetrics. In H. Bajraktari (Ed.), *Exploration of AI in Contemporary Legal Systems* (pp. 217-252). IGI Global. https://doi.org/DOI: 10.4018/979-8-3693-7205-0.ch011

Mortlock, D., Mosman, B., & El-Gamal, A. (2025, June 30). *OFAC and DOJ sanctions enforcement in the United States*. Global Investigations Review. https://globalinvestigationsreview.com/guide/the-guide-sanctions/sixth-edition/article/ofac-and-doj-sanctions-enforcement-in-the-united-states

Nadler, M., & Schär, F. (2023, April 10). Tornado Cash and blockchain privacy: A primer for economists and policymakers. *RE:view, 105*(2), 122–136. DOI: 10.20955/r.105.122-136

Ombu, A. (2023, June). Role of digital forensics in combating financial crimes in the computer era. *Journal of Forensic Accounting Profession*, *3*(1), 57–75. DOI: 10.2478/jfap-2023-0003

Pessarlay, W. (2023, November 19). *India: 3,000 police officers get training in blockchain forensics.* Coingeek. https://coingeek.com/india-3000-police-officers-get-training-in-blockchain-forensics

Pol, R. F. (2018, May 8). Anti-money laundering effectiveness: Assessing outcomes or ticking boxes? *Journal of Money Laundering Control, 21*(2), 215–230. DOI: 10.1108/JMLC-07-2017-0029

Press Information Bureau. (2025). *Financial Intelligence Unit (FIU IND) issues notices for non-compliance to 25 offshore Virtual Digital Assets Service Providers (VDA SPs) under Section 13 of the Prevention of Money Laundering Act (PML), 2002*. Government of India. https://www.pib.gov.in/PressReleasePage.aspx?PRID=2173758

Raj Goyal, H., & Prasad Mali, M. (2025). Digital evidence under the Indian legal system – Study of problems and perspective. *Journal of Neonatal Surgery*, *14*(32S), 10180–10189. DOI: 10.63682/jns.v14i32S.9809

Renda, A., & Caneppele, S. (2023, January). Compliant or not compliant? The challenges of anti-money laundering regulations in crypto assets: The case of Switzerland. *Journal of Money Laundering Control, 27*(2), 363–382. DOI: 10.1108/JMLC-04-2023-0078

Renuka, S. (2026, January 4). *Cryptocurrency fraud: Legal challenges in India.* Record of Law. https://recordoflaw.in/cryptocurrency-fraud-legal-challenges-in-india

Ron, D., & Shamir, A. (2014, October 8). How did Dread Pirate Roberts acquire and protect his bitcoin wealth? In *Lecture Notes in Computer Science, 8438,* 3-15. https://doi.org/DOI: 10.1007/978-3-662-44774-1_1

Sifat, I., Tariq, S. A., & van Donselaar, D. (2024, January). Suspicious trading in nonfungible tokens (NFTs). *Information & Management*, *61*(1), 103898. DOI: 10.1016/j.im.2023.103898

Sneha, C. S., Mohanta, A., & Shreya. (2024, November). Navigating AI liability in criminal law. In A. Ahmadi, A. Mna, & A. Slimani (Eds.), *Renewable Energy and the Economic Welfare of Society* (pp. 311-334). IGI Global. https://doi.org/DOI: 10.4018/979-8-3693-7580-8.ch014

Tackling crypto crime: 2023 survey of law enforcement. (2023, December 23). TRM Labs. https://www.trmlabs.com/reports-and-whitepapers/tackling-crypto-crime-2023-survey-of-law-enforcement

Turner, A. B., McCombie, S., & Uhlmann, A. J. (2020, November 30). Analysis techniques for illicit bitcoin transactions. *Frontiers of Computer Science*, *2*, 600596. DOI: 10.3389/fcomp.2020.600596

Updated guidance for a risk-based approach to virtual assets and virtual asset service providers. (2021, October). Financial Action Task Force. https://www.fatf-gafi.org/en/publications/Fatfrecommendations/Guidance-rba-virtual-assets-2021.html

U.S. Attorney's Office. Southern District of New York. (2019, November 21). *Former partner of Locke Lord LLP convicted in Manhattan Federal Court of conspiracy to commit money laundering and bank fraud in connection with scheme to launder $400 million of OneCoin fraud proceeds*. [Press release]. https://www.justice.gov/usao-sdny/pr/former-partner-locke-lord-llp-convicted-manhattan-federal-court-conspiracy-commit-money

The US and Canada join forces to combat scams, seizing millions in crypto. (2025, August 14). Chain analysis. https://www.chainalysis.com/blog/us-and-canada-join-forces-to-combat-crypto-scams

U.S. Department of Justice. (2021, June 7). *Department of Justice seizes $2.3 million in cryptocurrency paid to the ransomware extortionists Darkside*. [Press release]. https://www.justice.gov/archives/opa/pr/department-justice-seizes-23-million-cryptocurrency-paid-ransomware-extortionists-darkside

U.S. Department of the Treasury. (2022, August 8). *U.S. Treasury sanctions notorious virtual currency mixer Tornado Cash*. [Press release]. https://home.treasury.gov/news/press-releases/jy0916

van Roomen, T. (2025, November 28). Cross-border evidence gathering in criminal crypto investigations: A case study of the Netherlands. *Tilburg Law Review*, *30*(2), 120–146. DOI: 10.5334/tilr.423

Whitaker, R. (2025, July 31). *How blockchain forensics unraveled a $20 million crypto laundering scheme in China*. Merkle Science. https://www.merklescience.com/blog/how-blockchain-forensics-unraveled-a-20-million-crypto-laundering-scheme-in-china

Wollerton, M. (2023). Ransomware attacks. *CQ Press*, *33*(28). Advance online publication. DOI: 10.4135/cqresrre20230818

ADDITIONAL READINGS

Bancroft, A. (2020). *The darknet and smarter crime: Methods for investigating criminal entrepreneurs and the illicit drug economy*. Palgrave Studies in Cybercrime and Cybersecurity., DOI: 10.1007/978-3-030-26512-0

Campbell-Verduyn, M. (2018, January). Bitcoin, crypto-coins, and global anti-money laundering governance. *Crime, Law, and Social Change*, *69*(2), 283–305. DOI: 10.1007/s10611-017-9756-5

Dote-Pardo, J., & Espinosa-Jaramillo, M. T. (2025, October). Money laundering risks of cryptocurrencies: Towards coordinated regulatory and technological strategies. *Latin American Journal of Central Banking*, *100194*, 100194. Advance online publication. DOI: 10.1016/j.latcb.2025.100194

Foley, S., Karlsen, J. R., & Putniņš, T. J. (2019, May). Sex, drugs, and bitcoin: How much illegal activity is financed through cryptocurrencies? *Review of Financial Studies*, *32*(5), 1798–1853. DOI: 10.1093/rfs/hhz015

Harvey, A. I. (2019, June). *Anti-money laundering and counter-terrorism financing law and policy*. Nijhoff Law Specials. https://doi.org/DOI: 10.1163/9789004359109

Meiklejohn, S., Pomarole, M., Jordan, G., Levchenko, K., McCoy, D., Voelker, G. M., & Savage, S. (2013). A fistful of bitcoins: Characterizing payments among men with no names. [Conference paper]. *2013 Conference on Internet Measurement Conference* (pp. 127-140). https://doi.org/DOI: 10.1145/2504730.2504747

Teichmann, F. M. J., & Falker, M.-C. (2020, June 27). Cryptocurrencies and financial crime: Solutions from Liechtenstein. *Journal of Money Laundering Control*, *24*(4), 775–788. DOI: 10.1108/JMLC-05-2020-0060

Zetzsche, D. A., Buckley, R. P., Arner, D. W., & Föhr, L. (2019, Summer). The ICO Gold Rush: It's a scam, it's a bubble, it's a super challenge for regulators. *SSRN*, *60*(2), 267–315. DOI: 10.2139/ssrn.3072298

KEY TERMS AND DEFINITIONS

Blockchain Analytics: The use of data analysis, graph modeling, and heuristic techniques to examine blockchain transaction records for tracing fund flows and identifying patterns of illicit activity.

Cross-Border Enforcement: The coordinated investigation and prosecution of criminal activity involving multiple jurisdictions through legal assistance, intelligence sharing, and regulatory cooperation.

Cryptocurrency Laundering: The process of disguising the illicit origin of digital assets by routing them through blockchain transactions, exchanges, mixers, or decentralized protocols to obscure ownership and traceability.

Digital Forensics: The scientific process of identifying, acquiring, preserving, analyzing, and presenting digital evidence in a manner that is legally admissible in court.

Evidence Admissibility: The legal determination that a piece of evidence satisfies statutory and procedural standards of authenticity, relevance, and reliability for consideration in court.

Financial Crime: Illicit activities involving the unlawful acquisition, movement, concealment, or use of funds or financial assets in violation of criminal or regulatory law.

Forensic-First AML: An enforcement approach that prioritizes transaction reconstruction, attribution, and evidentiary reliability over procedural compliance metrics in combating money laundering.

Prevention of Money Laundering Act (India): India's principal anti-money laundering statute that criminalizes laundering of proceeds of crime and empowers authorities to investigate, attach, seize, and prosecute related offenses.

Chapter 12
The Use of Artificial Intelligence to Improve Access to Justice

Anton Limbo
http://orcid.org/0009-0006-5437-9716
University of Namibia, Namibia

Simon Iileka
http://orcid.org/0009-0009-5487-1964
University of Namibia, Namibia

Selma Limbo
http://orcid.org/0009-0008-4658-6277
University of Namibia, Namibia

ABSTRACT

The increase in technology has changed how we operate and conduct daily processes in our daily lives. One prominent technology that is increasingly becoming popular is the use or the application of Artificial Intelligence (AI) in many different sectors. However, some sectors have seen low rollout in the use of AI, one such sector is in the justice system. Therefore, this chapter will present an AI-based chatbot to assist with day-to-day legal inquiries based on the set parameters, such as the Constitution. The chatbot is developed based on the current limitations of accessing justice identified in the literature. The chatbot uses the Namibian constitution as the case study for the development of a prototype, with the idea that any legal framework of any nation can be used to guide the training of the AI model for a chatbot. Results show that this approach to improving access to justice systems has significant benefits to ordinary citizens, such as those in developing countries, who face barriers such as high legal costs, geographical isolation, and the lack of legal awareness.

INTRODUCTION

Access to justice is a foundational principle of law, yet for millions of people worldwide, it remains an elusive ideal rather than a lived reality (Rajendran et al., 2025). Structural barriers, such as the high cost of legal services, geographic distance from courts, limited legal literacy, and administrative inefficiencies,

DOI: 10.4018/979-8-3373-7660-8.ch012

continue to prevent individuals from effectively asserting their rights, particularly in developing and rural contexts (Peruginelli, 2009). Studies have also shown that, even in developed countries, the ratio of citizens per legal practitioner is high, with numbers as high as 1000 residents per legal practitioner in some countries, such as the United States of America (Appleby, 2024). This clearly demonstrates that current methods of enabling access to justice systems are not sufficient to cope with population growth, on top of the inherent challenges. This becomes even more apparent as many countries face backlogs of cases due to inefficient public defence systems (Munnang, 2024). Addressing this gap thus requires investigating innovative mechanisms that allow as many citizens as possible to access some form of legal information, regardless of current documented barriers.

Artificial Intelligence (AI) has emerged as one of the most transformative technologies with the potential to reshape how justice systems operate and how legal services are delivered. The rapid development of Natural Language Processing, Machine Learning, and conversational AI systems has made it technically conceivable for machines to perform tasks that once required years of legal training. These include conducting legal research, reviewing and interpreting documents, and providing preliminary guidance on legal rights and procedures (Choi & Schwarcz, 2024). These capabilities have sparked growing interest in the use of AI to democratise access to legal information and justice services, particularly for underserved populations.

One of the most promising applications of AI in this context is the deployment of AI-powered legal chatbots using digital platforms. Studies have shown that legal chatbots can improve access to justice by providing timely, low-cost, and user-friendly legal information, which ultimately helps users understand their rights and navigate legal procedures (Norchuk, 2025). The implementation of such technologies comes with its own challenges, however. Concerns around trust, accuracy, ethical considerations, digital literacy, and institutional readiness can significantly affect the effective adoption of AI-driven legal tools (Vassilopoulos, 2022).

Given the benefits that AI technology can offer to the justice system, many countries, including developing countries, have started with the introduction of this technology to aid access to justice systems. In Namibia, for example, the use of technology in the justice system has gained increasing attention. Namibia's legal system is shaped by a mix of Roman-Dutch common law, inherited statutory frameworks, and customary law systems that continue to have strong relevance in many communities (Odendaal, 2005). This legal pluralism means that citizens may engage with different forms of dispute resolution depending on their location and social context. Many Namibians live in rural areas, where access to formal courts, legal practitioners, and state-supported legal services is often limited (More, 2021). In these settings, distance, cost, and limited legal awareness can significantly affect the ability of individuals to pursue their rights through the formal justice system. Economic inequality further compounds these challenges, as many citizens cannot afford private legal representation. Taken together, these structural realities position Namibia as a particularly relevant case for exploring AI-driven interventions to expand access to legal information and justice services.

Initiatives such as e-justice systems aimed at improving records management in the High Court (Matongo & Jacobs, 2022) and mobile technology solutions designed to enhance justice service delivery in rural communities (Mendonca & Iyamu, 2024), demonstrate a growing recognition of technology's role in strengthening access to justice systems. Local studies on AI-powered chatbot applications, such as those conducted at the University of Namibia, illustrate the feasibility and potential impact of AI-driven solutions within Namibian institutions (Hashiyana & Kamati, 2024). Given Namibia's level of development, this approach can be adopted by any other developing country aiming to increase access to its justice system.

It is clear that exploring the use of Artificial Intelligence as a tool for improving access to justice is both timely and necessary, with a particular focus on AI-driven legal information systems and chatbots. The chatbot presented demonstrates how an AI legal chatbot can offer cost-effective, scalable solutions that provide real-time legal information, thereby bridging the knowledge gap between legal professionals and the public.

LITERATURE REVIEW

The Expanding Role of AI Across Industries

Artificial Intelligence (AI) is no longer merely a technological buzzword but a reflection of the expanding capabilities of modern computing systems. This has therefore led organisations and researchers to actively explore how AI can be applied across different areas to improve efficiency and quality of life (Raj & Kos, 2023). AI has consequently found application in Healthcare, Education, Agriculture, Automotive Industries, Finance, Surveillance, to mention a few, with the sole purpose of improving lives and enhancing productivity by automating tasks, uncovering insights from large data, answering questions, providing companionship, and even guiding humans in solving complex problems (Valavanidis, 2023).

AI Tools in the Justice System

AI has also found significant application in the justice system to improve operations and access. To this end, various studies have examined methods of using AI to aid current justice systems. One method is the use of AI legal chatbots. AI chatbots, in general, are computer programs that mimic human conversation by using Natural Language Processing and Machine Learning to understand questions and provide appropriate answers (Chang, 2021). These tools differ from simple chatbots because they learn from conversations and adjust based on user interactions (Gromova et al., 2023). In legal settings, they act like virtual helpers, advising on rights, procedures, and paperwork. For instance, applications like DoNotPay and LawBot help people write legal letters, fight parking tickets, and handle small claims (Queudot et al., 2020). These chatbots make it easier for people to get help without incurring the expenses of approaching lawyers, which is especially helpful in developing countries, where legal support and professionals are limited or expensive (Zongwe, 2022).

Other than the use of AI in chatbots, AI can also be used to aid law enforcement agencies in investigations to apprehend criminals, identify criminals through image recognition and to predict crime-prone areas or activities using historical data (Faghiri, 2022). Other studies have also outlined other important applications of AI in justice systems. These include its use in aiding legal research, reviewing documents such as contracts for due diligence, automating processes to further streamline legal tasks, predict legal outcomes based on historical data (Siani, 2024).

Despite these advantages of using AI in justice systems, it is important to note that AI is intended to aid, not replace, legal personnel, as documented by laws in various countries that have introduced the use of AI in their justice systems. For example, in China, the introduction of smart courts aimed to improve access and fast-track case resolution through technology (Papagianneas & Junius, 2023). These

Chinese smart court concepts, including the digitalisation of files, have been evolving since 1996, and in 2014 more sophisticated technologies were added to enable court proceedings and other services to be conducted online (Laptev & Feyzrakhmanova, 2024). The same sentiments can be observed in the United States of America, which has heavily invested in the development and implementation of AI in different areas, including the justice system. However, the regulatory board of AI emphasises that the purpose is to use AI to assist judges in making fair and unbiased decisions, rather than to replace the people performing these functions (Laptev & Feyzrakhmanova, 2024).

Among AI tools specifically designed to improve access to justice for ordinary citizens, conversational chatbots have attracted the most research interest. Unlike earlier rule-based systems that could only respond to pre-specified keywords and phrases, contemporary AI chatbots can handle varied phrasing, manage some degree of ambiguity, and adjust responses based on the context of an ongoing conversation (Gromova et al., 2023). In legal settings, this means a system that can explain rights, describe procedures, help users understand the significance of documents, and direct them toward appropriate resources and institutions. The same functions that, in a better-resourced environment, might be carried out by a paralegal or community legal worker. Tools like DoNotPay and LawBot have demonstrated these capabilities at scale, assisting hundreds of thousands of users with tasks ranging from contesting parking fines and appealing administrative decisions to pursuing small claims and understanding tenancy rights (Queudot et al., 2020).

Barriers to Legal Access in Developing Countries

The potential of AI-driven legal information becomes most crucial in contexts where access to existing systems is scarce, such as in many rural areas of developing countries. In many developing countries, obstacles to formal legal assistance are not minor inconveniences but are entrenched due to systemic characteristics of institutions that were never designed with equal access in mind. Namibia provides a clear example that is relatable to most developing countries. In Namibia as it is estimated that over 60% of the population cannot afford legal representation, as lawyers' hourly fees often exceed the monthly minimum wage (Zongwe, 2022). Although the Legal Aid Directorate is tasked with offering free legal services to those who qualify, it remains persistently under-resourced and understaffed. As a result, many individuals who cannot afford private counsel are also unable to rely on state support, leaving them to navigate complex legal procedures on their own (Matongo & Jacobs, 2022). For those living outside major urban areas, geographic barriers further intensify the problem, as legal institutions and professionals are largely concentrated in urban areas such as towns and cities. This makes access to legal services costly and logistically challenging to attain (Mendonca & Iyamu, 2024).

Despite these structural constraints, Namibia's digital environment has evolved in ways that open meaningful possibilities for technology-driven solutions. While only about 56% of the population has internet access, mobile phone penetration stands above 100%, largely due to widespread use of multiple SIM cards (Mendonca & Iyamu, 2024). This indicates that even individuals without access to desktop or laptop computers often possess mobile devices capable of using web-based services. This imbalance strongly supports a mobile-first approach as the most practical design strategy for legal access tools intended for use by underserved populations. This further reflects a key principle of technology design in the context of a developing country, where proposed solutions must align with the existing infrastructure, rather than introducing new technologies that the targeted user group is not familiar.

Ethical Considerations in AI-Driven Legal Systems

The need to regulate and limit the use of AI stems from ethical concerns regarding its introduction into justice systems. Gromova et al. (2023) points out that if the training data is biased, it can lead to wrong or unfair legal advice. This is because AI algorithms rely on training data to arrive at a conclusion or provide feedback. Thus, if the data used to train these algorithms has prejudices, the algorithm is likely to have the same prejudices in its feedback (Maphosa, 2024). A good example of this is JuridiQC, a Canadian chatbot that encountered challenges, such as providing ambiguous answers to complex legal questions (Vassilopoulos, 2022).

Transparency is also another closely related concern. Users should be aware that chatbots are designed to provide information based on the data used in training (Queudot et al., 2020). At the same time, developers of these chatbots should employ the "explainable AI" approach, where chatbots show how they arrive at their answers, such as pointing out the laws they are referencing (Vassilopoulos, 2022).

Data privacy is equally important, and any sensitive information shared with chatbots should be protected to prevent misuse (Gromova et al., 2023). This is further supported by Hermansyah et al. (2023), who stated that developers of AI technologies should conduct various tests to ensure that the privacy of the users is maintained, while considering the diversity of the users, such as race, gender and social background.

Matongo and Jacobs (2022) noted that people living in rural areas often have difficulty trusting automated systems, as they instead prefer talking to someone in person. For these technological solutions to be feasible and trustworthy, it is therefore necessary to investigate methods to build trust between users and the system being introduced. This implies designing interfaces with ethical considerations in mind and maintaining trust with users on the operations of these chatbots (Queudot et al., 2020). Providing user training on these technologies is equally important. There should, therefore, be digital literacy programs accompanying the rollout of these systems, such as AI legal chatbots (Mendonca & Iyamu, 2024).

Another ethical concern that has emerged in the implementation of AI systems is the question of who bears legal and ethical responsibility when a chatbot provides incorrect information. If a user acts on incorrect chatbot guidance and suffers a legal consequence as a result, the distribution of responsibility among the developer, the deploying organisation, and the user is unclear under existing law (Gromova et al., 2023). For legal practitioners and researchers building systems such as AI legal chatbots, the only responsible approach is to design in a way that minimises this risk. This can be achieved through rigorous and ongoing Knowledge Base verification by qualified legal practitioners, clearly worded disclaimers, built-in escalation pathways to human practitioners for queries that exceed the system's scope, and continuous monitoring and correction of identified errors.

Comparative Approaches: Chatbots, Mobile Clinics, and Paralegals

The solution to all these barriers is not limited to the use of AI legal chatbots as a realistic solution. Across several African contexts, mobile legal clinics, staffed by lawyers or paralegals who travel to underserved areas on a scheduled basis, have been used to deliver legal assistance directly to communities that cannot reach fixed legal institutions (Queudot et al., 2020). These approaches are especially important in settings where institutional capacity is constrained, and access to formal services remains uneven across regions (Mendonca & Iyamu, 2024). These approaches offer empathetic, face-to-face interaction that cannot be achieved with chatbots, as people in these communities are accustomed to human engagement rather than interacting with a computer system, such as a chatbot, for legal matters (Matongo & Jacobs, 2022). Human legal professionals are capable of handling the kind of complex, multi-layered, emotional legal situations that fall outside the scope of any structured information system, such as an AI legal chatbot.

The comparative advantage of AI legal chatbots, however, lies not in replicating what skilled legal professionals perform but in operating at a scale, consistency, and availability that a human being cannot match. This is true given that a chatbot does not take leave, does not have office hours, does not maintain a waiting list, and can handle simultaneous queries from a given number of users at very low marginal cost once implemented.

The literature outlined that AI legal chatbots can occupy a specific and bounded position within a wider ecosystem of addressing problems associated with the access to justice systems. They are not posed, however, as replacements for legal professionals such as lawyers, paralegals, or judges, nor do they aspire to be, at least for now and the foreseeable future. Their advantage in this case lies in scale, consistency, and round-the-clock availability that human beings cannot match at low cost.

Previous studies in this area also outlined that studies conducted in the context of developed countries significantly differ from the reality in developing countries, especially when assumptions are made on user literacy, language uniformity, and reliable connectivity. A limited number of studies also take into account the different conditions in developing countries, especially in rural areas, where governance is based on customary rather than statutory norms and where limited digital infrastructure is used in these settings.

The AI legal chatbot thus developed and presented directly addresses that gap. The chatbot is designed to integrate within the setting of a developing country. This is done by using Namibia as an example, while also laying the groundwork for implementation in any other country by aligning the chatbot's development with that country's laws. In the case of Namibia, this was achieved by developing the chatbot to interoperate with the already existing infrastructure of the country. The resulting AI legal chatbot employs a lightweight browser-based interface, has a clear disclaimer, relies on the frequently queried legal topics, and reflects lessons drawn from this literature.

PROTOTYPE DEVELOPMENT: THE NAMIBIAN AI LEGAL CHATBOT

Next to be explained is the development of a functional prototype, an AI legal chatbot. The chatbot was developed in the Namibian context to demonstrate that a computer system can improve access to legal information. The development of the chatbot was motivated by the persistent justice gap in developing countries such as Namibia, where many individuals cannot afford legal representation and may lack sufficient knowledge of legal procedures to navigate the justice system effectively (Zongwe, 2022). The chatbot was thus developed to serve as an accessible, low-cost information gateway that could help people understand basic laws and identify procedures to follow when faced with legal matters.

The prototype demonstrates how AI-enabled conversational systems can be adapted to local justice challenges, particularly those related to affordability, legal literacy, and geographic accessibility (Zongwe, 2022). The prototype was conceptualised as an AI legal information assistant rather than a legal advisory system, designed to provide basic guidance on legal matters such as criminal justice procedures and reporting mechanisms based on the Namibian Constitution. This design philosophy aligns with recommendations in AI-and-law research that emphasise decision-support and information-access roles for AI systems rather than autonomous legal reasoning (Choi & Schwarcz, 2024; Vassilopoulos, 2022). The chatbot, however, was not designed to replace professional legal advice.

The implementation approach was also informed by local research on chatbot-integrated applications developed at the University of Namibia, which demonstrated the feasibility of deploying AI conversational systems using web-based technologies within resource-constrained institutional environments (Hashiyana & Kamati, 2024).

Research Methodology

This study used the Design Science Research (DSR) approach, which focuses on creating practical and innovative solutions to make a real difference in society (Hevner & Chatterjee, 2010). According to De Sordi (2021), DSR has been proven to be an effective methodology for solving problems by developing innovative solutions. Following DSR, the prototype was developed using five phases: Analysis, Design, Implementation, Testing, and Deployment. These phases were aligned with the six fundamental steps of the DSR process as defined by De Sordi (2021), which are: 1. Identifying the Problem; 2. Defining Objectives; 3. Designing and Developing the Artefact; 4. Demonstrating the Developed Artefact; 5. Evaluating the Artefact; and 6. Communicating the Results Achieved by the Artefact.

Analysis Phase

The Analysis Phase forms part of the first two steps of DSR: Identifying the Problem; Defining Objectives. During this phase, the study focused on understanding the challenges faced by Namibians today in accessing justice. This involved considering the existing legal aid services, their limitations, such as high costs, geographical constraints, and a lack of legal literacy. This phase also included identifying the major legal matters in which citizens often sought legal advice on, based on the frequently asked questions sections of the Legal Assistance Centre and Office of the Judiciary websites.

The analysis began by re-examining the significant problems identified in the literature review, including inadequate access to affordable legal assistance, low legal literacy, and geographical constraints that make it difficult for rural citizens to access justice. These problems served as the basis for determining how the envisioned prototype could address them. From this analysis, it was determined that a chatbot will be able to address the identified problems. This would be achieved by developing a chatbot that is accessible, easy to use, and capable of dispensing accurate legal information in a comprehensible language.

A requirements analysis was also conducted to identify functional and non-functional system requirements. The functional requirements included the ability of the chatbot to receive user queries, process natural language inputs, query the Knowledge Base, and respond with relevant legal answers in accordance with Namibian laws and policies. The non-functional requirements included performance-related aspects such as usability, correctness of responses, reliability, and ethical data management to instil user trust.

To conduct a feasibility test, existing AI chatbot platforms and tools were examined to identify if they can be utilised to interface with Namibian legal data. The most appropriate technologies, Chatbase and Python, were identified as the most compatible and iterative capable technologies.

Design Phase

The Design Phase formed part of the third step of DSR, which is Designing and Developing the Artefact. In this phase, the requirements and insights from the analysis were translated into a system architecture. The chatbot was structured around three core modules, each serving a distinct functional role. The User Interface was responsible for receiving user input and presenting chatbot responses in a readable, navigable format. The AI Engine served as the processing core, interpreting user queries through Natural Language Processing and generating contextually appropriate responses. The Knowledge Base housed the curated Namibian legal materials that the AI Engine drew on to produce its responses.

The User Interface was designed with simplicity and accessibility as the guiding principles. Research on chatbot usability in contexts where users have limited digital literacy identifies uncluttered design, clearly labelled input fields, legible, well-formatted responses as the most important factors in enabling effective use (Queudot et al., 2020). The interface also opted for the use of conversational visual register to make the interaction feel natural by presenting responses in paragraph form, rather than dense legal text, while also avoiding technical terminology in both navigation and instructions. A clear, consistently visible disclaimer was incorporated at the start of each session, explicitly stating that the system provides general legal information only and does not constitute professional legal advice. The inclusion of this disclaimer reflects a commitment to transparency, as the literature identifies it as a requirement for ethical AI deployment in legal contexts (Vassilopoulos, 2022).

The Knowledge Base was compiled from authenticated Namibian legal documents, including the Constitution of Namibia, the Labour Act, provisions relating to criminal procedure, gender-based violence, and relevant policy documents from the Legal Assistance Centre. The curation process involved reviewing each document to identify the provisions most likely to be relevant to ordinary public queries, simplifying the language of complex statutory text to ensure accessibility for users without legal training. Finally, the content was structured in a form that the Chatbase Agent could index and retrieve effectively. The AI Engine used Natural Language Processing to identify user intent from the phrasing of queries, a process that involves translating natural language input into a structured representation that could be matched against the indexed knowledge base, before assembling responses that combined relevant legal provisions with plain-language explanations.

Implementation Phase

The Implementation Phase formed part of the third and fourth steps of the DSR process: Designing and Developing the Artefact; Demonstrating the Developed Artefact. This phase involved developing the artefact based on the design, followed by demonstrating the developed artefact. During this stage, the conceptual design of the chatbot was built into a functional prototype. An Agile, Iterative, and Incremental Model for prototype development was employed. Iterative development focuses on refining a working prototype in cycles, with each cycle enhancing existing features based on feedback. The Incremental Model builds the system module by module, delivering completed, functional subsets of the entire system sequentially until the whole product is built. The Agile Model combines aspects of both, implementing small, high-priority features within short development cycles (sprints) to produce working, adaptable software continuously (Anand et al., 2021).

The development was done using HyperText Markup Language (HTML) and Cascading Style Sheets (CSS) to construct the web-based front-end user interface. The backend functionality leveraged the

Chatbase Agent API to process natural language queries and generate context-aware responses. The chatbot's Knowledge Base was trained on a curated dataset of Namibian legal documents, including legislation, case law, and legal procedures, which were uploaded to the Chatbase platform to enable domain-specific responses. The Chatbase Agent processes user queries by first translating the question into a special code that it can decode. The agent then searches through its database of Namibian laws to find the most relevant legal information. Finally, it uses the language skills to combine this information into a clear, helpful answer in plain English to be presented to the user.

The Conversational Model was developed incrementally using an Agile Methodology, which enabled continuous refinement across multiple development stages. The first iteration established basic functionality with a minimal user interface for message exchange. The second iteration integrated the Chatbase Natural Language Processing model, enabling the retrieval of legally specific responses. Subsequent iterations focused on enhancing response accuracy through model training adjustments, reducing error rates, and improving the user interface design and styling. The AI Engine is the processing core that converts user queries into responses as needed. This engine was powered by the Chatbase Agent, which uses Natural Language Processing functionality to identify the intent of questions and link them to relevant legal data. The AI model was designed to learn from similar repetitive questions so that it could be more accurate over time.

Testing Phase

The Testing Phase was then conducted to evaluate the performance of the developed artefact. This formed part of DSR's fifth step, Evaluating the Artefact. Testing is crucial in ensuring that the developed artefact functions as intended by providing meaningful support to users seeking legal information. Testing was conducted in three modes: Benchmark Testing, Adversarial Testing, and User Evaluation.

Benchmark Testing involved presenting predefined legal questions derived from Namibian legal sources and comparing answers provided by the chatbot against validated reference answers. This process was designed to assess the completeness and accuracy of the knowledge base and the reliability of the Natural Language Processing engine in correctly identifying user intent. This was done using a sample from the University of Namibia student population to determine the chatbot's usability and performance in real-world scenarios. This group was selected because students represent a diverse user base with varying levels of digital literacy and legal knowledge.

Users were asked to rate the chatbot based on ease of use, clarity of responses, perceived correctness of the information, and overall satisfaction. In addition, the sample population was specifically asked to rate how accurately they believed the chatbot's responses were in relation to their expectations. This feedback provided valuable insight into how users experience the system and helped to identify areas where further improvement may be required. Their responses are summarised in Figure 1.

Figure 1. **Participants' response to the accuracy and relevancy of the answers given by the chatbot**

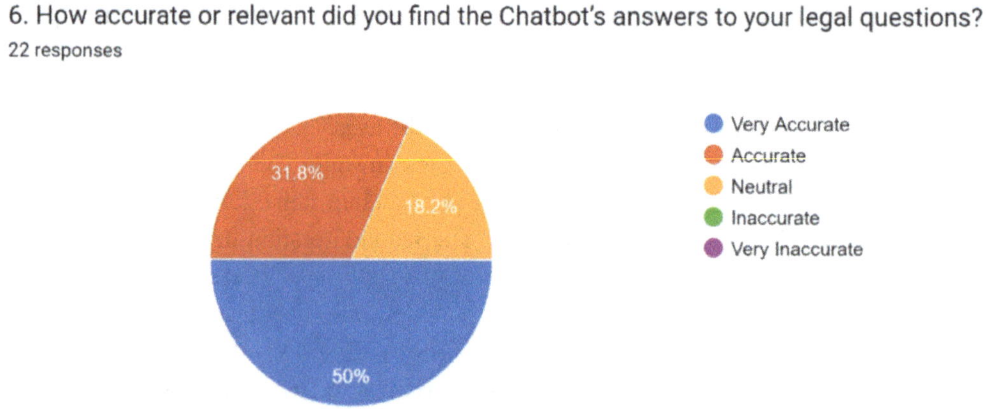

(image by the authors)

Adversarial Testing was subsequently conducted to measure the performance of the chatbot under unclear, poorly phrased, nonsensical questions and deliberately misleading queries. These types of queries simulate the kinds of inputs that users with limited literacy or low familiarity with formal legal language might generate. These queries also assist in assessing system robustness, such as identifying the conditions under which the chatbot would fail to provide useful responses, give misleading information, or simply decline to engage. This testing further determines how resilient the system is, precisely in the context of Namibia's varied levels of digital literacy. This is evident from the participant's response when asked how the chatbot responded to unclear questions. Their responses are summarised in Figure 2.

Figure 2. **Participants' response to the chatbot's performance to poorly worded prompts**

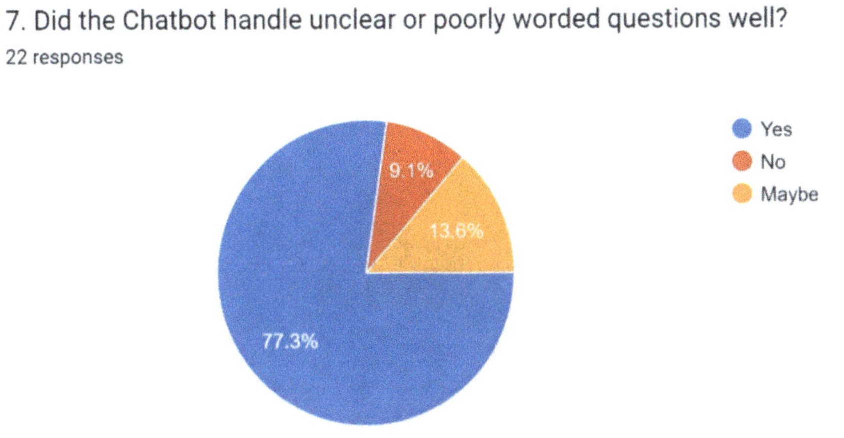

(image by the authors)

User Evaluation involved a random sample of students who interacted with the deployed chatbot and then completed the structured questionnaire after the interaction. One of the important aspects of the chatbot was the ease of use for the users. During the User Evaluation testing, the participants were asked to rate how easy it was to use the chatbot based on the instructions given and the responses given to the users based on the prompts, to which 90.9% agreed that it was easy enough to use the chatbot, as shown in Figure 3.

Figure 3. **Participants' response on the ease of use and understanding of the chatbot's instructions and prompts**

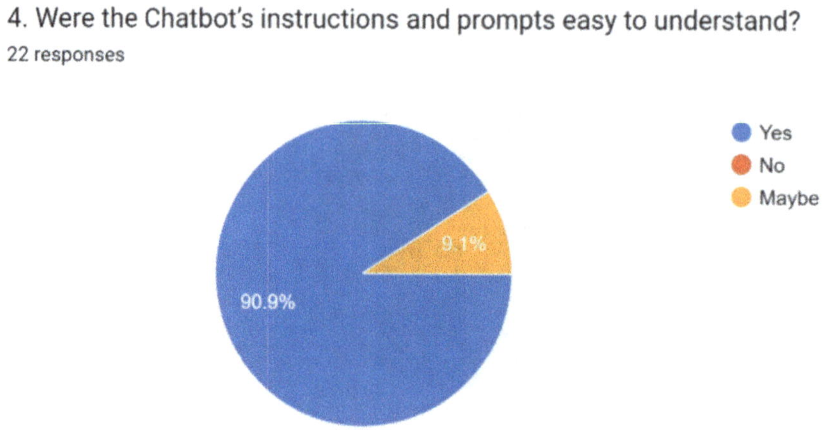

(image by the authors)

Deployment Phase

The Deployment Phase forms as the last step of DSR, which is Communicating the Results Achieved by the Artefact. The chatbot was deployed as a web-based application accessible through any standard web browser, without requiring additional software installation on the user's device. Initial deployment was carried out through a Flask-based local server to support structured testing with the student sample under controlled conditions. Following successful testing, the chatbot was made publicly accessible via the Netlify hosting platform, which provides free domain hosting suitable for prototyping and demonstration purposes. The web-based deployment architecture, combined with server-side AI processing, means that the computational demands on the user's device are kept to a minimum. This design choice ensures accessibility on lower-specification smartphones, which are the devices most likely to be used by the intended target population. The interface was also designed to minimise data consumption, using lightweight HTML and CSS without bandwidth-intensive multimedia elements, so that users on limited mobile data plans could access the service without incurring additional costs.

The choice of Netlify's free hosting tier for this prototype phase was appropriate for a proof-of-concept but not suitable for the full rollout of the system. This is because free hosting plans have usage limits that would become constrained as user numbers grow, and they provide no guarantees of uptime or technical support that a public-facing legal information service would require.

Knowledge base maintenance is a related and equally pressing concern. This is because legal materials can change in cases such as legislation amendments, updating of regulations, and alteration of interpretation of existing provisions based on court decisions. This implies that a knowledge base that is not actively maintained will, over time, become incomplete and misleading, as users receive information that no longer accurately reflects current laws and regulations. Addressing this requires a model of ongoing institutional engagement with legal institutions, government bodies, or civil society organisations, rather than a one-time development approach.

Resulting Prototype

The developed and iteratively tested prototype of a AI legal chatbot yielded tangible outputs, demonstrating that chatbots can also be developed for specific user-case applications in developing countries. The chatbot processing layer proved to be capable of handling user input interpretation and response generation. This was achieved by using Natural Language Processing techniques to identify keywords, user intent, and relevant legal topics. The prototype used a structured intent-matching approach to ensure reliability and minimise the risk of inaccurate legal information, instead of relying on generative AI models. This design choice reflects concerns raised in the literature regarding trust, accountability, and the risks associated with automated legal guidance (Vassilopoulos, 2022). This approach, based on controlled conversational architecture, is commonly used in early-stage legal chatbot systems designed for public legal education (Queudot et al., 2020).

The Knowledge Base contained simplified legal information structured into frequently asked questions and procedural guidance categories. Content in the Knowledge Base focused on foundational legal awareness topics, including reporting crimes, understanding arrest procedures, and accessing justice institutions. Organising legal information in structured, conversational formats aligns with recommended practices for legal chatbot design, aimed at improving accessibility and comprehension (Rajendran et al., 2025).

The chatbot prototype was designed to perform informational and guidance-oriented functions rather than legal reasoning or decision-making tasks. These functions align with the most common access-to-justice chatbot use cases identified in the literature (Queudot et al., 2020; Rajendran et al., 2025). Importantly, the chatbot interface included a clear disclaimer indicating that the system provided legal information only and did not constitute professional legal advice. This transparency measure is widely recommended to maintain ethical compliance and user trust in AI-supported legal systems (Vassilopoulos, 2022).

Access via a web browser enables the chatbot to be accessible from a variety of devices without the need to install additional software on the user's device. Using a web browser also allows for compatibility with mobile phones, further enhancing the accessibility of the chatbot. This is envisioned to make it more accessible and desirable for use, as other elements were added to the overall usage of the chatbot to reduce usage costs. Furthermore, because all the computation is done on the server, the chatbot requires very minimal computational resources from the user's device. Figure 4 shows the chatbot interface accessed from a web browser.

Figure 4. **Interface of the chatbot**

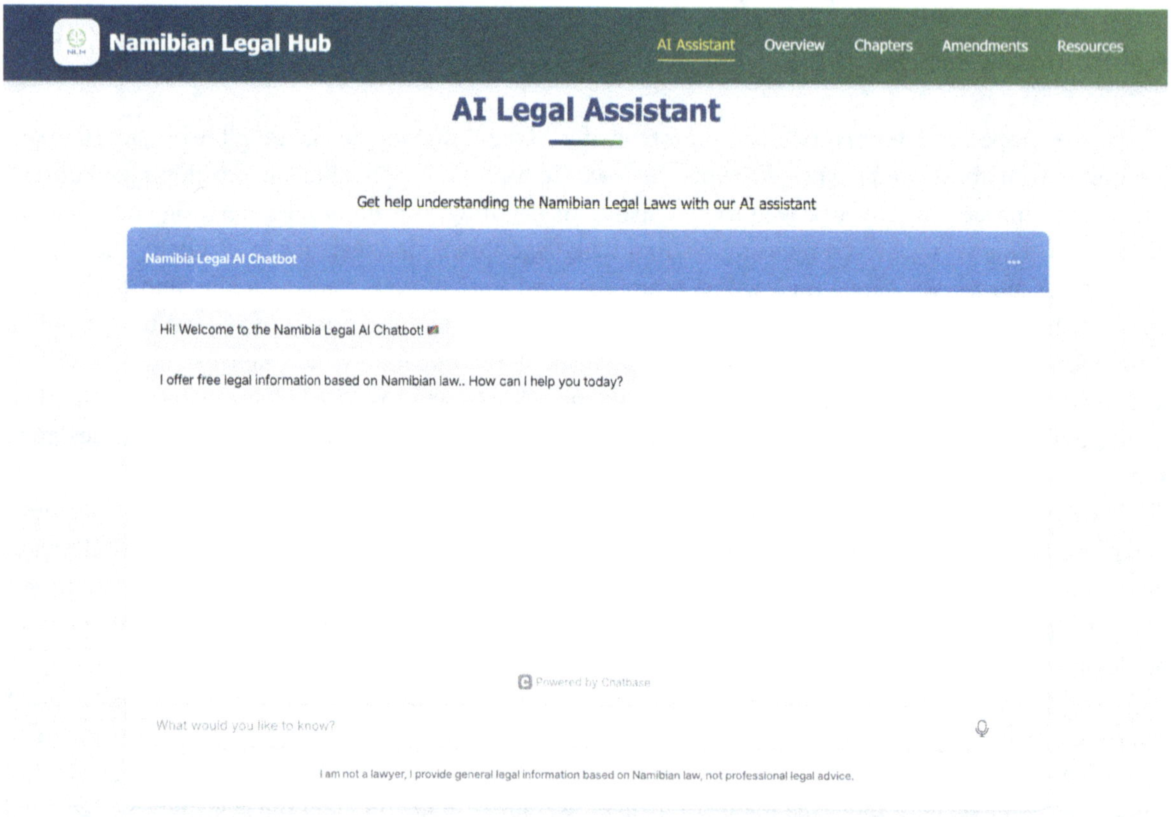

(image by the authors)

In addition to relying on the web server's computational power to reduce the burden on user devices, other elements were incorporated into the website's design. These elements include having a black and white interface with minimal multimedia, meaning that after loading the page, only small amounts of data will be used to send and receive text of the interactions between the user and the chatbot. This minimises the data transfer to/from the user device and the web server needed for performing tasks, resulting in reduced data costs on the user's end.

DISCUSSION

The results of the prototype testing indicate that an AI-supported legal chatbot can significantly help to improve access to legal information in a developing country. To validate this claim, a chatbot was developed based on an analysis and review of the literature around AI chatbots and other technologies within different justice systems. This process enabled a deeper understanding of the ability of AI systems to respond to legal questions from diverse jurisdictions. This then led to the development of a web-based AI legal chatbot that can be accessed through the internet.

The prototype provided a simple but functional interactive platform that was able to support users with low digital literacy. The chatbot demonstrated consistent accuracy and acceptable performance, substantiating its potential as a digital legal information tool, as shown in the user testing results. These findings are consistent with studies by Queudot et al. (2020) and Rajendran et al. (2025), that found that structured legal chatbots can effectively enhance legal awareness when designed within clearly defined informational boundaries. Unlike generative AI models, the structured intent-matching approach used in this prototype prioritised reliability over conversational flexibility, thereby reducing the risk of misinformation.

The Deployment Phase used free hosting services to prove the concept of internet accessible legal assistant in the form of a chatbot. Although there are limitations that come with free hosting, for purposes of testing and evaluating the chatbot, free hosting services were sufficient. When deploying similar services for public use, the approach will differ and depend on the deployment method. For example, the chatbot would be alongside the justice agency or within the Ministry of Justice website, if the deployment is government-sponsored, or it could be hosted within a legal aid centre or law firm whose mandate is to increase legal access to the people.

One of the identified challenges was the maintenance of the Knowledge Base with updated information. This is key as the Knowledge Base requires frequent updates based on activities such as legislative amendments, regulatory changes, and court decisions that alter how existing provisions are interpreted. This, therefore, requires adequate planning when deploying the chatbot, as there will be a need to have personnel responsible for updating the Knowledge Base to ensure accuracy of information. This update procedure will also be dependent on how and who deploys the chatbot.

One limitation of the chatbot evaluation is the composition of the test population, which was primarily university students. Although this population sample does not capture all demographics, it was used to evaluate key components that were used for the overall improvement of the chatbot. For the proof of concept, this population was adequate as the study was guided by the literature of studies performed in Namibia, and in comparison to those in the developed world, while also considering elements that need consideration when developing AI systems. Involving different population demographics can be done when implementing the full system after meeting requirements, such as hosting services and personnel responsible for maintaining the Knowledge Base. With a fully deployed system, it will then be possible to measure elements like network latency, computational load on the server, access methods, usage statistics and user databases.

CONCLUSION

This study presented the potential of using AI to power legal chatbots as a method for improving access to justice in developing countries, with Namibia as a case study. The relevance was motivated by the persistent challenges in accessing legal aid, caused by barriers such as high legal costs, distance from courts, and limited legal literacy, which are more common in developing countries and rural areas. The literature review showed that AI is increasingly being used in justice systems globally, from smart courts in China to AI-assisted research in the United States. Thus, legal chatbots have emerged as promising tools because they can provide timely, low-cost, and easy-to-understand legal information. Challenges such as ethical concerns around privacy, transparency, and bias in training data were also identified. Building user trust was also identified as crucial, especially in communities where people prefer face-to-face interactions with legal professionals.

Design Science Research was used as the research methodology using five phases: analysis, design, implementation, testing and deployment. The final prototype, a web-based chatbot accessible on the internet using a web browser, was developed. The chatbot contains the AI engine powered by Chatbase's Natural Language Processing, and a Knowledge Base containing Namibian legal materials.

User Testing of the developed chatbot produced encouraging results. With 90.9% of participants finding the chatbot easy to use, accurate and relevant. The chatbot was also tested on handling unclear or poorly phrased questions, which was an important test to represent varying digital literacy levels. In the end, the developed chatbot demonstrated that an AI legal chatbot can be developed in the context of a developing country by basing the Knowledge Base on the laws and regulations of that country. These results further suggest that with appropriate design choices, AI legal chatbots can effectively bridge the knowledge gap between legal professionals and the public.

AI-powered legal chatbots, when thoughtfully designed and ethically implemented, can meaningfully improve access to justice in developing countries. As AI continues to advance, its careful application in the justice sector offers hope for making the ideal justice system for all a reality, regardless of where they live or what they can afford. The developed chatbot in the Namibian context serves as further proof that such technology can be implemented without the significant financial investment that would otherwise be required to give citizens the same level of access to legal information from legal professionals.

FUTURE WORK

Several avenues for future research and development emerged from the findings. Future work will focus on significantly expanding the chatbot's Knowledge Base to cover a wider range of legal domains, including family law, inheritance law, and consumer rights. A critical step would be the formal inclusion and accurate representation of other components, such as customary law, and ensuring the tool is relevant across the entire multiple legal system. Future work will also include the implementation of more sophisticated security measures to protect user data and ensure system resilience against malicious attacks or the generation of legally harmful information.

Long-term deployment would also require collaboration with judicial institutions and legal aid organisations to ensure institutional legitimacy. Integration with mobile technologies such as SMS and USSD could significantly broaden accessibility, particularly in rural communities where users might not have access to smartphones. The addition of multilingual support would significantly extend the chatbot's reach, particularly among older users and those in communities where English is not the primary language of everyday life.

REFERENCES

Anand, A., Kaur, J., Singh, O., & Alhazmi, H., O. (. (2021, May 6). Optimal sprint length determination for Agile-based software development. *Computers, Materials & Continua, 68*(3), 3693–3712. DOI: 10.32604/cmc.2021.017461

Appleby, L. (2024). Breaking barriers: Exploring accessibility to legal advice and its implications for justice. *Wake Forest Journal of Law & Policy, 15*(1), 65–84.

Chang, C. (2021). Improving access to free online legal information through Universal Design: User personas, user journeys, a proposal, and a prototype. *Legal Reference Services Quarterly, 40*(4), 199–281. DOI: 10.1080/0270319X.2021.2003686

Choi, J. H., & Schwarcz, D. (2024). AI assistance in legal analysis: An empirical study. *Journal of Legal Education, 73*(2), 384–420.

De Sordi, J. O. (2021, September). *Design science research methodology: Theory development from artifacts*. Springer Nature.

Faghiri, A. K. (2022). The use of Artificial Intelligence in the criminal justice system (a comparative study). *Webology, 19*(5), 593–613.

Gromova, E. A., Brantes Ferreira, D., & Begishev, R., I. R. (. (2023). ChatGPT and other intelligent Chatbots: Legal, ethical and dipute resolution concerns. *Revista Brasileira de Alternative Dispute Resolution, 5*(10), 153–175. DOI: 10.52028/rbadr.v5i10.ART07.RU

Hashiyana, V., & Kamati, W. (2024). An Artificial Intelligence-powered chatbot-integrated web-based application: A case study of the University of Namibia. In Ertuğrul, D. Ç., & Elçi, A. (Eds.), *Cutting-Edge Technologies for Business Sectors* (pp. 205–244). IGI Global., DOI: 10.4018/979-8-3693-9586-8.ch008

Hermansyah, M., Najib, A., Farida, A., Sacipto, R., & Rintyarna, B. S. (2023, February 21). Artificial Intelligence and ethics: Building an Artificial Intelligence system that ensures privacy and social justice. *The International Journal of Science in Society, 5*(1), 154–168. DOI: 10.54783/ijsoc.v5i1.644

Hevner, A., & Chatterjee, S. (2010). *Design science research in Information Systems.*, DOI: 10.1007/978-1-4419-5653-8_2

Laptev, V. A., & Feyzrakhmanova, D. R. (2024). Application of Artificial Intelligence in justice: Current trends and future prospects. *Human-Centric Intelligent Systems, 4*(3), 394–405. DOI: 10.1007/s44230-024-00074-2

Maphosa, V. (2024, December). The rise of Artificial Intelligence and emerging ethical and social concerns. *AI. Computer Science and Robotics Technology, 3*(1), 1–20. DOI: 10.5772/acrt.20240020

Matongo, B., & Jacobs, L. (2022, June). E-justice to bridge records management gap at the High Court in Namibia. *Archiving : Final Program and Proceedings. IS & T's Archiving Conference, 19*(1), 25–29. DOI: 10.2352/issn.2168-3204.2022.19.1.6

Mendonca, H., & Iyamu, T. (2024). Improving the justice system services in Namibian rural communities through mobile technology. *Issues in Information Systems, 25*(4), 16–28. *Supplemental Index*, (180687392). Advance online publication. DOI: 10.48009/4_iis_2024_102

More, M. (2021). The institution of traditional authority in Okombahe, Erongo region of Namibia: Can the institution be reconciled with democratic values of justice? *Law, Democracy and Development, 25*(SPE), 146–166. https://doi.org/DOI: 10.17159/2077-4907/2020/ldd.v25.spe7

Munnang, S. (2024, November-December). Empowering access to justice through automated legal case management. *International Journal for Multidisciplinary Research, 6*(6), 1–13. DOI: 10.36948/ijfmr.2024.v06i06.31915

Norchuk, Y. (2025). The use of Artificial Intelligence and other technologies to improve legal communication and access to justice for different populations around the world. *Journal of International Legal Communication, 16*(1), 52–63. DOI: 10.32612/uw.27201643.2025.16.1.pp.52-63

Odendaal, W. (2005). *A place we want to call our own: A study on land tenure policy and securing housing rights in Namibia*. Legal Assistance Centre (LAC). http://www.lac.org.na/projects/lead/Pdf/aplacewewanttocallourown.pdf

Papagianneas, S., & Junius, N. (2023, November). Fairness and justice through automation in China's smart courts. *Computer Law & Security Review, 51*, 105897. DOI: 10.1016/j.clsr.2023.105897

Peruginelli, G. (2009). Accessing legal information across boundaries: A new challenge. *International Journal of Legal Information, 37*(3), 276–305. DOI: 10.1017/S0731126500005345

Queudot, M., Charton, É., & Meurs, M.-J. (2020). Improving access to justice with legal chatbots. *Stats, 3*(3), 356–375. DOI: 10.3390/stats3030023

Raj, R., & Kos, A. (2023). Artificial Intelligence: Evolution, developments, applications, and future scope. *Przeglad Elektrotechniczny, 1*(2), 3–15. DOI: 10.15199/48.2023.02.01

Rajendran, R. K. V., A. I., T., M. P., Vetrivel, S., & N. R., W. B. (2025). The role of AI in enhancing access to justice and legal services. In H. Bajraktari (Ed.), *Advances in Electronic Government, Digital Divide, and Regional Development* (pp. 139–162). IGI Global. https://doi.org/DOI: 10.4018/979-8-3693-7205-0.ch008

Siani, J. A. (2024). Empowering justice: Exploring the applicability of AI in the judicial system. *Journal of Law and Legal Research Development., 1*(1), 24–28. DOI: 10.69662/jllrd.v1i1.6

Valavanidis, A. (2023, April 10). *Artificial Intelligence (AI) applications*. University of Athens, University Campus Zografou, 15784.

Vassilopoulos, A. (2022). *Can AI chatbots improve access to legal information? A case study on the inhibitors of AI chatbots' implementation in the context of JuridiQC*. HEC Montréal.

Zongwe, D. (2022, November 11). Nobody can really afford legal services: The price of justice in Namibia. *Potchefstroom Electronic Law Journal/Potchefstroomse Elektroniese Regsblad, 24*(1). https://doi.org/DOI: 10.17159/1727-3781/2021/v24i0a6420

Chapter 13
Moving Faster Than the Rules:
Artificial Intelligence, Digital Evidence, and the Limits of Evidentiary Standards

Linnea Hall
http://orcid.org/0009-0004-1251-4794
Western Governors University, USA

Eric "Parkman" Speights
University of Mississippi School of Law, USA

ABSTRACT

This chapter provides a review of the constitutional and ethical concerns related to the evidentiary review of digital and AI derived evidence in the criminal justice system. First, the historical evolution of evidence from physical to scientific is introduced, and then the drastic shift to digital evidence including electronically stored information and algorithmic analysis is explored, focusing on the ethical and constitutional challenges. The limitations of existing standards including Rules 901 and 702 under the Daubert framework are analyzed as they relate to the differences between deterministic and probabilistic evidence and proprietary systems. The constitutional and ethical implications of using probabilistic evidence in sentencing and corrections are evaluated, and finally, a structured integration framework is proposed to ensure scientific validity, transparency, contestability, ethical safeguards, and institutional accountability to support lawful and equitable adoption of emerging technologies.

INTRODUCTION

The introduction of artificial intelligence (AI) and digital technologies to the legal system is challenging traditional evidentiary and procedural rules that were not conceived with sufficient foresight to adapt to these technologies while preserving justice and individuals' rights. These technologies provide convenience and expediency, while appearing to improve the judicial process through perceived fairness and unbiased adjudication. These technologies, however, are proving to be stochastic, opaque, and poorly understood by those who are relying on them. A critical examination of these tools, focusing on the use of AI and digital evidence and its admissibility, reliability and constitutional and ethical implications is required. A thorough research-based foundation is therefore presented to facilitate the creation and

DOI: 10.4018/979-8-3373-7660-8.ch013

adoption of regulatory frameworks and evidentiary standards that recognize the benefits of technological advancements while ensuring procedural fairness.

BACKGROUND

Historical Development of Evidentiary Practices

A conflict between scientific innovation in evidentiary practices and ensuring fairness and consistency is not new to the judicial process. The issue of introducing new forms of scientific evidence during trial has been addressed multiple times, each time focusing on the underlying fairness and reliability. Historically, forensic science was based on physical, observable characteristics, such as comparing handwriting and signatures for similarities, or looking at the patterns created by fingerprints that are left behind at a crime scene and comparing them to those of the defendant. Through time, the methods for examining forensic evidence evolved with experience, and training was introduced leading to clear methods, expert testimony, and forensic laboratories dedicated to forensic analysis in the late 19th and early 20th century, establishing consistency and clarity in forensic evaluation (Saks & Faigman, 2008). Although the processes were methodical, these pattern-based forensics lacked empirical validation, but their intuitive and observable nature supported widespread adoption in the courtroom.

In the United States, judges were the final arbitrators of the admissibility of evidence, ensuring relevance and reliability. In 1923, *Frye v. United States* introduced the "general acceptance test," which stated that the methods or principles used to determine evidence admissibility must be generally considered reliable within the relevant scientific community. This standard was considered the gold standard until science and technology began to change more rapidly, making *Frye* difficult to apply to emerging, and not yet widely known technologies. To allow courts to adapt to and allow new techniques that often allowed for more precise evidentiary analysis, the U.S. Supreme Court extended the general acceptance test to include empirical testing, peer review, and error rates in *Daubert v. Merrell Dow Pharmaceuticals* (1993). This represented a major shift toward incorporating scientific methodology and more complex forensic and digital techniques into judicial proceedings, allowing judges to use their judgement and proof of reliability to determine the admissibility of evidence, even when widespread acceptance was not available.

With the emergence and widespread adoption of electronically stored information (ESI), machine learning analytics, and artificial intelligence, the evidentiary landscape is again on the verge of major change and the introduction of challenges related to volatility, replicability, and invisibility of digital data. Unlike analysis of physical evidence, digital artifacts are more difficult to understand, and it is more difficult to observe identifying information that makes the digital evidence unique, such as metadata (Amadi, 2024; Ismail & Ariffin, 2025). Additionally, digital data is inherently mutable and often generated without conscious human input. This has forced courts to adopt new standards of authentication and chain of custody to ensure the data has not been changed from its original form (Ismail & Ariffin, 2025).

Establishing the integrity of digital evidence differs from physical evidence in that simply establishing a chain of custody is not sufficient to demonstrate that the data is authentic and has not been altered. In addition to these procedural guarantees such as data acquisition, storage, and analysis, technical mechanisms, such as hash verification are also required to demonstrate that the data has not been altered (Yadav, 2020).

The addition of digital evidence also requires an evolution in legal standards. For example, in May, 2025, an advisory committee on AI-related evidence issues began discussion on Proposed Rule 901(c) to the Federal Rules of Evidence (FRE), which would address AI-generated evidence. This would complement the proposed Rule 707 that would require "machine-generated" evidence to satisfy the requirements of Rule 702 (Advisory Committee, 2025). This is in addition to amendments to incorporate digital processes within the scope of admissible materials. Specifically, Federal Rule of Evidence 901 (2011), which governs authentication, now encompasses testimony from digital forensic examiners and verification using hash algorithms or metadata analysis. Federal Rule of Evidence 702 (2011) was also revised post-*Daubert* to require that expert opinions must derive from reliable principles, reliably applied, and this criteria must have been tested through digital forensics, where misapplication of tools can lead to significant evidentiary distortion.

These modifications demonstrate an increasing acknowledgement that digital data requires a different approach to evidentiary logic due to its transient and continuous nature, which raises unique ethical and procedural concerns. Surveillance by accumulation represents the routine data collection by law enforcement, which creates extensive data repositories that generally exceed the scope of original warrants creating concerns related to Fourth Amendment protections (Ferguson, 2024). To address this and ensure Fourth Amendment protections, standards need to be recalibrated for relevance and admissibility (Ferguson, 2024).

Changes in the way humans use technology have also resulted in data being collected twenty-four hours a day, seven days a week. This Data is often stored across distributed and cloud-based environments, creating jurisdictional and access challenges that complicate collection and admissibility (Ismail & Ariffin, 2025). Because data is collected from various platforms, evidence may be stored on multiple servers in jurisdictions all over the world complicating seizure and transfer (Handar, et al., 2021). To address this, bilateral and multilateral frameworks and agreements between nations (e.g. the CLOUD Act) help with the preservation and production of digital evidence. On the other hand, where conflicts exist (for example, GDPR, which may prevent the disclosure of certain types of evidence, even with agreements in place) procedural fairness issues remain (Ismail & Ariffin, 2025).

The introduction of artificial intelligence has complicated the underlying constitutional and ethical issues associated with digital evidence. After its introduction in 2023, artificial intelligence has seen widespread adoption in an effort to achieve greater efficiency and accuracy. It has been widely integrated into the judicial process though predictive analytics, image recognition, and natural language processing to interpret evidence, manage case files, and assess risk (Dmitrieva & Pastukhov, 2023). These tools have proven invaluable in interpreting the increasing quantities of available data, but the results are probabilistic rather than deterministic, which challenges evidentiary doctrines (Hefetz, 2025; Seng, 2025). As an example, consider profiling. AI is increasingly being used to identify likely perpetrators based on information like behavioral patterns or social network analysis. Unfortunately, there is a cognitive gap between legal professionals and digital forensic experts, which is creating issues in the adversarial process (Hefetz, 2025; Skaramuca, 2025). Judges, as gatekeepers, are responsible for determining the reliability and admissibility of evidence. However, the technical complexity and opacity of algorithmic and digital forensic systems limit their ability to independently evaluate methodological validity (Seng, 2025; Hefetz, 2025). Proprietary software makes the task even more difficult as neither judges nor defendants can access the underlying source code due to trade secret protections, preventing them from understanding the methods used to generate outputs and limiting their ability to challenge potentially flawed or biased evidence to superficial arguments (Seng, 2025; Ismail & Ariffin, 2025).

These black-box algorithms that hide the internal logic for determining outputs, raise serious due process concerns. Because this type of evidence is becoming more prominent, evidentiary practices must evolve to address both the technological and constitutional concerns that are raised. For example, when the defense cannot review an algorithm's logic, either for computational or proprietary reasons, due process concerns are raised under the Sixth and Fourteenth Amendments. Defendants must be able to confront the evidence against them and challenge its accuracy. If the outputs are not explainable, this is effectively prevented, as opaque systems restrict meaningful review and adversarial testing (Hefetz, 2025).

Although a consensus is beginning to build regarding the need to adapt to new types of evidence and some progress is being made through rule amendments and judicial standards, there are still gaps in how to address issues of fairness, transparency, and reliability. These gaps will need to ensure that progress improves and supports the legitimacy of the criminal justice system.

Historically, there have been many notable periods of change in evidentiary practices within the criminal justice system. Most of these are related to broader changes in the way that information is authenticated and evaluated.

From Physical Objects to Scientific Forensics

Historically, evidence was primarily tangible and observable, consisting of physical artifacts that could be directly examined and interpreted. It included easily detected proof such as fingerprints, blood stains, handwritten confessions, or physical documents. These items were subject to chain of custody rules, eyewitness authentication, or judicial discretion related to the relevance of the item or potential prejudice or bias introduced by its admission. In the 20th century, forensic techniques, such as ballistics, handwriting, bite marks, and friction ridge analysis was used by experts with training or experience in its use. These methods were typically reactive and intuitive making it relatively simple for judges and juries to understand the reasoning and explanations provided by expert testimony (Hefetz, 2025). Due to the intuitive nature of this type of evidence and direct observability, they seldom raised questions related to the likelihood of error or ethics of allowing its admission (Seng, 2025). As evidentiary practices evolved, forensic methods increasingly incorporated computational and probabilistic techniques, introducing opacity and reducing the ability of non-experts to independently evaluate results (Hefetz, 2025; Seng, 2025). These techniques increasingly relied on computational processes, including biometric analysis and digital tracking systems, which depend on complex data processing rather than direct observation (Seng, 2025). These techniques are characterized by a proactive rather than reactive investigative scope and are technically complex. They also raise ethical concerns regarding privacy implications, particularly where digital evidence and forensic analysis expose sensitive personal information and increase the risk of misuse or misinterpretation (Amadi, 2024; Ferguson, 2024).

The Digital Turn and Its Legal Implications

This shift from observable, pattern-based evidence to computational and data-driven analysis introduces fundamental challenges related to transparency, interpretability, and reliability, which directly inform the evidentiary and constitutional issues associated with digital and AI-generated evidence. The emergence of digital technologies also had a considerable impact on the nature of criminal evidence and how criminal adjudication was handled. Evidence was no longer considered a group of physical artifacts related to a crime, but rather data created, stored, and processed through networked systems and across jurisdictions (Ismail & Ariffin, 2025). This shift from analog to digital formats required the consideration of electronic evidence on a large scale rather than discrete artifacts that are more easily categorized. Electronic evidence encompasses data recorded or stored on any electronic medium. This is not limited to documents, but includes email headers, metadata, server logs, algorithmic inferences, and other information. Unlike physical or analog evidence, which is generally considered immutable, these digital footprints are ephemeral, malleable, and dependent on the integrity of the preservation system and processes (Ismail & Ariffin, 2025).

This ontological change resulted in transformational legal and ethical ramifications. Foundational concepts, such as originality, authenticity, and best evidence, were not easily adapted to the new digital evidence. For example, a digitized copy of a document may be indistinguishable from the original but susceptible to undetectable tampering. This led to the introduction of technical mechanisms such as cryptographic hashing and digital signatures to the traditional chain-of-custody logs to establish integrity (Dmitrieva & Pastukhov, 2023).

Judicial Standards for Admissibility

The increasing use of scientific and digital evidence has led to the need for clear standards governing admissibility. *Frye v. United States* (1923) required that evidence be "generally accepted" in its field, focusing more on consensus than empirical review. *Daubert v. Merrell Dow Pharmaceuticals* (1993) extended *Frye* by adding more scientifically based requirements, such as testability, peer review and error rates. *Kumho Tire Co. v. Carmichael* (1999) expanded these criteria to include expert testimony to explain more scientific and technical concepts to a jury lacking in the required expertise to properly analyze the evidence.

Mason and Seng (2021) explained that Daubert put trial judges in the position of gatekeepers, requiring them to evaluate the relevance and reliability of expert methods prior to admitting them into evidence. Judges unfortunately seldom have the required technical expertise to properly evaluate this type of evidence due to the "black box" and proprietary nature of digital systems and forensic software. In addition, there is a distinct asymmetry between the prosecution and defense related to access to these systems, adding an additional layer of "fairness" that the judge must consider when evaluating expert evidence and testimony.

The Rise of Electronically Stored Information (ESI)

With Frye, the court only had to adapt to new scientific techniques. The increasing use of new forms of digital data and electronically stored information (ESI) has created yet another layer of evidentiary adaptation. ESI is a broad category that encompasses all data created, recorded, manipulated, and stored in a digital format. This includes a plethora of potential evidence that grows by millions of terabytes every day. Thus, the courts need to consider how the data was collected, preserved, and stored, in addition to how it can be authenticated. According to Bakhtiar (2024), one of the first challenges with ESI was establishing authenticity in accordance with Federal Rule of Evidence 901. Unlike physical evidence, which can be authenticated visually with little expertise, digital evidence is authenticated through digital techniques, such as checksums, audit trails, or the testimony of digital forensic experts. Techniques such as hashing algorithms act like digital fingerprints to demonstrate that the file has not been altered since it was initially seized (Mason & Seng, 2021).

Due to its ephemeral nature, digital evidence is particularly vulnerable to manipulation (Ismail & Ariffin, 2025). Digital evidence can be altered without visible indicators, requiring technical validation methods and controlled forensic processes to ensure integrity (Ismail & Ariffin, 2025; Amadi, 2024); multistep protocols have therefore been developed for the seizure and preservation of digital evidence. These include procedures such as forensic imaging, preservation of original data, and strict documentation of access and handling processes to maintain evidentiary integrity (Law Enforcement Cyber Center, 2025; Ismail & Ariffin, 2025).

Epistemic Uncertainty and the Role of the Forensic Expert

The introduction of probabilistic and digital evidence has also complicated the traditional evidentiary process in criminal trials. Traditionally, physical evidence offers a level of certainty because it can be seen and touched, which provides assurances. Probabilistic conclusions, such as the probability that two separate DNA samples will match is one in 10 million, offers a less secure and verifiable result as it is contingent on variables such as database or algorithm design, error rates, and statistical assumptions, which are unclear to most jurors and add a distinct level of uncertainty to the overall conclusion.

This knowledge gap increases the need for a forensic expert, which has shifted from a person who interprets the meaning of physical evidence, to someone who represents an "epistemic corridor" by translating complex technical findings into understandable, legally grounded language while preserving the probabilistic nature of the evidence (Hefetz, 2025). However, conflicting expert testimony, proprietary software, and ambiguous admissibility standards continue to create issues.

EVIDENTIARY STANDARDS AND DIGITAL EVIDENCE

The increasing use of ESI has changed evidentiary analysis from direct inspection to process-based proof. Unlike physical evidence, which can be visually reviewed and intuitively interpreted, digital evidence cannot. The probative value lies in not just in what can be reviewed physically, but also in how they were created and preserved (Mason & Seng, 2021). This makes authentication, methodological reliability, and attribution increasingly important to admissibility of electronic and digital evidence (Ismail & Ariffin, 2025; Law Enforcement Cyber Center, 2025).

Authentication Under Rule 901

Federal Rule of Evidence 901 requires proof that an exhibit is what it is claimed to be. With traditional evidence, appearance alone is often sufficient (a knife, a fingerprint, a photograph); but in the case of digital evidence, while on its face, the evidence may appear simple (a letter, a photo, a social media post) that is rarely sufficient because the ability to manipulate or fabricate digital evidence adds an element of uncertainty that does not exist in traditional physical evidence (Mason & Seng, 2021; Dmitrieva, & Pastukhov, 2023).

When determining the admissibility of digital evidence, courts must not only evaluate the relevance of the item, but also the authenticity, including whether the evidence is being presented on the original storage media, whether additional data was collected, and how access was controlled and documented. Mason and Seng (2021) explained that authenticity in digital matters depends on continuous, legitimate custody supported by technical safeguards. Dmitrieva and Pastukhov (2023) also discussed the necessity of preservation practices and integrity verification in determining authenticity and admissibility of digital evidence.

A common form of authentication is hash-based integrity checks, though they are not self-authenticating. Their evidentiary value is based on when they were generated, who controlled the process, and whether there is a documented comparison history (Dmitrieva & Pastukhov, 2023).

Another problem with digital records is attribution; in other words, who created the record and what device they used, or what account is attached to the transmission or creation. In most cases, this can be demonstrated through multiple aspects rather than one single identifying feature. These aspects can include information such as account credentials, metadata, patterns of use, or contextual indicators that must be collectively evaluated to establish attribution and authenticity (Ismail & Ariffin, 2025; Amadi, 2024). This does not mean that proof is required with absolute certainty; instead, the court must be able to reasonably defend both integrity and attribution. Without both, admissibility can be challenged.

Chain of Custody and Preservation

Unlike physical evidence, which degrades through environmental exposure or handling, digital evidence does not physically decay; instead, its integrity degrades through procedural and system-level processes (Ismail & Ariffin, 2025). The routine functions of a computer system, such as file migration, remote storage, or overwriting, can alter or compromise digital evidence if not properly controlled (Ismail & Ariffin, 2025; Law Enforcement Cyber Center, 2025). Accordingly, digital chain of custody focuses on controlling system-level processes and documenting all interactions with the data to preserve integrity throughout its lifecycle (Ismail & Ariffin, 2025). The storage environment must be strictly controlled, including the use of forensic imaging, secure storage, duplication protocols, and audit logs that document access, handling, and verification activities (Law Enforcement Cyber Center, 2025; Ismail & Ariffin, 2025; Mason & Seng, 2021). Any break in the preservation or documentation process undermines the integrity and admissibility of digital evidence by introducing uncertainty regarding authenticity and potential alteration (Ismail & Ariffin, 2025; Dmitrieva & Pastukhov, 2023). Integrity is typically verified through cryptographic hashing and comparison processes, which ensure that the data remains unchanged from the point of acquisition through analysis and presentation (Law Enforcement Cyber Center, 2025; Ismail & Ariffin, 2025). Unlike physical evidence, where alteration is often visible, digital evidence can be modified without observable indicators, making procedural controls and technical validation essential to evidentiary reliability (Amadi, 2024; Ismail & Ariffin, 2025).

Reliability Under Rule 702 and Daubert

These challenges demonstrate that traditional chain-of-custody principles are insufficient when applied to digital environments without technical safeguards, reinforcing the need for enhanced evidentiary standards and judicial scrutiny. While authentication establishes that the evidence is being presented in substantially its original form, scientific reliability must be demonstrated through other means. This can include the use of specialized (often proprietary) forensic software or statistical modeling, and admissibility is governed by Federal Rule of Evidence 702 and Daubert (Daubert v. Merrell Dow Pharmaceuticals, Inc., 1993; Kumho Tire, 2024). These computer and software-driven techniques often operate in a "black-box" environment, meaning that the logic for reaching the result is often hidden, providing only the most basic information related to how the results were derived, making it difficult for the courts to fully evaluate (Hefetz, 2025), and the position of judicial gatekeeping more important, but challenging to administer reliably with the traditional frameworks (Hefetz, 2025). In many cases, once the evidence is admitted, it becomes a battle between experts and their interpretation of the evidence (Schwartz, 2024)

Proprietary systems exacerbate this issue by creating a black box with limited access to the source code and, thereby, restricting the ability to validate the results by independent verification. Experts may be able to describe system workflows at a high level, but limited access to source code, training data, and system architecture restricts independent validation of the assumptions underlying the output (Seng, 2025; Ismail & Ariffin, 2025). A court or judge's review thus depends on the information provided, whether that is documentation standards or error characterization. If information is absent, judges may resort to their overall impression of the reliability and authenticity of the data rather than a thoroughly documented methodological review.

Hearsay and System-Generated Records

Depending on the case, electronic evidence can consist of vast quantities of transactional data, system outputs, logs, and timestamps, raising a question of whether this information represents human assertion, constituting hearsay under rule 801 (Mason & Seng, 2021). If the data is completely automated, it lacks a declarant; although records that require user input, configuration, or discretion do not. How these are treated from an evidentiary standpoint will depend on system reliability and the admissibility of the embedded "assertions" and are relevant when confrontation requirements under Crawford are triggered (Mason & Seng, 2021).

Metadata and Provenance

Metadata, or data about the data, is often as important as the underlying content in establishing evidentiary value. Metadata can provide information about where and when the data was created or modified and by whom and are a foundational element of digital forensic proof, particularly in establishing authenticity, integrity, and provenance in digital environments (Ismail & Ariffin, 2025; Amadi, 2024). This becomes more complicated in distributed and networked environments, where metadata may be fragmented across multiple systems and storage locations (Ismail & Ariffin, 2025). Metadata artifacts may be distributed across multiple systems, requiring reconstruction of data provenance through aggregation of system logs, timestamps, and access records to establish a complete evidentiary narrative (Ismail & Ariffin, 2025; Law Enforcement Cyber Center, 2025). Metadata analysis also plays a critical role in identifying inconsistencies, anomalies, or potential manipulation, particularly where content may appear authentic but underlying data indicates alteration (Amadi, 2024). Courts thus rely on metadata not only for contextual understanding, but also to support authentication and admissibility determinations under evidentiary standards governing digital evidence (Ismail & Ariffin, 2025). The metadata itself may be incomplete, altered, or lost during routine system operations, however, requiring careful validation and corroboration with other evidentiary sources (Ismail & Ariffin, 2025). These limitations reinforce the broader challenge of relying on digital evidence, where authenticity and reliability depend on both technical processes and the ability to reconstruct and verify data provenance.

Procedural Fairness and Evidentiary Asymmetries

One major issue with the use of digital evidence is equal access to forensic software and technical expertise by all parties. Prosecutors and law enforcement generally have access to specialized tools that are not available to the defense, especially when limited funding is available such as in pro bono and pro se cases (Garrett & Rudin, 2024). This can have unfair consequences on the defendant as they may not be able to recreate the analyses or fully evaluate system behavior, limiting the defendant to superficial objections rather than providing clear objections supported by a methodological evaluation. Proprietary restrictions that limit access to source code, training data, and validation studies also make verification impractical, allowing expert testimony to substitute for verifiable review (Garrett & Rudin, 2024). Ultimately, this results in a less than perfect evaluation that is biased toward the introducing party leading to constitutional and ethical concerns.

THE JUDICIAL USE OF ARTIFICIAL INTELLIGENCE AND ALGORITHMIC DECISION-MAKING

The Technological Shift in Judicial Processes

The integration of artificial intelligence (AI) into judicial processes marks a fundamental evolution in the administration of justice. This transformation is characterized by the increasing use of algorithmic tools to facilitate legal research, assess risk, streamline workflow, and, in some jurisdictions, generate preliminary decisions. Although the application of AI promises significant efficiency and consistency, it simultaneously presents ethical, constitutional, and epistemological risks that courts are only beginning to address. These conflicts between innovation and integrity, utility and accountability require a deliberate legal response to ensure the judiciary remains independent, transparent, and fair.

Judicial Use of Artificial Intelligence in Adjudication

In recent years, artificial intelligence has been rapidly adopted across legal and institutional contexts (Skaramuca, 2025). It has been increasingly adopted across criminal justice institutions, including law enforcement agencies, legal practitioners, and courts (Skaramuca, 2025). Artificial intelligence systems are also capable of generating highly realistic synthetic content, raising concerns about evidentiary reliability and authenticity (Skaramuca, 2025). The ubiquity of this new technology must be addressed within the judiciary before it creates lasting and irreversible damage.

The judiciary and supporting tools… have increasingly incorporated artificial intelligence (Skaramuca, 2025). In many cases, these updates are made with the consent of users, and it is difficult to decouple the AI elements from the underlying tools. These tools are used to increase efficiency and ease the production load of often overworked individuals, with the intent of increasing both output and accuracy, often with minimal assistance or review from those using it (Lacqueur & Copus, 2022; Simmler & Canova, 2024; Villasenor & Foggo, 2020). Adoption has occurred through trial and error by individuals with very little oversight or guidance, resulting in a wide variation in use and often leading to errors from fabricated precedent to misidentified offenders. (Kaufmann, 2024; Lacqueur & Copus, 2022). And while there has been considerable discussion of the potential dangers of AI misuse, regulatory frameworks and standardization efforts remain underdeveloped relative to the pace of adoption (Vargas-Murillo et al., 2024).

Bias in sentencing has been a concern for decades due to the overrepresentation of minority males in the prison system. In an attempt to remove the sentencing bias, AI was introduced in adjudication using predictive and decision-support systems to estimate recidivism risk, flight risk, and supervision needs, relying on statistical and machine-learning models trained on historical criminal justice data (Singh & Devi, 2025; Brenner et al., 2020; Goel et al., 2021). These systems are designed to classify defendants using demographic, socioeconomic, and behavioral information that correlate with protected characteristics (Brenner et al., 2020). These efforts demonstrated that even when race is excluded, correlated values lead to racialized classification (Singh & Devi, 2025). Attempts to optimize predictions also often create unequal error distributions with higher false-positive rates on marginalized populations (Goel et al., 2021).

Unfortunately, these tools have been quickly adopted to attempt to ensure fairness in the adjudication process by removing human emotion, even though these tools are presented only as supportive and not meant to replace professional judgment. Research has found that, contradictory to their purpose, these tools often supplant decision making related to bail, sentencing, and supervision decisions, introducing the risk of reinforcing existing biases in decision-making processes (Hefetz, 2025). In practice, these tools may influence decision-making beyond their intended advisory role (Garrett & Rudin, 2024; Dancy & Zalnieriute, 2025).

Generative AI is also proving to be challenging. Judges, lawyers, and legal clerks are increasingly using it to draft memoranda, perform research, summarize precedent, and generate legal arguments (Smith et al., 2025; Lacqueur & Copus, 2022). There have been repeated instances where lawyers have been sanctioned for producing documents with fabricated citations, misstated holdings or precedent, and distorted doctrinal analysis (see e.g. Mata v. Avianca, Inc. (Federal Court, New York) where plaintiffs' attorneys submitted a motion with fabricated citations, *Clark Pear LLC. v MVP Realty Associates LLC.*, (United States District Court for the Middle District of Florida), where plaintiff's counsel submitted several filings with fabricated citations, and California's 2nd District Court of Appeal fined an attorney in September 2025 for submitting an appeal generated by AI. This is only a sample of the numerous issues that have been reported in the last year). Introducing these AI tools, whether by individuals trying to improve efficiency or accuracy, or institutionally, by an overburdened judiciary trying to do the same, introduces institutional risk when generated text is treated as reliable and verifiable without sufficient review (Lacqueur & Copus, 2022). Because generative systems operate through probabilistic pattern completion rather than legal reasoning, they do not retrieve or interpret law. They simulate legal discourse based on incomplete training data.

When unverified generative output enters judicial deliberation, it introduces the risk of incorporating inaccurate or unverifiable information into legal reasoning processes (Skaramuca, 2025). When parties respond without verifying citations that do not exist and courts rely on arguments that are inaccurate and unsupported, errors may propagate through subsequent filings and legal decisions if not identified and corrected (Skaramuca, 2025). This harm is not limited to isolated mistakes; it undermines the integrity of the adjudicative record.

Many AI systems operate as “black box” models, limiting transparency into how outputs are generated (Hefetz, 2025). While the AI can be asked to explain its “reasoning” and it can respond in a manner that appears logical on the surface, this does not provide insights into the algorithms or training data (which is often proprietary) that were used to create the output. These transparency deficits further complicate judicial reliance on AI systems (Jadidi, 2025; Villasenor & Foggo, 2020). This opacity restricts institutional control and prevents meaningful evaluation (Jadidi, 2025). Prioritizing functionality and cost over transparency and auditability undermines faith in the judicial process (Villasenor & Foggo, 2020, Vargas-Murillo et al., 2024). Dependence on private vendors further limits transparency and independent validation of system behavior (Vargas-Murillo et al., 2024). Contractual arrangements and high switching costs built-in by commercial vendors restrict system modification, and independent testing. These constraints also limit disclosure leading courts to rely on tools they neither control nor understand, while vendors retain authority over updates, error correction, and access policies (Socol De La Osa & Remolina, 2025). This shifts institutional power from public bodies to private developers, weakening accountability, and likewise, trust and fairness in the judicial process.

These developments introduce risks that may undermine the integrity of the adjudicatory process if not properly regulated. Generative systems influence legal reasoning. Management platforms determine case prioritization. Without requiring standards for validation, disclosure, and governance, AI systems can influence judicial processes in ways that are not fully transparent or subject to consistent oversight (Lacqueur & Copus, 2022; Jadidi, 2025; Smith et al., 2025; Villasenor & Foggo, 2020). Thus, algorithm mediation is increasingly shaping how judicial decisions are framed and evaluated.

CONSTITUTIONAL AND ETHICAL CHALLENGES OF ARTIFICIAL INTELLIGENCE AND DIGITAL EVIDENCE

The integration of artificial intelligence into evidentiary and adjudicative processes raises constitutional and ethical concerns related to the Due Process Clause, the Equal Protection Clause, and the Sixth Amendment (Skaramuca, 2025). These concerns are directly related to the limited transparency and vendor control typical of AI systems and growing institutional dependence.

Under the Due Process Clause, defendants are entitled to the opportunity to challenge the evidence that is used against them. AI outputs may limit a defendant's ability to meaningfully challenge the evidence when underlying systems are not transparent or accessible (Hefetz, 2025).

Due process requires that defendants have a meaningful opportunity to challenge the evidence used against them. AI-assisted systems undermine this requirement when proprietary forensic and algorithmic tools restrict access to source code and training data, which prevents defendants and their experts from evaluating the methods used to derive the output (Garrett & Rudin, 2024). When the opposing party is required to rely on limited vendor documentation or incomplete expert summaries, this limits the ability to develop fully informed counterarguments regarding system outputs (Hefetz, 2025). The defense is thus restricted to questioning the operator's use of the system, but not the system that performed the analysis and derived the results. Often, the operator can explain the inputs, and the steps taken to derive the results, but the underlying analysis remains in a black box, with only the software's designers knowing how the software works. Even then, many modeling processes, such as neural networks, rely on processes that are difficult to interpret in practice, though explainable AI (xAI) is attempting to bridge this gap.

Recent scholarship on xAI addresses the black-box issue by developing interpretability techniques that make the inner working of these models more apparent to users. This explainability is necessary to ensure due process and legality because it allows the opposing party (the person against whom the evidence is being introduced) to contest the automated results by identifying discriminatory or erroneous reasoning (Fornasier, 2022).

To adequately understand the issue, it is important to distinguish between inherently interpretable models and deep learning systems that sacrifice transparency for predictive accuracy (Fornasier, 2022). The decision pathways of deep learning systems that rely on black-box methods can be partially reconstructed, but they still fail to provide sufficient transparency for enabling a comprehensive objection because the explanations are generally selective and temporary; they also depend on the expertise of the recipient. Many deep learning systems are dynamic, allowing them to continuously update internal weights based on new data, so explanations may be valid only until the next analysis, thus lacking the ability to provide long-term accountability (Fornasier, 2022).

This limited explainability also does not alleviate the issues of asymmetry. Even if the explanation adequately describes the analytical methodology, proprietary restrictions still limit access to training data, parameter settings, and system architecture (Fornasier, 2022). Thus, xAI approaches may improve interpretability, but they do not fully resolve limitations related to transparency, validation, or independent review (Hefetz, 2025).

Legally, a substantial gap remains between transparency and the ability to substantially analyze and rebut the results leaving underlying normative or evidentiary errors (Fornasier, 2022). Explainability therefore is a necessary, but still insufficient safeguard of due process. Without full transparency and enforceable disclosure obligations, xAI tools risk legitimizing the use of black-box decision-making without providing sufficient constitutional protection.

The result is that the prosecution presents algorithmic outputs as objective and reliable, leaving the defense with insufficient information to adequately assess the legitimacy of the results, thus leaving that interpretation to the decision-maker and due process protections may be weakened where meaningful review of algorithmic evidence is not possible (Garrett & Rudin, 2024).

Machine-learning models are trained on historical data, which is typically comprised of previous sentencing decisions and patterns. This raises questions of equal protection because they may encode and reproduce existing biases present in historical data (Singh & Devi, 2025; Gravett, 2024; Bagaric et al., 2022; Brenner et al., 2020). For example, correlated inputs, such as education, marital status, number of parents in the household, and income reproduce protected characteristics while giving the appearance of neutrality (Singh & Devi, 2025). This apparent neutrality systematically masks structurally unequal outcomes (Bagaric et al., 2022). It also creates feedback loops where historical decisions result in classifications based on previous biases reinforce the disparity (Gravett, 2024). Unfortunately, because on their face, they appear neutral (the system never asks questions directly related to the bias being avoided, such as gender or race), they may be difficult to detect due to the indirect use of proxy variables (Skaramuca, 2025).

The Sixth Amendment provides the right of a defendant to confront witnesses against them. This becomes more difficult when the evidentiary output is generated by an automated system without a clearly identifiable human declarant. As previously explained, while the operator can be questioned, the results of the data (and how they were derived) lack sufficient transparency to adequately determine how the accusation was determined (Grimm et al., 2021). This issue cannot be resolved using xAI methodologies or expert analysis because the internal system reasoning remains in a black box (Garrett & Rudin, 2024). Questioning the operator without being able to assess the internal system would limit meaningful cross-examination because the underlying analytical process is not directly observable or testable.

Automation also creates issues, especially where the derivation of results is difficult to understand or determine. Decision-makers may defer to automated outputs, particularly when systems are perceived as objective or technically authoritative (Hefetz, 2025; Longinus, 2025).

This is especially apparent in sentencing and parole contexts (Dancy & Zalnieriute, 2025). Where these decisions are integrated into the regular workflow, they also become part of the process providing default decisions rather than an advisory basis for more advanced analysis effectively shifting human judgment from evaluation to confirmation (Jadidi, 2025).

The reliance on automated outputs without sufficient evaluation raises serious ethical questions. Lawyers have a duty to provide diligent, competent representation to their clients. Unfortunately, Many legal professionals lack the technical expertise necessary to fully evaluate algorithmic systems, limiting their ability to challenge or interpret AI-generated evidence (Skaramuca, 2025; Hefetz, 2025). The inability of an attorney to adequately understand how an algorithm applies precedent, or how it determines recidivism rates raises ethical questions as to the attorney's competency to use those tools, especially when access to validation materials and system assumptions are limited (O'Brien, 2021). Additionally, relying on these tools as administrative solutions to improve efficiency, prioritizing speed and cost over accountability, introduces risks that may undermine professional competency and diligence obligations (Skaramuca, 2025). While efficiency can benefit the client through lower fees, that should not be prioritized over accountability and competent and diligent representation (Olawade et al., 2025; Antwi, 2024). Especially when it results in fabricated citations and mischaracterized precedents. At least generative AI can be verified with sufficient review. Black box algorithms present a greater risk because even the software designer may not fully understand how the results are calculated, making independent verification difficult in practice (Ismail & Ariffin, 2025).

Generative AI systems introduce additional ethical risks. Smith et al. (2025) document fabricated citations and mischaracterized precedent produced by generative tools (Smith et al., 2025). Lacqueur and Copus (2022) links these failures to institutional legitimacy concerns. When such outputs enter judicial reasoning without verification, they corrupt the evidentiary record and distort adversarial engagement.

These recurring failures indicate gaps in governance and oversight of AI systems in legal contexts (Vargas-Murillo et al., 2024). As these tools become more embedded in the system, increasing issues are being identified and yet standards and controls remain underdeveloped relative to adoption (Vargas-Murillo et al., 2024; Skaramuca, 2025). The lack of adequate controls and technical competency is eroding trust in the courts and the ability to ensure a fair and unbiased trial. While there have been some limited efforts at reform to address these problems through disclosure obligations, validation requirements, and institutional reforms (Garrett & Rudin, 2024), sufficient and robust safeguards are still needed. The lack of transparency in AI-driven evidence creates due process concerns, equal protection is threatened by biased data, confrontation rights may be constrained, and professional responsibility obligations may be challenged by reliance on opaque systems (Skaramuca, 2025).

AI IN SENTENCING AND CORRECTIONS

AI is increasingly being used in key areas in the judicial process. This includes determining bail, sentencing, and parole/probation. These determinations are not limited to the individual crime, the laws that dictate minimum sentences and prior records. AI is now used with the premise of removing the bias of a judge looking at a young, male, minority defendant who is facing the judge maybe for a first or second time (Singh & Devi, 2025; Goel et al., 2021; Garrett & Rudin, 2024). Automation allows the judge to distance themselves from emotional judgment. The information is input (without considering bias markers, such as race) and a sentencing decision is automatically provided with the appearance of objectivity and fairness, eliminating the guesswork by determining statistically whether this young man is likely to offend again and passing judgment according to the recidivism likelihood.

This is a clear paradigmatic shift from previous sentencing decisions. Previous sentencing decisions asked, what did he do, does he have any priors, and what sentence does he deserve? Now the focus has shifted to what *might* he do in the future. The introduction of AI has shifted the focus from punishing people for their past behaviors to punishing them for what they might do in the future (based on a set of data that the defendant cannot access or challenge and a black box algorithmic process that nobody understands) (Garrett & Rudin, 2024). These risk assessments may be used across multiple decision points, influencing sentencing, supervision, and release determinations (Garrett & Rudin, 2024).

AI-based risk assessment tools are perhaps the most visible and controversial examples of algorithmic influence on sentencing. The Correctional Offender Management Profiling for Alternative Sanctions (COMPAS), developed by Northpointe (now Equivant) was developed to produce more consistent results by reducing the disparities and bias that often lead to sentencing challenges. The software evaluates defendants based on variables such as criminal history, employment status, and educational background while ignoring variables of high bias such as gender and race to produce recidivism risk scores (Brennan, Dieterich, & Ehret, 2009). The system was designed specifically to provide guidance on sentencing severity, parole eligibility, and pretrial detention. Concerns about the system's lack of transparency and potential bias have led to serious constitutional and ethical concerns, especially after an investigation by ProPublica revealed that COMPAS was more likely to overestimate recidivism risk for Black defendants while underestimating it for white defendants (Goel et al., 2021). Due to the lack of transparency, the courts who adopt these tools and the judges who use them may defer to the automated outputs when there is a difference in opinion, leading to "automation bias" over human judgment and context being ignored (Longinus, 2025). This also creates a due process concern when the defendant is given neither the means, nor the ability to challenge the risk categorization (Thomas, 2022).

They were not meant to replace the judge's experience, critical thinking skills, and ability to analyze context in widely varied situations, however. This is the theory. Reality has demonstrated that this is not how this software is being used. When advisory software is introduced, people tend to defer to the algorithms, allowing them to replace critical thinking and reasoning. Consider a case with a second time seventeen-year-old offender. The individual's mother testifies that the father has recently been deployed and because she works two jobs, he has fallen into spending time with a bad crowd. The mother has taken steps to enroll her son in an after-school mentoring and job skills training program. The judge considers the recidivism risk low due to the mother's involvement, but the software indicates a high recidivism risk because he is a repeat offender, he lives in a single parent household, and he is unemployed, among other factors. According to Garrett and Rudin (2024), this creates an anchoring effect that shades the judge's decision toward the software's recommendation. Dancy and Zalnieriute (2025) describe this effect as automation bias, where the judge defers their reasoning in favor of the algorithm, assuming that due to its process (which the judge neither knows, nor understands), its decision is more accurate. This then shades how the judge considers the presented information and their decision through the filter of the software's recommendation. This effect also creates an appearance of efficiency because the judge has a starting point, which speeds the decision-making process, though not necessarily to the benefit of the defendant.

Risk Assessment and Supervision

These models are not just used in the initial sentencing process. This recidivism risk assessment software may administratively result in a more efficient allocation of resources and lighter caseloads, but realistically, the assessments follow the supervisee through probation, parole, and post-release supervision, which may result in increased surveillance intensity and contribute to disparities in supervision and release outcomes(Taylor, 2023; Yazici, 2025). This approach has been used in Virginia, but the reliance on historical data leads to decisions consistently biased toward certain demographic and socioeconomic groups (Ross et al., 2023). Similarly, the use of algorithmic tools results in racialized disparities that begin with predictive policing and follow the accused offender through sentencing and parole decisions, compounding issues related to systemic discrimination (Thomas, 2022). In the previous example, due to the use of algorithmic risk determination, the 17-year-old repeat offender may be denied juvenile detention and early release in favor of general population in an adult facility. This is likely to have a catastrophic effect on future opportunities.

Outside of custody, the use of digital surveillance tools, such as GPS tracking and biometric check-ins, are the equivalent of digital incarceration, logging every movement and punishing every deviation (Ahmed et al., 2025). Compounded with the likelihood of increased surveillance on individuals determined as more likely to reoffend, this disproportionately affects marginalized communities and raises serious civil liberty concerns (Weisburd, 2020).

AI in Corrections

Predictive models are also increasingly being used in prisons to determine where inmates will be housed based on factors including prior misconduct, affiliations, and psychological evaluations (Jarldorn & Emery, 2024). These models are also used to identify inmates that are more likely to display aggressive behavior (Goel, et al., 2021). This software is justified on the premise that it helps reduce inmate violence, but raises questions related to an inmate's right to challenge the decision. Without knowing how those decisions are determined, the inmate cannot challenge a decision that puts them at higher risk, and the prison administration cannot determine whether a different assignment would be more appropriate.

In addition to violence prediction, many prisons are employing behavioral monitoring tools that use behavioral indicators, such as posture and facial expressions to predict when an inmate is more likely to become violent, resulting in preemptive "safety measures" that are more representative of punishment for something the inmate *might* do in the future (Weisburd, 2020). The problem here is that the prison administration relies on the judgement of the software without standards for validation or review. This may result in unwarranted punishment, but it also may have future consequences in parole decisions or participation opportunities.

The use of AI in prison management can affect parole opportunities. The initial risk assessment results in more strict supervision and heightened surveillance. This, in turn, may result in heightened behavioral scrutiny leading to more behavior alerts. The increased alerts may reduce opportunities to participate in work and rehabilitation programs. Each of these decisions is fed into the algorithm, reducing the opportunity for early release (Loudermilk Bhatia, 2024). Because there are no means to validate or challenge the algorithmic determinations at each level, they compound the civil liberty concerns related to their use.

Constitutional and Ethical Considerations

The automation bias that results when AI-based sentencing and correction systems are used raises serious constitutional concerns. The black box characteristic limits a defendant's ability to understand and challenge decisions affecting liberty, which raises questions of adequate due process (Thomas, 2022). Studies have documented that these systems systemically and unjustly disadvantage specific racial and socioeconomic groups (Brennan; Brenner et al., 2020) challenging the rights of defendants under the Equal Protection Clause. The Eighth Amendment's prohibitions on cruel and unusual punishment is challenged when punishments are administered based on what predictions of what a defendant *might* do.

Replacing human judgement, contextualized reasoning and empathy in decision-making also raises serious ethical concerns. The software should remain secondary to the role of the judge or parole officer, supplementing the decision, rather than becoming determinative (Olawade et al., 2025). While the software may offer a solution to the overload that pervades criminal justice reform, it is important to understand it cannot resolve the systemic issues of mass incarceration or inequality (Antwi, 2024).

The rapid and pervasive adoption of AI and algorithmic tools in the criminal justice system is increasing the tension between the need for efficiency and the preservation of constitutional guarantees, fairness, and justice. The introduction of risk assessment algorithms, predictive policing tools, and automated forensic analysis is significantly reshaping the criminal justice system (Vargas-Murillo et al., 2024). Uncontrolled adoption without clear standards and a foundational understanding of these tools has also raised constitutional and ethical challenges that have been identified but have not yet been adequately addressed.

Sentencing and predictive algorithms are opaque, shielding the mechanisms for calculating the result behind proprietary code and complex computational processes. This challenges a defendant's right of due process because they have no meaningful access to the adverse evidence (Garrett & Rudin, 2024). Equal protection is challenged by systems that are trained on historically biased datasets that apply racialized outcomes through proxy variables and feedback loops (Singh & Devi, 2025; Gravett, 2024). Confrontation rights are challenged when evidentiary assertions are presented without identifiable declarants (Grimm et al., 2021). This creates a foundational issue when defendants must respond to conclusions they cannot inspect and courts rely on results without adequate technical access to how those results were derived. In this case, constitutional safeguards may be weakened where transparency and access are limited.

Algorithmic tools also distort professional judgement. Automation bias encourages decision-makers to defer to the recommendations made by the tools, especially when systems are overloaded (Dancy & Zalnieriute, 2025; Villasenor & Foggo, 2020). Advisory tools anchor and shade decisions, reducing contextual consideration. Additionally, the individuals using the tools often lack technical competence to adequately understand and challenge the outputs creating dependency and reliance (Skaramuca, 2025; Hefetz, 2025). In practice this results in ethical failures related to contestability (O'Brien, 2021). This shift weakens trust as decision-making shifts from trained judges to vendors and software developers.

Judicial response to these issues remains fragmented. For example, *State v. Loomis* (2016) acknowledged the risks created by opacity but continued to allow its use. These weaknesses are also reinforced in scholarship. Lacambra, et al. (2018) address failures in efforts to regulate application in early bail systems, and Ismail & Ariffin (2025) argue that pre-deployment validation and independent audition should be mandated. This demonstrates the growing recognition of the systemic risk of widespread adoption of unregulated AI.

These issues with the undermining of constitutional rights, ethical standards, and fairness demonstrate that algorithmic tools are reshaping the judicial process without adequate constitutional controls. Limited disclosure, inconsistent validation, and weak oversight is having a detrimental effect on defendants' rights. Without adequate and widespread structural reform, technical dependance will continue to expand unchecked. To restore trust, regulatory controls capable of restoring transparency, accountability, and adversarial balance are necessary.

To allow the continued use of algorithmic tools, four specific areas must be addressed: full disclosure, mandatory transparency, the right to cross-examine algorithmic outputs, and professional standards of technological literacy. Decision-makers also must reclaim their gatekeeping role in regard to scientific admissibility and ensure that constitutional guarantees are preserved. The following frameworks are therefore recommended.

The criminal justice system is at the cusp of a transformative opportunity to fundamentally improve due to the integration of artificial intelligence and digital evidence. In their current state, AI tools are demonstrating their ability to enhance efficiency and consistency; but their opacity, demonstrated bias, and weak validation prevent constitutional and ethical concerns that must be addressed.

The introduction and use of scientific evidence throughout the criminal justice system have far outpaced the development of legal standards, resulting in a justice system that is unprepared to assess the reliability and effect they exert (Garrett & Rudin, 2024). The following framework proposes a structured integration model that allows for the introduction of new technologies while preserving constitution and ethical requirements through transparency and scientific integrity.

FRAMEWORK FOR STRUCTURED INTEGRATION

This framework integrates five related principles: (1) Scientific Reliability, (2) Transparency and Contestability, (3) Due Process and Individual Rights, (4) Ethical Safeguards, and (5) Institutional Accountability.

The foundations of scientific reliability cannot be abandoned simply because they were not available with those principles that were established. Thus, all AI and digital forensic tools must establish acceptable scientific validity thresholds prior to admission or use. The persistent use of AI systems without published error rates or external validation fundamentally violates the standards set forth in both *Daubert and Kumho Tire* (Garrett & Rudin, 2024; Booth et al., 2021; Grimm et al., 2021). To address this failure, courts should require independent testing and peer-reviewed validation of all AI and machine learning tools that are used in evidence analysis or decision support. Mandated disclosures should include false positive/negative rates and confidence intervals, especially as they relate to probabilistic tools (Garrett & Rudin, 2024). Codify admissibility rules that prioritize error rate transparency and cross-disciplinary evaluation of scientific inputs (Booth et al., 2021).

Next, courts need to address transparency and contestability. The black box characteristics of AI tools create issues of fairness and equity. To ensure the availability of adversarial testing, the defense needs to be able to challenge the methodology used for making a decision. If a challenge is not possible due to trade secrecy or technical complexity, the tool should be excluded (Morison & McInerney, 2024; O'Brien, 2021). Thus, to meet this requirement, the source code must be freely available for a third-party independent audit (Garrett & Rudin, 2024). However, simply making the code available for audit is not sufficient. If, due to technical complexity, it cannot be independently explained or contested, it should be excluded from use (Gravett, 2024). Judges must also apply heightened judicial scrutiny to algorithmic evidence in criminal cases to avoid the misuse of predictive tools (Grimm et al., 2021).

To ensure the protection of due process and individual rights, tools that can affect decisions related to an individual's liberty must be strictly scrutinized. The continued use of tools that provide automated risk scores and behavior prediction without allowing the results to be challenged violates constitutional rights and civil liberties. The use of these tools then must include clear notice of their use and afford the opportunity to contest the results to provide due process for any algorithmic input that affects or influences case outcomes (Skaramuca, 2025; Hefetz, 2025). Reliance on algorithmic evidence in high-stakes decisions, such as sentencing or bail, must be fully disclosed and subject to independent assessment to preserve due process protections (Ismail & Ariffin, 2025), and defendants must be afforded access to the data and logic used to generate algorithmic outputs (Grimm et al., 2021).

Ethical safeguards must also be in place to ensure equity and fairness. With or without AI support, bias remains a persistent issue, especially in criminal adjudication. Predictive tools may reinforce those biases if the models are trained using flawed or incomplete historical data (Gravett, 2024). Thus, safeguards need to be enforced to prevent these tools from amplifying persistent racial and socioeconomic disparities. To address this concern, bias auditing should be required for all AI tools that are used for law enforcement and sentencing (Singh & Devi, 2025). AI tools must be implemented only with extreme caution. If a tool demonstrates the potential for discriminatory outcomes, it should not be adopted, or if already in use, should be suspended pending an investigation and reform (Morison & McInerney, 2024). The use of demographically balanced datasets and clear statements regarding the limitation of the training data should be required (Meghwal, 2022).

Finally, the institution that adopts the AI tools must exercise substantial oversight and be fully accountable for its use. The lack of national standards and regulation enables unchecked, fragmented adoption of technologies without sufficient understanding or accountability (Garrett & Rudin, 2024; Ismail & Ariffin, 2025). To ensure institutional accountability, a national regulatory board must be established to certify tools and audit practices, and to maintain a public registry of validated technologies (Booth et al., 2021). Require all algorithmic by law enforcement and courts be publicly reported including success and error rates (Gravett, 2024). Implement sanctions for undisclosed AI use, or concealment of known limitations (Garrett & Rudin, 2024).

Unlike prior scientific advancements and evolution, digital and AI technologies are evolving at a rate that is difficult to follow. Legal frameworks governing their use must, therefore, be adaptable to future advancements. To accomplish this, interdisciplinary research is required to address the issues and provide recommendations as technologies evolve. Comparative legal studies must examine how different jurisdictions are integrating AI into judicial systems to identify effective governance models (Vargas-Murillo et al., 2024). Technical research needs to investigate interpretable machine learning and how it can be integrated into evidentiary rules to ensure that courts understand the methodology of how specific outputs are determined (Villasenor & Foggo, 2020, Vargas-Murillo et al., 2024). Empirical studies are also needed to determine how AI-informed decisions affect recidivism, fairness, and public trust in the justice system (Garrett & Rudin, 2024).

CONCLUSION

The rapid adoption and transition to AI digital evidence should not be continued ad hoc; rather, clear, systematic principles must be implemented to ensure a structured integration guided by transparency, fairness, and scientific integrity to ensure constitutional protections and civil rights are protected. A structured integration guided by transparency, fairness, and scientific integrity is necessary to successfully transition to AI and digital evidence without sacrificing constitutional protections. It is imperative that courts resist the promise of efficiency until the expense of individual rights can be thoroughly reviewed and addressed, particularly when technologies are untested or poorly understood. The future of justice in a digital era depends not on removing human discretion, but on enhancing it with tools that are lawful, ethical, and accountable.

REFERENCES

Advisory Committee on Evidence Rules. (2025, May 2). Minutes of the meeting of May 2, 2025 [Minutes of a meeting]. The Judicial Conference Advisory Committee on the Federal Rules of Evidence. https://www.uscourts.gov/sites/default/files/document/2025-05-02_evidence_committee_meeting_minutes_final.pdf

Ahmed, S. S., Rauf, S., & Ashraf, H. (2025). Human rights risks in tech-enhanced incarceration: A comparative analysis. *SSRN*, *5*(2), 304–311. DOI: 10.2139/ssrn.5554438

Amadi, P. (2024). Federal rules of evidence in the United States of America and the challenges of authentication in the age of deepfake technology. *UNILAG Law Review*, *7*(1), 1–29.

Antwi, N. (2024, September 30). Human rights and Constitutional law: Balancing security and freedom. *DME Journal of Law*, *5*(2), 108–119. DOI: 10.53361/dmejl.v5i02.11

Bagaric, M., Svilar, J., Bull, M., Hunter, D., & Stobbs, N. (2022). The solution to the pervasive bias and discrimination in the criminal justice system: transparent and fair artificial intelligence. *American Criminal Law Review, Georgetown Law*, *59*(1), 95–148. https://www.law.georgetown.edu/american-criminal-law-review/in-print/volume-59-number-1-winter-2022/the-solution-to-the-pervasive-bias-and-discrimination-in-the-criminal-justice-system-transparent-and-fair-artificial-intelligence

Bakhtiar, H. S. (2024). The evolution of scientific evidence theory in criminal law: A transformative insight. *Media Iuris*, *7*(2), 221–240. DOI: 10.20473/mi.v7i2.51095

Booth, B. M., Hickman, L., Subburaj, S. K., Tay, L., Woo, S. E., & D'Mello, S. K. (2021, October 18). Bias and fairness in multimodal machine learning: A case study of automated video interviews. [Conference paper]. *ICMI '21: Proceedings of the 2021 International Conference on Multimodal Interaction* (pp. 268–277). https://doi.org/DOI: 10.1145/3462244.3479897

Brenner, M., Gersen, J. S., Haley, M., Lin, M., Merchant, A., Millett, R. J., Sarkar, S. K., & Wegner, D. (2020). Constitutional dimensions of predictive algorithms in criminal justice. *Harvard Civil Rights-Civil Liberties Law Review*, *55*, 267–310. https://journals.law.harvard.edu/crcl/wp-content/uploads/sites/80/2020/09/Brenner-et-al.pdf

Dancy, T., & Zalnieriute, M. (2025, August 16). AI and transparency in judicial decision-making. *Oxford Journal of Legal Studies*, *41*(1), 1–34. DOI: 10.1093/ojls/gqaf030 PMID: 40123910

Daubert v. Merrell Dow Pharmaceuticals, Inc., 509 U.S. 579, 113 S. Ct. 2786 (1993)

Dmitrieva, A. A., & Pastukhov, P. S. (2023). Concept of electronic evidence in criminal legal procedure. *Journal of Digital Technologies and Law*, *1*(1), 270–295. DOI: 10.21202/jdtl.2023.11

Fed. R. Evid. 702 (2011). https://www.law.cornell.edu/rules/fre/rule_702

Fed. R. Evid. 901 (2011). https://www.law.cornell.edu/rules/fre/rule_901

Fornasier, M. de O. (2022). Deep learning and the right to explanation: Technological challenges to legality and due process of law in technology. *Revista De Direito Brasileira*, *32*(12), 218–235. DOI: 10.26668/IndexLawJournals/2358-1352/2022.v32i12.7547

Frye v. United States, 293 F. 1013 (D.C. Cir. 1923).

Garrett, B. L., & Rudin, C. (2024). The right to a glass box: Rethinking the use of artificial intelligence in criminal justice. *109. Cornell Law Review*, •••, 561–626. https://scholarship.law.duke.edu/faculty_scholarship/4297

Goel, S., Shroff, R., Skeem, J., & Slobogin, C. (2021, May 14). The accuracy, equity, and jurisprudence of criminal risk assessment. In *Research Handbook on Big Data Law*. Edward Elgar Publishing., DOI: 10.4337/9781788972826.00007

Gravett, W. H. (2024). Judicial decision-making in the age of artificial intelligence. In Antunes, H. S., Freitas, P. M., Oliveira, A. L., Pereira, C. M., Sequeira, E. V. D., & Xavier, L. B. (Eds.), *Multidisciplinary perspectives on artificial intelligence and the law* (Vol. 58, pp. 281–298). Springer Nature., DOI: 10.1007/978-3-031-41264-6_15

Grimm, P. W., Grossman, M. R., & Cormack, G. V. (2021, December). Artificial intelligence as evidence. *Northwestern Journal of Technology and Intellectual Property*, *19*(1), 9–106. https://scholarlycommons.law.northwestern.edu/njtip/vol19/iss1/2

Hefetz, I. (2025, October). Integrating AI Systems in criminal justice: The forensic expert as a corridor between algorithms and courtroom evidence. *Forensic Science*, *5*(4), 53. DOI: 10.3390/forensicsci5040053

Ismail, I., & Ariffin, K. A. Z. (2025, September 12). The admissibility of digital evidence from open-source forensic tools: Development of a framework for legal acceptance. *PLoS One*, *20*(9), e0331683. DOI: 10.1371/journal.pone.0331683 PMID: 40938950

Jadidi, V. (2025). The impact of Artificial Intelligence on judicial decision-making processes. *Advanced Journal of Management. Humanity and Social Science*, *1*(5), 271–281. DOI: 10.5281/zenodo.15660093

Jarldorn, M., & Emery, S. (2024, January 29). Using radical co-design to create and develop a technology-based solution to improve post-release outcomes for formerly incarcerated women: LindaBot. *International Journal of Communication*, *18*, 1246–1265. https://ijoc.org/index.php/ijoc/article/view/21208

Kaufmann, M. (2024, June 21). AI in policing and law enforcement. In R. Paul, E. Carmel, & J. Cobbe (Eds.), *Handbook on public policy and artificial intelligence* (pp. 295–306). Edward Elgar Publishing. https://doi.org/DOI: 10.4337/9781803922171.00031

Kumho Tire Co., Ltd. v. Carmichael, 526 U.S. 137, 119 S. Ct. 1167, 143 L. Ed. 2d 238 (1999).

Lacambra, S. J., Matthews, J., & Walsh, K. (2018, May). Opening the black box: Defendants' rights to confront forensic software. In *The Champion*. (pp. 28-39, 66). https://www.eff.org/files/2018/07/30/champion_article_-_lacambra_forensic_software_may_2018_07102018.pdf

Lacqueur, H., & Copus, R. W. (2022, October). An algorithmic assessment of parole decisions. *Journal of Quantitative Criminology*. https://irlaw.umkc.edu/faculty_works/496

Longinus, E. C. (2025). Smarter corrections and intelligence-driven innovations in correctional services in contemporary society. *International Journal of Business Ecosystem & Strategy*, *7*(6), 244–262. DOI: 10.36096/ijbes.v7i6.1036

Loudermilk Bhatia, P. (2024, April). *Artificial Intelligence and Recidivism: The use of risk assessment as prediction instruments in criminal sentencings* [Thesis, University of Chicago]. https://doi.org/DOI: 10.6082/uchicago.12260

Mason, S., & Seng, D. (2021, August 1). Hearsay. In *Electronic evidence and electronic signatures* (5th ed., pp. 85–111). Institute of Advanced Legal Studies., DOI: 10.14296/2108.9781911507246

Morison, J.Jr, & McInerney, T. (2024). When should a computer decide? Judicial decision-making in the age of automation, algorithms and generative artificial intelligence. In Turenne, S., & Moussa, M. (Eds.), *Research Handbook on Judging and the Judiciary*. Edward Elgar-Routledge.

O'Brien, T. (2021, Winter). Compounding injustice: The cascading effect of algorithmic bias in risk assessments. *Georgetown Journal of Law & Modern Critical Race Perspectives, 13*(1), 39–83. https://www.law.georgetown.edu/mcrp-journal/wp-content/uploads/sites/22/2021/05/GT-GCRP210003.pdf

Olawade, D. B., Ayoola, F. I., Ebo, T. O., Asaolu, A. J., Egbon, E., & David-Olawade, A. C. (2025). Artificial Intelligence in forensic mental health: A review of applications and implications. *Journal of Forensic and Legal Medicine, 113*, 102895. DOI: 10.1016/j.jflm.2025.102895 PMID: 40441026

Ross, S., Wood, M. A., Baird, R., & Lundberg, K. (2023). Digital service delivery applications in corrections: A scoping review. In *Report to the Criminology Research Advisory Council* [Report]. Australian Institute of Criminology., DOI: 10.52922/crg77109

Saks, M. J., & Faigman, D. L. (2008). Failed Forensics: How forensic science lost its way and how it might yet find it. *Annual Review of Law and Social Science, 4*(1), 149–171. DOI: 10.1146/annurev.lawsocsci.4.110707.172303

Schwartz, G. D. (2024). When disciplines disagree: The admissibility of computer-generated Forensic evidence in the criminal justice system. In Chappell, K., Dickerson, M., Dorsey, S., Gonzalez, V., McVoy, K., Orton, S., Siqueira, A., Stolmack, A., Vazquez, A., & Zahran, M. (Eds.), *UCLA Law Review, 72, 174–211.*

Simmler, M., & Canova, G. (2024). Facial recognition technology in law enforcement: Regulating data analysis of another kind. *Computer Law & Security Review, 56*, 106092. DOI: 10.1016/j.clsr.2024.106092

Singh, S., & Devi, L. (2025, December 17). *Reliability and admissibility of AI-Generated Forensic Evidence in criminal trials*. arXiv. https://arxiv.org/abs/2601.06048

Skaramuca, D. (2025). Evaluating the Admissibility of AI Evidence in Criminal Proceedings: Legal Standards and Ethical Implications. SPLITLAW, 155.

Smith, M. J., Harrington, M., Ross, B., Quinn, C. R., Musan, L. P., Brydon, D. M., Johnson, J. E., Cuddeback, G. S., Smith, J. D., Merle, J. L., Burke-Miller, J. K., Jordan, N., Bell, M. D., Friedman, B., Kryscio, P., & Suganuma, A. (2025). A pragmatic randomized controlled trial of virtual reality job interview training in prison employment services. *Journal of Experimental Criminology*. Advance online publication. DOI: 10.1007/s11292-025-09684-7

Socol De La Osa, D. U., & Remolina, N. (2025). AI at the Bench: Legal and ethical challenges of informing – or misinforming – judicial decision-making through generative AI. *International Journal for Research in Applied Science and Engineering Technology, 13*(5), 595–606. DOI: 10.22214/ijraset.2025.70243

State v. Loomis, 371 Wis. 2d 235, 881 N.W.2d 749 (Wis. 2016).

Thomas, C. (2022). Automating judicial discretion: How algorithmic risk assessments in pretrial adjudications violate equal protection rights on the basis of race. *Minnesota Journal of Law & Inequality, 40*(2), Article 5. https://scholarship.law.umn.edu/lawineq/vol40/iss2/5

Villasenor, J., & Foggo, V. (2020). Artificial Intelligence, due process, and criminal sentencing. *Michigan State University Law Review*, 295–354. https://doi.org/DOI: 10.17613/tp6fx-73531

Weisburd, K. (2020). Sentenced to surveillance: Fourth Amendment limits on electronic monitoring. *North Carolina Law Review, 98*(4), 3. https://scholarship.law.unc.edu/nclr/vol98/iss4/3

Yadav, A. (2020). Relevancy and admissibility of digital evidence: A comparative study. *International Journal of Integrated Law Review, 1*(1), 22–32.

Chapter 14
False Positives, Real Consequences:
The Accuracy Crisis in Automated Criminal Accusations

Mario DeSean Booker
http://orcid.org/0009-0002-0903-770X
Purdue University Global, USA

ABSTRACT

Criminal justice systems delegate fraud determinations to automated systems that generate immediate consequences—benefit termination, prosecution—before investigation. This work examines how fraud detection systems function as engines of false accusation: technical design mistakes poverty adaptation for fraud, vendor compensation rewards detection volume over accuracy, and constitutional protections fail against algorithmic accusers. Using Michigan's MiDAS system (40,000 falsely accused, 93% error rate), the work traces how contractual structures and opaque decision logic systematically generate wrongful accusations cascading into prosecution and poverty deepening. These harms flow from financial incentives to maximize detection regardless of accuracy. The work argues fraud detection systems require transparency, contestation, and accountability standards before continuing operation in criminal justice.

INTRODUCTION: THE ACCUSATION BEFORE THE EVIDENCE

When the State Comes Calling: Stories from MiDAS

In 2014, Carmelita Colvin received a letter from Michigan's Unemployment Insurance Agency stating she had committed unemployment fraud (Wykstra, 2020). Her immediate reaction was disbelief: "This has got to be impossible" (Wykstra, 2020, para. 6). She had collected benefits in 2013 after losing her cleaning job and knew she had been eligible. What Colvin did not realize was that thousands across the state were experiencing the same thing. The agency had introduced the Michigan Integrated Data Au-

DOI: 10.4018/979-8-3373-7660-8.ch014

tomated System (MiDAS), designed to automatically charge people with fraud and demand repayment (Wykstra, 2020).

Kevin Doss learned he was being penalized only after discovering his paycheck had been garnished in March 2015 (Roelofs, 2017). The system claimed he owed $84,000 for unemployment payments from six years earlier, payments he had already successfully contested before an administrative law judge (Roelofs, 2017). Brian Russell discovered the system had seized $11,000 from his 2015 tax refund and was charging him $22,000 total (Wykstra, 2020). Lindsay and Justin Perry faced similar devastation when Justin was accused of fraud and fined $10,000 after losing his chef job in 2014 (De La Garza, 2020). Their tax returns were seized for three years, their van was repossessed, and they filed for bankruptcy in 2017 (De La Garza, 2020).

These were not isolated mistakes. Between October 2013 and August 2015, MiDAS issued over 60,000 fraud determinations with a 93% error rate, wrongly accusing 40,000 Michigan residents (Kohl, 2024). The system flagged data discrepancies as fraud regardless of context, imposed quadruple penalties automatically, and triggered wage garnishment (Benefits Tech Advocacy Hub, n.d.). Many people learned they had been accused only when money vanished from their accounts. This is algorithmic accusation in practice: no detective investigated, no prosecutor reviewed files, and no hearing weighed credibility. A system scanned data, detected patterns it interpreted as fraud, and rendered judgment.

The Inversion of Justice

The MiDAS disaster reveals how fraud detection systems operate in criminal justice contexts. These systems do not predict future behavior; rather, they claim to identify specific acts of concrete fraud that already occurred. They position themselves as neutral fact-finding mechanisms. What they actually do is generate accusations absent the evidence required to prove fraud as a legal matter. As Citron and Pasquale (2014) demonstrate, the scored society reduces complex human situations to discrete numerical ratings assigned by algorithms no one can examine, with consequences imposed through administrative mechanism rather than adjudicated guilt.

Fraud requires intent. The person must have knowingly provided false information or deliberately concealed material facts (Grady, 2006). A data mismatch, reporting error, timing issue, or misunderstanding of complex rules: none of these constitute fraud without proof the person understood they were doing something wrong and did it anyway. Yet fraud detection systems routinely convert administrative irregularities into fraud determinations without establishing knowledge or intent.

MiDAS calculated the average of a claimant's entire income instead of examining individual paychecks, creating discrepancies between reported and system-determined income (Benefits Tech Advocacy Hub, n.d.). The agency's practice of "income spreading" led the state to falsely conclude workers were illegally receiving paychecks while collecting unemployment insurance (Roelofs, 2017). The system interpreted these statistical anomalies as intentional deception. The cascade mechanics were devastating: the system flagged an anomaly, triggering automatic consequences including benefit termination, overpayment demands, penalties, wage garnishment, and criminal referral. By the time a person realized they had been accused, punishment had already begun. The accusation preceded any investigation into whether fraud occurred. Punishment preceded any determination of guilt.

This inverts how justice is supposed to function. Constitutional protections presume accusation comes before punishment, evidence before conviction, notice and opportunity to defend before the state imposes consequences. Algorithmic fraud detection short-circuits all of this, accusing and punishing simultaneously. Michigan provides the clearest documentation, but the pattern extends far beyond one state's unemployment system. Welfare agencies use automated cross-matching to flag SNAP and TANF recipients based on income discrepancies that often reflect the chaotic reality of low-wage work (Soss et al., 2011). Court systems use automated payment processing that generates failure-to-pay warrants without assessing ability to pay. Probation agencies use GPS monitoring that interprets technical glitches as willful violations worthy of reincarceration.

In each context, the system claims to find fraud. What it actually does is convert uncertainty into accusation, correlation into culpability, and technical determination into legal fact. The people accused bear the burden of proving the system wrong, a burden requiring technical expertise, legal resources, and time most people lack.

Accusation Engines, Not Risk Assessments

Algorithmic accountability scholarship has documented serious problems with predictive systems in criminal justice. Risk assessment tools that predict recidivism embed racial bias and produce disparate impact (Dressel & Farid, 2018; Barocas & Selbst, 2016). Predictive policing concentrates enforcement in communities of color (Barocas & Selbst, 2016). These critiques are vital, but fraud detection systems operate differently and raise distinct concerns.

Predictive systems assess likelihood, estimating probability someone will commit a future crime. They do not claim someone already did something wrong; they claim someone *might*. Sentencing algorithms operate after conviction through adjudication. Due process protections have already applied. Fraud detection systems claim something categorically different. They assert factual determinations: this person committed fraud and this specific act happened. They do not predict behavior, instead purporting to identify it. Decisions are made, not supported. They operate at the accusation stage, before any adjudication, generating the charges that trigger criminal justice involvement.

This positioning as neutral fact-finding gives fraud detection dangerous legitimacy. When a predictive tool produces a risk score, people recognize it as contestable and probabilistic. When a fraud detection system flags someone, agencies and courts treat the determination as established fact (Citron & Pasquale, 2014). The algorithmic accusation carries the weight of evidence even though the system cannot prove the elements required for fraud: knowledge, intent, and willfulness. MiDAS did not predict who might commit fraud. It accused specific people of having already committed it. Those accusations triggered immediate consequences and criminal prosecution. People faced charges based on a technical system's determination they had knowingly lied, even though the system had no capacity to assess their mental state or whether discrepancies resulted from error rather than deception.

Technical Design, Financial Incentives, Constitutional Failures

Existing algorithmic accountability scholarship addresses bias, transparency, and fairness in automated systems that operate after someone enters the criminal justice system. What scholarship has given less attention to is how algorithmic systems generate the accusations that pull people into the criminal justice system in the first place. Fraud detection represents a specific and underexamined harm: false accusations that cascade into prosecution, conviction, and incarceration. These systems do not merely get decisions wrong; they manufacture accusations against innocent people with sufficient institutional weight to trigger criminal consequences (Eubanks, 2018). This work addresses that gap by examining how fraud detection systems function as engines of false accusation through three linked mechanisms: technical design that mistakes patterns for intent, financial incentives rewarding detection volume over accuracy, and constitutional protections that fail against algorithmic accusers. The goal is not to eliminate algorithms but to establish transparency, contestation, and accountability standards before continuing deployment. Michigan's MiDAS case illustrates these failures. Between 2013 and 2015, the system falsely accused 40,000 residents with a 93% error rate (Charette, 2018). The state eventually paid $20 million in settlement (Michigan Department of Attorney General, 2022), yet many victims continued facing wage garnishment and bankruptcy. As the system's false determinations accumulated, the state's fraud penalty fund ballooned to $155 million (Felton, 2016), money extracted from innocent people. MiDAS is not an outlier; similar systems operate across benefits administration, court payment processing, and parole monitoring in states and countries worldwide.

THE ARCHITECTURE OF ALGORITHMIC ACCUSATION

When Survival Looks Like Fraud

Fraud detection systems mistake patterns for intent. They scan for anomalies (income discrepancies, address changes, employment gaps, etc.) and categorize them as fraud indicators, but anomalies are not fraud. They are the texture of economic precarity. Pattern recognition is legitimate when consequence matches function. Banks decline suspicious transactions pending verification. Fraud detection systems in benefits administration function differently, because they determine not only that something looks suspicious, but that the person knowingly committed fraud, imposing penalties without human review. What gets flagged reveals systemic bias. A benefits recipient takes temporary cash work to make rent. The income does not immediately appear in state wage databases. The system flags fraud even if the person reported the work on their benefits form. The gap reflects timing misalignment with informal employment, not deception. Income volatility is inherent to low-wage work. Kalleberg (2011) documents contemporary employment precarity; people piece together survival from multiple part-time positions (Edin & Shaefer, 2015). MiDAS averaged a claimant's income across an entire quarter rather than examining individual paychecks. Someone earning a certain amount in two weeks then returning to unemployment appeared to the system as earning far less weekly, income that should have made them ineligible during weeks they received nothing. Australia's Centrelink "Robodebt" system employed identical flawed logic, issuing 470,000 incorrect debt notices before being declared unlawful in 2019; the government agreed to a $721 million settlement (Hayne & Doran, 2020). Housing instability and informal work similarly register as suspicious patterns, yet both are conditions of poverty, not fraud.

The Survival Problem and Systemic Design

Scholars documenting survival strategies among low-income populations identify what can be termed the survivability problem: the adaptive strategies people use to navigate poverty, such as taking temporary cash work, relocating frequently, and piecing together income from multiple informal sources, generate the very patterns fraud detection systems flag as suspicious (Kalleberg, 2011; Edin & Shaefer,

2015). When algorithms are trained on employment data reflecting middle-class stability, these survival adaptations register as anomalies rather than rational responses to precarious economic conditions.

This pattern repeats across jurisdictions. MiDAS flagged income volatility and address changes as fraud. Centrelink flagged the same patterns. The commonality is not coincidence. These systems share structural design choices: all resolve ambiguity against the accused, all prioritize volume over accuracy, all treat administrative errors as intentional fraud, and all lack pre-deprivation human review. The similarities suggest not isolated vendor failure but systemic design problems embedded in how fraud detection is built and deployed. As Soss et al. (2011) document, welfare administration has never been purely economic; instead, it embeds discipline and social control (Gilliom, 2001). Automated systems intensify rather than correct these dynamics.

What the System Sees (and What It Does Not)

Understanding how fraud detection systems work requires examining what they see, what they do not see, and how they convert data into accusations. These systems rely on input data from multiple sources: state wage databases, tax records, address verification systems, employment registries, and self-reported information. The system assumes these data sources are accurate, complete, and synchronized. They rarely are.

Input data quality varies dramatically. Employers report wages on different schedules. Tax records lag by months or years. Address databases contain outdated information. Self-reported data depends on applicants understanding complex questions. When systems cross-reference these sources, mismatches are inevitable, but the systems interpret mismatches as evidence of wrongdoing rather than data quality problems.

What the system does not see matters as much as what it does. It does not see explanations or context. Hypothetically, a person can report $500 in income one week and $0 the next. The system sees volatility. It does not see that the person worked a temporary job that ended, or that hours were cut, or that they were paid for two weeks in a single paycheck. If someone's address changes three times in six months, the system sees inconsistency. It does not see eviction, brief stays with family, and then a new apartment. This limitation exemplifies what Lipton (2018) identifies as the mythos of model interpretability, meaning the false assumption that automated systems can make determinations about complex human situations without access to context or explanation. When those systems accuse people of crimes, this interpretability gap becomes constitutionally problematic (Citron, 2008).

Decision thresholds determine when anomalies become accusations. Every fraud detection system has rules: if income discrepancy exceeds X dollars, flag for fraud; if address changes more than Y times in Z months, flag for review. These thresholds are policy choices, not natural facts. If the threshold is set low, the system generates false positives. Set it high, and the system misses genuine fraud. The pressure to demonstrate effectiveness pushes agencies toward lower thresholds and higher detection rates, which means more innocent people get flagged. Centrelink initially processed 20,000 debt letters weekly through Robodebt, a 50-fold increase over the manual system, ensuring that even a 20% error rate meant thousands of false accusations (Williams, 2017).

The training problem is fundamental. Machine learning systems learn to identify fraud by training on historical data, specifically cases previously determined to be fraud. That said, if historical data contains errors, the system learns to replicate those errors. If previous fraud determinations were biased against people with volatile incomes or frequent address changes, the system learns these characteristics predict fraud (Buolamwini & Gebru, 2018). When MiDAS trained on data from a benefits system that already disproportionately scrutinized poor people, it learned to flag poverty indicators as fraud indicators. This represents the disparate impact problem Barocas and Selbst (2016) identify: algorithms trained on biased historical data perpetuate and amplify existing inequities.

Uncertainty handling reveals system design priorities. When a fraud detection system encounters ambiguous data, such as income that might or might not be reportable or address changes that might or might not indicate ineligibility, it must decide how to handle uncertainty. MiDAS resolved uncertainty against claimants. When the system was not sure whether someone committed fraud, it accused them anyway. Centrelink made the identical design choice: when wage averaging produced ambiguous results, the system issued debt notices and shifted burden to recipients to disprove the debt within 21 days. The design choice in both systems was punitive, preferring to falsely accuse rather than risk missing fraud.

Black box architecture compounds every problem. Fraud detection systems are often proprietary, developed by private contractors who treat decision logic as trade secrets. The accused cannot examine how the system reached its determination. Public defenders cannot access the algorithm to challenge its reasoning. Courts defer to vendor confidentiality claims. As Mitchell et al. (2019) document in their framework for model transparency, this inscrutability is not technical necessity; it is a business model. Vendors protect intellectual property, and that protection makes the systems functionally unchallengeable. When Carmelita Colvin, Kevin Doss, and thousands of others tried to understand why MiDAS accused them, they encountered opacity. Centrelink recipients faced identical barriers, told they must provide documentation the system failed to obtain, without being able to examine the averaging calculation or understand the discrepancies that triggered the debt notice.

When Benefits Become Criminal Charges

Fraud detection systems are most extensively deployed in benefits administration, including SNAP, TANF, Medicaid, housing assistance, and unemployment insurance. These systems perform automated cross-matching: comparing applicant information against employment databases, tax records, Social Security data, wage files, and address verification systems. When discrepancies emerge, systems generate fraud determinations, often without human review. Overpayment calculations trigger automatically, penalties are assessed, and cases exceeding certain dollar thresholds are referred to prosecutors. The algorithmic determination is treated as established fact: the person committed fraud and so prosecution should proceed.

What Algorithms Cannot Prove: Intent and State of Mind

Fraud, as a legal concept, requires *mens rea*, or guilty mind. To prove fraud, prosecutors must establish that the defendant knowingly made false statements or deliberately concealed material facts with intent to deceive (Grady, 2006). A mistake or negligence is not fraud. Confusion about complex reporting requirements is not fraud. Fraud requires proof the person knew they were doing something wrong and did it anyway.

Algorithms cannot determine state of mind. They can identify discrepancies, detect patterns, and flag anomalies. They cannot assess whether the person understood reporting requirements, intended to deceive, or made an honest mistake. Yet fraud detection systems make fraud determinations, accusations that explicitly or implicitly claim the person acted with fraudulent intent. This represents what Citron

(2008) identifies as a fundamental constitutional problem: automated systems bypass the human judgment necessary for determinations requiring assessment of knowledge and intent.

Administrative violations and criminal fraud are legally distinct. Missing a reporting deadline or failing to update and address promptly is an administrative violation. Making an error on a benefits application is also an administrative violation. These may result in benefit adjustments or temporary ineligibility. Fraud on the other hand is criminal, as it requires intent. It subjects people to prosecution, fines, incarceration, and permanent criminal records.

Fraud detection systems blur this distinction. They identify administrative irregularities, including late reports, data discrepancies, and missing documentation, and categorize them as fraud. The categorization transforms administrative matters into criminal accusations. Someone who did not understand that temporary cash work needed reporting weekly rather than monthly faces not a correctable administrative error but a fraud determination with criminal referral. The system lacks capacity to distinguish between genuine fraud and people struggling to navigate complex bureaucratic requirements while surviving on precarious income.

This is the architecture of algorithmic accusation: systems that mistake patterns for intent, resolve ambiguity against the accused, operate in secrecy, and convert the conditions of poverty into evidence of crime. They cannot assess state of mind but make determinations that require it. They cannot distinguish fraud from error but impose criminal penalties for both. Importantly, they operate at scale, generating thousands of accusations built on technical determinations no human reviewed and logic no one can examine.

THE BUSINESS MODEL OF FALSE POSITIVES

How Vendors Get Paid and What Contracts Ignore

Fraud detection systems operate within a financial architecture that rewards volume over accuracy. Vendors structure compensation around detection metrics: payment tied to the number of fraud cases identified, dollar amounts flagged as fraudulent, or percentages of money recovered from accused individuals. Recovery percentage arrangements exemplify this misalignment: vendors receive a portion of money collected from people accused of fraud. The vendor's revenue depends entirely on collection volume, not on whether accusations were justified. This structural misalignment creates systematic incentive problems that cannot be solved through technical fixes alone.

Michigan's MiDAS: Documentation of the Model

Michigan's MiDAS provides clear documentation. The state paid Fast Enterprises $47 million to build the system (Wykstra, 2020). The system's "success" was measured by its dramatic increase in fraud detection. MiDAS flagged five times more fraud cases than the previous system and as fraud determinations surged, the state's penalty and interest fund grew from $3.1 million to $155 million in just five years (Wykstra, 2020). The financial incentives aligned perfectly: the vendor delivered a system that identified massive amounts of fraud, the state collected enormous sums, and no one bore contractual responsibility for the 93% error rate.

The Michigan contract with Fast Enterprises, publicly available through state procurement records, includes multiple extension options tied to system performance, a structure that incentivizes continued flagging regardless of accuracy. What the contract does not specify are accuracy thresholds, error rate caps, and independent audits to verify that flagged cases involve actual fraud. This procurement pattern is characteristic of government contracting for sensitive functions: absence of explicit performance standards coupled with financial reward for volume creates predictable misalignment between vendor interests and public benefit.

The Vendor Landscape: Industry-Wide Pattern

Fast Enterprises is not alone. Deloitte currently serves as the primary unemployment insurance technology vendor for 15 states. Deloitte's uFACTS platform includes uDetect, a fraud detection module marketed as identifying "likely fraud or overpayments early." However, Deloitte's track record reflects the same pattern as Fast Enterprises: large contracts with states seeking to modernize systems, coupled with problematic results. In California, a $110 million contract led to payment halts for 300,000 people (Brewster, 2022) Similar failures occurred in Florida and Massachusetts. IBM held comparable contracts in Pennsylvania and Indiana, both canceled due to erroneous benefit denials and other system failures. These failures illuminate what Kroll et al. (2017) identify as accountability gaps in algorithm-based governance: vendors retain significant discretion while bearing minimal accountability for errors. These are not isolated failures but structural features of how vendors are compensated and success is measured in government contracts.

What Contracts Specify and Ignore

Procurement documents reveal what agencies prioritize and what they ignore. Contracts specify detection deliverables and recovery targets. They define success through volume metrics: number of fraud determinations, dollars recovered, and efficiency gains measured by reduced staff requirements. What these contracts rarely specify is accuracy. Performance-based compensation tied to detection volume appears standard across the industry. Few contracts specify error rate thresholds or require vendor accountability for false positives.

Success metrics focus on outputs, not outcomes. A contract measures success by how many cases the system processes, how many fraud flags it generates, and how much money the jurisdiction collects, not by how many innocent people avoid false accusations. Few contracts require vendors to guarantee error rates below specified thresholds, or include provisions requiring independent audits to verify that flagged cases involve actual fraud. Reisman et al. (2018) propose algorithmic impact assessments as mechanism to evaluate whether systems produce harms before deployment, yet such assessments are rarely contractual requirements.

When appeals processes are mentioned in contracts, they are typically treated as procedural requirements to satisfy, not as mechanisms to catch and correct errors. The burden of proof falls on individuals to demonstrate the system made an error, despite lacking access to the system's logic, training data, or decision rules. This reversal of burden, coupled with contract structures that prioritize detection volume, creates conditions enabling systematic harm: profit motivation aligned with system opacity (Eubanks, 2018).

Liability and Risk Allocation

Vendors typically negotiate indemnification clauses protecting them from lawsuits arising from system errors. If someone falsely accused by the system sues, the jurisdiction, not the vendor, defends the claim and bears the cost of settlement. This allocation of risk removes any financial incentive for vendors to prioritize accuracy over detection volume. Risk allocation mechanisms shape incentive structures in government contracting. When vendors bear no cost for false positives, accuracy becomes irrelevant to profitability.

Michigan's $20 million settlement for MiDAS victims came from state coffers. Fast Enterprises bore no contractual liability for generating 40,000 false fraud determinations. The vendor's compensation structure, tied to detection rates and collection volume, was never adjusted to account for the system's 93% error rate (Kohl, 2024). Meanwhile, Deloitte was selected to replace the failed MiDAS system with a $78 million, 10-year contract for uFACTS . The pattern suggests that vendor failures trigger replacement contracts rather than accountability mechanisms.

This pattern demonstrates that fraud detection represents not a technical problem to be solved but a financial incentive structure that makes false accusations profitable for vendors and rewarding for states. Until contracts shift from rewarding volume to requiring accuracy, the systems will continue to generate accusations at scale. Mitchell et al. (2019) propose model cards and transparency requirements as contractual mechanisms, yet such transparency obligations remain rare in actual procurement practice.

The structural misalignment becomes visible when examining the financial flows: what incentivizes vendors and agencies to increase detection volume simultaneously punishes, and extracts wealth from, the people accused.

The image below visualizes how three actors respond to identical system activity with opposite financial outcomes. Vendor compensation tied to volume (not accuracy) means profit increases with false positives. State agencies grow their budgets through penalty collection from the falsely accused. Accused individuals bear 100% of costs (lost wages, seized refunds, bankruptcy, housing loss) with no contractual recourse and delayed compensation only after years of litigation.

Figure 1. Perverse Incentive Alignment Diagram

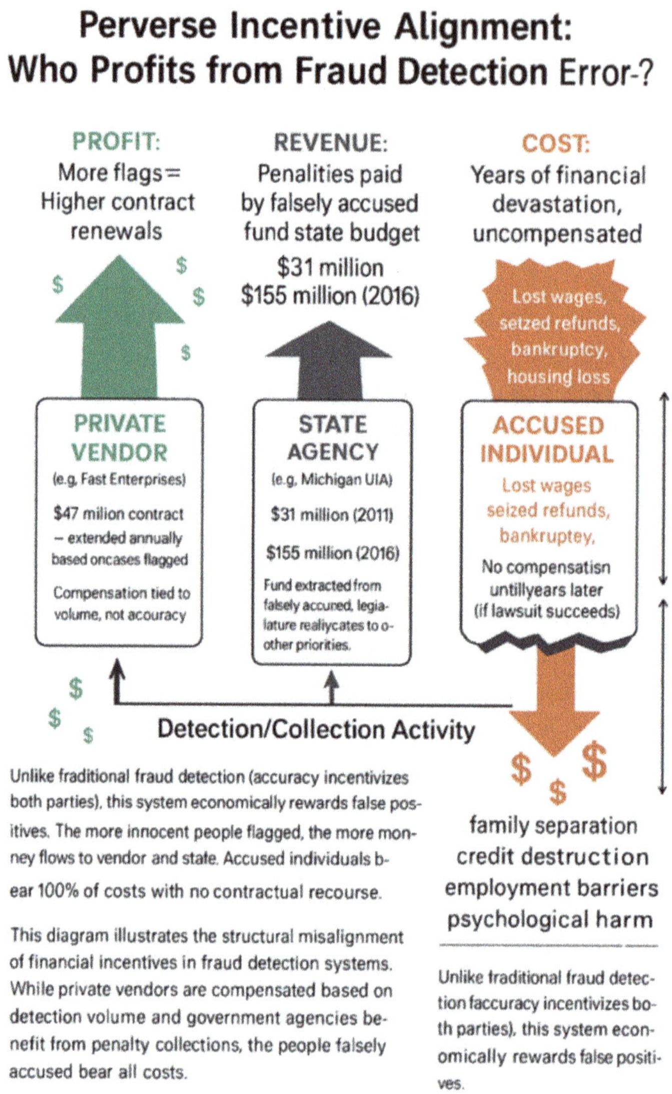

(graphic by the author)

This is not accidental misalignment. Contract structures shape incentive alignment in government procurement. In fraud detection systems, each contractual provision reinforces the misalignment: compensation tied to detection volume rather than accuracy, indemnification protecting vendors from liability, performance metrics measuring dollars recovered rather than wrongful accusation prevention, and appeals mechanisms treated as compliance requirements rather than error-correction mechanisms. Kroll et al. (2017) document how such accountability gaps in algorithm-based governance allow vendors to retain discretion while bearing minimal responsibility for errors.

Marketing That Sidesteps Accuracy

Vendor marketing materials position fraud detection systems as solutions to budget crises. The pitch emphasizes revenue recovery, essentially claiming the jurisdiction is losing millions to fraud but the system will find those errors. This framing transforms fraud detection from a compliance function into a revenue generation opportunity. Barocas and Selbst (2016) observe how algorithmic systems become adopted based on marketing claims about efficiency without corresponding scrutiny of accuracy claims or potential harms.

Cost-recovery promises dominate sales presentations. Vendors present projections showing that increased fraud detection will pay for the system within months. These projections rarely account for false positive rates or acknowledge that aggressive detection might impose costs on innocent people. The marketing strategy, as Eubanks (2018) documents, positions technological solutions as efficiency gains while obscuring who efficiency is achieved through, often poor populations bearing costs that enable cost savings for agencies.

Efficiency rhetoric positions automation as the solution to resource constraints. Agencies struggling with case backlogs hear that automated systems can process thousands of cases without human review. The vendor emphasizes what the system can do (scan millions of records, cross-reference multiple databases, flag discrepancies in seconds) not what it cannot do: assess intent, evaluate context, and distinguish error from deception. This selective emphasis on capabilities while obscuring limitations represents what Kroll et al. (2017) identify as accountability gaps in algorithmic governance.

Accuracy questions get sidestepped through focus on "detection capabilities." Marketing materials highlight the sophistication of pattern recognition, the comprehensiveness of data sources, and the speed of processing. Vendors present detection volume as evidence of effectiveness. The assumption is that detection equals accuracy, that what the system flags is fraud by definition. This assumption collapses under scrutiny: detection and accuracy are distinct measures, yet marketing materials conflate them.

The Financial Logic of Harm

The business model creates perverse incentives at every level. Vendor profit increases with detection volume. Hypothetically, a system that flags 50,000 cases generates more revenue than a system that flags 5,000 cases, regardless of error rates. Agencies measure success by dollars recovered and so a jurisdiction that collects $100 million from fraud determinations considers the system successful, even if $80 million came from people who committed no fraud.

No contractual penalty exists for wrongful accusations. Vendors face no financial consequences when their systems generate high false positive rates. The costs of false accusations, including prosecution expenses, public defender resources, detention costs, appeals processing, and settlement payments, often come from different budget lines than the revenue fraud detection generates. This cost externalization is systematic: financial benefits accrue to vendors and agencies while harms distribute to accused individuals and criminal justice systems.

The harm is externalized. When MiDAS falsely accused 40,000 people, those individuals bore the consequences: lost wages, seized refunds, bankruptcies, damaged credit, housing loss, and family separation. The vendor collected its fees. The state grew its fraud fund from $3.1 million to $155 million. The legislature transferred $10 million of that money, extracted from innocent people, to plug budget holes caused by tax giveaways to business (Felton, 2016, Wykstra, 2020).

The fundamental misalignment is structural, not incidental, but inherent to how fraud detection systems are built and compensated. Every actor benefits from aggressive detection except the people accused: vendors profit from high detection rates regardless of accuracy, agencies grow budgets through penalty collection, and policymakers claim fraud-fighting success. Barocas and Selbst (2016) demonstrate that algorithmic systems inherit and amplify the structural inequities embedded in their training data and design incentives. The MiDAS case illustrates this principle applied to financial incentives: technical accuracy improvements cannot overcome business models designed to reward detection volume over accuracy.

CONSTITUTIONAL GAPS: WHEN MACHINES BECOME WITNESSES

The Confrontation Clause Crisis

The Sixth Amendment guarantees that "in all criminal prosecutions, the accused shall enjoy the right to be confronted with the witnesses against him." This protection, applicable to states through the Fourteenth Amendment, has been interpreted by the Supreme Court as a fundamental safeguard against wrongful conviction. In *Crawford v. Washington*, the Court held that testimonial statements, those made for the purpose of establishing or proving facts in criminal proceedings, cannot be admitted against a defendant unless the witness is unavailable and the defendant had a prior opportunity for cross-examination (Sanders, 2022).

Crawford rejected the previous framework that allowed admission of out-of-court statements if judges deemed them reliable. Instead, the Court held that where testimonial evidence is at issue, the Sixth Amendment demands unavailability and a prior opportunity for cross-examination (Sanders, 2022). The decision emphasized that the Confrontation Clause was designed to prevent *ex parte* examinations, meaning statements made outside the defendant's presence, from being used as evidence. Reliability could only be assessed through cross-examination, not through judicial determination.

It is not clear who the defendant cross-examines when an algorithm accuses someone of fraud: the system that generated the determination, the vendor that built it, the data scientists who trained it, and/or the government employees who deployed it. None of these provide meaningful confrontation. The algorithm itself cannot be questioned about its reasoning. It cannot explain why it interpreted a data discrepancy as intentional fraud rather than administrative error. It cannot be challenged on its assumptions or pressed on its limitations. Citron (2008) identifies this problem as fundamental to technological due process. The constitutional framework presumes human decision-makers whose reasoning can be examined, but automated systems bypass that framework entirely.

Trade secret protections create insurmountable discovery barriers. Vendors claim their algorithms constitute proprietary business information, refusing to disclose decision logic even when liberty is at stake. Courts routinely defer to these confidentiality claims, accepting vendor assertions that revealing how the system works would compromise competitive advantage. This leaves defendants unable to examine the accuser's methodology, unable to challenge its accuracy, and unable to expose its errors. As Brauneis and Goodman (2018) document, confrontation rights become meaningless when discovery barriers prevent access to system logic. The constitutional right exists on paper but not in practice.

In the MiDAS litigation, attorneys struggled to obtain basic information about how the system made fraud determinations. The state and its vendors resisted disclosure, citing trade secrets and system security. Public defenders lacked technical resources to challenge algorithmic determinations even when they suspected errors. The "witness" remained hidden behind claims of proprietary protection. This inverts the constitutional design: the accuser remains invisible while the accused must prove innocence without access to the evidence against them.

Due Process in the Age of Automation

The Fifth Amendment prohibits deprivation of life, liberty, or property without due process of law. The question arises as to the process due when an algorithm accuses someone of fraud. The Supreme Court's framework in *Mathews v. Eldridge* weighs three factors: the private interest affected, the risk of erroneous deprivation, and the government's interest in alternative procedures. Applying this test to algorithmic fraud detection reveals profound due process failures. Citron (2008) argues that technological systems require distinct due process protections precisely because they operate differently from human decision-makers.

The private interests are substantial. People accused by fraud detection systems face benefit termination, wage garnishment, tax refund seizure, criminal prosecution, and permanent consequences. These rival what courts demand in traditional criminal proceedings. The risk of erroneous deprivation is demonstrably high. MiDAS achieved a 93% error rate (Wykstra, 2020). Yet the procedures used (automated determination without human review, notice posted only online, appeals processed by independent judges who lack technical capacity to examine algorithmic logic) provide minimal protection. The government's interest in efficiency cannot justify procedures that fail to protect against known high error rates.

The Appeals Process: Carmelita Colvin's Six-Year Struggle

Carmelita Colvin received a letter in 2014 stating she had committed unemployment fraud and owed over $13,000, approximately four times what she had actually claimed in benefits (Wykstra, 2020). She had collected benefits in 2013 after losing her cleaning job and knew she was eligible. Her reaction was disbelief: "This has got to be impossible" (Wykstra, 2020, para. 2). What Colvin did not know was that thousands across Michigan were experiencing identical accusations from MiDAS.

When MiDAS flagged someone, the person typically learned about the accusation after consequences had already begun. The state seized Colvin's $3,500 tax refund and demanded repayment. Colvin had no access to information showing what data the system examined or what discrepancies triggered the fraud flag. To appeal, Colvin had to file within 30 days and appear before an administrative law judge through Michigan's Office of Administrative Hearings and Rules (MOAHR), a separate agency from the UIA established by MCL 421.33. Although structurally independent, MOAHR judges lacked technical expertise to examine how MiDAS reached its determination. They could verify the system followed its programmed rules but could not assess whether those rules were valid. When MiDAS averaged Colvin's entire quarterly income to create statistical artifacts it then interpreted as fraud evidence, the judge could confirm the calculation was performed correctly without evaluating whether income averaging was a sound fraud detection method.

The appeal's scope was narrowly defined and questioned if the system followed its own rules. Not whether the rules themselves were valid. The burden fell on Colvin to prove the system wrong without access to its logic, training data, or decision thresholds. She faced this hearing without legal resources, though nonprofit advocacy organizations assisted hundreds of MiDAS victims, most people could not obtain such help. As Crenshaw (1989) documents through her framework of intersectionality, procedural protections that presume equal access become mechanisms of discrimination when some populations lack resources to navigate them.

The appeal became a six-year ordeal while consequences continued. In 2017, three years into her appeals process, Colvin completed her bachelor's degree in criminal justice. That same year, she applied for a position with the Wayne County Sheriff's office. She was rejected, not for job performance, but because the fraud charge remained on her record despite her ongoing appeal. The determination was still pending. Not until early 2020, six years after MiDAS flagged her, did an administrative judge finally dismiss her case. Even winning brought no immediate relief. Colvin later stated she had not received her refund. The damage persisted: lost employment opportunity, years of anxiety, and damaged reputation. She described the impact: "they suggested that I was a criminal" (Wykstra, 2020, para. 42).

The Constitutional Failure

The timing inverts due process fundamentally. *Mathews v. Eldridge* presumes notice and hearing precede deprivation. For algorithmic systems, deprivation occurs first. MiDAS seized refunds and terminated benefits immediately. Only then could appeals begin. While Colvin pursued her appeal (six years), consequences continued. The system did not pause. Citron (2008) argues that the constitutional framework governing due process was designed for sequential decision-making: investigation, notice, hearing, then deprivation. Algorithmic systems collapse this sequence, imposing consequences first and creating appeals as afterthought rather than protection.

The appeal system assumes procedural protections can operate without access to decision logic. This assumption collapses when the accuser is code. Hearing officers cannot examine algorithmic design, assess whether training data was biased, or evaluate decision thresholds. They cannot determine whether activity MiDAS flagged actually constitutes fraud under law. Pre-deprivation hearings, when they occur, lack technical capacity. Post-deprivation appeals cannot challenge system design. The burden falls on accused individuals to prove the system wrong while lacking information necessary for that proof. Vendors claim proprietary protection, courts defer to confidentiality claims, and appellants, particularly poor people navigating this alone, face expertise asymmetry they cannot overcome.

The constitutional framework governing due process was designed for human decision-makers whose reasoning can be examined and errors corrected. When the decision-maker is algorithmic, the entire framework fails. Colvin's six-year journey of accusation, appeal during which consequences continued, employment rejection mid-appeal, vindication years later, and then still awaiting refunds illustrates what that failure costs. The cascading timeline of her experience mirrors patterns documented across thousands of falsely accused individuals.

The following image shows how algorithmic accusations trigger immediate consequences that persist throughout the entire appeals process, inverting constitutional protections that presume notice and hearing before deprivation.

Figure 2. Cascade of consequences flowchart

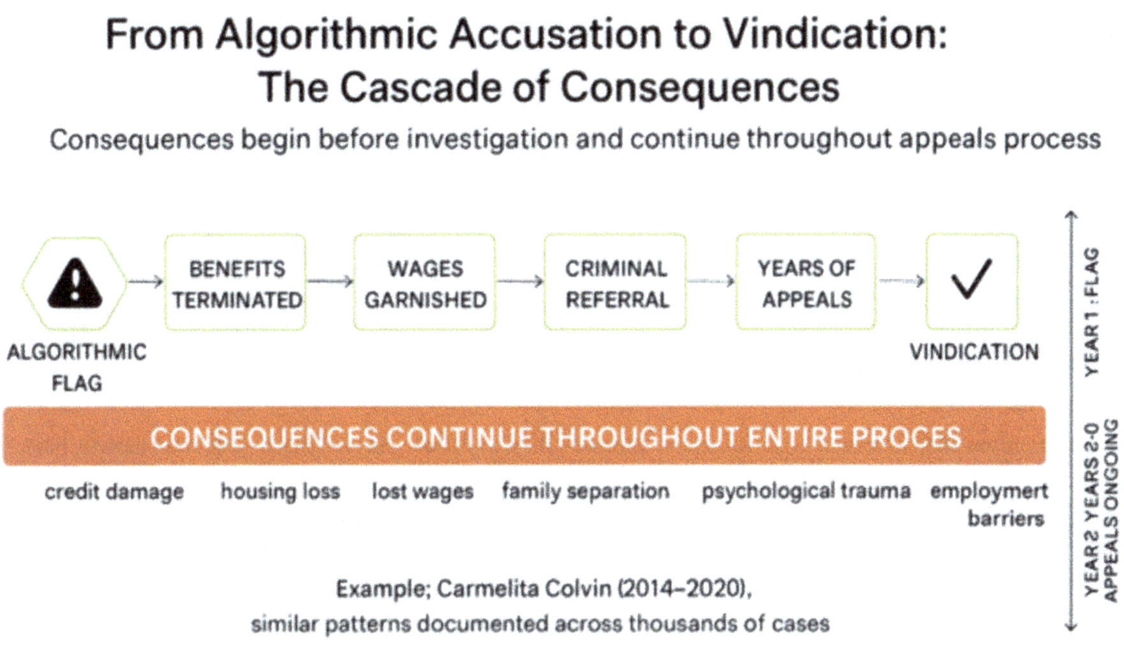

(graphic by the author)

This temporal inversion, deprivation preceding investigation, violates the foundational constitutional principle that due process requires notice and hearing before the state imposes consequences. Yet for people accused by algorithms, that principle is suspended. Citron and Pasquale (2014) document how the scored society creates conditions where algorithmic determinations trigger cascading consequences before due process protections can operate.

The Evidentiary Standard Problem

Fraud requires proof beyond reasonable doubt in criminal cases or clear and convincing evidence in civil proceedings. Both standards demand that the state prove the defendant knowingly made false statements or deliberately concealed material facts with intent to deceive. Algorithms produce correlation, not causation. They identify discrepancies, not intent. Courts increasingly treat algorithmic determinations as expert evidence without applying scrutiny required for expert testimony. Under *Daubert v. Merrell Dow Pharmaceuticals*, expert evidence must be based on scientifically valid reasoning and methodology. The Supreme Court established that judges must determine both relevance and reliability of expert testimony, asking whether the testimony helps the jury resolve the case and whether it is derived through scientific method (Grady, 2006). The Court identified four key factors for assessing reliability: whether the theory can be tested through scientific method, whether it has been subjected to peer review, what the error rate is, and whether it has gained general acceptance in the relevant field (Grady, 2006).

Fraud detection systems rarely face such scrutiny. Courts admit algorithmic determinations based on claims that the system is sophisticated, that it processes vast amounts of data, that it was built by technical experts. The system is presented as a neutral arbiter, an objective fact-finder that simply identifies fraud without bias or error. This myth of neutrality obscures that every design choice in the system reflects policy decisions about what counts as suspicious, what level of false positives is acceptable, and whose interests matter. Under rigorous *Daubert* analysis, fraud detection systems would fail: error rates are not measured, peer review is absent, decision logic is proprietary, and general acceptance is questionable.

Defense attorneys lack resources to challenge technical determinations effectively. Hiring expert witnesses to examine algorithms requires funding most public defender offices cannot provide. Even when experts are available, they may be denied access to system details due to trade secret protections. The expertise asymmetry in courtrooms, where prosecution is backed by state resources and vendor technical support while the defense operates without access to the system or funds to challenge it, ensures most algorithmic determinations go uncontested.

Transparency Law Failures

Some states have passed algorithmic accountability statutes. New York's law requires impact assessments for automated decision systems used by city agencies. Vermont and Washington, D.C. have similar provisions. These laws however typically exempt criminal justice applications or lack enforcement mechanisms. They require transparency about system deployment without guaranteeing individual access to decision logic when accused. Reisman et al. (2018) propose algorithmic impact assessments as mechanism to evaluate systems before deployment, yet most existing statutes lack effectiveness: they require reporting without mandating changes.

Freedom of Information Act requests face trade secret exemptions. When attorneys seek information about how fraud detection systems work, agencies invoke FOIA exceptions protecting proprietary information and commercial secrets. Even when code is disclosed, most defendants lack the technical expertise to interpret it meaningfully. Providing source code to someone without computer science training does no more for their defense than providing a chemistry textbook does for someone wrongly accused based on lab results. As Brauneis and Goodman (2018) argue, transparency about system existence differs fundamentally from transparency enabling contestation. The former satisfies disclosure requirements; the latter requires discovery rights comparable to those in criminal procedure.

No statutory right exists to independent technical evaluation. Defendants cannot compel the state to provide expert analysis of whether the system correctly processed their case. They cannot demand access to training data to determine if the system learned to discriminate against people with their characteristics or require testing of the system's error rates across different populations. The result is expertise asymmetry that ensures unequal justice. Wealthy defendants might hire technical experts, obtain independent evaluation, challenge system validity. Poor defendants, the overwhelming majority of those accused by fraud detection systems in benefits and court payment contexts, face algorithmic accusations without resources to mount technical defense.

Cascading Consequences Beyond Criminal Charges

The accusation itself becomes punishment. Administrative penalties are imposed without criminal conviction. Someone flagged by a fraud detection system faces immediate wage garnishment and tax refund seizure, consequences that begin before any court reviews the case. The state collects money based solely on the algorithmic determination. Credit damage follows automatically. When benefits agencies report fraud determinations to credit bureaus, credit scores plummet. People cannot qualify for housing, get approved for car loans, and access credit necessary for basic needs. The fraud determination appears on background checks, blocking employment opportunities. Employers see the accusation and refuse to hire, unwilling to risk employing someone flagged for fraud regardless of whether charges were proven.

Housing instability accelerates. Lost income from garnishment makes rent payments impossible and evictions follow. Someone who had precarious but functional housing becomes homeless because an algorithm flagged their file. Child welfare agencies respond to housing loss by investigating whether children are being properly cared for, opening another front of state intervention triggered by the initial algorithmic accusation. Employment barriers from fraud accusations persist even when criminal charges are dismissed. The person may successfully contest the determination, may prove the system made an error, or may have charges dropped, but the accusation appears in public records, in background checks, and in credit reports. Employers, landlords, and creditors see that the person was accused of fraud. The ultimate disposition (charges dismissed and determination reversed) receives far less attention than the initial accusation.

These cascading consequences disproportionately affect poor populations and communities of color, who are overrepresented among those dependent on benefits systems and subject to criminal justice involvement (Crenshaw, 1989). The compounding harms from a single algorithmic error demonstrate what intersectional analysis reveals: those already marginalized by multiple systems face exponentially greater consequences from technological failures.

MiDAS victims experienced these cascading consequences. People filed for bankruptcy, lost homes, and faced years of damaged credit. Some dealt with child welfare investigations prompted by housing and income instability. Those who successfully appealed their cases still struggled to repair the damage the false accusation caused. The state eventually paid $20 million in settlement, but money cannot restore the years of hardship, the family separations, and the opportunities lost.

This is the constitutional crisis of algorithmic accusation: the Confrontation Clause offers no protection when the witness is code, due process fails when deprivation precedes review, evidentiary standards collapse when courts treat technical determinations as proof, transparency laws provide no meaningful access, and consequences cascade far beyond what any criminal conviction would impose. The Constitution protects people against certain forms of state action. Those protections however were written for human accusers, human decision-makers, and human witnesses. When machines accuse, the constitutional framework fails.

IMPLICATIONS AND NECESSARY REFORMS

Immediate Safeguards and Structural Reforms

The crisis of algorithmic false accusation demands immediate action. Jurisdictions should impose a moratorium on criminal referrals based solely on algorithmic determinations. No prosecution should proceed unless human investigators have reviewed the case and independently established probable cause. This requirement addresses what Citron (2008) identifies as the fundamental failure of technological due process: the absence of human review before deprivation. Secondly, mandatory human review must precede any deprivation, including benefit termination, wage garnishment, or tax refund seizure. The system can flag cases, but humans must verify before consequences begin. This reverses the current architecture where consequences precede review.

A third actionable item is that consequences should be suspended pending meaningful appeal. Someone flagged by a fraud detection system should maintain benefits, avoid garnishment, and remain free from prosecution until technical review confirms the determination's validity. As Reisman et al. (2018) document through their framework for algorithmic impact assessments, pre-deployment review should include evaluation of what happens when systems produce errors. Current practice assumes errors are acceptable; necessary reform presumes they are not.

Trade secret exceptions for criminal defense discovery must be established immediately. When liberty is at stake, vendor claims about proprietary protection cannot block access to system logic. Defendants need the right to examine how the system reached its determination. Brauneis and Goodman (2018) argue that algorithmic transparency requires discovery rights comparable to those in criminal procedure, meaning meaningful access to decision logic, not merely notice that a system exists. Additionally, indigent defendants must receive automatic right to independent technical experts at public expense. The state provides counsel for those who cannot afford attorneys; it must provide technical expertise for those who cannot afford to challenge algorithmic accusations.

Structural reforms require deeper policy changes. Contracts must be restructured to eliminate compensation tied to detection volume. Vendors should not profit from high false positive rates. Payment models must shift to accuracy-based performance metrics with financial penalties when systems wrongly accuse people. Without explicit accuracy requirements and vendor liability in procurement standards, systems will continue prioritizing volume. Vendor liability for wrongful prosecution and associated harms would create proper incentives: if vendors face lawsuits and damage awards when their systems destroy innocent lives, they will prioritize accuracy over aggressive flagging.

Independent oversight boards with technical expertise should review fraud detection systems before deployment and conduct ongoing audits. These boards, composed of computer scientists, civil rights advocates, public defenders, and affected community members, would assess system design, examine training data, test for disparate impact, and require corrections before systems go "live." Reisman et al. (2018) propose algorithmic impact assessments as mechanism for such review; Buolamwini and Gebru (2018) demonstrate methodologies for testing disparate impact across demographic groups. Mandatory public reporting of false positive rates and demographic disparities would enable accountability. Agencies should publish annual reports detailing system performance and include how many cases flagged, how many determinations are overturned on appeal, and what error rates exist across different populations. Transparency of this magnitude is rare but essential. Mitchell et al. (2019) propose model cards as framework for systematic documentation of algorithmic system behavior.

Constitutional Protections and Limits of Automation

Constitutional protections require judicial or legislative action. Statutes should establish clear rights to examine system logic in all criminal proceedings. Defendants must access source code, training data, and decision rules. This represents what Brauneis and Goodman (2018) identify as discovery rights necessary for meaningful confrontation. Heightened evidentiary standards for algorithmic accusations would require prosecutors to prove not only that the system flagged the defendant, but that the system's determination meets *Daubert* standards for reliability. Courts must recognize the legal distinction between correlation and proof of intent; a data discrepancy is not evidence of fraudulent purpose. Barocas and Selbst (2016) demonstrate that algorithmic fairness problems rooted in structural design cannot be solved through technical modification alone; reliability standards must account for this limitation.

Due process protections must account for algorithmic opacity. Pre-deprivation hearings should include technical review capacity. Post-deprivation appeals should involve independent experts, not agency staff reviewing their own system's determinations. The Confrontation Clause should apply to algorithmic witnesses: if a system's determination forms the basis for prosecution, defendants must be able to challenge that system's methodology, examine its error rates, and expose its failures. As Citron and Pasquale (2014) document in their analysis of the scored society, constitutional protections designed for human decision-makers fail when applied to algorithmic systems without modification.

Some determinations should be prohibited from automation entirely. Fraud detection serves as test case for algorithmic governance limits. As Eubanks (2018) documents, automated systems deployed in governance contexts create conditions enabling systematic harm when they operate without meaningful oversight; the solution includes not just better regulation of automated systems but recognition that certain decisions cannot be automated at all. Systems that provide decision support, highlighting cases for human review, differ fundamentally from systems that make final determinations. The former is permissible but the latter raises constitutional concerns when it generates criminal accusations.

A constitutional floor must exist. Systems that accuse people of crimes must be transparent, challengeable, and accountable. Lipton (2018) argues that the mythos of model interpretability obscures fundamental limits on what algorithmic systems can explain about their own reasoning. When those systems accuse people of crimes, this inability to provide explanation violates constitutional principles. The efficiency argument has limits. Cost savings cannot justify false imprisonment. Some determinations, specifically those requiring assessment of intent, knowledge, and culpability, require human judgment that algorithms cannot provide. This is not a technical problem to be solved but a governance boundary to be established: fraud determinations should not be automated.

The reforms outlined above address immediate harms while establishing structural safeguards against systematic false accusation. Their implementation requires commitment across executive, legislative, and judicial branches. Without such commitment, fraud detection systems will continue operating as accusation engines, converting patterns into crimes and poverty into evidence of wrongdoing.

CONCLUSION: THE ACCUSATION AS PUNISHMENT

Synthesis and Systemic Harm

Fraud detection systems function as engines of false accusation through convergence of three failures. Technical architecture mistakes patterns for intent. Systems identify statistical anomalies (income volatility, address changes, data discrepancies) and categorize them as fraud without capacity to assess whether the person acted knowingly and deceptively. The survivability problem is fundamental: adaptation strategies people use to navigate poverty look, to algorithms trained on middle-class employment patterns, like criminal behavior (Kalleberg, 2011; Edin & Shaefer, 2015). This is not incidental bias; it is structural misalignment between how systems are designed and how poor people survive.

Financial incentives also reward volume over accuracy. Vendors profit from high detection rates regardless of error rates. Agencies measure success by dollars recovered, not by whether accusations are justified. Contracts specify detection deliverables without accuracy guarantees. Performance bonuses reward aggressive flagging. No contractual penalty exists for false positives. The business model is structured so that every actor benefits from wrongful accusations except the people accused. When fundamental incentive structures create misalignment between detection volume and accuracy, technical improvements alone cannot remedy the problem (Barocas & Selbst, 2016).

Constitutional protections fail when the accuser is composed of code. The Confrontation Clause provides no meaningful protection when defendants cannot cross-examine algorithms (*Crawford v. Washington*, 541 U.S. 36, 2004; Sanders, 2022). Due process collapses when deprivation precedes review and appeals lack technical scrutiny capacity (Citron, 2008; Citron & Pasquale, 2014). Evidentiary standards erode when courts admit algorithmic determinations without *Daubert* analysis (Grady, 2006). Trade secrets block discovery. Expertise asymmetries prevent effective defense. The constitutional framework, written for human accusers, offers inadequate safeguards against machine-generated charges.

These elements converge to manufacture false accusations at scale. MiDAS demonstrates the mechanism clearly: technical design converted income averaging into fraud evidence, financial incentives drove the state to flag aggressively and collect penalties, and constitutional gaps left 40,000 people unable to effectively challenge determinations (Roelogs, 2017). MiDAS is notably exemplar, not an outlier. Eubanks (2018) documents how automated systems targeting poor populations become tools of social control rather than neutral administration. Similar fraud detection systems operate across benefits administration, court payment processing, and supervision monitoring. The pattern is expanding, not contracting, as jurisdictions adopt automation to address budget constraints and fraud prevention mandates.

What Justice Requires

The question is not whether algorithms should exist in criminal justice. The question is how they must operate if they are to exist at all. Justice requires three things aligned with established legal and ethical frameworks: transparency, contestation, and accountability. To be transparent, systems that accuse people of crimes must be examinable. Trade secrets cannot shield decision logic from scrutiny when liberty is at stake (Brauneis & Goodman, 2018). Defendants must access source code, understand thresholds, examine training data, and challenge methodology. This reflects what Mitchell et al. (2019) propose as essential to algorithmic accountability: transparent documentation of system behavior sufficient for meaningful scrutiny.

Next is contestation: accused individuals must have meaningful ability to challenge algorithmic determinations. This means technical review before consequences, independent expert access, burden on the state to prove system accuracy, and appeals with genuine scrutiny rather than perfunctory review by the same agency that deployed the system (Reisman et al., 2018). The *Mathews v. Eldridge* framework requires this level of process protection when deprivation is this severe.

Accountability includes consequences for vendors and agencies when systems falsely accuse. Vendors should face liability for wrongful prosecution. Agencies should bear costs when their systems destroy innocent lives. Performance metrics should penalize false positives. Contracts should include accuracy guarantees with financial penalties for failures. Without accountability mechanisms, the financial incentive structure remains fundamentally misaligned with justice.

The constitutional crisis hiding in automation is that technical systems bypass fundamental protections designed to prevent wrongful prosecution. Someone loses everything from one algorithmic flag (income, savings, housing, custody, liberty, etc.) without opportunity to confront their accuser, without due process, and without meaningful review (Citron & Pasquale, 2014). The accusation becomes the punishment. By the time the person proves the system wrong, irreparable damage has occurred. Crenshaw's (1989) framework of intersectionality illuminates how these harms concentrate on populations already marginalized by multiple systems: poor people, people of color, and people dependent on state benefits are most vulnerable to algorithmic false accusation.

Reform is urgent. Every day these systems operate without transparency, without contestation mechanisms, without accountability, more people face false accusations that cascade into prosecution, poverty, and family separation. What is at stake extends beyond individual liberty. The integrity of justice itself is threatened when we allow machines to accuse people of crimes using logic no one can examine, producing errors no one measures, destroying lives while vendors profit and agencies claim success (Eubanks, 2018).

Michigan paid $20 million to settle claims from 3,200 people who joined the Bauserman lawsuit. Thousands more were falsely accused and never joined the litigation. Money cannot restore what was taken: years of financial stability, relationships severed, and opportunities lost. The only adequate response is structural change that prevents these harms before they occur, including accuracy requirements, transparency mandates, contestation rights, and clear limits on when automation may be used at all. Until fraud detection systems meet these standards, they should not operate. The efficiency they promise is not worth the injustice they produce. The constitutional framework and moral imperative are clear: systems that accuse people of crimes must operate transparently and with accountability for the accuracy of their determinations. Anything less represents abandonment of the justice system's fundamental purpose.

REFERENCES

Barocas, S., & Selbst, A. D. (2016). Big data's disparate impact. *SSRN*, *104*, 671–732. DOI: 10.2139/ssrn.2477899

Benefits Tech Advocacy Hub. (n.d.). Michigan unemployment insurance false fraud determinations [Case study]. https://www.btah.org/case-study/michigan-unemployment-insurance-false-fraud-determinations.html

Brauneis, R., & Goodman, E. P. (2018). Algorithmic transparency for the smart city. *SSRN*, *20*(1), 103–176. DOI: 10.2139/ssrn.3012499

Brewster, T. (2022, October 31). States spent millions on Deloitte's 'Anti-Fraud' Covid unemployment systems. They suffered billions in fraud. Forbes. https://www.forbes.com/sites/thomasbrewster/2022/10/31/covid-pandemic-fraud-hits-billions-despite-deloitte-contracts-worth-hundreds-of-millions

Buolamwini, J., & Gebru, T. (2018). Gender shades: Intersectional accuracy disparities in commercial gender classification. [Conference paper]. In Conference on Fairness, Accountability and Transparency (pp. 77–91). Proceedings of Machine Learning Research. https://proceedings.mlr.press/v81/buolamwini18a.html

Charette, R. N. (2018, January 24). Michigan's MiDAS unemployment system: Algorithm alchemy that created lead, not gold. IEEE Spectrum. https://spectrum.ieee.org/michigans-midas-unemployment-system-algorithm-alchemy-that-created-lead-not-gold

Citron, D. K. (2008). Technological due process. Washington University Law Review, 85, 1249–1313. https://journals.library.wustl.edu/lawreview/article/id/6697

Citron, D. K., & Pasquale, F. (2014, March 1). The scored society: Due process for automated predictions. *Washington Law Review (Seattle, Wash.)*, *89*(1), 1–33. https://digitalcommons.law.uw.edu/wlr/vol89/iss1/2

Crawford v. Washington, 541 U.S. 36 (2004).

Crenshaw, K. (1989). Demarginalizing the intersection of race and sex: A Black feminist critique of antidiscrimination doctrine, feminist theory and antiracist politics. *University of Chicago Legal Forum*, *1989*(1), 139–167. https://chicagounbound.uchicago.edu/uclf/vol1989/iss1/8

Daubert v. Merrell Dow Pharmaceuticals, Inc., 509 U.S. 579 (1993).

de la Garza, A. (2020, May 28). States' automated systems are trapping citizens in bureaucratic nightmares with their lives on the line. Time. https://time.com/5840609/algorithm-unemployment

Dressel, J., & Farid, H. (2018, March 30). The accuracy, fairness, and limits of predicting recidivism. *Science Advances*, *4*(1), eaao5580. Advance online publication. DOI: 10.1126/sciadv.aao5580 PMID: 29376122

Edin, K. J., & Shaefer, H. L. (2015). *2.00 a day: Living on almost nothing in America*. Houghton Mifflin Harcourt.

Eubanks, V. (2018, January). Automating inequality: How high-tech tools profile, police, and punish the poor. St. Martin's Press.

Felton, R. (2016, December 18). Michigan unemployment agency made 20,000 false fraud accusations—report. The Guardian. https://www.theguardian.com/us-news/2016/dec/18/michigan-unemployment-agency-fraud-accusations

Gilliom, J. (2001). *Overseers of the poor: Surveillance, resistance, and the limits of privacy*. University of Chicago Press.

Grady, A. (2006, February). Daubert and expert testimony. *AMA Journal of Ethics*, *8*(2), 97–100. DOI: 10.1001/virtualmentor.2006.8.2.hlaw1-0602 PMID: 23228539

Hayne, J., & Doran, M. (2020, May 29). Government to pay back $721m as it scraps Robodebt for Centrelink welfare recipients. ABC News Australia. https://www.abc.net.au/news/2020-05-29/federal-government-refund-robodebt-scheme-repay-debts/12299410

Kalleberg, A. L. (2011). *Good jobs, bad jobs: The rise of polarized and precarious employment systems in the new economy*. Russell Sage Foundation.

Kohl, R. (2024, April 22). Automated stategraft: Faulty programming and improper collections in Michigan's unemployment insurance program. [Conference paper]. Wisconsin Law Review/ 2023 Symposium on Stategraft. https://wlr.law.wisc.edu/automated-stategraft-faulty-programming-and-improper-collections-in-michigans-unemployment-insurance-program

Kroll, J. A., Huey, J., Barocas, S., Felten, E. W., Reidenberg, J. R., Robinson, D. G., & Yu, H. (2017). Accountable algorithms. *University of Pennsylvania Law Review*, *165*(3), 633–705. https://papers.ssrn.com/sol3/papers.cfm?abstract_id=2765268

Lipton, Z. C. (2018, June 1). The mythos of model interpretability: In machine learning, the concept of interpretability is both important and slippery. *ACM Queue; Tomorrow's Computing Today*, *16*(3), 31–57. DOI: 10.1145/3236386.3241340

Michigan Department of Attorney General. (2022, October 20). State of Michigan announces settlement of civil rights class action alleging false accusations of unemployment fraud [Press release]. https://www.michigan.gov/ag/news/press-releases/2022/10/20/som-settlement-of-civil-rights-class-action-alleging-false-accusations-of-unemployment-fraud

Mitchell, S., Wu, S., Zaldivar, A., Barnes, P., Vasserman, L., Hutchinson, B., Spitzer, E., Raji, I. D., & Gebru, T. (2019, January). Model cards for model reporting. In *Conference on Fairness, Accountability and Transparency* (pp. 220–229). PMLR. DOI: 10.1145/3287560.3287596

Reisman, D., Schultz, J. M., Crawford, K., & Whittaker, M. (2018, April 9). Algorithmic impact assessments: A practical framework for public agency accountability. AI Now Institute. https://ainowinstitute.org/publications/algorithmic-impact-assessments-report-2

Roelofs, T. (2017, February 7). Broken: The human toll of Michigan's unemployment fraud saga. Bridge Michigan. https://bridgemi.com/michigan-government/broken-human-toll-michigans-unemployment-fraud-saga

Sanders, S. (2022, January 25). Justices affirm Crawford's application of Sixth Amendment confrontation clause to testimonial evidence. SCOTUSblog. https://www.scotusblog.com/2022/01/justices-affirm-crawfords-application-of-sixth-amendment-confrontation-clause-to-testimonial-evidence

Soss, J., Fording, R. C., & Schram, S. F. (2011). *Disciplining the poor: Neoliberal paternalism and the persistent power of race*. University of Chicago Press. DOI: 10.7208/chicago/9780226768786.001.0001

Williams, S. (2017, February 13). Errors in Centrelink's debt recovery system were inevitable, as in all complex systems. The Conversation. https://theconversation.com/errors-in-centrelinks-debt-recovery-system-were-inevitable-as-in-all-complex-systems-71409

Wykstra, S. (2020, June 1). Government's use of algorithm serves up false fraud charges. Undark. https://undark.org/2020/06/01/michigan-unemployment-fraud-algorithm

Chapter 15
Deepfake Forensics: Threats and Detection of AI-Manipulated Media

Pedro M. C. Cardoso
http://orcid.org/0009-0003-5056-2191
School of Science and Technology, Higher Polytechnic Institute Gaya, Portugal

Rúben S. Oliveira
http://orcid.org/0009-0000-4232-866X
School of Science and Technology, Higher Polytechnic Institute Gaya, Portugal

Tiago F. N. Gomes
http://orcid.org/0009-0003-1695-719X
School of Science and Technology, Higher Polytechnic Institute Gaya, Portugal

Eduardo S. Bastos
http://orcid.org/0009-0004-8613-7469
School of Science and Technology, Higher Polytechnic Institute Gaya, Portugal

Sérgio F. S. F. Lopes
http://orcid.org/0000-0003-4039-9979
INSIGHT - Research Center for Ecological Human Development, Portugal

ABSTRACT

The development of Artificial Intelligence has enabled the creation of artificially altered multimedia content known as deepfakes. These manipulated images, videos, and audio pose a growing threat to criminal justice systems, where the integrity of digital evidence is paramount. This chapter presents a narrative review of deepfake forensics, tracing the evolution of media manipulation from analogue techniques to modern generative models, and examining the threat landscape across political, financial, and personal domains, including non-consensual intimate imagery. Detection methodologies are surveyed, from artefact-based and statistical approaches to the operational tools accessible to law enforcement. Beyond the technical dimension, the chapter addresses chain of custody requirements, evidentiary standards

DOI: 10.4018/979-8-3373-7660-8.ch015

across jurisdictions, the fragmented legislative landscape, and the role of Explainable AI in bridging detection outputs and courtroom admissibility. The psychological factors influencing how investigators and jurors assess synthetic media are also considered.

INTRODUCTION AND SCOPE

The remarkable advancement of Artificial Intelligence (AI) and, more specifically, Generative Artificial Intelligence, has revolutionised the process of creating digital content during the past decade (Abdullah et al., 2024; Babaei et al., 2025; Bisht & Pooja, 2025). Traditionally, image and video editing have always required specialised knowledge and involved labour-intensive processes to create manipulated content (Delp et al., 2020; Goyal et al., 2025; Waseem et al., 2023). With the advent of generative models such as Generative Adversarial Networks (GANs) and Diffusion Probabilistic Models (DPMs), it is now possible to create highly realistic synthetic images, videos, and even audio recordings, popularly known as deepfakes, that can manipulate existing media or generate entirely new content, potentially deceiving both humans and automated systems (Acim et al., 2025; Liu et al., 2025; Lyu, 2020; Meckel & Steinacker, 2021; Xu et al., 2025).

Aside from their genuine uses in the realms of entertainment, creative industry, and education, deepfakes have also created several ethical, security-related, and human rights concerns that go beyond the usual issues of misinformation (Babaei et al., 2025; Goyal et al., 2025; Shamsabadi et al., 2022). In the context of politics, deepfakes have been used as a tool in information warfare, that can manipulate public discourse and the legitimacy of democratic processes in a country (Harris, 2024a; Masood et al., 2021; Meckel & Steinacker, 2021; Miotti & Wasil, 2024). In the context of the financial industry, "Phishing 2.0" has been used to carry out sophisticated forms of social engineering, through the use of voice cloning and avatars (Mathew & Rodas, 2025; Frankovits & Mirsky, 2023; Mai et al., 2023). In the context of the individual user, deepfake technology has been used in several unethical ways to produce forms of non-consensual sexual content, that can cause harm to one's reputation (Lyu, 2020; Meckel & Steinacker, 2021; Pawelec, 2022; Shamsabadi et al., 2022).

At the same time, the availability of such realistic synthetic media undermines the public's trust in digital communications (Fallis, 2020; Harris, 2024a; Harris, 2024b). Merely being aware of the existence of such believable deepfakes, provides the so-called "liar's dividend," in the sense that unscrupulous individuals can easily deny the legitimacy of genuine audio-visual information as being manipulated (Harris, 2024b; Pawelec, 2022). This naturally undermines the traditional notion of video as an objective "silent witness" in various scenarios (Akhtar et al., 2024; Sandoval et al., 2024). In general, this creates significant issues in the realm of digital forensics, where the legitimacy of audio-visual information is of primary importance (Akhtar et al., 2024; Lei et al., 2025; Masood et al., 2021).

In this context of increasing concern about deepfakes, the detection of such forgeries has become the primary focus of AI security and digital forensics (Amerini et al., 2024; Qureshi et al., 2024). However, with the increasing sophistication of these generation tools, the detection methods have failed to keep up with the challenge, highlighting the "arms race" between content generators and detection specialists (Babaei et al., 2025; Qureshi et al., 2024). Indeed, the detection methods have consistently demonstrated impressive results on the widely used evaluation sets, yet the results have failed to translate to real-world scenarios (Amerini et al., 2024; Hwang, 2020; Le et al., 2025; Ramanaharan et al., 2025). For instance, "media laundering" operations such as compression, resampling, and transcoding can mask the traces many detectors rely on, and cross-dataset generalisation often remains weak, when models face unseen generation methods or distribution platforms (Lyu, 2020; Ramanaharan et al., 2025; Rössler et al., 2018).

In the case of forensic and legal usage, however, technical performance is only half the story (Kraetzer et al., 2022). A further layer of complexity stems from the "black box" nature of deep learning-based detectors, whose decision making is difficult to interpret and explain, which is particularly problematic in legal settings as discussed by Qian et al. (2025). In other words, verifiable evidence is needed, rather than simply high numerical accuracy (Lyu, 2020; Masood et al., 2021). This creates tension between the sophistication of state-of-the-art detection systems and the transparency required in legal settings, highlighting the need for Explainable AI (XAI) approaches, including process-based models, that can bridge advanced machine learning and evidentiary requirements (Amerini et al., 2025; Kraetzer et al., 2022).

While the body of literature on deepfakes has expanded at a rapid pace, the surveys that have been carried out have either concentrated on the technical classifications of the processes of creation and detection or have taken a general approach to the ethics and law of deepfakes. There is a gap that needs to be filled with a discussion that ties all the elements together and assesses the detection of deepfakes, not just as a matter of pattern recognition, but as a part of the larger picture of digital content verification. Equally important, existing reviews rarely address the operational realities facing criminal justice practitioners, such as the procedural demands of chain of custody documentation, the evidentiary standards governing the admissibility of AI-derived forensic evidence, or the fragmented legislative landscape that currently applies to synthetic media across jurisdictions.

This narrative review on deepfake forensic science aims to fulfil four major requirements. First, it traces the development process from early stages of digital manipulation to modern AI-based media synthesis, positioning deepfakes within the context of modern threat patterns, including their impact on political processes, financial systems, and the growing criminal justice challenge of non-consensual intimate imagery. There is an overview of major detection and authentication methodologies for AI-generated multimedia content, focusing on their robustness and practical usability, and assessing the operational tools currently accessible to law enforcement and forensic practitioners. An examination of the operational and legal challenges that deepfakes create for criminal proceedings is included, with chain of custody requirements for digital evidence, evidentiary standards governing the admissibility of AI-derived forensic conclusions, the emerging legislative frameworks across jurisdictions, and the role of XAI in making detection outputs comprehensible within legal settings. Finally, the human and institutional dimensions of the problem are highlighted, from the cognitive biases that influence how jurors and investigators assess synthetic media to the policy and technological directions, such as hardware-level authentication and international cooperation, that may shape the field in the coming years.

METHODOLOGY

A narrative overview of the deepfake forensics field is thus offered. It looks at how synthetic media generation has developed, the main threat settings in which deepfakes are used, and the detection methods that are currently being applied. A narrative review was chosen instead of a systematic review or a meta-analysis for several practical reasons: (1) The field of deepfake forensics encompasses a broad spectrum of methods, ranging from traditional artefact-based image analysis to modern machine learning-based models. A narrative review allows the different strands of the literature and the connections between different approaches to be synthesised in an organic manner, without the need for inclusion criteria that could limit the range of the literature being considered (de Cassai et al., 2025; Wang and Guo, 2022). (2) The field of deepfake technology is constantly evolving. The meaning of state of the art moves quickly as generative models improve and detection techniques adapt. A narrative format allows the literature to be grouped according to thematic rather than strictly chronological themes (de Cassai et al., 2025). (3) The impact of deepfakes is not limited to technical performance. Their consequences stretch across information warfare, financial fraud, privacy harms, and the wider weakening of digital trust. A narrative framework allows these issues to be considered alongside forensic practice and developing policy thinking, within a single coherent structure.

To establish a firm starting point that can serve as a basis for the following literature review, a preliminary bibliometric mapping exercise was carried out (Acim et al., 2025; Wang & Guo, 2022). An exploratory search of the Scopus database, accessed via an institutional subscription, utilised a general query and returned a total of 850 records. The intention behind this process was to capture the intersection between synthetic media and forensic sciences, using the following search string:

TITLE-ABS-KEY (deepfake* AND ("digital forensics" OR "content verification") OR ("Watermarking" OR "Provenance tracking"))) OR (TITLE-ABS-KEY (("image manipulation" OR "video manipulation") AND ("machine learning" OR "artificial intelligence"))) OR (TITLE-ABS-KEY (deepfake AND ("digital evidence" OR "forensic readiness" OR "legal implications"))) AND (PUBYEAR > 2015)

These records were processed using VOSviewer to identify high-frequency keyword clusters, which served as a thematic framework for the review (Acim et al., 2025; Passas, 2024; Wang & Guo, 2022). These were not intended as strict prerequisites for inclusion in the review, but rather as a framework. This approach ensured complete coverage of the research landscape, while allowing for the necessary flexibility in the discourse.

A temporal overlay analysis further revealed a clear shift in research priorities over a short period. Earlier terms, clustering around 2022, centre on foundational technical concepts such as image classification, support vector machines, and computer vision. By 2023, the focus moves toward machine learning, deep learning, and deepfake detection methods. The most significant shift appears around 2024, where the literature pivots toward advanced generative AI, diffusion models, and forensic countermeasures, suggesting an accelerating "arms race" between generation and detection.

To promote the reproducibility and accessibility that are now a fundamental criterion of scholarly work, the Scopus database entries were validated and supplemented by a corresponding verification from a variety of open-access databases (Acim et al., 2025; Passas, 2024). From October 2025 to March 2026, a systematic search was performed across IEEE Xplore, The Lens.org, MDPI, arXiv and Google Scholar databases, using Boolean operators analogous to the initial Scopus search. Such a method effectively overcomes the long-standing dilemma of academic publication, by providing access to reliable indexed databases while allowing readers or researchers to access the literature independently, regardless of their institutional affiliations (de Cassai et al., 2025; Stephen et al., 2025).

The overall approach taken in the narrative review, remained practical and focused in nature. Relevant sources were those that were written in English or Portuguese, and discussed the key elements related to deepfakes, including the creation, detection, or overall social implications related to deepfake forensics. Documents without a solid empirical or theoretical contribution to deepfake forensics were excluded to maintain academic rigour. Rather than setting a fixed number of sources in advance, the review followed a saturation approach, continuing to include relevant studies until the main themes became consistent and additional papers added little new insight.

The main analysis covers 2016 to 2025, reflecting the timeframe captured by the search strategy and the period in which AI generated synthetic media, became a sustained focus within both research and practice.

Although the body of research on the topics of image forensics, manipulation detection, and the ethics of digital photography is relevant as background information, the year of 2016 is used as the starting point of the analysis of contemporary problems related to AI-generated synthetic media, rather than the year in which the issue of manipulation was introduced (Acim et al., 2025; Masood et al., 2021; Munhoz, 2014; Sugiyama & Kataoka, 2025; Verdoliva, 2020).

HISTORICAL CONTEXT

Long before digital editing became common, photographers were already retouching images, making darkroom adjustments and combining elements from different negatives (Munhoz, 2014). Almeida and Boni note that these practices could enhance an image but also raised ethical concerns, particularly in photojournalism where credibility depends on public trust (Almeida & Boni, 2006).

One striking historical example comes from a photograph taken in 1937 by Heinrich Hoffmann, Hitler's official photographer, in the park of the Reich Chancellery in Berlin. The original image shows Hitler alongside actress Leni Riefenstahl and Joseph Goebbels, the Minister of Propaganda. A later version found in Hoffmann's archives, shows that Goebbels had been removed, as documented in Figures 13-14 (pp. 26-27) of "A ética no fotojornalismo da era digital" (Almeida & Boni, 2006; Meckel & Steinacker, 2021). Jaubert had already recorded this kind of deliberate alteration, illustrating that concerns about the trustworthiness of images are not new (Almeida & Boni, 2006).

This case is part of a much larger ongoing discussion about the accuracy of visual representations (Munhoz, 2014; Verdoliva, 2020). Since the first illustrations based on photographs appeared in 1842, depicting the aftermath of a big fire in the city of Hamburg, questions about accuracy have followed photography. Early reproduction techniques often required engravers to interpret photographs by hand for printing, and that process could change what was shown (Almeida & Boni, 2006). Two centuries later, the debate continues, albeit not in the same way, as the question now concerns the many possibilities that digital editing allows. Hoffmann's image and its altered version demonstrate how meaning can be shaped. The original composition reinforces Hitler's presence and authority, while the removal of Goebbels appears designed to steer interpretation (Almeida & Boni, 2006; Meckel & Steinacker, 2021). It therefore draws attention to enduring questions about truth, perception and ethical responsibility in visual media (Flattery & Miller, 2024; Munhoz, 2014)

Other authors help frame this history in a more structured way. Peixoto (2014) emphasises the artistic potential of the initial manipulation methods. He points out that darkroom work, multiple exposures, and retouching, were commonly used to create artistic photographs rather than to mislead the viewer. Such methods blurred the line between photography and art, shaping the visual culture that later fed into digital and AI-based practices (Peixoto, 2014). In Batori's work, the author provides the necessary differentiation between technical adjustments and those intended to mislead the viewer. He also introduces the concept of photographic illocutionary acts, to explain how viewers interpret edited images and why ethics cannot be separated from perception (Batori, 2018). Munhoz focuses on the professional standards in photojournalism, noting that acceptable technical correction can slide into content changes that violate journalistic codes. Even before the digital era, photographers and editors had to navigate this tension, which shows why ethical scrutiny has remained central (Munhoz, 2014). Hausken develops this dual perspective further, by describing manipulation both as a morally charged act of deception and as a neutral technical process. He also provides an explanation for the cultural and academic definitions of the word "manipulation," thus connecting the historical background to the current debates on the use of deepfakes and the ethics of AI-based images (Hausken, 2024).

From a digital forensic perspective, historical context is important because the technology has changed over time (Batori, 2018; Verdoliva, 2020). Many analogue manipulations left traces, such as physical marks from retouching or chemical anomalies from development processes (Batori, 2018; Munhoz, 2014). Today's digital technology can remove or bypass many of the traditional signs of manipulation, creating a problem in evaluating authenticity (Hwang, 2020; N. Khan et al., 2025; Verdoliva, 2020). The fundamental issues have remained consistent throughout history, and as technology becomes more complex, questions around trust, authenticity and ethical conduct become more pressing (Harris, 2024a; Hausken, 2024; Meckel & Steinacker, 2021; Munhoz, 2014).

HOW DEEPFAKES ARE MADE

Generative Models: From GANs to Diffusion

Manipulation has moved to a new stage in recent times with the advent of AI, that can create convincing images rather than just editing existing ones (Alanazi & Asif, 2024; Masood et al., 2021; Meckel & Steinacker, 2021). Deepfake has been strongly linked with the development of generative modelling, especially using GANs (Acim et al., 2025; Le et al., 2025).

Goodfellow introduced GANs as a system in which a generator produces synthetic data, while a discriminator evaluates whether the output appears real. Through this competitive feedback loop, the generator learns to create increasingly realistic results (Goodfellow et al., 2014; Hwang, 2020; Patel et al., 2023). Once trained, the GANs have the capability to produce images with features related to the statistical characteristics learned from the dataset. As shown in Figure 2 (p. 6) of the article Generative Adversarial Networks by Goodfellow et al. (2014), the generated images are compared to their nearest training examples, demonstrating that the model does not memorise the data but produces novel outputs. These samples, drawn from datasets such as MNIST, TFD, and CIFAR-10, demonstrate how adversarial training allows the generator to iteratively improve its outputs based on feedback from the discriminator, forming the foundation for modern AI-based deepfake generation (Goodfellow et al., 2014; Le et al., 2025). This adversarial approach became central to many image-based deepfakes, especially for generating realistic faces and scenes (Karras et al., 2020; Kaur et al., 2024; Meckel & Steinacker, 2021).

Subsequent advances have improved both control and quality. Specifically, the use of style generators in both StyleGAN and StyleGAN2, has facilitated more control over image features on multiple dimensions, thus enabling more accurate and realistic results in terms of image textures and identities (Karras et al., 2020). DPMs have also been used as an alternative to GANs, to ensure high-quality image generation while addressing some instabilities during the training process (Ho et al., 2020). Meanwhile, motion-driven methods have been used to expand image synthesis from still images to videos. Specifically, the First Order Motion Model (FOMM) has been used to animate an image using motion patterns from an input video, highlighting the significant expansion in image and video synthesis (Siarohin et al., 2020). Overall, these advances show how modern deepfake techniques support both creative applications and increasingly serious challenges for reliable detection and verification in digital forensics (Thies et al., 2019; Verdoliva, 2020).

Video, Audio, and Full-Body Synthesis

The move from static image manipulation to fully dynamic video synthesis represents a major step forward in the evolution of deepfakes (Khan et al., 2025; Rössler et al., 2018). Face2Face led the way in real-time facial reenactment by capturing expressions from a source actor and transferring them to a target in RGB video sequences. This demonstrated that manipulating video content in live or recorded settings was entirely feasible (Thies et al., 2020). Later innovations like Deep Video Portraits expanded on these abilities by synthesising full head and upper body movements, while maintaining accurate expressions and lip synchronisation (Kim et al., 2018). The FOMM framework also brought improvements by allowing static images to be animated using reference motion. This approach enabled the creation of flexible and realistic videos across a wide range of subjects (Siarohin et al., 2020).

These advancements highlight the increasing realism found in modern deepfake videos, where even subtle facial expressions and body movements appear natural (Goyal et al., 2025; Tan et al., 2025). Such high-quality video increases the risk of misinformation campaigns and highlights the need for strong forensic methods to verify content (Alamayreh et al., 2024; Garcia, 2025; Hashmi et al., 2024). Researchers eventually looked beyond facial imagery to incorporate voice and full-body movements for a more immersive effect. Recent progress in generative AI has pushed deepfakes past simple face swaps. The technology now includes realistic audio synthesis and multimodal manipulation, that combines voice with face and body data (Hashmi et al., 2024; Khan et al., 2025; Liu et al., 2025).

Modern voice cloning and text-to-speech systems, capture timbre and rhythm well enough to deceive human listeners (Masood et al., 2021; Zhang et al., 2025). Reviews confirm that this specific type of falsification poses a growing threat to privacy and information security (Khan et al., 2025; Tan et al., 2025). Research into full-body movement synthesis is perhaps even more concerning from a forensic standpoint. For instance, the study titled "Just Dance: Detection of Human Body Reenactment Fake Videos," created a specific dataset called FakeDance to analyse AI-generated videos featuring full-body movement. Such work proves that multimodal deepfake technology, combining image and audio with body movement is already under active development (Alamayreh et al., 2024). This reality significantly expands the potential for malicious use (Goyal et al., 2025).

Text-to-Video Generation

The leap from static photos to realistic videos has happened almost overnight, driven by advances no one fully predicted (Khan et al., 2025; Liu et al., 2025). OpenAI's Sora model and Google DeepMind's Veo aim to take video generation from text to another level, combining moving images, sounds, and narrative clues in ways that, until recently, seemed impossible (Sharan et al., 2025; Sugiyama & Kataoka, 2025; Wiedemer et al., 2025). A clear example is a historian, using one of these tools to recreate an old street from archival photographs, restoring textures, lighting, and small features in a way that makes the scene feel immediate and lived in (Alanazi & Asif, 2024; Goyal et al., 2025; Kammari et al., 2025). The same realism, however, makes the detection of manipulated video far more demanding than it once was, because subtle changes can blend seamlessly into otherwise plausible footage (Liu et al., 2024; Sharan et al., 2025; Tan et al., 2025).

Researchers are currently trying to understand these difficulties. Diffusion-based systems show that many traditional detectors lose their sense of perspective when the video changes rapidly, such as a cut from a rainy alley to a sunlit café (Liu et al., 2024; Sugiyama & Kataoka, 2025). Some studies have found that detectors tuned to static frame gaps, often allow discrete signals that only appear over time to pass through (Nguyen-Le et al., 2025; Ramanaharan et al., 2025). It is no longer just a matter of detector failure, but rather the need for a change in detection. Nowadays, patterns unfold over seconds or minutes, not just in a single frame (Kaur et al., 2024; Liu et al., 2024; Ramanaharan et al., 2025).

These models present a dual-use challenge: while they offer considerable value for creative and educational applications, they simultaneously lower the barrier to producing convincing synthetic media (Hashmi et al., 2024; Mubarak et al., 2023). No consensus has yet emerged on appropriate evaluation metrics for text-to-video deepfakes, and traditional unimodal detection systems struggle to generalise across modalities, which has prompted a shift toward multimodal approaches that jointly analyse audio and visual information (Liu et al., 2025; Tan et al., 2025). It is now widely recognised that frame-level analysis is insufficient, detection must also assess temporal coherence and narrative consistency across the entire sequence (Gao et al., 2024; Sharan et al., 2025).

Emerging models such as Veo 3.1 further complicate forensic analysis through improved audio-video synchronisation and narrative continuity, although peer-reviewed research on their detection remains limited (Wiedemer et al., 2025). In response, multimodal frameworks such as Cross-Modal Alignment and Distillation, and multi-agent fusion architectures, have been proposed to reconcile semantic synchronisation and modality-specific artefact cues across audio and video streams (Du et al., 2025; Zaman et al., 2025).

THE THREAT LANDSCAPE AND CRIMINAL JUSTICE IMPLICATIONS

The wide availability of generative AI tools has made the creation of visual and audio deepfakes accessible even to users with very little technical knowledge (Akhtar et al., 2024; Alanazi & Asif, 2024; Goyal et al., 2025). Pre-trained models and software for facial manipulation are now easily obtainable, and this reality amplifies concerns about potential misuse (A. Khan et al., 2025; Qureshi et al., 2024). Although the technology was first used for entertainment, its malicious applications are now evident and pose serious threats across political and personal sectors (Alanazi & Asif, 2024; Firc et al., 2023; Goyal et al., 2025; Hwang, 2020).

This technological shift arrives at a difficult moment, when facts play a smaller role in public life. A decline in trust towards traditionally respected sources, creates an audience that is susceptible to AI-generated disinformation (Helmus, 2022). Deepfakes worsen existing weaknesses in the digital world and present a specific challenge for digital forensics and the criminal justice system, where the integrity of evidence is crucial (Sandoval et al., 2024). The issues are complex and the resulting impact on the concept of truth is severe (Meckel & Steinacker, 2021; Sandoval et al., 2024).

The Evolving Threat Landscape

The dangers posed by deepfakes extend far beyond simple misinformation, covering a spectrum of high-impact criminal and social harms (Veerasamy & Pieterse, 2022). In the political sphere, deepfakes have emerged as a powerful instrument of information warfare, capable of manipulating public opinion, distorting democratic discourse, and eroding trust in institutions (Helmus, 2022; Meckel & Steinacker, 2021). Malicious actors can leverage synthetic means to destabilise elections or intensify social divisions (Pawelec, 2022). Notable incidents include a deepfake video of Ukrainian president Volodymyr Zelensky, seeming to surrender at the beginning of the Russian invasion (Harris, 2024a), and a robocall generated by AI impersonating Joe Biden, that urged voters to abstain from the New Hampshire primary (Amerini et al., 2025; Miotti & Wasil, 2024). These incidents threaten not only to mislead the public but also to compromise national security and democratic processes (Sandoval et al., 2024).

Concurrently, the financial sector faces a new generation of sophisticated social engineering attacks, frequently designated as "Phishing 2.0" (Mathew & Rodas, 2025). In the corporate sphere, attackers have used voice phishing to perpetrate major fraud. In one example, the CEO of a UK-based energy company was deceived by a phone call from someone sounding like his boss, resulting in a fraudulent wire transfer of 220.000 euros (Helmus, 2022; Sar et al., 2025). An even larger heist involved deceiving a bank manager into transferring 35 million dollars, by using a deepfake voice clone of a customer (Cinar, 2023; Mai et al., 2023). Beyond financial theft, deepfake technology facilitates corporate infiltration. There are reports of attackers using fake personas in video interviews, to secure remote work positions and gain insider access to sensible corporate information (Frankovits & Mirsky, 2023). Furthermore, the most prevalent and damaging use of this technology belongs in the personal scope, for the creation of non-consensual pornography (Leone, 2023; Shamsabadi et al., 2022). Reports indicate that the vast majority of online deepfake videos are pornographic, vastly targeting women (Sandoval et al., 2024). This phenomenon, which has expanded to include the exploitation of minors, is frequently used for blackmail, harassment and deep reputational damage (Miotti & Wasil, 2024).

Non-Consensual Intimate Images as a Criminal Justice Issue

Of the many ways in which deepfake technology has been used for harmful purposes, the creation and distribution of Non-Consensual Intimate Imagery (NCII) is arguably the most widespread and the most personally damaging. The scale of the problem is difficult to overstate. Studies consistently report that the vast majority of deepfake content circulating online is pornographic, with women bearing a disproportionate share of the harm (Miotti & Wasil, 2024; Sandoval et al., 2024; Umbach et al., 2024).

What sets deepfake NCII apart from earlier forms of image-based sexual abuse is a structural difference in how the material is produced. There is no need for the perpetrator to obtain genuine intimate imagery of the victim. Publicly available photographs, often taken from social media profiles, are sufficient to generate sexually explicit synthetic content. The implication is that the threat is no longer confined to individuals whose private images have been compromised. Anyone with an online presence is, in principle, vulnerable (Shamsabadi et al., 2022; Umbach et al., 2024; van der Sloot & Wagensveld, 2022).

The consequences for victims frequently extend beyond reputational harm and include severe psychological distress, withdrawal from social and professional life, and in a number of documented instances, coercion and blackmail (Hall et al., 2023; Miotti & Wasil, 2024; Pawelec, 2022).

Legislatures have responded to deepfake-related harms, though not uniformly (Chawki, 2024; Miotti & Wasil, 2024). In the United Kingdom, Parliament has tightened the regulation of intimate image abuse through several instruments. The Online Safety Act 2023 imposes safety duties on platforms regarding illegal content and, alongside amendments to the Sexual Offences Act 2003, criminalises the non-consensual sharing of fabricated sexual and intimate material. The proposed Crime and Policing Bill goes further, addressing not only dissemination but also the taking and recording of intimate images, reflecting a growing recognition that the wrong begins at the point of creation (Chawki et al., 2026).

In the United States, responses have been fragmented across jurisdictions. California's Assembly Bill 602 (AB 602) established a private right of action for victims of sexually explicit deepfakes, while states such as Virginia and New York have introduced comparable measures addressing non-consensual synthetic pornography and digital replicas, though the specifics differ considerably (Akhtar et al., 2024; Chawki, 2024; Helmus, 2022).

At the European level, the 2024 Directive on Combating Violence Against Women and Domestic Violence classifies non-consensual deepfakes as image-based violence, obliging Member States to criminalise their creation and distribution, although national transposition remains uneven (Chawki et al., 2026). The Artificial Intelligence Act complements this framework by imposing transparency obligations, requiring artificially generated or manipulated content to be clearly disclosed (Rijsbosch et al., 2025; Sousa Antunes et al., 2024).

The investigative challenges posed by NCII cases are considerable and, in certain respects, distinct from those of other deepfake-related offences. Attribution remains a persistent difficulty (Chawki, 2024; Chawki et al., 2026). The tools used to produce synthetic intimate content are widely available, often open-source, and tend to leave few traces that would allow an investigator to identify the creator with confidence (Alkhatib, 2025; Masood et al., 2021; Miotti & Wasil, 2024). Evidence preservation is complicated by the speed at which content can spread across platforms, often reaching thousands of users before any takedown procedure has been initiated (Miotti & Wasil, 2024; Qureshi et al., 2024).

Cross-jurisdictional issues compound the problem further. It is common for the perpetrator, the victim, and the platform hosting the material to be located in different countries, each governed by its own legal framework for handling such cases (Hall et al., 2023; Sousa Antunes et al., 2024; van der Sloot & Wagensveld, 2022).

Taken together, these factors highlight the need for forensic approaches that can both establish the synthetic nature of the imagery and satisfy the attribution standards required by criminal proceedings (Amerini et al., 2025; Nguyen-Le et al., 2025; Sar et al., 2025).

Implications for Forensic Science and Legal Admissibility

The proliferation of these threats poses new challenges to the criminal justice system, as they compromise the integrity of digital evidence and demand a critical revaluation of forensic techniques (Sandoval et al., 2024). A critical outcome of this situation is the "liar's dividend." In this situation, the existence of deepfake technology makes it easier for malicious actors to deny genuine and incriminating footage, by claiming it has been fabricated (Harris, 2024b; Helmus, 2022; Pawelec, 2022). As a result, trust in audiovisual evidence can weaken even when the material is authentic (Fallis, 2020; Harris, 2024a). This loss of confidence has direct implications for judicial proceedings. It places strain on the idea of the video record as a "silent witness," where footage is often treated as a neutral account of events rather than a statement from an interested party (Sandoval et al., 2024). In practical terms, it can reduce the perceived value and, in some cases, the admissibility of digital media more broadly, creating a significant challenge for systems that depend on evidence-based decision making (Harris, 2024b; van der Sloot & Wagensveld, 2022).

Law enforcement agencies in different areas of South Asia, like India and Pakistan, have seen deepfakes being used in extortion and political activities. There have been many such incidents that ended in arrests or filing of complaints, before it was realized that the images were manipulated (Pawelec, 2022). Investigators in the field often face what seems to be irrefutable facts but later realize that the facts were not reliable (Flattery & Miller, 2024; Leone, 2023).

These events demonstrate the logic of the "liar's dividend," whereby the authenticity of both the counterfeit and the authentic media is suspect (Harris, 2024b). Sandoval and colleagues suggest these incidents point to a gradual erosion of confidence in digital evidence across criminal justice systems (Pawelec, 2022; Sandoval et al., 2024).

Courts are beginning to acknowledge these issues with a degree of caution (Alanazi & Asif, 2024). Legal rulings increasingly recognise the harm caused by AI-manipulated media, regarding evidentiary integrity and procedural fairness (Sandoval et al., 2024; van der Sloot & Wagensveld, 2022). While the courts implicitly recognized the problem of authentication that exists today, by ordering the deletion of the content that has been manipulated, most of these judgments fall within the realm of civil law and thus cannot be compared directly (Sousa Antunes et al., 2024). However, these judgments represent an emerging judicial understanding, that deepfakes pose the possibility of challenging the assumptions that exist, regarding evidence that can be used in criminal courts (van der Sloot & Wagensveld, 2022).

All these examples serve to undermine the legitimacy of the audiovisual evidence as an effective witness (Sandoval et al., 2024; Sousa Antunes et al., 2024). That traditional view made sense when recording technologies were stable and manipulation required specialist skills, but it feels less convincing today (Delp et al., 2020; Fallis, 2020; A. Khan et al., 2025). Nevertheless, this perception appears to be unsustainable (Sandoval et al., 2024). There exists an emerging need for effective and technically sound methods of forensic analysis, that are also transparent within the legal framework. This remains an area of concern for the broader community of scholars, who work within the domain of forensic science (Amerini et al., 2025; Kraetzer et al., 2022; Mansoor & Iliev, 2025). While the cases do not address the matter conclusively, it becomes evident that the roots of the legitimacy of the domain of digital evidence are undergoing change (Sandoval et al., 2024; Sousa Antunes et al., 2024; van der Sloot & Wagensveld, 2022). Legal systems are only just beginning to understand the full implications.

Currently the judicial system remains poorly equipped to manage the technical and legal complexities of synthetic media. Forensic practitioners lack established standards or procedures for addressing deepfakes in court proceedings, creating significant difficulties in establishing attribution and building robust legal cases (Sandoval et al., 2024). Innovation in digital forensics is essential to counter the growing complexity of content generated by AI (Qureshi et al., 2024). Yet a noticeable gap separates academic research from practical application. Studies often focus on creating new detection algorithms, while investigators specifically need methods that are fully prepared for courtroom use (Kraetzer et al., 2022). Academic models frequently operate as "black boxes," but forensic tools must offer clear interpretability (Amerini et al., 2025; Hermosilla et al., 2025; Mansoor & Iliev, 2025). Expert witnesses need to articulate the investigative method and the factors driving the results in a way that judges or juries can understand (Hermosilla et al., 2025; Richmond et al., 2023). It is vital that these explanations remain accessible to legal practitioners who lack specialist technical training (Amerini et al., 2025; Khan et al., 2025).

Future research should therefore prioritise process-driven modelling that relies on transparency and standardisation as well as human oversight. This strategy ensures detection methods are not just technically accurate but also forensically sound and legally defensible during adversarial proceedings (Amerini et al., 2025; Hermosilla et al., 2025; Kraetzer et al., 2022).

Deepfake Detection in Active Investigations

To give a clearer picture of the operational reality facing forensic practitioners, it is useful to walk through a concrete scenario. A law enforcement agency receives a complaint involving what appears to be a video recording of a public official accepting a bribe. The recording has surfaced during a politically sensitive period and has already been shared widely across social media before anyone in authority has had the chance to assess whether it is genuine. The investigator's first task is straightforward in theory but difficult in practice: secure the original file, or at least the earliest version that can still be accessed, and document the chain of custody from the moment the file is acquired. Any gap in this record, no matter how small, risks undermining the evidentiary value of everything that follows (Alam & Altiparmak, 2024; Celebi et al., 2022).

From that point, the recording is subjected to a series of forensic examinations. Artefact-based analysis might reveal lighting inconsistencies, problems with facial geometry, or blending boundaries that are typical of face-swap manipulations (Hashmi et al., 2024; Le et al., 2025; Waseem et al., 2023). Statistical approaches could flag unusual frequency-domain signatures or the absence of the sensor noise patterns that a genuine camera would produce (Sar et al., 2025; Waseem et al., 2023). If the investigator uses deep learning classifiers, the confidence scores that come out of those models need to be placed in context, ideally with the help of explainability tools like SHAP or LIME, which can identify the regions or features that drove the classification decision (Alam & Altiparmak, 2024; Ge et al., 2024; Samek & Müller, 2019).

What matters just as much as the analysis itself is the documentation. Every analytical step, the tools used, the parameters chosen, the reasoning behind each conclusion, needs to be recorded in enough detail to support expert testimony that a judge or jury without any technical background can follow (Alam & Altiparmak, 2024; Hermosilla et al., 2025; Kraetzer et al., 2022; Singh & Devi, 2025).

The reality, at present, is that no widely adopted protocol exists for this kind of forensic work. Investigators are left to construct their own procedural frameworks on a case-by-case basis, which only reinforces the urgency of developing formalised forensic readiness guidelines for synthetic media (Kraetzer et al., 2022; Sandoval et al., 2024; Singh et al., 2022).

FORENSIC DETECTION METHODOLOGIES

The threats and forensic implications already explained underscore the need for reliable detection strategies (Abbasi et al., 2025; Verdoliva, 2020). As generative models continue to produce increasingly realistic content, and newer systems such as diffusion models and hybrid architectures defeat many established detectors, forensic techniques must evolve accordingly (Liu et al., 2025; Passos et al., 2024; Xu et al., 2025).

Benchmark datasets such as FaceForensics++ and initiatives such as the DeepFake Detection Challenge reflect this rapid pace (Goyal et al., 2025; Rössler et al., 2018, 2019). In the case of multimodal deepfakes that incorporate video, audio, and body movement, detection becomes particularly challenging, given that many existing mechanisms remain primarily oriented toward visual artefacts (Hashmi et al., 2024; Tan et al., 2025; Zaman et al., 2025). Forensic detection is generally organised into two broad families of approach: artefact-based methods and statistical or feature-based methods, which offer complementary capabilities (Waseem et al., 2023).

Artefact-Based Detection Methods

Forensic methods based on the investigation of artefacts, aim to recognize irregularities caused during the synthesis of the media contents (Luo & Wang, 2025). These irregularities are different from the ones caused by authentic camera sensors (Verdoliva, 2020). They are considered a forensic "fingerprint," which can be used to differentiate between synthetic and authentic contents (Marra et al., 2018; Say et al., 2025). For instance, the "fingerprints" of GANs can be detected through the artefacts left by upsampling and convolutional filtering (Passos et al., 2024; Q. Xu et al., 2025). It is often characterised by repeating patterns or subtle irregularities in image texture and frequency content. These irregularities are still noticeable even in the case of well-created synthetic images (Neves et al., 2020; Rössler et al., 2019). Additionally, synthetic pipelines often skip sensor-specific artefacts such as Photo-Response Non-Uniformity (PRNU) or demosaicing patterns, which typically appear in genuine camera outputs (Qian et al., 2025; Verdoliva, 2020).

Many deepfake systems also have difficulty replicating realistic light interactions, which leads to inconsistencies in shadows and highlights that offer forensic clues (Edwards et al., 2024; Guo et al., 2022). Boundary and blending artefacts represent another characteristic feature of synthetic content, because overlays frequently produce subtle colour mismatches, distorted edges or misaligned facial structures, especially under occlusion or motion (Du et al., 2025; Liu et al., 2025; Sar et al., 2025). This has been observed in datasets such as the DeepFake Detection Challenge (Dolhansky et al., 2020). Methods based on artefact analysis offer the benefit of interpretability, which makes them especially well-suited for legal and forensic applications where explanatory evidence becomes necessary (Hermosilla et al., 2025; Kraetzer et al., 2022; Qian et al., 2025).

Statistical and Feature-Based Detection

While artefact-based methods can provide clear and explainable indicators, they may be less reliable when manipulations are subtle or deliberately hidden (Bisht & Pooja, 2025; Frankovits & Mirsky, 2023). In these situations, statistical and feature based approaches can complement artefact analysis by examining the underlying properties of the content, rather than focusing only on visible defects (Marra et al., 2018; Waseem et al., 2023). Noise residual modelling, for example, isolates high frequency components to identify departures from typical sensor behaviour, and synthetic images may show unusual statistical distributions, that can be recognised using classical classifiers (Guarnera et al., 2020; Wang et al., 2023). Frequency domain analysis using techniques such as the Fast Fourier Transform, the Discrete Cosine Transform and wavelet transforms, has also been shown to reveal spectral patterns associated with GAN generated content (Luo & Wang, 2025; Sar et al., 2025; Wolter et al., 2022).

More recent work combines frequency domain masking with spatial interactions through Vision Transformers, which can improve generalisation to generative models, not seen during training (Luo & Wang, 2025; Say et al., 2025; Wolter et al., 2022). Texture and co-occurrence analysis methods such as

Local Binary Patterns, can highlight abnormal relationships between neighbouring pixels, adding further discriminatory power when identifying synthetic textures (Ramanaharan et al., 2025; Waseem et al., 2023; Zhao et al., 2021). In addition, features inspired by steganalysis, including Spatial Rich Models and the Subtractive Pixel Adjacency Matrix, were originally developed to detect hidden payloads, yet they remain effective for deepfake detection when paired with classifiers such as Support Vector Machines (Nguyen-Le et al., 2025; Rössler et al., 2019; Wang et al., 2023).

When paired effectively, statistical and feature-based techniques do a great deal to improve model robustness. It is best to view these as partners to artefact-based methods, rather than replacements (Guo et al., 2022; Lei et al., 2025; Nguyen-Le et al., 2025). Looking to the future, research is heavily pivoting towards a mix of frequency domain analysis, multimodal detection, and interpretable frameworks (Cao et al., 2025; Du et al., 2025). This combination is essential for ensuring digital evidence remains reliable, especially as synthetic media becomes the norm. Ultimately, these strategies provide a comprehensive toolkit for spotting deepfakes, reinforcing the value of evidence in contemporary investigations (Lee et al., 2025; Verdoliva, 2020).

Detection Tools Available to Law Enforcement

Academic research on deepfake detection has advanced at an impressive pace, yet the tools actually available to law enforcement officers and forensic analysts remain far more limited than the literature might suggest (Amerini et al., 2024; Chawki et al., 2026; Wang et al., 2025). A number of initiatives have attempted to bridge this gap, with varying degrees of success. In the United States, the Defense Advanced Research Projects Agency (DARPA) invested in two large-scale programmes focused on media forensics (Helmus, 2022).

The first, the Media Forensics (MediFor) programme, began in 2016 and aimed to develop algorithms for the automated integrity assessment of images and video (Helmus, 2022; Verdoliva, 2020). Its successor, the Semantic Forensics (SemaFor) programme, launched in 2020 and expanded the scope to semantic analysis across modalities, addressing not only the detection of manipulated content but also its attribution and characterisation. Following the conclusion of SemaFor, DARPA began transitioning the resulting technologies to government and commercial partners, while also launching open community research challenges to sustain detection research (Defense Advanced Research Projects Agency, 2025).

On the commercial side, a small number of tools have been developed with law enforcement needs in mind. Microsoft released Video Authenticator in 2020, which returns a confidence score indicating the likelihood that a given image or video has been manipulated (Celebi et al., 2022; Tipper et al., 2024). Intel's FakeCatcher takes a different approach, using photoplethysmography to analyse subtle blood-flow signals visible in facial video, on the assumption that synthetic faces do not reproduce these physiological cues faithfully (Kammari et al., 2025; Waseem et al., 2023). Both represent genuine progress, but their limitations are significant. Accuracy drops sharply once media have been compressed, re-encoded, or passed through multiple platforms, which is precisely how law enforcement typically encounters video evidence in real investigations (Masood et al., 2021; Tan et al., 2025; Tipper et al., 2024).

More broadly, the field of deepfake detection still lacks the standardised validation protocols and the level of explainability that forensic testimony in criminal proceedings demands (Alam & Altiparmak, 2024; Lyu, 2020; Masood et al., 2021; Qian et al., 2025). Efforts such as the European FF4ALL consortium and DARPA's open-source analytic catalogue are designed to address this gap, but the field remains some distance from a mature, forensically certified toolkit for routine law enforcement use (Amerini et al., 2025; Defense Advanced Research Projects Agency, 2025).

OPERATIONAL AND LEGAL CHALLENGES

The "Arms Race" and Operational Gaps

The detection landscape is defined by an accelerating asymmetry between generation and forensic analysis. Generative models, including GANs, diffusion models, and derivatives such as StyleGAN and SimSwap, continue to advance in realism, speed, and multimodal synthesis, while forensic tools struggle to maintain pace (Amerini et al., 2024; Goyal et al., 2025; Pei et al., 2024). Improvements in fidelity and multimodal synthesis frequently outpace detector adaptation (Du et al., 2025; Meckel & Steinacker, 2021). Compounding this challenge, platforms such as Facebook, Twitter, and TikTok process millions of uploads daily, and the routine re-encoding and compression that occurs during cross-platform sharing can eliminate the subtle traces on which detectors rely (Amerini et al., 2024; Lyu, 2020; Ramanaharan et al., 2025).

A related challenge concerns training data quality (Edwards et al., 2024). Detectors that achieve high accuracy on curated benchmarks frequently underperform when confronted with low-quality mobile recordings, re-shared and cropped content, or audio processed through consumer-grade filters. These routine degradations reveal a fundamental limitation: training on controlled, synthetic collections can produce models that are brittle in operational conditions (Amerini et al., 2024; Le et al., 2025; Nguyen-Le et al., 2025). The problem is compounded by the fact that many datasets are narrow, poorly documented, or restricted by proprietary access, preventing researchers from conducting meaningful comparative evaluations (Edwards et al., 2024; Le et al., 2025). A model that performs well in a published study may therefore face justified scepticism from prosecutors, forensic examiners, or security analysts confronted with real-world evidence (Kraetzer et al., 2022; Lyu, 2020; Qian et al., 2025).

The field remains caught in a form of practical paralysis because academic gains do not automatically translate into trustworthy tools for those making high-stakes decisions (Le et al., 2025; Qian et al., 2025; Wang et al., 2025). Achieving detectors that function beyond controlled settings requires two significant steps that are far from simple. The first is the creation of diverse and well-curated public datasets that truly reflect how media is captured, shared, and degraded in the wild. The second involves clearer standards for reproducibility, so that research teams can compare methods honestly and build upon the work of others. Without these changes, the divide between academic advances and operational reliability is likely to widen (Amerini et al., 2025; Rana et al., 2022).

The community can no longer afford to worry only about obvious fakes. Small, almost imperceptible edits, a shifted micro-expression, a barely off lip sync, a subtle audio splice, can do real damage to the credibility of digital evidence (Amerini et al., 2025; Hashmi et al., 2024; Sandoval et al., 2024). Such changes might go unnoticed when a clip is viewed on a mobile device, yet a court, a newsroom, or a security team could be misled by those very same inconsistencies (Sandoval et al., 2024). Because modern deepfakes stitch together visual, auditory, and biometric cues, detection that looks at only one stream is increasingly inadequate (Tan et al., 2025). Researchers argue for integrated, multimodal approaches that analyse audio, video, and physiological signals at once. In practice, this means systems that check whether lip movements match speech acoustics, whether micro-expressions align with vocal prosody, and whether biometric markers behave as expected (Amerini et al., 2024; Kammari et al., 2025; Masood et al., 2021).

A further complication arises from the adversarial nature of the threat itself. Malicious actors now deliberately design adversarial perturbations and anti-forensic techniques to exploit vulnerabilities in deep learning detectors (Nguyen-Le et al., 2025; Xu et al., 2025). Self-supervised and zero-shot methods, while promising for reducing dependence on labelled data, still struggle with the variability of real-world artefacts and can be defeated by novel manipulation techniques or simple re-encoding (Sar et al., 2025; Yan et al., 2025). Xu et al. (2025) demonstrate that generative attacks extend beyond forensic evasion, posing a systemic risk to Zero Trust Architecture by targeting identity governance and adaptive trust mechanisms. A convincing synthetic voice or forged biometric signal can compromise systems that rely on identity verification, thereby destabilising the trust infrastructure that underpins modern network security (Xu et al., 2025). These dynamics contribute to persistent rates of false positives and false negatives in operational detection settings (Amerini et al., 2024; Dolhansky et al., 2020; Harris, 2024a).

The opaque, "black box" nature of many deep learning models further compounds these operational gaps, creating an urgent need for explainable forensic approaches (Hermosilla et al., 2025; Samek & Müller, 2019).

Explainability and the Black Box Problem

There is currently a patchwork of governance tools, such as the EU AI Act, NIST's AI RMF, and ISO 42001, yet these various frameworks do not align neatly. Furthermore, none of them focus specifically on the unique problems that deepfakes create. The result is regulatory fragmentation, which leaves forensic teams and courts without clear guidance on what standards to follow and how to admit AI-derived evidence with confidence (Finch & Butt, 2025; Kyrychenko et al., 2026; D. Xu et al., 2025). The legal and ethical questions compound this uncertainty. Concerns about accountability, privacy, and the potential for surveillance or political misuse are not theoretical, they are practical challenges for institutions trying to respond responsibly (Amerini et al., 2025; Naitali et al., 2023; Sandoval et al., 2024).

At the same time, the so-called "liar's dividend" creates a significant challenge. This dynamic does not stop at the courthouse, as it seeps into public trust in platforms and institutions and makes the task of communicating forensic findings much harder (Fallis, 2020; Helmus, 2022; Pawelec, 2022). A prosecutor explaining why a clip is genuine, faces a very different conversation when jurors have already heard that almost anything can be fabricated (Feigenson & Carney, 2025; Sandoval et al., 2024). Deepfakes also exploit human vulnerabilities that technical fixes often ignore (Meckel & Steinacker, 2021; Sousa Antunes et al., 2024). Naitali et al. (2023) and D. Xu et al. (2025) warn that the real vulnerabilities are often human: insider threats, sophisticated social engineering, and the slow erosion of trust within organisations. These represent more than just technical failures, as they are fundamentally failures of people, process, and culture (Frankovits & Mirsky, 2023; Naitali et al., 2023; D. Xu et al., 2025). Forensic readiness, therefore, cannot be only about better detectors, it must include training, policy, and governance (Alkhatib, 2025; Babaei et al., 2025; Veerasamy & Pieterse, 2022).

That is where XAI comes in, at least partly. XAI offers a way to make AI-driven forensic outputs intelligible to judges, juries, and lawyers who are not machine learning specialists (Alam & Altiparmak, 2024; Richmond et al., 2023; Samek & Müller, 2019). "Black box" confidence scores rarely persuade a judge or jury (Akhtar et al., 2024; Amerini et al., 2025). Methods such as SHAP and LIME can, however, improve this situation by indicating which pixels, audio features, or temporal segments mattered, and flagging possible biases for lawyers and experts to examine (Alam & Altiparmak, 2024; Hermosilla et al., 2025; Qian et al., 2025).

A necessary caveat remains that while interpretability tools do help, they are not a cure-all (Alam & Altiparmak, 2024; Qian et al., 2025). People can misread the visualizations, lawyers or experts might overinterpret what a highlighted feature means, and bad actors can deliberately game explanations to create a misleading veneer of legitimacy (Alam & Altiparmak, 2024; Lakkaraju & Bastani, 2019; Qian et al., 2025). Courts will therefore need clear, agreed rules about how to treat these outputs alongside traditional forms of evidence, because a colourful chart or a feature ranking alone will not settle a legal question (Alam & Altiparmak, 2024; Delfino, 2025). When explanations are produced carefully, with full context and transparent limitations, they do offer something valuable, a way to translate model behaviour into terms that judges, jurors, and counsel can interrogate. When handled carefully and with clear limits, XAI can close the gap between technical detection and legal reasoning, helping judges and juries understand why a model flagged a clip and making AI-derived evidence easier to defend in court (Alam & Altiparmak, 2024; Amerini et al., 2025).

When opaque probability scores are translated into concrete, contestable features, such as a highlighted waveform indicating a suspicious audio splice or a recurring pixel pattern linked to synthesis, XAI can serve as an instrument for safeguarding due process. Provided that explanations are presented with appropriate caveats regarding uncertainty, such evidence may contribute to restoring confidence in decisions that rely on AI-assisted forensic analysis (Alam & Altiparmak, 2024; Mansoor & Iliev, 2025; Qian et al., 2025; Richmond et al., 2023).

Chain of Custody and Digital Evidence Handling

When deepfake detection is brought into a criminal investigation, a set of procedural concerns arises that goes well beyond the question of whether the detector itself is accurate. In traditional digital forensic practice, every piece of evidence must be documented from the point of acquisition through to its presentation in court (Alam & Altiparmak, 2024; Celebi et al., 2022; Meinen et al., 2025). The chain of custody for deepfake-related evidence needs to cover not just the suspect media file, but also the tools used during analysis, the procedures followed at each step, and the intermediate outputs that were produced along the way. A single gap in this documentation, however minor it may appear, can give the defence grounds to challenge the admissibility of the forensic conclusions entirely, regardless of how technically sound they might be (Alam & Altiparmak, 2024; Siegel et al., 2022; Singh & Devi, 2025).

Synthetic media creates a number of specific difficulties in this regard. The provenance of the suspect file is often uncertain from the outset, since content shared across social media platforms routinely undergoes re-encoding and metadata stripping, both of which obscure the file's origin and its processing history (Amerini et al., 2024; Lyu, 2020; Masood et al., 2021). An investigator therefore needs to document not only the file itself, but also the platform it came from, the date and method of acquisition, and whatever is known about any intermediary steps (Alam & Altiparmak, 2024; Celebi et al., 2022; Singh et al., 2022).

The detection tools are another area that demands careful attention. The software version, model architecture, the characteristics of the training data, and the specific parameters used during analysis all need to be recorded in enough detail for an independent party to verify the work (Siegel et al., 2022; Singh & Devi, 2025). When more than one method is applied in sequence, which is common in practice, the examiner must also explain why those particular methods were chosen, in what order they were run, and how any inconsistencies between their outputs were resolved (Hermosilla et al., 2025; Siegel et al., 2022; Verdoliva, 2020).

Process-driven forensic models, of the kind proposed by Kraetzer et al. (2022), offer a structured way to handle all of this, by defining standardised workflows that link each analytical decision to an evidentiary conclusion. Wider adoption of these frameworks would go a long way toward strengthening both the procedural integrity and the legal defensibility of deepfake forensic work (Kraetzer et al., 2022; Siegel et al., 2022).

Evidentiary Standards by Jurisdiction

The question of how courts should treat forensic evidence derived from AI-based detection tools does not have a straightforward answer, and the difficulty is compounded by the fact that different legal traditions approach the admissibility of expert testimony in quite different ways (Lorch et al., 2022; Richmond et al., 2023; Singh & Devi, 2025). In the United States, two standards dominate. The first is the Daubert standard, applied in federal courts and most state jurisdictions since the Supreme Court's 1993 decision in Daubert v. Merrell Dow Pharmaceuticals. Under Daubert, expert testimony must rest on methods that are testable, that have been subjected to peer review, that possess known or quantifiable error rates, and that enjoy general acceptance within the relevant scientific community (Delfino, 2025; Kraetzer et al., 2022; Singh & Devi, 2025).

A smaller number of states continue to apply the older Frye standard, which focuses solely on whether a methodology has gained general acceptance among practitioners in the field. Deepfake detection methods sit uncomfortably under both frameworks (Singh & Devi, 2025). The most effective current approaches tend to rely on deep learning architectures whose internal reasoning is difficult to articulate in terms that satisfy either standard, and independent validation studies that would permit a credible statement of error rates remain scarce (Alam & Altiparmak, 2024; Feigenson & Carney, 2025; Lyu, 2020).

In civil law jurisdictions the formal structure is different, though the practical concerns overlap considerably. Courts in the European Union, for instance, do not typically apply a Daubert-style gatekeeping test; instead, the presiding judge evaluates the scientific reliability and methodological transparency of expert evidence when determining the weight it should receive (Lorch et al., 2022; Rijsbosch et al., 2025; Sousa Antunes et al., 2024).

The EU AI Act has introduced transparency and risk-management obligations for high-risk AI systems, and these may, over time, come to bear on the presentation of AI-derived forensic conclusions in court, even though the Act does not treat deepfake detection as a separate regulatory category (Lorch et al., 2022; Rijsbosch et al., 2025). In India, where deepfake technology has already surfaced in extortion cases and political manipulation, questions of digital evidence authenticity have been addressed largely through the provisions of the Indian Evidence Act. Case law dealing specifically with AI-generated synthetic media, however, remains limited (Fallis, 2020; Sar et al., 2025; Singh & Devi, 2025).

A common thread runs through all of these jurisdictions: there is, at present, a lack of standardized validation protocols and no established set of forensic standards designed specifically for deepfake analysis (Lorch et al., 2022; Singh & Devi, 2025). Until comparable structures and AI-specific admissibility criteria are developed and adopted, the admission of AI-derived forensic evidence in criminal proceedings will continue to depend on ad hoc judicial assessments rather than on a stable and predictable evidentiary foundation (Delfino, 2025; van der Sloot & Wagensveld, 2022).

Legislation and Criminal Liability

As discussed in the context of NCII, several jurisdictions have begun to criminalise specific deepfake harms. The wider legislative picture, however, remains uneven, and criminal liability for the creation and distribution of synthetic media extends well beyond intimate imagery into areas such as electoral manipulation and financial fraud (Miotti & Wasil, 2024; Rosen, 2025).

In the United States, there is no comprehensive federal statute that addresses deepfakes directly, though the TAKE IT DOWN Act, signed into law in May 2025, marked the first nationwide attempt to tackle NCII by criminalising its distribution and requiring platforms to implement takedown procedures within 48 hours (Rosen, 2025). At the state level, a separate strand of legislative activity has targeted electoral manipulation. California's AB 730 prohibited the distribution of deepfake videos depicting political candidates within 60 days of an election, though that provision has since expired (Helmus, 2022; Tashman, 2021).

Texas Senate Bill 751 (SB 751) took a more durable approach, making it a Class A misdemeanour to create or distribute deepfake videos intended to influence elections, punishable by up to one year of imprisonment (Helmus, 2022; Rahman & Anggriawan, 2025). Other states have moved in different directions, with Virginia, California, and Georgia passing laws that specifically criminalize non-consensual deepfake pornography (Rosen, 2025; Umbach et al., 2024). The result, across the country, is an uneven patchwork in which the same behaviour may be heavily penalized in one state and entirely unregulated in another, leaving many victims without any avenue of redress (Miotti & Wasil, 2024; Rosen, 2025).

Within the European Union, the AI Act mandates transparency and the clear labelling of AI-generated content, such as deepfakes, but avoids explicitly classifying deceptive deepfakes as high-risk or criminalising their production and distribution (Gabor, 2025; Romero Moreno, 2024). The broader regulatory architecture, including the 2024 Directive on combating violence against women discussed earlier, is still being transposed into national law (Chawki et al., 2026). For practitioners and law enforcement working across borders, this fragmentation creates tangible difficulties, as the cross-border nature of the technology, divergent offence definitions, and varying procedural routes across jurisdictions severely complicate investigations, cooperation, and prosecutions (Akilal & Kechadi, 2025; Chawki et al., 2026; van der Sloot & Wagensveld, 2022).

POLICY AND FUTURE DIRECTIONS

Societal and Policy Considerations

Integrating real-time detection into social platforms could, in practice, stop many manipulated clips from going viral before they reach huge audiences (Amerini et al., 2025; A. Khan et al., 2025; Qureshi et al., 2024). Still, technology on its own will not be enough to accomplish this task. Legal and regulatory measures are needed alongside detection (Alanazi & Asif, 2024; Miotti & Wasil, 2024). Emerging frameworks such as the European Union AI Act and parallel international efforts are already pushing for greater transparency, traceability, and accountability around AI-generated content (Knott et al., 2024; Rijsbosch et al., 2025). Given this context, treating watermarking or provenance labels for AI-created images and videos as a legal obligation, rather than a voluntary measure makes sense (Neekhara et al., 2022). Platforms should be mandated to deploy detection, watermarking, and provenance systems to meet those obligations and to be held accountable when they fail to do so (Knott et al., 2024; Rijsbosch et al., 2025; van der Sloot & Wagensveld, 2022).

Global cooperation is crucial. Initiatives like FF4ALL show why shared datasets, common protocols, and coordinated international responses are useful, no single country can police this alone (Amerini et al., 2025). Public education also has a role to play. Individuals who are able to recognise indicators of manipulation, such as lip-sync inconsistencies or visual artefacts, are less likely to be misled, which in turn reduces the social impact of disinformation (Alkhatib, 2025; Naitali et al., 2023).

On the technical side, a few concrete paths are starting to look promising. Visible and invisible watermarking, provenance ledgers built on blockchain, and cryptographic stamps such as JPEG Trust all, offer practical ways to assert that an image or video has not been tampered with (Alkhatib, 2025; Amerini et al., 2024; Neekhara et al., 2022; Rijsbosch et al., 2025). There are also hardware-based approaches to lock in authenticity at the source, relying on secure camera pipelines and minute sensor noise fingerprints, that act as unique device signatures when a clip is recorded (Helmus, 2022; Qian et al., 2025).

These ideas are promising, yet they only work if camera makers, app developers, and platforms adopt common standards. It is equally necessary to account for the adaptive behaviour of malicious actors, who employ adversarial noise, fully synthetic personas, and anti-forensic techniques specifically designed to degrade or eliminate the traces on which detectors rely. Often enough, these tactics do not just confuse an algorithm, they fundamentally alter the detection landscape, requiring defenders to adapt continuously and in near real time (Amerini et al., 2024; Lyu, 2020; Sar et al., 2025). This dynamic creates an "arms race" in which detectors cannot remain static. They must learn continuously and operate in near real time if they are to keep pace (Akhtar et al., 2024; Amerini et al., 2024; Helmus, 2022).

Emerging Research Directions

Another practical lesson is that single-modality checks are becoming inadequate (Hashmi et al., 2024; Liu et al., 2025). A fake that merely appears plausible no longer represents the primary threat, because the most convincing examples also sound authentic and move in ways that align with human physiology (Amerini et al., 2025; Kammari et al., 2025). So, robustness increasingly means thinking multimodally, cross-checking lip motion against audio, comparing micro expressions with vocal prosody, or even looking for subtle pulse signals in the skin (Ahmed et al., 2024; Hashmi et al., 2024; Kammari et al., 2025).

Putting continuous learning pipelines together with multimodal frameworks and then subjecting them to rigorous benchmarks and standardized stress tests, will make forensic tools noticeably more resilient and better able to generalize beyond the lab (Amerini et al., 2024; Rana et al., 2022). In practice, that means systems that keep updating from fresh adversarial examples, cross check audio, video, and subtle physiological cues, like micro expressions or pulse signals, and are measured against messy, real-world datasets rather than pristine academic ones (Ahmed et al., 2024; Amerini et al., 2024; Kammari et al., 2025; Masood et al., 2021). That approach will not magically solve every problem, but it moves detectors from brittle prototypes toward operational tools, that can actually survive the kinds of degradation and trickery they encounter in the wild (Amerini et al., 2024; Patel et al., 2023; Zhang et al., 2025).

Such considerations suggest a simple yet uncomfortable truth that incremental technical patches will not be enough (Alkhatib, 2025; Le et al., 2025; Meckel & Steinacker, 2021). Progress requires an integrated strategy that is both explainable and internationally coordinated, combining evolving detection, provenance, and authentication protocols embedded into the processes of capture and distribution (Alkhatib, 2025; Amerini et al., 2025; Helmus, 2022; Knott et al., 2024; Le et al., 2025). This approach must be supported by legal requirements to enforce these practices, alongside public education to help individuals identify manipulation and shared standards to ensure that tools and evidence remain valid across borders. Only then does preserving trust in digital evidence become a realistic goal (Akhtar et al., 2024; Alkhatib, 2025; Miotti & Wasil, 2024; Qureshi et al., 2024; Sandoval et al., 2024).

Psychology of Deepfake Susceptibility

Whether a deepfake achieves its intended effect has as much to do with the people who encounter it as with the sophistication of the underlying technology (Hashmi et al., 2024; Hwang, 2020; Meckel & Steinacker, 2021). Psychology has long recognised that individuals do not process information, visual or auditory, in an entirely rational way. Cognitive shortcuts such as confirmation bias, anchoring, and the illusory truth effect shape how evidence is perceived and weighed, often without the observer being aware of the distortion (Hashmi et al., 2024; Meckel & Steinacker, 2021; Riesthuis & Woods, 2024).

In forensic contexts, these tendencies carry particular consequences (Delfino, 2025; Pfefferkorn, 2020). Jurors asked to determine whether a piece of audiovisual evidence is authentic or fabricated face a task for which most have no relevant background (Delfino, 2025; Singh & Devi, 2025). A juror who has read press coverage about convincing deepfakes may approach genuine footage with unwarranted scepticism, while another, less familiar with the technology, may accept a synthetic recording at face value. In either case, the verdict may turn less on the evidence itself than on prior assumptions about what AI can and cannot do (Delfino, 2025; Pfefferkorn, 2020).

The dynamics of social media compound the problem. Platform algorithms are designed to maximise engagement, not accuracy, which means that a sensational deepfake can circulate widely before any verification takes place (Germano et al., 2026; Meckel & Steinacker, 2021; Mubarak et al., 2023). Controlled experiments by Mai et al. (2023) have demonstrated that human listeners are unable to distinguish reliably between authentic and synthetic speech, a result with clear implications for the treatment of audio evidence in criminal proceedings. More broadly, Naitali et al. (2023) and Xu et al. (2025) argue that the deepfake threat is as much an institutional and human problem as it is a technical one.

Insider threats, social engineering, and the gradual erosion of organisational trust all create conditions in which synthetic media can cause serious harm, even when the quality of the manipulation is far from perfect (Harris, 2024a; Hwang, 2020; Naitali et al., 2023). What follows for the criminal justice system is that forensic readiness cannot be reduced to a question of better detection tools. Programmes aimed at strengthening the media literacy of investigators, prosecutors, judges, and jurors need to be treated as an integral part of the forensic infrastructure, rather than as a secondary concern (Akhtar et al., 2024; Delfino, 2025; Shoderu et al., 2024).

Hardware-Level Authentication

A different line of research tries to address the deepfake problem at the source, by building authentication directly into the process of capturing media. Every camera sensor produces characteristic noise patterns, known as PRNU, which are unique enough to serve as a kind of device fingerprint (Manisha et al., 2021; Qian et al., 2025). Secure capture pipelines can take advantage of this by embedding cryptographic signatures at the moment a recording is made, creating a verifiable link between the content and the device that produced it (Xie et al., 2022). Several standardisation efforts, including the Coalition for Content Provenance and Authenticity (C2PA) and the JPEG Trust initiative, aim to establish interoperable provenance frameworks that would allow content integrity to be tracked all the way from creation to distribution (Amerini et al., 2024; Helmus, 2022; Rijsbosch et al., 2025; Simmons & Winograd, 2024).

The appeal of this approach is obvious. Rather than trying to catch manipulations after the fact, hardware-based authentication would establish that a piece of content is genuine from the moment it is recorded. In practice, however, serious limitations remain. The whole scheme depends on widespread adoption by device manufacturers, which in turn requires standardisation agreements and commercial incentives that have not yet materialised in a meaningful way (Simmons & Winograd, 2024). There is also a more fundamental fragility. Once content leaves a controlled environment, the provenance chain can easily be broken. Re-encoding, screen recording, or redistribution through platforms that strip metadata will sever the link between the content and its authenticated origin, and these are precisely the operations that digital media routinely undergoes (Lyu, 2020; Masood et al., 2021; Rijsbosch et al., 2025). For this reason, hardware-level authentication is probably best understood not as a standalone solution, but as one layer within a broader strategy that also includes detection-based and policy-based approaches to content verification (Alkhatib, 2025; Amerini et al., 2025).

CONCLUSION

It is important to draw together the forensic difficulties that deepfakes present, moving across the historical origins of media manipulation, the generative technologies behind contemporary synthetic content, the threats now facing criminal justice systems, and the detection methods open to forensic practitioners. In doing so, strands that the existing literature often keeps apart have been connected, linking the technical side of deepfake creation and detection with the operational, legal, and human considerations that shape whether forensic conclusions can genuinely be trusted when they matter most.

History reminds us that manipulating visual media is hardly new. What is new, and strikingly so, is how quickly the tools have become more powerful, more accessible, and more convincing. GANs, diffusion models, and text-to-video systems such as Sora and Veo now allow people with minimal technical skill to produce synthetic material that neither human observers nor automated classifiers can reliably tell apart from genuine recordings. The consequences of this shift reach well beyond the spread of false information. They touch political stability, financial crime through cloned voices, and the mass production of NCII. Perhaps most corrosive of all is the so-called liar's dividend: the fact that the mere availability of deepfake technology gives individuals grounds to dismiss authentic evidence as fabricated, undermining judicial proceedings and eroding wider public confidence in digital media.

Detection considers both artefact-based and statistical approaches, each of which brings real strengths but also shared vulnerabilities. Results that appear persuasive under controlled laboratory conditions tend to deteriorate once practitioners encounter the material they actually work with: compressed files, re-encoded footage, and content that has passed through several rounds of sharing across platforms. The tools currently available to law enforcement are improving, not least through programmes such as DARPA's MediFor and SemaFor, yet they remain some way short of what routine forensic casework demands. Few offer the degree of explainability that courtroom testimony requires, and none has yet been tested against the kind of standardised benchmarks that would satisfy a judge as to their reliability.

The operational and legal obstacles are, in many respects, more formidable than the technical ones. For deepfake forensic evidence to carry weight, it must meet the procedural demands of chain-of-custody documentation, satisfy evidentiary thresholds that differ from one jurisdiction to another, and withstand adversarial challenge in court. At present, there are no dedicated forensic standards for synthetic media, which leaves practitioners without an agreed procedural framework and leaves courts without settled criteria for evaluating forensic conclusions. Legislative responses, for their part, remain uneven. Some jurisdictions have introduced targeted provisions; others have adapted existing law; many have nothing specific to deepfakes at all. The resulting patchwork poses real problems for cross-border investigations and for practitioners operating across different regulatory landscapes.

Looking forward, there are several directions that seem necessary if meaningful progress is to be made. Multimodal detection, which examines audio, video, and physiological signals in combination rather than in isolation, promises a more robust route to identifying synthetic content than approaches confined to a single modality. Hardware-level authentication, grounded in provenance standards such as C2PA, may help to establish the integrity of content from the moment it is captured, although how widely such standards will be adopted remains an open question. Just as important, the psychological dimensions of deepfake susceptibility, including the cognitive biases that influence how jurors, investigators, and the public interpret digital evidence, need to be built into forensic readiness frameworks rather than left as an afterthought. No single measure will be enough on its own. Safeguarding trust in digital evidence will call for a sustained and coordinated effort, one that brings together technical innovation, legal reform, institutional training, international cooperation, and a level of public understanding that most societies are only now beginning to develop.

AI DISCLOSURE STATEMENT

During the preparation of this chapter, the authors used Anthropic's Claude solely as a writing assistant to support the revision process. Specifically, the tool was utilized to restructure and reorganize the authors' existing content based on reviewer recommendations, improve the readability and formal register of selected passages, and identify inconsistencies in spelling and terminology. No AI tools were used to generate new scholarly content, ideas, or references. After using this tool, the authors carefully reviewed and edited the text, manually verified all references for accuracy and completeness, and assume full responsibility for the final published content.

REFERENCES

Abbasi, M., Váz, P., Silva, J., & Martins, P. (2025, January). Comprehensive evaluation of deepfake detection models: Accuracy, generalization, and resilience to adversarial attacks. *Applied Sciences (Basel, Switzerland), 15*(3), 1225. DOI: 10.3390/app15031225

Abdullah, S. M., Cheruvu, A., Kanchi, S., Chung, T., Gao, P., Jadliwala, M., & Viswanath, B. (2024, April 24). An analysis of recent advances in deepfake image detection in an evolving threat landscape (arXiv:2404.16212v1). *arXiv*. /arXiv.2404.16212DOI: 10.1109/SP54263.2024.00194

Acim, B., Boukhlif, M., Ouhnni, H., Kharmoum, N., & Ziti, S. (2025, October 1). A decade of deepfake research in the generative AI era, 2014–2024: A bibliometric analysis. *Publications / MDPI, 13*(4), 50. DOI: 10.3390/publications13040050

Ahmed, N., Ur, R., Badshah, A., Adeel, H., Tajammul, A., Daud, A., & Alsahfi, T. (2024). Visual deepfake detection: Review of techniques, tools, limitations, and future prospects. *IEEE Access : Practical Innovations, Open Solutions, 13*, 1923–1961. DOI: 10.1109/ACCESS.2024.3523288

Akhtar, Z., Pendyala, T. L., & Athmakuri, V. S. (2024, July 12). Video and audio deepfake datasets and open issues in deepfake technology: Being ahead of the curve. *Forensic Science, 4*(3), 289–377. DOI: 10.3390/forensicsci4030021

Akilal, A., & Kechadi, M.-T. (2025, July). Cloud digital forensic readiness: An open source approach to law enforcement request management (arXiv:2507.04174v1). *arXiv*. /arXiv.2507.04174DOI: 10.48550

Alam, S., & Altiparmak, Z. (2024, February). XAI-CF — Examining the role of explainable Artificial Intelligence in cyber forensics (arXiv:2402.02452). *arXiv*. /arXiv.2402.02452DOI: 10.2139/ssrn.4833246

Alamayreh, O., Fascella, C., Mandelli, S., Tondi, B., Bestagini, P., & Barni, M. (2024, August). Just dance: Detection of human body reenactment fake videos. *EURASIP Journal on Image and Video Processing, 2024*(1), 21. DOI: 10.1186/s13640-024-00635-2

Alanazi, S., & Asif, S. (2024, September). Exploring deepfake technology: Creation, consequences and countermeasures. *Human-Intelligent Systems Integration, 6*(1), 49–60. DOI: 10.1007/s42454-024-00054-8

Alkhatib, M. (2025, November 7). A multifaceted deepfake prevention framework integrating blockchain, post-quantum cryptography, hybrid watermarking, human oversight, and policy governance. *Computers, 14*(11), 488. DOI: 10.3390/computers14110488

Amerini, I., Barni, M., Battiato, S., Bestagini, P., Boato, G., Bonaventura, T. S., Bruni, V., Caldelli, R., Natale, F. D., Nicola, R. D., Guarnera, L., Mandelli, S., Marcialis, G. L., Micheletto, M., Montibeller, A., Orru', G., Ortis, A., Perazzo, P., Puglisi, G., . . . Vitulano, D. (2024. August). Deepfake media forensics: State of the art and challenges ahead (arXiv:2408.00388). *arXiv*. /arXiv.2408.00388DOI: 10.48550

Amerini, I., Barni, M., Battiato, S., Bestagini, P., Boato, G., Bruni, V., Caldelli, R., De Natale, F., De Nicola, R., Guarnera, L., Mandelli, S., Majid, T., Marcialis, G. L., Micheletto, M., Montibeller, A., Orrù, G., Ortis, A., Perazzo, P., Puglisi, G., & Vitulano, D. (2025, February). Deepfake media forensics: Status and future challenges. *Journal of Imaging, 11*(3), 73. DOI: 10.3390/jimaging11030073 PMID: 40137185

Babaei, R., Cheng, S., Duan, R., & Zhao, S. (2025). Generative Artificial Intelligence and the evolving challenge of deepfake detection: A systematic analysis. *Journal of Sensor and Actuator Networks, 14*(1), 17. DOI: 10.3390/jsan14010017

Batori, Z. (2018). Photographic manipulation and photographic deception. *Aisthesis. Pratiche, Linguaggi e Saperi Dell'estetico, 11*(2), 35–47. DOI: 10.13128/Aisthesis-23863

Bisht, U. & Pooja. (2025, July-December). Evolving deepfake technologies: Advancements, detection techniques, and societal impact. *Don Bosco Institute of Technology Delhi Journal of Research, 1*(2), 38–43. https://acspublisher.com/journals/index.php/dbitdjr/article/view/20696

Cao, H., Mci, Q., Li, Z., Li, Y., Mcng, Z., Zhang, Y., Li, C., Zhang, Z., Ding, X., Wang, Y., Lyu, J., & Wu, F. (2025, November 28). REVEAL: Reasoning-enhanced forensic evidence analysis for explainable AI-generated image detection (arXiv:2511.23158). *arXiv.* /arXiv.2511.23158DOI: 10.48550

Celebi, N., Liu, Q., & Karatoprak, M. (2022, May). A survey of deep fake detection for trial courts. *Artificial Intelligence and Applications (Commerce, Calif.)*, •••, 227–238. DOI: 10.5121/csit.2022.120919

Chawki, M. (2024). Navigating legal challenges of deepfakes in the American context: A call to action. *Cogent Engineering, 11*(1), 2320971. DOI: 10.1080/23311916.2024.2320971

Chawki, M., Basu, S., & Choi, K.-S. (2026, February). Deepfake sextortion in England, Wales and Northern Ireland: A doctrinal and regulatory analysis. *Laws, 15*(1), 11. DOI: 10.3390/laws15010011

Cinar, B. (2023, October 25). Deepfakes in cyber warfare: Threats, detection, techniques and countermeasures. *Asian Journal of Research in Computer Science, 16*(4), 178–193. DOI: 10.9734/ajrcos/2023/v16i4381

de Almeida, C. M. T., & Boni, P. C. (2006, December). A ética no fotojornalismo da era digital. *Discursos Fotograficos, 2*(2), 11–42. DOI: 10.5433/1984-7939.2006v2n2p11

de Cassai, A., Dost, B., Tulgar, S., & Boscolo, A. (2025, August). Methodological standards for conducting high-quality systematic reviews. *Biology (Basel), 14*(8), 973. DOI: 10.3390/biology14080973 PMID: 40906182

Defense Advanced Research Projects Agency. (2025, March 5). *Furthering deepfake defenses.* https://www.darpa.mil/news/2025/furthering-deepfake-defenses

Delfino, R. (2025). Deepfakes on trial 2.0: A revised proposal for a new Federal rule of evidence to mitigate deepfake deceptions in court. *Loyola Law School, Los Angeles. Legal Studies*, •••, 2025–10. DOI: 10.2139/ssrn.5188767

Delp, E., Huang, J., Memon, N., Rocha, A., Turek, M., & Verdoliva, L. (2020). Editorial: Media authentication and forensics—New solutions and research opportunities. *IEEE Journal of Selected Topics in Signal Processing, 14*(5), 906–909. DOI: 10.1109/JSTSP.2020.3011085

Dolhansky, B., Bitton, J., Pflaum, B., Lu, J., Howes, R., Wang, M., & Ferrer, C. C. (2020, October). The DeepFake Detection Challenge (DFDC) dataset (arXiv:2006.07397). *arXiv.* /arXiv.2006.07397DOI: 10.48550

Du, Y., Wang, Z., Luo, Y., Piao, C., Yan, Z., Li, H., & Yuan, L. (2025, May). CAD: A general multimodal framework for video deepfake detection via cross-modal alignment and distillation (arXiv:2505.15233). *arXiv*. /arXiv.2505.15233DOI: 10.48550

Edwards, P., Nebel, J.-C., Greenhill, D., & Liang, X. (2024, October). A Review of Deepfake Techniques: Architecture, Detection, and Datasets. *IEEE Access : Practical Innovations, Open Solutions, 12*, 154718–154742. DOI: 10.1109/ACCESS.2024.3477257

Fallis, D. (2020). The epistemic threat of deepfakes. *Philosophy & Technology, 34*(4), 623–643. DOI: 10.1007/s13347-020-00419-2 PMID: 32837868

Feigenson, N., & Carney, B. (2025). Generative AI as courtroom evidence: A practical guide. *Mitchell Hamline Law Review, 52*(1), 3. https://open.mitchellhamline.edu/mhlr/vol52/iss1/3

Finch, W. W., & Butt, M. (2025, November 17). Gaps in AI-compliant complementary governance frameworks' suitability (for low-capacity actors), and structural asymmetries (in the compliance ecosystem)—A systematic review. *Journal of Cybersecurity and Privacy, 5*(4), 101. DOI: 10.3390/jcp5040101

Firc, A., Malinka, K., & Hanáček, P. (2023, April). Deepfakes as a threat to a speaker and facial recognition: An overview of tools and attack vectors. *Heliyon, 9*(4), e15090. DOI: 10.1016/j.heliyon.2023.e15090 PMID: 37089334

Flattery, T., & Miller, C. B. (2024, October). Deepfakes and dishonesty. *Philosophy & Technology, 37*(4), 120. DOI: 10.1007/s13347-024-00812-1

Frankovits, G., & Mirsky, Y. (2023, June). Discussion paper: The threat of real time deepfakes (arXiv:2306.02487v1). *arXiv*. /arXiv.2306.02487DOI: 10.1145/3595353.3595881

Gabor, D. (2025, December 22). Labelling deepfakes in terms of EU law: The AI Act and beyond. *Ruch Prawniczy, Ekonomiczny i Socjologiczny, 87*(4), 139–160. DOI: 10.14746/rpeis.2025.87.4.08

Gao, Y., Wang, X., Zhang, Y., Zeng, P., & Ma, Y. (2024, August). Temporal feature prediction in audio–visual deepfake detection. *Electronics (Basel), 13*(17), 3433. DOI: 10.3390/electronics13173433

Garcia, J. M. S. (2025, March 6). Exploring deepfakes and effective prevention strategies: A critical review. *Psychology and Education: A Multidisciplinary Journal, 33*(1), 93-96.. DOI: 10.2139/ssrn.5168131

Ge, W., Patino, J., Todisco, M., & Evans, N. (2024, April 26). Explaining deep learning models for spoofing and deepfake detection with SHapley Additive exPlanations (arXiv:2110.03309). *arXiv*. /arXiv.2110.03309DOI: 10.48550

Germano, F., Gomez, V., & Sobbrio, F. (2026, March). Ranking for engagement: How social media algorithms fuel misinformation and polarization. *Journal of Public Economics, 255*, 105589. DOI: 10.1016/j.jpubeco.2026.105589

Goodfellow, I. J., Pouget-Abadie, J., Mirza, M., Xu, B., Warde-Farley, D., Ozair, S., Courville, A., & Bengio, Y. (2014, June 10). Generative adversarial networks (arXiv:1406.2661). *arXiv*. /arXiv.1406.2661DOI: 10.48550

Goyal, H., Wajid, M. S., Wajid, M. A., Khanday, A. M. U. D., Neshat, M., & Gandomi, A. (2025, January 2). State-of-the-art AI-based learning approaches for deepfake generation and detection, analyzing opportunities, threading through pros, cons, and future pospects (arXiv:2501.01029). *arXiv*. /arXiv.2501.01029DOI: 10.48550

Guarnera, L., Giudice, O., & Battiato, S. (200, September). Fighting deepfake by exposing the convolutional traces on images. *IEEE Access, 8*, 165085–165098. DOI: 10.1109/ACCESS.2020.3023037

Guo, Z., Yang, G., Chen, J., & Sun, X. (2022). Exposing deepfake face forgeries with guided residuals (arXiv:2205.00753). *arXiv*. /arXiv.2205.00753DOI: 10.48550

Hall, M., Hearn, J., & Lewis, R. (2023, March 11). Image-based sexual abuse: Online gender-sexual violations. *Encyclopedia, 3*(1), 327–339. DOI: 10.3390/encyclopedia3010020

Harris, K. R. (2024a). AI or your lying eyes: Some shortcomings of artificially intelligent deepfake detectors. *Philosophy & Technology, 37*(1), 7. DOI: 10.1007/s13347-024-00700-8

Harris, K. R. (2024b). Synthetic media detection, the wheel, and the burden of proof. *Philosophy & Technology, 37*(4), 131. DOI: 10.1007/s13347-024-00821-0

Hashmi, A., Shahzad, S. A., Lin, C.-W., Tsao, Y., & Wang, H.-M. (2024, November 12). Understanding audiovisual deepfake detection: Techniques, challenges, human factors and perceptual insights (arXiv:2411.07650). *arXiv*. /arXiv.2411.07650DOI: 10.48550

Hausken, L. (2024, December 11). Untangling photographic manipulation: Exploring a dual concept and its societal implications. *Journalism and Media, 5*(4), 1881–1900. DOI: 10.3390/journalmedia5040114

Helmus, T. C. (2022, July 6). *Artificial Intelligence, deepfakes, and disinformation: A primer.* RAND Corporation. DOI: 10.7249/PEA1043-1

Hermosilla, P., Berríos, S., & Allende-Cid, H. (2025, June 29). Explainable AI for forensic analysis: A comparative study of SHAP and LIME in intrusion detection models. *Applied Sciences (Basel, Switzerland), 15*(13), 7329. DOI: 10.3390/app15137329

Ho, J., Jain, A., & Abbeel, P. (2020). Denoising diffusion probabilistic models (arXiv:2006.11239). *arXiv*. /arXiv.2006.11239DOI: 10.48550

Hwang, T. (2020, July). *Deepfakes: A grounded threat assessment.* Center for Security and Emerging Technology. DOI: 10.51593/20190030

Kammari, K. S., Khanna, M., Annambhotla, Y. L., Anuradha, K. D., Namrata, P. N. S., Nagaraja, K. V., Smitha, T. V., Jan, T., & Naik, G. R. (2025, October 30). A comprehensive review of deepfake detection techniques utilizing remote photoplethysmography. *IEEE Access : Practical Innovations, Open Solutions, 13*, 183557–183578. DOI: 10.1109/ACCESS.2025.3624284

Karras, T., Laine, S., Aittala, M., Hellsten, J., Lehtinen, J., & Aila, T. (2020, June). Analyzing and improving the image quality of StyleGAN. [Conference paper]. *2020 IEEE/CVF Conference on Computer Vision and Pattern Recognition (CVPR)* (pp. 8107–8116). DOI: 10.1109/CVPR42600.2020.00813

Kaur, A., Hoshyar, A. N., Saikrishna, V., Firmin, S., & Xia, F. (2024, May). Deepfake video detection: Challenges and opportunities. *Artificial Intelligence Review, 57*(6), 159. DOI: 10.1007/s10462-024-10810-6

Khan, A., Laghari, A., Inam, S., Ullah, S., Shahzad, M., & Syed, D. (2025, April). A survey on multimedia-enabled deepfake detection: State-of-the-art tools and techniques, emerging trends, current challenges & limitations, and future directions. *Discover Computing, 28*(1), 48. DOI: 10.1007/s10791-025-09550-0

Khan, N., Nguyen, T., Bermak, A., & Khalil, I. (2025, July). Unmasking synthetic realities in generative AI: A comprehensive review of adversarially robust deepfake detection systems (arXiv:2507.21157). *arXiv.* /arXiv.2507.21157DOI: 10.48550

Kim, H., Garrido, P., Tewari, A., Xu, W., Thies, J., Nießner, M., Pérez, P., Richardt, C., Zollhöfer, M., & Theobalt, C. (2018, May). Deep video portraits (arXiv:1805.11714). *arXiv.* /arXiv.1805.11714DOI: 10.48550

Knott, A., Pedreschi, D., Jitsuzumi, T., Leavy, S., Eyers, D., Chakraborti, T., Trotman, A., Sundareswaran, S., Baeza-Yates, R., Biecek, P., Weller, A., Teal, P. D., Basu, S., Haklidir, M., Morini, V., Russell, S., & Bengio, Y. (2024, September). AI content detection in the emerging information ecosystem: New obligations for media and tech companies. *Ethics and Information Technology, 26*(4), 63. DOI: 10.1007/s10676-024-09795-1

Kraetzer, C., Siegel, D., Seidlitz, S., & Dittmann, J. (2022, April 19). Process-driven modelling of media forensic investigations-considerations on the example of DeepFake detection. *Sensors (Basel), 22*(9), 3137. DOI: 10.3390/s22093137 PMID: 35590827

Kyrychenko, M., Mudryi, M., & Chaklosh, M. (2026, January 18). Global AI governance overview: Understanding regulatory requirements across global jurisdictions (arXiv:2512.02046). *arXiv.* /arXiv.2512.02046DOI: 10.48550

Lakkaraju, H., & Bastani, O. (2019, November). "How do I fool you?": Manipulating user trust via misleading black box explanations (arXiv:1911.06473). *arXiv.* /arXiv.1911.06473DOI: 10.48550

Le, B. M., Kim, J., Woo, S. S., Moore, K., Abuadbba, A., & Tariq, S. (2025, March 2). SoK: Systematization and benchmarking of deepfake detectors in a unified framework (arXiv:2401.04364). *arXiv.* /arXiv.2401.04364DOI: 10.1109/EuroSP63326.2025.00055

Lee, R. W., Jun, T. J., Lee, J.-M., Cho, S. I., Park, H. J., & Suh, J. (2025, December). Vulnerability of Large Language Models to prompt injection when providing medical advice. *JAMA Network Open, 8*(12), e2549963. DOI: 10.1001/jamanetworkopen.2025.49963 PMID: 41632124

Lei, S., Song, J., Feng, F., Yan, Z., & Wang, A. (2025, June 10). Deepfake face detection and adversarial attack defense method based on multi-feature decision fusion. *Applied Sciences (Basel, Switzerland), 15*(12), 6588. DOI: 10.3390/app15126588

Leone, M. (2023, January 19). The spiral of digital falsehood in deepfakes. *International Journal for the Semiotics of Law - Revue Internationale de Sémiotique Juridique, 36*(2), 385–405. DOI: 10.1007/s11196-023-09970-5

Liu, P., Tao, Q., & Zhou, J. T. (2025, April 3). Evolving from single-modal to multi-modal facial deepfake detection: Progress and challenges (arXiv:2406.06965). *arXiv*. /arXiv.2406.06965DOI: 10.48550

Liu, Q., Shi, P., Tsai, Y.-Y., Mao, C., & Yang, J. (2024, June 13). Turns out I'm not real: Towards robust detection of AI-generated videos (arXiv:2406.09601). *arXiv*. /arXiv.2406.09601DOI: 10.48550

Lorch, B., Scheler, N., & Riess, C. (2022, March 1). Compliance challenges in forensic image analysis under the Artificial Intelligence Act (arXiv:2203.00469). *arXiv*. /arXiv.2203.00469DOI: 10.23919/EUSIPCO55093.2022.9909723

Luo, X., & Wang, Y. (2025, March 25). Frequency-domain masking and spatial interaction for generalizable deepfake detection. *Electronics (Basel)*, *14*(7), 1302. DOI: 10.3390/electronics14071302

Lyu, S. (2020, March 11). DeepFake detection: Current challenges and next steps (arXiv:2003.09234). *arXiv*. /arXiv.2003.09234DOI: 10.1109/ICMEW46912.2020.9105991

Mai, K. T., Bray, S., Davies, T., & Griffin, L. D. (2023, August 2). Warning: Humans cannot reliably detect speech deepfakes. *PLoS One*, *18*(8), e0285333. DOI: 10.1371/journal.pone.0285333 PMID: 37531336

Manisha, L. C.-T., Lin, X., & Kotegar, K. A. (2021, November 3). Beyond PRNU: Learning robust device-specific fingerprint for source camera identification (arXiv:2111.02144). *arXiv*. /arXiv.2111.02144DOI: 10.48550

Mansoor, N., & Iliev, A. I. (2025, January 12). Explainable AI for DeepFake detection. *Applied Sciences (Basel, Switzerland)*, *15*(2), 725. Advance online publication. DOI: 10.3390/app15020725

Marra, F., Gragnaniello, D., Verdoliva, L., & Poggi, G. (2018, December 31). Do GANs leave artificial fingerprints? (arXiv:1812.11842). *arXiv*. /arXiv.1812.11842DOI: 10.48550

Masood, M., Nawaz, M., Malik, K. M., Javed, A., & Irtaza, A. (2021). Deepfakes generation and detection: State-of-the-art, open challenges, countermeasures, and way forward (arXiv:2103.00484). *arXiv*. /arXiv.2103.00484DOI: 10.48550

Mathew, A., & Rodas, F. (2025, February). Phishing 2.0: Leveraging cyber threat intelligence to combat deepfake-enhanced social engineering. *International Journal of Innovative Research in Science, Engineering and Technology*, *14*(2), 1016–1022. DOI: 10.15680/IJIRSET.2025.1402003

Meckel, M., & Steinacker, L. (2021). Hybrid reality: The rise of deepfakes and diverging truths. *Morals & Machines*, *1*(1), 10–21. DOI: 10.5771/2747-5182-2021-1-10

Meinen, L., Schomäcker, A., Wiedemann, S., Hartmann, M., Speith, T., Kästner, L., Kühl, N., & Rückert, C. (2025, July 4). Deepfakes in criminal investigations: Interdisciplinary research directions for CMC research (arXiv:2507.03457). *arXiv*. /arXiv.2507.03457DOI: 10.48550

Miotti, A., & Wasil, A. (2024, February). Combatting deepfakes: Policies to address national security threats and rights violations (arXiv:2402.09581). *arXiv*. /arXiv.2402.09581DOI: 10.48550

Mubarak, R., Alsboui, T., Alshaikh, O., Inuwa-Dutse, I., Khan, S., & Parkinson, S. (2023, December). A survey on the detection and impacts of deepfakes in visual, audio, and textual formats. *IEEE Access : Practical Innovations, Open Solutions*, *11*, 144497–144529. DOI: 10.1109/ACCESS.2023.3344653

Munhoz, P. (2014, June 25). Manipulation, professional practices and deontology in informational photography: Identifying new parameters. *Brazilian Journalism Research, 10*(1), 210–237. DOI: 10.25200/BJR.v10n1.2014.632

Naitali, A., Ridouani, M., Salahdine, F., & Kaabouch, N. (2023, October 22). Deepfake attacks: Generation, detection, datasets, challenges, and research directions. *Computers, 12*(10), 216. DOI: 10.3390/computers12100216

Neekhara, P., Hussain, S., Zhang, X., Huang, K., McAuley, J., & Koushanfar, F. (2022, April 5). FaceSigns: Semi-fragile neural watermarks for media authentication and countering deepfakes (arXiv:2204.01960). *arXiv*. /arXiv.2204.01960DOI: 10.48550

Neves, J. C., Tolosana, R., Vera-Rodriguez, R., Lopes, V., Proença, H., & Fierrez, J. (2020, July). GANprintR: Improved fakes and evaluation of the state of the art in face manipulation detection. *IEEE Journal of Selected Topics in Signal Processing, 14*(5), 1038–1048. DOI: 10.1109/JSTSP.2020.3007250

Nguyen-Le, H.-H., Tran, V.-T., Nguyen, D.-T., & Le-Khac, N.-A. (2025, April 5). Passive deepfake detection across multi-modalities: A comprehensive survey (arXiv:2411.17911). *arXiv*. /arXiv.2411.17911DOI: 10.48550

Passas, I. (2024, June 19). Bibliometric analysis: The main steps. *Encyclopedia, 4*(2), 1014–1025. DOI: 10.3390/encyclopedia4020065

Passos, L. A., Jodas, D., Costa, K. A. P., Souza Júnior, L. A., Rodrigues, D., Ser, J. D., Camacho, D., & Papa, J. P. (2024, February 22). A review of deep learning-based approaches for deepfake content detection. *Expert Systems: International Journal of Knowledge Engineering and Neural Networks, 41*(8), e13570. DOI: 10.1111/exsy.13570

Patel, Y., Tanwar, S., Gupta, R., Bhattacharya, P., Davidson, I. E., Nyameko, R., Aluvala, S., & Vimal, V. (2023, December). Deepfake generation and detection: Case study and challenges. *IEEE Access : Practical Innovations, Open Solutions, 11*, 143296–143323. DOI: 10.1109/ACCESS.2023.3342107

Pawelec, M. (2022, September). Deepfakes and democracy (theory): How synthetic audio-visual media for disinformation and hate speech threaten core democratic functions. *Digital Society : Ethics, Socio-Legal and Governance of Digital Technology, 1*(2), 19. DOI: 10.1007/s44206-022-00010-6 PMID: 36097613

Pei, G., Zhang, J., Hu, M., Zhang, Z., Wang, C., Wu, Y., Zhai, G., Yang, J., & Tao, D. (2024, March). Deepfake generation and detection: A benchmark and survey (arXiv:2403.17881). *arXiv*. /arXiv.2403.17881DOI: 10.48550

Peixoto, I. de M. (2014, December). Arte da Manipulação: As interações entre fotografia e arte na era digital. [Conference proceedings]. *XVII Conference of the Iberoamerican Society of Digital Graphics - SIGraDi: Knowledge-based Design, 1*(7), 655–658. DOI: 10.5151/despro-sigradi2013-0129

Pfefferkorn, R. (2020, October 1). 'Deepfakes' in the courtroom. *The Boston University Public Interest Law Journal, 29*(2), 245–276. https://ssrn.com/abstract=4321140

Qian, H., Xia, L., Ge, R., Fan, Y., Wang, Q., & Jing, Z. (2025, September 25). From black boxes to glass boxes: Explainable AI for trustworthy deepfake forensics. *Cryptography*, *9*(4), 61. DOI: 10.3390/cryptography9040061

Qureshi, S. M., Saeed, A., Almotiri, S. H., Ahmad, F., & Al Ghamdi, M. A. (2024, May 27). Deepfake forensics: A survey of digital forensic methods for multimodal deepfake identification on social media. *PeerJ. Computer Science*, *10*, e2037. DOI: 10.7717/peerj-cs.2037 PMID: 38855214

Rahman, R. A., & Anggriawan, R. (2025, June). Deepfake and election crimes: Comparative perspectives from Indonesia, India, Pakistan, and the U.S. *Indonesian Comparative. Law Review*, *7*(2), 132–146.

Ramanaharan, R., Guruge, D. B., & Agbinya, J. I. (2025, December). DeepFake video detection: Insights into model generalisation — A systematic review. *Data and Information Management*, *9*(4), 100099. DOI: 10.1016/j.dim.2025.100099

Rana, M., Nobi, M. N., Murali, B., & Sung, A. H. (2022, February 24). Deepfake detection: A systematic literature review. *IEEE Access : Practical Innovations, Open Solutions*, *10*, 25494–25513. DOI: 10.1109/ACCESS.2022.3154404

Richmond, K. M., Muddamsetty, S. M., Gammeltoft-Hansen, T., Olsen, H. P., & Moeslund, T. B. (2023, December 19). Explainable AI and law: An evidential survey. *Digital Society : Ethics, Socio-Legal and Governance ofDigital Technology*, *3*(1), 1. Advance online publication. DOI: 10.1007/s44206-023-00081-z

Riesthuis, P., & Woods, J. (2024, June 10). "That's just like, your opinion, man": The illusory truth effect on opinions. *Psychological Research*, *88*(1), 284–306. DOI: 10.1007/s00426-023-01845-5 PMID: 37300704

Rijsbosch, B., van Dijck, G., & Kollnig, K. (2025). Adoption of watermarking for generative AI systems in practice and implications under the new EU AI Act (arXiv:2503.18156). *arXiv*. /arXiv.2503.18156DOI: 10.48550

Romero Moreno, F. (2024). Generative AI and deepfakes: A human rights approach to tackling harmful content. *International Review of Law Computers & Technology*, *38*(3), 297–326. DOI: 10.1080/13600869.2024.2324540

Rosen, L. Z. (2025). Deepfakes and intimate partner violence: The TAKE IT DOWN Act and other proposed federal legislation. *NYU Annual Survey of American Law*. https://annualsurveyofamericanlaw.org/wp-content/uploads/2025/07/02_Note-Rosen_FINAL-1.pdf

Rössler, A., Cozzolino, D., Verdoliva, L., Riess, C., Thies, J., & Nießner, M. (2018, March 24). FaceForensics: A large-scale video dataset for forgery detection in human faces (arXiv:1803.09179). *arXiv*. /arXiv.1803.09179DOI: 10.48550

Rössler, A., Cozzolino, D., Verdoliva, L., Riess, C., Thies, J., & Nießner, M. (2019, August 26). FaceForensics++: Learning to detect manipulated facial images (arXiv:1901.08971). *arXiv*. /arXiv.1901.08971DOI: 10.1109/ICCV.2019.00009

Samek, W., & Müller, K.-R. (2019). Towards explainable Artificial Intelligence. In W. Samek, G. Montavon, A. Vedaldi, L. Hansen, & K.-R. Müller (Eds.), *Explainable AI: Interpreting, explaining and visualizing deep learning* (pp. 5-22). Spring Nature. DOI: 10.1007/978-3-030-28954-6_1

Sandoval, M.-P., de Almeida Vau, M., Solaas, J., & Rodrigues, L. (2024, November). Threat of deepfakes to the criminal justice system: A systematic review. *Crime Science, 13*(1), 41. DOI: 10.1186/s40163-024-00239-1

Sar, A., Roy, S., Choudhury, T., & Abraham, A. (2025, August 28). Zero-shot visual deepfake detection: Can AI predict and prevent fake content before it's created? *Foundations and Trends in Signal Processing, 19*(3), 212–370. DOI: 10.1561/2000000136

Say, T., Alkan, M., & Kocak, A. (2025, January 17). Advancing GAN deepfake detection: Mixed datasets and comprehensive artifact analysis. *Applied Sciences (Basel, Switzerland), 15*(2), 923. DOI: 10.3390/app15020923

Shamsabadi, A., Mojdeganlou, H., Barzegary, A., Fakhfouri, A., Azad, K., Heydari, M., Pashaei, Z., & Mehraeen, E. (2022, March 12). Opportunities, threats and solution techniques of deep-fake technology: A systematic review. [Conference proceedings]. *20th International Conference on E-Society and 18th International Conference on Mobile Learning* (pp. 19-25). DOI: 10.33965/ES_ML2022_202202L003

Sharan, S. P., Choi, M., Shah, S., Goel, H., Omama, M., & Chinchali, S. (2025, April 25). Neuro-symbolic evaluation of text-to-video models using formal verification (arXiv:2411.16718). *arXiv.* /arXiv.2411.16718DOI: 10.1109/CVPR52734.2025.00786

Shoderu, G., Baror, S., & Venter, H. (2024, March). A privacy-compliant process for digital forensics readiness. [Conference proceedings]. *International Conference on Cyber Warfare and Security, 19*(1), 337–347. DOI: 10.34190/iccws.19.1.2055

Siarohin, A., Lathuilière, S., Tulyakov, S., Ricci, E., & Sebe, N. (2020, October). First order motion model for image animation (arXiv:2003.00196). *arXiv.* /arXiv.2003.00196DOI: 10.48550

Siegel, D., Krätzer, C., Seidlitz, S., & Dittmann, J. (2022, January). Forensic data model for artificial intelligence based media forensics - Illustrated on the example of DeepFake detection. *IS&T International Symposium on Electronic Imaging, 34*(4), 324. DOI: 10.2352/EI.2022.34.4.MWSF-324

Simmons, J. C., & Winograd, J. M. (2024, May 20). Interoperable provenance authentication of broadcast media using open standards-based metadata, watermarking and cryptography (arXiv:2405.12336v1). *arXiv.* /arXiv.2405.12336DOI: 10.48550

Singh, A., Ikuesan, R. A., & Venter, H. (2022, February 14). Secure storage model for digital forensic readiness. *IEEE Access : Practical Innovations, Open Solutions, 10*, 19469–19480. DOI: 10.1109/ACCESS.2022.3151403

Singh, S., & Devi, L. (2025, December 17). Reliability and admissibility of AI-generated forensic evidence in criminal trials. *arXiv.* /arXiv.2601.06048DOI: 10.48550

Sousa Antunes, H., Freitas, P. M., Oliveira, A. L., Martins Pereira, C., Vaz de Sequeira, E., & Barreto Xavier, L. (Eds.). (2024). *Multidisciplinary perspectives on Artificial Intelligence and the law*. Springer International, Law, Governance and Technology Series 58. DOI: 10.1007/978-3-031-41264-6

Stephen, D., Schniedermann, A., Lovakov, A., Schmidt, M., Ottaviani, M., Sorgatz, N., Romero, R. C., Möller, T., Aman, V., & Stahlschmidt, S. (2025, August 22). Implicit reporting standards in bibliometric research: What can reviewers' comments tell us about reporting completeness? *arXiv*. 10.48550/arXiv.2508.16276 DOI: 10.51408/issi2025_132

Sugiyama, M., & Kataoka, H. (2025, April 30). Simple visual artifact detection in Sora-generated videos (arXiv:2504.21334). *arXiv*. /arXiv.2504.21334DOI: 10.48550

Tan, D., Yang, Y., Niu, C., Li, S., Yang, D., & Tan, B. (2025, August). A review of deep learning based multimodal forgery detection for video and audio. *Discover Applied Sciences*, *7*(9), 987. DOI: 10.1007/s42452-025-07629-3

Tashman, A. (2021, December 1). "Malicious Deepfakes"—How California's A.B. 730 tries (and fails) to address the internet's burgeoning political crisis. *Loyola of Los Angeles Law Review*, *54*(4), 8. https://digitalcommons.lmu.edu/llr/vol54/iss4/8

Thies, J., Zollhöfer, M., & Nießner, M. (2019, April 28). Deferred neural rendering: Image synthesis using neural textures (arXiv:1904.12356). *arXiv*. /arXiv.1904.12356DOI: 10.48550

Thies, J., Zollhöfer, M., Stamminger, M., Theobalt, C., & Nießner, M. (2020, July 29). Face2Face: Real-time face capture and reenactment of RGB videos (arXiv:2007.14808v1). /arXiv.2007.14808DOI: 10.48550

Tipper, S., Atlam, H. F., & Lallie, H. S. (2024, October 24). An investigation into the utilisation of CNN with LSTM for video deepfake detection. *Applied Sciences (Basel, Switzerland)*, *14*(21), 9754. DOI: 10.3390/app14219754

Umbach, R., Henry, N., Beard, G., & Berryessa, C. (2024, May). Non-consensual synthetic Intimate imagery: Prevalence, attitudes, and knowledge in 10 countries. [Conference proceedings]. *CHI Conference on Human Factors in Computing Systems,* 779 (pp. 1–20). DOI: 10.1145/3613904.3642382

van der Sloot, B., & Wagensveld, Y. (2022, September). Deepfakes: Regulatory challenges for the synthetic society. *Computer Law & Security Review*, *46*, 105716. DOI: 10.1016/j.clsr.2022.105716

Veerasamy, N., & Pieterse, H. (2022, March). Rising above misinformation and deepfakes. [Conference proceedings]. *International Conference on Cyber Warfare and Security, 17*(1), 340–348. DOI: 10.34190/iccws.17.1.25

Verdoliva, L. (2020, June 12). Media forensics and DeepFakes: An overview. *IEEE Journal of Selected Topics in Signal Processing*, *14*(5), 910–932. DOI: 10.1109/JSTSP.2020.3002101

Wang, B., Wu, X., Tang, Y., Ma, Y., Shan, Z., & Wei, F. (2023, February 5). Frequency domain filtered residual network for deepfake detection. *Mathematics*, *11*(4), 816. DOI: 10.3390/math11040816

Wang, K., & Guo, F. (2022, October 16). Towards sustainable development through the perspective of Construction 4.0: Systematic literature review and bibliometric analysis. *Buildings (Basel, Switzerland)*, *12*(10), 1708. DOI: 10.3390/buildings12101708

Wang, T., Liao, X., Chow, K. P., Lin, X., & Wang, Y. (2025, March). Deepfake detection: A comprehensive survey from the reliability perspective. *ACM Computing Surveys, 57*(3), 1–35. DOI: 10.1145/3699710

Waseem, S., Abu Bakar, S. A. R. S., Ahmed, B. A., Omar, Z., Eisa, T. A. E., & Dalam, M. E. E. (2023, October 13). DeepFake on face and expression swap: A review. *IEEE Access : Practical Innovations, Open Solutions, 11*, 117865–117906. DOI: 10.1109/ACCESS.2023.3324403

Wiedemer, T., Li, Y., Vicol, P., Gu, S. S., Matarese, N., Swersky, K., Kim, B., Jaini, P., & Geirhos, R. (2025, September). Video models are zero-shot learners and reasoners (arXiv:2509.20328). *arXiv*. / arXiv.2509.20328DOI: 10.48550

Wolter, M., Blanke, F., Heese, R., & Garcke, J. (2022, August 31). Wavelet-packets for deepfake image analysis and detection. *Machine Learning, 111*(11), 4295–4327. DOI: 10.1007/s10994-022-06225-5

Xie, M., Kulshrestha, M., Wang, S., Yang, J., Chakrabarti, A., Zhang, N., & Vorobeychik, Y. (2022, January). PROVES: Establishing image provenance using semantic signatures. [Conference paper]. *2022 IEEE/CVF Winter Conference on Applications of Computer Vision* (pp. 3017-3026). DOI: 10.1109/WACV51458.2022.00307

Xu, D., Gondal, I., Yi, X., Susnjak, T., Watters, P., & McIntosh, T. R. (2025, October 14). The erosion of cybersecurity zero-trust principles through generative AI: A survey on the challenges and future directions. *Journal of Cybersecurity and Privacy, 5*(4), 87. DOI: 10.3390/jcp5040087

Xu, Q., Chen, D., Chen, J., Lyu, S., & Wang, C. (2025, February 27). Recent advances on generalizable diffusion-generated image detection (arXiv:2502.19716). *arXiv*. /arXiv.2502.19716DOI: 10.48550

Yan, B., Liu, P., Yang, Y., Guo, Y., Yan, B., Liu, P., Yang, Y., & Guo, Y. (2025, June 18). Self-supervised feature disentanglement for deepfake detection. *Mathematics, 13*(12), 2024. DOI: 10.3390/math13122024

Zaman, S. B., Karim, W., Abian, A. I., Mohamed, R. E., & Islam, Md. R., Karim, A., & Azam, S. (2025, December 8). DeepAgent: A dual stream multi agent fusion for robust multimodal deepfake detection (arXiv:2512.07351). *arXiv*. /arXiv.2512.07351DOI: 10.48550

Zhang, B., Cui, H., Nguyen, V., & Whitty, M. (2025, March 21). Audio deepfake detection: What has been achieved and what lies ahead. *Sensors (Basel), 25*(7), 1989. DOI: 10.3390/s25071989 PMID: 40218502

Zhao, T., Xu, X., Xu, M., Ding, H., Xiong, Y., & Xia, W. (2021, July 26). Learning self-consistency for deepfake detection (arXiv:2012.09311). *arXiv*. /arXiv.2012.09311DOI: 10.1109/ICCV48922.2021.01475

KEY TERMS AND DEFINITIONS

Artefact-Based Detection: A forensic approach designed to identify visual, acoustic, or structural inconsistencies. These flaws appear during media synthesis or manipulation and include abnormal textures, lighting errors, or missing camera sensor traces.

Black Box: This term refers to AI models with opaque internal logic where only inputs and outputs are visible to the observer. Such lack of transparency makes it difficult for experts to explain specific results to non-technical audiences such as juries or legal panels.

Chain of Custody: The documented process of tracking digital evidence from its point of acquisition through analysis, storage, and presentation in court. Each transfer or handling step must be recorded to ensure the integrity of the evidence and to prevent challenges to its admissibility during legal proceedings.

Deepfake: Artificially generated or manipulated multimedia content that convincingly imitates real people, events, or environments using artificial intelligence. The primary goal is often to mislead viewers regarding the veracity of the material.

Deepfake Detection: The process of identifying synthetic or manipulated media relies on forensic, statistical, or machine learning techniques. These tools distinguish authentic content from AI-generated forgeries.

Diffusion Probabilistic Model (DPM): A generative artificial intelligence technique that produces synthetic content through a step-by-step denoising process. It transforms random noise into structured and highly realistic data.

Digital Forensics: The scientific discipline concerned with the identification, preservation, analysis, and presentation of digital evidence. Its main focus involves ensuring the integrity and admissibility of evidence in legal and investigative contexts.

Evidentiary Standards: The legal criteria that courts apply when determining whether expert testimony or novel scientific evidence is admissible in proceedings. In common law systems, these are typically governed by frameworks such as the Daubert or Frye standards, which assess factors including testability, peer review, error rates, and general acceptance within the relevant scientific community.

Explainable Artificial Intelligence (XAI): These methods make artificial intelligence systems transparent and interpretable. They allow human experts to understand, verify, and justify how algorithms produce specific decisions or classifications.

Forensic Readiness: Systems and organisations use this capability to collect, preserve, and manage digital evidence proactively. Such preparation supports efficient forensic investigations and ensures legal accountability when necessary.

Generative Adversarial Network (GAN): A machine learning architecture composed of competing generator and discriminator networks. They improve each other iteratively to enable the creation of extremely realistic synthetic media.

Generative Artificial Intelligence (GAI): A category of artificial intelligence focused on producing new content such as images, audio, video, or text. It operates by learning patterns and distributions from large pre-existing datasets.

Liar's Dividend: The mere existence of deepfakes allows individuals to plausibly deny authentic digital evidence. A person might falsely claim that real evidence was manipulated or artificially generated to avoid culpability.

Media Laundering: Repeated processing of digital media causes the degradation of forensic evidence. Actions such as compression, resizing, or redistribution on platforms obscure the traces used for manipulation detection.

Multimodal Deepfake: Synthetic media forgeries that combine multiple modalities of manipulated data. The fusion of video, audio, facial expressions, and body movement increases realism and reduces detectability.

Non-Consensual Intimate Imagery (NCII): Sexually explicit visual content depicting an identifiable individual, created or distributed without that person's consent. In the context of deepfakes, such material is generated synthetically from publicly available photographs, requiring no access to genuine intimate imagery of the victim.

Silent Witness: This legal doctrine treats photographic or video evidence as an independent record of events that requires no human testimony to be admissible. It relies on the inherent reliability of the recording process, though this link is increasingly challenged by the rise of synthetic media.

Chapter 16
Punishment in a Digital Society:
Tablet Use and Public Perception in Corrections

Gulsebnem Bishop
http://orcid.org/0009-0009-4520-9143
Campbellsville University, USA

ABSTRACT

This chapter examines the use of tablets in correctional facilities. It argues that digital competence is essential for reentry and that incarceration intensifies the digital divide by isolating individuals from rapidly changing technologies. Using survey evidence from Cape Vincent, New York, the chapter summarizes the findings and analyzes public awareness and attitudes toward tablet functions, including education, rehabilitation, family communication, recreation, and free access. Referring to the findings, the analysis show conditional support: residents approve when tablets are framed as educational and rehabilitative infrastructure, and resist when tablets are seen as luxury items, entertainment, or "free" privileges. The chapter also addresses policy implications, privatization, surveillance, and ethical commitments to human dignity and equity. Overall, it concludes that digital rehabilitation can strengthen reintegration when tablet programs are transparent and purpose-driven.

INTRODUCTION: TABLETS, PUNISHMENT, AND DIGITAL SOCIETY

Contemporary society is fundamentally digital. Everyday activities, such as seeking employment, accessing health care, maintaining social relationships, managing finances, or participating in civic life, are now mediated through digital technologies. Competence with devices, interfaces, and digital systems is no longer optional; it is a prerequisite for meaningful participation in modern life. Yet access to these technologies and the skills required to use them remain unevenly distributed, producing persistent forms of digital exclusion. While the digital divide is often discussed in relation to education, income, age, or geographic location, it is rarely examined through the lens of incarceration.

Correctional facilities occupy a unique position within the digital divide. Incarcerated individuals are physically and socially separated from a society undergoing rapidly accelerating technological change. As a result, many of them leave prison not only with the stigma of incarceration but also with diminished digital literacy and limited exposure to contemporary technologies. This gap can significantly hinder

DOI: 10.4018/979-8-3373-7660-8.ch016

reintegration, exacerbate social exclusion, and increase vulnerability to recidivism. In a digital society, rehabilitation that ignores technological competence is incomplete.

In response to these challenges, correctional systems have increasingly turned to technology as a rehabilitative tool. Among the most visible and contested of these technologies are tablets. Unlike traditional prison technologies, such as television or telephones, tablets are multifunctional devices. They can support education, provide access to legal and mental health resources, facilitate communication with family, and offer limited forms of recreation, all within secure and controlled environments. At the same time, tablets closely resemble consumer technologies used in everyday life outside prison walls. This resemblance makes them symbolically powerful and politically sensitive. Therefore, tablets sit at the intersection of two competing logics: rehabilitation and punishment. From a rehabilitative perspective, tablets can be framed as tools that build skills, reduce isolation, and prepare individuals for successful reentry into a digital society. From a punitive perspective, the same devices may be interpreted as undeserved privileges or "luxury items" that undermine the purpose of incarceration. These competing interpretations shape not only public discourse but also policy decisions regarding what technologies are introduced, how they are funded, and how access is regulated.

Public opinion plays a central role in this tension. In democratic societies, perceptions of crime, punishment, and rehabilitation influence political priorities and correctional policy. Public attitudes toward inmate amenities have historically contributed to cycles of punitiveness, in which demands for harsher conditions lead to the restriction or elimination of programs perceived as too permissive. Technologies that resemble everyday consumer goods, such as tablets, are particularly susceptible to these dynamics. Even when such technologies are deployed primarily for education or rehabilitation, their symbolic association with leisure and personal enjoyment can trigger resistance.

Here, tablet use in correctional facilities is examined through the lens of public perception. Rather than focusing solely on the technical design or institutional outcomes of tablet programs in correctional facilities, this is instead a study of how members of the public evaluate tablet access and how these evaluations vary depending on the perceived purpose of the technology. Specifically, it considers whether tablets are viewed differently when framed as tools for education, rehabilitation, or family communication versus when they are associated with entertainment or free access.

Understanding public opinion in this context is not a superficial exercise. Public perceptions shape the political environment in which correctional leaders and policymakers operate. When technologies are framed as rehabilitative tools aligned with public safety and reintegration, they are more likely to gain legitimacy and sustained support. When they are framed as indulgences, they risk becoming targets of punitive reform, despite the empirical evidence of their benefits. As a result, the success or failure of correctional technology initiatives often depends as much on public narrative as on program effectiveness.

The empirical foundation is a community-based survey conducted in Cape Vincent, New York, a small town that has a correctional facility. Proximity to incarceration does not necessarily translate into familiarity with prison life, but it does offer a meaningful context in which to examine public attitudes. Residents in such communities are often exposed to local discourse about prisons, employment, and public safety, making their perspectives particularly relevant to discussions of correctional policy. The survey explored residents' awareness of tablet use in prisons, their general support or opposition, and their attitudes toward specific tablet functions (Bishop, 2021). Demographic factors, including age, gender, education level, and employment connection to the facility, were examined to identify patterns in support and resistance.

The findings reveal a nuanced and conditional form of public support. Tablets are not rejected outright. Instead, support depends heavily on how tablets are used and how access is framed. Educational and rehabilitative uses receive substantially more approval than recreational uses, while free access provokes strong resistance regardless of demographic group. Education level emerges as a particularly important factor in shaping perceptions, suggesting that familiarity with technology and its role in modern life influences how tablets are interpreted within correctional settings.

Beyond reporting these findings, there is broader debate about digital rehabilitation, punishment culture, and the symbolic meaning of technology in prisons. It argues that tablets should be understood not as luxury amenities, but as rehabilitative infrastructure, as tools that support reintegration in a society where digital competence is essential. At the same time, the ethical and economic tensions surrounding tablet programs are acknowledged, including concerns about cost, surveillance, and equity.

Bringing public opinion into conversation with correctional technology and digital rehabilitation contributes to a more comprehensive understanding of why tablet programs remain contested despite evidence of their potential benefits. It highlights the importance of framing, transparency, and education—not only for incarcerated individuals but also for the public, whose perceptions ultimately shape policy. In doing so, it invites readers to reconsider how punishment, rehabilitation, and technology intersect in a digital society, and what it means to prepare individuals for life beyond prison walls.

TECHNOLOGY AND THE DIGITAL DIVIDE IN CORRECTIONS

The digital divide is most often discussed as a problem of unequal access to devices, connectivity, and digital skills across socioeconomic, geographic, and demographic lines. In this framing, the divide affects students without broadband, older adults unfamiliar with digital platforms, and communities lacking technological infrastructure. What is less frequently acknowledged is that incarceration itself functions as a structural amplifier of the digital divide. Prison walls do not simply restrict physical movement; they also interrupt technological exposure despite digital competence becoming increasingly central to everyday life.

Correctional facilities are, by design, environments of restriction and control. Access to information, communication, and technology is tightly regulated, often justified through security concerns. Historically, this has resulted in a technological ecosystem that is static, slow to evolve, and disconnected from developments in the outside world. While society has transitioned through multiple waves of technological change—from desktop computing to mobile devices, cloud platforms, and app-based services—many incarcerated individuals experience these changes only indirectly or not at all. As a result, incarceration produces a form of temporal digital displacement, where individuals reenter society technologically "out of sync" with contemporary norms. This displacement has concrete consequences. As mentioned before, employment searches, housing applications, health care portals, and even basic communication increasingly require digital literacy. Tasks that were once completed in person or on paper are now mediated through online systems that assume familiarity with interfaces, passwords, document uploads, and real-time communication tools. Individuals who lack these skills face compounded disadvantages upon release, particularly when combined with the stigma of incarceration and limited employment opportunities. In this sense, the digital divide in corrections is not merely about access to devices; it is about functional exclusion from digital citizenship. The concept of digital rehabilitation has emerged as a response to this challenge.

Digital rehabilitation reframes technology access in correctional settings as a preparatory intervention rather than a privilege. From this perspective, exposure to digital tools during incarceration can support skill development, reduce reentry shock, and promote autonomy. Importantly, digital rehabilitation does not imply unrestricted access to the Internet or consumer technologies. Instead, it emphasizes structured, secure, and purposeful access aligned with rehabilitative goals.

Within this framework, tablets have gained prominence because they bridge several gaps simultaneously. Technically, tablets are adaptable to secure environments: They can operate on closed networks, restrict content, and be centrally monitored. Pedagogically, they support modular learning, self-paced education, and multimedia content delivery. Socially, they facilitate communication with family and service providers in ways that reduce isolation. Symbolically, however, tablets complicate the rehabilitative narrative because they resemble everyday consumer devices associated with leisure, entertainment, and personal choice. This symbolic dimension matters. Technologies are not neutral objects; they carry cultural meanings shaped by everyday use. In the free world, tablets are associated with convenience, entertainment, and discretionary consumption. When similar devices appear in prisons, they can trigger moral judgments about deservingness. This is particularly true in punishment-oriented cultures, where incarceration is understood primarily as deprivation rather than preparation. As a result, the same device can be interpreted in two opposing ways: as a rehabilitative tool or as an indulgence.

The correctional system has long relied on limited technologies to manage inmate behavior and institutional order. Televisions, radios, and telephones have been justified as mechanisms to reduce tension and maintain routine, even when they offer little rehabilitative value. These technologies are largely passive; they do not require skill development or interaction beyond consumption. Tablets differ because they are interactive. They require engagement, decision-making, and navigation. This interactivity is precisely what makes them valuable for rehabilitation—and controversial in the public imagination. Public discomfort with interactive technologies in prisons reflects broader anxieties about control and autonomy. Granting inmates the ability to choose content, communicate asynchronously, or engage in self-directed learning challenges traditional assumptions about what incarceration should look like. For some members of the public, such autonomy appears inconsistent with punishment, even when it demonstrably supports rehabilitation. This tension reveals an underlying contradiction in correctional policy: Society expects individuals to reenter as capable, self-sufficient citizens yet resists providing the tools necessary to develop those capacities during incarceration.

The digital divide in corrections is further complicated by economic structures surrounding prison technology. Many tablet programs operate through cost-recovery or fee-based models, where access to certain services requires payment. While these models reduce direct taxpayer burden, they shift costs onto incarcerated individuals and their families—groups that are often already economically vulnerable. From an equity perspective, this raises important questions about who benefits from digital rehabilitation and who is excluded. From a public perception perspective, however, fee-based access may increase acceptability by aligning with beliefs that inmates should "pay their own way." This dynamic creates a paradox. Public support may increase when tablet access is framed as earned or paid, yet such models can exacerbate inequality within the incarcerated population. Those with external financial support gain greater access to educational and communicative resources, while others remain digitally marginalized. In this sense, the digital divide does not disappear inside prison; it is reproduced and reshaped by institutional and economic arrangements.

Another critical aspect of the digital divide in corrections is skill decay. Digital competence is not static; it requires continuous exposure and adaptation. Individuals serving long sentences may experience not only a lack of new skill acquisition but also the erosion of previously held competencies. Interfaces change, norms evolve, and platforms disappear. Upon release, individuals may encounter technologies that are conceptually unfamiliar even if they once used earlier versions. Tablets, when used consistently during incarceration, can serve as transitional technologies that mitigate this decay by maintaining baseline familiarity with digital interaction.

Despite these potential benefits, the introduction of tablets alone does not resolve the digital divide. Access without guidance can be insufficient, and poorly implemented programs may reinforce surveillance rather than empowerment. Digital rehabilitation requires intentional design: educational content aligned with real-world demands, opportunities for guided learning, and policies that balance security with meaningful use. Importantly, it also requires public legitimacy. Programs that lack public support are vulnerable to political reversal, regardless of their effectiveness. This is where public opinion becomes central. The digital divide in corrections is not solely a technical or institutional problem; it is also a social and political one. Public beliefs about punishment, rehabilitation, and technology shape what forms of access are deemed acceptable. When the public views tablets primarily as entertainment devices, support erodes. When tablets are framed as tools for education, job readiness, and reintegration, support increases. These distinctions are not incidental; they reflect deeply held assumptions about the purpose of incarceration and the moral boundaries of rehabilitation.

Understanding the digital divide in corrections thus requires moving beyond access metrics and examining interpretive frameworks. How technologies are described, justified, and communicated matters as much as how they are implemented. Tablets are not merely devices placed in prisons; they are symbols through which society negotiates its expectations of punishment and reform in a digital age.

That insight is built upon through examining how members of the public interpret tablet use in correctional facilities and how those interpretations vary depending on perceived function. By situating tablet programs within the broader context of the digital divide and public punitiveness, one continues to argue that successful digital rehabilitation depends not only on secure technology and institutional leadership but also on reshaping the narratives that define what incarcerated individuals are allowed to learn, use, and become.

TABLETS AS REHABILITATIVE INFRASTRUCTURE IN CORRECTIONAL FACILITIES

Rehabilitation in correctional facilities has traditionally been framed around education, vocational training, and behavioral programs. In recent decades, however, rehabilitation has become inseparable from technology. Employment, health care, education, communication, and civic participation increasingly depend on digital tools. As a result, rehabilitation without digital skill development risks leaving incarcerated individuals unprepared for life after release. Within this context, tablets have emerged not simply as devices but as rehabilitative infrastructure that supports education, communication, mental health, and reentry readiness.

Rehabilitation is commonly defined as the process of preparing incarcerated individuals to reintegrate into society as law-abiding and productive members (Hudson, 2003; Raynor & Robinson, 2009). In a digital society, this preparation necessarily includes technological competence. Many daily tasks that were once completed in person, such as job applications, banking, health care appointments, and government services, are now conducted online. Individuals who lack familiarity with these systems therefore face significant disadvantages upon release (Jewkes & Reisdorf, 2016).

Research consistently shows that incarcerated individuals experience prolonged periods of technological exclusion. While society has rapidly transitioned through multiple waves of digital innovation, prison environments have largely remained static (Reisdorf & Rikard, 2018). This gap creates what scholars describe as a form of digital isolation, where individuals are released into a society that operates through technologies they have never used or no longer recognize. Tablets, when used in structured and controlled ways, offer a practical response to this challenge.

Unlike consumer devices, which have unrestricted Internet access, tablets in correctional facilities are typically deployed on closed or highly restricted networks. These systems are designed to limit risk while enabling specific rehabilitative functions, such as access to educational materials, legal resources, mental health programs, and communication platforms (Johnson & Hail-Jares, 2016). Tablets are often preloaded with approved content and monitored by correctional authorities, allowing institutions to balance security with access. This controlled design is significant. It challenges the perception that tablets represent unchecked privileges or entertainment devices. Instead, they function as structured platforms that support institutional goals. Studies have shown that digital distribution of educational and informational content reduces reliance on physical materials, limits contraband, and improves operational efficiency within facilities (Cournoyer & Stanton, 2016). From an institutional perspective, tablets are also scalable. They can deliver consistent programming across facilities, reduce printing and staffing costs, and allow for standardized access to learning resources. From a rehabilitative perspective, they offer inmates opportunities to engage in purposeful activities that mirror how information is accessed outside prison walls.

Education has long been associated with reduced recidivism, particularly when it is aligned with employable skills (Hall & Bannatyne, 2000). Tablets expand the reach of correctional education by making learning materials more accessible and adaptable. Digital textbooks, self-paced courses, literacy programs, and certification preparation can all be delivered through tablet platforms. Several studies indicate that inmates engage more consistently with educational content when it is delivered digitally. Tablets allow learners to revisit materials, track progress, and develop independent study habits. These behaviors are consistent with lifelong learning skills expected in modern workplaces. Importantly, digital learning environments also reduce logistical barriers associated with classroom scheduling, space limitations, and instructor availability. Vocational training similarly benefits from tablet-based delivery. Instructional videos, simulations, and job readiness modules introduce inmates to workplace technologies and expectations. Even basic familiarity with navigating menus, completing forms, and managing digital content can ease the transition into employment settings after release (Jewkes & Reisdorf, 2016).

Correctional facilities face persistent challenges related to mental health, stress, and behavioral management. Tablets have increasingly been used to support mental health services through guided programs, self-help resources, and access to counseling materials. Research suggests that structured digital engagement can reduce idle time, which is often associated with increased tension and conflict in correctional settings (Cournoyer & Stanton, 2016). Evidence from facilities that have implemented tablet programs shows reductions in behavioral incidents, including assaults and self-harm (Stewart, 2017). While tablets are not substitutes for professional mental health care, they can supplement existing services by providing consistent access to coping strategies, mindfulness programs, and crisis resources. From a rehabilitative standpoint, this contributes to emotional regulation and self-management skills that are critical both during incarceration and after release.

Maintaining family and community ties is a well-documented factor in successful reentry and reduced recidivism. Tablets facilitate communication through secure messaging and video conferencing systems that allow inmates to remain connected to family members, legal representatives, and support networks (Johnson & Hail-Jares, 2016). These tools are particularly important for individuals housed far from their communities or those with limited access to in-person visitation. Research indicates that communication technologies can reduce feelings of isolation and support prosocial identity development (Kerr & Willis, 2018). Tablets, when used for communication, reinforce relational stability rather than entertainment. However, public support for these functions varies. While educational and rehabilitative uses receive broader approval, communication tools, especially video conferencing, often generate mixed reactions due to perceptions of comfort or privilege. The Cape Vincent study (Bishop, 2021) illustrates this gap by demonstrating that public support increases when tablet functions are framed as rehabilitative rather than recreational. This distinction is critical for policy development and program sustainability.

Another important dimension of tablet use is its role in behavioral management. Access to tablets is often contingent on compliance with institutional rules. This creates a structured incentive system that encourages positive behavior. Inmates are motivated to maintain privileges by avoiding infractions, which can contribute to calmer and more orderly environments (Cournoyer & Stanton, 2016). From a correctional management perspective, this aligns rehabilitation with institutional safety. Tablets become tools that support both individual development and facility stability. Importantly, this dual function challenges the assumption that rehabilitative technologies undermine security. Instead, evidence suggests that well-designed digital programs enhance it.

Despite their rehabilitative functions, tablets are frequently perceived by the public as luxury items. This perception is rooted in broader cultural associations between tablets and leisure, entertainment, and consumer convenience (Lenz, 2002; Wozniak, 2014). As the Cape Vincent study (Bishop, 2021) shows, this framing significantly affects public support, particularly when tablet use includes games or free access. This creates what can be described as an infrastructure paradox. Tablets function as essential rehabilitative tools within correctional systems, yet they are judged by external audiences through a consumer lens. Public discomfort arises not from the outcomes tablets produce, but from what they symbolize. This symbolic conflict places pressure on policymakers and correctional administrators, who must justify rehabilitative technologies within punitive political climates. Understanding this tension is essential. Without public support, even effective programs risk defunding or restrictions. The Cape Vincent study findings underscore the importance of reframing tablets not as amenities, but as infrastructure, tools necessary for education, rehabilitation, and reintegration in a digital society.

Tablets represent a significant shift in how rehabilitation can be operationalized within correctional facilities. When deployed as controlled, purpose-driven tools, they support education, mental health, communication, and behavioral stability. The evidence suggests that tablets contribute to safer facilities and better reentry outcomes. However, their success depends not only on institutional implementation but also on public understanding. Tablets may also be positioned as rehabilitative infrastructure rather than discretionary privileges, providing a foundation for examining public opinion, policy resistance, and the broader implications of digital rehabilitation.

PUBLIC OPINION, PUNISHMENT, AND THE MEANING OF "LUXURY"

Public opinion plays a central role in shaping correctional policy. Decisions about inmate amenities, programming, and technology are rarely made in isolation from public sentiment. In democratic societies, politicians respond to voters' perceptions of crime, punishment, and fairness. As a result, the success or failure of rehabilitative initiatives, such as tablet programs, often depends less on empirical evidence and more on how these initiatives are interpreted by the public.

For much of the twentieth century, criminal justice policy in the United States oscillated between rehabilitative ideals and punitive approaches. Beginning in the 1970s, public discourse shifted sharply toward punishment, driven by rising crime rates, political rhetoric, and media portrayals of offenders (Cullen et al., 2000; Ramirez, 2013). This shift produced policies emphasizing long sentences, reduced amenities, and limited rehabilitative programming. Research shows that public punitiveness is not static. Survey data indicates that while Americans continue to support punishment, they also express strong support for rehabilitation, particularly for nonviolent offenders (Blizzard, 2018; O'Hear & Wheelock, 2016). This duality creates tension. The public often endorses rehabilitation in principle but resists specific rehabilitative tools when they appear to reduce the harshness of incarceration. This contradiction is especially visible in reactions to technology. Educational programs, job training, and mental health services tend to receive support when framed as necessities. When these same programs rely on technologies associated with comfort or leisure, however, public approval declines sharply (Lenz, 2002; Wozniak, 2014).

Amenities in prisons carry symbolic meaning. Items such as televisions, recreational equipment, and now tablets are often interpreted not by their function, but by what they represent. Johnson (2005) described this phenomenon as time envy, where free individuals resent perceived leisure in prison because it contrasts with their own time-constrained lives. This resentment fuels the perception that prisons are "too comfortable," despite evidence to the contrary. Tablets amplify this symbolic conflict. In everyday life, tablets are associated with entertainment, convenience, and personal choice. Consequently, when these devices appear in correctional settings, they challenge deeply held beliefs about what punishment should look like. Even when tablets are restricted and used primarily for education or communication, their appearance triggers resistance because they resemble consumer luxuries.

The Cape Vincent study (Bishop, 2021) reflects this dynamic clearly. While respondents supported educational and rehabilitative uses of tablets, a majority also described tablets as luxury items. This finding aligns with earlier research showing that public support declines as amenities become more "luxurious" in perception, regardless of their rehabilitative value (Lenz, 2002).

Another critical factor shaping public opinion is limited knowledge of prison conditions. Most members of the public have never visited a correctional facility. Their understanding of prison life is shaped largely by media portrayals, political messaging, and anecdotal narratives (Cullen et al., 2000; Wozniak, 2014). These portrayals often exaggerate comfort and minimize deprivation. As a result, technologies introduced for rehabilitation are interpreted as rewards rather than tools. Tablets, despite operating on closed networks and offering limited content, are frequently assumed to provide unrestricted Internet access or entertainment, a misunderstanding that contributes to resistance and fuels demands for restriction. However, research consistently shows that when members of the public receive accurate information about prison conditions and program outcomes, their attitudes become more nuanced and less punitive (Enns, 2017). This suggests that opposition to tablet use is not rooted in opposition to rehabilitation itself, but in misconceptions about how technology functions within prisons.

The Cape Vincent study (Bishop, 2021) highlights the importance of education level in shaping attitudes toward tablet use. Respondents with higher education levels were more likely to support tablets for educational purposes and communication with family and friends. This pattern mirrors earlier studies showing that education correlates with greater support for rehabilitative policies and alternatives to incarceration (O'Hear & Wheelock, 2016).

Education appears to influence how individuals interpret technology. Those with higher educational attainment may be more likely to view tablets as functional tools rather than leisure devices. They may also have greater familiarity with how digital platforms support learning, work, and communication, making it easier to imagine tablets as rehabilitative infrastructure rather than indulgences. This distinction is critical for policymakers. It suggests that public resistance may be mitigated through targeted education efforts that explain the purpose, restrictions, and outcomes of tablet programs.

Gender differences in attitudes toward punishment have been documented across multiple studies. Women tend to express less punitive attitudes and greater support for rehabilitative approaches, particularly those emphasizing education and social connection (Cullen et al., 2000). The study reflects this pattern, with female respondents showing stronger support for educational uses of tablets. These differences may stem from moral frameworks emphasizing care, relationality, and long-term social outcomes. Communication with family, educational growth, and mental health support align with these values. However, even among supportive groups, resistance emerges when tablet use is framed as free access or entertainment, reinforcing the power of the luxury narrative.

Labeling matters. When tablets are framed as luxuries, they become politically vulnerable. Policymakers seeking public approval may limit access, impose fees, or eliminate programs altogether, even when evidence supports their effectiveness. This pattern has been observed repeatedly in corrections, where amenities perceived as indulgent are among the first to be reduced during policy shifts (Johnson, 2005). The Cape Vincent study demonstrates that while the public differentiates between rehabilitative and recreational uses, the device itself remains symbolically charged. This creates a policy dilemma: how to deliver digital rehabilitation without triggering backlash rooted in moral judgments rather than outcomes. One solution lies in reframing. When tablets are presented as educational platforms, communication tools, and safety-enhancing infrastructure, support increases. When they are described vaguely or associated with entertainment, resistance dominates. This underscores the importance of transparent communication among correctional institutions, policymakers, and the public.

Public opinion does not merely reflect attitudes; it actively shapes correctional policy. Enns (2017) demonstrated that shifts in public punitiveness correlate strongly with incarceration rates, prison spending, and reform efforts. Politicians respond to voter sentiment, even when that sentiment is based on incomplete information. The Cape Vincent study illustrates this process at the local level. In a small community near a correctional facility, opinions about tablet use were divided, nuanced, and strongly influenced by framing. These micro-level findings mirror national trends and highlight the importance of understanding public attitudes when implementing technological reforms.

Public reactions to tablet use in correctional facilities are shaped less by evidence of effectiveness and more by symbolic interpretations of punishment and luxury. While support for rehabilitation is widespread, technologies associated with comfort provoke resistance. Education level, gender, and framing significantly influence attitudes, revealing opportunities for informed policy engagement. The debate over tablets is not simply about technology. It is about values, perceptions, and the meaning society assigns to punishment and rehabilitation in a digital age.

TABLETS, CONTROL, AND PRIVATIZATION IN CORRECTIONS

The introduction of tablets into correctional facilities does not occur in a neutral policy environment. Tablet programs are embedded within broader systems of institutional control, surveillance, and privatization. While tablets are often framed as rehabilitative tools, their implementation raises important questions about power, governance, cost, and accountability. Understanding these dimensions is essential for evaluating whether tablet use advances rehabilitation or reinforces existing inequities within the correctional system.

Correctional facilities are fundamentally structured around control. Every aspect of daily life—movement, communication, access to information—is regulated. Technology introduced into this environment is therefore not simply a tool; it becomes part of the control architecture. Tablets exemplify this dual function. On the one hand, they provide access to education, communication, and mental health resources. On the other hand, they operate within tightly managed systems that monitor use, restrict content, and enforce compliance (Johnson & Hail-Jares, 2016).

Tablet access is often conditional. In many facilities, privileges are tied to behavior, disciplinary records, or program participation. This creates a behavioral incentive structure in which technology becomes a mechanism of governance rather than solely rehabilitation. While this structure can promote institutional order, it also raises ethical questions about whether access to education and communication should be contingent upon compliance rather than treated as foundational rehabilitative supports.

Scholars have noted that digital tools in prisons frequently serve administrative efficiency goals alongside rehabilitative ones (Knight, 2016). Tablets reduce staff workload, streamline information distribution, and minimize physical interactions. These efficiencies benefit institutions, but they also reinforce asymmetrical power relationships between incarcerated individuals and the correctional system.

Tablet systems generate extensive data. Usage patterns, communication logs, content access, and behavioral indicators can all be tracked. From an administrative standpoint, this data offers valuable insight into inmate behavior and program engagement. It can inform interventions, identify risks, and support safety planning (McDougall et al., 2017).

The collection of digital data also introduces concerns about surveillance and privacy. Incarcerated individuals have limited autonomy over how their data is collected, stored, and used. Communication through tablets, whether messaging or video conferencing, is monitored. While monitoring is justified on security grounds, it may discourage open communication and reinforce feelings of constant observation. This tension highlights a broader issue within digital rehabilitation: Technology can empower, but it can also extend institutional oversight into new domains. The challenge lies in balancing legitimate security needs with respect for dignity and rehabilitation goals.

One of the most significant aspects of tablet implementation is the role of private corporations. The correctional technology market has expanded rapidly, with companies such as JPay and Global Tel*Link becoming dominant service providers. These companies supply hardware, software, communication platforms, and content, often under exclusive contracts with state departments of corrections (Arguelles & Ortiz-Luis, 2021). Privatization introduces market logic into correctional environments. While private companies can provide innovation and scalability, their profit motives may conflict with rehabilitative goals. Many tablet services operate on fee-based models, meaning that inmates or their families must pay for music downloads, messaging, video calls, and other services. Consequently, even when devices are provided at no cost, ongoing access frequently depends on the ability to pay. Research has shown that these costs disproportionately affect low-income families, exacerbating existing inequalities (Arguelles

& Ortiz-Luis, 2021). In this context, technology intended to bridge the digital divide may inadvertently reinforce economic barriers.

Communication is one of the most valued tablet functions. Secure messaging and video conferencing allow incarcerated individuals to maintain family ties, which are critical for emotional well-being and successful reentry. However, these services are often among the most expensive features offered through tablet platforms (Johnson & Hail-Jares, 2016). Unfortunately, the Cape Vincent study's findings reflect public discomfort with free access to tablet services (Bishop, 2021). While respondents supported educational and rehabilitative uses, they largely opposed providing tablets or services at no cost. This aligns with broader public attitudes toward prison amenities but conflicts with evidence that family contact reduces recidivism and supports rehabilitation (Kerr & Willis, 2018). This contradiction places policymakers in a difficult position. Charging for services satisfies public concerns about fairness but risks undermining rehabilitative outcomes. Eliminating or restricting access reduces costs but increases isolation. Tablet programs thus sit at the intersection of moral judgment, economic policy, and correctional goals.

Tablet systems can create stratification within prisons. Individuals with financial resources can access more content, communicate more frequently, and engage more fully with digital programs, whereas those without resources may be limited to basic functions or excluded altogether. This demonstrates that broader patterns of digital inequality in society are mirrored and intensified within correctional settings.

Jewkes and Reisdorf (2016) warned that such stratification risks producing a two-tiered rehabilitative system. In this model, technological engagement becomes uneven, potentially influencing reentry outcomes. Those with greater access may leave prison better prepared, while others remain digitally marginalized. This outcome challenges the rehabilitative promise of tablet programs. If access is uneven, technology may widen rather than narrow the digital divide. Addressing this requires careful policy design, including subsidized access for educational and rehabilitative content.

Correctional staff play a critical role in the success of tablet programs. Their attitudes toward technology influence implementation, enforcement, and inmate engagement. While some studies report positive staff perceptions, particularly where technology reduces workload and improves safety, others identify resistance rooted in increased administrative demands or inadequate training (Mufarreh et al., 2021). The findings indicate that correctional officers were less supportive of tablet use than their family members. It suggests that daily operational realities may shape attitudes differently than indirect exposure. Tablets may represent additional responsibilities, troubleshooting, or perceived loss of authority. Without adequate training and inclusion in program development, staff may view technology as a burden rather than a benefit. This is also directly related to the institutional culture. Facilities that frame tablets as tools supporting both staff and inmates are more likely to achieve positive outcomes. Where technology is imposed without consultation, resistance is likely to persist.

Finally, the governance of tablet programs raises questions of accountability. Private contracts, pricing structures, data ownership, and service quality are often opaque. Public scrutiny is limited, and incarcerated individuals have little recourse when systems fail or costs escalate. Transparency is essential for maintaining public trust. Clear communication about how tablets are used, what content is available, how data is handled, and how costs are determined can reduce suspicion and resistance. This transparency also supports informed public debate, which this study shows is currently shaped by limited information.

Tablet programs in correctional facilities exist at the intersection of rehabilitation, control, and privatization. While tablets offer meaningful opportunities for education, communication, and behavioral support, they also extend institutional surveillance, introduce market dynamics, and risk reinforcing inequality. Public resistance to free access reflects broader moral judgments about punishment, yet fee-based systems raise serious equity concerns. Understanding these tensions is essential for designing tablet programs that truly support rehabilitation. Empirical findings of this study will show how these dynamics are reflected in local public opinion and what they reveal about broader societal attitudes.

WHAT THE DATA REVEALS: PUBLIC ATTITUDES TOWARD TABLET USE

It is important to interpret the empirical findings of the Cape Vincent study (Bishop, 2021) within the broader themes of punishment, rehabilitation, and digital access already discussed. Rather than presenting results as isolated statistics, the data is examined as an indicator of how members of the public conceptualize tablet use in correctional facilities. The findings reveal a nuanced pattern: Respondents differentiate strongly between how tablets are used and what tablets symbolize.

One of the most striking findings of the study is the limited public awareness of tablet use in correctional facilities. A majority of respondents were unaware that inmates at the nearby Cape Vincent Correctional Facility had access to tablets. This lack of awareness is consistent with prior research indicating that the public possesses limited knowledge of prison conditions and correctional programming (Cullen et al., 2000; Wozniak, 2014). This knowledge gap is consequential. Public opinion is often formed without direct exposure to correctional realities, relying instead on assumptions or media narratives. When new technologies are introduced into prisons, they are judged through existing beliefs about punishment rather than through an understanding of their function. The data suggests that opposition to tablet use may stem less from informed disagreement and more from unfamiliarity.

When respondents were asked directly whether they supported tablet use in correctional facilities, responses were nearly evenly split. This initial division reflects ambivalence rather than outright opposition. However, as the survey moved from general questions to specific uses of tablets, patterns of conditional support emerged. Support increased significantly when tablets were framed as tools for education, rehabilitation, and communication with family and friends. More than half of respondents agreed that tablets could serve educational purposes, and nearly half supported their use for rehabilitation. These findings align with national surveys showing strong public endorsement of rehabilitation in principle, even among individuals who favor punishment (Blizzard, 2018; O'Hear & Wheelock, 2016). This conditional support reinforces a key argument: the public does not reject rehabilitation. Instead, it evaluates rehabilitative tools based on perceived purpose. Tablets are acceptable when they are clearly instrumental and goal oriented.

Educational use of tablets received the strongest support among respondents in this study. This finding is significant because education has long been viewed as a legitimate function of correctional systems. Educational programming is often perceived as a means of self-improvement rather than reward, making it more politically and socially acceptable (Hall & Bannatyne, 2000).

Gender and education level influenced support for educational tablet use. Female respondents and individuals with higher levels of education were more likely to agree that tablets could be used effectively for learning. This aligns with prior research suggesting that education is associated with greater support for rehabilitative policies and alternatives to incarceration.

Age, however, was not a significant factor. This suggests that attitudes toward educational technology in prisons are shaped more by values and knowledge than by generational differences.

Support for rehabilitative use of tablets was moderate but notable. Nearly half of respondents believed tablets could contribute to rehabilitation, while a substantial portion remained neutral. This neutrality is important. It indicates uncertainty rather than resistance.

The lack of statistically significant relationships between demographic variables and rehabilitative support suggests that rehabilitation is broadly endorsed across groups but not deeply understood. This mirrors findings from Cullen et al. (2000), who observed that while rehabilitation enjoys widespread support, the public often lacks clarity about what rehabilitation entails or how it should be implemented. Tablets, as relatively new rehabilitative tools, appear to occupy this space of uncertainty. The data suggests that clearer communication about outcomes and mechanisms could increase public confidence.

Support for tablet-based communication revealed another layer of complexity. While a plurality of respondents supported video conferencing with family and friends, a substantial minority opposed it. Education level again played a significant role, with higher educational attainment associated with greater support. This pattern reflects broader public ambivalence about social connection in prisons. On the one hand, maintaining family ties is recognized as beneficial for rehabilitation and reentry (Kerr & Willis, 2018). On the other hand, communication technologies can be perceived as reducing the punitive nature of incarceration. The data suggests that public acceptance of communication tools depends heavily on framing. When communication is framed as emotional support and reintegration, it gains legitimacy. When it is framed as comfort or convenience, resistance increases.

The strongest resistance emerged around perceptions of tablets as luxury items. A majority of respondents agreed that tablets constitute a luxury for inmates. This perception had direct implications for support of free access and recreational use. Respondents overwhelmingly opposed free tablet privileges, regardless of gender, age, or education level. This finding is consistent with earlier research demonstrating that public support declines sharply when amenities are perceived as luxurious or unearned (Lenz, 2002).

Games and entertainment functions triggered similar resistance. Even when respondents acknowledged that inmates might pay for these features themselves, many opposed access. This reinforces the symbolic nature of opposition: Resistance is driven less by cost and more by moral judgment.

One of the most intriguing findings involves respondents connected to the correctional facility. Family members of correctional officers were more supportive of tablet use than correctional officers themselves, contrasting with recent research indicating generally positive staff attitudes toward technology (Mufarreh et al., 2021). This divergence may reflect role-based experiences. Correctional officers interact with tablet programs operationally, experiencing potential burdens related to monitoring, troubleshooting, or enforcement. Family members, by contrast, may observe outcomes indirectly, such as reduced stress, improved communication, or safer environments. This finding underscores the importance of including staff voices in implementation and training. Without institutional buy-in, even effective technologies may face resistance.

Taken together, the data reveals several consistent patterns. First, purpose matters more than the device: tablets are supported when their function aligns with education, rehabilitation, or reintegration. Luxury framing also undermines support: when tablets are associated with entertainment or free access, resistance increases sharply. Education shapes interpretation: higher education levels are associated with greater acceptance of tablet-based rehabilitation and communication. Lastly, public opinion is conditional, not punitive: respondents do not reject rehabilitation but demand clear boundaries around what is acceptable. These patterns support the broader argument: Public opinion is not an obstacle to digital rehabilitation, but it is highly sensitive to framing, symbolism, and understanding.

As a conclusion, the Cape Vincent data provides valuable insight into how members of the public evaluate tablet use in correctional facilities. Support is neither uniform nor dismissive. Instead, it reflects careful distinctions between education and entertainment, rehabilitation and reward, necessity and luxury. These findings reinforce the need for policymakers and correctional leaders to communicate clearly about the goals and limitations of tablet programs. Public opinion, when informed, has the potential to support meaningful rehabilitation in a digital society.

POLICY IMPLICATIONS AND REFRAMING TABLETS FOR PUBLIC ACCEPTANCE

The findings of the Cape Vincent study point to an important conclusion: Public opinion does not inherently oppose rehabilitation or technology use in correctional facilities. Rather, public acceptance depends on how technology, specifically tablets, is framed, explained, and governed. For policymakers, correctional leaders, and legislators, the challenge is not whether to adopt tablet programs, but how to design and communicate them in ways that align with public values while preserving rehabilitative effectiveness.

In democratic systems, correctional policy is inseparable from public sentiment. Legislators respond to voter attitudes, particularly on issues related to crime and punishment (Enns, 2017). Even when evidence supports rehabilitative initiatives, programs perceived as excessive or indulgent may face resistance, defunding, or elimination. Tablet programs are especially vulnerable because they are highly visible and symbolically charged. The study demonstrates that public support is conditional. Respondents were more likely to approve of tablet use when it was associated with education, rehabilitation, and communication. Opposition intensified when tablets were framed as free amenities or entertainment devices. These distinctions matter for policy design. Programs that fail to differentiate clearly between rehabilitative and recreational functions risk losing public support.

One of the most significant policy implications of the study is the need to reframe tablets as rehabilitative infrastructure rather than inmate amenities. Infrastructure implies necessity, functionality, and long-term benefit. Amenities imply comfort and excess. This distinction shapes public perception and political viability. When tablets are presented as platforms for education, job readiness, mental health support, and family communication, they align with publicly endorsed goals of rehabilitation and reduced recidivism (Cullen et al., 2000; O'Hear & Wheelock, 2016). Policymakers should emphasize outcomes rather than devices. Tablets are not the benefit; preparation for reintegration is. This reframing also addresses misconceptions. Many members of the public assume tablets provide unrestricted Internet access or entertainment. Clear communication about closed networks, restricted content, and monitoring can reduce resistance and increase trust.

The Cape Vincent study highlights a substantial gap in public knowledge regarding prison technology. Most respondents were unaware that tablets were used in the correctional facilities. This lack of awareness allows assumptions to dominate public opinion. Policy responses must therefore include proactive public education. Transparency should be built into tablet initiatives. Correctional agencies can publish clear descriptions of tablet functionality, costs, restrictions, and program goals. Reports that link tablet use to educational completion, reduced behavioral incidents, or improved reentry outcomes can further legitimize these programs (Stewart, 2017). Public education does not require persuasion. It requires information. Research indicates that when the public is informed about correctional realities and program effectiveness, punitive attitudes tend to soften (Enns, 2017). Tablets, when explained accurately, may be perceived less as luxuries and more as necessary tools.

One of the strongest sources of opposition identified in this study relates to free access and paid services. Respondents overwhelmingly rejected the idea of free tablet privileges. At the same time, research shows that excessive fees for communication and content place disproportionate burdens on low-income families (Arguelles & Ortiz-Luis, 2021). Policymakers must navigate this tension carefully. A balanced approach involves distinguishing between core rehabilitative functions and optional recreational services. Educational content, mental health resources, legal materials, and reentry preparation tools should be universally accessible, while entertainment features can remain optional and fee-based, consistent with public expectations. This tiered model preserves equity while respecting public concerns. It also prevents digital rehabilitation from becoming dependent on an individual's financial resources, which would undermine its purpose.

The mixed findings regarding correctional staff support underscore the importance of including frontline employees in policy development. Tablet programs affect daily operations. If staff perceive technology as increasing workload or reducing authority, resistance is likely. Training is essential. Staff should understand not only how tablet systems function but also why they matter. When officers see reductions in behavioral incidents, improved communication, and safer environments, support increases (Mufarreh et al., 2021). Policies that include staff feedback, training, and clear protocols are more sustainable and effective. Correctional officers are also members of the public, and their perceptions influence broader community attitudes. Positive staff experiences with technology can gradually reshape public opinion from within.

From a policy perspective, the most compelling argument for tablet use lies in reentry outcomes. Employment, housing, health care, and civic participation increasingly require digital literacy. Rehabilitation that ignores this reality is incomplete. Policymakers should frame tablet programs as part of reentry preparation rather than inmate recreation. This shift moves the conversation away from comfort during punishment and toward readiness for release. Research consistently links education, skill development, and family support to lower recidivism (Hall & Bannatyne, 2000; Kerr & Willis, 2018). Tablet programs should thus be evaluated not by their presence, but by their outcomes. Metrics such as program completion, post-release employment, and recidivism rates provide evidence that can justify continued investment.

For legislators, this study offers a clear message: Public opinion is nuanced, not hostile. Voters support rehabilitation when it is clearly defined and responsibly implemented. Policies that articulate boundaries, emphasize accountability, and demonstrate outcomes are more likely to gain support. Legislation governing correctional technology should address pricing transparency, data privacy, and equitable access. Oversight mechanisms can ensure that privatization does not undermine rehabilitative goals or exploit incarcerated populations. These measures protect both public trust and program integrity.

It has been demonstrated that tablet programs in correctional facilities succeed or fail not solely on their effectiveness but additionally on their alignment with public values and policy narratives. Reframing tablets as rehabilitative infrastructure, increasing transparency, addressing equity, and incorporating staff perspectives are essential steps toward sustainable implementation. Public opinion is not an obstacle to digital rehabilitation. It is a variable that can be shaped through evidence, transparency, and responsible policy design. To broaden this discussion, tablet use within the future of digital rehabilitation and correctional reform must be examined.

THE FUTURE OF DIGITAL REHABILITATION IN CORRECTIONS

Digital rehabilitation is no longer a speculative concept. It is an emerging necessity shaped by technological change, labor market expectations, and evolving views on punishment and reintegration. Tablet use in correctional facilities represents an early but significant step toward aligning rehabilitation practices with the realities of a digital society. The future of digital rehabilitation will depend on how effectively correctional systems balance security, equity, public acceptance, and long-term reintegration outcomes.

Correctional systems cannot remain technologically static while society continues to advance. Employment applications, housing systems, health care portals, and government services increasingly assume digital competence. Individuals released from incarceration who lack these skills face compounded barriers to reintegration (Jewkes & Reisdorf, 2016; Reisdorf & Rikard, 2018). Tablets provide a scalable and adaptable platform for addressing this challenge. Unlike fixed computer labs, they can support individualized learning, flexible programming, and continuous engagement. Therefore, as correctional systems evolve, tablets are likely to become standard components of rehabilitative infrastructure rather than exceptional initiatives.

Future rehabilitation models will need to integrate technology intentionally. Digital skill development should be treated as foundational, alongside literacy, vocational training, and behavioral programs. This approach reframes technology not as an optional enhancement, but as a core competency for reentry. While tablets currently dominate digital rehabilitation efforts, they are unlikely to remain the sole technological focus. Emerging tools such as virtual reality training modules, secure learning management systems, and AI-assisted educational platforms may eventually supplement or replace tablet-based programs. These technologies can simulate workplace environments, support adaptive learning, and provide personalized feedback. However, the lessons learned from tablet implementation are instructive. Public acceptance, equity, staff training, and governance will remain central concerns regardless of the technology used. The tablet debate demonstrates that technological capability alone does not guarantee success. Social perception and policy framing are equally important.

The study reinforces the idea that public opinion is not fixed. Attitudes toward rehabilitation, punishment, and inmate amenities have shifted over time and continue to evolve (Cullen et al., 2000; Enns, 2017). As digital technology becomes increasingly normalized across all areas of life, devices once considered luxuries may eventually be viewed as necessities. Tablets themselves illustrate this trajectory. Once regarded as optional consumer devices, they are now common tools in education, health care, and professional settings. As their societal role changes, public perceptions of their use in correctional facilities may also shift. Future policy efforts should anticipate and guide this transition rather than react to resistance.

Public education will play a critical role. Transparent communication about how technology is used, what it achieves, and how it is controlled can reduce fear-based opposition. Over time, demonstrated outcomes, such as reduced recidivism or improved post-release employment, can further legitimize digital rehabilitation initiatives.

The future of digital rehabilitation must address equity directly. If access to digital tools depends on an individual's financial resources, digital rehabilitation risks reproducing the same inequalities it seeks to resolve (Arguelles & Ortiz-Luis, 2021). Ensuring that educational, legal, and rehabilitative content is universally accessible is essential.

Ethical considerations also extend to data privacy and surveillance. As digital systems collect increasing amounts of behavioral data, correctional institutions must establish clear policies governing data use, retention, and oversight. Respect for dignity and proportionality should guide technological expansion, even within environments of control.

Leadership will be decisive in shaping the future of digital rehabilitation. Correctional administrators must move beyond reactive implementation toward strategic planning. This includes evaluating technology not only for cost and security but also for rehabilitative impact and staff integration.

Training and professional development will be essential. Staff confidence in technology influences both implementation quality and institutional culture (Mufarreh et al., 2021). Leaders who invest in training, solicit staff feedback, and align technology use with institutional goals are more likely to achieve sustainable outcomes.

The Cape Vincent study highlights the need for continued empirical research. While tablet programs are expanding, systematic evaluation remains limited. Future research should examine long-term outcomes, including digital skill retention, employment trajectories, and recidivism rates. Comparative studies across regions and populations can further refine best practices.

Public opinion research should also continue. Understanding how attitudes shift over time—and how they respond to education and evidence—can inform more responsive policy design. As new technologies emerge, the insights gained from tablet adoption will remain relevant.

In light of research, the evidence suggests that digital rehabilitation should be understood as a framework rather than a single intervention. Tablets are one component of a broader effort to prepare incarcerated individuals for life in a digital society. This framework integrates education, communication, mental health support, and digital literacy within secure and equitable systems. The future of correctional rehabilitation lies not in resisting technology, but in governing it responsibly. Digital tools, when implemented with clarity and purpose, can support safer institutions and more successful reintegration.

Tablet use in correctional facilities clearly sits at the intersection of technology, punishment, rehabilitation, and public opinion. Tablets are not merely devices; they are symbols, tools, and policy instruments. Their effectiveness depends on how they are framed, implemented, and evaluated. Looking forward, digital rehabilitation will continue to shape correctional reform. The question is not whether technology belongs in prisons, but how it can be used to support human development, public safety, and social reintegration. This study contributes to that conversation by grounding future directions in empirical evidence and public perspective.

ETHICAL CONSIDERATIONS, HUMAN DIGNITY, AND CULTURAL CHANGE IN DIGITAL REHABILITATION

The use of tablets in correctional facilities raises ethical questions that extend beyond technology, cost, or public opinion. At its core, the debate about digital access in prisons reflects deeper concerns about human dignity, fairness, and the moral purpose of punishment. As correctional systems increasingly adopt digital tools, it becomes essential to examine not only what these technologies do but also what they represent within a society committed to justice, rehabilitation, and social reintegration. Modern theories of punishment generally recognize multiple goals: deterrence, incapacitation, retribution, and rehabilitation. While these goals may coexist, democratic societies increasingly acknowledge that incarceration should not strip individuals of their fundamental dignity (Hudson, 2003). Rehabilitation, in particular, presumes that incarcerated individuals retain the capacity for growth, learning, and change.

Digital rehabilitation aligns closely with this premise. Access to educational materials, mental health resources, and communication tools affirms the idea that incarcerated individuals are more than the crimes they committed. Tablets, when used responsibly, can support autonomy, self-improvement, and psychological well-being. Denying access to basic digital tools in a highly technological society risks reinforcing social exclusion and undermining the rehabilitative mission of incarceration (Jewkes & Reisdorf, 2016). Ethically, the question is not whether incarcerated individuals deserve comfort, but whether society has an obligation to prepare them for lawful participation upon release. From this perspective, digital literacy is not a luxury; it is a prerequisite for functioning in contemporary social and economic systems.

Equity is a central ethical concern in digital rehabilitation. As discussed earlier, many tablet programs rely on fee-based models for communication and content access. While public opinion often supports charging inmates for optional services, this approach raises fairness concerns. Incarcerated populations disproportionately come from low-income backgrounds, and many families already bear significant financial burdens related to incarceration (Arguelles & Ortiz-Luis, 2021). When access to educational or rehabilitative content depends on an individual's ability to pay, digital rehabilitation risks replicating the same inequalities present outside prison walls. Ethical implementation therefore requires clear distinctions between essential rehabilitative functions and optional recreational services. Educational materials, legal resources, and reentry preparation should be accessible regardless of financial status. This approach balances public concerns with ethical responsibility.

Digital technologies inevitably introduce surveillance. Tablet use in correctional facilities is closely monitored, with communication logged and content access tracked. While security concerns justify a degree of oversight, ethical tensions arise when surveillance becomes pervasive or opaque. Incarcerated individuals have limited control over how their data is collected or used. Ethical governance requires transparency about monitoring practices, limits on data retention, and safeguards against misuse. Respect for autonomy should not disappear in prison; while constrained, it must not be extinguished. Digital rehabilitation should therefore aim to support self-regulation and responsibility rather than reinforce constant observation as a behavioral control mechanism (Knight, 2016).

The ethical challenges surrounding tablet use are closely tied to cultural perceptions of punishment. Public resistance to digital access often reflects deeply ingrained beliefs that punishment must involve deprivation and discomfort. Technologies that resemble consumer devices challenge this belief system and provoke moral unease. The study demonstrates that this resistance is not absolute. When tablet use is framed as educational or rehabilitative, public support increases, suggesting that cultural change is possible, but gradual. Ethical reform in corrections rarely occurs through abrupt policy shifts; it emerges through sustained dialogue, evidence, and transparency (Cullen et al., 2000). Correctional staff play a crucial role in this cultural transformation. Officers and administrators who witness positive outcomes, such as reduced behavioral incidents, calmer environments, and improved inmate engagement, become informal ambassadors of change. Their experiences can influence both institutional culture and broader public attitudes.

Ethically, society bears some responsibility for the outcomes of incarceration. High recidivism rates reflect not only individual failure but also systemic shortcomings in preparation for reentry. Digital exclusion is one such shortcoming. Releasing individuals into a society that operates digitally, without adequate preparation, sets them up for failure (Reisdorf & Rikard, 2018). Tablets, as part of a broader digital rehabilitation framework, offer a means of addressing this responsibility by allowing incarcerated individuals to develop familiarity with digital interfaces, communication norms, and self-directed learning. These skills contribute to agency and self-efficacy, both of which are associated with successful reintegration.

For policymakers and correctional leaders, ethical considerations must inform decision-making alongside cost, security, and public opinion. Policies that restrict digital access purely to satisfy punitive sentiment risk undermining long-term public safety. Ethical leadership requires balancing immediate political pressures with evidence-based practices that promote rehabilitation. This includes resisting simplistic narratives that equate technology with indulgence. It also requires acknowledging that digital rehabilitation is not about comfort, but competence. Ethical policy frames tablet use as an investment in reduced recidivism, safer communities, and social reintegration.

Ultimately, the ethical case for tablets in correctional facilities is grounded in inclusion. Digital exclusion exacerbates marginalization. Digital inclusion, when implemented responsibly, supports dignity, opportunity, and accountability. The transition toward digital rehabilitation reflects broader societal shifts toward recognizing the importance of skills, access, and equity in achieving justice. Cultural change is slow, but evidence suggests it is possible. As tablets become normalized as educational and rehabilitative tools—rather than symbols of luxury—public resistance may diminish. Ethical clarity, transparency, and outcome-focused communication will be essential in guiding this transition.

As a result, tablet use in correctional facilities raises fundamental ethical questions about dignity, equity, surveillance, and social responsibility. Digital rehabilitation is not simply a technological innovation; it is a moral statement about how society understands punishment and reintegration in a digital age. Incorporating tablets into correctional systems ethically requires careful governance, equitable access, respect for autonomy, and sustained cultural engagement. When these conditions are met, digital rehabilitation can contribute not only to individual transformation but also to broader societal goals of justice and inclusion.

CONCLUSION

Tablet use in correctional facilities has been examined through the lenses of digital rehabilitation, public opinion, and empirical evidence drawn from a community closely situated to a correctional institution. The analysis demonstrated that while tablets are often perceived as luxury items, public support increases significantly when their use is clearly framed around education, rehabilitation, and maintaining family connections. These findings reinforce the importance of how technology is presented, governed, and communicated within correctional systems.

The results of the Cape Vincent study indicate that residents generally support the educational and rehabilitative functions of tablet use in correctional facilities, though perceptions vary by gender and education level. Female participants and individuals with higher educational attainment were more likely to support tablet use for educational purposes, while broader resistance emerged when tablet access was associated with entertainment or free privileges. These distinctions highlight a persistent tension between rehabilitative goals and punitive attitudes toward incarceration.

Beyond empirical patterns, the ethical dimensions of digital rehabilitation are also emphasized. Tablet use in correctional facilities is not merely a technological or administrative decision; it reflects societal beliefs about punishment, dignity, and responsibility in a digital age. Ethical considerations such as equity of access, respect for human dignity, surveillance, and cultural resistance play a critical role in shaping both public opinion and policy outcomes. As societies become increasingly dependent on digital skills, excluding incarcerated individuals from meaningful technological engagement risks reinforcing the very conditions that contribute to recidivism.

The findings suggest that digital technologies, when implemented transparently, ethically, and with a rehabilitative focus, can serve as powerful tools for reintegration rather than symbols of excessive privilege. Public support is not inherently opposed to technology in prisons; rather, it is contingent upon purpose, accountability, and perceived fairness. Correctional leaders and policymakers therefore face the dual challenge of designing effective digital rehabilitation programs while also addressing public concerns through evidence, education, and ethical clarity.

Tablet use in correctional facilities sits at the critical intersection of technology, punishment, and social reintegration. When framed and governed appropriately, tablets can contribute to safer facilities, more effective rehabilitation, and stronger community outcomes. At the same time, understanding and engaging public opinion, while grounding policy decisions in ethical principles, remains essential for advancing correctional practices that align with both justice and societal well-being.

REFERENCES

Arguelles, C., & Ortiz-Luis, I. (2021, May). Bars behind bars: Digital technology in the prison system. *SSRN*, *32*(1), 1–18. DOI: 10.2139/ssrn.3812046

Bishop, G. (2021). *Tablet use in Cape Vincent Correctional Facility, NY: Its effects on the community.* [Master's thesis, Campbellsville University].

Blizzard, B. (2018, January 25). *National poll results.* [Memorandum]. Justice Action Network. https://www.politico.com/f/?id=00000161-2ccc-da2c-a963-efff82be0001

Cournoyer, J., & Stanton, S. (2016, January 19). *In jail, tablets calm and educate inmates.* Governing. https://www.governing.com/archive/tns-tablets-jail-sacramento.html

Cullen, F. T., Fisher, B. S., & Applegate, B. K. (2000). Public opinion about punishment and corrections. *Crime and Justice*, *27*, 1–79. DOI: 10.1086/652198

Enns, P. K. (2017). *Incarceration nation: How the United States became the most punitive democracy in the world.* Cambridge University Press.

Hall, R. A., & Bannatyne, M. W. McK. (2000, December). Technology education and the convicted felon: How it works behind prison walls. *Journal of Correctional Education*, *51*(4), 320–323. https://www.jstor.org/stable/41971950

Hudson, B. (2003). *Understanding justice: An introduction to ideas, perspectives, and controversies in modern penal theory.* Open University Press.

Jewkes, Y., & Reisdorf, B. C. (2016, November). A brave new world: The problems and opportunities presented by new media technologies in prisons. *Criminology & Criminal Justice*, *16*(5), 534–551. DOI: 10.1177/1748895816654953

Johnson, H. J., & Hail-Jares, K. (2016). Technology and prisons. In Jewkes, Y., Bennett, J., & Crewe, B. (Eds.), *Handbook on prisons* (2nd ed., pp. 273–291). Routledge. DOI: 10.4324/9781315797779-17

Johnson, R. (2005). *Hard time: Understanding and reforming the prison* (3rd ed.). Wadsworth.

Kerr, A., & Willis, M. (2018, October). Prisoner use of information and communications technology. *Trends and Issues in Crime and Criminal Justice*, *560*, 1–19. DOI: 10.52922/ti107289

Knight, V. (2016). *Remote control: Television in prisons.* Palgrave Macmillan. DOI: 10.1057/9781137443915

Lenz, N. (2002, October). "Luxuries" in Prison: The relationship between amenity funding and public support. *Crime and Delinquency*, *48*(4), 499–525. DOI: 10.1177/001112802237127

McDougall, C., Pearson, D. A. S., Torgerson, D. J., & Garcia-Reyes, M. (2017, October). The effect of digital technology on prisoner behavior and reoffending: A natural stepped-wedge design. *Journal of Experimental Criminology*, *13*(1), 455–482. DOI: 10.1007/s11292-017-9303-5

Mufarreh, A., Waitkus, J., & Booker, T. A. (2021, February). Prison official perceptions of technology in prison. *Punishment & Society*, *24*(3), 410–432. DOI: 10.1177/1462474521990777

O'Hear, M. M., & Wheelock, D. (2016). Public attitudes toward punishment, rehabilitation, and reform: Lessons from the Marquette Law School Poll. *Faculty Publications,* 678. https://scholarship.law.marquette.edu/facpub/678

Ramirez, M. D. (2013, March). Punitive sentiment. *Criminology, 51*(2), 329–364. DOI: 10.1111/1745-9125.12007

Raynor, P., & Robinson, G. (2009). *Rehabilitation, crime, and justice*. Palgrave Macmillan.

Reisdorf, B. C., & Rikard, R. V. (2018, May). Digital rehabilitation: A model of reentry into the digital age. *The American Behavioral Scientist, 62*(9), 1273–1290. DOI: 10.1177/0002764218773817

Stewart, S. T. (2017, September 19). How tablets are helping clean up one Ariz. prison. *Corrections1*. https://www.corrections1.com/products/corrections/articles/how-tablets-are-helping-clean-up-one-ariz-prison-pcpVlpSvZVVGHICO

Wozniak, K. H. (2014, September). American public opinion about prisons. *Criminal Justice Review, 39*(3), 305–324. DOI: 10.1177/0734016814529968

Chapter 17

Supporting the Community Reintegration of People Leaving Prison:

Measuring Digital Skills as a Tool for Inclusion

Karlie E. Stonard
http://orcid.org/0000-0001-7431-6225
University of Wolverhampton, UK

Laura Caulfield
University of Wolverhampton, UK

Kyros Hadjisergis
http://orcid.org/0009-0000-2575-9329
University of Wolverhampton, UK

Siobhan Sadlier
University of Wolverhampton, UK

ABSTRACT

This mixed methods case study presents research conducted with the innovative Tech4PrisonLeavers pilot project that provided digital and employability skills training to male former prisoners. The research utilised a Digital Literacy Assessment (DLA) along with psychological scales, and voice diaries or a reflective survey, to measure digital literacy and the impact of the digital skills programme. Participants completed a DLA (n=23) and psychological scales before and after (n=12) the project. Participants (n=9) also completed the qualitative element, detailing their thoughts and experiences of the digital skills training received. The combination of a digital skills assessment with qualitative insights has the potential to be a model for measuring the impact of digital skills programmes across and beyond the criminal justice context however the use of voice diaries did raise some challenges. Participants discussed the value of the training in having a wider impact on their lives and goals for the future.

DOI: 10.4018/979-8-3373-7660-8.ch017

INTRODUCTION

This case study is based on a wider study of an innovative digital skills project for people leaving prison: Tech4PrisonLeavers. The pilot project aimed to reduce reoffending rates and associated costs by providing digital and employability skills training to 20-25 male former prisoners aged 18-44 (although originally aimed at men aged 18-44, in practice older men were accepted onto the pilot.). The project focused on improving participants' digital skills and enhancing their employment opportunities, leading to sustainable employment and a brighter future for themselves, their families, and their communities (Digital Poverty Alliance, 2023). Tech4PrisonLeavers was overseen by the Digital Poverty Alliance, with funding from Intel, and delivered by Radical Recruit, who offered a series of interventions, workshops, and training sessions aimed at increasing the men's digital literacy (reducing the digital skills gap) and employability, thereby contributing to desistence from crime. The men were provided with devices (laptops and dongles) to access the internet and given support in key areas such as setting up email accounts and accessing Microsoft packages, video conference call facilities (Zoom, Teams), developing their curriculum vitae. They were allowed to keep these devices upon completion of the project. Practical assistance was provided through training, and mentorship by CapGemini, Vodafone, CGI, Nacro, iDEA, and We Are Digital. It is noted that contention with the term “prison leavers” used in the title of the pilot was not intended to reinforce stigmatisation. The terms “individual,” “participant,” or “men” hereafter are used where possible unless using the name of the pilot.

The authors were the researchers for this project and were involved from the outset to embed research and evaluation into the project design. A summary of the full qualitative and quantitative findings can be found in a White Paper (Digital Poverty Alliance, 2024). Positive outcomes are reported in terms of the men either securing paid employment upon completion or having success at being invited for interviews. The men reported positive improvements on various psychological and personal measures of wellbeing, feelings of competence in finding future employment and participants' aspirations for personal growth. This current research is focused on the digital literacy element of Tech4PrisonLeavers, reporting a case study of how the impact of the project on digital literacy was measured and understood. Given the nature of the project as an exploratory pilot with people leaving prison (which is a hard-to-reach population), there are several limitations explained later, but these do not negate the value of the lessons learned from this research which are important findings to share.

A summary of emerging research is first provided concerning digital literacy within the context of the criminal justice system. The methodology is outlined and the development and use of a Digital Literacy Assessment (DLA) as a quantitative measure of the impact of the digital skills programme, alongside three psychological scales to measure mental wellbeing, perceived confidence, and aspirations for the future. This was complemented with reflective voice diaries or written survey responses to qualitatively explore experiences of the project and to understand how this had an impact on participants' digital skills and outlook for the future. The quantitative findings from the DLA and psychological scales are provided followed by the key themes from the qualitative voice diaries or survey responses, demonstrating that the combination of a digital skills assessment with qualitative insights has the potential to be a model for measuring the impact of digital skills programmes across and beyond the criminal justice context.

LITERATURE REVIEW

The core theoretical frameworks underpinning this case study are that of social exclusion, social harm, and digital literacy. Individuals leaving prison often experience social and economic exclusion because of their criminal label, such exclusion may also be experienced prior to incarceration (Young, 1999). Incarcerated people may experience further exclusion from access to resources and opportunities outside such as access to technology and the internet. The digital literacy of individuals who have been incarcerated for a significant time is of concern and is fundamental to their participation in modern society and their subsequent successful reintegration and inclusion once released (Digital Poverty Alliance, 2024). Not providing men leaving prison with education and skills to navigate a digital world upon their release could be described as socially harmful and what Salmi (2004) terms as an indirect violation of the right to survival (violence by omission). Without the ability to navigate a digital world, men leaving prison will be disadvantaged when searching for and applying for jobs amongst other daily essential activities such as banking, paying bills, applying for benefits, housing, employment, or making and accessing appointments. Research has shown a link between digital literacy and (long-term) employability and in influencing career decision-making and self-efficacy (Gao, 2024). For example, Lloyds Bank (2021) reported that around 11 million people in the UK lack the digital skills needed for everyday life, 36% of the workforce lack Essential Digital Skills for work, and only 74% of those who earn up to £13,500 per year have Essential Digital Skills for life vs. 95% of those who earn over £75,000. Furthermore, over 75% of modern jobs require digital literacy to some extent (Caroline et al., 2025). However, the lack of access to the internet in prisons - the "digital wall" - can lead to difficult transitions into a world that relies on the internet for basic essential services once released and therefore impacts on rehabilitation and resettlement (Prison Reform Trust 2025). A further consideration here is the issue of access (i.e. inclusion) after release which might be affected by practical issues such as unstable housing or the ability to access a safe and private space in the community to use the internet, which may present a further barrier causing stress and undermining confidence, even for digitally literate individuals (Prison Reform Trust 2025).Van De Steene and Knight (2017) note that "there is a societal responsibility to ensure all citizens can flourish" (p. 258). Ultimately, without such skills, individuals leaving prison will undoubtedly be excluded from full participation in social, educational and employment opportunities, leaving them vulnerable to further exclusion and risks of poverty and reoffending.

What is "Digital Literacy"?

Digital literacy refers to "the knowledge, skills and attitudes that underpin the ability to make confident, creative, and effective use of technologies and systems, and make well-informed critical judgements about the implications and impact of how digital technology is used" (British Computer Society, n.d.). The BCS argues the definition extends beyond common applications identified in the UK Government's Essential Digital Skills Framework to provide a wider understanding of digital participation in the modern world. UNESCO also previously defined digital literacy as "the ability to access, manage, understand, integrate, communicate, evaluate and create information safely and appropriately through digital technologies for employment, decent jobs and entrepreneurship. It includes competences that are variously referred to as computer literacy, ICT literacy, information literacy and media literacy" (Law et al., 2018, p. 6). Digital literacy thus moves beyond simple "digital skills" in that it refers to cognitive ability and an understanding of using these skills in an ethical manner, instead of simple skill competence (OECD, 2023). Basic ICT-based skills include things like searching for information online, word processing, using spreadsheets, or online communication tools (OECD 2023). "Digital inclusion" means accessibility to digital tools and opportunities to learn skills for full inclusion and equal participation in modern society. Many have been critical of attempts to standardise definitions of "digital literacy" due to notable regional and cultural differences in definitions as well as the politics of education (Pangrazio et al., 2020; Global Digital Compact 2023).

Digital Literacy and Prisons

New skills are needed to access and utilise new technologies, digital tools and the internet. Foundational literacies (such as the ability to read and write) are also essential for accessing digital information effectively and ethically (Leu et al., 2013; Julien, 2019). This is a challenge for the prison population who often have lower levels of educational achievements and literacy than the general population (Ministry of Justice, 2021). The Centre for Social Justice (2021) reports that only 18 out of 117 prisons possess in-cell cabling or hardware to support broadband and many older prisoners serving longer sentences have never held a digital device. Arguably, prison institutions need to do more to develop their digital provision using a needs-based and human-centred approach to support rehabilitation, desistance, societal integration and to reduce digital exclusion (Van De Steene & Knight, 2017). Improving the digital literacy of those in prison can have social and psychological benefits such as engaging prisoners in active learning, time management, increased autonomy and self-esteem (Knight, 2015; Knight, 2017). Such benefits are not limited to men in prison but can also lead to positive outcomes for prison staff through establishing a calmer and more productive prison environment creating opportunities for constructive activities to take place that can better prepare men for release and resettlement, as well as alleviating boredom which can amplify loneliness and harmful outcomes (Knight, 2015; Knight, 2017). This digital lag prisoners may experience interrupts their successful transition back into society. Control and regulations contrast with the provision of opportunities for digital literacy, which in turn assists rehabilitation and reintegration (Knight & Van De Steene, 2017a). The Prison Reform Trust (2025) reports an emerging digital culture in prisons after its earlier recommendation for more "interactive, updated and secure web content" to be made available in prisons which includes better access to virtual methods of communication with families and self-services. The issue of the "digital wall" cannot be underestimated.

Digital Education and Reducing Reoffending

Diminished access to technology can enhance the distance between prisoners and society in a rapidly changing digital world. A feedback loop emerges where "social exclusion leads to digital exclusion, which in turn perpetuates and exacerbates that social exclusion" (Monteiro et al., 2015, p. 1038). The literature presents a picture of prisoners having inconsistent and often inadequate access to education both before and during prison, and inadequate access to technology exacerbates the educational award gap and its impact on employability (Grierson et al., 2022; Barreiro-Gen & Novo-Corti, 2015).

Low education levels and poor employment experiences are statistically linked to an increased risk of recidivism (Bonta et al., 2013). Most people in contact with the criminal justice system (CJS), both in the UK and globally, have few educational or professional qualifications (McLauchlan & Farley, 2019; Barreiro-Gen & Novo-Corti, 2015). There are a range of barriers such as: previous experiences of education impacting future decisions around engagement with education; undiagnosed learning difficulties

(Maroney et al., 2019; Jones & Manger, 2019); and the fear of not being proficient in this area or being seen as "dumb" (Ricciardelli et al., 2015). Basic skills boost employability, but a comprehensive educational experience has a wider impact framed as "secondary desistance from crime" (McNeil, 2014, in McFarlane & Pike, 2019, p. 3). Education serves to reduce recidivism but also has a developmental effect on prisoners and creates safer environments (Farley & Pike, 2016). Education offers a "student identity" and opportunity to bolster resilience inside and outside of prison.

Unfortunately, prison management and delivery of educational opportunities can reduce the potential for education to become a pathway to societal reintegration. The risk management approach of the CJS can potentially limit the quality of delivery, with internet access a security concern and online learning resources therefore unavailable for many learners unless they meet criteria to be accepted onto "whitelists" (Monteiro et al., 2015; Pike & Adams, 2012). Further organisational barriers to accessing education include ineffective leadership and policy decision making, the quality and use of teaching and learning support staff as well as how they are employed and trained, short term sentencing, lack of fast track enrolment for prisoners on short term sentences, continuity of curriculum between prisons and the community, lack of quality interactive multimedia learning materials, and restricted access to technology (Monteiro et al., 2015).

Addressing the Digital Needs of Former Prisoners

There are examples in the literature of the digital needs of former prisoners, in a basic sense, as they leave prison and re-enter the community. For example, a phone for contacting professionals or a laptop for continuing learning started in prison (Kaun & Stiernstedt, 2020; Capece, 2020; McFarlane & Pike, 2019). There are examples of technology being weaved into the lives of (former) prisoners for educational (Pike & Adams, 2012), wellbeing (Kaun & Stiernstedt, 2020), and security purposes (Smith, 2020). Many of these are isolated pilots globally and do not reflect policy changes in criminal justice.

There is evidence within prisons of self-service technology enabling a sense of control and confidence in returning to a digital world, as well as impacting a prisoner's outlook and behaviour (McDougall et al., 2017). In the UK, self-service kiosks can be used for a range of purposes, such as to "arrange family or legal visits, order certain products or choose their canteen food" (Kaun & Stiernstedt, 2020, p. 1585), and enable prisoners to build a sense of independence. When comparing the frequency of disciplinary processes in settings with and without kiosks, McDougall et al. (2017) found that there was a reduction in re-offending of 5.36%, compared to 0.78% in comparison prisons. Jewkes and Reisdorf (2016) argue that the use of kiosks enables responsibilisation.

There are examples of being offered devices to enable learning. For example, the Open University (UK) developed a scheme to lend laptops to former prison students to support continued studying post release (McFarlane & Pike, 2019), although no publicly available data yet exist concerning the impact of this scheme. In 2022, the House of Commons Education Committee recommended that the Ministry of Justice enable prisoners to have access to devices and 'in cell technology' for education purposes, that was envisaged to "allow prisoners to have greater access to courses and tutors, enabling them to work at their own pace, and would provide continuity when they moved prison" (House of Commons Education Committee, 2022, p. 28).

Post-prison, there are some examples of digital tools that exist aiming to mitigate the challenges of engaging with probation services. An app used by former prisoners in Sweden, Utsikt, aims to improve engagement with probation from tracking attendance at required meetings through to cognitive training exercises (Kaun & Stiernstedt, 2020). These exercises are designed to help former prisoners prepare for challenging environments. Critically, use is voluntary. In the US, the Missouri Community Corrections and Rehabilitative Services started using Skype for communication between prisoners, former prisoners, and probation staff (National Institute of Justice, 2014). A key benefit for former prisoners was not having to travel to appointments, "which can be a significant amount of time" (Capece, 2020, p. 387). In Australia, an app is being used to improve the experience of probation, co-designed with probationers. An app that would support independent living skills and self-management was needed, but was not connected to probation practitioners or the CJS as a whole because "if there's a perception that Corrections could access it, they wouldn't use it" (Grierson et al., 2022, p. 509). This app was regarded by some as a "reintegration road map" helping with practical tasks of getting a bank account, planning meals, and getting a driver's licence, and thus amounting to a "digital transition plan" that is further helpful to temporarily share with professionals. It must be noted that many former prisoners may not be able to afford smartphones, particularly those who have been released from longer sentences (Kaun & Stiernstedt, 2020).

In researching design considerations of digital services aiming to support former prisoners, peer support emerged as a key element (Grierson et al., 2022, p. 509). There was a connection to the value of lived experience and one participant noted the value of interacting with former prisoners through a "message board that they can bounce ideas of … [to] seek advice from others who had left prison" (Grierson et al., 2022, p. 509). Destigmatisation can be enabled through peer support.

It is therefore vital that former prisoners have appropriate digital skills to enable them to seek and secure employment (as such skills are essential for searching and applying for jobs) thus reducing risk of reoffending. Emerging evidence suggests that digital skills programmes should also involve peer and mentoring support (Grierson et al., 2022; Hadjisergis et al., in prep.). While some examples exist internationally of digital support for former prisoners, little evidence yet exists of the impact of these programmes, particularly within England. This provides reasons for exploring the use of a DLA as a tool to measure digital literacy in men leaving prison who were enrolled on a programme designed to support their digital and employment skills. Using voice diary or open survey responses, the research also qualitatively explored how the men in the pilot viewed the impact of the programme.

METHODOLOGY

Approach and Design

This case study used a mixed methods convergent design where the quantitative and qualitative data analysis is considered together providing a more thorough and comprehensive understanding of the impact of a digital skills programme than could be achieved through either method if used alone. The boundary between mixed methods and case study research is fluid, meaning this methodology is flexible (Carolan et al., 2016) and particularly suitable for in-depth research assessing the impact of a programme (Creswell, 2014). In the current study, the quantitative element included the DLA to assess digital skills and change over time, while the qualitative element explored how and where this change occurred, in addition to the impact of such changes in skills because of the programme.

The research was undertaken by researchers with considerable experience in conducting research in the CJS and community projects. Ethical approval was granted by the University of Wolverhampton Ethics Committee and the research adheres to the ethical guidelines of the British Psychological Society.

Design of Measures and Data Collection

Digital Literacy Assessment (DLA)

The DLA used as the primary quantitative measure was developed from the Department for Education's (2018) Essential Digital Skills Framework, which has not been used as a measure of digital skills in this context before. The DLA consisted of 21 questions with subthemes, each including 2-4 questions relating to their confidence in: foundational skills, communicating, handing information and content, transacting, problem solving, being safe and legal online, and other (relating to searching and applying for jobs online). Participants were asked to rate how they felt on a scale from 1–5 with 1 being not confident and 5 being very confident. DLAs were completed via JISC Online Surveys; first during the face-to-face launch of the project (Time 1) using devices provided and then at the end of the project (Time 2). The survey was sent via a weblink and mentors supported those who needed it to complete it. The Cronbach's alpha for the Time 1 and Time 2 DLA surveys showed good reliability (.98 and .97 respectively). The Essential Digital Skills Framework was used as the basis for the DLA based on group discussions with the research team and project partners (i.e. Digital Poverty Alliance) and subsequent shared decision this was an appropriate tool to use. This framework is highlighted by the UK government, specifically, the Department for Education in their guidance (GOV.UK 2019)

Further measures of primary outcomes of the project

In addition to the DLA, this research also utilised three validated psychological quantitative measures of further primary outcomes (1) well-being; (2) perceived competence (i.e. with finding future employment and doing well at work); and (3) aspirations for the future. Both questionnaires were completed via JISC Online Surveys. Again, participants completed the surveys first during a face-to-face launch of the project, using devices provided as part of the project. Surveys were then completed online at the end of the project.

Wellbeing: Warwick Edinburgh Mental Wellbeing Scale: short version (SWEMWBS)

The Short Warwick Edinburgh Mental Well-being Scale (SWEMWBS; Tennant et al., 2007) is designed to monitor well-being in the general population. SWEMWBS is a shorter version of the 14-item WEMWBS. The seven items relate to functioning rather than to feeling, such as measurement of elements of positive affect, satisfying interpersonal relationships and positive functioning. The SWEMWBS is scored by first summing the scores for each of the seven items, which are scored from 1 to 5. The total raw scores are then transformed into metric scores using a SWEMWBS conversion table. The shorter length of SWEMWBS makes it particularly suitable for evaluations (Warwick Medical School, 2020) and SWEMWBS has been successfully used with several study populations (e.g. Breslin et al., 2018).

Perceived Competence Scale (PCS)

Competence is proposed to be a fundamental psychological need (Williams & Deci, 1996) and perceptions of competence facilitate goal attainment. The perception of one's competence may affect behaviour and be predictive of other areas of performance. Any significant changes in participant scores on the Perceived Competence Scale (PCS) would indicate changes in the likelihood of behavioural changes and levels of effective performance. The PCS is a short, four-item questionnaire devised to be specific to the behaviour or activity being studied. Individuals rate each item on a 7-point Likert scale where 1 = not at all true, 4 = somewhat true and 7 = very true. This scale has demonstrated good psychometric properties of validity and reliability across a variety of settings (Williams & Gill, 1995; Williams et al., 2006; Williams et al., 2004). In this research, the PCS assesses participants' feelings of competence in finding future employment and doing well at work. PCS has been successfully used with multiple study populations (e.g. Caulfield et al., 2023).

Aspirations Index (AI)

The Aspirations Index (AI) (Kasser & Ryan, 1996) was developed to assess individual aspirations. The Aspirations Index includes seven categories of aspirations within the full scale. This assessment has demonstrated good psychometric properties of reliability and validity across a range of settings (Bernard & Taffesse, 2014; Utvaer et al., 2014). The intrinsic aspirations scale of personal growth was used in this research. Participants rate (a) the importance to themselves of each aspiration, (b) their beliefs about the likelihood of attaining each, and (c) the degree to which they have already attained each. For example, participants are asked to think about their actions, and rate the importance, likelihood of attaining goals, and the current level of attainment, on a 7-point Likert rating scale. There are a total of five items for importance, five for likelihood, and five for attainment for the personal growth subscale. As noted above, attainment of personal growth is positively associated with well-being (Sheldon & Kasser, 1998). The AI with multiple study populations, including people leaving prison, has been successfully used (e.g. McGuire-Snieckus & Caulfield, 2018).

Reflective voice diary / survey questions

The reflective voice diary/survey questions were developed for the purpose of this study. To understand participant's experiences and the impact of the project, a set of questions was designed to be asked at both the start and the end of the project, plus four sets of questions to be asked during (bi-weekly) participation in the project. The questions included a focus on the impact of technology and training, access to Education/Training/Employment (ETE), engagement with ETE opportunities, wellbeing, barriers and levers in the project, plus open-ended questions about elements of the project participants most worried about, enjoyed, or found useful. The men completed this with a Radical Recruit mentor.

Voice diaries (or audio diaries) are a flexible qualitative approach to capturing individuals' experiences and have the potential to yield rich qualitative data while empowering participants to share their reflections (Williamson et al., 2015; Verma, 2021). The diary method has been used successfully in research in other contexts such as higher education (Sabharwal et al., 2021) and health settings (Coolbrandt et al., 2017; Williamson et al., 2012). Negative aspects, however, have also been highlighted relating to ethical and methodological concerns (e.g., confidentiality, participant reservations related to self-consciousness, lack of participant support and ability to offer prompts, and the varied length and quality of recordings) which can be influenced by the skill and motivation of participants (Williamson et al., 2015). Only five (from four men) of the 12 responses to the qualitative questions were provided in this way, the other seven responses (from five men) were transferred to a survey format, indicating some barriers or issues for this participant group that need to be further explored. Although these questions were asked and recorded in different formats, the same questions were asked, and mentors assisted the mentees in both instances ensuring comparability in that sense.

Radical Recruit worked with the participants, assisting them when needed to complete both the DLA online surveys and the qualitative voice diaries/surveys. It is important to note that participants were not all recruited at the same time but as and when they were released from prison, meaning some men were engaged with the programme for longer than others and may therefore have completed more frequent responses to the qualitative questions.

Setting and Participants

The organisation delivering the project introduced the research to the participants, gained their consent, and recorded demographic information that was shared with consent with the research team for the purpose of the wider study. The participants were purposively selected by Radical Recruit working with men leaving prison in the London (UK) area based on the criteria that they were male and had been released from prison during the timeframe of the Tech4PrisonLeavers pilot project (2023).

27 men enrolled in the pilot project and 15 of these completed the project. Demographic data were provided for the 27 men who initially enrolled in the pilot: Mean age=38.4 years (SD=12.3, Min=19 years, Max=59 years); 37% described themselves as White British, 14.8% British Pakistani or British Caribbean, 7.4% British Indian, British African, White and Caribbean, or Other White, and 3.7% as Any Other. Most of the men reported having a low level of education, training and employment (40.7%), followed by being educated and having a work history (33%), highly educated and extensive work history (22.2%), and unknown (3.7%). Most men rated their health as good (66.7%) followed by average (18.5%), poor or unknown (7.4%). The most important resettlement factors (criminogenic needs) identified for the men were attitudes, thinking and behaviour (74.1%), drugs and alcohol (14.8%), finance, benefit and debt (7.4%), and unknown (3.7%). Finally, the self-rated digital skills collected by the pilot programme delivery team (not the DLA measure used in the data collection phase of this research) indicated most of the men felt that they had a poor level of digital skills (40.7%), followed by average (25.9%), good (22.2%), and excellent (3.7%); in 7.4% of cases this was noted as unknown.

23 out of 27 men completed the initial quantitative self-assessed DLA measure at Time 1 and 12 out of 15 at Time 2 (52% completion rate). Unfortunately, the research team were not provided with unique participant reference codes by the pilot programme team so were unable to determine which of the 27 men for whom demographic data were available went on to complete the initial DLA. Nine men engaged with the qualitative element (submitting a total of 12 responses) which sought to gain insight into how the men were experiencing the programme and its potential benefits or challenges. These were either completed using the voice diary format or the responses were written up in a survey format, supported by their Radical Recruit mentor. The mixed methods research process therefore started with the quantitative data collection, followed by a series of qualitative data collection, with a final collection of quantitative data (Creswell & Plano Clark, 2018).

Data Analysis

The Statistical Package for the Social Sciences (SPSS) was used to analyse the quantitative data. Basic descriptive analyses were undertaken to calculate mean scores and standard deviations for the available Time 1 and Time 2 data. Insufficient Time 2 data were available to test for any statistical differences between mean scores at Time 1 and Time 2, therefore only the overall scores for the samples at each time point are reported. Qualitative data from the reflective voice diaries/survey responses were organised using a thematic process (Braun & Clarke, 2006). These responses were grouped into related themes that are of relevance to the success and impact of the digital skills training received by one of the authors. These themes were then checked by the other team members to ensure accuracy and relevance. As this study was exploratory, saturation was determined by the sample size, and all responses were read multiple times and coded into themes. Verbatim extracts from the men's responses are provided to get a deeper understanding of how the men felt about the project before, during and after completion in relation to these themes.

FINDINGS

Quantitative findings: Digital Literacy Assessment (DLA)

As can be seen in Table 1, the Mean shows an overall score on this DLA measure slightly above the average or neutral response option. The highest Mean score at Time 1 was for the "foundational skills" subscale (e.g. using a laptop, getting connected to the internet and opening a browser), suggesting relative confidence with more basic digital skills prior to the project. The lowest levels of confidence were reported for being safe and legal online. Mean scores improved on all measures between Time 1 (start of the project) and Time 2 (end of the project), which is promising. There was insufficient data to test, however, if the findings are statistically significant and likely to be generalisable beyond this participant group.

Table 1. Digital Literacy Assessment (DLA)

	T1		T2	
	Mean	**SD**	**Mean**	**SD**
Overall score	3.73	1.00	4.31	0.59
Foundation skills	4.07	0.93	4.52	0.60
Communicating	3.79	0.99	4.47	0.39
Handing information and content	3.77	1.01	4.28	0.55
Transacting	3.72	1.12	4.42	0.64
Problem solving	3.84	1.00	4.13	0.64
Being safe and legal online	3.47	1.10	4.02	0.77
Other	3.67	0.90	4.30	0.60

Notes: Overall Time 1 based on 19/23 responses. Subscales range from 22-23/23 responses.
Time 2 based on 12 responses

Quantitative Findings: Psychological Scales for Other Primary Outcome Variables

As can be seen in Table 2, there was an improvement in participant's self-reported well-being over the course of the project, in addition to an improvement in participant's feelings of competence in finding future employment and doing well at work over the course of the project. Finally, there was an improvement in participant's aspirations for personal growth over the course of the project. As with the DLA, while mean scores improved on all measures between Time 1 (start of project) and Time 2 (end of project), there was insufficient data to conduct robust statistical analyses to test if the findings are likely to be generalisable beyond this participant group.

Table 2. Psychological Scales

	T1		T2	
	Mean	**SD**	**Mean**	**SD**
Wellbeing (overall score)	23.6	3.79	27.9	5.18
Perceived Competence Scale (overall score)	5.38	1.15	5.95	1.09
Aspirations Index (overall score)	5.29	0.85	6.05	0.93
Life-goal 1: To grow and learn new things	5.35	0.89	6.12	0.89
Life-goal 2: At the end of my life, to be able to look back on my life as meaningful and complete	5.14	0.88	5.91	1.20
Life-goal 3: To choose what I do, instead of being pushed along by life	5.25	1.06	6.18	1.12
Life-goal 4: To know and accept who I really am	5.54	1.10	5.90	1.15
Life-goal 5: To gain increasing insight into why I do the things I do	5.30	1.05	6.12	1.15

Notes: Time 1: Wellbeing and Aspirations overall scores are based on 20/23 responses, and the Perceived Competence overall score is based on 21/23 responses. Life goal overall scores are based on 20-21/23 responses. Time 2 overall scores are based on 11 responses.

Qualitative Findings: Voice and Survey Diary Responses

The qualitative findings are summarised below and organised based on four prominent themes relating to the digital skills training offered on the programme and its impact: the programme and training content; the confidence and competence in digital skills learned and feeling digitally included; challenges and barriers; and the wider impact of the digital skills learned beyond digital literacy and inclusion.

Key things that the men were looking forward to at the start of the project were learning and using new skills; meeting new people; engaging with potential employers; and applying and securing employment. The value of networking with volunteers and mentors was also acknowledged and is discussed in more depth in another paper (Hadjisergis et al., in prep). The findings below may allude to the overall programme which included elements of training beyond purely digital skills, including employability skills such as CV writing and preparing for interviews, but the digital skills are integral to these elements as searching for and applying for jobs requires the use of technology.

The programme and training content

The men highlighted several things that they felt were useful in terms of the programme and training content (e.g. having access to a laptop and dongle, learning new skills, networking, the employability sessions), and the opportunity to earn "badges" to evidence achievements. When asked what they enjoyed the most, learning new digital and employment skills, and meeting and networking with new people in a non-judgemental environment were widely noted:

> "I would say the information to do with preparing myself for employment mainly to develop and build skills, using emails, teams, jobsites, and making effective job searches especially using LinkedIn." (RAD013)

> "I think what I'm enjoying about the project is the interaction with different people that I've never kind of come across before. One obviously, is the other people on the groups so them kind of conversations we've had there but more so the professionals because you're getting to speak with people and getting feedback from people that in my position would never get, so that door already opened from that perspective." (RAD003)

The non-judgemental environment in which this interaction occurred was praised as being useful and provided hope to the men, particularly the role of those supporting the delivery of the project:

> "The enthusiasm and encouragement of the mentors and volunteers, because it makes me feel hopeful that someone may be interested in employing me eventually". (RAD002)

Participants mentioned that they had learned a range of new skills including using and accessing Microsoft Word and Excel files, using Teams/Zoom and online chat functions, better understanding of social media platforms such as LinkedIn, how to apply for roles relevant to their skills/qualifications, creating and optimising their CVs, searching for jobs, and attending interviews. Such skills were attributed to the project and the support received from Radical Recruit, which gave them opportunities, and the practical experience needed to develop more confidence in using technology, as well as enabling them to identify what skillsets they needed to continue to work on to gain employment.

Importantly, having access to a laptop and the internet was extremely valuable to the men in terms of giving them inclusive opportunities to access further information and courses, which they could not have done without this equipment. While the men found the training offered during the programme helpful, some highlighted that they would like some additional support with education/training courses to develop digital skills further. For example, more advanced IT skills sessions through iDEA or options to tailor sessions to their interests and future employment goals:

> "Regarding a Digital Marketing course, I would like additional support, in finding my feet with this." (RAD013)

Another man mentioned it would be helpful if *"a list was provided of potential employment opportunities"* (RAD002) (e.g. actual job vacancies) that could be used to then tailor CVs to work towards applying for jobs.

The confidence and competence in digital skills learned and feeling digitally included

Despite some men feeling initially worried about their current level of IT skills, and some experiencing challenges with getting to grips with using technology and navigating new tools such as Teams and Zoom, they felt that their skills were improving over the course of the programme and with this their confidence in using such devices and tools:

"I feel that I have more of an understanding of the digital world and workplace. The advice in relation to CVs and interviews have in particular given me more confidence in terms of future employment prospects and my employability." (RAD007)

"Yeah, it has boosted my confidence and ability to deal with life things with the laptop – emails, filling in forms, etc." (RAD017)

"Yes, as I am more competent to cope in the digital world." (RAD001)

The men identified feeling more competent in the digital world having learnt these new skills since taking part in the project which has made practical tasks of life more manageable such access to information, as well as applying for jobs, and inspired them to pursue new qualifications and training, as one man put it, *"it has opened up the world for me a bit more and I want to learn things again now" (RAD007).* Similar points are echoed in the following extracts:

"Having the laptop and dongle helped a hell of a lot otherwise I would have no access to using internet other than my phone, iDEA has helped me gain knowledge and insight into using digital. Has made me want to pursue courses." (RAD007)

"Yes, because I am confident in applying for jobs online, and use the internet in ways I didn't previously have the knowledge to do, and helping to write my CV, and search for work." (RAD013)

Specifically, one man mentioned he would now feel much more confident in attending an interview online:

"Yes, although I would be happier in a F2F interview, I feel I could probably attend one via MS Teams." (RAD002)

The men directly attributed their newly developed skills and confidence to the project and the training offered by Radical Recruit which was highly valued.

"I have developed them through iDEA badges and workshops, it stimulated my interests and got my brain working, if I never got this opportunity, I would have probably been looking for a delivery job and not thinking about graphic design or any other employment I have the skills for!" (RAD007)

Challenges and barriers

For some men, technological challenges were mentioned as a barrier to their engagement with the programme. For example, one man mentioned that *"Getting involved with the computers and navigating new technologies like Teams and Zoom was challenging at first" (RAD012).* Another man identified an issue with his Wi-Fi dongle and having to use the local library for internet access and, for another, the internet connection at his residence was an issue at times. One man expressed being self-conscious about his dyslexia which he identified as a slight challenge but having technical tools (e.g. speaker text software) to help with this was beneficial. For others, a mixture of technical difficulties and confidence in approaching or talking to others was a particular challenge, however such issues were addressed and their confidence increased over the course of the programme. As expressed by this man:

"At the beginning it was talking to people, a few tech issues that have now been sorted with Teams, but the last few sessions everything has worked perfectly!" (RAD007)

Some early problems were mentioned regarding setting up accounts for iDEA or other technical difficulties. It was also mentioned by one man that he would have liked more time to complete the iDEA courses. Three men mentioned committing to online workshops was difficult at times due to work, family or probation commitments during the day. These are some considerations for future programmes to address in the interests of a more inclusive provision.

The wider impact of the digital skills learned beyond digital literacy and inclusion

The experience of the programme was viewed as having a great impact on the men's lives and well-being beyond the digital skills element. Importantly, most men responded that their new skills had a wider impact on their improved mental health:

> "Yeah, this project has kept me busy, I am learning new things, and it makes me feel positive, it's a good thing to do after going through what I've been through it helps a lot." (RAD007)

> "I enjoy the conversation I have with the volunteers at the workshop as each time after a workshop I feel more empowered and gain a confidence boost, it's really gradual but as we have kept going, I can see a big improvement in my mental health. It makes life enjoyable! I feel so much better about myself."(RAD022)

The men agreed that their new digital skills had improved their outlook on life and their hopes for the future:

> "The help and advice I have received, together with the added knowledge and experience I have gained these past few months has given me more confidence and hope for the future." (RAD007)

Self-reflection and having broader aspirations appeared to be a valuable personal skill developed:

> "... boosted my confidence, and allowed me to see other issues I had that I could work on to help me get employment, I broke a lot of comfort zones within, and that's ongoing." (RAD022)

Some men discussed wanting to change jobs to move away from labouring roles into digital and technological roles (e.g. digital marketing, digital artwork, cyber security) showing an interest in furthering their skills and qualifications to succeed in such aspirations:

> "It's really got me thinking about courses and learning new things, outside my normal comfort zone, I nearly went online to do a cybersecurity course, but it was a lot of money, but I would love to get a qualification and learn something especially because I have a laptop to use." (RAD007)

One man felt although it had not directly improved his future aspirations, it had given him more skills for his "*toolbox*" (RAD002). For five of the men who responded to these questions, they felt the project had helped to reduce their risk of reoffending, an ultimate impact that the project aimed to achieve:

> "The help I have received, and the hope I now have for the future has reduced the risk of me reoffending." (RAD007)

The qualitative findings complement the results from the DLA and psychological scales to provide a deeper understanding of how the digital skills programme had impacted on the participants' digital literacy. In particular, the men also highlighted the wider impact of the opportunity to take part in the project, receive the training and technological support, including access to devices and the internet, and the added benefits that this had beyond their digital skills. This included positive impacts on their well-being, confidence, self-esteem, mental health, feelings of inclusion, brighter aspirations for the future and employment goals, which aligns with the quantitative findings. This would not have been possible without both the practical access to IT equipment and the internet (which was highly valued and appreciated) and the training in how to use such devices and various platforms that are used for everyday tasks as well as searching for and applying for jobs and further education opportunities.

Discussion

The findings of this case study explored the use of a DLA along with psychological scales and qualitative insights from participants as a method to measure digital literacy and the impact of a digital skills programme for men who had recently left prison. The findings indicate that the programme helped to improve the men's digital literacy, competence and confidence, in addition to having a wider impact on their quality of life, self-esteem, educational and employment opportunities, aspirations, and goals for the future, including supporting their desistance from crime. Working towards inclusive access to employment through education, the pilot echoes both the Social Exclusion Unit's skills and employment pathway to reducing recidivism (Office of the Deputy Prime Minister, 2002) and Bonta et al.'s (2013) education and employment factor for reducing reoffending.

Successful community reintegration is vital for people leaving prison, and being able to engage with the digital world has become central to social equality. Undoubtedly, the impact of this is not only of benefit to the individual, but also to society and the state in terms of the economic cost of crime and criminal justice. Engagement in the programme and the newly acquired skills, as well as the opportunity to have access to digital technology and the internet, also appears to improve the mental health and wellbeing of the participants. Importantly, the DLA appears to be a useful and successful tool to measure digital skills while the qualitative elements provided a contextual understanding for how and where those skills were learned and the impact of such skills on the men's lives.

Interestingly, there was something of a disconnect when comparing the findings of the DLA to the self-rated digital skills rating collected by Radical Recruit upon recruitment to the project, where 41% of participants rated themselves as "poor." Both data sources were based on self-report, so it seems likely that the higher scores on the DLA used as the quantitative measure relate to the breakdown of topics/areas of digital literacy. The self-rated score collected by Radical Recruit were based on high-level questions about digital literacy and did not delve into detailed questions relating to specific skills. This suggests that the men actually had higher skill levels to begin with than they might have realised after a period in prison and supports the use of the more detailed DLA to understand participants' baseline.

While the use of the DLA appears to be an effective and inclusive tool to measure the impact of the digital skills programme, the use of voice diaries as a method to collect qualitative data did not prove to be as successful with many participants reluctant to engage in this way. There is certainly potential in the use of voice diaries to gather rich, personal information regarding the training experience and its impact that can be conducted longitudinally (Coolbrandt et al., 2017; Sabharwal et al., 2021; Williamson et al., 2012), with the potential to complement and enhance the results from the quantitative measure. However, reflecting on this study, the presence of mentors might have made participants feel self-conscious in recording their thoughts if not done entirely privately and confidentially. Further research should explore the use of voice diaries as a method for working with people leaving prison and explore what factors (i.e. privacy, confidentiality, digital skills) would promote or hinder participants engagement with such approaches. When the research team responded to low uptake with the voice diaries by providing an open-ended survey with the same questions, response rates improved.

Implications, reflections, and future directions

Given the current priorities for criminal justice reform concerned with the prison population and reducing recidivism, along with the need to provide effective services and opportunities (such as those that tackle educational, employment and mental health issues) that support rehabilitation (Rowland 2025; GOV.UK 2026), the findings highlight important implications for strategies to enhance rehabilitation and resettlement through digital inclusion and improved opportunities for employability. The implications for policy, practice, and future research arising from these findings will now be considered. First, the men who participated in the project reported finding the experience very beneficial. They placed value on being given IT equipment and learning new digital and employment-related skills, networking, and meeting new people. Participants reported increased self-esteem and confidence beyond that of their digital skills, something that was echoed in the wider psychological measures and as reported in the Tech4PrisonLeavers White Paper (Digital Poverty Alliance, 2024). The programme appeared to result in perceived greater potential social mobility and reduced inequality for participants through increased access to employment and education opportunities. The perceived positive impact on the mental health and wellbeing of participants also provided them with a sense of purpose and direction which is a promising signal. Policy attention should be given to the role of digital skills training for men leaving prison as standard practice (Digital Poverty Alliance, 2024), as most current programmes are isolated pilots from around the world and do not reflect policy changes in criminal justice. The findings provide further support for the provision of digital skills within prisons before release, allowing time to complete courses or training and to develop individualised pathways. The DLA could be implemented as standard mandatory practice to assess digital skills and needs upon entry to prison, during, prior to, and post release to identify support and training needs required for successful resettlement. The methodological contribution of the DLA could be useful in identifying needs earlier and therefore providing more time and opportunity to engage individuals in training or programmes that will assist in addressing gaps in knowledge and skills in preparation for release. This, in addition to any digital skills training or courses, would need to be resourced and training provided to those conducting the assessments and training to ensure it is being used consistently and that data is recorded and stored in a way that is practical and useful for analysis to track progress, evaluate the impact of any training or support received, and to make further referrals where gaps in skills or literacy are identified. Indeed, the Prisoner's Education Trust (2025) has called for the development of a national long-term strategy for consistent digital learning in prison to support employment prospects after release as well as basic digital skills that are needed for everyday tasks and resettling into modern society. In terms of the content of the digital skills training, policy makers and practitioners should consider developing customised pathways and courses that build on the individual needs of participants (person centred), supporting progression, or ensure clear sign-posting to more advanced and inclusive learning. As highlighted by McGuire-Snieckus and Caulfield (2018) for sustained change when working with prisoners, "interventions should focus on improving individual motivations associated with employment" (p. 3461). Employment that fits an individual's interests, strengths and skills is related to greater motivation (Noe et al., 1990). Using the DLA as a baseline and to prompt skills-based discussions with participants would be valuable to individualised pathways. The men also made suggestions for areas they would like to see developed. These included: more advanced IT skills sessions through iDEA; options to tailor sessions to their interests and future employment goals; having a list of job vacancies; meeting more potential employers; and more face-to-face in person workshops and support.

As such skills training likely has wider impacts beyond employability and potential influence on reducing recidivism, such programmes could also be targeted at other marginalised or digitally excluded individuals. This could help to reduce digital inequality/exclusion via access to information and resources, education and employment opportunities, in addition to having the potential to improve quality of life, health and social needs, reduce poverty, and increase access to statutory services. The creation of a successful blueprint or model for digital skills and employment support for individuals in the CJS that can be scaled up and replicated in the future would be ideal. This could also be adapted for non-criminal justice involved populations who may be digitally excluded or lacking in digital literacy.

The research reported in this case study is one of the first to explore the use of this DLA as a method to collect data as part of a study of this type. The tool, combined with qualitative insights, produced rich findings regarding the men's thoughts, experiences, and the impact of the project. Further research should consider utilising the DLA developed for this study as a tool to map and evaluate the level and needs of individuals. Future research should explore whether there are any gendered forms of digital exclusion as there is a wider gap in research with females leaving prison and their level of digital literacy and its impact on rehabilitation and resettlement. Research should also examine the use of the DLA as a measure of digital literacy on a longer-term basis. Additional testing and validation of this tool as an instrument to measure impact would be beneficial. Research should continue to explore the use of voice diaries as a method for measuring impact when evaluating similar programmes as such tools have been found to be useful in other marginalised groups (Sabharwal et al., 2021).

Limitations

As with any research, there are some limitations that should be considered. First, the sample was small and not representative of the wider population of people leaving prison (e.g. the participants were all male, from one geographical area/prison, recruited from one organisation). This impacts the generalisation of the findings beyond the study population. Collecting data with a broader demographic range (including women, who have very different needs in the CJS), would allow for a deeper analysis and understanding of digital skills needs. A larger sample would also mean greater statistical power and a comparison group design could be used to test whether any changes could reliably be attributed to the project.

The attrition rate was also a limitation. Given the nature of the population in the pilot, this attrition rate was not surprising. There are several reasons that may explain the high attrition rate, for example, study fatigue, a lack of incentive (although the men were provided with laptops and internet dongles), the data collection tools themselves (voice diaries may have required further training for mentors and mentees), or simply due to life factors or other circumstances affecting people as they reintegrate into society (issues with housing or changes in location of residence), or perhaps these men had already achieved employment. Future evaluations of similar projects can build on this and address such limitations.

There was also limited uptake of the voice diaries to collect the qualitative data and participants had to be prompted by their mentors or turn to a survey format for these questions. Further research should consider what would encourage engagement and inclusivity in such data collection methods and evaluate this as a data collection tool. Voice diaries clearly have potential benefits; however, these may be time consuming and challenging to get participants to engage in remotely without incentives or training.

Additionally, although tracking people leaving prison over the long-term is challenging, extending this pilot over a longer period to capture longer term outcomes for the men would be advantageous. It may be desirable to track reoffending data over the next two years and compare rates for this group against average reoffending rates for a similar profile cohort. It is important for researchers and programme delivery teams to work together to measure longer-term impact, and projects should include clear monitoring of participant progression towards employment as well as reoffending. Recording participant outcomes in the short, medium, longer term would allow for more rigorous understanding of the impact of digital skills programme on men leaving prison and their reintegration into society. Including a comparison or control group in future research would be beneficial, if practical, to strengthen the analysis to ascertain more specific impacts from the programme being delivered, adding weight to the resulting impactions and recommendations.

CONCLUSION

The DLA appears to be successful in measuring the changes in digital literacy in the sample, which showed some degree of improvement by the end of the programme. The use of voice/survey diaries helped to understand how and why the programme improved digital skills and highlighted the wider impact that such skills had provided the men beyond digital literacy and feeling digitally included into the modern societies in which they had been recently released. This enabled them to engage in activities such as finding information and resources online, increasing accessibility to educational and employment opportunities, and ultimately, improving their positive outlooks for the future and in some cases their state of mental health. The need for more training and guidance on the use of a voice diary is apparent. While this was assessed among a sample of men within a criminal justice context, this method has the potential to assess the impact of similar programmes aimed at other groups that may be marginalised or digitally excluded. Future research should continue to evaluate such methods and tools on a wider scale and with a broader demographic of participants. Given government priorities for criminal justice reform and increasing recognition of technology's role in enhancing practice and outcomes in criminal justice settings - themes explored in this edited collection - the findings herein can inform future strategies to improve rehabilitation and reduce recidivism, particularly through developing interventions and opportunities that support digital inclusion, assess digital skills, and address broader factors underpinning rehabilitation.

ACKNOWLEDGMENT

Research funding: This project was funded through the Learning Foundation.

REFERENCES

Barreiro-Gen, M., & Novo-Corti, I. (2015, October). Collaborative learning in environments with restricted access to the internet: Policies to bridge the digital divide and exclusion in prisons through the development of the skills of inmates. *Computers in Human Behaviour, 51*(B), 1172-1176. https://doi.org/DOI: 10.1016/j.chb.2015.01.076

Bernard, T., & Taffesse, A. S. (2014, January). Aspirations: An approach to measurement with validation using Ethiopian data. *Journal of African Economies, 23*(2), 189–224. DOI: 10.1093/jae/ejt030

Bonta, J., Blais, J., & Wilson, H. A. (2013, January). *The prediction of risk for mentally disordered offenders: A quantitative synthesis.* Public Safety Canada. https://www.publicsafety.gc.ca/cnt/rsrcs/pblctns/prdctn-rsk-mntlly-dsrdrd/index-en.aspx

Braun, V., & Clarke, V. (2006). Using thematic analysis in psychology. *Qualitative Research in Psychology, 3*(2), 77–101. DOI: 10.1191/1478088706qp063oa

Breslin, G., Haughey, T., O'Brien, W., Caulfield, L. S., Robertson, A., & Lawlor, M. (2018). Increasing athlete knowledge of mental health and intentions to seek help: The State of Mind Ireland (SOMI) pilot program. *Journal of Clinical Sport Psychology, 12*(1), 39–56. DOI: 10.1123/jcsp.2016-0039

British Computer Society (BCS). The Chartered Institute for IT (n.d.). *Digital literacy.* https://www.bcs.org/policy-and-influence/education/digital-literacy

Capece, J. (2020, July). The effects of probation stipulations on employment quality among people on probation. *Journal of Offender Rehabilitation, 59*(7), 375–388. DOI: 10.1080/10509674.2020.1784348

Carolan, C. M., Forbat, L., & Smith, A. (2016, April). Developing the DESCARTE Model: The design of case study research in health care. *Qualitative Health Research, 26*(5), 626–639. DOI: 10.1177/1049732315602488 PMID: 26336896

Caroline, A., Coun, M. J. H., Gunawan, A., & Stoffers, J. (2025, January 16). A systematic literature review on digital literacy, employability, and innovative work behavior: Emphasizing the contextual approaches in HRM research. *Frontiers in Psychology, 15*, 1448555. DOI: 10.3389/fpsyg.2024.1448555 PMID: 39895978

Caulfield, L. S., Brooks-Wilson, S., Booth, J., & Monaghan, M. (2023, September). Engaging parents to reduce youth violence: Evidence from a youth justice board pathfinder programme. *Crime Prevention and Community Safety, 25*(4), 401–426. DOI: 10.1057/s41300-023-00190-4

The Centre for Social Justice. (2021, January). *Digital technology in prisons: Unlocking relationships, learning and skills in UK prisons.* https://www.centreforsocialjustice.org.uk/wp-content/uploads/2021/01/CSJJ8671-Digital-In-Prisons-210604.pdf

Coolbrandt, A., Steffens, E., Wildier, H., Bruyninckx, E., Verslype, C., & Milisen, J. (2017, December). Use of a symptom diary during chemotherapy: A mixed-methods evaluation of the patient perspective. *European Journal of Oncology Nursing*, *31*, 37–45. DOI: 10.1016/j.ejon.2017.09.003 PMID: 29173825

Creswell, J. W. (2014). *Educational research: Planning, conducting, and evaluating quantitative and qualitative research* (5th ed.). Pearson.

Creswell, J. W., & Plano Clark, V. L. (2018). *Designing and conducting mixed methods research* (3rd ed.). Sage.

Department for Education. (2018). *Essential digital skills framework.* https://assets.publishing.service.gov.uk/government/uploads/system/uploads/attachment_data/file/738922/Essential_digital_skills_framework.pdf

Digital Poverty Alliance. (2023, July 14). *Tech4PrisonLeavers.* https://digitalpovertyalliance.org/projects/tech4prisonleavers

Digital Poverty Alliance. (2024, April). *Tech4PrisonLeavers white paper. Improving access and digital skills for prison leavers: Challenges and opportunities.* https://digitalpovertyalliance.org/wp-content/uploads/2024/05/Tech4PrisonLeavers-White-Paper-2024-website.pdf

Farley, H., & Pike, A. (2016). Engaging prisoners in education: Reducing risk and recidivism. *Journal of the International Corrections and Prisons Association*, *1*, 65–73. https://oro.open.ac.uk/46511/1/Final_Farley_Pike_Advancing_Corrections.pdf

Gao, M. (2024, December 30). Relationship between digital literacy and employment ability of vocational undergraduate students: The parallel mediating role of future time perspective and career decision self-efficacy. *Journal of Contemporary Educational Research*, *8*(12), 82–87. DOI: 10.26689/jcer.v8i12.9155

Global Digital Compact. (2023, March). *Digital literacy: The great divide.* UN Digital Compact Consultation. https://www.un.org/digital-emerging-technologies/sites/www.un.org.techenvoy/files/GDC-submission_Digital-National-Alliance-Bulgaria.pdf

GOV. UK Justice Data. (2026). *Prisons data: Reform.* Retrieved April 21, 2026 from https://data.justice.gov.uk/prisons/prison-reform

Gov.UK. (2019, April 23). *Guidance: Essential digital skills framework.* https://www.gov.uk/government/publications/essential-digital-skills-framework)

Grierson, M., Varghese, D., Bolton, M., & Olivier, P. (2022*). Design considerations for a digital service to support prison leavers.* [Conference paper]. ACM Designing Interactive Systems Conference. https://doi.org/DOI: 10.1145/3532106.3533567

Hadjisergis, K., Caulfield, L. S., Stonard, K. E., & Sadlier, S. (in prep). *The 'Human Factor': Mentoring, peerage, and community in the development of digital literacy of prison leavers.*

House of Commons Education Committee Report. (2022, May 18). *Not just another brick in the wall: Why prisoners need an education to climb the ladder of opportunity.* https://publications.parliament.uk/pa/cm5803/cmselect/cmeduc/56/report.html

Jewkes, Y., & Reisdorf, B. C. (2016, November). A brave new world: The problems and opportunities presented by new media technologies in prisons. *Criminology & Criminal Justice, 16*(5), 534–551. DOI: 10.1177/1748895816654953

Jones, L. Ø., & Manger, T. (2019). Literacy skills, academic self-efficacy, and participation in prison education. In D. Perin, *The Wiley Handbook of Adult Literacy* (pp. 151-169). John Wiley & Sons. https://doi.org/DOI: 10.1002/9781119261407.ch7

Julien, H. (2019). Digital literacy in theory and practice. In Khosrow-Pour, M. (Ed.), *Advanced Methodologies and Technologies in Library Science, Information Management, and Scholarly Inquiry* (4th ed., pp. 22–32). IGI Global., DOI: 10.4018/978-1-5225-2255-3.ch195

Kasser, T., & Ryan, R. M. (1996, March). Further examining the American dream: Differential correlates of intrinsic and extrinsic goals. *Personality and Social Psychology Bulletin, 22*(3), 20–287. DOI: 10.1177/0146167296223006

Kaun, A., & Stiernstedt, F. (2020, September). Doing time, the smart way? Temporalities of the smart prison. *New Media & Society, 22*(9), 1580–1599. DOI: 10.1177/1461444820914865

Knight, V. (2015, July). Some observations on the digital landscape of prisons today. *Prison Service Journal, 220*, 3–9.

Knight, V., & Van De Steene, S. (2017a). The capacity and capability of digital innovation in prisons: Towards smart prisons. *Advancing Corrections, 4*(8), 88–101.

Law, N., Woo, D., de la Torre, J., & Wong, G. (2018, June). *A global framework of reference on digital literacy skills for indicator 4.4.2.* UNESCO. UIS Information Paper, 51. https://unesdoc.unesco.org/ark:/48223/pf0000265403

Leu, D. J., Kinzer, C. K., Coiro, J., Castek, J., & Henry, L. A. (2013). New literacies: A dual-level theory of the changing nature of literacy, instruction and assessment. In Alvermann, D. E., Unrau, N. J., & Ruddell, R. B. (Eds.), *Theoretical models and processes of reading* (6th ed., pp. 1150–1181). International Reading Association. DOI: 10.1598/0710.42

Lloyds Bank. (2021). *Essential digital skills report 2021: Third Edition—Benchmarking the essential digital skills of the UK.* https://www.lloydsbank.com/assets/media/pdfs/banking_with_us/whats-happening/210923-lb-essential-digital-skills-2021-report.pdf

Maroney, N., Williams, B. J., Thomas, A., Skues, J., & Moulding, R. (2019). A stress-coping model of problem online video game use. *International Journal of Mental Health and Addiction, 17*(4), 845–858. DOI: 10.1007/s11469-018-9887-7

McDougall, C., Pearson, D. A. S., Torgerson, D. J., & Garcia-Reyes, M. (2017, October). The effect of digital technology on prisoner behavior and reoffending: A natural stepped-wedge design. *Journal of Experimental Criminology, 13*(4), 455–482. DOI: 10.1007/s11292-017-9303-5

McFarlane, R., & Pike, A. (2019). From prisoner to student. In R. Earle, & J. Mehigan, *Degrees of Freedom: Prison Education and The Open University.* Policy Press.

McGuire-Snieckus, R., & Caulfield, L. S. (2018, August). An evaluation of Talent 4 . . .: A programme to identify talent and skills for prisoners, disadvantaged, unemployed, and vulnerable groups. *International Journal of Offender Therapy and Comparative Criminology, 62*(11), 3460–3484. DOI: 10.1177/0306624X17740556 PMID: 29160124

McLauchlan, J., & Farley, H. (2019, December). Fast cars and fast learning: Using Virtual Reality to learn literacy and numeracy in prison. *Journal of Virtual Worlds Research, 12*(3), 1–11. DOI: 10.4101/jvwr.v12i3.7391

Ministry of Justice. (2021, August 5). *Prison education statistics April 2019 to March 2020.* https://assets.publishing.service.gov.uk/media/610ba7b48fa8f506a5bf1325/Prisoner_Education_2019_20.pdf

Monteiro, A., Barros, R., & Leite, C. (2015, March). Lifelong learning through e-learning in European prisons: Rethinking digital and social inclusion. [Conference paper]. *Inted2015 Madrid.* (pp. 1038-1046).

National Institute of Justice. (2014). *National Institute of Justice annual report.* https://www.ojp.gov/pdffiles1/nij/249533.pdf

Office of the Deputy Prime Minister. (2002, July). *Reducing re-offending by ex-prisoners.* Social Exclusion Unit. https://www.bristol.ac.uk/poverty/downloads/keyofficialdocuments/Reducing%20Reoffending.pdf

Organisation for Economic Co-operation and Development (OECD). (2023). *Digital skills and digital inclusion: Briefing note.* https://www.oecd.org/content/dam/oecd/en/about/projects/cfe/oecd-city-network-on-jobs-and-skills/Briefing-note-Digital-skills-and-digital-inclusion.pdf

Pangrazio, L., Godhe, A.-L., & López Ledesma, A. G. (2020, November). What is digital literacy? A comparative review of publications across three language contexts. *E-Learning and Digital Media, 17*(6), 442–459. DOI: 10.1177/2042753020946291

Pike, A., & Adams, A. (2012). Digital exclusion or learning exclusion? An ethnographic study of adult male distance learners in English prisons. *Research in Learning Technology, 20*(4), 363–376. DOI: 10.3402/rlt.v20i0.18620

Prison Reform Trust. (2025, June 9). *Update and restart: Post-pandemic prison digitisation in England and Wales.* https://prisonreformtrust.org.uk/wp-content/uploads/2025/06/Update_and_Restart.pdf

Prisoner's Education Trust. (2025, December 10). *Getting connected: Digital provision and education in prison.* https://prisonerseducation.org.uk/wp-content/uploads/2025/12/Getting-Connected-December-2025.pdf

Ricciardelli, R., Maier, K., & Hannah-Moffat, K. (2015, November). Strategic masculinities: Vulnerabilities, risk and the production of prison masculinities. *Theoretical Criminology, 19*(4), 491–513. DOI: 10.1177/1362480614565849

Rowland, C. (2025, October). *Public services performance tracker 2025: The criminal justice system.* Nuffield Foundation Institute for Government. https://www.instituteforgovernment.org.uk/sites/default/files/2025-10/performance-tracker-2025-criminal-justice-system.pdf

Sabharwal, N. S., Joseph, R. S., Bankar, A. C., & Talmale, A. V. (2021, March). Accessing silenced voices? Diary method as a source of data for understanding higher education experiences of students from socially excluded groups. In Cao, X., & Henderson, E. F. (Eds.), *Exploring Diary Methods in Higher Education Research: Opportunities, Choices, Challenges* (pp. 131–144). Routledge., DOI: 10.4324/9780429326318-13

Sheldon, K. M., & Kasser, T. (1998, December). Pursuing personal goals: Skills enable progress but not all progress is beneficial. *Personality and Social Psychology Bulletin, 24*(12), 1319–1331. DOI: 10.1177/01461672982412006

Smith, V. S. (2020, June). *Exploring the potential of digital technology to reduce recidivism: A Delphi study on the digitalisation of prison education.* [PhD Dissertation, Ashford University].

Tennant, R., Hiller, L., Fishwick, R., Platt, S., Joseph, S., Weich, S., Parkinson, J., Secker, J., & Stewart-Brown, S. (2007, November). The Warwick-Edinburgh Mental Well-being Scale (WEMWBS): Development and UK validation. *Health and Quality of Life Outcomes, 5*(1), 63. DOI: 10.1186/1477-7525-5-63 PMID: 18042300

Utvaer, B. K. S., Hammervold, R., & Haugan, G. (2014). The Aspiration Index in vocational students: Dimensionality, reliability, and construct validity. *Education Enquiry, 5*(3), 359–383. DOI: 10.3402/edui.v5.24612

Van De Steene, S., & Knight, V. (2017, September). Digital transformation for prisons: Developing a needs-based strategy. *Probation Journal, 64*(3), 256–268. DOI: 10.1177/0264550517723722

Verma, A. (2021). Using audio-diaries for research and education: AMEE Guide No. 144. *Medical Teacher, 43*(12), 1346–1352. DOI: 10.1080/0142159X.2021.1972954 PMID: 34499842

Warwick Medical School. (2020, November 6). *WEMWBS: 14-item vs 7-item scale.* https://warwick.ac.uk/fac/sci/med/research/platform/wemwbs/about/wemwbsvsswemwbs

Williams, G. C., & Deci, E. L. (1996). Internalization of biopsychosocial values by medical students: A test of self-determination theory. *Journal of Personality and Social Psychology, 70*(4), 767–779. DOI: 10.1037/0022-3514.70.4.767 PMID: 8636897

Williams, G. C., McGregor, H. A., Sharp, D., Levesque, C., Kouides, R. W., Ryan, R. M., & Deci, E. L. (2006). Testing a self-determination theory intervention for motivating tobacco cessation: Supporting autonomy and competence in a clinical trial. *Health Psychology, 25*(1), 91–101. DOI: 10.1037/0278-6133.25.1.91 PMID: 16448302

Williams, G. C., McGregor, H. A., Zeldman, A., Freedman, Z. R., & Deci, E. L. (2004). Testing a self-determination theory process model for promoting glycemic control through diabetes self-management. *Health Psychology, 23*(1), 58–66. DOI: 10.1037/0278-6133.23.1.58 PMID: 14756604

Williams, L., & Gill, D. L. (1995, January). The role of perceived competence in the motivation of physical activity. *Journal of Sport & Exercise Psychology, 17*(4), 363–378. DOI: 10.1123/jsep.17.4.363

Williamson, I., Leeming, D., Lyttle, S., & Johnson, S. (2012). It should be the most natural thing in the world: Exploring first-time mothers' breastfeeding difficulties in the UK using audio-diaries and interviews. *Maternal and Child Nutrition*, *8*(4), 434–447. DOI: 10.1111/j.1740-8709.2011.00328.x PMID: 21696542

Williamson, I., Leeming, D., Lyttle, S., & Johnson, S. (2015, February 2). Evaluating the audio-diary method in qualitative research. *Qualitative Research Journal*, *15*(1), 20–34. DOI: 10.1108/QRJ-04-2014-0014

Young, J. (1999, December 13). The exclusive society: Social exclusion, crime and difference in late modernity. *Sage (Atlanta, Ga.)*.

Compilation of References

2026. *trends every public safety leader should watch.* (2026). Versaterm. https://www.versaterm.com/resource/2026-trends-every-public-safety-leader-should-watch

9th global conference on criminal finances and cryptoassets. (2025, October). Basel Institute on Governance. https://baselgovernance.org/9crc

A new era of safety. (n.d.). Tended. https://www.tended.co.uk

A novel solution to public security: Japan's AI-based crime prediction. (2024, June 7). KIZUNA. https://www.japan.go.jp/kizuna/2024/06/japans_ai-based_crime_prediction.html

Abbasi, M., Váz, P., Silva, J., & Martins, P. (2025, January). Comprehensive evaluation of deepfake detection models: Accuracy, generalization, and resilience to adversarial attacks. *Applied Sciences (Basel, Switzerland), 15*(3), 1225. DOI: 10.3390/app15031225

Abdullah, Q. A. (n.d.). GEOG 892- Geospatial applications of Unmanned Aerial Systems: Classification according to size. *PennState College of Earth and Mineral Science.* https://courses.ems.psu.edu/geog892/node/642

Abdullah, S. M., Cheruvu, A., Kanchi, S., Chung, T., Gao, P., Jadliwala, M., & Viswanath, B. (2024, April 24). An analysis of recent advances in deepfake image detection in an evolving threat landscape (arXiv:2404.16212v1). *arXiv.* /arXiv.2404.16212DOI: 10.1109/SP54263.2024.00194

Abe, K. (2004, June). Everyday policing in Japan: Surveillance, media, government and public opinion. *International Sociology, 19*(2), 215–231. DOI: 10.1177/0268580904042901

Acim, B., Boukhlif, M., Ouhnni, H., Kharmoum, N., & Ziti, S. (2025, October 1). A decade of deepfake research in the generative AI era, 2014–2024: A bibliometric analysis. *Publications / MDPI, 13*(4), 50. DOI: 10.3390/publications13040050

Adamson, T. (2025, October 19). Thieves steal crown jewels in 4 minutes from Louvre Museum. AP News. https://apnews.com/article/france-louvre-museum-robbery-a3687f330a43e0aaff68c732c4b2585b

Admass, W. S., Munaye, Y. Y., & Diro, A. A. (2024). Cyber security: State of the art, challenges and future directions. *Cyber Security and Applications, 2*, 100031. DOI: 10.1016/j.csa.2023.100031

Advisory Committee on Evidence Rules. (2025, May 2). Minutes of the meeting of May 2, 2025 [Minutes of a meeting]. The Judicial Conference Advisory Committee on the Federal Rules of Evidence. https://www.uscourts.gov/sites/default/files/document/2025-05-02_evidence_committee_meeting_minutes_final.pdf

Agboola, V., Osamor, J., & Olajide, F. (2024). Evaluating the efficiency of FTK, autopsy, and mobile forensic tools: A comparative study in criminal investigations. [IJICR]. *International Journal of Intelligent Computing Research, 15*(1), 1279–1291. DOI: 10.20533/ijicr.2042.4655.2024.0156

Ahmad, A. A., Jusoh Yusoff, A. F., Mat Zain, M. N., & Ahmad, S. (2023, June 30). Conspiracy of Silk Road: Dread Pirate Roberts to cybercrime and money laundering. [MJSSH]. *Malaysian Journal of Social Sciences and Humanities*, *8*(6), e002354. DOI: 10.47405/mjssh.v8i6.2354

Ahmed, N., Ur, R., Badshah, A., Adeel, H., Tajammul, A., Daud, A., & Alsahfi, T. (2024). Visual deepfake detection: Review of techniques, tools, limitations, and future prospects. *IEEE Access : Practical Innovations, Open Solutions*, *13*, 1923–1961. DOI: 10.1109/ACCESS.2024.3523288

Ahmed, S. S., Rauf, S., & Ashraf, H. (2025). Human rights risks in tech-enhanced incarceration: A comparative analysis. *SSRN*, *5*(2), 304–311. DOI: 10.2139/ssrn.5554438

Ahmed, S., Alshater, M. M., El Ammari, A., & Hammami, H. (2022, October). Artificial intelligence and machine learning in finance: A bibliometric review. *Research in International Business and Finance*, *61*, 101646. DOI: 10.1016/j.ribaf.2022.101646

AI-powered cameras in LA: Are DUI arrests going high-tech? (2025, April 30). Werksman Jackson Quinn, Los Angeles Criminal Defense Blog. https://werksmanjackson.com/blog/ai-powered-cameras-in-la-are-dui-arrests-going-high-tech

Akhtar, Z., Pendyala, T. L., & Athmakuri, V. S. (2024, July 12). Video and audio deepfake datasets and open issues in deepfake technology: Being ahead of the curve. *Forensic Science*, *4*(3), 289–377. DOI: 10.3390/forensicsci4030021

Akshaya, R., & Devadharshini, V. V. (2025, April 26). An analysis on artificial intelligence and data privacy in India. *Indian Journal of Law and Legal Research*, *7*(2), 4917–4921. https://3fdef50c-add3-4615-a675-a91741bcb5c0.usrfiles.com/ugd/3fdef5_0a790d1ad05548dfa0758fd7c6586057.pdf

Akumba, B. O., Iorliam, A., Agber, S., Okube, E. O., & Kwaghtyo, K. D. (2021, April). Authentication of Video evidence for forensic investigation: A case of Nigeria. *Journal of Information Security*, *12*(2), 163–176. DOI: 10.4236/jis.2021.122008

Alam, S., & Altiparmak, Z. (2024, February). XAI-CF — Examining the role of explainable Artificial Intelligence in cyber forensics (arXiv:2402.02452). *arXiv.* /arXiv.2402.02452DOI: 10.2139/ssrn.4833246

Alamayreh, O., Fascella, C., Mandelli, S., Tondi, B., Bestagini, P., & Barni, M. (2024, August). Just dance: Detection of human body reenactment fake videos. *EURASIP Journal on Image and Video Processing*, *2024*(1), 21. DOI: 10.1186/s13640-024-00635-2

Alanazi, S., & Asif, S. (2024, September). Exploring deepfake technology: Creation, consequences and countermeasures. *Human-Intelligent Systems Integration*, *6*(1), 49–60. DOI: 10.1007/s42454-024-00054-8

Alexander, A. (2021, July). Location monitoring for greater plant safety: Location monitoring devices and geofencing can help reduce risks of injury or exposure for plant personnel. *Processing*, *34*(7), 26–27.

Aliieva, E., & Gao, L. (2025, December 16). Video shows elderly couple trying to stop and disarm Bondi gunman. *NBC News.* https://www.nbcnews.com/world/australia/new-video-shows-elderly-couple-disarm-bondi-beach-gunman-rcna249446

Ali, S., Wang, J., & Leung, V. C. M. (2025, June). AI-driven fusion with cybersecurity: Exploring current trends, advanced techniques, future directions, and policy implications for evolving paradigms- A comprehensive review. *Information Fusion, 118*, 102922. DOI: 10.1016/j.inffus.2024.102922

Aljahdali, A., Alsaidi, N., Alsafri, M., Alsulami, A., & Almutairi, T. (2021). Mobile device forensics. *Romanian Journal of Information Technology & Automatic Control, 31*(3), 81–96. DOI: 10.33436/v31i3y202107

Alkhatib, M. (2025, November 7). A multifaceted deepfake prevention framework integrating blockchain, post-quantum cryptography, hybrid watermarking, human oversight, and policy governance. *Computers, 14*(11), 488. DOI: 10.3390/computers14110488

Almeida, D., Shmarko, K., & Lomas, E. (2022, August). The ethics of facial recognition technologies, surveillance, and accountability in an age of artificial intelligence: A comparative analysis of US, EU, and UK regulatory frameworks. *AI and Ethics, 2*(3), 377–387. DOI: 10.1007/s43681-021-00077-w PMID: 34790955

Alqahtany, S. S., & Syed, T. A. (2024, February 12). ForensicTransMonitor: A comprehensive blockchain approach to reinvent digital forensics and evidence management. *Information (Basel), 15*(2), 109. DOI: 10.3390/info15020109

Alrashoud, M. (2025, June). Deepfake video detection methods, approaches, and challenges. *Alexandria Engineering Journal, 125*, 265–277. DOI: 10.1016/j.aej.2025.04.007

Alvarado, A. (2024). The mosaic theory in Fourth Amendment jurisprudence: The last bastion of privacy in a camera-surveilled world. *St. Mary's Law Journal, 55*(3), 849–884. https://commons.stmarytx.edu/thestmaryslawjournal/vol55/iss3/5

Amadi, P. (2024). Federal rules of evidence in the United States of America and the challenges of authentication in the age of deepfake technology. *UNILAG Law Review, 7*(1), 1–29.

Amendments I and IV. (1791, December 15). Constitution of the United States. https://constitution.congress.gov/constitution

American Civil Liberties Union. (2022 May 11). *Court cases: ACLU v. Clearview AI.* https://www.aclu.org/cases/aclu-v-clearview-ai

Amerini, I., Barni, M., Battiato, S., Bestagini, P., Boato, G., Bruni, V., Caldelli, R., De Natale, F., De Nicola, R., Guarnera, L., Mandelli, S., Majid, T., Marcialis, G. L., Micheletto, M., Montibeller, A., Orrù, G., Ortis, A., Perazzo, P., Puglisi, G., & Vitulano, D. (2025, February). Deepfake media forensics: Status and future challenges. *Journal of Imaging, 11*(3), 73. DOI: 10.3390/jimaging11030073 PMID: 40137185

Amster, H., & Diehl, B. (2022, February). Against geofences. *Stanford Law Review, 74*(2), 385–445.

Anand, A., Kaur, J., Singh, O., & Alhazmi, H., O. (. (2021, May 6). Optimal sprint length determination for Agile-based software development. *Computers, Materials & Continua, 68*(3), 3693–3712. DOI: 10.32604/cmc.2021.017461

András, H. L., & Bélai, G. (2025). The impact of recordings of police actions on organisational culture. *Academic Journal of Internal Affairs / Belügyi Szemle, 73*(6), 1287–1300. https://doi.org/DOI: 10.38146/bsz-ajia.2025.v73.i6.pp1287-1300

Antwi, N. (2024, September 30). Human rights and Constitutional law: Balancing security and freedom. *DME Journal of Law, 5*(2), 108–119. DOI: 10.53361/dmejl.v5i02.11

Appleby, L. (2024). Breaking barriers: Exploring accessibility to legal advice and its implications for justice. *Wake Forest Journal of Law & Policy, 15*(1), 65–84.

Aracri, C. (2024, September 12). *Supreme Court of Maryland discusses authentication of video evidence.* Maryland State Bar Association. https://www.msba.org/site/site/content/News-and-Publications/News/General-News/Supreme-Court-of-Maryland-Discusses-Authentication-of-Video-Evidence.aspx

Arguelles, C., & Ortiz-Luis, I. (2021, May). Bars behind bars: Digital technology in the prison system. *SSRN, 32*(1), 1–18. DOI: 10.2139/ssrn.3812046

Ariel, B., Farrar, W. A., & Sutherland, A. (2015). The effect of police body-worn cameras on use of force and citizens' complaints against the police: A randomized controlled trial. *Journal of Quantitative Criminology, 31*(3), 509–535. DOI: 10.1007/s10940-014-9236-3

Arietti, R. (2024, January-February). Do real-time crime centers improve case clearance? An examination of Chicago's strategic decision support centers. *Journal of Criminal Justice, 90*, 102145. DOI: 10.1016/j.jcrimjus.2023.102145

Arizona Attorney General. (2022, October 4). *Attorney General Mark Brnovich achieves historic $85 million settlement with Google*. [Press release]. https://www.azag.gov/press-release/attorney-general-mark-brnovich-achieves-historic-85-million-settlement-google

Arora, P., & Deswal, S. (2025, March 10). Geofence-based boundary violation detection algorithms in Unmanned Aerial Vehicles. *International Journal of Communication Systems, 38*(4), 1–11. DOI: 10.1002/dac.6035

Arun, P. (2021). In pursuit of personal data: A survey on state surveillance and democracy in India. In P. R. deSouza, Mohd. S. Alam, & H, Ahmed (Eds.), *Companion to Indian democracy: Resilience, fragility, ambivalence* (pp. 234-255). Routledge India. https://doi.org/DOI: 10.4324/9781003219477

Arun, P. (2025). Regressive and authoritarian: Surveillance powers in the Telecommunications Act 2023 and Post Office Act 2023. *Indiana Law Review, 9*(1), 80–96. DOI: 10.1080/24730580.2024.2440943

Asgari, S. (2024, March 27). *The threat of geofence warrants: Why courts should deem geofence warrants unconstitutional under the Fourth Amendment*. NYU Proceedings. https://proceedings.nyumootcourt.org/2024/03/the-threat-of-geofence-warrants-why-courts-should-deem-geofence-warrants-unconstitutional-under-the-fourth-amendment

Ashe, A. (2023, September 25). Digital perimeters. *Journal of Commerce, 24*(20), 37–38.

Atlam, H. F., Ekuri, N., Azad, M. A., & Lallie, H. S. (2024, September 7). Blockchain forensics: A systematic literature review of techniques, applications, challenges, and future directions. *Electronics (Basel), 13*(17), 3568. DOI: 10.3390/electronics13173568

Atlas of surveillance. (n.d.). Electronic Frontier Foundation. https://atlasofsurveillance.org

Attri, A., & Tripathi, M. K. (2025). Police reform and human rights: Bridging the gap in protection of minority communities. *International Journal of Political Science and Governance, 7*(8, 8A), 27–32. DOI: 10.33545/26646021.2025.v7.i8a.617

Atwood, J. R. (2015). The encryption problem: Why the courts and technology are creating a mess for law enforcement. *Saint Louis University Public Law Review, 34*(2), 407–434.

Auteri, S. (2023). The ripple effect of Dobbs on geofence warrants. *Northern Kentucky Law Review, 50*(2), 181–203.

Awati, R. (2022, December). *Geofencing.* TechTarget. https://www.techtarget.com/whatis/definition/geofencing

Ayoub, E., & Griffiths, H. (2023, November 20). *We're suing the NYPD to uncover its online surveillance practices.* Brennan Center for Justice. https://www.brennancenter.org/our-work/analysis-opinion/were-suing-nypd-uncover-its-online-surveillance-practices

Babaei, R., Cheng, S., Duan, R., & Zhao, S. (2025). Generative Artificial Intelligence and the evolving challenge of deepfake detection: A systematic analysis. *Journal of Sensor and Actuator Networks, 14*(1), 17. DOI: 10.3390/jsan14010017

Babwin, D., & Tareen, S. (2019, June 25). Chicago police release more than 1,000 files from Smollett investigation. *PBS/Associated Press.* https://www.pbs.org/newshour/nation/chicago-police-release-more-than-1000-files-from-smollett-investigation

Bagaric, M., Svilar, J., Bull, M., Hunter, D., & Stobbs, N. (2022). The solution to the pervasive bias and discrimination in the criminal justice system: transparent and fair artificial intelligence. *American Criminal Law Review, Georgetown Law, 59*(1), 95–148. https://www.law.georgetown.edu/american-criminal-law-review/in-print/volume-59-number-1-winter-2022/the-solution-to-the-pervasive-bias-and-discrimination-in-the-criminal-justice-system-transparent-and-fair-artificial-intelligence

Bailey, R., & Parsheera, S. (2021, October). Data localization in India: Paradigms and processes. *CSI Transactions on ICT, 9*(3), 137–150. DOI: 10.1007/s40012-021-00337-4

Bakhtiar, H. S. (2024). The evolution of scientific evidence theory in criminal law: A transformative insight. *Media Iuris, 7*(2), 221–240. DOI: 10.20473/mi.v7i2.51095

Bandara, P. (2023, July 21). *Japan tests 'minority report' style cameras to stop crime before it happens.* PetaPixel. https://petapixel.com/2023/07/21/japan-tests-minority-report-style-cameras-to-stop-crime-before-it-happens

Barocas, S., & Selbst, A. D. (2016). Big data's disparate impact. *SSRN, 104*, 671–732. DOI: 10.2139/ssrn.2477899

Barreiro-Gen, M., & Novo-Corti, I. (2015, October). Collaborative learning in environments with restricted access to the internet: Policies to bridge the digital divide and exclusion in prisons through the development of the skills of inmates. *Computers in Human Behaviour, 51*(B), 1172-1176. https://doi.org/DOI: 10.1016/j.chb.2015.01.076

Basheer, I. P. (2025, January). Bias in the algorithm: Issues raised due to use of facial recognition in India. *Journal of Development Policy and Practice*, *10*(1), 61–79. Advance online publication. DOI: 10.1177/24551333241283992

Bathke, B. (2024, Spring). Google and the role of surveillance intermediaries in geofence warrants. *Tulane Journal of Technology and Intellectual Property*, *26*, 111–134.

Batori, Z. (2018). Photographic manipulation and photographic deception. *Aisthesis. Pratiche, Linguaggi e Saperi Dell'estetico, 11*(2), 35–47. DOI: 10.13128/Aisthesis-23863

Bayley, D. H. (1994). *Police for the future*. Oxford University Press. DOI: 10.1093/oso/9780195091168.001.0001

Bello, I. A., Bashir, A., Kamba, M. I., Ibahim, S., & Bena, A. A. (2023, November). Smart watch technology as a solution to insecurity in northern Nigeria: A case study of kidnapping. *The 9th National Conference on skill acquisition as a solution to insecurity and unemployment in Nigeria, Kebbi.*

Bellovin, S. M., Hutchins, R. M., Jebara, T., & Zimmeck, S. (2014). When enough is enough: Location tracking, Mosaic theory, and Machine Learning. *New York University Journal of Law & Liberty*, *8*(2), 555–628.

Bender, J. (2013, February 17). *Good "geofences" make good neighbors in age of mobile alerts.* New England Board of Higher Education. https://nebhe.org/journal/good-geofencing-makes-good-neighbors-the-age-of-mobile-alerts

Bendett, S., & Kirichenko, D. (2025, January 10). *Battlefield drones and the accelerating autonomous arms race in Ukraine.* Modern War Institute at West Point. https://mwi.westpoint.edu/battlefield-drones-and-the-accelerating-autonomous-arms-race-in-ukraine

Benefits Tech Advocacy Hub. (n.d.). Michigan unemployment insurance false fraud determinations [Case study]. https://www.btah.org/case-study/michigan-unemployment-insurance-false-fraud-determinations.html

Bengart, A. A. (2024). Always a suspect: Law enforcement's violative use of geofence warrants and geolocation data in criminal investigations and proceedings. *Cardozo International & Comparative Law Review*, *7*(2), 639–673.

Benson, J. (2021, February 15). *Smartphone recordings as evidence in family law proceedings.* Berryman Partners. https://www.berrymanpartners.com.au/smartphone-recordings-as-evidence

Bernard, T., & Taffesse, A. S. (2014, January). Aspirations: An approach to measurement with validation using Ethiopian data. *Journal of African Economies*, *23*(2), 189–224. DOI: 10.1093/jae/ejt030

Bhalla, K. (2019, November 8). Gurugram startup Staqu develops AI surveillance system for monitoring Uttar Pradesh prisons. *Inc42.* https://inc42.com/buzz/gurugram-startup-staqu-develops-ai-surveillance-system-for-uttar-pradesh-prisons/

Bhandari, V., & Lahiri, K. (2020). The surveillance state: Privacy and criminal investigation in India: Possible futures in a post-Puttaswamy world. *University of Oxford Human Rights Hub Journal, 3*(2), 15-46. https://papers.ssrn.com/abstract=3580630

Bhat, P. I. (2020, January 23). Doctrinal legal research as a means of synthesizing facts, thoughts, and legal principles. In *Idea and Methods of Legal Research* (pp. 143-168). DOI: 10.1093/oso/9780199493098.003.0005

Biale, N. (2008, June 25). *What criminologists and others studying cameras have found.* ACLU Technology and Liberty Program. https://www.aclu.org/sites/default/files/images/asset_upload_file708_35775.pdf

Bild, E., Redman, A., Newman, E. J., Muir, B. R., Tait, D., & Schwarz, N. (2021, October). Sound and credibility in the virtual court: Low audio quality leads to less favorable evaluations of witnesses and lower weighting of evidence. *Law and Human Behavior, 45*(5), 481–495. DOI: 10.1037/lhb0000466 PMID: 34871019

Biometric Information Privacy Act. (740 ILCS 14, Section 10). (2024, August 2). Illinois State Government. https://www.ilga.gov/Legislation/ILCS/Articles?ActID=3004&ChapterID=57

Bischoff, P. (2024, January 8). *CCTV surveillance in the most populated cities in the United States.* Comparitech. https://www.comparitech.com/blog/vpn-privacy/us-surveillance-camera-statistics

Bishop, G. (2021). *Tablet use in Cape Vincent Correctional Facility, NY: Its effects on the community.* [Master's thesis, Campbellsville University].

Bisht, U. & Pooja. (2025, July-December). Evolving deepfake technologies: Advancements, detection techniques, and societal impact. *Don Bosco Institute of Technology Delhi Journal of Research, 1*(2), 38–43. https://acspublisher.com/journals/index.php/dbitdjr/article/view/20696

Blizzard, B. (2018, January 25). *National poll results.* [Memorandum]. Justice Action Network. https://www.politico.com/f/?id=00000161-2ccc-da2c-a963-efff82be0001

Block, A. (2023, November 8). *What we know about CPD social media technology and monitoring.* ACLU Illinois. https://www.aclu-il.org/en/news/what-we-know-about-cpd-social-media-technology-and-monitoring

Bonifazi, G., Cauteruccio, F., Corradini, E., Marchetti, M., Montella, D., Scarponi, S., Ursino, D., & Virgili, L. (2023, February 20). Performing wash trading on NFTs: Is the game worth the candle? *Big Data and Cognitive Computing, 7*(1), 38. DOI: 10.3390/bdcc7010038

Bonta, J., Blais, J., & Wilson, H. A. (2013, January). *The prediction of risk for mentally disordered offenders: A quantitative synthesis.* Public Safety Canada. https://www.publicsafety.gc.ca/cnt/rsrcs/pblctns/prdctn-rsk-mntlly-dsrdrd/index-en.aspx

Booth, B. M., Hickman, L., Subburaj, S. K., Tay, L., Woo, S. E., & D'Mello, S. K. (2021, October 18). Bias and fairness in multimodal machine learning: A case study of automated video interviews. [Conference paper]. *ICMI '21: Proceedings of the 2021 International Conference on Multimodal Interaction* (pp. 268–277). https://doi.org/DOI: 10.1145/3462244.3479897

Bowers, K., & Johnson, S. (2024, July/September). Facing the future of crime: A framework for police use of technology. *The Political Quarterly*, *95*(3), 480–488. DOI: 10.1111/1467-923X.13426

Bradbury, S. (2024, May 26). Police drones responding to 911 calls in Colorado? "This really is the future of law enforcement." *The Denver Post.* https://www.denverpost.com/2024/05/26/colorado-police-drones-first-responders

Brauneis, R., & Goodman, E. P. (2018). Algorithmic transparency for the smart city. *SSRN*, *20*(1), 103–176. DOI: 10.2139/ssrn.3012499

Braun, V., & Clarke, V. (2006). Using thematic analysis in psychology. *Qualitative Research in Psychology*, *3*(2), 77–101. DOI: 10.1191/1478088706qp063oa

Brayne, S., & Christin, A. (2021, August). Technologies of crime prediction: The reception of algorithms in policing and criminal courts. *The Sociological Review*, *68*(3), 608–624. DOI: 10.1093/socpro/spaa004 PMID: 38250480

Brenner, M., Gersen, J. S., Haley, M., Lin, M., Merchant, A., Millett, R. J., Sarkar, S. K., & Wegner, D. (2020). Constitutional dimensions of predictive algorithms in criminal justice. *Harvard Civil Rights-Civil Liberties Law Review*, *55*, 267–310. https://journals.law.harvard.edu/crcl/wp-content/uploads/sites/80/2020/09/Brenner-et-al.pdf

Breslin, G., Haughey, T., O'Brien, W., Caulfield, L. S., Robertson, A., & Lawlor, M. (2018). Increasing athlete knowledge of mental health and intentions to seek help: The State of Mind Ireland (SOMI) pilot program. *Journal of Clinical Sport Psychology*, *12*(1), 39–56. DOI: 10.1123/jcsp.2016-0039

Brewster, T. (2022, October 31). States spent millions on Deloitte's 'Anti-Fraud' Covid unemployment systems. They suffered billions in fraud. Forbes. https://www.forbes.com/sites/thomasbrewster/2022/10/31/covid-pandemic-fraud-hits-billions-despite-deloitte-contracts-worth-hundreds-of-millions

British Computer Society (BCS). The Chartered Institute for IT (n.d.). *Digital literacy.* https://www.bcs.org/policy-and-influence/education/digital-literacy

Brown, R. L., & Harmon, R. R. (2014, October). Viral geofencing: An exploration of emerging big-data driven direct digital marketing services. *Proceedings of PICMET '14 Conference: Portland International Center for Management of Engineering and Technology; Infrastructure and Service Integration*, Kanazawa, Japan, pp. 3300-3308.

Brown, I. (2012, November). Government access to private-sector data in the United Kingdom. *International Data Privacy Law*, *2*(4), 230–238. DOI: 10.1093/idpl/ips018

Browning, J. G. (2020, July). Should judges have a duty of tech competence? *St. Mary's Journal on Legal Malpractice & Ethics*, *10*(2), 176-196.

Bunce, E. C. (2022, May 2). *#MyrtleMondays: Victorian police equipment.* Elizabeth C. Bunce. https://elizabethcbunce.com/2022/05/02/myrtlemondays-victorian-police-equipment

Buolamwini, J., & Gebru, T. (2018). Gender shades: Intersectional accuracy disparities in commercial gender classification. [Conference paper]. In Conference on Fairness, Accountability and Transparency (pp. 77–91). Proceedings of Machine Learning Research. https://proceedings.mlr.press/v81/buolamwini18a.html

Bureau of Justice Assistance. (2018). *Implementing a body-worn camera program: Recommendations and lessons learned.* U.S. Department of Justice. https://www.justice.gov/iso/opa/resources/472014912134715246869.pdf

Bureau of Justice Assistance. (2025). *Implementation, body-worn camera toolkit.* https://bja.ojp.gov/program/bwc/topics/implementation

Burman, A. (2023, October 3). *Understanding India's new data protection law.* Carnegie Endowment for International Peace. https://carnegieendowment.org/research/2023/10/understanding-indias-new-data-protection-law?lang=en&utm_source=chatgpt.com

Butler, J. (2025, December 29). CCTV suggests alleged Bondi shooters acted alone and did not receive training in Philippines, AFP says. *The Guardian.* https://www.theguardian.com/australia-news/2025/dec/30/alleged-bondi-shooters-did-not-receive-training-philippines-ntwnfb

Butler, R. (2025, February 7). *2025 Predictions: How will the interplay of AI and fraud play out?* Thomson Reuters Institute. https://www.thomsonreuters.com/en-us/posts/corporates/2025-predictions-interplay-fraud-ai

Caggiani, L., Camporeale, R., Di Bari, D., & Ottomanelli, M. (2025, July). A geofencing-based methodology for speed limit regulation and user safety in e-scooter sharing systems. *Journal of Intelligent Transport Systems, 29*(4), 401–416. DOI: 10.1080/15472450.2023.2201681

Calacci, D., Shen, J. J., & Pentland, A. (2022, November 11). The cop in your neighbor's doorbell: Amazon Ring and the spread of participatory mass surveillance. *Proceedings of the ACM on Human-Computer Interaction, 6*(CSCW2), 400. https://doi.org/DOI: 10.1145/3555125

Calams, S. (2024, February 13). *Leading the digital beat: LAPD's deputy chief talks technology's role in shaping the future of policing.* Police1. https://www.police1.com/tech-pulse/leading-the-digital-beat-lapds-deputy-chief-talks-technologys-role-in-shaping-the-future-of-policing

California v. Ciraolo, 476 U.S. 207. (1986, May 19). *Justia U.S. Supreme Court.* https://supreme.justia.com/cases/federal/us/476/207

Callaghan, R. (2025, February). *How home CCTV can help keep our suburbs safer.* Horizons. https://rac.com.au/horizons/lifestyle/perth-cctv-program

Campbell, C. (n.d.). *What is 'smart' technology?* Williams College Office for Information Technology. https://oit.williams.edu/ats-posts/what-is-smart-technology

Cancela-Outeda, C. (2024, October). The EU's AI act: A framework for collaborative governance. *Internet of Things : Engineering Cyber Physical Human Systems, 27,* 101291. DOI: 10.1016/j.iot.2024.101291

Capece, J. (2020, July). The effects of probation stipulations on employment quality among people on probation. *Journal of Offender Rehabilitation*, *59*(7), 375–388. DOI: 10.1080/10509674.2020.1784348

Carolan, C. M., Forbat, L., & Smith, A. (2016, April). Developing the DESCARTE Model: The design of case study research in health care. *Qualitative Health Research*, *26*(5), 626–639. DOI: 10.1177/1049732315602488 PMID: 26336896

Caroline, A., Coun, M. J. H., Gunawan, A., & Stoffers, J. (2025, January 16). A systematic literature review on digital literacy, employability, and innovative work behavior: Emphasizing the contextual approaches in HRM research. *Frontiers in Psychology*, *15*, 1448555. DOI: 10.3389/fpsyg.2024.1448555 PMID: 39895978

Carpenter v. United States, 585 U.S. 296. (2018, June 22). *Oyez*. https://www.oyez.org/cases/2017/16-402

Carpenter v. United States. 484 U.S. 19 (2018). https://casetext.com/case/carpenter-v-united-states-10

Case study: Geofencing technology trialled with Defence Digital. (2022, January 13). GovUK. https://www.gov.uk/government/case-studies/geofencing-technology-trialled-with-defence-digital

Caulfield, L. S., Brooks-Wilson, S., Booth, J., & Monaghan, M. (2023, September). Engaging parents to reduce youth violence: Evidence from a youth justice board pathfinder programme. *Crime Prevention and Community Safety*, *25*(4), 401–426. DOI: 10.1057/s41300-023-00190-4

Celebi, N., Liu, Q., & Karatoprak, M. (2022, May). A survey of deep fake detection for trial courts. *Artificial Intelligence and Applications (Commerce, Calif.)*, •••, 227–238. DOI: 10.5121/csit.2022.120919

Center for Human Security Studies. (2021, October 19). *Using Artificial Intelligence for smart policing*. https://chss.org.in/using-artificial-intelligence-for-smart-policing/

Chadha, V., & Sivaraman, J. (2024, June 25). Critical analysis of the law on admissibility of electronic evidence in India. *Jindal Global Law Review*, *15*(1), 119–132. DOI: 10.1007/s41020-024-00219-1

Chang, R. (2024, April 11). *What happened to the white Ford Bron*co. Biography. https://www.biography.com/crime/oj-simpson-bronco-chase-car-museum

Chang, C. (2021). Improving access to free online legal information through Universal Design: User personas, user journeys, a proposal, and a prototype. *Legal Reference Services Quarterly*, *40*(4), 199–281. DOI: 10.1080/0270319X.2021.2003686

Charette, R. N. (2018, January 24). Michigan's MiDAS unemployment system: Algorithm alchemy that created lead, not gold. IEEE Spectrum. https://spectrum.ieee.org/michigans-midas-unemployment-system-algorithm-alchemy-that-created-lead-not-gold

Chaturvedi, S. (2025, March 5). The DPDP rules unveiled: Progress, shortcomings and the road ahead. *Harvard Journal of Law & Technology*. https://jolt.law.harvard.edu/digest/the-dpdp-rules-unveiled-progress-shortcomings-and-the-road-ahead

Chawki, M. (2024). Navigating legal challenges of deepfakes in the American context: A call to action. *Cogent Engineering*, *11*(1), 2320971. DOI: 10.1080/23311916.2024.2320971

Chawki, M., Basu, S., & Choi, K.-S. (2026, February). Deepfake sextortion in England, Wales and Northern Ireland: A doctrinal and regulatory analysis. *Laws, 15*(1), 11. DOI: 10.3390/laws15010011

Chen, Y.-C., & Huang, C. (2021, January 6). Smart data-driven policy on unmanned aircraft systems (UAS): Analysis of drone users in U.S. cities. *Smart Cities, 4*(1), 78–92. DOI: 10.3390/smartcities4010005

Cheong, B. C. (2024, July 2). Transparency and accountability in AI systems: Safeguarding wellbeing in the age of algorithmic decision-making. *Frontiers in Human Dynamics, 6*, 1421273. DOI: 10.3389/fhumd.2024.1421273

Chhina, M. A. S. (2025, March 13). How Mohali police are integrating AI into day-to-day crime detection and resolution. *The Indian Express*. https://indianexpress.com/article/cities/chandigarh/mohali-police-integrating-ai-crime-detection-resolution-9884590

Chiao, V. (2019, June 20). Fairness, accountability and transparency: Notes on algorithmic decision-making in criminal justice. *International Journal of Law in Context, 15*(2), 126–139. DOI: 10.1017/S1744552319000077

Chidambaram, A. S., Suthendran, K., & Kumar, M. S. (2022, March). Forensic investigation on electronic evidences using encase and autopsy. *Sustainable Development in Engineering and Technology*, 117-124.

Choi, J. H., & Schwarcz, D. (2024). AI assistance in legal analysis: An empirical study. *Journal of Legal Education, 73*(2), 384–420.

Chowdhary, S., Kawakami, A., Gray, M. L., Suh, J., Olteanu, A., & Saha, K. (2023, June*). Can workers meaningfully consent to workplace wellbeing technologies?* [Conference paper]. ACM Conference on Fairness, Accountability, and Transparency (pp. 569-582). https://doi.org/DOI: 10.1145/3593013.3594023

Chowdri, P. (2024, January 4). *Emerging tech and law enforcement: What are geofences and how do they work?* Lexipol. https://www.lexipol.com/resources/blog/emerging-tech-and-law-enforcement-what-are-geofences-and-how-do-they-work

Christoff, T., & Patterson, Q. (2025, September). *Drones as first responders (DFR): National landscape, operational considerations, and future directions.* CNA Corporation. https://www.cna.org/reports/2025/09/Drones-as-First-Responders.pdf

Christopher Mooney vs. State of Maryland. (2024, August 13). Maryland Courts. https://www.mdcourts.gov/data/opinions/coa/2024/32a23.pdf

Chula Vista Police Department. (n.d.). *Drone as first responder (DFR) operations and de-escalation dashboard.* Retrieved March 30, 2026 from https://app.powerbigov.us/view?r=eyJrIjoiNWNiYmI5ZTEtMzVjZi00NjNjLTkzNzgtNjg5NDQ3Yzk1NzEzIiwidCI6IjU2ZmM0NjE4LWM4M2QtNDAxZS1hNTMxLWZlYTEyNGI2NDZhNyJ9

Cinar, B. (2023, October 25). Deepfakes in cyber warfare: Threats, detection, techniques and countermeasures. *Asian Journal of Research in Computer Science, 16*(4), 178–193. DOI: 10.9734/ajrcos/2023/v16i4381

Cindrapole, A. C., & Rosmini, S. (2024, May). The legal and ethical implications of surveillance in criminal law: A literatur review. *eScience Humanity Journal 4*(2), 448-455. https://doi.org/DOI: 10.37296/esci.v4i2.164

Citron, D. K. (2008). Technological due process. Washington University Law Review, 85, 1249–1313. https://journals.library.wustl.edu/lawreview/article/id/6697

Citron, D. K., & Pasquale, F. (2014, March 1). The scored society: Due process for automated predictions. *Washington Law Review (Seattle, Wash.)*, *89*(1), 1–33. https://digitalcommons.law.uw.edu/wlr/vol89/iss1/2

City of Chicago. (n.d.). *Facts & statistics.* https://www.chicago.gov/city/en/about/facts.html

City of Chula Vista. (n.d.). *Drone program.* https://www.chulavistaca.gov/departments/police-department/programs/uas-drone-program

City of Jamestown. (n.d.). *Police department history.* https://www.jamestownny.gov/police-department/history

Clarke, A. (2023, July 10). *The most overlooked feature in a police car.* CivicEye. https://www.civiceye.com/overlooked-feature-in-police-cars

Cochran, C. (2025, September 3). *Emerging technologies in law enforcement.* Right on crime: Texas Public Policy Foundation. https://rightoncrime.com/emerging-technologies-in-law-enforcement

Connolly, K. (2016, November 5). Documentary casts doubt on guilty verdict in 1990 Virginia murder trial. *The Guardian.* https://www.theguardian.com/us-news/2016/nov/05/jens-soring-elizabeth-haysom-virginia-murders-documentary

Const, U. S. Amend. IV. https://constitution.congress.gov/constitution/amendment-4

Constitution Annotated. (n.d.). *Katz and reasonable expectation of privacy test.* https://constitution.congress.gov/browse/essay/amdt4-3-3/ALDE_00013717

Conti, M., Kumar, G., Lal, C., & Saha, R. (2023, August). Blockchain-based distributed and secure digital forensic investigation systems. *Advances in Information Security*, *105*, 337–362. DOI: 10.1007/978-3-031-32146-7_11

Coolbrandt, A., Steffens, E., Wildier, H., Bruyninckx, E., Verslype, C., & Milisen, J. (2017, December). Use of a symptom diary during chemotherapy: A mixed-methods evaluation of the patient perspective. *European Journal of Oncology Nursing*, *31*, 37–45. DOI: 10.1016/j.ejon.2017.09.003 PMID: 29173825

Coomaraswamy, R., & de los Reyes, C. (2004, April). Rule by emergency: Sri Lanka's postcolonial constitutional experience. *International Journal of Constitutional Law*, *2*(2), 272–295. DOI: 10.1093/icon/2.2.272

Cordner, A., & Cordner, G. (2025). Overview of law enforcement technology. In Moriarty, L. J. (Ed.), *Criminal Justice in the 21st Century*. Charles C. Thomas Publisher.

Cournoyer, J., & Stanton, S. (2016, January 19). *In jail, tablets calm and educate inmates.* Governing. https://www.governing.com/archive/tns-tablets-jail-sacramento.html

Court of Appeals in Iowa. (2025, February 19). State of Iowa v. Terence Edward Manning Jr. (Case 23-1390). Iowa Courts. https://www.iowacourts.gov/courtcases/22746/embed/CourtAppealsOpinion

Crawford v. Washington, 541 U.S. 36 (2004).

Create and monitor geofences. (2024, June 17). Android Developers. https://developer.android.com/develop/sensors-and-location/location/geofencing

Crenshaw, K. (1989). Demarginalizing the intersection of race and sex: A Black feminist critique of antidiscrimination doctrine, feminist theory and antiracist politics. *University of Chicago Legal Forum, 1989*(1), 139–167. https://chicagounbound.uchicago.edu/uclf/vol1989/iss1/8

Creswell, J. W. (2014). *Educational research: Planning, conducting, and evaluating quantitative and qualitative research* (5th ed.). Pearson.

Creswell, J. W., & Plano Clark, V. L. (2018). *Designing and conducting mixed methods research* (3rd ed.). Sage.

Crispin, M. (2025, October 16). *Fraud Detection with Machine Learning & AI.* SEON. https://seon.io/resources/fraud-detection-with-machine-learning

Croce, J. (2025, Spring). Addressing and overcoming the top digital transformation challenges for correctional facilities. *Corrections Today*, *87*(1), 32–36.

Cryptocurrencies: Tracing the evolution of criminal finances. (2021, December). Publication Office of the European Union: Europol. https://doi.org/DOI: 10.2813/75468

Cullen, F. T., Fisher, B. S., & Applegate, B. K. (2000). Public opinion about punishment and corrections. *Crime and Justice*, *27*, 1–79. DOI: 10.1086/652198

Curvey, E. (2024, June 27). *Tips for improving truck turn times.* Tideworks Technology. https://tideworks.com/tips-for-improving-truck-turn-times

Cybercrime roadmap 2026: Nearly 2,500 law enforcement personnel trained on latest forensic tools, techniques. (2025, December 31). *The Economic Times.* https://economictimes.indiatimes.com/tech/technology/cybercrime-roadmap-2026-nearly-2500-law-enforcement-personnel-trained-on-latest-forensic-tools-techniques/articleshow/126270912.cms

Czymara, C. S., Dochow-Sondershaus, S., Drouhot, L. G., Simsek, M., & Spörlein, C. (2023, January). Catalyst of hate? Ethnic insulting on YouTube in the aftermath of terror attacks in France, Germany and the United Kingdom 2014–2017. *Journal of Ethnic and Migration Studies*, *49*(2), 535–553. DOI: 10.1080/1369183X.2022.2100552

D'Avino, C. (2022, November 6). Money laundering and AML regulatory and judicial system regimes: Investigation of FinCEN files. *European Journal of Law and Economics*, *55*, 195–223. DOI: 10.1007/s10657-022-09756-3

Damon, S. (2025). The constitutionality of geofence warrants. *Student Journal of Information Privacy Law, 3*(1), 76-98. https://digitalcommons.mainelaw.maine.edu/sjipl/vol3/iss1/6

Dancy, T., & Zalnieriute, M. (2025, August 16). AI and transparency in judicial decision-making. *Oxford Journal of Legal Studies*, *41*(1), 1–34. DOI: 10.1093/ojls/gqaf030 PMID: 40123910

Daniel, L. (2025, January 29). Judge throws out facial recognition evidence in murder case. *Forbes*. https://www.forbes.com/sites/larsdaniel/2025/01/29/judge-throws-out-facial-recognition-evidence-in-murder-case/

Daraghmi, Y.-A., & Shawahna, I. (2023, August). Digital forensic analysis of vehicular video sensors: Dashcams as a case. *Sensors (Basel)*, *23*(17), 7548. DOI: 10.3390/s23177548 PMID: 37688004

Darwis, D., Fernando, Y., Mehta, A. R., Wamiliana, , & Setiawansyah, . (2025, October). Metadata-based video steganography: Development of a new model for secure information embedding. *Engineering, Technology &. Applied Scientific Research*, *15*(5), 27076–27088. DOI: 10.48084/etasr.11937

Dashcam shows truck rushing towards Berlin Christmas market. (2016, December 22). *Reuters*. https://www.reuters.com/article/world/exclusive-dashcam-shows-truck-speed-into-berlin-christmas-market-idUSKBN14B2FG

Daubert v. Merrell Dow Pharmaceuticals, Inc., 509 U.S. 579 (1993).

Daubert v. Merrell Dow Pharmaceuticals, Inc., 509 U.S. 579, 113 S. Ct. 2786 (1993)

Dauvergne, P. (2022). Facial recognition technology for policing and surveillance in the Global South: A call for bans. *Third World Quarterly*, *43*(9), 2325–2335. DOI: 10.1080/01436597.2022.2080654

Davies, A., & Krame, G. (2023, December 13). Integrating body-worn cameras, drones, and AI: A framework for enhancing police readiness and response. *Policing. Policing (Oxford, England)*, *17*, paad083. Advance online publication. DOI: 10.1093/police/paad083

de Almeida, C. M. T., & Boni, P. C. (2006, December). A ética no fotojornalismo da era digital. *Discursos Fotograficos*, *2*(2), 11–42. DOI: 10.5433/1984-7939.2006v2n2p11

de Cassai, A., Dost, B., Tulgar, S., & Boscolo, A. (2025, August). Methodological standards for conducting high-quality systematic reviews. *Biology (Basel)*, *14*(8), 973. DOI: 10.3390/biology14080973 PMID: 40906182

De Donà, M. (2025, December). Multistakeholder governance through epistemic authority: exploring the role of the Climate and Clean Air Coalition in the global climate regime. *International Environmental Agreements Politics Law and Economics*. DOI: 10.1007/s10784-025-09708-7

de la Garza, A. (2020, May 28). States' automated systems are trapping citizens in bureaucratic nightmares with their lives on the line. Time. https://time.com/5840609/algorithm-unemployment

De La Rue, L., Ortega, L., & Castro Rodriguez, G. (2023, January). System-based victim advocates identify resources and barriers to supporting crime victims. *International Review of Victimology*, *29*(1), 16–26. DOI: 10.1177/02697580221088340 PMID: 36644331

De Sordi, J. O. (2021, September). *Design science research methodology: Theory development from artifacts*. Springer Nature.

Defense Advanced Research Projects Agency. (2025, March 5). *Furthering deepfake defenses.* https://www.darpa.mil/news/2025/furthering-deepfake-defenses

Del Prete, S., Barbiroli, M., & Fuschini, F. (2025, February). Frequency diverse array for signal geofencing in wireless communications: Does it work? *IEEE Open Journal of Antennas and Propagation*, *6*(1), 51–63. DOI: 10.1109/OJAP.2024.3465652

Delfino, R. (2025). Deepfakes on trial 2.0: A revised proposal for a new Federal rule of evidence to mitigate deepfake deceptions in court. *Loyola Law School, Los Angeles. Legal Studies*, **•••**, 2025–10. DOI: 10.2139/ssrn.5188767

Delgado, R. (2024, Winter). Doorbell monitors, pest alarms, neighborhood chat groups, and a second fundamental contradiction. *Case Western Reserve Law Review*, *75*(2), 521–529.

Delhi Police. (2019, July 24). *Best practices in Delhi Police.* https://delhipolice.gov.in/doc/Best_practices-English.pdf

Delp, E., Huang, J., Memon, N., Rocha, A., Turek, M., & Verdoliva, L. (2020). Editorial: Media authentication and forensics—New solutions and research opportunities. *IEEE Journal of Selected Topics in Signal Processing*, *14*(5), 906–909. DOI: 10.1109/JSTSP.2020.3011085

Dempsey, R. P., Brunet, J. R., & Dubljević, V. (2023, March). Exploring and understanding law enforcement's relationship with technology: A qualitative interview study of police officers in North Carolina. *Applied Sciences (Basel, Switzerland)*, *13*(6), 3887. DOI: 10.3390/app13063887

Department for Education. (2018). *Essential digital skills framework.* https://assets.publishing.service.gov.uk/government/uploads/system/uploads/attachment_data/file/738922/Essential_digital_skills_framework.pdf

Department of Homeland Security. (2024, January). *Virtual Reality (VR) training systems for first responders market survey report.* System Assessment and Validation for Emergency Responders (SAVER) Program. https://www.dhs.gov/sites/default/files/2024-07/2024_0709_st_vrmsr%20%282%29.pdf

Department of War. (n.d.). *Privacy, civil liberties, and transparency.* https://pclt.defense.gov/DIRECTORATES/Privacy-and-Civil-Liberties-Directorate/Civil-Liberties

Detention of four defendants was renewed, including Chocalata and Warda; and activist Wessam Salah was released, The. (2023, May 21). Association for Freedom of Thought and Expression (AFTE) Egypt Weekly Legal Bulletin. https://afteegypt.org/en/legal-profiles-en/weekly-legal-bulletin-en-2/2023/05/21/34502-afteegypt.html

Devi, G. G., & Radha, R. (2024, September 20). Smart alerting services; Safeguarding women and children in the digital age. *The Scientific Temper*, *15*(3), 2683–2691. DOI: 10.58414/SCIENTIFICTEMPER.2024.15.3.36

Dhir, S., & Sarraf, S. (2016, January-June). Crime and criminal tracking networks & systems using agile methodology. *BVICAM's. International Journal of Information Technology : an Official Journal of Bharati Vidyapeeth's Institute of Computer Applications and Management*, *8*(1), 930–933. https://www.proquest.com/openview/b2e2634c6c517fa3ad98ff1e939bebca/1?pq-origsite=gscholar&cbl=2034493

Diel, A., Lalgi, T., Mellis, F. S., Teufel, A., & Bäuerle, A. (2025, December). The harm of deepfakes: A scoping review of deepfakes' negative effects on human mind and behavior. *AI & Society*. Advance online publication. DOI: 10.1007/s00146-025-02774-0

Digital Poverty Alliance. (2023, July 14). *Tech4PrisonLeavers.* https://digitalpovertyalliance.org/projects/tech4prisonleavers

Digital Poverty Alliance. (2024, April). *Tech4PrisonLeavers white paper. Improving access and digital skills for prison leavers: Challenges and opportunities.* https://digitalpovertyalliance.org/wp-content/uploads/2024/05/Tech4PrisonLeavers-White-Paper-2024-website.pdf

Dmitrieva, A. A., & Pastukhov, P. S. (2023). Concept of electronic evidence in criminal legal procedure. *Journal of Digital Technologies and Law, 1*(1), 270–295. DOI: 10.21202/jdtl.2023.11

Dolata, M., & Schwabe, G. (2023, October). Moving beyond privacy and airspace safety: Guidelines for just drones in policing. *Government Information Quarterly, 40*(4), 101874. DOI: 10.1016/j.giq.2023.101874

Dominguez, C. (2025, October 19). How is AI used in Houston law enforcement? The sheriff's office and a prosecutor weigh in. *Houston Chronicle.* https://www.houstonchronicle.com/news/houston-texas/trending/article/montgomery-county-ai-crimes-21017304.php

Donohue, L. K. (2015). The Fourth Amendment in a digital world. *Annual Survey of American Law, 71*, 553–685.

Dressel, J., & Farid, H. (2018, March 30). The accuracy, fairness, and limits of predicting recidivism. *Science Advances, 4*(1), eaao5580. Advance online publication. DOI: 10.1126/sciadv.aao5580 PMID: 29376122

Drone delivery FAQs. (n.d.). Amazon. https://www.amazon.com/gp/help/customer/display.html?nodeId=T3jxhuvPfQ629BOIL4

Ducas, E., & Wilner, A. (2017, December). The security and financial implications of blockchain technologies: Regulating emerging technologies in Canada. *International Journal (Toronto, Ont.), 72*(4), 538–562. DOI: 10.1177/0020702017741909

Dukowitz, Z. (2026, January 3). *Selfie drones: A comprehensive guide for drone pilots.* Drone Pilot Ground School. https://www.dronepilotgroundschool.com/selfie-drone

Durston, G. J. (2012). *Burglars and bobbies: Crime and policing in Victorian London.* Cambridge Scholars Publishing.

Dwyer, M. P. (2021, September 8). *LAPD documents reveal use of social media monitoring tools.* Brennan Center for Justice. https://www.brennancenter.org/our-work/analysis-opinion/lapd-documents-reveal-use-social-media-monitoring-tools

Dyson, I., Milner, Y., & Griffiths, H. (2024, April 30). *Documents reveal how DC police surveil social media profiles and protest activity.* Brennan Center for Justice. https://www.brennancenter.org/our-work/analysis-opinion/documents-reveal-how-dc-police-surveil-social-media-profiles-and-protest

Dywaba, Z., Horne, J., & Thenga, G. (2025, March 27). Unlocking the investigative potential: The role of Closed-Circuit Television footage in combating ATM card fraud. *OIDA International Journal of Sustainable Development, 18*(6), 53–70.

Eckman, S. J. (2016). Video broadcasting from the federal courts: Issues for Congress. In M. Davis (ed.), *Cameras in Federal Courts* (pp. 1-25). Nova Science.

Edin, K. J., & Shaefer, H. L. (2015). *2.00 a day: Living on almost nothing in America*. Houghton Mifflin Harcourt.

Edvardsen, A. (2025, October 1). *Russia's violations of Norwegian and allied airspace: "Sign of desperation," says professor.* High North News. https://www.highnorthnews.com/en/russias-violations-norwegian-and-allied-airspace-sign-desperation-says-professor

Edwards, M., Rashid, A., & Rayson, P. (2015, September). A systematic survey of online data mining technology intended for law enforcement. *ACM Computing Surveys, 48*(1), 1–54. DOI: 10.1145/2811403

Edwards, P., Nebel, J.-C., Greenhill, D., & Liang, X. (2024, October). A Review of Deepfake Techniques: Architecture, Detection, and Datasets. *IEEE Access : Practical Innovations, Open Solutions, 12*, 154718–154742. DOI: 10.1109/ACCESS.2024.3477257

Egypt: Three TikTok influencers arrested after parody video of jail visit. (2023, January 30). Middle East Eye. https://www.middleeasteye.net/news/egypt-tiktok-influencers-arrested-parody-video-jail-visit

Ehrlinger, L., & Wöß, W. (2022, March 30). A survey of data quality measurement and monitoring tools. *Frontiers in Big Data, 5*, 850611. DOI: 10.3389/fdata.2022.850611 PMID: 35434611

Ehtesham, H. (2025, December 25). *AI cyberattack statistics 2025: What the data warns us about.* All About AI. https://www.allaboutai.com/resources/ai-statistics/ai-cyberattack

Elm, D. L. (2020, Summer). Geofence warrants: Challenging digital dragnets. *Criminal Justice, 35*(2), 7–13.

Elm, D. L. (2024, August 8). Are geofence warrants headed for extinction? *Criminal Justice, 39*(2), 48–60.

Enemark, C. (2021, June 19). Armed drones and ethical policing: Risk, perception, and the Tele-present officer. *Criminal Justice Ethics, 40*(2), 124–144. DOI: 10.1080/0731129X.2021.1943844 PMID: 34413570

Enns, P. K. (2017). *Incarceration nation: How the United States became the most punitive democracy in the world.* Cambridge University Press.

Epstein, B., Emerson, J. J., & Chat, G. P. T. (2024, April 3). *Navigating the future of policing: Artificial intelligence (AI) use, pitfalls, and considerations for executives.* Police Chief Online. https://www.policechiefmagazine.org/navigating-future-ai-chatgpt

Erickson, D., & Merkle, D. (2025, July 24). *How facial recognition assists criminal investigations.* Police1. https://www.police1.com/police-products/police-technology/police-software/facial-recognition/facial-recognition-is-solving-crimes-heres-how-to-use-it-the-right-way

Erickson, P. (2025, September 18). *Biometrics for law enforcement: Transforming public safety with fast, accurate identification.* HID Global Corporation. https://blog.hidglobal.com/biometrics-law-enforcement-transforming-public-safety-fast-accurate-identification

E-scooters & e-bikes. (n.d.). City of Darwin. https://www.darwin.nt.gov.au/community/about-darwin/getting-around/e-scooters-e-bikes

Eubanks, V. (2018, January). Automating inequality: How high-tech tools profile, police, and punish the poor. St. Martin's Press.

European Transportation Safety Council. (2019, February 18). *In-vehicle technology vital to tackling speeding in Europe.* [Press release]. https://etsc.eu/in-vehicle-technology-vital-to-tackling-speeding-in-europe

Ezzat, W. (2025, December 30). New petition targets license-plate reader cameras in the Quad Cities. *KWQC News.* https://www.kwqc.com/2025/12/31/new-petition-targets-license-plate-reader-cameras-quad-cities

Faghiri, A. K. (2022). The use of Artificial Intelligence in the criminal justice system (a comparative study). *Webology, 19*(5), 593–613.

Fairbanks, R. (2021, June 23). Masterpiece or mess: The Mosaic theory of the Fourth Amendment post-Carpenter. *Berkeley Journal of Criminal Law, 26*(1), 71-119. https://doi.org/DOI: 10.15779/Z38DZ03287

Falcón-López, S. A., Tobarra, L., Robles-Gómez, A., & Pastor-Vargas, R. (2025, November 29). Forensic analysis of manipulated images and videos. *Applied Sciences (Basel, Switzerland), 15*(23), 12664. DOI: 10.3390/app152312664

Fallis, D. (2020). The epistemic threat of deepfakes. *Philosophy & Technology, 34*(4), 623–643. DOI: 10.1007/s13347-020-00419-2 PMID: 32837868

Famili, A., Sun, S., Atalay, T., & Stavrou, A. (2025). Harnessing Meta-Reinforcement Learning for Enhanced Tracking in Geofencing Systems. *IEEE Open Journal of the Communications Society, 6*, 944–960. DOI: 10.1109/OJCOMS.2025.3531318

Fangary, F., & Mahfouz, S. (2025, August 3). *Seven TikTokers arrested on immorality charges as authorities respond to campaign against 'vulgar' content.* Mada. https://www.madamasr.com/en/2025/08/03/news/u/seven-tiktok-creators-arrested-on-moral-charges-as-authorities-respond-to-campaign-against-vulgar-content

Fan, M. D. (2024, April). Big data searches and the future of criminal procedure. *Texas Law Review, 102*(5), 877–936.

Faqir, R. S. A. (2023, December). Digital criminal investigations in the era of artificial intelligence: A comprehensive overview. *International Journal of Cyber Criminology, 17*(2), 77–94.

Farivar, C., & Brewster, T. (2023, December 14). Google just killed warrants that give police access to location data. *Forbes.* https://www.forbes.com/sites/cyrusfarivar/2023/12/14/google-just-killed-geofence-warrants-police-location-data

Farley, H., & Pike, A. (2016). Engaging prisoners in education: Reducing risk and recidivism. *Journal of the International Corrections and Prisons Association*, *1*, 65–73. https://oro.open.ac.uk/46511/1/Final_Farley_Pike_Advancing_Corrections.pdf

Fed. R. Evid. 702 (2011). https://www.law.cornell.edu/rules/fre/rule_702

Fed. R. Evid. 901 (2011). https://www.law.cornell.edu/rules/fre/rule_901

Federal Aviation Administration. (2020, October 6). *Small Unmanned Aircraft Systems (UAS) Regulations, Part 107*. https://www.faa.gov/newsroom/small-unmanned-aircraft-systems-uas-regulations-part-107

Federal Aviation Administration. (2024, December 19). *Getting started*. https://www.faa.gov/uas/getting_started

Federal Aviation Administration. (2025a, August 6). *Beyond visual line of sight (BVLOS): Normalizing drone operations in the national airspace*. https://www.faa.gov/newsroom/beyond-visual-line-sight-bvlos

Federal Aviation Administration. (2025b, May). *Drone integration: concept of operations*. https://www.faa.gov/uas/resources/policy_library/Drone-Integration-Concept-of-Operations-May-2025.pdf

Federal Aviation Administration. (2025c, March 19). *Remote ID for drone pilots: Compliance and enforcement standards*. https://www.faa.gov/uas/getting_started/remote_id

Feigenson, N. (2023, Spring). Adjudication on Zoom and beyond: Human interaction in virtual courts. *Washburn Law Journal*, *62*(3), 461–506.

Feigenson, N., & Carney, B. (2025). Generative AI as courtroom evidence: A practical guide. *Mitchell Hamline Law Review*, *52*(1), 3.

Felton, R. (2016, December 18). Michigan unemployment agency made 20,000 false fraud accusations—report. The Guardian. https://www.theguardian.com/us-news/2016/dec/18/michigan-unemployment-agency-fraud-accusations

FEMA. (2023, February 22). *Geographic accuracy of Wireless Emergency Alerts (WEAs)*. https://www.fema.gov/emergency-managers/practitioners/integrated-public-alert-warning-system/public/wireless-emergency-alerts/geographic-accuracy-wea

FEMA. (2024, April 4). *IPAWS myths vs. facts*. https://www.fema.gov/emergency-managers/practitioners/integrated-public-alert-warning-system/public/myths-facts

Ferguson, A. G. (2017). *The rise of Big Data policing: Surveillance, race, and the future of law enforcement*. NYU Press. DOI: 10.18574/nyu/9781479854608.001.0001

Ferguson, A. G. (2021). Facial recognition and the Fourth Amendment. *Minnesota Law Review*, *105*(3), 1105–1210. DOI: 10.24926/265535.4104

Ferguson, A. G. (2025, May). Video analytics and Fourth Amendment vision. *Texas Law Review*, *103*(6), 1253–1319.

Fifth Circuit rules that geofence warrants are inherently unconstitutional. (2024, August 13). EPIC. https://epic.org/fifth-circuit-rules-that-geofence-warrants-are-inherently-unconstitutional

Financial Action Task Force. (2019, June). *Guidance for a risk-based approach to virtual assets and virtual asset service providers.* https://www.fatf-gafi.org/en/publications/Fatfrecommendations/Guidance-rba-virtual-assets.html

Financial Action Task Force. (2023, March). *Countering ransomware financing: Report of the Financial Action Task Force.* https://www.fatf-gafi.org/content/dam/fatf-gafi/reports/Countering-Ransomware-Financing.pdf.coredownload.pdf

Financial Crimes Enforcement Network. (2021). *Financial trend analysis: Ransomware trends in bank secrecy act data.* https://www.fincen.gov/system/files/2022-11/Financial%20Trend%20Analysis_Ransomware%20FTA%202_508%20FINAL.pdf

Financial Stability Board (FSB). (2025, October 16). *Thematic review on FSB global regulatory framework for crypto-asset activities.* https://www.fsb.org/uploads/P161025-1.pdf

Finch, W. W., & Butt, M. (2025, November 17). Gaps in AI-compliant complementary governance frameworks' suitability (for low-capacity actors), and structural asymmetries (in the compliance ecosystem)—A systematic review. *Journal of Cybersecurity and Privacy*, *5*(4), 101. DOI: 10.3390/jcp5040101

Finklea, K. (2023). Law enforcement and technology: Use of unmanned aircraft systems. *Library of Congress.* https://www.congress.gov/crs-product/R47660

Finklea, K. (2023, August 22). *Law enforcement and technology: Use of unmanned aircraft systems.* Congressional Research Service. https://www.congress.gov/crs-product/R47660

Firc, A., Malinka, K., & Hanáček, P. (2023, April). Deepfakes as a threat to a speaker and facial recognition: An overview of tools and attack vectors. *Heliyon*, *9*(4), e15090. DOI: 10.1016/j.heliyon.2023.e15090 PMID: 37089334

Flattery, T., & Miller, C. B. (2024, October). Deepfakes and dishonesty. *Philosophy & Technology*, *37*(4), 120. DOI: 10.1007/s13347-024-00812-1

Florida v. Riley, 488 U.S. 445. (1989). *Justia U.S. Supreme Court.* https://supreme.justia.com/cases/federal/us/488/445

Flower, L. (2025). *The digital courtroom: Participation, attendance, engagement and consumption.* Taylor & Francis., DOI: 10.4324/9781003344643

Flowers, V. (2025, May 24). Jussie Smollett to make charitable donations to settle Chicago's hoax attack lawsuit. *NBC News.* https://www.nbcnews.com/news/us-news/jussie-smollett-settle-chicago-lawsuit-rcna208880

Fornasier, M. de O. (2022). Deep learning and the right to explanation: Technological challenges to legality and due process of law in technology. *Revista De Direito Brasileira*, *32*(12), 218–235. DOI: 10.26668/IndexLawJournals/2358-1352/2022.v32i12.7547

Forsyth County, GA and Avive Solutions celebrate a life saved by citizen volunteer through Avive's 4 minute community program. (2025). Avive. https://www.avive.life/news/forsyth-county-avive-life-saved

Frankovits, G., & Mirsky, Y. (2023, June). Discussion paper: The threat of real time deepfakes (arXiv:2306.02487v1). *arXiv.* /arXiv.2306.02487DOI: 10.1145/3595353.3595881

Fröwis, M., Gottschalk, T., Haslhofer, B., Rückert, C., & Pesch, P. (2020, June). Safeguarding the evidential value of forensic cryptocurrency investigations. *Forensic Science International Digital Investigation, 33*, 200902. DOI: 10.1016/j.fsidi.2019.200902

Frye v. United States, 293 F. 1013 (D.C. Cir. 1923).

FTC proposes new protections to combat AI impersonation of individuals. (2024, February 15). [Press release]. Federal Trade Commission. https://www.ftc.gov/news-events/news/press-releases/2024/02/ftc-proposes-new-protections-combat-ai-impersonation-individuals

Fudge, T. P. (2026a, January 2). *Circular geofence.* [Image]. Fudgelink: The simple geometry of geofencing. https://fudgelink.com/geofencing

Fudge, T. P. (2026b, January 2). *Isochrone geofence.* [Image]. Fudgelink: The simple geometry of geofencing. https://fudgelink.com/geofencing

Fudge, T. P. (2026c, January 2). *Polygonal geofence.* [Image]. Fudgelink: The simple geometry of geofencing. https://fudgelink.com/geofencing

Fudge, T. P. (2022, October). Ethics and risks associated with self-driving automobiles. In Fudge, T. P. (Ed.), *Exploring ethical problems in today's technological world* (pp. 289–314). IGI Global., DOI: 10.4018/978-1-6684-5892-1.ch015

Fudge, T. P., & Ferebee, S. S. (2024). Search and Rescue drones: Balancing security & privacy with preserving life. In Shah, I., & Jhanjhi, N. (Eds.), *Cybersecurity issues and challenges in the drone industry* (pp. 108–127). IGI Global., DOI: 10.4018/979-8-3693-0774-8.ch005

Furizal, N., Ma'arif, A., Maghfiroh, H., Suwarno, I., Prayogi, D., Kariyamin, N., Lonang, S., & Sharkawy, A. (2025). Social, legal, and ethical implications of AI-Generated deepfake pornography on digital platforms: A systematic literature review. *Social Sciences & Humanities Open, 12*, 101882. DOI: 10.1016/j.ssaho.2025.101882

Furnell, S. (2017). The evolving landscape of technology-dependent crime. In McGuire, M. R., & Holt, T. J. (Eds.), *The Routledge Handbook of Technology, Crime and Justice* (pp. 65–77). Routledge., DOI: 10.4324/9781315743981-4

Gabor, D. (2025, December 22). Labelling deepfakes in terms of EU law: The AI Act and beyond. *Ruch Prawniczy, Ekonomiczny i Socjologiczny, 87*(4), 139–160. DOI: 10.14746/rpeis.2025.87.4.08

Galante, N., Cotroneo, R., Furci, D., Lodetti, G., & Casali, M. B. (2023). Applications of artificial intelligence in forensic sciences: Current potential benefits, limitations and perspectives. *International Journal of Legal Medicine, 137*(2), 445–458. DOI: 10.1007/s00414-022-02928-5 PMID: 36507961

Galarraga Gortázar, N. (2025, May 10). In São Paulo, 'Big Brother' is watching, with 25,000 cameras and facial recognition technology. *El País.* https://english.elpais.com/international/2025-05-10/in-sao-paulo-big-brother-is-watching-with-25000-cameras-and-facial-recognition-technology.html

Ganguli, P. (2025). Digital policing: Using social media surveillance to tackle cybercrime. *Indian Journal of Legal Review, 5*(1), 324–334. https://ijlr.iledu.in/wp-content/uploads/2025/02/V5I136.pdf

Gantenapalli, S. R., Choppala, P. B., & Teal, P. D. (2024, June). Securing vehicles with Arduino: Implementing geo-fencing technology for theft prevention. *IEEE International Conference on Information Technology, Electronics and Intelligent Communication Systems (ICITEICS),* Karnataka, India. https://doi.org/DOI: 10.1109/ICITEICS61368.2024.10625496

Gao, M., Peng, J., & Wang, H. (2025, December). Algorithmic transparency, financial stability, and enterprise digital transformation. *Finance Research Letters, 86*(B), 108481. DOI: 10.1016/j.frl.2025.108481

Gao, M. (2024, December 30). Relationship between digital literacy and employment ability of vocational undergraduate students: The parallel mediating role of future time perspective and career decision self-efficacy. *Journal of Contemporary Educational Research, 8*(12), 82–87. DOI: 10.26689/jcer.v8i12.9155

Gao, Y., Wang, X., Zhang, Y., Zeng, P., & Ma, Y. (2024, August). Temporal feature prediction in audio–visual deepfake detection. *Electronics (Basel), 13*(17), 3433. DOI: 10.3390/electronics13173433

Garcia, J. M. S. (2025, March 6). Exploring deepfakes and effective prevention strategies: A critical review. *Psychology and Education: A Multidisciplinary Journal, 33*(1), 93-96.. DOI: 10.2139/ssrn.5168131

Garrett, B. L., & Rudin, C. (2024). The right to a glass box: Rethinking the use of artificial intelligence in criminal justice. *109. Cornell Law Review,* •••, 561–626. https://scholarship.law.duke.edu/faculty_scholarship/4297

Garzon, S. R., & Deva, B. (2014, September). Geofencing 2.0: Taking location-based notifications to the next level. *UbiComp '14: Proceedings of the 2014 ACM International Joint Conference on Pervasive and Ubiquitous Computing*, pp. 921-932. https://doi.org/DOI: 10.1145/2632048.2636093

Gaub, J. E., Choate, D. E., Todak, N., Katz, C. M., & White, M. D. (2016). Officer perceptions of body-worn cameras before and after deployment: A study of three departments. *Police Quarterly, 19*(3), 275–302. DOI: 10.1177/1098611116653398

Gautam, K. (2017, October 12). The unfair operation principle and the exclusionary rule: On the admissibility of illegally obtained evidence in criminal trials in India. *Indiana International & Comparative Law Review, 27*(2), 147–189. DOI: 10.18060/7909.0049

Geofence API. (n.d.). NetBillion.ai. https://docs.nextbillion.ai/docs/tracking/api/geofence

Geofencing iOS: Understanding the limitations. (2024, September 18). Radar. https://radar.com/blog/limitations-of-ios-geofencing

Geofencing: An in-depth overview. (2024, August 2). NetBillion.ai. https://nextbillion.ai/post/geofencing

George, P. (2025, February 6). *India's surveillance landscape after the DPDPA*. IAPP. https://iapp.org/news/a/india-s-surveillance-landscape-after-the-dpdpa

Germano, F., Gomez, V., & Sobbrio, F. (2026, March). Ranking for engagement: How social media algorithms fuel misinformation and polarization. *Journal of Public Economics, 255*, 105589. DOI: 10.1016/j.jpubeco.2026.105589

Ghouri, M. F., Malahim, M., Shaikh, S. M., & Fattima, Z. (2020, December 17). GSM and IoT based smart traffic system with geofencing. *Journal of Independent Studies and Research on Computing*, *18*(2). Advance online publication. DOI: 10.31645/16

Gillin, P. (2024, February 25). *Geofencing helps construction firm avoid $2.5M in equipment theft.* Silicon Angle. https://siliconangle.com/2024/02/25/geofencing-helps-construction-firm-avoid-2-5m-equipment-theft

Gilliom, J. (2001). *Overseers of the poor: Surveillance, resistance, and the limits of privacy.* University of Chicago Press.

Gillis, A., Lutkevich, B., & Earls, A. (2024). *What is a drone (UAV)?* TechTarget. https://www.techtarget.com/iotagenda/definition/drone

Gips, M., Goldenberg, P., & Grantham, D. A. (2025). A response to the concerns of civil liberties groups on law enforcement's use of uncrewed aerial systems. https://www.scribd.com/document/849957571/Drone-White-Paper

Glaser, P. (2025, October 1). Dumping the fence: Unifying tower dumps and geofence searches as reverse location searches. *University of Baltimore Law Review*, *54*(2), 5. https://scholarworks.law.ubalt.edu/ublr/vol54/iss2/5

Global Digital Compact. (2023, March). *Digital literacy: The great divide.* UN Digital Compact Consultation. https://www.un.org/digital-emerging-technologies/sites/www.un.org.techenvoy/files/GDC-submission_Digital-National-Alliance-Bulgaria.pdf

Godwin, F. O. (2025, April 26). The role of Artificial Intelligence and Robotic Process Automation (RPA) in fraud detection: Enhancing financial security through automation. *International Journal of Finance*, *10*(3), 80–100. DOI: 10.47941/ijf.2671

Goel, S., Shroff, R., Skeem, J., & Slobogin, C. (2021, May 14). The accuracy, equity, and jurisprudence of criminal risk assessment. In *Research Handbook on Big Data Law*. Edward Elgar Publishing., DOI: 10.4337/9781788972826.00007

Go, J. (2020, March). The imperial origins of American policing: Militarization and imperial feedback in the early 20th century. *American Journal of Sociology*, *125*(5), 1193–1254. DOI: 10.1086/708464

Gómez Fuentes, Á. (2025, June 3). Un padre desbloquea el móvil de su hijo apuñalado en Italia y encuentra al asesino. *ABC*. https://www.abc.es/sociedad/padre-desbloquea-movil-hijo-apunalado-italia-encuentra-20250602191600-nt.html

GOV. UK Justice Data. (2026). *Prisons data: Reform.* Retrieved April 21, 2026 from https://data.justice.gov.uk/prisons/prison-reform

Gov.UK. (2019, April 23). *Guidance: Essential digital skills framework.* https://www.gov.uk/government/publications/essential-digital-skills-framework)

Government of India. (2023, August 11). *The Digital Personal Data Protection Act, 2023* (Act No. 22 of 2023). https://www.meity.gov.in/static/uploads/2024/06/2bf1f0e9f04e6fb4f8fef35e82c42aa5.pdf

Govindarajan, B., Jaganraj, R., Srinivasan, V., & Kumaran, T. (2025). Evolution of UAV technology: From early innovations to future horizons. In Mellal, M. (Ed.), *Innovations and developments in Unmanned Aerial Vehicles* (pp. 53–94). IGI Global., DOI: 10.4018/979-8-3693-8462-6.ch004

GPS Act. (n.d.). Ron Wyden, United States Senator for Oregon. https://www.wyden.senate.gov/priorities/gps-act

Grady, A. (2006, February). Daubert and expert testimony. *AMA Journal of Ethics*, *8*(2), 97–100. DOI: 10.1001/virtualmentor.2006.8.2.hlaw1-0602 PMID: 23228539

Grant, S. (2024, November 3). *How does a doorbell camera work?* Abode. https://goabode.com/blog/how-doorbell-camera-works

Graves, D. (1979, June-July). Cameras in the courts: The situation today. *Judicature*, *63*(1), 24–27.

Gravett, W. H. (2024). Judicial decision-making in the age of artificial intelligence. In Antunes, H. S., Freitas, P. M., Oliveira, A. L., Pereira, C. M., Sequeira, E. V. D., & Xavier, L. B. (Eds.), *Multidisciplinary perspectives on artificial intelligence and the law* (Vol. 58, pp. 281–298). Springer Nature., DOI: 10.1007/978-3-031-41264-6_15

Greitens, S. C. (2020). Surveillance, security, and liberal democracy in the post-COVID world. *International Organization*, *74*(S1), 169–190. DOI: 10.1017/S0020818320000417

Grierson, M., Varghese, D., Bolton, M., & Olivier, P. (2022*). Design considerations for a digital service to support prison leavers.* [Conference paper]. ACM Designing Interactive Systems Conference. https://doi.org/DOI: 10.1145/3532106.3533567

Grimm, P. W., Grossman, M. R., & Cormack, G. V. (2021, December). Artificial intelligence as evidence. *Northwestern Journal of Technology and Intellectual Property*, *19*(1), 9–106. https://scholarlycommons.law.northwestern.edu/njtip/vol19/iss1/2

Gromova, E. A., Brantes Ferreira, D., & Begishev, R., I. R. (. (2023). ChatGPT and other intelligent Chatbots: Legal, ethical and dipute resolution concerns. *Revista Brasileira de Alternative Dispute Resolution*, *5*(10), 153–175. DOI: 10.52028/rbadr.v5i10.ART07.RU

Guarnera, L., Giudice, O., & Battiato, S. (200, September). Fighting deepfake by exposing the convolutional traces on images. *IEEE Access, 8,* 165085–165098. DOI: 10.1109/ACCESS.2020.3023037

Gu, H., Chandrasegaran, S., & Lloyd, P. (2025, January 27). Synthetic users: Insights from designers' interactions with persona-based chatbots. *Artificial Intelligence for Engineering Design, Analysis and Manufacturing*, *39*, e2. DOI: 10.1017/S0890060424000283

Gunawardana, V. (2023, June). Criminalising dissent: Sri Lanka's Prevention of Terrorism Act and its use in suppressing social movements - 2022. *Asian Journal of Management Studies*, *1*(1), 83–99. http://repo.lib.sab.ac.lk:8080/xmlui/handle/susl/4050

Gupta, N., & Agarwal, B. B. (2023, April). Recognition of suspicious human activity in video surveillance: A review. *Engineering, Technology &. Applied Scientific Research*, *13*(2), 10529–10534. DOI: 10.48084/etasr.5739

Gurumurthy, K. M., Auld, J., & Kockelman, K. (2021). A system of shared autonomous vehicles for Chicago: Understanding the effects of geofencing the service. *Journal of Transport and Land Use, 14*(1), 993–948. DOI: 10.5198/jtlu.2021.1926

Hadjisergis, K., Caulfield, L. S., Stonard, K. E., & Sadlier, S. (in prep). *The 'Human Factor': Mentoring, peerage, and community in the development of digital literacy of prison leavers.*

Haley, P., & Burrell, D. N. (2025). Integrating artificial intelligence into law enforcement: Socioeconomic and ethical challenges. *SocioEconomic Challenges, 9*(2), 60–77. https://armgpublishing.com/wp-content/uploads/2025/07/SEC_2_2025_4.pdf

Haley, P. (2025, May 16). The impact of biometric surveillance on reducing violent crime: Strategies for apprehending criminals while protecting the innocent. *Sensors (Basel), 25*(10), 3160. DOI: 10.3390/s25103160 PMID: 40431950

Hall, M., Hearn, J., & Lewis, R. (2023, March 11). Image-based sexual abuse: Online gender-sexual violations. *Encyclopedia, 3*(1), 327–339. DOI: 10.3390/encyclopedia3010020

Hall, R. A., & Bannatyne, M. W. McK. (2000, December). Technology education and the convicted felon: How it works behind prison walls. *Journal of Correctional Education, 51*(4), 320–323. https://www.jstor.org/stable/41971950

Handa, S., & Thakur, S. (2024, November). Role of artificial intelligence in admissibility of electronic evidence. *International Journal of Research Publication and Reviews, 5*(11), 1323–1328. https://ijrpr.com/uploads/V5ISSUE11/IJRPR34777.pdf

Hanisch, M., Goldsby, C. M., Fabian, N. E., & Oehmichen, J. (2023, July). Digital governance: A conceptual framework and research agenda. *Journal of Business Research, 162*, 113777. DOI: 10.1016/j.jbusres.2023.113777

Hansen Löfstrand, C., & Backman, C. (2021). Control or protection? Work environment implications of police body-worn cameras. *New Technology, Work and Employment, 36*(3), 327–347. DOI: 10.1111/ntwe.12201

Hanspal, M. S., & Behera, B. (2026). Privacy and data protection in AI-driven legal services: An analysis of India's emerging challenges and solutions. *Journal of Trends and Challenges in Artificial Intelligence, 3*(1), 73–82. https://jai.aspur.rs/archive/v3/n2/2.php

Harris, D. A. (2010, Fall). Picture this: Body worn video devices ('head cams') as tools for ensuring Fourth Amendment compliance by police. *Legal studies Research. Pittsburgh University School of Law.* https://hdl.handle.net/2346/103656

Harris, L. (2025, May 3). *New York MTA quietly turns to AI surveillance to predict crime before it happens.* Newstarget. https://www.newstarget.com/2025-05-03-mta-turns-to-ai-surveillance-to-predict-crime.html

Harris, K. R. (2024a). AI or your lying eyes: Some shortcomings of artificially intelligent deepfake detectors. *Philosophy & Technology, 37*(1), 7. DOI: 10.1007/s13347-024-00700-8

Harris, K. R. (2024b). Synthetic media detection, the wheel, and the burden of proof. *Philosophy & Technology, 37*(4), 131. DOI: 10.1007/s13347-024-00821-0

Harvard Law School & Stanford Law School. (2020). *Emerging police technology: A policy toolkit.* https://law.stanford.edu/wp-content/uploads/2020/01/Emerging-Police-Technology-A-Policy-Toolkit.pdf

Harvey, C. R., Ramachandran, A., & Santoro, J. (2020). DeFi and the future of finance. SSRN *Electronic Journal.* https://doi.org/DOI: 10.2139/ssrn.3711777

Hasan, A., & Vijayaraghavan, J. (2019, May). *Geospatial data science quick start guide.* Packt. https://research.ebsco.com/linkprocessor/plink?id=22cfc18b-1285-31e3-8a0f-1fc176486ed2

Hashiyana, V., & Kamati, W. (2024). An Artificial Intelligence-powered chatbot-integrated web-based application: A case study of the University of Namibia. In Ertuğrul, D. Ç., & Elçi, A. (Eds.), *Cutting-Edge Technologies for Business Sectors* (pp. 205–244). IGI Global., DOI: 10.4018/979-8-3693-9586-8.ch008

Hastie, R., & Pennington, N. (1996). The O.J. Simpson stories: Behavioral scientists' reflections on the people of the State of California v. Orenthal James Simpson. *University of Colorado Law Review, 67*(4), 957–976.

Hausken, L. (2024, December 11). Untangling photographic manipulation: Exploring a dual concept and its societal implications. *Journalism and Media, 5*(4), 1881–1900. DOI: 10.3390/journalmedia5040114

Hayne, J., & Doran, M. (2020, May 29). Government to pay back $721m as it scraps Robodebt for Centrelink welfare recipients. ABC News Australia. https://www.abc.net.au/news/2020-05-29/federal-government-refund-robodebt-scheme-repay-debts/12299410

Hazardous. (n.d.) Merriam-Webster. https://www.merriam-webster.com/dictionary/hazardous

Hefetz, I. (2025, October). Integrating AI Systems in criminal justice: The forensic expert as a corridor between algorithms and courtroom evidence. *Forensic Science, 5*(4), 53. DOI: 10.3390/forensicsci5040053

Hegde, M. (2017, April 10). Espionage in Kautilya's Arthaśāstra. *Pragyata.* https://pragyata.com/espionage-in-kautilyas-arthasastra

Helmus, T. C. (2022, July 6). *Artificial Intelligence, deepfakes, and disinformation: A primer.* RAND Corporation. DOI: 10.7249/PEA1043-1

Hemdan, E. E.-D., & Manjaiah, D. H. (2016, October). A cloud forensic strategy for investigation of cybercrime. In *2016 International Conference on Emerging Technological Trends (ICETT)* (pp. 1-5). IEEE. https://doi.org/DOI: 10.1109/ICETT.2016.7873667

Herman, M., Iorga, M., Salim, A. M., Jackson, R. H., Hurst, M. R., Leo, R. A., Mishra, A. K., Landreville, N. M., & Wang, Y. (2024, July). *NIST Cloud Computing Forensic Reference Architecture* (NIST Special Publication 800-201). National Institute of Standards and Technology. https://doi.org/DOI: 10.6028/NIST.SP.800-201

Hermansyah, M., Najib, A., Farida, A., Sacipto, R., & Rintyarna, B. S. (2023, February 21). Artificial Intelligence and ethics: Building an Artificial Intelligence system that ensures privacy and social justice. *The International Journal of Science in Society, 5*(1), 154–168. DOI: 10.54783/ijsoc.v5i1.644

Hermosilla, P., Berríos, S., & Allende-Cid, H. (2025, June 29). Explainable AI for forensic analysis: A comparative study of SHAP and LIME in intrusion detection models. *Applied Sciences (Basel, Switzerland), 15*(13), 7329. DOI: 10.3390/app15137329

Hernandez, J. (2021, May 26). Read this powerful statement from Darnella Frazier, who filmed George Floyd's murder. *NPR.* https://www.npr.org/2021/05/26/1000475344/read-this-powerful-statement-from-darnella-frazier-who-filmed-george-floyds-murd

Hetzel, D., & Strickland, R. A. (2025, March 31). *Cameras in the courtroom.* Middle Tennessee State University Free Speech Center. https://firstamendment.mtsu.edu/article/cameras-in-the-courtroom

Hevner, A., & Chatterjee, S. (2010). *Design science research in Information Systems.*, DOI: 10.1007/978-1-4419-5653-8_2

Hicks, J. (2022, August 1). *Export of digital surveillance technologies from China to developing countries* [Report]. Institute of Development Studies. https://doi.org/DOI: 10.19088/K4D.2022.123

Hill, D., O'Connor, C. D., & Slane, A. (2022). Police use of facial recognition technology: The potential for engaging the public through co-constructed policy-making. *International Journal of Police Science & Management, 24*(3), 325–335. DOI: 10.1177/14613557221089558

History and use of the billy club. (2015, November 16). Police 1. https://www.police1.com/police-history/articles/history-and-use-of-the-billy-club-lCrwpOflpDTkHY2B

Hoang Hop, H. (2025, February 28). *The peace of Japan and the AI.* Japan Up Close. https://japanupclose.web-japan.org/policy/p20250228_1.html

Hoffman, S. (2022, April). China's tech-enhanced authoritarianism. *Journal of Democracy, 33*(2), 76–89. DOI: 10.1353/jod.2022.0019

Holtzblatt, A., Varghese, G. P., Aiken, E., Russell, W., & Gelbort, H. (2024, August 27). *The impact and future of the Fifth Circuit's new hard-line stance on geofence warrants.* WilmerHale. https://www.wilmerhale.com/en/insights/client-alerts/20240827-the-impact-and-future-of-the-fifth-circuits-new-hard-line-stance-on-geofence-warrants

Honey, L. (2022, July 25). *Collecting police truncheons & tipstaves.* Homes and Antiques. https://www.homesandantiques.com/antiques/collecting-guides-antiques/experts/luke-honeys-cabinet-of-curiosities-truncheons-yipstaves

Hopkins, M., & Mahr, J. (2024, September 29). *Many cameras. Little focus. Blurry results.* Illinois Answers Project. https://illinoisanswers.org/2024/09/29/chicago-police-camera-surveillance-fail-deliver-promise-fight-crime

House of Commons Education Committee Report. (2022, May 18). *Not just another brick in the wall: Why prisoners need an education to climb the ladder of opportunity.* https://publications.parliament.uk/pa/cm5803/cmselect/cmeduc/56/report.html

Houston. (n.d.). World Population Review. https://worldpopulationreview.com/us-cities/texas/houston

How policing agencies use AI. (2024, November 12). Policing Project. https://www.policingproject.org/ai-explained-articles/2024/9/6/how-policing-agencies-use-ai

How virtual reality is transforming the way Phoenix PD trains. (2026, February 24). Axon Enterprise. https://www.axon.com/resources/articles-source/how-virtual-reality-is-transforming-the-way-phoenix-pd-trains

Hudson, B. (2003). *Understanding justice: An introduction to ideas, perspectives, and controversies in modern penal theory*. Open University Press.

Hwang, T. (2020, July). *Deepfakes: A grounded threat assessment.* Center for Security and Emerging Technology. DOI: 10.51593/20190030

Iboshi, K. (2025, July 22). Why former US Army soldier went 'sword in hand' in alleged traffic cam shooting spree across Portland. *KGW8 News*. https://www.kgw.com/article/news/investigations/portland-man-chase-grijalva-allegedly-shoot-traffic-cameras/283-e86307df-49ec-4393-85df-4b3874e97cbb

Ilbiz, E., & Kaunert, C. (2022, May 27). Sharing economy for tackling crypto-laundering: The Europol associated 'Global Conference on Criminal Finances and Cryptocurrencies.'. *Sustainability (Basel), 14*(11), 6618. DOI: 10.3390/su14116618

Iliadis, M., Harris, B., Vakhitova, Z., Flynn, A., & Tyson, D. (2024, November). Police body-worn cameras as a response to domestic and family violence: Practitioner insights into the consequences for victim/survivors. *Violence Against Women, 30*(14), 3536–3557. DOI: 10.1177/10778012231185541 PMID: 37487222

Illicit finance risk assessment of decentralized finance. (2023, April). U.S. Department of the Treasury. https://home.treasury.gov/system/files/136/DeFi-Risk-Full-Review.pdf

Illinois General Assembly. (2024, June 14). Freedom from Drone Surveillance Act (725 ILCS 167). https://www.ilga.gov/Legislation/ILCS/Articles?ActID=3520&ChapterID=54

Impact of artificial intelligence on fraud and scams. (2023, December). Stop Scams UK. https://www.pwc.co.uk/forensic-services/assets/impact-of-ai-on-fraud-and-scams.pdf

Indian police expand AI facial recognition system, arrest 70 suspects in Delhi. (2024, December 24). ID Tech Wire. https://idtechwire.com/indian-police-expand-ai-facial-recognition-system-arrest-70-suspects-in-delhi

Information Commissioner's Office. (n.d.). Video surveillance (including guidance for organisations using CCTV). https://ico.org.uk/for-organisations/uk-gdpr-guidance-and-resources/cctv-and-video-surveillance/guidance-on-video-surveillance-including-cctv

International Association of Chiefs of Police. (2012, August). *Recommended guidelines for the use of unmanned aircraft.* https://www.theiacp.org/sites/default/files/all/i-j/IACP_UAGuidelines.pdf

International Trade Administration. (n.d.). Unmanned aircraft systems. https://www.trade.gov/unmanned-aircraft-systems

Internet Crime Complaint Center. (n.d.). *Internet Crime Complaint Center*. Federal Bureau of Investigation. https://www.ic3.gov

Ionova, A. (2025, October 3). Brutal killing of 3 women, livestreamed on social media, shocks Argentina. *The New York Times*. https://www.nytimes.com/2025/09/26/world/americas/argentina-women-murder-instagram.html

Iowa Supreme Court. (2025, October 3). State of Iowa v. Terence Edward Manning Jr. (No. 23-1390). Iowa Courts. https://www.iowacourts.gov/courtcases/22746/embed/SupremeCourtOpinion

Ismail, I., & Ariffin, K. A. Z. (2025, September 12). The admissibility of digital evidence from open-source forensic tools: Development of a framework for legal acceptance. *PLoS One*, *20*(9), e0331683. DOI: 10.1371/journal.pone.0331683 PMID: 40938950

Jadidi, V. (2025). The impact of Artificial Intelligence on judicial decision-making processes. *Advanced Journal of Management. Humanity and Social Science*, *1*(5), 271–281. DOI: 10.5281/zenodo.15660093

Jaeger, P. T., Lin, J., Grimes, J. M., & Simmons, S. N. (2009, April 8). Where is the cloud? Geography, economics, environment, and jurisdiction in cloud computing. *First Monday*, *14*(5). Advance online publication. DOI: 10.5210/fm.v14i5.2456

Jahankhani, H., Kendzierskyj, S., Jamal, A., Epiphaniou, G., & Al-Khateeb, H. (2019). Blockchain and clinical trial. In *Advanced sciences and technologies for security applications*. Springer International Publishing., DOI: 10.1007/978-3-030-11289-9

Jansen, F., Sánchez-Monedero, J., & Dencik, L. (2021, July). Biometric identity systems in law enforcement and the politics of (voice) recognition: The case of SiiP. *Big Data & Society*, *8*(2), 20539517211063604. Advance online publication. DOI: 10.1177/20539517211063604

Japan. (n.d.). World Population Review. https://worldpopulationreview.com/countries/japan

Jarldorn, M., & Emery, S. (2024, January 29). Using radical co-design to create and develop a technology-based solution to improve post-release outcomes for formerly incarcerated women: LindaBot. *International Journal of Communication*, *18*, 1246–1265. https://ijoc.org/index.php/ijoc/article/view/21208

Jedličková, A. (2024, August). Ethical approaches in designing autonomous and intelligent systems: A comprehensive survey towards responsible development. *AI & Society*, *40*(4), 2703–2716. DOI: 10.1007/s00146-024-02040-9

Jenkins, M., & Shields, C. (2024, April 10). *Taking a principled approach to AI in policing*. Police Chief Online. https://www.policechiefmagazine.org/principled-approach-ai

Jennings, W. G., Fridell, L. A., & Lynch, M. D. (2014, November-December). Cops and cameras: Officer perceptions of the use of body-worn cameras in law enforcement. *Journal of Criminal Justice*, *42*(6), 549–556. DOI: 10.1016/j.jcrimjus.2014.09.008

Jennings, W. G., Lynch, M. D., & Fridell, L. A. (2015). Novmber-December). Evaluating the impact of police officer body-worn cameras (BWCs) on response-to-resistance and serious external complaints: Evidence from the Orlando Police Department (OPD) experience utilizing a randomized controlled experiment. *Journal of Criminal Justice*, *43*(6), 480–486. DOI: 10.1016/j.jcrimjus.2015.10.003

Jewkes, Y., & Reisdorf, B. C. (2016, November). A brave new world: The problems and opportunities presented by new media technologies in prisons. *Criminology & Criminal Justice*, *16*(5), 534–551. DOI: 10.1177/1748895816654953

Jha, A. C. (2025, June 10). A comprehensive review of challenges in cybersecurity systems across digital infrastructures. In A. C. Jha & S. K. Dandapat (Eds.), *CyberFusion: The Strategic Integration of Cybersecurity for Digital Transformation in Tech Environment* (pp. 16-25). QTanalytics. DOI: 10.48001/978-81-980647-2-1-2

Johnson, A., Egan, E., & Londoño, J. (2023, January 9). Police tech: exploring the opportunities and fact-0checking the criticisms. *Information Technology & Innovation Foundation.* https://itif.org/publications/2023/01/09/police-tech-exploring-the-opportunities-and-fact-checking-the-criticisms

Johnson, H. J., & Hail-Jares, K. (2016). Technology and prisons. In Jewkes, Y., Bennett, J., & Crewe, B. (Eds.), *Handbook on prisons* (2nd ed., pp. 273–291). Routledge. DOI: 10.4324/9781315797779-17

Johnson, R. (2005). *Hard time: Understanding and reforming the prison* (3rd ed.). Wadsworth.

Johnson, T. L., Johnson, N. N., Topalli, V., McCurdy, D., & Wallace, A. (2024, December). Police facial recognition applications and violent crime control in U.S. cities. *Cities (London, England)*, *155*, 105472. DOI: 10.1016/j.cities.2024.105472

Jones, L. Ø., & Manger, T. (2019). Literacy skills, academic self-efficacy, and participation in prison education. In D. Perin, *The Wiley Handbook of Adult Literacy* (pp. 151-169). John Wiley & Sons. https://doi.org/DOI: 10.1002/9781119261407.ch7

Jones, C. (2021, October). Law enforcement use of facial recognition: Bias, disparate impacts on people of color, and the need for federal legislation. *North Carolina Journal of Law & Technology*, *22*(4), 777–814. https://scholarship.law.unc.edu/ncjolt/vol22/iss4/6

Jones, E. (2023, Spring). Digital disruption: Artificial intelligence and international trade policy. *Oxford Review of Economic Policy*, *39*(1), 70–84. DOI: 10.1093/oxrep/grac049

Jordan, A. (2017, October 27). "Ninja" burglar revealed to be 74-year-old man. *Tokyo Weekender.* https://www.tokyoweekender.com/japan-life/ninja-burglar-revealed-74-year-old-man

Joseph, S. (2023, Spring). The unconstitutionality of geofence warrants. *University of Central Florida Department of Legal Studies Law Journal*, *6*, 71–112.

Josey, V. (2025, August 10). Deepfake: The new face of financial fraud. *Deccan Herald.* https://www.deccanherald.com/opinion/deepfake-the-new-face-of-financial-fraud-3674748

Joshi, N. (2025, February 4). *Sebi takes its investor-protection crusade to algo trading turf.* Mint. https://www.livemint.com/market/sebi-framework-algo-algorithmic-trading-rules-retail-investors-api-market-11738681654852.html

Julien, H. (2019). Digital literacy in theory and practice. In Khosrow-Pour, M. (Ed.), *Advanced Methodologies and Technologies in Library Science, Information Management, and Scholarly Inquiry* (4th ed., pp. 22–32). IGI Global., DOI: 10.4018/978-1-5225-2255-3.ch195

Kabir, M. S., & Alam, M. N. (2023, May). IoT, big data and AI applications in the law enforcement and legal system: A review. *International Research Journal of Engineering and Technology (IRJET), 10*(5), 1777-1789. https://www.irjet.net/archives/V10/i5/IRJET-V10I5271.pdf

Kalaam, S. A. (2025, July 8). *The legality of public filming and pranks in India*. LawBro. https://www.lawbro.net/blog/law-5/the-legality-of-public-filming-and-pranks-in-india-18

Kalleberg, A. L. (2011). *Good jobs, bad jobs: The rise of polarized and precarious employment systems in the new economy*. Russell Sage Foundation.

Kammari, K. S., Khanna, M., Annambhotla, Y. L., Anuradha, K. D., Namrata, P. N. S., Nagaraja, K. V., Smitha, T. V., Jan, T., & Naik, G. R. (2025, October 30). A comprehensive review of deepfake detection techniques utilizing remote photoplethysmography. *IEEE Access : Practical Innovations, Open Solutions, 13*, 183557–183578. DOI: 10.1109/ACCESS.2025.3624284

Kansal, K., Wong, Y., & Kankanhalli, M. S. (2025, July). Implications of privacy regulations on video surveillance systems. *ACM Transactions on Multimedia Computing Communications and Applications, 21*(7), 1–27. DOI: 10.1145/3706108

Karras, T., Laine, S., Aittala, M., Hellsten, J., Lehtinen, J., & Aila, T. (2020, June). Analyzing and improving the image quality of StyleGAN. [Conference paper]. *2020 IEEE/CVF Conference on Computer Vision and Pattern Recognition (CVPR)* (pp. 8107–8116). DOI: 10.1109/CVPR42600.2020.00813

Kasser, T., & Ryan, R. M. (1996, March). Further examining the American dream: Differential correlates of intrinsic and extrinsic goals. *Personality and Social Psychology Bulletin, 22*(3), 20–287. DOI: 10.1177/0146167296223006

Kaufmann, M. (2024, June 21). AI in policing and law enforcement. In R. Paul, E. Carmel, & J. Cobbe (Eds.), *Handbook on public policy and artificial intelligence* (pp. 295–306). Edward Elgar Publishing. https://doi.org/DOI: 10.4337/9781803922171.00031

Kaun, A., & Stiernstedt, F. (2020, September). Doing time, the smart way? Temporalities of the smart prison. *New Media & Society, 22*(9), 1580–1599. DOI: 10.1177/1461444820914865

Kaur, A., Hoshyar, A. N., Saikrishna, V., Firmin, S., & Xia, F. (2024, May). Deepfake video detection: Challenges and opportunities. *Artificial Intelligence Review, 57*(6), 159. DOI: 10.1007/s10462-024-10810-6

Kaur, M., & Saini, M. (2024, July). Role of Artificial Intelligence in the crime prediction and pattern analysis studies published over the last decade: A scientometric analysis. *Artificial Intelligence Review, 57*(8), 202. DOI: 10.1007/s10462-024-10823-1

Kavenna, J. (2019, October 4). Shoshana Zuboff: 'Surveillance capitalism is an assault on human autonomy.' *The Guardian*. https://www.theguardian.com/books/2019/oct/04/shoshana-zuboff-surveillance-capitalism-assault-human-automomy-digital-privacy

Kelling, G. L., & Coles, C. M. (1998). Fixing broken windows: Restoring order and reducing crime in our communities. *Touchstone (Nashville, Tenn.)*.

Kelly, S. P. (2021, Winter). Internet searching, geo-tagging, geo-fencing and open source investigations: A plaintiff's perspective. *Trial Journal, 23*(1), 32–39.

Kennedy, G., & Wong, J. K. C. (2025, December 15). *Hong Kong issues new PCPD guidelines and leaflets on CCTV, drones and in-vehicle cameras.* Mayer Brown. https://www.mayerbrown.com/en/insights/publications/2025/12/new-guidance-on-cctv-drones-and-in-vehicle-cameras-in-hong-kong

Kerr, A., & Willis, M. (2018, October). Prisoner use of information and communications technology. *Trends and Issues in Crime and Criminal Justice, 560*, 1–19. DOI: 10.52922/ti107289

Kerr, O. (2012). The Mosaic theory of the Fourth Amendment. *Michigan Law Review, 111*(3), 311–354. https://repository.law.umich.edu/mlr/vol111/iss3/1. DOI: 10.36644/mlr.111.3.mosiac

Kethineni, S., & Cao, Y. (2019, February). The rise in popularity of cryptocurrency and associated criminal activity. *International Criminal Justice Review, 30*(3), 325–344. DOI: 10.1177/1057567719827051

Ketzner, R., Ravindra, V., & Bramble, M. (2022, October). A robust, fast, and accurate algorithm for point in spherical polygon classification with applications in geoscience and remote sensing. *Computers & Geosciences, 167*, 105185. DOI: 10.1016/j.cageo.2022.105185

Khalil, R. F. (2023). Aerial trespass and the Fourth Amendment. *Michigan Law Review, 121*(7), 1269–1299. https://repository.law.umich.edu/mlr/vol121/iss7/4. DOI: 10.36644/mlr.121.7.aerial

Khan, A., Laghari, A., Inam, S., Ullah, S., Shahzad, M., & Syed, D. (2025, April). A survey on multimedia-enabled deepfake detection: State-of-the-art tools and techniques, emerging trends, current challenges & limitations, and future directions. *Discover Computing, 28*(1), 48. DOI: 10.1007/s10791-025-09550-0

Khanna, R. (2025, June 2). ED slaps PMLA in 1,500-crore digi-arrest fraud run from Dubai. *The Times of India*. https://timesofindia.indiatimes.com/city/kolkata/ed-slaps-pmla-in-1500-crore-digi-arrest-fraud-run-from-dubai/articleshow/121576275.cms

Kielbowicz, R. B. (1979, June-July). The story behind the adoption of the ban on courtroom cameras. *Judicature, 63*(1), 14–23.

Kilbane, S. M. (2019, January 30). Drones and Jones: Rethinking curtilage flyover in light of the revived Fourth Amendment trespass doctrine. *Capital University Law Review, 42*, 249–285. https://www.capitallawreview.org/article/7273-drones-and-jones-rethinking-curtilage-flyover-in-light-of-the-revived-fourth-amendment-trespass-doctrine

Kim, T., & Im, I. (2025, January). Understanding users' AI manipulation intention: An empirical investigation of the antecedents in the context of AI recommendation algorithms. *Information & Management, 62*(1), 104061. DOI: 10.1016/j.im.2024.104061

Kishore, M. B., Reddy, S., Sujihelen, L., Sivasangari, A., & Christy, A. (2023, May). Artificial Intelligence based detection of traffic violations by two-wheeler vehicles. [Conference paper]. *2023 7th International Conference on Intelligent Computing and Control Systems (ICICCS)* (pp. 1788-1792). https://doi.org/ DOI: 10.1109/ICICCS56967.2023.10142605

Klepper, D. (2025, July 28). Scammers are impersonating CEOs and Trump officials using AI deepfakes. *AP News*. https://apnews.com/article/artificial-intelligence-deepfake-trump-espionage-hack-scammers-da90ad1e5298a9ce50c997458d6aa610

Kleygrewe, L., Hutter, R. I. V., Koedijk, M., & Oudejans, R. R. D. (2024, July). Changing perspectives: Enhancing learning efficacy with the after-action review in virtual reality training for police. *Ergonomics, 67*(5), 628–637. DOI: 10.1080/00140139.2023.2236819 PMID: 37440434

Knight, V. (2015, July). Some observations on the digital landscape of prisons today. *Prison Service Journal, 220*, 3–9.

Knight, V. (2016). *Remote control: Television in prisons*. Palgrave Macmillan. DOI: 10.1057/9781137443915

Knight, V., & Van De Steene, S. (2017a). The capacity and capability of digital innovation in prisons: Towards smart prisons. *Advancing Corrections, 4*(8), 88–101.

Knott, A., Pedreschi, D., Jitsuzumi, T., Leavy, S., Eyers, D., Chakraborti, T., Trotman, A., Sundareswaran, S., Baeza-Yates, R., Biecek, P., Weller, A., Teal, P. D., Basu, S., Haklidir, M., Morini, V., Russell, S., & Bengio, Y. (2024, September). AI content detection in the emerging information ecosystem: New obligations for media and tech companies. *Ethics and Information Technology, 26*(4), 63. DOI: 10.1007/s10676-024-09795-1

Koerner, M. R. (2015). Drones and the Fourth Amendment: Redefining expectations of privacy. *Duke Law Journal, 64*(6), 1129–1172. https://scholarship.law.duke.edu/dlj/vol64/iss6/3

Kohl, R. (2024, April 22). Automated stategraft: Faulty programming and improper collections in Michigan's unemployment insurance program. [Conference paper]. Wisconsin Law Review/ 2023 Symposium on Stategraft. https://wlr.law.wisc.edu/automated-stategraft-faulty-programming-and-improper-collections-in-michigans-unemployment-insurance-program

Koops, B.-J., Newell, B. C., & Škorvánek, I. (2019, March 1). Location tracking by police: The regulation of "tireless and absolute surveillance." *UC Irvine Law Review, 9*(3), 635–698. https://escholarship.org/uc/item/62r710t0

Kotagiri, A., & Bammidi, T. R. (2024). Sustainable safeguarding: Implementing fraud defense systems for authorized push payments through robotics process automation and AI integration. [Conference paper]. In P. Whig, N. Silva, A. A. Elngar, N. Aneja, & P. Sharma, P. (Eds.), *Sustainable Development through Machine Learning, AI and IoT. Communications in Computer and Information Science, 2196* (pp. 130–140). DOI: 10.1007/978-3-031-71729-1_13

Kraetzer, C., Siegel, D., Seidlitz, S., & Dittmann, J. (2022, April 19). Process-driven modelling of media forensic investigations-considerations on the example of DeepFake detection. *Sensors (Basel), 22*(9), 3137. DOI: 10.3390/s22093137 PMID: 35590827

Kroll, J. A., Huey, J., Barocas, S., Felten, E. W., Reidenberg, J. R., Robinson, D. G., & Yu, H. (2017). Accountable algorithms. *University of Pennsylvania Law Review, 165*(3), 633–705. https://papers.ssrn.com/sol3/papers.cfm?abstract_id=2765268

Kulhari, S. (2018). Data protection, privacy and identity: A complex triad. In *Building-Blocks of a Data Protection Revolution: The Uneasy Case for Blockchain Technology to Secure Privacy and Identity* (1st ed., pp. 23-37). Nomos Verlagsgesellschaft mbH. https://www.jstor.org/stable/j.ctv941qz6.7

Kumho Tire Co., Ltd. v. Carmichael, 526 U.S. 137, 119 S. Ct. 1167, 143 L. Ed. 2d 238 (1999).

Kyllo v. United States, 533 U.S. 27. (2001). *Oyez.* https://www.oyez.org/cases/2000/99-8508

La Vigne, N. G., Lowry, S. S., Markman, J. A., & Dwyer, A. M. (2011). *Evaluating the use of public surveillance cameras for crime control and prevention.* U.S. Department of Justice, Office of Community Oriented Policing Services. Urban Institute, Justice Policy Center. https://www.urban.org/sites/default/files/publication/27556/412403-evaluating-the-use-of-public-surveillance-cameras-for-crime-control-and-prevention.pdf

Lacambra, S. J., Matthews, J., & Walsh, K. (2018, May). Opening the black box: Defendants' rights to confront forensic software. In *The Champion.* (pp. 28-39, 66). https://www.eff.org/files/2018/07/30/champion_article_-_lacambra_forensic_software_may_2018_07102018.pdf

Lacqueur, H., & Copus, R. W. (2022, October). An algorithmic assessment of parole decisions. *Journal of Quantitative Criminology.* https://irlaw.umkc.edu/faculty_works/496

Lallie, H. S. (2023, July). Dashcam forensic investigation guidelines. *Forensic Science International Digital Investigation, 45*, 301558. DOI: 10.1016/j.fsidi.2023.301558

Laptev, V. A., & Feyzrakhmanova, D. R. (2024). Application of Artificial Intelligence in justice: Current trends and future prospects. *Human-Centric Intelligent Systems, 4*(3), 394–405. DOI: 10.1007/s44230-024-00074-2

Law enforcement requests. (n.d.). Uber Transparency Report. https://www.uber.com/us/en/about/reports/transparency/law-enforcement

Law, N., Woo, D., de la Torre, J., & Wong, G. (2018, June). *A global framework of reference on digital literacy skills for indicator 4.4.2.* UNESCO. UIS Information Paper, 51. https://unesdoc.unesco.org/ark:/48223/pf0000265403

Le, B. M., Kim, J., Woo, S. S., Moore, K., Abuadbba, A., & Tariq, S. (2025, March 2). SoK: Systematization and benchmarking of deepfake detectors in a unified framework (arXiv:2401.04364). *arXiv.* l arXiv.2401.04364DOI: 10.1109/EuroSP63326.2025.00055

Leatherdale, D., & Lake, E. (2025, April 30). Video shows felling of much-loved tree, jury told. *BBC.* https://www.bbc.com/news/articles/c3v90z17k74o

Lederer, F. I. (2023). Courtroom technology from the judge's perspective: A 2022-23 update. *Court Review, 59*(2), 52–56.

Lee, G.-L., Yun, N.-Y., & Park, S.-H. (2013, October 1). A smart electronic tagging system based on context awareness and machine to machine internetworking. *International Journal of Distributed Sensor Networks, 9*(10), 392083. Advance online publication. DOI: 10.1155/2013/392083

Lee, R. W., Jun, T. J., Lee, J.-M., Cho, S. I., Park, H. J., & Suh, J. (2025, December). Vulnerability of Large Language Models to prompt injection when providing medical advice. *JAMA Network Open, 8*(12), e2549963. DOI: 10.1001/jamanetworkopen.2025.49963 PMID: 41632124

Lefoane, M., Ghafir, I., Kabir, S., & Awan, I.-U. (2025, April). Internet of Things botnets: A survey on Artificial Intelligence based detection techniques. *Journal of Network and Computer Applications, 236*, 104110. DOI: 10.1016/j.jnca.2025.104110

Lei Geral de Proteção de Dados Pessoais. Law n. 13.709/2018 (2018, August). https://www.lgpdbrasil.com.br/wp-content/uploads/2019/06/LGPD-english-version.pdf

Lei, S., Song, J., Feng, F., Yan, Z., & Wang, A. (2025, June 10). Deepfake face detection and adversarial attack defense method based on multi-feature decision fusion. *Applied Sciences (Basel, Switzerland), 15*(12), 6588. DOI: 10.3390/app15126588

Lenahan-Pfahlert, K. A. (2024, March 18). *Blockchain analysis and related expert testimony admissible in criminal trial.* Money Laundering Watch. https://www.moneylaunderingnews.com/2024/03/blockchain-analysis-and-related-expert-testimony-admissible-in-criminal-trial

Lenz, N. (2002, October). "Luxurics" in Prison: The relationship between amenity funding and public support. *Crime and Delinquency, 48*(4), 499–525. DOI: 10.1177/001112802237127

Leone, M. (2023, January 19). The spiral of digital falsehood in deepfakes. *International Journal for the Semiotics of Law - Revue Internationale de Sémiotique Juridique, 36*(2), 385–405. DOI: 10.1007/s11196-023-09970-5

Leu, D. J., Kinzer, C. K., Coiro, J., Castek, J., & Henry, L. A. (2013). New literacies: A dual-level theory of the changing nature of literacy, instruction and assessment. In Alvermann, D. E., Unrau, N. J., & Ruddell, R. B. (Eds.), *Theoretical models and processes of reading* (6th ed., pp. 1150–1181). International Reading Association. DOI: 10.1598/0710.42

Levenson, E., & Cooper, A. (2021, March 31). Derek Chauvin's body camera video shows his reaction just after George Floyd left in an ambulance. *CNN.* https://www.cnn.com/2021/03/31/us/derek-chauvin-trial-george-floyd-day-3

Levi, M., & Reuter, P. (2006). Money laundering. *Crime and Justice, 34*(1), 289–375. DOI: 10.1086/501508

Levi, M., & Soudijn, M. (2020). Understanding the laundering of organized crime money. *Crime and Justice, 49*, 579–632. DOI: 10.1086/708047

Lexington Sheriff's Department. (n.d.). *Taking flight: meet the team controlling the drones at LCSD.* https://joinlcsd.com/taking-flight-meet-the-team-controlling-the-drones-at-lcsd

Lezama, F. (2022, August 28). A guide to video analytics: Applications and opportunities. TryOLabs. https://tryolabs.com/guides/video-analytics-guide

Libell, H. P., Sorensen, M. S., Alami, A., & Callimachi, R. (2018, December 22). Video of tourist's killing in Morocco is most likely real, Norway says. *The New York Times.* https://www.nytimes.com/2018/12/22/world/europe/scandinavian-tourists-morocco.html

Liju, A. (2025, September 5). *Recovering metadata & telemetry from drones & legal implications of seizing UAV evidence.* Cyint Technologies. https://www.cyint.in/post/recovering-metadata-telemetry-from-drones-legal-implications-of-seizing-uav-evidence

Lillich, R. B. (1991, January 1). The Soering Case. *The American Journal of International Law, 85*(1), 128–149. DOI: 10.1017/S0002930000011398

Lipton, B. (2025, November 12). *Washington court rules that data collected on flock safety cameras are public record.* Electronic Frontier Foundation. https://www.eff.org/deeplinks/2025/11/washington-court-rules-data-captured-flock-safety-cameras-are-public-records

Lipton, Z. C. (2018, June 1). The mythos of model interpretability: In machine learning, the concept of interpretability is both important and slippery. *ACM Queue; Tomorrow's Computing Today, 16*(3), 31–57. DOI: 10.1145/3236386.3241340

Lloyds Bank. (2021). *Essential digital skills report 2021: Third Edition—Benchmarking the essential digital skills of the UK.* https://www.lloydsbank.com/assets/media/pdfs/banking_with_us/whats-happening/210923-lb-essential-digital-skills-2021-report.pdf

Lohre, R., Bois, A. J., Pollock, J. W., Lapner, P., McIlquham, K., Athwal, G. S., & Goel, D. P. (2020). Effectiveness of immersive virtual reality on orthopedic surgical skills and knowledge acquisition among senior surgical residents. *JAMA Network Open, 3*(12), e2031217. DOI: 10.1001/jamanetworkopen.2020.31217 PMID: 33369660

Longinus, E. C. (2025). Smarter corrections and intelligence-driven innovations in correctional services in contemporary society. *International Journal of Business Ecosystem & Strategy, 7*(6), 244–262. DOI: 10.36096/ijbes.v7i6.1036

Lorch, B., Scheler, N., & Riess, C. (2022, March 1). Compliance challenges in forensic image analysis under the Artificial Intelligence Act (arXiv:2203.00469). *arXiv.* /arXiv.2203.00469DOI: 10.23919/EUSIPCO55093.2022.9909723

Los Angeles (n.d.). World Population Review. https://worldpopulationreview.com/us-cities/california/los-angeles

Loudermilk Bhatia, P. (2024, April). *Artificial Intelligence and Recidivism: The use of risk assessment as prediction instruments in criminal sentencings* [Thesis, University of Chicago]. https://doi.org/DOI: 10.6082/uchicago.12260

Loux, M., & Loux, B. (2025, October 28). *Technology in criminal justice: Efficiency and fairness.* American Military University. https://www.amu.apus.edu/area-of-study/criminal-justice/resources/technology-in-criminal-justice

Lucas, K. (2016, January 26). *Stay tuned for a brief history of television. Video* Caption Corporation. https://www.vicaps.com/blog/brief-history-television

Lum, C., Merola, L., Willis, J., & Cave, B. (2010, September). *License plate recognition technology (LPR): Impact evaluation and community assessment.* Center for Evidence-Based Crime Policy, George Mason University. https://cebcp.org/wp-content/evidence-based-policing/LPR_FINAL.pdf

Lum, C., & Isaac, W. (2016, October). To predict and serve? *Significance, 13*(5), 14–19. DOI: 10.1111/j.1740-9713.2016.00960.x

Lum, C., Koper, C. S., Lee, H., Nagin, D. S., & Sherman, L. (2025, December 11). Measuring the cost-effectiveness of new technologies in policing: The case of automatic license plate readers (ALPR). *Cambridge Journal of Evidence-Based Policing, 9*(1), 1–19. DOI: 10.1007/s41887-025-00099-y

Lum, C., Koper, C. S., & Willis, J. J. (2016). Understanding the limits of technology in policing. *Police Quarterly*, *20*(2), 1–29. DOI: 10.1177/1098611116667279

Luo, X., & Wang, Y. (2025, March 25). Frequency-domain masking and spatial interaction for generalizable deepfake detection. *Electronics (Basel)*, *14*(7), 1302. DOI: 10.3390/electronics14071302

Ly, D. (2025, August 21). Facial recognition in policing and smart cities: Balancing innovation with responsibility. *Forbes*. https://www.forbes.com/councils/forbestechcouncil/2025/08/21/facial-recognition-in-policing-and-smart-cities-balancing-innovation-with-responsibility

Lyft's law enforcement support. (n.d.). Lyft. https://help.lyft.com/hc/ko/all/articles/115012925607-Lyft-s-law-enforcement-support

Lyu, S. (2020, March 11). DeepFake detection: Current challenges and next steps (arXiv:2003.09234). *arXiv*. /arXiv.2003.09234DOI: 10.1109/ICMEW46912.2020.9105991

M, R. (2025, October 5). *Blockchain crime typologies: 32 case studies bridging traditional and crypto laundering (Part-1)*. LinkedIn. https://www.linkedin.com/pulse/blockchain-crime-typologies-32-case-studies-bridging-traditional-m-45epc

Mahajan, S., & Chaudhary, R. (2025, July). Technological evolution of Indian policing from traditional to SMART technology. *International Research Journal of Multidisciplinary Scope*, *6*(3), 800–812. DOI: 10.47857/irjms.2025.v06i03.04072

Mai, K. T., Bray, S., Davies, T., & Griffin, L. D. (2023, August 2). Warning: Humans cannot reliably detect speech deepfakes. *PLoS One*, *18*(8), e0285333. DOI: 10.1371/journal.pone.0285333 PMID: 37531336

Malhotra, D., & Goyal, K. (2025, March 5). Balancing liberty and surveillance: The intersection of digital monitoring and bail jurisprudence in India. *SSRN*, *1*, 163–197. https://jccj.in/2025/03/05/balancing-liberty-and-surveillance-the-intersection-of-digital-monitoring-and-bail-jurisprudence-in-india/. DOI: 10.2139/ssrn.5589250

Malik, A. A., Azeem, W., & Asad, M.Dr Aftab Ahmad MalikDr Waqar AzeemDr Mujtaba Asad. (2022, September 10). The child kidnapping and abuse by gang criminals and the legitimate custody of minors to parents after rescue and use of geo-fencing to arrest the absconding criminals. *International Journal for Electronic Crime Investigation*, *6*(3), 3–10. DOI: 10.54692/ijeci.2022.0603136

Mandalapu, V., Elluri, L., Vyas, P., & Roy, N. (2023, June 14). Crime prediction using machine learning and deep learning: A systematic review and future directions. *IEEE Access : Practical Innovations, Open Solutions*, *11*, 60153–60170. Advance online publication. DOI: 10.1109/ACCESS.2023.3286344

Mandela, N., Manna, F., Garibado, D. A., Musaka, S., Mutara, M., & Mistry, N. R. (2024, February). Exploring the use of Tails Operating System in cybercrime and its impact on law enforcement investigations. *In 2024 11th International Conference on Computing for Sustainable Global Development (INDIACom)* (pp. 1109-1114). IEEE. https://doi.org/DOI: 10.23919/INDIACom61295.2024.10499122

Maneke, J., & Morasch, C. (2020, August 3). Show-me surveillance: Law enforcement navigation of Missouri's Sunshine Law requirements. *Journal of the Missouri Bar*, *76*(4), 160–183. https://news.mobar.org/show-me-surveillance-law-enforcement-navigation-of-missouris-sunshine-law-requirements

Manky, D., & Baram, G. (2025, January 16). *Beyond Phishing: Exploring the rise of AI-enabled cybercrime*. University of California Berkeley Center for Long-Term Cybersecurity. https://cltc.berkeley.edu/2025/01/16/beyond-phishing-exploring-the-rise-of-ai-enabled-cybercrime/

Mansoor, N., & Iliev, A. I. (2025, January 12). Explainable AI for DeepFake detection. *Applied Sciences (Basel, Switzerland)*, *15*(2), 725. Advance online publication. DOI: 10.3390/app15020725

Maphosa, V. (2024, December). The rise of Artificial Intelligence and emerging ethical and social concerns. *AI. Computer Science and Robotics Technology*, *3*(1), 1–20. DOI: 10.5772/acrt.20240020

Marathe, I. (2024, August 30). *Tech providers, not courts, may have last word on geofence warrants.* LegalTech. https://www.law.com/legaltechnews/2024/08/30/tech-providers-not-courts-may-have-the-last-word-on-geofence-warrants

Marginalized community surveillance. (n.d.). Sustainability directory. https://lifestyle.sustainability-directory.com/area/marginalized-community-surveillance/resource/1

Maroney, N., Williams, B. J., Thomas, A., Skues, J., & Moulding, R. (2019). A stress-coping model of problem online video game use. *International Journal of Mental Health and Addiction*, *17*(4), 845–858. DOI: 10.1007/s11469-018-9887-7

Martin, K. (2025, May 27). *AI cyber attack statistics 2025.* Tech Advisors. https://tech-adv.com/blog/ai-cyber-attack-statistics

Marturana, F., Tacconi, S., Bertè, R., & Me, G. (2012, June). Triage-based automated analysis of evidence in court cases of copyright infringement. In *2012 IEEE International Conference on Communications (ICC)* (pp. 6668-6672). IEEE. https://doi.org/DOI: 10.1109/ICC.2012.6364819

Mas'ud, M. Z., Hassan, A., Shah, W. M., Abdul-Latip, S. F., Ahmad, R., Ariffin, A., & Yunos, Z. (2021, January). A review of digital forensics framework for blockchain in cryptocurrency technology. [Conference paper]. *2021 3rd International Cyber Resilience Conference (CRC).* DOI: 10.1109/CRC50527.2021.9392563

Mason, S., & Seng, D. (2021, August 1). Hearsay. In *Electronic evidence and electronic signatures* (5th ed., pp. 85–111). Institute of Advanced Legal Studies., DOI: 10.14296/2108.9781911507246

Mathew, A., & Rodas, F. (2025, February). Phishing 2.0: Leveraging cyber threat intelligence to combat deepfake-enhanced social engineering. *International Journal of Innovative Research in Science, Engineering and Technology*, *14*(2), 1016–1022. DOI: 10.15680/IJIRSET.2025.1402003

Matongo, B., & Jacobs, L. (2022, June). E-justice to bridge records management gap at the High Court in Namibia. *Archiving : Final Program and Proceedings. IS & T's Archiving Conference*, *19*(1), 25–29. DOI: 10.2352/issn.2168-3204.2022.19.1.6

Mazzanti, C. (2022, March 28). Securing the perimeter: How geofences can make good neighbors. *Regional Business News*, *35*(12), 7.

McClain, S. (1996, Spring/Summer). A history of aerial cinematography. *The Operating Cameraman*, *6*(1), 32–49.

McComas, J., MacKay, M., & Pivik, J. (2002). Effectiveness of virtual reality for teaching pedestrian safety. *Cyberpsychology & Behavior, 5*(3), 185–190. DOI: 10.1089/109493102760147150 PMID: 12123238

McDougall, C., Pearson, D. A. S., Torgerson, D. J., & Garcia-Reyes, M. (2017, October). The effect of digital technology on prisoner behavior and reoffending: A natural stepped-wedge design. *Journal of Experimental Criminology, 13*(1), 455–482. DOI: 10.1007/s11292-017-9303-5

McFarlane, R., & Pike, A. (2019). From prisoner to student. In R. Earle, & J. Mehigan, *Degrees of Freedom: Prison Education and The Open University*. Policy Press.

McGuire-Snieckus, R., & Caulfield, L. S. (2018, August). An evaluation of Talent 4 . . .: A programme to identify talent and skills for prisoners, disadvantaged, unemployed, and vulnerable groups. *International Journal of Offender Therapy and Comparative Criminology, 62*(11), 3460–3484. DOI: 10.1177/0306624X17740556 PMID: 29160124

McGuirk, R. (2025, December 22). Australian police release documents showing Bondi Beach shooting suspect conducted firearms training with his father. *PBS.* https://www.pbs.org/newshour/world/australian-police-release-documents-showing-bondi-beach-shooting-suspect-conducted-firearms-training-with-his-father

McKay, C. (2026). Digital criminology, vulnerability theories and digital vulnerability. In *Digital Vulnerability in Criminal Justice Vulnerable People and Communication Technologies* (pp. 23–43). Palgrave MacMillan., DOI: 10.1007/978-3-032-10028-3_2

McKenna, F. (2024, December 17). 5 AI scams set to surge in 2025: What you need to know. *Forbes.* https://www.forbes.com/sites/frankmckenna/2024/12/16/5-ai-scams-set-to-surge-in-2025-what-you-need-to-know

McKinnon, M. E. (2026, January 5). Counter-drone technology coming to your town. *Fox Rothschild: Plane-ly Spoken.* Fox-Rothschild. https://plane-lyspoken.foxrothschild.com/2026/01/05/counter-drone-technology-coming-to-your-town

McLauchlan, J., & Farley, H. (2019, December). Fast cars and fast learning: Using Virtual Reality to learn literacy and numeracy in prison. *Journal of Virtual Worlds Research, 12*(3), 1–11. DOI: 10.4101/jvwr.v12i3.7391

McMennamy, A. (2024, May 15). *GPS pet tracking devices versus microchips: Which tracks pets better?* Tracki. https://tracki.com/blogs/post/pet-gps-tracking-devices-vs-microchipping

Meckel, M., & Steinacker, L. (2021). Hybrid reality: The rise of deepfakes and diverging truths. *Morals & Machines, 1*(1), 10–21. DOI: 10.5771/2747-5182-2021-1-10

Melendez, H., & Christoff, T. (2024). *Sacramento (California) Police Department's virtual reality system: Addressing crime through innovative technology*. Office of Community Oriented Policing Services. https://portal.cops.usdoj.gov/resourcecenter/content.ashx/cops-r1174-pub.pdf

Mendonca, H., & Iyamu, T. (2024). Improving the justice system services in Namibian rural communities through mobile technology. *Issues in Information Systems, 25*(4), 16–28. Supplemental Index, (180687392). Advance online publication. DOI: 10.48009/4_iis_2024_102

Mental Health America. (2024, September 16). *Responding to behavioral health crises.* https://mhanational.org/position-statements/responding-to-behavioral-health-crises

Meyers, H. E. (2023, January 19). *Destroyed by discovery: How New York State's discovery law destabilizes the criminal justice system.* Manhattan Institute. https://manhattan.institute/article/destroyed-by-discovery-how-new-york-states-discovery-law-destabilizes-the-criminal-justice-system

Michigan Department of Attorney General. (2022, October 20). State of Michigan announces settlement of civil rights class action alleging false accusations of unemployment fraud [Press release]. https://www.michigan.gov/ag/news/press-releases/2022/10/20/som-settlement-of-civil-rights-class-action-alleging-false-accusations-of-unemployment-fraud

Millcarek, L. (2012, July). Eighteenth century law, twenty-first century problems: *Jones*, GPS tracking, and the future of privacy. *Florida Law Review, 64*(4), 1101–1111. https://scholarship.law.ufl.edu/flr/vol64/iss4/7

Miller, L., & Toliver, J. (2014). *Implementing a body-worn camera program: Recommendations and lessons learned.* U.S. Department of Justice. https://www.justice.gov/iso/opa/resources/472014912134715246869.pdf

Milliner, C. (2024, December 13). New Jersey drone mystery: What to know and what can be done. *ABC News.* https://abcnews.go.com/US/new-jersey-drone-mystery/story?id=116719847

Ministry of Justice. (2021, August 5). *Prison education statistics April 2019 to March 2020.* https://assets.publishing.service.gov.uk/media/610ba7b48fa8f506a5bf1325/Prisoner_Education_2019_20.pdf

Mishra, P., Varadharajan, V., Tupakula, U., & Pilli, E. S. (2018). A detailed investigation and analysis of using machine learning techniques for intrusion detection. *IEEE Communications Surveys and Tutorials, 21*(1), 686–728. DOI: 10.1109/COMST.2018.2847722

Mitchell, S., Wu, S., Zaldivar, A., Barnes, P., Vasserman, L., Hutchinson, B., Spitzer, E., Raji, I. D., & Gebru, T. (2019, January). Model cards for model reporting. In *Conference on Fairness, Accountability and Transparency* (pp. 220–229). PMLR. DOI: 10.1145/3287560.3287596

Modise, J. M. (2023, June). Community engagement in policing: A path to more meaningful, knowledgeable, and successful public consultation. *International Journal of Innovative Science and Research Technology, 8*(6), 3894–3906. DOI: 10.5281/zenodo.10060950

Mohanta, A. Sneha, Garikapati, K., Mohanty, S., & Samanta, S. (2025, June). Forensic linguistics and DBN: Automating the analysis of witness statements and testimonies in AI-driven policing. In M. A. Abdelmottlep (Ed.), *AI-Driven Policing and Urban Security in Smart Cities* (pp. 171-202). IGI Global. https://doi.org/DOI: 10.4018/979-8-3373-0245-4.ch007

Mohanta, A., & Garikapati, K. Sneha, Mohanty, S., & Shreya. (2024, December). Predictive justice in criminal proceedings: The role of AI jurimetrics. In H. Bajraktari (Ed.), *Exploration of AI in Contemporary Legal Systems* (pp. 217-252). IGI Global. https://doi.org/DOI: 10.4018/979-8-3693-7205-0.ch011

Molnar, T. G., Kannan, S. K., Cunningham, J., Dunlap, K., Hobb, K. L., & Ames, A. D. (2024, March). Collision avoidance and geofencing for fixed-wing aircraft with control barrier functions. *IEEE Transactions on Control System Technology.* https://doi.org//arXiv.2403.02508DOI: 10.48550

Montañez, R., Golob, E., & Xu, S. (2020, September 29). Human cognition through the lens of social engineering cyberattacks. *Frontiers in Psychology, 11*, 1755. DOI: 10.3389/fpsyg.2020.01755 PMID: 33101096

Monteiro, A., Barros, R., & Leite, C. (2015, March). Lifelong learning through e-learning in European prisons: Rethinking digital and social inclusion. [Conference paper]. *Inted2015 Madrid.* (pp. 1038-1046).

More, M. (2021). Thc institution of traditional authority in Okombahe, Erongo region of Namibia: Can the institution be reconciled with democratic values of justice? *Law, Democracy and Development, 25*(SPE), 146–166. https://doi.org/DOI: 10.17159/2077-4907/2020/ldd.v25.spe7

Moriarty, L. J. (2025). *Criminal justice in the 21st century* (4th ed.). Charles C. Thomas Publisher.

Morison, J.Jr, & McInerney, T. (2024). When should a computer decide? Judicial decision-making in the age of automation, algorithms and generative artificial intelligence. In Turenne, S., & Moussa, M. (Eds.), *Research Handbook on Judging and the Judiciary*. Edward Elgar-Routledge.

Morte di Michael, B. in aula Giacomo Friso si avvale della facoltà di non rispondere. (2025, December 12). *Padova Oggi.* https://www.padovaoggi.it/cronaca/udienza-processo-friso-boschetto-padova-11-dicembre-2025.html

Mortlock, D., Mosman, B., & El-Gamal, A. (2025, June 30). *OFAC and DOJ sanctions enforcement in the United States*. Global Investigations Review. https://globalinvestigationsreview.com/guide/the-guide-sanctions/sixth-edition/article/ofac-and-doj-sanctions-enforcement-in-the-united-states

Mubarak, R., Alsboui, T., Alshaikh, O., Inuwa-Dutse, I., Khan, S., & Parkinson, S. (2023, December). A survey on the detection and impacts of deepfakes in visual, audio, and textual formats. *IEEE Access : Practical Innovations, Open Solutions, 11*, 144497–144529. DOI: 10.1109/ACCESS.2023.3344653

Mufarreh, A., Waitkus, J., & Booker, T. A. (2021, February). Prison official perceptions of technology in prison. *Punishment & Society, 24*(3), 410–432. DOI: 10.1177/1462474521990777

Muhly, F., Chizzonic, E., & Leo, P. (2025, February 24). AI-deepfake scams and the importance of a holistic communication security strategy. *International Cybersecurity Law Review, 6*(1), 53–61. DOI: 10.1365/s43439-025-00143-7

Mulkerrin, E. C., & Keeffe, O, S. T. (2025, September 18). In-room surveillance of residents in long term care: It's complicated. *Irish Medical Journal, 118*(8), 127. PMID: 40982312

Mulrooney, K., & Harkness, A. (2023, September 27). Farm crime and security: Evaluating smart tag technology for preventing, tracking and recovering stolen livestock. *International Journal of Rural Criminology, 8*(1), 108–123. DOI: 10.18061/ijrc.v8i1.9619

Munhoz, P. (2014, June 25). Manipulation, professional practices and deontology in informational photography: Identifying new parameters. *Brazilian Journalism Research, 10*(1), 210–237. DOI: 10.25200/BJR.v10n1.2014.632

Munnang, S. (2024, November-December). Empowering access to justice through automated legal case management. *International Journal for Multidisciplinary Research, 6*(6), 1–13. DOI: 10.36948/ijfmr.2024.v06i06.31915

Muñoz, J. E., Lavoie, J. A., & Pope, A. T. (2024, September 4). Psychophysiological insights and user perspectives: Enhancing police de-escalation skills through full-body VR training. *Frontiers in Psychology, 15*. Advance online publication. DOI: 10.3389/fpsyg.2024.1390677 PMID: 39295763

Munson, A. (2026, January 28). Mike Brennan appointed new police chief. *The Register, 82*(29). https://register.turley.com/lr-archives/LUD012826.pdf

Murphy, J. H. (1997, February 14). Feasibility demonstration of a second-generation electronic monitoring system. *SPIE Conference Proceedings,* 2935, pp. 143-152. https://doi.org/DOI: 10.1117/12.266794

Murugesan, B. (2025, March 10). AI-driven phishing and deep fakes: The future of digital fraud. *Forbes*. https://www.forbes.com/councils/forbestechcouncil/2025/03/10/ai-driven-phishing-and-deep-fakes-the-future-of-digital-fraud

Murugesan, R. (2021, April 16). *Predictive policing in India: Deterring crime or discriminating minorities?* LSE Human Rights Blog. https://blogs.lse.ac.uk/humanrights/2021/04/16/predictive-policing-in-india-deterring-crime-or-discriminating-minorities

Myhand, T. (2023). Once the jury sees it, the jury can't unsee it: The challenge trial judges face when authenticating video evidence in the age of deepfakes. *Widener Law Review, 29*(2), 171–189.

Nadler, M., & Schär, F. (2023, April 10). Tornado Cash and blockchain privacy: A primer for economists and policymakers. *RE:view, 105*(2), 122–136. DOI: 10.20955/r.105.122-136

Naitali, A., Ridouani, M., Salahdine, F., & Kaabouch, N. (2023, October 22). Deepfake attacks: Generation, detection, datasets, challenges, and research directions. *Computers, 12*(10), 216. DOI: 10.3390/computers12100216

Narayan, S. (2023). CCTVs and the criminal city. *Surveillance & Society, 21*(4), 363–374. DOI: 10.24908/ss.v21i4.15779

NASA. (n.d.). *Ingenuity Mars helicopter.* https://science.nasa.gov/mission/mars-2020-perseverance/ingenuity-mars-helicopter

Nath, S., & Barman, A. (2024). AI-Policing in India - Existing research and where to begin future research? [IJIRCST]. *International Journal of Innovative Research in Computer Science and Technology, 12*(5), 14–23. DOI: 10.55524/ijircst.2024.12.5.3

National Air and Space Museum. (2023, June 21). *The beginnings and basics of aerial photography.* Smithsonian. https://airandspace.si.edu/stories/editorial/beginnings-and-basics-aerial-photography

National Association of Criminal Defense Lawyers. (n.d.). *Geofence warrant primer.* https://www.nacdl.org/getattachment/816437c7-8943-425c-9b3b-4faf7da24bba/nacdl-geofence-primer.pdf

National Conference of State Legislatures. (2021, April 30). *Body-worn camera laws database.* https://www.ncsl.org/civil-and-criminal-justice/body-worn-camera-laws-database

National Conference of State Legislatures. (2023, March 27). *Current unmanned aircraft state law landscape.* https://www.ncsl.org/transportation/current-unmanned-aircraft-state-law-landscape

National Institute of Justice. (2014). *National Institute of Justice annual report.* https://www.ojp.gov/pdffiles1/nij/249533.pdf

National Institute of Justice. (2023, August 7). *Law 101: Legal guide for the forensic expert: Daubert and Kumho decisions.* https://nij.ojp.gov/nij-hosted-online-training-courses/law-101-legal-guide-forensic-expert/pretrial/pretrial-rules-evidence/daubert-and-kumho-decisions

NATO Stability Policing Centre of Excellence. (n.d.). *French Republic: Gendarmerie.* https://www.nspcoe.org/about-us/sponsoring-nations/french-republic/french-gendarmerie

Neves, J. C., Tolosana, R., Vera-Rodriguez, R., Lopes, V., Proença, H., & Fierrez, J. (2020, July). GANprintR: Improved fakes and evaluation of the state of the art in face manipulation detection. *IEEE Journal of Selected Topics in Signal Processing, 14*(5), 1038–1048. DOI: 10.1109/JSTSP.2020.3007250

New York City Police Department. (2023, October 26). *Facial recognition: Impact and use policy.* https://www.nyc.gov/assets/nypd/downloads/pdf/public_information/post-final/facial-recognition-nypd-impact-and-use-policy_10.26.23.pdf

New York State Senate. (2025, August 8). *New York State Penal Law, Section 245.20.* https://www.nysenate.gov/legislation/laws/CPL/245.20

New York. (n.d.). World Population Review. https://worldpopulationreview.com/us-cities/new-york/new-york

Newberry, B. (2022, July 19). New ordinance requires some Houston businesses to have surveillance cameras, share footage if HPD asks. *Click2Houston.* https://www.click2houston.com/news/local/2022/07/19/new-ordinance-requires-some-houston-businesses-to-have-surveillance-cameras-share-footage-if-hpd-asks

Ng, A. (2022, July 13). *Amazon gave Ring videos to police without owners' permission.* Politico. https://www.politico.com/news/2022/07/13/amazon-gave-ring-videos-to-police-without-owners-permission-00045513

Nix, E. (2025, May 27). *Why are British police officers called "Bobbies"?* History.com. https://www.history.com/articles/why-are-british-police-officers-called-bobbies

Nofer, M., Gomber, P., Hinz, O., & Schiereck, D. (2017). Blockchain. *Business & Information Systems Engineering, 59*(3), 183–187. DOI: 10.1007/s12599-017-0467-3

Norchuk, Y. (2025). The use of Artificial Intelligence and other technologies to improve legal communication and access to justice for different populations around the world. *Journal of International Legal Communication, 16*(1), 52–63. DOI: 10.32612/uw.27201643.2025.16.1.pp.52-63

Northern Illinois University Continuing and Professional Education. (2021, June 15). *Virtual reality and lean…the good, the bad, and the ugly.* https://cpelearn.niu.edu/virtual-reality-and-leanthe-good-the-bad-and-the-ugly

North-Samardzic, A. (2020, December). Biometric technology and ethics: Beyond security applications. *Journal of Business Ethics*, *167*(3), 433–450. DOI: 10.1007/s10551-019-04143-6

Nova Scotia's 1990 report about 'grisly trial' of Jens Soering. (2023, November 8). [Video]. CBC News. https://www.cbc.ca/player/play/video/1.7022295

Nuckolls, C. (2023). Houston security camera ordinance: Reasonable safety measure or Orwellian surveillance. *SMU Science & Technology Law Review*, *26*(1), 8. DOI: 10.25172/smustlr.26.1.8

Nunes, E. (2025, June 3). Selfie killer: I unlocked my murdered son's phone after his death…& found his grinning 'killer' posing in selfie moments after stabbing. *The Sun*. https://www.thesun.co.uk/news/35227135/unlocked-murdered-sons-phone-grinning-killer

O'Brien, T. (2021, Winter). Compounding injustice: The cascading effect of algorithmic bias in risk assessments. *Georgetown Journal of Law & Modern Critical Race Perspectives*, *13*(1), 39–83. https://www.law.georgetown.edu/mcrp-journal/wp-content/uploads/sites/22/2021/05/GT-GCRP210003.pdf

O'Connor, M., & Giovannini, A. V. (2024, January). *USA: New geofence technology laws*. OneTrust DataGuidance. https://www.dataguidance.com/opinion/usa-new-geofence-technology-laws

O'Hear, M. M., & Wheelock, D. (2016). Public attitudes toward punishment, rehabilitation, and reform: Lessons from the Marquette Law School Poll. *Faculty Publications*, 678. https://scholarship.law.marquette.edu/facpub/678

O'Malley, P., & Smith, G. J. D. (2022, February). 'Smart' crime prevention? Digitization and racialized crime control in a Smart City. *Theoretical Criminology*, *26*(1), 40–56. DOI: 10.1177/1362480620972703

Odendaal, W. (2005). *A place we want to call our own: A study on land tenure policy and securing housing rights in Namibia*. Legal Assistance Centre (LAC). http://www.lac.org.na/projects/lead/Pdf/aplacewewanttocallourown.pdf

Office of Community Oriented Policing Services. (2020). *Drones: A report on the use of drones by public safety agencies – and a wake-up call about the threat of malicious drone attacks*. U.S. Department of Justice. https://portal.cops.usdoj.gov/resourcecenter/content.ashx/cops-w0894-pub.pdf

Office of the Deputy Prime Minister. (2002, July). *Reducing re-offending by ex-prisoners*. Social Exclusion Unit. https://www.bristol.ac.uk/poverty/downloads/keyofficialdocuments/Reducing%20Reoffending.pdf

Oh, H., & Son, W. (2022). Cybersickness and its severity arising from virtual reality content: A comprehensive study. *Sensors (Basel)*, *22*(4), 1314. DOI: 10.3390/s22041314 PMID: 35214216

Okandeji, E. (2024, October 2). *The ethics of surveillance technologies*. Federal Character. https://federalcharacter.com/the-ethics-of-surveillance-technologies

Olawade, D. B., Ayoola, F. I., Ebo, T. O., Asaolu, A. J., Egbon, E., & David-Olawade, A. C. (2025). Artificial Intelligence in forensic mental health: A review of applications and implications. *Journal of Forensic and Legal Medicine*, *113*, 102895. DOI: 10.1016/j.jflm.2025.102895 PMID: 40441026

Oliver, W. M. (2017). *August Vollmer: The father of America policing*. Carolina Academic Press.

Oloke, O. C., Keke, O. V., Mushanga, S., & Nwokolo, B. O. (2024, December). Efficacy of closed circuit television in security management of commercial properties in Lagos Metropolis, Nigeria. *International Journal of Safety and Security Engineering*, *14*(6), 1719–1727. DOI: 10.18280/ijsse.140607

Ölvecký, M., Huraj, L., & Brlej, I. (2025, February). Evaluating the Effectiveness of Deepfake Video Detection Tools: A Comparative Study. *TEM Journal, 14*(1), 64–77. https://doi.org/DOI: 10.18421/TEM141-07

Ombu, A. (2023, June). Role of digital forensics in combating financial crimes in the computer era. *Journal of Forensic Accounting Profession*, *3*(1), 57–75. DOI: 10.2478/jfap-2023-0003

Organisation for Economic Co-operation and Development (OECD). (2023). *Digital skills and digital inclusion: Briefing note.* https://www.oecd.org/content/dam/oecd/en/about/projects/cfe/oecd-city-network-on-jobs-and-skills/Briefing-note-Digital-skills-and-digital-inclusion.pdf

Overbreadth. (2023, July). Cornell Law School Legal Information Institute. https://www.law.cornell.edu/wex/overbreadth

Owsley, B. L. (2022, June 1). The best offense is a good defense: Fourth Amendment implications of geofence warrants. *Hofstra Law Review*, *50*(4), 829–894.

Ozaki, A. (2022, September). The use of live facial recognition technology by private entities in public places: A study of recent case in Japan. [Conference paper]. In D. Kreps, R. Davison, T. Komukai, & K. Ishii (Eds.), *Human choice and digital by default: Autonomy vs digital determination. 15th IFIP International Conference on Human Choice and Computers* (pp. 27–35). Springer. https://doi.org/DOI: 10.1007/978-3-031-15688-5_3

Özdal Oktay, S., Heitmann, S., & Kray, C. (2023). Linking location privacy, digital sovereignty and location-based services: A meta review. *Journal of Location Based Services*, *18*(1), 1–52. DOI: 10.1080/17489725.2023.2239180

Pallavicini, F., Argenton, L., Toniazzi, N., Aceti, L., & Mantovani, F. (2016, December). Virtual reality applications for stress management training in the military. *Aerospace Medicine and Human Performance*, *87*(12), 1021–1030. https://asma.kglmeridian.com/downloadpdf/view/journals/amhp/87/12/article-p1021.pdf PMID: 28323588

Pandian, M. P. (2010). RFID issues. *RFID for Libraries: A Practical Guide* (p. 133-149). https://doi.org/DOI: 10.1016/B978-1-84334-545-9.50005-7

Pangrazio, L., Godhe, A.-L., & López Ledesma, A. G. (2020, November). What is digital literacy? A comparative review of publications across three language contexts. *E-Learning and Digital Media*, *17*(6), 442–459. DOI: 10.1177/2042753020946291

Paoline, E. A.III, Elligson, R., & Gau, J. M. (2025, May). Police culture and body-worn cameras: Examining how cultural values impact officers' acceptance of technology. *Policing. Policing (Oxford, England)*, *19*, paaf007. Advance online publication. DOI: 10.1093/police/paaf017

Papagianneas, S., & Junius, N. (2023, November). Fairness and justice through automation in China's smart courts. *Computer Law & Security Review*, *51*, 105897. DOI: 10.1016/j.clsr.2023.105897

Parry, M. M., Dario, L. M., & Moule, R. K.Jr. (2021, July). Is seeing believing? On the content validity of video recordings for use in criminological research. *Deviant Behavior, 42*(7), 807–820. DOI: 10.1080/01639625.2019.1699259

Parten, J. L. (2022, June). *Police use of drone surveillance technology.* Law Enforcement Management Institute of Texas (LEMIT). https://hdl.handle.net/20.500.11875/4139

Passalaqua, C. (1995, August 15). Post-Trial, Is There Life for the Soaps?: Television: The past decade has seen steadily dropping ratings for daytime soap operas. Simpson trial has only caused further erosion. Los Angeles Times. https://www.latimes.com/archives/la-xpm-1995-08-15-ca-35367-story.html

Passas, I. (2024, June 19). Bibliometric analysis: The main steps. *Encyclopedia, 4*(2), 1014–1025. DOI: 10.3390/encyclopedia4020065

Passos, L. A., Jodas, D., Costa, K. A. P., Souza Júnior, L. A., Rodrigues, D., Ser, J. D., Camacho, D., & Papa, J. P. (2024, February 22). A review of deep learning-based approaches for deepfake content detection. *Expert Systems: International Journal of Knowledge Engineering and Neural Networks, 41*(8), e13570. DOI: 10.1111/exsy.13570

Patel, Y., Tanwar, S., Gupta, R., Bhattacharya, P., Davidson, I. E., Nyameko, R., Aluvala, S., & Vimal, V. (2023, December). Deepfake generation and detection: Case study and challenges. *IEEE Access : Practical Innovations, Open Solutions, 11*, 143296–143323. DOI: 10.1109/ACCESS.2023.3342107

Pawelec, M. (2022, September). Deepfakes and democracy (theory): How synthetic audio-visual media for disinformation and hate speech threaten core democratic functions. *Digital Society : Ethics, Socio-Legal and Governance of Digital Technology, 1*(2), 19. DOI: 10.1007/s44206-022-00010-6 PMID: 36097613

Peeler, T. (2022, September 19). *Nanny/babysitter cam law.* LegalMatch. https://www.legalmatch.com/law-library/article/babysitternanny-camera-legality.html

Peixoto, I. de M. (2014, December). Arte da Manipulação: As interações entre fotografia e arte na era digital. [Conference proceedings]. *XVII Conference of the Iberoamerican Society of Digital Graphics - SIGraDi: Knowledge-based Design, 1*(7), 655–658. DOI: 10.5151/despro-sigradi2013-0129

People of the State of Illinois v. Jussie Smollett. (2024, November 21). https://law.justia.com/cases/illinois/supreme-court/2024/130431.html

Perry, N. (2024, September 3). *How D.C. police launched a real time crime center in 8 months.* Police1. https://www.police1.com/tech-pulse/how-d-c-police-launched-a-real-time-crime-center-in-8-months

Personal Data (Privacy) Ordinance. Cap. 486. (2022, January 10). Hong Kong e-Legislation. https://www.elegislation.gov.hk/hk/cap486!en-zh-Hant-HK.pdf

Peruginelli, G. (2009). Accessing legal information across boundaries: A new challenge. *International Journal of Legal Information, 37*(3), 276–305. DOI: 10.1017/S0731126500005345

Pessarlay, W. (2023, November 19). *India: 3,000 police officers get training in blockchain forensics.* Coingeek. https://coingeek.com/india-3000-police-officers-get-training-in-blockchain-forensics

Pfefferkorn, R. (2020, October 1). 'Deepfakes' in the courtroom. *The Boston University Public Interest Law Journal*, *29*(2), 245–276. https://ssrn.com/abstract=4321140

Pieper, O. (2021, December 19). *Germany remembers Christmas market attack victims*. Deutsche Welle. https://www.dw.com/en/5-years-later-germany-remembers-victims-of-berlin-christmas-market-terror-attack/a-60148540

Pierobon, M. (2025, December 10). *Training with virtual reality*. Flight Safety Foundation. https://flightsafety.org/asw-article/training-with-virtual-reality

Pike, A., & Adams, A. (2012). Digital exclusion or learning exclusion? An ethnographic study of adult male distance learners in English prisons. *Research in Learning Technology*, *20*(4), 363–376. DOI: 10.3402/rlt.v20i0.18620

Pisarić, M. (2022, March). Communications encryption as an investigative obstacle. *The Journal of Criminal Law & Criminology*, *60*(1), 61–74. DOI: 10.47152/rkkp.60.1.4

Pisarić, M. M. (2020). Encryption as an obstacle for criminal investigation and evidence collection. *Zbornik Radova*, *54*(3), 1079–1094. DOI: 10.5937/zrpfns54-26929

Piza, E. L. (2024, February 21). *Learning about ShotSpotter and gun violence - from Chicago*. Vital City. https://www.vitalcitynyc.org/articles/learning-about-shot-spotter-from-chicago

Pol, R. F. (2018, May 8). Anti-money laundering effectiveness: Assessing outcomes or ticking boxes? *Journal of Money Laundering Control*, *21*(2), 215–230. DOI: 10.1108/JMLC-07-2017-0029

Pongpaichet, S., Singh, V. K., Jain, R., & Pentland, A. (2013, October). Situation fencing: Making geofencing personal and dynamic. In V. K. Singh, T. Chua, R. Jain (Eds.), PDM '13 *Proceedings of the 1st ACM International Workshop on Personal Data Meets Distributed Multimedia* (3-10). ACM. https://doi.org/DOI: 10.1145/2509352.2509401

Potluri, S. (2025, July 12). Policy-Aware secure data governance in distributed information systems using explainable AI models. *International Journal of AI, BigData. Computational and Management Studies*, *6*(3), 1–10. DOI: 10.63282/3050-9416.IJAIBDCMS-V6I3P101

Pottle, J. (2019, October). Virtual reality and the transformation of medical education. *Future Healthcare Journal*, *6*(3), 181–185. DOI: 10.7861/fhj.2019-0036 PMID: 31660522

Prasad, S. K., & Aravindakshan, S. (2021). Playing catch up – privacy regimes in South Asia. In Çınar, Ö., & Vanberg, A. D. (Eds.), *The right to privacy revisited*. Routledge. DOI: 10.4324/9781003252191-5

Pratama, E. R., Renaldi, F., Umbara, F. R., & Djamal, E. D. (2020, September). Geofencing technology in monitoring of geriatric patients suffering from dementia and Alzheimer. In D. Sensuse, E. C. Djamal, A. A. Agus, F. Nugraha, & L. M. Hasani (Eds.), *2020 3rd International Conference on Computer and Informatics Engineering (IC2IE)*, Yogyakarta, Indonesia, pp. 106-111. IEEE. https://doi.org/DOI: 10.1109/IC2IE50715.2020.9274637

Prayatno, C., Tohari, M., & Susilowati, T. (2024, August 29). The impact of using technology and innovation in law enforcement in the era of digitalization. [JETBIS]. *Journal of Economics, Technology, and Business*, *3*(8), 1026–1033. DOI: 10.57185/jetbis.v3i8.127

Prayatno, C., Tohari, M., & Susilowati, T. (2024, August). The impact of using technology and innovation in law enforcement in the era of digitalization. *Journal of Economics. Technology & Business, 3*(8), 1026–1033.

Predictive policing: Leveraging AI and Machine Learning for crime prevention. (2024, November 18). New Media Communication. https://newmediacomm.com/predictive-policing-leveraging-ai-and-machine-learning-for-crime-prevention

Press Information Bureau, Government of India. (2025, February 25). *Integrating AI in India's judiciary and law enforcement.* [Press release]. https://www.pib.gov.in/PressReleasePage.aspx?PRID=2106239

Press Information Bureau. (2025). *Financial Intelligence Unit (FIU IND) issues notices for non-compliance to 25 offshore Virtual Digital Assets Service Providers (VDA SPs) under Section 13 of the Prevention of Money Laundering Act (PML), 2002.* Government of India. https://www.pib.gov.in/PressReleasePage.aspx?PRID=2173758

Price v. The Superior Court of Riverside County 93 Cal. App. 5th 13 (2023). https://casetext.com/case/price-v-the-superior-court

Price, L. (2021). Platform responsibility for online harms: Towards a duty of care for online hazards. *Journal of Medicine and Law, 13*(2), 238–261. DOI: 10.1080/17577632.2021.2022331

Prison Reform Trust. (2025, June 9). *Update and restart: Post-pandemic prison digitisation in England and Wales.* https://prisonreformtrust.org.uk/wp-content/uploads/2025/06/Update_and_Restart.pdf

Prisoner's Education Trust. (2025, December 10). *Getting connected: Digital provision and education in prison.* https://prisonerseducation.org.uk/wp-content/uploads/2025/12/Getting-Connected-December-2025.pdf

Privacy International. (2019, January 26). *State of privacy Pakistan.* https://privacyinternational.org/state-privacy/1008/state-privacy-pakistan

Pulley, J., Claflin, K., & Thompson, A. (2025, August 4). A review of virtual reality applications in agriculture education and recommendations for future research. *Journal of Agricultural Education, 66*(3), 15. DOI: 10.5032/jae.v66i3.3195

Qabajeh, I., Thabtah, F., & Chiclana, F. (2018, August). A recent review of conventional vs. automated cybersecurity anti-phishing techniques. *Computer Science Review, 29*, 44–55. DOI: 10.1016/j.cosrev.2018.05.003

Qawqzeh, Y., Shraah, A. A., Rizwan, A., Sánchez-Chero, M., More, L. A. V., & Shabaz, M. (2025, August 7). Exploring the effectiveness of virtual reality-based training for sustainable health and occupational safety in Industry 4.0. *Scientific Reports, 15*, 28930. DOI: 10.1038/s41598-025-14173-y PMID: 40775014

Qian, H., Xia, L., Ge, R., Fan, Y., Wang, Q., & Jing, Z. (2025, September 25). From black boxes to glass boxes: Explainable AI for trustworthy deepfake forensics. *Cryptography, 9*(4), 61. DOI: 10.3390/cryptography9040061

Qinjun, L., Tianwei, C., Zhao, Y., & Yuying, W. (2023). Facial recognition technology: A comprehensive overview. *Academic Journal of Computing & Information Science*, *6*(7), 15–26. DOI: 10.25236/AJCIS.2023.060703

Queudot, M., Charton, É., & Meurs, M.-J. (2020). Improving access to justice with legal chatbots. *Stats*, *3*(3), 356–375. DOI: 10.3390/stats3030023

Qureshi, S. M., Saeed, A., Almotiri, S. H., Ahmad, F., & Al Ghamdi, M. A. (2024, May 27). Deepfake forensics: A survey of digital forensic methods for multimodal deepfake identification on social media. *PeerJ. Computer Science*, *10*, e2037. DOI: 10.7717/peerj-cs.2037 PMID: 38855214

Raflesia, S. P., Taufiqurrahman, T., Lestarini, D., & Bardadi, A. (2021, March). A context-aware mobile-based system for crime prevention and emergencies. [IJEEI]. *Indonesian Journal of Electrical Engineering and Informatics*, *9*(1), 153–162. DOI: 10.52549/ijeei.v9i1.2624

Rahman. Md, A., & Rashid, H.-O. (2020, July 15). Digital Security Act and investigative journalism in Bangladesh: A critical analysis. *CenRaPS Journal of Social Sciences*, *2*(2), 216–236. DOI: 10.46291/cenraps.v2i2.32

Rahman, R. A., & Anggriawan, R. (2025, June). Deepfake and election crimes: Comparative perspectives from Indonesia, India, Pakistan, and the U.S. *Indonesian Comparative. Law Review*, *7*(2), 132–146.

Raj Goyal, H., & Prasad Mali, M. (2025). Digital evidence under the Indian legal system – Study of problems and perspective. *Journal of Neonatal Surgery*, *14*(32S), 10180–10189. DOI: 10.63682/jns.v14i32S.9809

Raja, A. (2024, April 26). Meet Crime GPT, the UP Police Department's AI tool for fighting crime. *India AI*. https://indiaai.gov.in/article/meet-crime-gpt-the-up-police-department-s-ai-tool-for-fighting-crime

Rajendran, R. K. V., A. I., T., M. P., Vetrivel, S., & N. R., W. B. (2025). The role of AI in enhancing access to justice and legal services. In H. Bajraktari (Ed.), *Advances in Electronic Government, Digital Divide, and Regional Development* (pp. 139–162). IGI Global. https://doi.org/DOI: 10.4018/979-8-3693-7205-0.ch008

Raji, I., & Sholademi, D. B. (2024). Predictive policing: The role of AI in crime prevention. *International Journal of Computer Applications Technology and Research*, *13*(10), 66–78. DOI: 10.7753/IJCATR1310.1006

Raj, R., & Kos, A. (2023). Artificial Intelligence: Evolution, developments, applications, and future scope. *Przeglad Elektrotechniczny*, *1*(2), 3–15. DOI: 10.15199/48.2023.02.01

Raj, R., & Patel, H. (2023, December). Predictive policing and the emerging contours of law enforcement in India: A study. *International Journal of Innovative Science and Research Technology*, *8*(2), 16–29. https://rru.ac.in/wp-content/uploads/2024/04/Volume-8-Issue-2-SMART-Policing-Innovations.pdf

Ramanaharan, R., Guruge, D. B., & Agbinya, J. I. (2025, December). DeepFake video detection: Insights into model generalisation — A systematic review. *Data and Information Management*, *9*(4), 100099. DOI: 10.1016/j.dim.2025.100099

Ramirez, M. D. (2013, March). Punitive sentiment. *Criminology, 51*(2), 329–364. DOI: 10.1111/1745-9125.12007

Rana, M., Nobi, M. N., Murali, B., & Sung, A. H. (2022, February 24). Deepfake detection: A systematic literature review. *IEEE Access : Practical Innovations, Open Solutions, 10*, 25494–25513. DOI: 10.1109/ACCESS.2022.3154404

Rana, P., Nagvekar, P., Agarwal, P., Savla, Y., Mishra, R., Gawade, A., & Rathod, N. (2025). AI courtroom: An AI-powered legal learning & trial prepbot. *Lex Localis: Journal of Local Self-Government, 23*(S6), 1480–1503. DOI: 10.52152/801995

Rani, M. (2024, September 12). Impacts and ethics of using Artificial Intelligence by the Indian Police. *Public Administration and Policy, 27*(2), 182–192. DOI: 10.1108/PAP-06-2023-0081

Rao, R. S., & Pais, A. R. (2017, April). Detecting phishing websites using automation of human behavior. [Conference proceedings]. *3rd ACM Workshop on Cyber-Physical System Security* (pp. 33–42). DOI: 10.1145/3055186.3055188

Ratzan, S. (2021, May 17). *Cell phone videos are ubiquitous, but are they admissible?* Ratzan Weissman & Bolt. https://www.rwblawyers.com/news/cell-phone-videos-are-ubiquitous-but-are-they-admissible

Ravishankar, K., & Anand, P. (2023, August 8). *AI judges: The question of AI's role in Indian judicial decision-making.* Centre for Comparative Constitutional Law and Administrative Law. https://www.calj.in/post/ai-judges-the-question-of-ai-s-role-in-indian-judicial-decision-making

Raynor, P., & Robinson, G. (2009). *Rehabilitation, crime, and justice.* Palgrave Macmillan.

Ready, J. T., & Young, J. T. (2015, June 14). The impact of on-officer video cameras on police-citizen contacts: Findings from a controlled experiment in Mesa, AZ. *Journal of Experimental Criminology, 11*(3), 445–458. https://link.springer.com/article/10.1007/s11292-015-9237-8. DOI: 10.1007/s11292-015-9237-8

Reaves, B. A. (2015, July). *Local police departments, 2013: Equipment and technology.* Bureau of Justice Statistics. https://bjs.ojp.gov/content/pub/pdf/lpd13et.pdf

Reclus, F., & Drouard, K. (2009). Geofencing for fleet & freight management. *2009 9th International Conference on Intelligent Transport Systems Telecommunications (ITST),* Lille, France, pp. 352-356. https://doi.org/DOI: 10.1109/ITST.2009.5399328

Rector, K., & Winton, R. (2020, September 21). Despite past denials, LAPD has used facial recognition software 30,000 times in last decade, records show. *Los Angeles Times.* https://www.latimes.com/california/story/2020-09-21/lapd-controversial-facial-recognition-software

Redmond, Washington. (n.d.). *Drone program.* https://www.redmond.gov/2161/Drone-Program

Regulation (EU) 2016/679 of the European Parliament and of the Council of 27 April 2016 on the protection of natural persons with regard to the processing of personal data and on the free movement of such data, and repealing Directive 95/46/EC (General Data Protection Regulation). (2016). *Official Journal of the European Union*, L119, 1–88. https://gdpr-info.eu/art-5-gdpr

Regulation (EU) 2018/302 of the European Parliament and of the Council. (2018, February 28). Official Journal of the European Union. LI 60/1. https://eur-lex.europa.eu/legal-content/EN/TXT/?uri=CELEX:32018R0302

Regulation 2016/679 OJ L 119 of the European Parliament and of the Council of 27 April 2016 on the protection of natural persons with regard to the processing of personal data and on the free movement of such data, and repealing Directive 95/46/EC (General Data Protection Regulation). *Official Journal of the European Union, 59,* 1-88. https://eur-lex.europa.eu/legal-content/EN/TXT/PDF/?uri=CELEX:32016R0679

Reisdorf, B. C., & Rikard, R. V. (2018, May). Digital rehabilitation: A model of reentry into the digital age. *The American Behavioral Scientist, 62*(9), 1273–1290. DOI: 10.1177/0002764218773817

Reisman, D., Schultz, J. M., Crawford, K., & Whittaker, M. (2018, April 9). Algorithmic impact assessments: A practical framework for public agency accountability. AI Now Institute. https://ainowinstitute.org/publications/algorithmic-impact-assessments-report-2

Rempel, E., Hamovitch, L., Zannella, L., & Burke, T. M. (2019, November). The power of technology: Examining the effects of digital visual evidence on jurors' processing of trial information. *Applied Cognitive Psychology, 33*(6), 1288–1295. DOI: 10.1002/acp.3598

Renda, A., & Caneppele, S. (2023, January). Compliant or not compliant? The challenges of anti-money laundering regulations in crypto assets: The case of Switzerland. *Journal of Money Laundering Control, 27*(2), 363–382. DOI: 10.1108/JMLC-04-2023-0078

Renuka, S. (2026, January 4). *Cryptocurrency fraud: Legal challenges in India.* Record of Law. https://recordoflaw.in/cryptocurrency-fraud-legal-challenges-in-india

Revolutionizing employee training: six benefits of virtual and augmented reality in the workplace. (2023, May 11). *Forbes.* https://www.forbes.com/councils/forbeshumanresourcescouncil/2023/05/11/revolutionizing-employee-training-six-benefits-of-virtual-and-augmented-reality-in-the-workplace

Ricciardelli, R., Maier, K., & Hannah-Moffat, K. (2015, November). Strategic masculinities: Vulnerabilities, risk and the production of prison masculinities. *Theoretical Criminology, 19*(4), 491–513. DOI: 10.1177/1362480614565849

Ricci, J. (2022). No drone zones: Assessing the FAA's role in implementing geofencing and the future of drone regulations in the United States. *University of Illinois Journal of Law. Technology & Policy, 2022*(1), 161–181.

Richardson, R., Schultz, J., & Crawford, K. (2019, May). Dirty data, bad predictions: How civil rights violations impact police data, predictive policing systems, and justice. *Big Data & Society, 10*(1), 192–233. https://ssrn.com/abstract=3333423

Riches, S., Iannelli, H., Reynolds, L., Fisher, H. L., Cross, S., & Attoe, C. (2022, July 19). Virtual reality-based training for mental health staff: A novel approach to increase empathy, compassion, and subjective understanding of service user experience. *Advances in Simulation (London, England), 7,* 19. DOI: 10.1186/s41077-022-00217-0 PMID: 35854343

Richmond, K. M., Muddamsetty, S. M., Gammeltoft-Hansen, T., Olsen, H. P., & Moeslund, T. B. (2023, December 19). Explainable AI and law: An evidential survey. *Digital Society : Ethics, Socio-Legal and Governance of Digital Technology, 3*(1), 1. Advance online publication. DOI: 10.1007/s44206-023-00081-z

Ridderbusch, K. (2025, August 25). Case study: How Dunwoody Police use drones to speed response and improve officer safety. *Police (Springfield), 1*, •••. https://www.police1.com/drones/case-study-how-dunwoody-police-use-drones-to-speed-response-and-improve-officer-safety

Riesthuis, P., & Woods, J. (2024, June 10). "That's just like, your opinion, man": The illusory truth effect on opinions. *Psychological Research, 88*(1), 284–306. DOI: 10.1007/s00426-023-01845-5 PMID: 37300704

Riley v. California, 573 U.S. 373 (2014).

Rind, A. (2026, February 25). *Video evidence Authentication: Standards courts expect in 2026*. Vidizmo Digital Evidence Management System. https://digitalevidence.ai/blog/video-evidence-authentication-standards-courts

Ring Alarm monitoring services for your location. (2024, March 7). Ring. https://ring.com/gb/en/support/articles/xk0je/Ring-Alarm-availability-in-Europe

Rizzo, A., Princiotta, E., & Iuele, G. (2023, December). Exploring the link between smartphone use, recorded violence, and social sharing in 80 case studies in Italy. *Psych, 5*(4), 1241–1255. DOI: 10.3390/psych5040082

Rodman, D. (2010, September). Unmanned aerial vehicles in the service of the Isreal Air Force: "They will soar on wings like eagles.". *Middle East Review of International Affairs (Online), 14*(3), 77–87.

Roelofs, T. (2017, February 7). Broken: The human toll of Michigan's unemployment fraud saga. Bridge Michigan. https://bridgemi.com/michigan-government/broken-human-toll-michigans-unemployment-fraud-saga

Roffel, M., & Lin, X. (2023, August). Write Blocker for Internet of Things Flash technologies. In *2023 20th Annual International Conference on Privacy, Security and Trust* (PST) (pp. 1-10). IEEE. https://doi.org/DOI: 10.1109/PST58708.2023.10320158

Rogers, E. M. (2003, August 16). *Diffusion of innovations* (5th ed.). Free Press.

Rohilla, N. (2025, June). History and evolution of police system in India. *Journal of International Research for Engineering and Management, 5*(6), 1. https://joirem.com/wp-content/uploads/journal/published_paper/volume-05/issue-6/J_mbEhydGj.pdf

Role of video evidence in modern legal practices, The. (2025, July 28). Marko Law. https://www.markolaw.com/post/the-role-of-video-evidence-in-modern-legal-practices

Romero Moreno, F. (2024). Generative AI and deepfakes: A human rights approach to tackling harmful content. *International Review of Law Computers & Technology, 38*(3), 297–326. DOI: 10.1080/13600869.2024.2324540

Ron, D., & Shamir, A. (2014, October 8). How did Dread Pirate Roberts acquire and protect his bitcoin wealth? In *Lecture Notes in Computer Science, 8438,* 3-15. https://doi.org/DOI: 10.1007/978-3-662-44774-1_1

Rosen, L. Z. (2025). Deepfakes and intimate partner violence: The TAKE IT DOWN Act and other proposed federal legislation. *NYU Annual Survey of American Law.* https://annualsurveyofamericanlaw.org/wp-content/uploads/2025/07/02_Note-Rosen_FINAL-1.pdf

Rössler, A., Cozzolino, D., Verdoliva, L., Riess, C., Thies, J., & Nießner, M. (2019, August 26). FaceForensics++: Learning to detect manipulated facial images (arXiv:1901.08971). *arXiv.* /arXiv.1901.08971DOI: 10.1109/ICCV.2019.00009

Ross, S., Wood, M. A., Baird, R., & Lundberg, K. (2023). Digital service delivery applications in corrections: A scoping review. In *Report to the Criminology Research Advisory Council* [Report]. Australian Institute of Criminology., DOI: 10.52922/crg77109

Rowland, C. (2025, October). *Public services performance tracker 2025: The criminal justice system.* Nuffield Foundation Institute for Government. https://www.instituteforgovernment.org.uk/sites/default/files/2025-10/performance-tracker-2025-criminal-justice-system.pdf

Royo, P., Asenjo, À., Trujillo, J., Çetin, E., & Barrado, C. (2022, November 17). Enhancing drones for law enforcement and capacity monitoring at open large events. *Drones (Basel), 6*(11), 359. DOI: 10.3390/drones6110359

Ryan, M. (2025, September 22). *Lockheed Martin unveils stealth combat drone.* AVWeb. https://avweb.com/aviation-news/lockheed-martin-new-stealth-combat-drone

Sabharwal, N. S., Joseph, R. S., Bankar, A. C., & Talmale, A. V. (2021, March). Accessing silenced voices? Diary method as a source of data for understanding higher education experiences of students from socially excluded groups. In Cao, X., & Henderson, E. F. (Eds.), *Exploring Diary Methods in Higher Education Research: Opportunities, Choices, Challenges* (pp. 131–144). Routledge., DOI: 10.4324/9780429326318-13

Sadler, L. (2020, October 22). *Geofencing guidance for Urban Vehicle Access Regulations* (working document). ReVeAL Project. https://civitas-reveal.eu/wp-content/uploads/2020/08/Note-on-Geofencing-for-UVAR_Lucy-Sadler-Sadler-Consultants-1.pdf

Saks, M. J., & Faigman, D. L. (2008). Failed Forensics: How forensic science lost its way and how it might yet find it. *Annual Review of Law and Social Science, 4*(1), 149–171. DOI: 10.1146/annurev.lawsocsci.4.110707.172303

Salawu, R. O., Bolatito, A.-O. S., & Masibo, S. (2023). Theoretical and conceptual frameworks in clarification. *European Chemical Bulletin, 12*(12), 2103–2117. DOI: 10.48047/ecb/2023.12.12.139

Saluja, D., Kukreja, H., Saini, A., Tegwal, D., Nagrath, P., & Hemanth, J. (2023, November). Analysis and comparison of various deep learning models to implement suspicious activity recognition in CCTV surveillance. *Intelligent Decision Technologies, 17*(4), 917–942. DOI: 10.3233/IDT-230469

Samek, W., & Müller, K.-R. (2019). Towards explainable Artificial Intelligence. In W. Samek, G. Montavon, A. Vedaldi, L. Hansen, & K.-R. Müller (Eds.), *Explainable AI: Interpreting, explaining and visualizing deep learning* (pp. 5-22). Spring Nature. DOI: 10.1007/978-3-030-28954-6_1

Sanders, S. (2022, January 25). Justices affirm Crawford's application of Sixth Amendment confrontation clause to testimonial evidence. SCOTUSblog. https://www.scotusblog.com/2022/01/justices-affirm-crawfords-application-of-sixth-amendment-confrontation-clause-to-testimonial-evidence

Sanders, C. B., & Henderson, S. (2013). Police 'empires' and information technologies: Uncovering material and organizational barriers to information sharing in Canadian police services. *Policing and Society*, *23*(2), 243–260. DOI: 10.1080/10439463.2012.703196

Sandoval, M.-P., de Almeida Vau, M., Solaas, J., & Rodrigues, L. (2024, November). Threat of deepfakes to the criminal justice system: A systematic review. *Crime Science*, *13*(1), 41. DOI: 10.1186/s40163-024-00239-1

Sar, A., Roy, S., Choudhury, T., & Abraham, A. (2025, August 28). Zero-shot visual deepfake detection: Can AI predict and prevent fake content before it's created? *Foundations and Trends in Signal Processing*, *19*(3), 212–370. DOI: 10.1561/2000000136

Sarkar, A., Mishra, A. K., Singh, U. P., Hassan, S., Munda, G. S., & Singh, P. (2025, July). Real-Time crime prediction in India using machine learning. *International Journal for Research in Applied Science and Engineering Technology*, *13*(7), 641–646. DOI: 10.22214/ijraset.2025.73053

Sasaki, I., Arikawa, M., Lu, M., Utsumi, T., & Sato, R. (2025, September). *Activating location-based storytelling in a city: Geofence identification from crowdsourced mobile sensing*. [Conference paper]. The International Archives of the Photogrammetry, Remote Sensing and Spatial Information Sciences, *48*(4), 9th International Conference on Smart Data and Smart Cities. https://doi.org/DOI: 10.5194/isprs-archives-XLVIII-4-W16-2025-99-2025

Sathilkumar, A., & Graham, N. (2018). Cryptocurrency: Law enforcement challenges and opportunities. A risk perspective. *Australia and New Zealand Society of Evidence Based Policing*, *3*(1), 11–13.

Saunders, J., Hunt, P., & Hollywood, J. S. (2016, August). Predictions put into practice: A quasi-experimental evaluation of Chicago's predictive policing pilot. *Journal of Experimental Criminology*, *12*(3), 347–371. DOI: 10.1007/s11292-016-9272-0

Sauser, M. K. (2025, July-August). Unmanned aircraft and the revolution in operational warfare: Preparing the U.S. Army for the age of unmanned systems. *Military Review*, •••, 54–64. https://www.armyupress.army.mil/Journals/Military-Review/English-Edition-Archives/July-August-2025/Unmanned-Aircraft-Revolution

Sawyers, R. (2022, Spring). For geofences: An originalist approach to the Fourth Amendment. *George Mason Law Review*, *29*(3), 787–826. https://lawreview.gmu.edu/print__issues/for-geofences-an-originalist-approach-to-the-fourth-amendment

Sayal, A., Gupta, A., & Vasundhara, C., M, Y. B., Gupta, V., & Maheshwari, H. (2024, April). Crime detection using data mining techniques. In *2024 Sixth International Conference on Computational Intelligence and Communication Technologies (CCICT)* (pp. 200-204). IEEE. https://doi.org/DOI: 10.1109/CCICT62777.2024.00041

Sayler, K. (2015, June). *A world of proliferated drones: A technology primer.* Center for a New Americal Security. https://drones.cnas.org/wp-content/uploads/2016/03/CNAS-World-of-Drones_052115.pdf

Say, T., Alkan, M., & Kocak, A. (2025, January 17). Advancing GAN deepfake detection: Mixed datasets and comprehensive artifact analysis. *Applied Sciences (Basel, Switzerland), 15*(2), 923. DOI: 10.3390/app15020923

Sayyed, H. (2024, April). Artificial intelligence and criminal liability in India: Exploring legal implications and challenges. *Cogent Social Sciences, 10*(1), 2343195. DOI: 10.1080/23311886.2024.2343195

Schembri, T. J. (2023, Autumn). The rise of technology and its effect on search and seizure analysis: The constitutionality of geofencing warrants under the Supreme Court's Fourth Amendment jurisprudence. *SSRN, 75*(1), 129–154. DOI: 10.2139/ssrn.4430269

Schmerber v. California, 384 U.S. 757. (1966). *Justia U.S. Supreme Court.* https://supreme.justia.com/cases/federal/us/384/757

Schmitt, M., & Flechais, I. (2024, October). Digital deception: Generative artificial intelligence in social engineering and phishing. *Artificial Intelligence Review, 57*(12), 324. DOI: 10.1007/s10462-024-10973-2

Schwartz, G. D. (2024). When disciplines disagree: The admissibility of computer-generated Forensic evidence in the criminal justice system. In Chappell, K., Dickerson, M., Dorsey, S., Gonzalez, V., McVoy, K., Orton, S., Siqueira, A., Stolmack, A., Vazquez, A., & Zahran, M. (Eds.), *UCLA Law Review, 72, 174–211.*

Scott, T., & Cunningham, C. (1996, Summer). *John Barnes of Plymouth.* The Plymouth Colony Archive Project. http://www.histarch.illinois.edu/plymouth/BARNES2.htm

Segall, S. (2013). Jurisdictional challenges in the United States government's move to cloud computing technology. *Fordham Intellectual Property. Media and Entertainment Law Journal, 23*(3), 1105–1153.

Shaath, S. (2019, March 27). Decline of soap operas: was OJ Simpson to blame? *BBC.* https://www.bbc.com/news/world-us-canada-47585335

Shahid, M. K., Shou-lian, T., & Liu, C. (2007). Competition and liberalization policies and regulations for telecommunications industries in China and Pakistan: A comparative analysis. *International Journal of Management Science and Engineering Management, 2*(4), 268–277. DOI: 10.1080/17509653.2007.10671026

Shamsabadi, A., Mojdeganlou, H., Barzegary, A., Fakhfouri, A., Azad, K., Heydari, M., Pashaei, Z., & Mehraeen, E. (2022, March 12). Opportunities, threats and solution techniques of deep-fake technology: A systematic review. [Conference proceedings]. *20th International Conference on E-Society and 18th International Conference on Mobile Learning* (pp. 19-25). DOI: 10.33965/ES_ML2022_202202L003

Sharan, S. P., Choi, M., Shah, S., Goel, H., Omama, M., & Chinchali, S. (2025, April 25). Neuro-symbolic evaluation of text-to-video models using formal verification (arXiv:2411.16718). *arXiv*. /arXiv.2411.16718DOI: 10.1109/CVPR52734.2025.00786

Sharma, A., & Gupta, S. (2022). Origin of police system in India and the world. *International Journal of Law, Management, &. Humanities (Washington)*, *5*(2), 792–806. https://doij.org/10.10000/IJLMH.112900

Shavers, B. (2013). Physical investigations. *Placing the suspect behind the keyboard: using digital forensics and investigative techniques to identify cybercrime suspects*. (p. 53-84)(. https://doi.org/DOI: 10.1016/B978-1-59-749985-9.00003-4

Shekhar, C. (2025, July 12). *Jane Street case marks a turning point in SEBI's index governance strategy*. Zenodo (CERN European Organization for Nuclear Research). DOI: 10.2139/ssrn.5341047

Sheldon, K. M., & Kasser, T. (1998, December). Pursuing personal goals: Skills enable progress but not all progress is beneficial. *Personality and Social Psychology Bulletin*, *24*(12), 1319–1331. DOI: 10.1177/01461672982412006

Sheppard, K. G., & Welsh, B. C. (2022, May-June). Can police use of less-than-lethal weapons reduce harm during violent police-citizen encounters? A systematic review and directions for future research. *Aggression and Violent Behavior*, *64*, 101748. DOI: 10.1016/j.avb.2022.101748

Shoderu, G., Baror, S., & Venter, H. (2024, March). A privacy-compliant process for digital forensics readiness. [Conference proceedings]. *International Conference on Cyber Warfare and Security, 19*(1), 337–347. DOI: 10.34190/iccws.19.1.2055

Shoemaker, P. (2025, November 6). *Deepfakes and identity verification: What's at risk*. Identity. https://www.identity.org/the-growing-threat-of-deepfakes-to-identity-verification-processes

Shuai, T., Beng, S., Khalid, F. B., & Rahmat, R. W. B. O. K. (2025, October 8). Advances in facial micro-expression detection and recognition: A comprehensive review. *Information (Basel)*, *16*(10), 876. DOI: 10.3390/info16100876

Siani, J. A. (2024). Empowering justice: Exploring the applicability of AI in the judicial system. *Journal of Law and Legal Research Development.*, *1*(1), 24–28. DOI: 10.69662/jllrd.v1i1.6

Siegel, D., Krätzer, C., Seidlitz, S., & Dittmann, J. (2022, January). Forensic data model for artificial intelligence based media forensics - Illustrated on the example of DeepFake detection. *IS&T International Symposium on Electronic Imaging*, *34*(4), 324. DOI: 10.2352/EI.2022.34.4.MWSF-324

Sifat, I., Tariq, S. A., & van Donselaar, D. (2024, January). Suspicious trading in nonfungible tokens (NFTs). *Information & Management*, *61*(1), 103898. DOI: 10.1016/j.im.2023.103898

Silalahi, J. A. S. (2023, May 20). The application of criminal law in the digital age: A literature review of challenges and opportunities. *Innovative: Journal of Social Science Research, 3*(2), 3658-3668. https://j-innovative.org/index.php/Innovative/article/view/678

Silver, C. (2025). Is the data collected by license plate readers public record? Here's what Florida law says. *News6*. https://www.clickorlando.com/news/local/2025/11/25/is-the-data-collected-by-license-plate-readers-public-record-heres-what-florida-law-says

Simmler, M., & Canova, G. (2024). Facial recognition technology in law enforcement: Regulating data analysis of another kind. *Computer Law & Security Review*, *56*, 106092. DOI: 10.1016/j.clsr.2024.106092

Singh, I. (2022, October 19). *Norway detains 7 Russian drone pilots, including Putin associate's son.* Drone DJ. https://dronedj.com/2022/10/19/norway-russian-drone-pilot-arrest

Singh, A., Ikuesan, R. A., & Venter, H. (2022, February 14). Secure storage model for digital forensic readiness. *IEEE Access : Practical Innovations, Open Solutions*, *10*, 19469–19480. DOI: 10.1109/ACCESS.2022.3151403

Singh, R. K. (2024). The evolution of the Indian police: From colonial legacy to contemporary challenges. *International Journal of Multidisciplinary Trends*, *6*(8, 8A), 50–54. DOI: 10.22271/multi.2024.v6.i8a.467

Singh, S., & Devi, L. (2025, December 17). *Reliability and admissibility of AI-Generated Forensic Evidence in criminal trials.* arXiv. https://arxiv.org/abs/2601.06048

Sinha, N., & Dutta, M. (2025). Proportionality in Indian and South African review jurisprudence – A comparative analysis. *Global Journal of Comparative Law*, *14*(3), 326–358. DOI: 10.1163/2211906X-14030004

Skaramuca, D. (2025). Evaluating the Admissibility of AI Evidence in Criminal Proceedings: Legal Standards and Ethical Implications. SPLITLAW, 155.

Skogan, W. G. (2017). Stop-and-frisk and trust in police in Chicago. In Oberwittler, D., & Roché, S. (Eds.), *Police-citizen relations: A comparative investigation of sources and impediments of legitimacy around the world* (pp. 246–265). Routledge. DOI: 10.4324/9781315406664-11

Slobogin, C. (2012, June). Making the most of United States v. Jones in a surveillance society: A statutory implementation of Mosaic theory. *Duke Journal of Constitutional Law & Public Policy*. https://scholarship.law.vanderbilt.edu/faculty-publications/260

Smith, V. S. (2020, June). *Exploring the potential of digital technology to reduce recidivism: A Delphi study on the digitalisation of prison education.* [PhD Dissertation, Ashford University].

Smith, M. J., Harrington, M., Ross, B., Quinn, C. R., Musan, L. P., Brydon, D. M., Johnson, J. E., Cuddeback, G. S., Smith, J. D., Merle, J. L., Burke-Miller, J. K., Jordan, N., Bell, M. D., Friedman, B., Kryscio, P., & Suganuma, A. (2025). A pragmatic randomized controlled trial of virtual reality job interview training in prison employment services. *Journal of Experimental Criminology*. Advance online publication. DOI: 10.1007/s11292-025-09684-7

Smith, M., & Miller, S. (2021). *Biometric identification, law and ethics*. Springer., DOI: 10.1007/978-3-030-90256-8

Smurfing in money laundering: Understanding smurfing techniques and AML responses across regulated sectors. (2025, June 12). Dilisense. https://dilisense.com/en/insights/what-is-smurfing-in-money-laundering

Snap Inc. law enforcement guide. (2025, July 1). Snapchat. https://www.snapchat.com/lawenforcement

Sneha, C. S., Mohanta, A., & Shreya. (2024, November). Navigating AI liability in criminal law. In A. Ahmadi, A. Mna, & A. Slimani (Eds.), *Renewable Energy and the Economic Welfare of Society* (pp. 311-334). IGI Global. https://doi.org/DOI: 10.4018/979-8-3693-7580-8.ch014

Socol De La Osa, D. U., & Remolina, N. (2025). AI at the Bench: Legal and ethical challenges of informing – or misinforming – judicial decision-making through generative AI. *International Journal for Research in Applied Science and Engineering Technology, 13*(5), 595–606. DOI: 10.22214/ijraset.2025.70243

Sokler, B. D., Hecht, A., Fjeld, C. R., & Tikhonovsky, M. (2024, October 3). *FTC launches Operation AI Comply with five enforcement actions involving AI misuse -AI: The Washington Report.* Mintz. https://www.mintz.com/insights-center/viewpoints/54731/2024-10-03-ftc-launches-operation-ai-comply-five-enforcement

Solomon, T. (2025, October 20). French audit reveals that major parts of the Louvre have no cameras, and other security flaws. *Art News.* https://www.artnews.com/art-news/news/french-audit-louvre-robbery-security-flaws-no-cameras-1234757968

Soni, T., Kaur, R., Gupta, D., Sharma, A., & Gupta, G. (2023, April). The cybersecurity ecosystem: challenges, risk and emerging technologies. [Conference paper]. *7th International Conference on Trends in Electronics and Informatics (ICOEI), Tirunelveli, India* (pp. 699–703). DOI: 10.1109/ICOEI56765.2023.10125775

Sood, Y. (2022, October 30). Addressing algorithmic bias in India: Ethical implications and pitfalls. SSRN *Electronic Journal.* https://dx.doi.org/DOI: 10.2139/ssrn.4466681

Soss, J., Fording, R. C., & Schram, S. F. (2011). *Disciplining the poor: Neoliberal paternalism and the persistent power of race.* University of Chicago Press. DOI: 10.7208/chicago/9780226768786.001.0001

Sousa Antunes, H., Freitas, P. M., Oliveira, A. L., Martins Pereira, C., Vaz de Sequeira, E., & Barreto Xavier, L. (Eds.). (2024). *Multidisciplinary perspectives on Artificial Intelligence and the law.* Springer International, Law, Governance and Technology Series 58. DOI: 10.1007/978-3-031-41264-6

Spunta il video selfie choc del killer con il rivale ancora Morente. (2025, June 3). *Padova Oggi.* https://www.padovaoggi.it/cronaca/villafrancapadovana-video-delitto-processo-3-giugno-2025.html

Starks, M. A. (2025, November 19). Integration of drone-delivered AEDs into emergency response: A multi-center trial. *Cardiovascular Business.* https://cardiovascularbusiness.com/topics/clinical/heart-rhythm/drones-deliver-aeds-first-time-united-states

State v. Contreras-Sanchez, A22-1579, 5 N.W.3d 151 (Minn. Ct. App. 2024). https://casetext.com/case/state-v-contreras-sanchez

State v. Loomis, 371 Wis. 2d 235, 881 N.W.2d 749 (Wis. 2016).

Steinmetz, K. F., Schaefer, B. P., & Kurtz, D. L. (2025). Computer crime units and task forces. In *Policing the Digital Void: Cybercrime Investigations in the US* (pp. 47-59). Springer Nature Switzerland. https://doi.org/DOI: 10.1007/978-3-031-98040-4_4

Stender, S. (2024). Circumventing the Fourth Amendment: The unconstitutional nature of geofence warrants. *Utah Law Review, 2024*(3), 733–759. DOI: 10.63140/rv3lhh.e-i

Stephen, D., Schniedermann, A., Lovakov, A., Schmidt, M., Ottaviani, M., Sorgatz, N., Romero, R. C., Möller, T., Aman, V., & Stahlschmidt, S. (2025, August 22). Implicit reporting standards in bibliometric research: What can reviewers' comments tell us about reporting completeness? *arXiv*. 10.48550/arXiv.2508.16276 DOI: 10.51408/issi2025_132

Stewart, S. T. (2017, September 19). How tablets are helping clean up one Ariz. prison. *Corrections1*. https://www.corrections1.com/products/corrections/articles/how-tablets-are-helping-clean-up-one-ariz-prison-pcpVlpSvZVVGHICO

Stiernströmer, E. (2026, January). Facial recognition technology in law enforcement- a scoping review of existing empirical studies. *Police Practice and Research*, *1*(25), 1–25. Advance online publication. DOI: 10.1080/15614263.2026.2627208

Stockwell, S., Hughes, M., Ashurst, C., & Ní Loideáin, N. (2024, March). *The future of biometric technology for policing and law enforcement: Informing UK regulation*. Centre for Emerging Technology and Security (CETaS), Alan Turing Institute. https://cetas.turing.ac.uk/sites/default/files/2024-03/cetas_research_report_-_the_future_of_biometric_technology_for_policing_and_law_enforcement_0.pdf

Storbeck, M. (2022, June). *Artificial intelligence and predictive policing: Risks and challenges*. European Crime Prevention Network. https://eucpn.org/sites/default/files/document/files/PP%20%282%29.pdf

Stubbs, G. (2025, June 12). Addressing the potential for training scars: Investigating the risk of using extended reality in police training. *Policing. Journal of Policy Practice*, *19*, paaf019. Advance online publication. DOI: 10.1093/police/paaf019

Substance Abuse and Mental Health Services Administration. (2023, April 24). *What is mental health?* https://www.samhsa.gov/mental-health/what-is-mental-health

Sullivan, D. (2019, November 8). *Digital transformation and law enforcement: How smart technology can reduce response times, improve public safety and save lives*. LinkedIn. https://www.linkedin.com/pulse/digital-transformation-law-enforcement-how-smart-can-reduce-sullivan

Sur, A. (2022, January 19). Delhi Police deploys facial recognition systems, CCTV cameras ahead of Republic Day: Report. *Medianama*. https://www.medianama.com/2022/01/223-facial-recognition-systems-republic-day-report

Surveillance Devices Act 2007 No 64. (2024). New South Wales Government. https://legislation.nsw.gov.au/view/whole/pdf/inforce/2024-07-01/act-2007-064

Synthetic identity fraud & its importance in a digital world. (2025, February 18). Moody's. https://www.moodys.com/web/en/us/kyc/resources/insights/synthetic-identities-and-why-they-are-important-in-todays-digital-landscape.html

Tackling crypto crime: 2023 survey of law enforcement. (2023, December 23). TRM Labs. https://www.trmlabs.com/reports-and-whitepapers/tackling-crypto-crime-2023-survey-of-law-enforcement

Taher, M. A. (2025). Right to access the internet vis-à-vis freedom of expression: Bangladesh in context. In *The Asian Yearbook of Human Rights and Humanitarian Law* (pp. 35–60). Brill Nijhoff., DOI: 10.1163/9789004748736_003

Tampa Police Department. (2026, January 8). *New year, new tech for Tampa Police Department* [Press release]. https://www.tampa.gov/news/2026-01/new-year-new-tech-tampa-police-department-178786

Tan, D., Yang, Y., Niu, C., Li, S., Yang, D., & Tan, B. (2025, August). A review of deep learning based multimodal forgery detection for video and audio. *Discover Applied Sciences*, *7*(9), 987. DOI: 10.1007/s42452-025-07629-3

Tang, J., Cui, Y., Li, Q., Ren, K., Liu, J., & Buyya, R. (2016, June 6). Ensuring security and privacy preservation for cloud data services. *ACM Computing Surveys*, *49*(1), 1–39. DOI: 10.1145/2906153

Tanimu, J. A., & Abada, W. (2025, December). Addressing cybersecurity challenges in robotics: A comprehensive overview. *Cyber Security and Applications*, *3*, 100074. DOI: 10.1016/j.csa.2024.100074

Tashman, A. (2021, December 1). "Malicious Deepfakes"—How California's A.B. 730 tries (and fails) to address the internet's burgeoning political crisis. *Loyola of Los Angeles Law Review*, *54*(4), 8. https://digitalcommons.lmu.edu/llr/vol54/iss4/8

Tavawalla, H., & Majumdar, A. (2024, August 19), Impact of India's new privacy law on the geospatial industry. *The National Law Review, XIV*(336). https://natlawreview.com/article/impact-indias-new-privacy-law-geospatial-industry

Technology. (n.d.). New York City Police Department. https://www.nyc.gov/site/nypd/about/about-nypd/equipment-tech/technology.page

Tennant, R., Hiller, L., Fishwick, R., Platt, S., Joseph, S., Weich, S., Parkinson, J., Secker, J., & Stewart-Brown, S. (2007, November). The Warwick-Edinburgh Mental Well-being Scale (WEMWBS): Development and UK validation. *Health and Quality of Life Outcomes*, *5*(1), 63. DOI: 10.1186/1477-7525-5-63 PMID: 18042300

Termanini, R. (2023). *Drone delivery methods and how to communicate with the destination*. Biomedical Defense Principles to Counter DNA Deep Hacking., DOI: 10.1016/B978-0-323-99914-4.00004-7

Thacker, H. (2025, April 17). How Mumbai Police are using technology to prevent crime. *The CSR Journal*. https://thecsrjournal.in/mumbai-police-artificial-intelligence-ai-technology-prevent-crime/

The Centre for Social Justice. (2021, January). *Digital technology in prisons: Unlocking relationships, learning and skills in UK prisons*. https://www.centreforsocialjustice.org.uk/wp-content/uploads/2021/01/CSJJ8671-Digital-In-Prisons-210604.pdf

The Nigeria Data Protection Act of 2023. (2023, July 1). *Federal Republic of Nigeria Official Gazette, 110*(119), A719-758. https://cert.gov.ng/ngcert/resources/Nigeria_Data_Protection_Act_2023.pdf

The US and Canada join forces to combat scams, seizing millions in crypto. (2025, August 14). Chain analysis. https://www.chainalysis.com/blog/us-and-canada-join-forces-to-combat-crypto-scams

The use of surveillance technology in law enforcement. (2023, February 23). Criminal Justice - iResearchNet. https://criminal-justice.iresearchnet.com/criminal-justice-process/impact-of-technology/the-use-of-surveillance-technology-in-law-enforcement

Thomas, C. (2022). Automating judicial discretion: How algorithmic risk assessments in pretrial adjudications violate equal protection rights on the basis of race. *Minnesota Journal of Law & Inequality, 40*(2), Article 5. https://scholarship.law.umn.edu/lawineq/vol40/iss2/5

Thomas, A. (2020, Winter). No place to hide: Private implications of geolocation tracking and geofencing. *SciTech Lawyer, 16*(2), 20–23.

Thompson, S. K., Sandhu, A., & Koziol, C. (2025, June). 'History is written by the victor ... but in some cases, it's also now written by the recordings': Body-worn cameras and the double-edged nature of police visibility. *Theoretical Criminology*, •••, 1–20. DOI: 10.1177/13624806251342569 PMID: 41799372

ical, G.-M. (2025). Facial recognition and biometric systems: Benefits and challenges for law enforcement. *Land Forces Academy Review, 30*(2), 249–259. DOI: 10.2478/raft-2025-0024

Tipper, S., Atlam, H. F., & Lallie, H. S. (2024, October 24). An investigation into the utilisation of CNN with LSTM for video deepfake detection. *Applied Sciences (Basel, Switzerland), 14*(21), 9754. DOI: 10.3390/app14219754

Tobler, W. R. (1970, June). A computer movie simulating urban growth in the Detroit region. *Economic Geography, 26*, 234–240. DOI: 10.2307/143141

Tóth, D., & Gáspár, Z. (2020, December 1). Jurisdictional challenges of cybercrime. *Journal of Eastern European Criminal Law, 7*(2), 101–118.

Tozi, F. (2024, June). Ride-hailing corporations, territorial selectivity, and urban algorithmic inequalities in Brazil. In Vale, M., Ferreira, D., & Rodrigues, N. (Eds.), *Geographies of the Platform Economy. Economic Geography* (pp. 33–48). Springer., DOI: 10.1007/978-3-031-53594-9_3

Transforming urban living: The expansion of smart city infrastructure in Chicago. (2025, April 15). The Chicago Journal. https://thechicagojournal.com/the-expansion-of-smart-city-infrastructure

Trigger, R. (2025, December 14). Moment Ahmed Al Ahmed disarms gunman Sajid Akram captured on film. *ABC News.* https://www.abc.net.au/news/2025-12-14/bondi-shooter-tackled-and-disarmed-by-possible-civilian/106141690

Truck plows through crowd at Christmas market in Berlin, killing 12. (2016, December 19). *CBS News.* https://www.cbsnews.com/news/truck-plows-through-crowd-christmas-market-berlin-germany

Tuhin, M. (2025, April 9). What is facial recognition technology? How it works and why it matters in 2025. *Science News Today.* https://www.sciencenewstoday.org/what-is-facial-recognition-technology-how-it-works-and-why-it-matters-in-2025

Turner, A. B., McCombie, S., & Uhlmann, A. J. (2020, November 30). Analysis techniques for illicit bitcoin transactions. *Frontiers of Computer Science, 2*, 600596. DOI: 10.3389/fcomp.2020.600596

Tursi, R. (2023, March). Gone fishing: Casting a wide net using geofence warrants. *Washington Law Review (Seattle, Wash.), 98*(1), 323–362.

Turyn, N. (2025, October 23). Convicted killer Jens Soering reacts to Netflix docuseries 'Till Murder Do Us Part'. *ABC13 News.* https://wset.com/news/local/convicted-killer-jens-soering-reacts-to-netflix-docuseries-till-murder-do-us-part-november-2023

U.S. Attorney's Office. Southern District of New York. (2019, November 21). *Former partner of Locke Lord LLP convicted in Manhattan Federal Court of conspiracy to commit money laundering and bank fraud in connection with scheme to launder $400 million of OneCoin fraud proceeds.* [Press release]. https://www.justice.gov/usao-sdny/pr/former-partner-locke-lord-llp-convicted-manhattan-federal-court-conspiracy-commit-money

U.S. Customs and Border Protection. (2023, August 18). *Air and marine operations' unmanned aircraft system.* https://www.cbp.gov/about/history/cbp-20-20-establishment/air-and-marine-operations-unmanned-aircraft-system

U.S. Department of Homeland Security. (2025, July). *TechNote: Drone as first responder.* https://www.dhs.gov/sites/default/files/2025-07/25_0708_st_dfrtn.pdf

U.S. Department of Justice. (2021, June 7). *Department of Justice seizes $2.3 million in cryptocurrency paid to the ransomware extortionists Darkside.* [Press release]. https://www.justice.gov/archives/opa/pr/department-justice-seizes-23-million-cryptocurrency-paid-ransomware-extortionists-darkside

U.S. Department of Justice. (2024, December 3). *Artificial intelligence and criminal justice: Final report.* https://www.justice.gov/olp/media/1381796/dl

U.S. Department of Justice. Federal Aviation Administration, Department of Homeland Security, & Federal Communications Commission. (2020, August). *Advisory on the application of Federal laws to the acquisition and use of technology to detect and mitigate Unmanned Aircraft Systems.* https://www.faa.gov/sites/faa.gov/files/uas/resources/c_uas/Interagency_Legal_Advisory_on_UAS_Detection_and_Mitigation_Technologies.pdf

U.S. Department of the Treasury. (2022, August 8). *U.S. Treasury sanctions notorious virtual currency mixer Tornado Cash.* [Press release]. https://home.treasury.gov/news/press-releases/jy0916

Ueno, H. (2023). Artificial Intelligence as dual-use technology. In Hatzilygeroudis, I. K., Tsihrintzis, G. A., & Jain, L. C. (Eds.), *Intelligent systems reference library* (pp. 7–32)., DOI: 10.1007/978-3-031-22371-6_2

Ulvin, O. E., Skjærseth, E. Å., Krüger, A. J., Thorsen, K., Nordseth, T., & Haugland, H. (2023, October 3). Can video communication in the emergency medical communication Centre improve dispatch precision? A before–after study in Norwegian helicopter emergency medical services. *BMJ Open, 13*(10), e077395. DOI: 10.1136/bmjopen-2023-077395 PMID: 37899141

Umbach, R., Henry, N., Beard, G., & Berryessa, C. (2024, May). Non-consensual synthetic Intimate imagery: Prevalence, attitudes, and knowledge in 10 countries. [Conference proceedings]. *CHI Conference on Human Factors in Computing Systems,* 779 (pp. 1–20). DOI: 10.1145/3613904.3642382

Understanding India's cybersecurity policy Frameworks: IT Act, national cybersecurity policy, and strategy. (2025, January 10). RSM India. https://www.rsm.global/india/insights/consulting-insights/cybersecurity-policy-frameworks

Understanding the nuances between 'film,' 'movie,' and 'video.' (2024, June 12). WeVideo. https://www.wevideo.com/blog/film-movie-video-comparison

United States Courts. (n.d.) *History of cameras, broadcasting, and remote public access in courts.* https://www.uscourts.gov/court-records/access-court-proceedings/remote-public-access-proceedings/history-cameras-broadcasting-and-remote-public-access-courts

United States of America v. Jamarr Smith, Thomas Iroko Ayodele, Gilbert McThunel II (2024, August 29). US Court of Appeals, Fifth Circuit. No. 23-60321. https://caselaw.findlaw.com/court/us-5th-circuit/116472182.html

United States v. Causby, 328 U.S. 256. (1946). *Justia U.S. Supreme Court.* https://supreme.justia.com/cases/federal/us/328/256

United States v. Chatrie, 590 F. Supp 3d 901 (2022). https://casetext.com/case/united-states-v-chatrie

United States v. Chatrie, 590 F. Supp. 3d 901 (E.D. Va. 2020).

United States v. Dunn, 480 U.S. 294. (1987). *Jusita U.S. Supreme Court.* https://supreme.justia.com/cases/federal/us/480/294

United States v. Jones, 565 U.S. 400. (2012). *Oyez.* https://www.oyez.org/cases/2011/10-1259

United States v. Knights, 534 U.S. 112 (2001). https://supreme.justia.com/cases/federal/us/534/112

United States v. LaChance, 788 F.2d 856 (1986). https://casetext.com/case/united-states-v-lachance

United States v. Morris, 928 F.2d 504 (2d Cir. 1991)

United States v. Rhine, 652 F. Supp. 3d 38 (2023). https://casetext.com/case/united-states-v-rhine-11

United States v. Ulbricht, 31 F. Supp. 3d 540 (S.D.N.Y. 2014).

Updated guidance for a risk-based approach to virtual assets and virtual asset service providers. (2021, October). Financial Action Task Force. https://www.fatf-gafi.org/en/publications/Fatfrecommendations/Guidance-rba-virtual-assets-2021.html

USA: Amnesty International, S.T.O.P. lawsuit reveals NYPD surveillance abuses. (2025, November 13). Amnesty International. https://www.amnesty.org/en/latest/news/2025/11/amnesty-and-s-t-o-p-reveal-nypd-surveillance-abuses

Utvaer, B. K. S., Hammervold, R., & Haugan, G. (2014). The Aspiration Index in vocational students: Dimensionality, reliability, and construct validity. *Education Enquiry, 5*(3), 359–383. DOI: 10.3402/edui.v5.24612

Vakhitova, Z., Iliadis, M., Harris, B., Tyson, D., & Flynn, A. (2022, June 22). The merits and risks of body-worn camera footage in domestic and family violence incidents and legal proceedings: A study of police perceptions and experiences. *Policing and Society, 33*(2), 170–186. DOI: 10.1080/10439463.2022.2082421

Valavanidis, A. (2023, April 10). *Artificial Intelligence (AI) applications.* University of Athens, University Campus Zografou, 15784.

Van De Steene, S., & Knight, V. (2017, September). Digital transformation for prisons: Developing a needs-based strategy. *Probation Journal*, *64*(3), 256–268. DOI: 10.1177/0264550517723722

van der Sloot, B., & Wagensveld, Y. (2022, September). Deepfakes: Regulatory challenges for the synthetic society. *Computer Law & Security Review*, *46*, 105716. DOI: 10.1016/j.clsr.2022.105716

van Roomen, T. (2025, November 28). Cross-border evidence gathering in criminal crypto investigations: A case study of the Netherlands. *Tilburg Law Review*, *30*(2), 120–146. DOI: 10.5334/tilr.423

Varma, B. (2019, March 15). Column: Fruit of the poisonous tree. *Bar and Bench*. https://www.barandbench.com/columns/column-fruit-of-the-poisonous-tree

Varner, C., Wood, D. P., & Young, D. (2021, August 19). A report from the 2015 United States–United Kingdom legal exchange. *Judicare International, 100*(2). https://judicature.duke.edu/articles/a-report-from-the-2015-united-states-united-kingdom-legal-exchange/

Vaseashta, A. (2025). Dual-use Artificial Intelligence: Trends, security challenges, and mitigation strategies. In Vaseashta, A., & Rocha, A. (Eds.), *Information systems engineering and management, 6* (pp. 3–37). Springer., DOI: 10.1007/978-3-032-00202-0_1

Vassilopoulos, A. (2022). *Can AI chatbots improve access to legal information? A case study on the inhibitors of AI chatbots' implementation in the context of JuridiQC*. HEC Montréal.

Vasudev, E., & Hansen, T. B. (2024, March 1). *Citizens and the state: Policing, impunity, and the rule of law in India.* The Hindu Centre for Politics and Public Policy. https://www.thehinducentre.com/profile/author/Eklavya-Vasudev-17224

Veerasamy, N., & Pieterse, H. (2022, March). Rising above misinformation and deepfakes. [Conference proceedings]. *International Conference on Cyber Warfare and Security, 17*(1), 340–348. DOI: 10.34190/iccws.17.1.25

Verdoliva, L. (2020, June 12). Media forensics and DeepFakes: An overview. *IEEE Journal of Selected Topics in Signal Processing*, *14*(5), 910–932. DOI: 10.1109/JSTSP.2020.3002101

Verma, A. (2021). Using audio-diaries for research and education: AMEE Guide No. 144. *Medical Teacher*, *43*(12), 1346–1352. DOI: 10.1080/0142159X.2021.1972954 PMID: 34499842

Vickers, C. (2024, April 7). How AI risks creating a 'black box' at the heart of US legal system. *The Hill.* https://thehill.com/business/personal-finance/4571982-ai-black-box-legal-system

Victim Support Europe. (n.d.). *Help for victims: Info for cross border victims*. https://victim-support.eu/help-for-victims/info-on-specific-types-of-victims/domestic-violence-victims

Villasenor, J. (2013). Observations from above: Unmanned aircraft systems and privacy. *Harvard Journal of Law & Public Policy*, *36*(2), 457–517. https://journals.law.harvard.edu/jlpp/wp-content/uploads/sites/90/2013/04/36_2_457_Villasenor.pdf

Villasenor, J., & Foggo, V. (2020). Artificial Intelligence, due process, and criminal sentencing. *Michigan State University Law Review*, 295–354. https://doi.org/DOI: 10.17613/tp6fx-73531

Virginia Law. (n.d.). *Code of Virginia § 19.2-60.1. Use of unmanned aircraft systems by public bodies; search warrant required.* https://law.lis.virginia.gov/vacode/19.2-60.1

Vizzini, A. (2022). The technological wedge in law enforcement. *Florida Department of Law Enforcement.* https://www.fdle.state.fl.us/getContentAsset/38e05ac5-7e0f-41b1-bfac-6738458bf7c4/73aabf56-e6e5-4330-95a3-5f2a270a1d2b/Vizzini-Anthony-paper.pdf

von Münchow, S. (2017, July). *Aftermath of the terror attack on Breitscheid Platz Christmas Market: Germany's security architecture and parliamentary inquiries.* George C. Marshall European Center for Security Studies, Occasional Papers, No. 028. https://www.marshallcenter.org/en/publications/occasional-papers/aftermath-terror-attack-breitscheid-platz-christmas-market-germanys-security-architecture-and

Wahab, M. I. (2025, July 10). *AI in policing: Trends, applications, and challenges.* Legal Service India. https://www.legalserviceindia.com/Legal-Articles/ai-in-policing-trends-applications-and-challenges

Walden, I. (2018, August). 'The Sky is Falling!'–Responses to the 'Going Dark' problem. *Computer Law & Security Review, 34*(4), 901–907. DOI: 10.1016/j.clsr.2018.05.013

Walker, R. T. (2021, April). Geography, Von Thünen, and Tobler's first law: Tracing the evolution of a concept. *Geographical Review, 112*(4), 591–607. DOI: 10.1080/00167428.2021.1906670

Wall, D. S. (2017, May 13). Towards a conceptualisation of cloud (cyber) crime. In *International Conference on Human Aspects of Information Security, Privacy, and Trust* (pp. 529-538). Springer International Publishing. DOI: 10.1007/978-3-319-58460-7_37

Walsh, P. (2021, June 10). 2nd Derek Chauvin juror who deliberated comes forward, breaks down what worked for prosecution and what didn't for defense in George Floyd murder case. *Minnesota Star Tribune.* https://www.startribune.com/2nd-derek-chauvin-juror-who-deliberated-comes-forward-breaks-down-what-worked-for-prosecution-and-wh/600066839

Wang, C., Musaev, A., Sheinidashtegol, P., & Atkison, T. (2019, June 20). Towards detection of abnormal vehicle behavior using traffic cameras. In K. Chen, S. Seshadri, & L.-J. Zhang (Eds.), *Big Data – BigData 2019. Lecture Notes in Computer Science* (pp. 125-136), 11514. Springer. https://doi.org/ DOI: 10.1007/978-3-030-23551-2_9

Wang, X. (2025, November 14). Rights groups claim 2,700 NYPD documents disclosed in lawsuit reveal 'surveillance abuses'. *JURISTnews.* https://www.jurist.org/news/2025/11/rights-groups-claims-2700-nypd-documents-disclosed-from-lawsuit-reveal-surveillance-abuses

Wang, B., Wu, X., Tang, Y., Ma, Y., Shan, Z., & Wei, F. (2023, February 5). Frequency domain filtered residual network for deepfake detection. *Mathematics, 11*(4), 816. DOI: 10.3390/math11040816

Wang, K., & Guo, F. (2022, October 16). Towards sustainable development through the perspective of Construction 4.0: Systematic literature review and bibliometric analysis. *Buildings (Basel, Switzerland), 12*(10), 1708. DOI: 10.3390/buildings12101708

Wang, T., Liao, X., Chow, K. P., Lin, X., & Wang, Y. (2025, March). Deepfake detection: A comprehensive survey from the reliability perspective. *ACM Computing Surveys, 57*(3), 1–35. DOI: 10.1145/3699710

Wang, X., Wu, Y. C., Zhou, M., & Fu, H. (2024, July 2). Beyond surveillance: Privacy, ethics, and regulations in face recognition technology. [REMOVED HYPERLINK FIELD]. *Frontiers in Big Data*, *7*, 1337465. DOI: 10.3389/fdata.2024.1337465 PMID: 39027377

Warwick Medical School. (2020, November 6). *WEMWBS: 14-item vs 7-item scale*. https://warwick.ac.uk/fac/sci/med/research/platform/wemwbs/about/wemwbsvsswemwbs

Waseem, S., Abu Bakar, S. A. R. S., Ahmed, B. A., Omar, Z., Eisa, T. A. E., & Dalam, M. E. E. (2023, October 13). DeepFake on face and expression swap: A review. *IEEE Access : Practical Innovations, Open Solutions*, *11*, 117865–117906. DOI: 10.1109/ACCESS.2023.3324403

Washington, District of Columbia. (n.d.). World Population Review. https://worldpopulationreview.com/us-cities/district-of-columbia/washington

Watts, K. (2024, November 4). *Geofencing demystified: Understanding the virtual boundaries in marketing*. Raincross. https://raincross.com/what-is-geofencing

Wawrzyniak, N., & Hyla, T. (2016, June). *Application of geofencing technology for the purpose of spatial analysis in focuses on geofencing in mobile navigation for hazard alerts*. Inland mobile navigation. 2016 Baltic Geodetic Congress (BGC Geomatics), Gdansk, Poland, pp. 34-39. https://doi.org/DOI: 10.1109/BGC.Geomatics.2016.15

Wazzan, M., Algazzawi, D., Bamasaq, O., Albeshri, A., & Cheng, L. (2021, June). Internet of Things botnet detection approaches: Analysis and recommendations for future research. *Applied Sciences (Basel, Switzerland)*, *11*(12), 5713. DOI: 10.3390/app11125713

Wearable geofencing approval. (2022, November). *Railway Gazette International*, *178*(11), 16.

Wegner, D., Borba da Silveira, A., Marconatto, D., & Mitrega, M. (2023, September). A systematic review of collaborative digital platforms: Structuring the domain and research agenda. *Review of Managerial Science*, *18*(9), 2663–2695. DOI: 10.1007/s11846-023-00695-0

Weikmann, T., Egelhofer, J. L., & Lecheler, S. (2025, December). Beyond credibility: The effects of different forms of visual disinformation. *Journalism & Mass Communication Quarterly*, *102*(4), 1020–1043. DOI: 10.1177/10776990251357299

Weisburd, K. (2020). Sentenced to surveillance: Fourth Amendment limits on electronic monitoring. *North Carolina Law Review*, *98*(4), 3. https://scholarship.law.unc.edu/nclr/vol98/iss4/3

Wessels, M. (2023). Algorithmic policing accountability: Eight sociotechnical challenges. *Policing and Society*, *34*(3), 124–138. DOI: 10.1080/10439463.2023.2241965

West, J. P., Klofstad, C. A., Uscinski, J. E., & Connolly, J. M. (2018). Citizen support for domestic drone use and regulation. *American Politics Research*, *47*(1), 119–151. DOI: 10.1177/1532673X18782208

What are carbon emissions & why do they matter? (n.d.). Constellation. https://www.constellation.com/energy-101/energy-innovation/what-are-carbon-emissions.html

What is an unmanned aircraft system (UAS)? (n.d.). Federal Aviation Administration. https://www.faa.gov/faq/what-unmanned-aircraft-system-uas

Wheatley, M. C. (2024, November). Ethics of surveillance technologies: Balancing privacy and security in a digital age. *Premier Journal of Data Science, 2024.* Advance online publication. DOI: 10.70389/PJDS.100001

Whitaker, R. (2025, July 31). *How blockchain forensics unraveled a $20 million crypto laundering scheme in China.* Merkle Science. https://www.merklescience.com/blog/how-blockchain-forensics-unraveled-a-20-million-crypto-laundering-scheme-in-china

White, M. D. (2014). *Police officer body-worn cameras: Assessing the evidence.* Office of Community Oriented Policing Services. https://portal.cops.usdoj.gov/resourcecenter/content.ashx/cops-p289-pub.pdf

Willey, J. (2024, June 13). Houston city council OKs $178K to expand HPD's surveillance network. *ABC13 Houston.* https://abc13.com/post/houston-police-artificial-intelligence-video-surveillance-airship-ai/14942179

Williams, C. (2024, December 10). *How geofencing technology is transforming business in 2024.* Tech-Times. https://www.techtimes.com/articles/308656/20241210/how-geofencing-technology-transforming-business-2024.htm

Williams, M. C., Jr., Weil, N., Rasich, E. A., Ludwig, J., Chang, H., & Egrari, S. (2021, March). *Body-worn cameras in policing: Benefits and costs (Working Paper No. 2021-38).* Becker Friedman Institute. University of Chicago. https://bfi.uchicago.edu/wp-content/uploads/2021/04/BFI_WP_2021-38.pdf

Williams, S. (2017, February 13). Errors in Centrelink's debt recovery system were inevitable, as in all complex systems. The Conversation. https://theconversation.com/errors-in-centrelinks-debt-recovery-system-were-inevitable-as-in-all-complex-systems-71409

Williams, G. C., & Deci, E. L. (1996). Internalization of biopsychosocial values by medical students: A test of self-determination theory. *Journal of Personality and Social Psychology*, *70*(4), 767–779. DOI: 10.1037/0022-3514.70.4.767 PMID: 8636897

Williams, G. C., McGregor, H. A., Sharp, D., Levesque, C., Kouides, R. W., Ryan, R. M., & Deci, E. L. (2006). Testing a self-determination theory intervention for motivating tobacco cessation: Supporting autonomy and competence in a clinical trial. *Health Psychology*, *25*(1), 91–101. DOI: 10.1037/0278-6133.25.1.91 PMID: 16448302

Williams, G. C., McGregor, H. A., Zeldman, A., Freedman, Z. R., & Deci, E. L. (2004). Testing a self-determination theory process model for promoting glycemic control through diabetes self-management. *Health Psychology*, *23*(1), 58–66. DOI: 10.1037/0278-6133.23.1.58 PMID: 14756604

Williams, K. L. (2003, April). Peel's Principles and their acceptance by American police: Ending 175 years of reinvention. *The Police Journal*, *76*(2), 97–120. DOI: 10.1177/0032258X0307600202

Williams, L., & Gill, D. L. (1995, January). The role of perceived competence in the motivation of physical activity. *Journal of Sport & Exercise Psychology*, *17*(4), 363–378. DOI: 10.1123/jsep.17.4.363

Williamson, I., Leeming, D., Lyttle, S., & Johnson, S. (2012). It should be the most natural thing in the world: Exploring first-time mothers' breastfeeding difficulties in the UK using audio-diaries and interviews. *Maternal and Child Nutrition*, *8*(4), 434–447. DOI: 10.1111/j.1740-8709.2011.00328.x PMID: 21696542

Williamson, I., Leeming, D., Lyttle, S., & Johnson, S. (2015, February 2). Evaluating the audio-diary method in qualitative research. *Qualitative Research Journal, 15*(1), 20–34. DOI: 10.1108/QRJ-04-2014-0014

Williams, R., Ali, S., Devasia, N., DiPaola, D., Hong, J., Kaputsos, S. P., Jordan, B., & Breazeal, C. (2023, August). AI+ ethics curricula for middle school youth: Lessons learned from three project-based curricula. *International Journal of Artificial Intelligence in Education, 33*(2), 325–383. DOI: 10.1007/s40593-022-00298-y PMID: 35935456

Wilson, O. W. (1950). *Police administration.* McGraw-Hill Series in Political Science.

Wolfrum, R. (2015, September). Combatants. *Max Planck Encyclopedias of International Law (MPIL).* https://opil.ouplaw.com/display/10.1093/law:epil/9780199231690/law-9780199231690-e272

Wollerton, M. (2023). Ransomware attacks. *CQ Press, 33*(28). Advance online publication. DOI: 10.4135/cqresrre20230818

Wolter, M., Blanke, F., Heese, R., & Garcke, J. (2022, August 31). Wavelet-packets for deepfake image analysis and detection. *Machine Learning, 111*(11), 4295–4327. DOI: 10.1007/s10994-022-06225-5

Worgul, M. (2025, October 22). *Can cell phone video be used as evidence in court?* Worgul, Sarna & Ness. https://www.pittsburghcriminalattorney.com/can-cell-phone-video-be-used-as-evidence-in-court

World Economic Forum. (2025, January). *Global cybersecurity outlook 2025.* https://reports.weforum.org/docs/WEF_Global_Cybersecurity_Outlook_2025.pdf

Wozniak, K. H. (2014, September). American public opinion about prisons. *Criminal Justice Review, 39*(3), 305–324. DOI: 10.1177/0734016814529968

Wright, I. (2019, October 8). *History of American police cars.* Car Buzz. https://carbuzz.com/features/history-of-american-police-cars

Wu, Y., Sun, I. Y., & Hu, R. (2021, January). Cooperation with police in China: Surveillance cameras, neighborhood efficacy and policing. *Social Science Quarterly (Wiley-Blackwell), 102*(1), 433–453. https://doi.org/DOI: 10.1111/ssqu.12903

Wu, G., Wang, X., & Zhang, J. (2024, May). PeerG: A P2P botnet detection method based on representation learning and graph contrastive learning. *Computers & Security, 140*, 103775. DOI: 10.1016/j.cose.2024.103775

Wykstra, S. (2020, June 1). Government's use of algorithm serves up false fraud charges. Undark. https://undark.org/2020/06/01/michigan-unemployment-fraud-algorithm

Xie, M., Kulshrestha, M., Wang, S., Yang, J., Chakrabarti, A., Zhang, N., & Vorobeychik, Y. (2022, January). PROVES: Establishing image provenance using semantic signatures. [Conference paper]. *2022 IEEE/CVF Winter Conference on Applications of Computer Vision* (pp. 3017-3026). DOI: 10.1109/WACV51458.2022.00307

Xu, D., Gondal, I., Yi, X., Susnjak, T., Watters, P., & McIntosh, T. R. (2025, October 14). The erosion of cybersecurity zero-trust principles through generative AI: A survey on the challenges and future directions. *Journal of Cybersecurity and Privacy*, *5*(4), 87. DOI: 10.3390/jcp5040087

Yadav, R., & Varshney, R. (2024, July-December). Right to be forgotten amidst data protection, right to privacy and cyber security. *Library Progress International, 44*(2), 1750–1757. https://bpasjournals.com/library-science/index.php/journal/article/view/2092

Yadav, A. (2020). Relevancy and admissibility of digital evidence: A comparative study. *International Journal of Integrated Law Review*, *1*(1), 22–32.

Yan, B., Liu, P., Yang, Y., Guo, Y., Yan, B., Liu, P., Yang, Y., & Guo, Y. (2025, June 18). Self-supervised feature disentanglement for deepfake detection. *Mathematics*, *13*(12), 2024. DOI: 10.3390/math13122024

Yang, S., Nakajima, H., Yang, Y., Shin, Y., & Koizumi, H. (2024, November 15). The impact of surveillance cameras and community safety activities on crime prevention: Evidence from Kakogawa City, Japan. *Sustainable Cities and Society*, *115*, 105858. DOI: 10.1016/j.scs.2024.105858

Ybarra v. Illinois, 444 U.S. 85 (1979). https://casetext.com/case/ybarra-v-illinois

Yebra, M., Galarza-Vallejo, A., Soto-León, V., Gonzalez-Rosa, J. J., de Berker, A. O., Bestmann, S., Oliviero, A., Kroes, M. C. W., & Strange, B. A. (2019, August 6). Action boosts episodic memory encoding in humans via engagement of a noradrenergic system. *Nature Communications*, *10*(1), 1–12. DOI: 10.1038/s41467-019-11358-8 PMID: 31388000

Young, J. (1999, December 13). The exclusive society: Social exclusion, crime and difference in late modernity. *Sage (Atlanta, Ga.).*

Zaib, H. U., Shaheen, M. B., & Chaudhary, H. K. (2025, July-September). Constitutional validity of surveillance technologies in Pakistan: Reconciling national security with individual privacy rights in the digital age. *Social Science Review Archives*, *3*(3), 1653–1665. DOI: 10.70670/sra.v3i3.991

Zalnieriute, M. (2025). Facial recognition surveillance and public space: Protecting protest movements. *International Review of Law Computers & Technology*, *39*(1), 116–135. DOI: 10.1080/13600869.2023.2295690

Završnik, A. (2021). Algorithmic justice: Algorithms and big data in criminal justice settings. *European Journal of Criminology*, *18*(5), 623–642. DOI: 10.1177/1477370819876762

Zhang, L. (2024, January 9). *Deciphering cybersecurity vulnerabilities requires context.* Security Boulevard. https://securityboulevard.com/2024/01/deciphering-cybersecurity-vulnerabilities-requires-context

Zhang, B., Cui, H., Nguyen, V., & Whitty, M. (2025, March 21). Audio deepfake detection: What has been achieved and what lies ahead. *Sensors (Basel)*, *25*(7), 1989. DOI: 10.3390/s25071989 PMID: 40218502

Zhao, J., & Zhang, Y. (2022, June). A longitudinal study of police differential response team impact on crime in Houston: A test of broken windows thesis. *Police Quarterly, 26*(2), 143–168. https://doi.org/ DOI: 10.1177/10986111221092947

Zhao, T., Xu, X., Xu, M., Ding, H., Xiong, Y., & Xia, W. (2021, July 26). Learning self-consistency for deepfake detection (arXiv:2012.09311). *arXiv.* /arXiv.2012.09311DOI: 10.1109/ICCV48922.2021.01475

Zhuhao Wang, H. (2025). Asynchronous trials: A new approach to high-volume civil adjudication. *Denver Law Review, 102*(3), 659–713.

Ziosi, M., & Pruss, D. (2024, June). Evidence of what, for whom? The socially contested role of algorithmic bias in a predictive policing tool. [Conference proceedings] In *Proceedings of the 2024 ACM Conference on Fairness* (pp. 1596–1608). Accountability, and Transparency., https://dl.acm.org/doi/pdf/10.1145/3630106.3658991 DOI: 10.1145/3630106.3658991

Zipline, Pfizer and BioNTech collaboration paves the way for automated, on-demand delivery of first mRNA COVID-29 vaccines in Ghana. (2021, November 11). Pfizer. https://www.pfizer.com/news/press-release/press-release-detail/zipline-pfizer-and-biontech-collaboration-paves-way

Zongwe, D. (2022, November 11). Nobody can really afford legal services: The price of justice in Namibia. *Potchefstroom Electronic Law Journal/Potchefstroomse Elektroniese Regsblad, 24*(1). https://doi.org/DOI: 10.17159/1727-3781/2021/v24i0a6420

Zuboff, S. (2019). *The age of surveillance capitalism: The fight for a human future at the new frontier of power*. PublicAffairs.

About the Contributors

Tamara Phillips Fudge is a full-time professor in the graduate technology programs at Purdue University Global. She has won fellowships and awards for innovation and teaching, and has taught a wide variety of topics, including web development, human-computer interaction, systems analysis and design, and those featuring documentation, diagramming, problem-solving, and presentation. Her career started with music degrees from Indiana University and her doctorate from Florida State University. She sang opera, oratorio, and in recital; her compositions have been heard on Public Radio, at various universities, and a state choral convention. She taught vocal and choral music, piano, pedagogy, foreign language diction, opera production, music theory, composition, and related courses in the traditional college classroom for 20-odd years. For 7 years, she was a weekend correspondent for the Quad-City Times (Davenport, IA). Following a brief stint as an agent/registered representative selling life and health insurance and variable products, she returned to school and teaching with a keen interest in technology and has since distinguished herself in online teaching, coordination of large projects, and curriculum development. She has had several book chapters published through IGI Global, and both journal articles and conference presentations elsewhere; she also previously served as editor for two other IGI volumes.

***

Bhagyashree Agarwal is an Assistant Professor at the School of Law, UPES, Dehradun. She is currently pursuing her Ph.D. at Dharmashastra National Law University (DNLU), Jabalpur, specializing in the regulatory approach to pornography in India. Her academic journey includes an LL.M in Human Rights Law from NLUJAA and an LL.B. and a B.A. (Hons.) from University of Delhi. At UPES, she serves as a member of the Gender Champions Committee. Previously, she served as Faculty of Law at DNLU, where she co-directed the Centre for Constitutional Law and served on multiple editorial boards. Her work on reproductive rights, gender-based digital crimes, and criminal law has been published by Bloomsbury India and various indexed journals. She has participated and presented her work at various global conferences. A UGC-NET qualified scholar, she has also worked with Bachpan Bachao Andolan, a child rights movement founded and spearheaded by Nobel Peace Laureate Kailash Satyarthi.

Eduardo Silva Bastos holds a Bachelor's degree in Computer Engineering from the Instituto Superior Politécnico Gaya (ISPGAYA), Portugal, obtained in 2025. He is currently pursuing a Master's degree in Cybersecurity and IT Systems Auditing at the same institution, while working as a Quality Assurance Engineer. He has professional experience in software testing, automation, and performance analysis, focusing on ensuring reliability and security in mobile and distributed systems. His research interests include lightweight cryptography, IoT security, and secure software development practices.

Gulsebnem (Sheb) Bishop is currently teaching at Campbellsville University as an Assistant Professor of Computer Information Systems in the Department of Business, Economics, and Technology. She graduated with a doctorate in Computer Science and Information Systems from Pace University, NY, in 2006. She holds an MBA and a Cybersecurity degree from Stratford University in VA, and an MS in Criminology from Campbellsville University in KY. She is a certified PMP. Her area of interest is software development, design and security, data warehousing, database administration, and data analytics. Dr. Bishop worked in non-profit IT, specifically in database administration, for over thirteen years and in other IT areas, such as web design, systems integration/conversion, and IT project management. She worked for several non-profits in New York and Washington, DC (American Museum of Natural History, NAACP, Legal Defense and Education Fund, and Human Rights Campaign). Dr. Bishop is currently working on incorporating VR and AI technologies into her classes and experimenting with different platforms.

Mario DeSean Booker stands at the nexus of technological innovation and social justice, wielding his Ph.D. in Information Technology, he challenges systems of algorithmic discrimination and digital colonialism. His interdisciplinary approach fuses rigorous technical analysis with community-centered advocacy, creating frameworks that expose how emerging technologies perpetuate structural inequalities while providing actionable solutions for democratic governance. Currently serving as a Full-Time Professor in Graduate Information Technology at Purdue University Global, Dr. Booker has taught across multiple institutions including the University of Michigan-Flint, Trine University, ect. His pedagogical expertise spans cybersecurity, network management, cloud computing, and data science, while his research penetrates the deeper implications of AI infrastructure on environmental justice and community autonomy. Dr. Booker's scholarly contributions have established him as a leading voice in the emerging field of critical technology studies. His 2025 book 404: Justice Not Found synthesizes years of interdisciplinary research into a comprehensive framework examining how algorithmic discrimination, cybersecurity vulnerabilities, and digital colonialism converge to shape contemporary governance. This work builds upon his extensive publication record, including peer-reviewed articles on digital redlining, automated crisis negotiation systems, and the environmental impact of AI infrastructure. Dr. Booker holds multiple advanced degrees, including an M.S. in Technology and Innovation Management from Northcentral University and dual B.A.S. degrees in Information Systems Engineering and Networking and Security from American Business Technology University. Active in community engagement. His commitment to bridging academic research with community organizing reflects his belief that technological inquiry and social justice are mutually reinforcing endeavors. Dr. Booker's research agenda continues to evolve across three primary directions: large-scale algorithmic auditing applications, comparative studies of AI infrastructure in the Global South with emphasis on resistance movements, and policy model development that aligns technical resilience with democratic accountability. His work provides essential frameworks for policymakers, scholars, and organizers confronting the challenges of building equitable and sustainable technology futures.

Pedro Miguel Correia Cardoso holds a Bachelor's degree in Computer Engineering from the Instituto Superior Politécnico Gaya (ISPGAYA), Portugal. He is currently pursuing a Master's degree in Cybersecurity and IT Systems Auditing at the same institution, while working as a Systems Analyst, focusing on the development and maintenance of secure systems and data analysis solutions. His areas of interest include cybersecurity, systems administration, and network infrastructure.

Laura Caulfield PhD is Dean of Research Culture and Postgraduate Research at the University of Wolverhampton. Laura is an expert in the evaluation of programmes designed to reduce risk of crime. She has designed and conducted over 45 research evaluations and has received funding from the Home Office, Economic and Social Research Council, the NHS, the Ministry of Justice, and several third-sector organisations. Her latest book, 'Criminological Skills and Research for Beginners', is published by Routledge

Tyler Cranmore is an academic advisor and graduate researcher whose work focuses on cybercrime, digital forensics, and the intersection of technology and the criminal justice system. He holds a Master of Science in Cybersecurity, with formal training in digital forensics, cloud security, and cyber investigations, and is completing a Master of Science in Criminology and Criminal Justice. His academic interests center on how emerging technologies reshape investigative practices, evidentiary standards, and constitutional protections, particularly in cases involving digital evidence, encryption, and online criminal activity. Tyler's research bridges technical cybersecurity concepts with criminological and legal analysis, emphasizing practical challenges faced by law enforcement and courts in addressing cyber-enabled crime. His work draws on federal case law, forensic standards, and contemporary research to examine how investigative tools evolve alongside concerns about privacy, oversight, and legitimacy. His broader scholarly interests include cybercrime investigations, forensic evidence handling, algorithmic decision-making in justice systems, and the ethical implications of digital surveillance. Tyler plans to pursue doctoral study in criminology, with the goal of teaching and conducting interdisciplinary research on cybercrime and digital justice.

Susan Ferebee earned her Ph.D. in Information Systems at Nova Southeastern University in Ft Lauderdale, Florida. She also has an Executive Juris Doctorate from Concord Law School and a Master's in Educational Psychology from Purdue University Global. She serves as a Dissertation Chair for several universities and has also served as a consultant with more than 30 years of experience working directly with organizations and higher education institutions. Susan has published many peer-reviewed articles. Her current research in progress includes studies on geofencing in criminal justice, drone use for search and rescue, machine learning in environmental forecasting, metaverse ethics, and effective AI use for people with disabilities. Susan also served as a guest editor for a special issue of the International Journal of Conceptual Structures and Smart Applications. Susan serves as an Editorial Review Board member for the International Journal of Cognitive Informatics and Natural Intelligence. She is an active presenter at international and national conferences. Susan has received numerous teaching and outstanding contributor awards and has been awarded several research grants.

Anwesha Ghosh is an Assistant Professor of Law at Amity Law School, Amity University Mumbai. A gold medalist in both LL.B. and LL.M., Dr. Ghosh holds a UGC NET-JRF qualification and has submitted her Ph.D. thesis on Legislative Governance Towards Gender Diversity in Indian Corporate Boards at the Central University of Punjab, India. Her research emphasizes the role of women directors in fostering inclusive corporate governance. Ms. Ghosh's academic journey includes accolades like the Endowment Medal for excellence in Corporate and Commercial Laws and significant contributions to projects on HIV/AIDS and the criminal justice system in India. She has authored An Introspection of Corporate Criminal Liability in India and published in Scopus-indexed and UGC Care journals.

Puranjoy Ghosh is the Associate Professor of Law at the School of Law, KIIT (Deemed to be University), Bhubaneswar, Odisha, India. He started his career in legal profession as an Advocate and professed Advocacy in Civil Proceeding at various Trial & Appellate Courts. He joined the Teaching Profession in the year 2002 in his academic journey he has gained experience in Procedural Laws, Property Laws, Insolvency Laws, Laws on International Commercial Arbitration, Investment Laws, Capital Market Regulations, International Trade Laws. Till date under his supervision one Research Scholar is awarded with Ph.D. His area of interests for research projects are on intersection of Investment, Healthcare, Agriculture, Corporate Laws.

Tiago Filipe Neto Gomes holds a Bachelor's degree in Computer Engineering from the Instituto Superior Politécnico Gaya (ISPGAYA), Portugal, where he is currently pursuing a Master's degree in Cybersecurity and IT Systems Auditing. His professional experience has focused on software development and quality assurance, including system design, testing, and validation, with an emphasis on building and securing reliable information systems, as well as cybersecurity-related projects.

Kyros Hadjisergis is a Senior Lecturer in Criminology and Criminal Justice and member of the Institute for Community Research and Development at the University of Wolverhampton. He has conducted research in the areas of probation and human rights, offender rehabilitation, organised crime and community justice, human trafficking, and has expertise in qualitative research methods. His wider research interests relate to probation, rehabilitation and desistance, community crime prevention, restorative justice, and human rights. He has undertaken research and impact evaluations for criminal justice agencies and other associated government organisations.

Linnea Hall is an evaluator at WGU. She earned a doctorate in law from California Western School of Law in San Diego, CA and a doctorate in computer science from Colorado Technical University in Colorado Springs, CO. Her research interests include artificial intelligence, computational neuroscience, and ethics.

Simon Iileka is a scholar at the University of Namibia and an aspiring Solution Architect with a strong interest in cybersecurity, artificial intelligence, and digital innovation. His academic and project work focuses on developing practical, technology-driven solutions, including secure web applications, AI-powered systems, and cybersecurity awareness platforms. Simon is particularly passionate about leveraging modern technologies to improve systems design, security, and accessibility in developing contexts. Through hands-on projects and research, he continues to build expertise in software development, infrastructure security, and intelligent systems.

Pradeep Kulshreshtha, Dean, Bennett School of Law is the senior academician with over 30+ years of extensive expertise in academic affairs, legal research & advisory services. He is an alumnus of Kurukshetra University and Jodhpur University. He has been awarded Honorary Doctorate (Law) by National American University, South Dakota, USA for his contribution to the field of legal education. He is also a recipient of the UP Government merit scholarship. He has authored and edited 21 books, 46 research papers and conference papers. He has successfully guided three PhD scholars. His teaching and research interests include Constitutional Law of India, Comparative Constitution, Comparative

Public Law, Criminal Justice and Human Rights, Law of Tort, Consumer Protection Laws, Labour Laws, Industrial Relations, and Clinical legal education.

Mary K. Lannon is a professor of graduate public safety at Purdue University Global. Dr. Lannon has over 13 years of experience in online higher education and previously worked for 12 years in public safety communications. Dr. Lannon's research interests include emergency preparedness and response, online teaching and learning, and ethics in research and academia.

Anton Limbo is a Senior Lecturer and Researcher at the University of Namibia's Department of Computing, Mathematics, and Statistics. His research is centred on the innovative applications of IoT within the field of ICT for Development (ICT4D), with a particular emphasis on Smart Agriculture, Smart Healthcare, Smart Home-Care Giving, and Home Automation. Through his work, Anton has significantly contributed to the academic community by publishing numerous papers that underscore the critical need for ongoing research in applying IoT technologies to improve the quality of life in the developing world. In addition to his research, Anton plays other roles such as coordinating and administering the University of Namibia's High-Performance Computing (HPC) system, which is instrumental in advancing computational research, including data modelling, simulations, and training artificial intelligence models. His efforts are paving the way for enhanced research capabilities and technological advancements in Namibia. Anton also serves as a member on various boards, such as the Computer Science and Cybersecurity Curriculum Advisory Boards, Namibia 4th Industrial Revolution Taskforce.

Selma Limbo is a Coordinator for Digital Learning Systems at the University of Namibia's Centre for Innovation in Learning and Teaching. She holds a Master of Philosophy in IT Governance, with a focus on the applications of IT frameworks to manage eLearning systems in Southern Africa. Selma's research focuses on barriers preventing the successful rollout of eLearning systems in the developing world, as well as mechanisms to improve access to learning materials using modern technologies such as Artificial Intelligence, the Internet of Things, Educational Technologies and Blended Learning. To date, she has published papers on improving healthcare using the Internet of Things, deploying eLearning systems in resource-constrained environments using embedded devices, and now on improving access to legal services using Artificial Intelligence.

Cassie Longhart-Thomas is a healthcare professional, educator, and researcher with extensive experience in health administration, quality improvement, data analytics, and public health systems. She currently serves as Assistant Department Chair and Graduate Professor in the School of Business and Information Technology at Purdue Global University, where she supports curriculum development, assessment activities, faculty mentoring, and student success initiatives. Dr. Longhart-Thomas teaches graduate and undergraduate courses across analytics, database systems, information systems management, workplace safety, and capstone research, bridging theory with applied practice. Dr. Longhart-Thomas earned her Doctor of Health Administration with a specialization in Quality and Analytics from Capella University. Her doctoral capstone focused on improving instructor communication, record-keeping, and tracking through the integration of new software systems. Dr. Longhart-Thomas has published peer-reviewed research in Issues in Information Systems and contributed to white papers on zero trust gap analysis for health technology. She is an active conference presenter at various venues, with recent invited presentations on generative AI, emotional intelligence in higher education, cybersecurity education, and emergency medical services (EMS) systems. Her academic work brings significant applied leadership experience from healthcare operations, public health, and emergency medical services. She has served as a Data Manager for a state Department of Public Health, where she improved regulatory data compliance, led statewide data initiatives, managed federally funded grants, and produced annual EMS reports. Her professional background also includes roles as a business data analyst, clinic manager, and EMT-Intermediate. Dr. Longhart-Thomas is actively engaged in professional volunteer service. She serves as a peer reviewer for the International Journal of Paramedicine and participates on the Transportation Research Board panels with the National Academies of Sciences, Engineering, and Medicine. Through her combined work in education, research, healthcare leadership, and analytics, Dr. Longhart-Thomas is committed to advancing data-driven decision-making, innovative learning environments, and high-quality, equitable healthcare systems.

Lara Lucas, MS, is an IT Manager at American Airlines with more than two decades of experience in the industry. She earned her BS in Business/CIS from WVU and her MS in Operations Research from George Mason University. Currently, she teaches Human-Computer Interaction at Purdue Global University. Her professional interests focus on the future of AI and the innovations it brings to corporate IT and educational settings. An avid tennis player, Lara also volunteers with Southwest English Setter Rescue and lives with her two setters.

Jaylen B. Moody is a Bowie State University alumna with a Bachelor of Science degree in Computer Technology, specializing in networking infrastructure. She currently serves as a Systems Engineer at BAE Systems, where she applies her expertise to configure, manage, and secure enterprise-level environments across Azure, AWS, and Oracle platforms. Her responsibilities include deploying scalable cloud infrastructures, enforcing access controls and security policies, managing system performance, and supporting integration across hybrid architectures. Jaylen's understanding of systems and platforms enables her to ensure operational continuity, system reliability, and security compliance across diverse IT ecosystems. Jaylen holds a Master's degree in the Internet of Things (IoT) from Bowie State University, further expanding her expertise in emerging technologies. Her professional background includes experience in customer service, database engineering, and IT support, complemented by strong skills in programming (Python, Java), automation, and cloud platforms such as GitHub. She is proficient in network administration, cybersecurity, and database administration, and is well-versed with tools like Jenkins, Ansible (AWX), Nexus, and SonarQube. In addition to her Systems Engineering experience, Jaylen has served in capacities aligned with DevOps as a DevOps Engineer Associate at Chubb Insurance, where she automated application processes, enhanced software development lifecycles (SDLC), and implemented robust security governance practices. In her previous role, Jaylen contributed to the design and execution of strategies related to collaboration, code management, infrastructure automation, source control, compliance, CI/CD pipelines, testing, and monitoring.

Vernice J. Moody is an Adjunct Professor at Purdue University Global. She is also an Associate Part-time Professor at National University. She taught at Prince Georges Community College in Largo, Md as an Adjunct Professor. Dr. Moody was also an Academic Coach where she assisted instructors. Dr. Moody received her Doctorate's degree in Management and Organizational Leadership/ Information Systems & Technology from the University of Phoenix. She received her Master of Science in Information Technology and Bachelor of Science in Information Systems from the University of

Maryland. Dr. Moody also received her Associate of Arts in Computer and Information Science at Prince Georges Community College. Dr. Moody is currently a Cyber Security Officer. Her previous positions throughout her professional career included Engineer, Operations Specialist, Executive Secretary, and Telecommunications Specialist. Dr. Moody's expertise spans both technical and managerial roles, allowing her to bridge the gap between complex IT solutions and effective organizational strategies.

Kathi Nicholson is an Assistant Academic Department Chair at Purdue University Global with over 20 years of expertise in UX design, web development, and database architecture. An advocate for ethical AI and student mentorship, she focuses on the practical application of emerging technologies in the workplace. Her career began in the 1990s in law enforcement, where she served in patrol and undercover narcotics. Today, she translates that experience into a passion for protecting integrity and fostering innovation within the BSIT program.

Rúben dos Santos Oliveira holds a Bachelor's degree in Computer Engineering from the Instituto Superior Politécnico Gaya (ISPGAYA), Portugal, and previously completed the Professional Higher Education Course in Networks and Computer Systems at the same institution. Over the past few years, his work has focused on software development, with a specialization in enterprise management systems across various industries, as well as financial software. He has recently begun a Master's degree in Cybersecurity and IT Systems Auditing, aiming to build a career in cybersecurity.

Naresh Prajapati is an Assistant Professor of Law at the School of Law, Bennett University, India. He holds a Ph.D. in Law from the Central University of Punjab, with research focusing on climate change, human rights, international environmental law, and comparative constitutional approaches in South Asia. He is the recipient of the Chancellor's Award for Best Ph.D. Scholar at the Central University of Punjab. His academic interests include climate justice, sustainable development, environmental governance, corporate accountability, and human rights protection. He has presented research at national and international platforms and contributed to scholarly publications, book chapters, and academic reviews.

Sangeeta Rani serves as an Assistant Professor in the Department of Computer Science & Engineering at Chaudhary Devi Lal University (CDLU), Sirsa, Haryana, India, since October 2010. Her academic qualifications include advanced degrees in computer science, supporting her teaching and research contributions in the Faculty of Engineering & Technology. Dr Rani has earned a B.Tech, MTech and a doctorate, all in Computer Science and Engineering. She is actively involved in WSN and machine learning research.

Siobhan Sadlier is a PhD student and Research Assistant in the Institute for Community Research and Development at the University of Wolverhampton. Siobhan is an experienced researcher, previously employed at several research and evaluation agencies and thinktanks. Her doctoral research explores understandings of how communities respond to domestic abuse, using a community asset and network mapping methodology.

Smruti Ranjan Sahoo is a legal practitioner and researcher who completed his B.A.LL.B. (Hons.) from University Law College in 2015 and his LL.M. from the P.G. Department of Law, Berhampur University, in 2017. He enrolled in the Ph.D. programme in Law at KIIT Deemed to be University in 2018 and is currently pursuing his doctoral research in the area of anti-money laundering. Since the completion of his LL.M., he has been practicing before the Orissa High Court and the courts at Bhubaneswar.

Sergio Francisco Sargo Ferreira Lopes, Professor at Higher Polytechnic Institute Gaya (ISPGAYA), Researcher at INSIGHT Research Centre for Ecological Human Development and Researcher at Laboratory of Distance Education and e-Learning at Open University of Portugal, Trainer, and Manager of the ICT area, Ph.D. in Information Sciences (specialty Information Systems, Technologies, and Management), M.Sc in Teaching and Educational Management, MBA in ICT Management, Specialist in Higher Education Teaching and Bachelor in Information Systems. Reserve Officer of the Brazilian Army, having held the position of Manager of the Telecommunications and Information Technology area (Telematics). Decorated with the Patriarca da Independência medal, for relevant services rendered to the Brazilian Army. Certified IT professional by Microsoft, ISACA, and EXIN (Holland) in MIE, ITIL, COBIT, ISO/IEC 27002 (Information Security Management), and Green IT Citizen, working with ITC department management and project management. Trainer accredited by the Scientific-Pedagogical Council of Continuous Training of the Ministry of Education (Portugal). Corresponding Associate Member of the Brazilian Association of Distance Education (ABED).

Siddharth Saxena is an Assistant Professor at Maharashtra National Law University (MNLU), Nagpur. Previously, he served as Faculty of Law at Dharmashastra National Law University (DNLU), Jabalpur, where he is currently pursuing a Ph.D. in Online Gaming Law. His expertise spans Civil, Procedural, Labour, Gaming, Evidence, and Criminal Law. His research on modernizing Indian policing is published internationally, and he has participated and presented his work at various global conferences. He has served as a Resource Person for police training workshops and is a reviewer for the SCOPUS-indexed Journal of Intellectual Property Rights (CSIR-NIScPR). His policy work includes research on the Bharatiya Sakshya Adhiniyam, 2023, submitted to the Ministry of Law and Justice, Government of India and research on Artificial Intelligence submitted to the 22nd Law Commission of India. A UGC-NET qualified scholar, he is an alumnus of National Law University, Jodhpur (LL.M) and UPES, Dehradun (BA.LLB).

Joshua T. Shadwick is an Associate Professor at Southeast Missouri State University in the Department of Criminal Justice, Social Work and Sociology. He teaches both undergraduate and graduate courses on topics ranging from research methods to gangs. His research interests include the justice system's response to social problems, police investigations, and wildlife crime. Dr. Shadwick's research has been published in peer-reviewed journals such as, Policing: An International Journal, Deviant Behavior, and Criminal Justice Policy Review. Prior to his current occupation, he served a total of seven years in law enforcement. These years of service were comprised of four years as a Sheriff Deputy for the Montgomery County Sheriff's Office and three years as a Conservation Agent for the Missouri Department of Conservation.

Vikram Singh is an academician, researcher, and administrator at Chaudhary Devi Lal University (CDLU), Sirsa, Haryana, India, serving as a full Professor in the Department of Computer Science and Engineering since Dec 2008. He has dispensed the duties of Dean, Academic Affairs, Dean of Engineering & Technology, Dean of Research, Dean of Colleges, and Director of University Computer Centre at his University. He holds an MSc in Physics (1989), Post B.Sc. Diploma in Computer Science (1990), MCA

(1992), and PhD in Computer Science (2004), all from Kurukshetra University, India, along with recent certifications in Cyber Security from Udemy (2020) and eLearning College (2020). His research interests include system simulation, cyber security, Indian IT and Data Privacy Laws, Data Mining, Artificial Intelligence and Machine Learning and related ethics.

Parkman Speights is a law student from Jackson, Mississippi. He graduated from Mississippi State University with a Bachelor's Degree in Psychology in 2023. He is currently a 3L at the University of Mississippi School of Law and expects to graduate in May of 2026. As a Law Student, he is a member of the Pi Beta Phi Legal Honors Society, the former Executive Manager and current Chair of the University of Mississippi School of Law's Negotiation and Alternative Dispute Resolution Board.

Karlie Stonard is a Senior Lecturer in Criminology and member of the Institute for Community Research and Development at the University of Wolverhampton. Karlie's expertise is in Intimate Partner Violence (IPV), in particular, violence that occurs via technology. She has conducted several research evaluations for local organisations in Wolverhampton as well as for Wolverhampton City Council individually and as part of a research team. She has received funding from the AHRC for her current project exploring the role of technology in inclusive access to support for deaf survivors of IPV: SmartSafeSigning.. Karlie has research expertise in quantitative and qualitative research methods.

Holli Vah Seliskar has more than twenty years of experience in higher education. Dr. Vah Seliskar has taught at the undergraduate, graduate, and doctoral levels, and has led academic departments as an Academic Department Chair, and Assistant Academic Department Chair. Dr. Vah Seliskar's previous experience includes working as a Program Coordinator for the United Way of Greater Cleveland, the Cleveland Metropolitan School District, and the Mandel Foundation in Ohio. Dr. Vah Seliskar received her Ph.D. in Curriculum and Instruction from Kent State University in Ohio. Dr. Vah Seliskar's research interests include restorative justice, restorative practices in K-12 and higher education, restorative practices in the workplace, subjectivity in qualitative research, and best practices in online learning, teaching, and mentoring.

David Alan White has taught criminal justice at the undergraduate and graduate levels, first as an adjunct and now as a full-time professor. At Purdue Global, he teaches various graduate criminal justice courses. He is also a course lead. In addition to teaching, he is on numerous committees, including the Institutional Review Board and Professional Competency Committee. Before joining Purdue Global, White was a law enforcement officer with over 25 years of service, working in the Ludlow (MA) Police Department and Collier County (FL) Sheriff's Office. He was a criminal investigator for many years, investigating property and violent crime, then supervised an Economic Crimes Unit. Education: PhD, Northcentral University; MPA, Florida Gulf Coast University; MS, American International College; Graduate Certificate, Kaplan University (now Purdue Global); and BA, Western New England University. Certifications: Certified Fraud Investigator

Index

A

B

C

D

E

F

G

I

J

L

V

www.ingramcontent.com/pod-product-compliance
Lightning Source LLC
LaVergne TN
LVHW060256011026
849161LV00011B/2721
9798337376608